# HAMMURABI'S LAWS

## Text, Translation and Glossary



*M.E.J. Richardson*

Sheffield Academic Press

*HORA FUGIT STAT IUS*



Published by Sheffield Academic Press Ltd
Mansion House
19 Kingfield Road
Sheffield S11 9AS
England
www.shef-ac-press.co.uk

Typeset by Sheffield Academic Press
and
Printed on acid-free paper in Great Britain
by Bookcraft Ltd
Midsomer Norton, Bath

British Library Cataloguing in Publication Data

A catalogue record for this book is available
from the British Library

ISBN 1-84127-030-X (cloth)
1-84127-139-X (paper)

# CONTENTS

## PREFACE

This book has its origin long ago when I first began teaching Akkadian at the University of Manchester. I soon realized that my students, as well as most of the others who were studying elsewhere, could not easily find for themselves the essential meaning of a given word in a given passage of Hammurabi's laws, the text that is used as the standard introduction to Akkadian in most of the world's academic institutions where the language is taught.

To compare any given occurrence of a word with others elsewhere in the text was, to say the least, tedious. In other ancient Semitic languages the problem is not so great, because handy dictionaries and concordances are readily available. Therefore, like many other teachers, I encouraged my students to make their own simple word lists and cross-reference tables, which would serve them well for later advanced searching in the prestigious multi-volume Akkadian dictionaries.

But the more I talked with colleagues the more I realized that not only students of Akkadian but also biblical scholars and ancient historians are very interested in the actual words that are used in these laws, in order to see how those words reflect the basic concept of good behaviour in a civilized community. To what extent the laws were observed we shall probably never really know, but to have had them set out as a god-given ideal standard means that we can begin to draw some conclusions about the relationship between faith and works in Mesopotamian society at the beginning of the second millennium BCE.

And then there was the question of the later manuscripts, which showed that at various times and in various places ancient scribes had copied out parts of the law, apparently not because they were dealing with a legal problem but because for many, many centuries after the glory of Old Babylon had departed it was considered worthwhile to preserve a knowledge of the ancient laws of the land. Such a veneration of texts like this has clear parallels in later Semitic cultures.

My own word list began to expand to cover not just the parts of the text prescribed by the University syllabus but all the laws, and the prologue and the epilogue, and the major variant readings, without which there can be no real understanding of the high value placed on the content of the laws. I had hoped that my notes would be ready to be published while I was still teaching, but with one thing and another, that could not happen. Reading through the work as a whole now that I am retired, I have become aware of how easy it is for inconsistencies to find their way into writing that has been through so many stages of partial revision. I have tried to iron them out, and do hope that any creases that remain will not prove annoying.

In these last stages of preparation I have become more and more aware of how much I owe to those who first taught me the discipline of cuneiform studies, and also to those who have attended my classes who raised questions demanding disciplined answers. They know who they are and that my thanks are heartfelt.

I have also been aware of the constant love and support and tolerance of my family; they must have thought for many a year that the piles of notes on my desk would never be compressed between hard covers.

Special thanks are due to the Sheffield Academic Press for agreeing to take on the responsibility of publishing what I know was a difficult manuscript, and particularly to Professor Clines, who requested Professor Healey to include it in the Semitic Studies Series.

Current affairs have clouded over the earlier long years of cordial diplomatic relations between Britain and Iraq, and it now becomes harder and harder to see the light. So it is perhaps appropriate to recall the remark of the French revolutionary Robespierre, when he wrote, 'La volonté générale gouverne la société, comme la volonté particulière gouverne chaque individu isolé.'

Mervyn Richardson
Leiden, The Netherlands
1 March 2000

## ABBREVIATIONS

| | |
|---|---|
| *AHw* | Wolfram von Soden, *Akkadisches Handwörterbuch* (Wiesbaden: Otto Harrassowitz, 1965–81; Fascicules 1–16). |
| *ANET* | James B. Pritchard (ed.), *Ancient Near Eastern Texts Relating to the Old Testament* (Princeton, NJ: Princeton University Press, 1950) |
| *BAL* | Rykle Borger, *Babylonische-Assyrische Lesestücke* (Analecta Orientalia, 54; Rome: Biblical Institute Press, 2nd edn, 1979). |
| *BL* | G.R. Driver and J.C. Miles, *The Babylonian Laws, Edited with Translation and Commentary* (2 vols.; Oxford: Clarendon Press, 1952–55). |
| *CAD* | Chicago University (The Oriental Institute), *The Assyrian Dictionary* (Chicago: The Oriental Institute). The first volume published was vol. VI (Ḫ) in 1956, since when others have been published at irregular intervals. Vol. I (A/1) appeared in 1964, and most recently vol. XVII/iii (Š/iii) has appeared (1992). It is now almost complete. |
| Caplice | R. Caplice (with the assistance of D. Snell), *Introduction to Akkadian* (Rome: Biblical Institute Press, 3rd edn, 1988). Considerably modified from the first edition, 1980. |
| CH | Codex Hammurabi. The conventional abbreviation in English to refer to the text of Hammurabi's Laws. |
| Finet | A. Finet, *Le code d'Hammurapi* (Paris: Cerf, 1973). |
| Finkelstein | J.J. Finkelstein, 'The Hamurapi Law Tablet BE xxxi: 22', *Revue d'Assyriologie 63* (1969), 20. |
| Fish | T. Fish, *Letters of the First Babylonian Dynasty in the John Rylands Library, Manchester* (Manchester: Manchester University Press, 1936). |
| Meek | Theophile J. Meek, 'The Code of Hammurabi', in James B. Pritchard (ed.), *Ancient Near Eastern Texts Relating to the Old Testament* (Princeton, NJ: Princeton University Press, 1950), pp. 163-80; see also 3rd edn (1969). |
| Roth | Martha T. Roth, *Law Collections from Mespotamia and Asia Minor* (SBL Writings from the Ancient World Series, 6; Atlanta: Scholars Press, 2nd edn, 1997); in particular Chapter 8, pp. 71-142, 'Laws of Hammurabi'; this chapter is unchanged from the first edition (1995). |

| | |
|---|---|
| Scheil | V. Scheil, *Mémoires de la délegation en Perse*, IV (Paris: Leroux, 1902); see also V. Scheil, *La loi de Hammourabi* (Paris: Leroux, 3rd edn, 1906). |
| Stele | The main text of CH, as recorded on the stele recovered from French excavations at Susa in south-western Iran at the end of the nineteenth century. This stele is now conserved in the Musée du Louvre, Paris. As far as possible variant manuscripts are compared to the readings on this stele. |
| Stol | Marten Stol, *Studies in Old Babylonian History* (Istanbul: Nederlands Historisch-Archaeologisch Institut, 1976). |
| Szlechter | Emile Szlechter, *Codex Hammurapi* (Rome: Pontifica Universitas Lateranensis, 1977). |
| Ungnad | Arthur Ungnad, *Gesetze Ḫammurapis* (Leipzig: J.C. Hinrichs, 1909). |

# INTRODUCTION

I have prepared this handbook with a view to making the text of the Laws of Hammurabi more easily accessible to students of Hebrew and Arabic. Although I use what has become the standard abbreviation for the text adopted by English-speaking scholars of CH, standing for Codex Hammurabi, most now agree that the document is really a collection of laws rather than a code of law.

The diorite stele on which these laws are recorded came to light as a result of French archaeological research in south-western Iran at the end of the nineteenth century. It had evidently been captured from Babylon and taken home as one of the spoils of war by Elamite aggressors. It can now be seen on display in the Musée du Louvre, Paris, where it has been kept ever since that discovery. Reference has often been made to the content of the stele in all kinds of historical, sociological and theological treatises in subsequent scholarly literature.

Translations into English of the Old Babylonian original (either the whole text or a part of it) are not impossible to obtain, but access to the text itself is not so easy. Until recently it was possible to buy the standard edition of the text edited by Driver and Miles, which incorporated a complete annotated translation as well as an extensive textual, grammatical and legal commentary. But that book is now out of print, and also out of date. The best alternative is Borger's edition of CH in his beginners' chrestomathy, *Babylonisch-Assyrische Lesestücke* (*BAL*), a book that includes much Akkadian literature that enjoys only a remote (if any) connection with Hammurabi. While there is absolutely no question that this is a magnificent chrestomathy, unfortunately it has a limited use for someone who knows only a little German and no Akkadian.

Akkadian is unquestionably the most important language for the general Semitist to learn, along with Arabic and Hebrew; since CH embodies excellent textual material through which to learn this language, there is clearly a need for a concise presentation of what was actually written on the original stele, together with an easily usable glossary. That is what I have set out to prepare. Bearing in mind the importance of the text in later Akkadian literary tradition I have also sought to provide a synopsis of the major textual variants, for they have so many interesting parallels with the development of the more familiar Biblical Hebrew literary tradition.

## THE TEXT AND TRANSLATION

I have presented the text in transcription rather than transliteration, because that is the format preferred by the general Semitist. But since Assyriologists frequently disagree about the best system of transliteration, I have had to decide what is best for the beginner. My choice has naturally been influenced by the decisions taken by Caplice in his *Introduction to Akkadian*, which is probably the most convenient manual for the beginner to use in English, and my original draft transcription of the text was marked according to the principles adopted by Borger (*BAL*) and von Soden (*AHw*). This seemed to be the best procedure, since those were the only modern sources that could give fuller grammatical information for all the words in the text of CH, and they were based on sound philological principles. It was only after I had completed this task, and the draft of the whole Glossary had been prepared, that a new transcription was published by Professor Martha T. Roth in her *Law Collections from Mesopotamia and Asia Minor*, where she used a somewhat different system of transcription. In order to avoid too much confusion I decided to revise the draft of my transcription so that as far as I felt able it would agree with hers; I have included a note of the few points where I have taken a different course from her (see below, p. 22). I have felt able to take a less literal line in the translation that is presented alongside the text since all individual words are given their literal meanings in the Glossary.

The whole text has been divided into three sections (the Prologue, the Laws and the Epilogue) and then by subsection number; this is in preference to the alternative complicated column and line system. Since there is an agreed (though not altogether satisfactory) system of numbering the Laws for this part of the text, there was no problem; but for the Prologue and Epilogue there is no agreed system, so they have been divided into a number of manageable sections to make reference to them easier. Unfortunately, the section breaks I have made do not agree with those (unnumbered) paragraphs suggested by Finet or Roth, but to have changed them would have been too tedious. In general I have preferred shorter sections, for it seemed to me important that the reader should be able to find a particular word within the text as quickly as possible. I do not regard this difference as important, though of course it is desirable that in the future, when a deeper analysis of the whole discourse is completed, textual boundaries should be agreed. It was necessary to have some working system of divisions for the purpose of convenient citation in a book like this, and details of the divisions I have used are as listed below.

| | |
|---|---|
| Prologue | |
| *Stele ref.* | *Text ref.* |
| I:1-13 | P1 |
| I:14-26 | P2 |
| I:27-49 | P3 |
| I:50-62 | P4 |
| I:63-II:12 | P5 |
| II:13-21 | P6 |
| II:22-31 | P7 |
| II:32-54 | P8 |
| II:55-67 | P9 |
| II:68-III:12 | P10 |
| III:13-23 | P11 |
| III:24-35 | P12 |
| III:36-54 | P13 |
| III:55-64 | P14 |
| III:65-IV:6 | P15 |
| IV:7-22 | P16 |
| IV:23-37 | P17 |
| IV:38-52 | P18 |
| IV:53-59 | P19 |
| IV:60-66 | P20 |
| IV:67-V:13 | P21 |
| V:14-25 | P22 |
| Laws | |
| V:26--XLVI (= Rv. XXIII):102 | L1–L282 |
| Epilogue | |
| XLVII (Rv. XXIV):1-8 | E1 |
| XLVII (Rv. XXIV):9-14 | E2 |
| XLVII (Rv. XXIV):15-21 | E3 |
| XLVII (Rv. XXIV):22-31 | E4 |
| XLVII (Rv. XXIV):32-39 | E5 |
| XLVII (Rv. XXIV):40-45 | E6 |
| XLVII (Rv. XXIV):46-58 | E7 |
| XLVII (Rv. XXIV):59-78 | E8 |
| XLVII (Rv. XXIV):79-83 | E9 |
| XLVII (Rv. XXIV):84- XLVIII (Rv. XXV):2 | E10 |
| XLVIII (Rv. XXV):3-19 | E11 |
| XLVIII (Rv. XXV):20-47 | E12 |
| XLVIII (Rv. XXV):48-58 | E13 |
| XLVIII (Rv. XXV):59-74 | E14 |
| XLVIII (Rv. XXV):75-85 | E15 |
| XLVIII (Rv. XXV):86-94 | E16 |
| XLVIII (Rv. XXV):95- XLIX (Rv. XXVI):1 | E17 |
| XLIX (Rv. XXVI):2-17 | E18 |
| XLIX (Rv. XXVI):18-44 | E19 |
| XLIX (Rv. XXVI):45-52 | E20 |
| XLIX (Rv. XXVI):53-80 | E21 |
| XLIX (Rv. XXVI):81-97 | E22 |
| XLIX (Rv. XXVI):98- L (Rv. XXVII):13 | E23 |
| L (Rv. XXVII):14-40 | E24 |
| L (Rv. XXVII):41-63 | E25 |
| L (Rv. XXVII):64-80 | E26 |
| L (Rv. XXVII):81-91 | E27 |
| L (Rv. XXVII):92- LI (Rv. XXVIII):23 | E28 |
| LI (Rv. XXVIII):24-39 | E29 |
| LI (Rv. XXVIII):40-49 | E30 |
| LI (Rv. XXVIII):50-69 | E31 |
| LI (Rv. XXVIII):70-83 | E32 |
| LI (Rv. XXVIII):84-91 | E33 |

## The Glossary

From its beginnings as a simple list of words this Glossary has developed into a mini-dictionary. It is presented with the model of *CAD* in mind. To have individual words cited within their full context for their different occurrences makes accurate learning of any language easier. But it has been prepared so that it can be used in conjunction with *AHw* or *CAD*. For the general Semitist there is no doubt that the frequent reference to roots in *AHw* is an advantage, but the immediate citation of individual words in their full contexts is indispensable for a study of meaning. Even though *CAD* is still incomplete, it has been decided to use the citation forms chosen there as the primary reference here, but cross-references are given to *AHw* citation forms where these are significantly different. It is because the claims of convenience seemed to outstrip those of accuracy that mimation was ignored, for there is no doubt that strictly speaking these forms would have been more correct for CH.

Verbs have been separated according to theme and not grouped under one theme. This practice is different from normal and has been adopted from my experience in teaching Akkadian, where I have found that students almost always find it easier to identify the stem of a word than to identify its root. What this means is, for example, that the causative (Š-theme) of *aṣû* will here be found as a separate item under *šūṣû*, that 'to turn' (intransitive) will be found under *târu*, while 'to turn' (transitive) is under *turru*, and that N-themes will all be listed under an actual or hypothetical N-infinitive.

Within verbal entries *-t-* and *-tan-* forms have not usually been treated separately. These forms most often seem to possess a modal or perfective nuance, and if this is not obvious it is the subject of (often inconclusive) discussion, and this requires fuller commentary than can be justified in a dictionary. It would probably have been desirable to treat all such forms separately if this glossary had had to cover a wider range of literature, but, with only one text under consideration, it seemed to be a more appropriate solution to take infixed and non-infixed forms together. But there were occasions, such as with the forms of the verbs *abālu* and *tabālu*, where a particular semantic idea seems to be conveyed by the infix; in such cases the different forms are treated separately under the one headword.

I have also decided as far as possible to separate verbal forms from nominal forms. This has implications for infinitives and participles, which often have verbal force but nominal inflection. All verbal forms have been listed under the infinitive as headword according to normal practice, and therefore any occurrence of the infinitive itself, whether used verbally or nominally, is included under that same headword; but participles are treated as separate items. What this means is, for example, that the essentially nominal form *muštēmiqu*, 'supplicant' will be found under its own lemma rather than under *emēqu*; similarly, the essentially verbal *mugarrinu*, 'heaping up' will be found under its own lemma rather than under *gurrunu,* the D-theme of *garānu.* Appropriate cross-references will be given, and an overall view of all the attested themes of a given root can be found in the Index of Roots and Stems. I hope this new arrangement will be more convenient for learners without being disturbing to teachers. Within the Glossary and Indexes a number of abbreviations are regularly used:

| | |
|---|---|
| adj. | adjectival |
| adv. | adverbial |
| impv. | imperative |
| inf. | infinitive |
| num. | numeral |
| part. | particle |
| prs. | present |
| prt. | preterite |
| ptcp. | participle |
| sbst. | substantival |
| stv. | stative |
| vb. | verbal (including infinitive) |
| vnt. | variant |

There will be several occasions where a given quotation will be translated differently under different headwords. This is usually because a different element in the sentence is under close consideration, but it may sometimes reflect different interpretations. This whole exercise is not designed so much to provide definitive translations of awkward passages as to make the reader aware that translation is no substitute for the subtleties of the original language.

## VARIANT READINGS

The text on which this transcription is based is that of *BAL* (2nd edition, 1979, considerably changed since the first edition of 1963). While it is essentially that of the Stele, there have been a number of points where Borger has restored or improved the reading from other manuscripts.

In addition to the Stele text, there are 34 manuscripts formally denoted in *BAL* by the letters A-Z and a-t; one or two other manuscripts are also mentioned that have not been formally incorporated into that work; these are referred to with the prefix 'z-a...'). The significance of most of the manuscripts has been recognized in Driver's edition (1955) and Meek's translation (1950, revised 1969). Borger's sequence of sigla is essentially based on the sequence of the text preserved on the manuscripts in question: A-F preserve parts of the Prologue with or without the early Laws; G-e preserve parts of the Laws with or without the Epilogue; f-h preserve parts of the Epilogue only; i-t are manuscripts discovered after 1963, when the first edition of *BAL* was published. The sigla for the manuscripts that he uses are maintained, but not all the variant readings he notes have been included here. For the most part the variant readings are of relatively minor importance, but one or two show a substantial change.

The manuscript tradition is interesting because many of the late Assyrian copies from Kouyunjik seem to reflect a text that is earlier than the Stele itself. They sometimes contain scribal notes that raise important questions about how particular words were understood by later literary scholars in antiquity; it also suggests that the text was being copied not primarily for the purposes of the administration of justice but rather to educate scribes in the art of good writing. Such questions can properly be answered only by a comprehensive study of all the text variants, including the homographs, but the major variants from the Stele that can be observed in one or two of the later manuscripts deserve to be given special attention. Three passages in the Prologue (see P16; 18; 20) are omitted by the Old Babylonian manuscript A, and since they can be excluded without disturbing the grammar or the sense (in fact, the grammar may be improved by omitting them), it is sensible to conclude that Stele evolved from the shorter text exemplified by manuscript A.

For these sections of the Prologue other manuscripts diverge from both Stele and MS A: MS F (Middle Assyrian) and MS C (Late Babylonian) represent an intermediary tradition; they both omit the first of the passages (P16); F omits the second (P18) but includes the third (P20); C omits the third and includes the second. It seems therefore that the first passage was the last of the three to be incorporated into the main text (i.e. Stele), and the consequent wide separation of the subordinating pronoun *šu* (which seems to have begun its life as the particle *ša* in MS A) from its associated verb *išīmu* can be explained as inelegant syntax resulting from textual amplification.

The Late Babylonian MS B agrees with Stele so far as these three passages are concerned (showing that this was the accepted text of that period), but differs noticeably from it for the first 15 lines of the Prologue. The beginning of the tablet is broken, but presumably Anu and Enlil are mentioned before the first legible word, which is *erṣetim* (cf. I:5). There is room for only about six signs in the break before the next legible word *niši* (cf. I:12), which is separated from the restored words *Ḫammurabi* (MS B line 3, but which is not written on the Stele until I:28 and I:50), *Sinmuballiṭ* (MS B line 4, which is presumably preceded by a word for 'son of'), and *re'um* (MS B line 5, cf. Stele I:51) by only two or three more signs. The rest of the text corresponding to Stele I:16 is completely different and reads thus:

> *lipit qātišun rē'ūtim* [read *rē'ūt*] *mīšarium* [read *-im*] *ana širikti išrukūšu ušatlimūšu ḫaṭṭim* [read *-am*] *u agī* [read *-am*] *sīmāt šarrūtim.*
>
> By the touch of their hands they endowed him with the gift of the pastorship of justice; they presented him with the sword and the crown as signs of kingship.

The last sentence seems to echo a passage from the Epilogue (cf. Stele XLVII).

The special interest of MS B is further emphasized by its substitution of the name of Ellil for Marduk at P22, which suggests that it may come from the tradition of Nippur rather than Babylon, where Ellil rather than Marduk would naturally be considered as the source of the divine inspiration for the laws.

The other variant readings that are considered here depend on a hierarchical ordering of all the variants according to their significance for lexicography. The order adopted here is as follows:

| | | |
|---|---|---|
| 1. | Homophonic | A different sign but with the same phonetic value. |
| 2. | Allophonic | The different phonetic value is one which is known to be allophonic in Akkadian. |
| 3. | Phonetic | A different phoneme that appears to have no morphemic significance. |
| 4. | Morphemic | Morphemic variation on the same lexical base. |
| 5. | Lexical | Lexical substitution. |
| 6. | Textual | Lexical addition or omission |

Variants in categories 1 and 2 have not been noted here since homographs are in principle excluded. Category 3 variants have been noted, but many of them are best regarded as errors. Category 4 variants are all noted, except for the omission of mimation on nouns, and similarly for category 5, except where different Sumerograms reflect the same Akkadian lexeme. All variants in category 6 have been noted without exception.

While it was clearly inappropriate in a work like this to provide a full list of variant readings, it would have been negligent to ignore those with morphological or lexicographical significance. In the notes to the transcribed text such variants are recorded. The existence of a variant is noted in the relevant Glossary entry by annotation of the citation. By cross-checking with *BAL* more precise details of the variant can easily be traced. Proposed emendations to the text are marked by the symbol (!), and restorations by square brackets, but these are not always noted in the Glossary. Where it was felt necessary to draw the reader's attention to a discrepancy between Roth and Borger (or others) the remark has been added to the footnotes to the Laws, where it can be studied together with any manuscript variants noted there.

The following conventions are observed in the footnotes to the transcribed text:

| | |
|---|---|
| * | A footnote number placed before a word (and after any associated punctuation mark) refers to the text as far as the next post-fixed asterisk; a footnote number placed after a word (and before any associated punctuation mark) refers only to that word. |
| ! | A reading that is considered to be a mistake; a conjectural emendation will be offered if one is not obvious. |
| ? | A reading that is uncertain. |
| [...] | Signs to be restored in a damaged manuscript. |
| <...> | Sign(s) that have evidently been omitted and are to be restored. |
| {...} | Sign(s) that have evidently been written by mistake and are to be deleted. |
| ø | Text that has been omitted by the scribe in an otherwise intact manuscript, but which is attested in the Stele or elsewhere. |

The tablets that conserve these parallel texts are presently located in various museums, including Paris (Musée du Louvre), Berlin (Archaeological Museum), Istanbul (Archaeological Museum) and London (British Museum). As other manuscripts are found it will be straightforward for the moment to extend the sequence of sigla. Explicit details about the circumstances of the composition of most of the manuscripts have been preserved in colophons, for which see *BL* II, pp. 113-14.

## THE LACUNA

Because the Stele is destroyed at the end of its sixteenth column (which closes with all but the last word of L65) and seven columns are missing, some (but there is no way of knowing just how many) Laws are missing. A few (but by no means all) of them can be restored from parallel manuscripts, written at different times and in different places on clay tablets. After the break, at the top of col. XXIV, the Stele continues with the closing words of a Law that, by convention, is referred to as L100 (the beginning of it is restored from MS S 1-11). But there has been no agreement on how best to number the Laws that can be restored in the break from the variant manuscripts. The words and phrases that can be restored in these sections have been summarily listed in the Glossary, but full citations have not always been included.

For the missing sections Driver (*BL*) used letters §§A-V, which corresponded to the manuscripts from which the restorations were made, and this has been followed by Finet. Meek (*ANET*) preferred to use numbers for four groups of Laws (66–71; 78; 88–91; 93–100). Borger (*BAL*), the results of whose work was used as the basis for this text, has recognised six lacuna of undetermined length, and refers to these lacunae by the sigla a-f. He is then able to provide a new continuous numerical sequence, augmented as appropriate by a letter. But his system does not take account of the important manuscript discovered after his work was published and now incorporated into Roth's text. Having decided to adopt Borger's system as standard, it now needs to be amplified by sigla used by Roth. The table below summarizes the sigla used by previous scholars.

There is also disagreement on how best to number the columns on the Stele after the break. Borger has introduced new column numbers, showing his preference for a continuous sequence rather than renumbering from 1 on the reverse. So what others refer to as column Rv.1 is for Borger column 24 (augmenting by 23 to allow for the first 16 preserved columns and the 7 that are calculated as lost on the obverse). Meek does not use column references in *ANET* for the Laws themselves, but refers to column 'reverse xxiv' at the beginning of the epilogue, which corresponds to Borger's col. XLVII. It is important when

| *BAL* | *BL* | *Meek* | *Manuscript* | *Roth* |
|---|---|---|---|---|
| 66 | A | 66 | P, Q | gap §a |
| 67 | B | 67 | P | gap §b |
| 67+a | C | 70, 71 | P, Q | gap §c |
| 68+a | D | [72–77] | Q | gap §d |
| 68+b | H, G | [72–77] | P, R | gap §e |
| 68+c | J | [72–77] | R | gap §f |
| 69+c | J, E | 78 | P, R | gap §g |
| – | – | – | – | gap §h-r |
| 69d | K | [79–87] | S | gap §s |
| 70+d | L | 88 | S | gap §t |
| 71+d | M | 89–90 | S | gap §u |
| 72+d | N | 91 | S | gap §v |
| 72+e | O | 93 | S | gap §w |
| 73+e | P | 94 | S | gap §x |
| 74+e | Q | 95 | S | gap §y |
| 75+e | R | 96 | P, S | gap §z |
| '76+e' | S | – | T | gap §aa |
| 76+f | T | 97 | S | gap §bb |
| 77+f | U | 98 | S | gap §cc |
| 78+f = 100 | V | 99–100 | S | 100 |

consulting very early studies to remember that in his edition Scheil had estimated that only 5 columns were broken; it was Ungnad (1909) who later showed that 7 was a more exact number.

That opinions on this issue still vary can be seen clearly when consulting *CAD*. Like Borger, the editors prefer a continuous sequence of column numbers, but they ignore the break after col. XVI. For them the next preserved column is XVII. In order to accord with Borger's col. XXIV–LI, the numbers of *CAD* col. XVII–XLIV must all therefore be augmented by seven. Even though Borger's proposed renumeration has not been universally accepted, because of its simplicity it is the best system for the student to learn first. But for the absolute beginner it will be sufficient to refer to the Laws by their traditional number, without any reference to Stele column number, and to adopt a convenient set of references for manageable units of text in the Prologue and the Epilogue, such as is suggested here.

## TRANSCRIPTION

While there is an agreed method for the transliteration of Babylonian cuneiform, there is no clear consensus about transcription. A Glossary has to deal with transcription, and the system adopted here is intended to help the beginner as much as possible. Standard forms that would be expected to be found in a teaching grammar are used rather than aberrant forms that may be suggested in the text itself. So the substantive formed from the D-participle of *rabû* is presented as *murabbīšu,* 'his foster father', and not transcribed as *murābīšu*, which may perhaps be the more correct phonetic transcription of the word suggested by the writing *mu-ra-bi-šu* (L192; 193).

Vowel length, whether for phonological or morphological cause, has been marked with macron but the circumflex has been retained for lemmata and other instances where it has become usual among Assyriologists. There seemed no good cause to change the spelling of words that very soon the reader will need to check with *CAD* or *AHw*. While it is important to learn eventually the philological arguments that justify using both macron and circumflex in Akkadian transcription, in a work that has been designed primarily for beginners, it seemed more important to indicate consistently where a vowel was likely to be long rather than make philological judgments that could be fully explained only in a grammar. Intervocalic ʾ is not normally marked.

In general, since this text is written primarily for readers in English and unnecessary differences inevitably lead to confusion, I have changed my text to conform to the one published by Roth. But the differences between the American system (established by *CAD* and naturally followed by Roth) and the German system (adopted by Borger following von Soden) affect several words and morpho-syntactic features of the text that sometimes need special notes. So where Roth's transliteration has failed to record grammatical features that are of particular importance for the beginner (especially the marking of the *-ū* of 3rd person plural verbs as long, to distinguish from the short *-u* marking a subjunctive) then I have reverted to the German method. In addition I have used *y* instead of *j* (even though *CAD* also uses *j)* as a much more acceptable transcription for anglophones of Semitic semiconsonant *y*.

Three commonly occurring problems of transcription that concern theoretical phonological rules affecting the marking of vowel length are not always noted in the text. While it is helpful on the one hand to mark all vowels involving a contracted ʾ as long, on the other hand it has to be recognized that some such vowels would lose that length by the loss of stress in particular morpho-syntactic contexts. The second problem concerns whether to mark vowel length that results from phonetic contraction differently from length that is purely a feature of morphology (the former by the circumflex, the latter by the macron). The third frequently recurring problem is whether to use /i/ or /e/ in particular words where the cuneiform uses homographs. There are also some problems with the consonants of some lexemes, mostly about whether to transcribe as voiced or unvoiced. While some of these can easily be solved by simple cross-references, others remain a source of disagreement.

Not only is there a difference between American and European practice, there are also differences among individual scholars belonging to any one of the Assyriological camps. Because of the importance of Roth's edition to my own work, and the desire to cause as little confusion to the beginner as possible, I have tended to follow her solutions wherever I have noticed divergence from others. Such differences deserve a thorough explanation in a study of the grammar of CH in the light of General Semitic, but to have published within the compass of the present work the detailed set of notes on this and other Old Babylonian grammatical features that it was necessary to prepare would have been premature and also a diversion. But a selection of words in CH that show where the American transliterations (as found in Roth) differ from those preferred in Continental Europe can be used to illustrate some of the problems involved.

| *BAL; AHw* | *Roth; CAD* | *Reason for Variation* |
|---|---|---|
| *ṭabû* | *tabu* | contracted /ʾ/ in III-weak verb. |
| *mūdē* | *mudē* | contracted /ʾ/ in I-weak verb |
| *izzazu* | *izzazzu* | defective verb |
| *iḫiāṭ* | *iḫiʾaṭ* | intervocalic /ʾ/ |
| *Ellil* | *Enlil* | partial or full assimilation of consonant |
| *ellilūt* | *illilūt* | /e/ instead of /i/ |
| *ekišnugal* | *egišnugal* | voiced or unvoiced phoneme |
| *Hammurapi* | *Hammurabi* | etymology of personal name |
| *Kută* | *Kutî* | inflexion of proper name |
| *lā* and *lū* | *la* and *lu* | monosyllable with long vowel |
| *rikis* | *markas* | variant Akk. equivalent for *DUR AN KI* |
| *entum* | *ugbabtum* | *AHw* in contrast to *CAD* E, pp. 173 |
| *ZI.IK.RU.UM* | *sekretum* | see *CAD* S, pp. 215-17 |

## INDEX

The Index of Verbal Forms is intended to provide a bridge between the study of lexemes and the study of grammar; even though full parsing has not been given (that would have been monotonous to writer and reader alike), it is hoped that enough information has been provided to facilitate further study of the use of particular moods and tenses. The List of Roots and Stems will primarily be of interest to those lexicographers who prefer the traditional approach to Semitic philology, where words are listed according to root rather than stem. Older Akkadian dictionary makers (as well as Driver in his Glossary) regarded this as normal, and *CAD* succeeds in avoiding the issue. The fact of the matter is that Akkadian has been permeated more than any other ancient Semitic language by non-Semitic lexemes so that a modification of the traditional approach is required. The lists of key words derived from each identified root at the head of every letter entry in *AHw* would have been an acceptable model to follow in a larger glossary, but it seemed to me best for the purposes of studying a relatively small body of text to provide a completely separate index of roots and stems. Root transformations are so fundamental to understanding the structure of all Semitic languages that I felt they could not be ignored in a work such as this, which I hope will prove useful even to those who know about them already.

# OUTLINE CONTENTS OF HAMMURABI'S LAWS

# THE LAWS: TEXT AND TRANSLATION

## TEXT

### Prologue

**P1 (= I:1-13)**
*īnu*[1] *Anum, ṣīrum, šar Anunnakī,*
*Ellil, bēl šamê u erṣetim, šā'im šīmāt mātim,*
*ana Marduk, mārim rēštîm ša Ea,*
*ellilūt*[2] *kiššat nišī išīmūšum.*

**P2 (= I:14-26)**
*in*[3] *Igigī ušarbiūšu, Bābilam*[4] *šumšu ṣīram ibbiū,*
*in*[5] *kibrātim ušāterūšu, ina*[6] *libbišu šarrūtam*[7] *dārītam*[8]
*ša kīma šamê u erṣetim išdāša*[9] *šuršudā*
*ukinnūšum*[10].

**P3 (I:27-49)**
*inūmišu*[11]
*Ḫammurabi*[12], *rubâm na'dam*[13], *pāliḫ ilī,*

---

1. A: *inūma*; B: major textual variant, see Introduction.
2. A: *ililūt.*
3. A: *ina.*
4. B: *lipit qātišun rē'ūtim* [read *rē'ūt*] *mīšarium* [read *mīšarim*] *ana širikti išrukūšu ušatlimūšu ḫaṭṭim* [read *ḫaṭṭam*] *u agī* [read *agâm*] *sīmāt šarrūtim*; see Introduction.
5. A: *ina.*
6. B: *in.*
7. B: *šarrūtim.*
8. B: *dārīti.*
9. B: *išdāšu.*
10. B: *ukinnūšu.*
11. A: *ina ūmišu*; B: ø.
12. B: + *šarra*(!) *mīšaram*(!) (for *šar mīšarim*).
13. B: *rubâm na'da*(!).

# THE LAWS: TEXT AND TRANSLATION

## TRANSLATION

### Prologue

**(P1)** There was a time[1] when exalted Anu, the king of the Anunnaku,
and Enlil, the lord of heaven and earth,
who determines the destinies of the nation,
determined that Marduk, the first son born to Ea,
should govern as Enlil all the peoples of the world.

**(P2)** They exalted him among among the Igigi,
and gave Babylon its illustrious name,
and made it pre-eminent throughout the earth;
with its foundations as secure as heaven and earth,
they established for him an everlasting reign within it.

**(P3)** It was then that Anu and Enlil ordained Hammurabi,
a devout prince who fears the gods,
to demonstrate justice within the land,

---

1. P1+2 together are really adverbial clauses to the main clause in P3, and so the first word of P1 should properly be seen as anticipating the first word of P3, so that a more literal translation would be 'It was when…that Anu ordained me…' Separate sentences are clearer in English.

*iâti,*
*mīšaram*[14] *ina mātim ana šūpîm,*
*raggam u ṣēnam ana ḫulluqim*[15]*,*
*dannum enšam ana la ḫabālim,*
*kīma Šamaš ana ṣalmāt qaqqadim waṣêmma*[16] *mātim nuwwurim,*
*Anum u Ellil ana šīr nišī ṭubbim šumī*[17] *ibbû.*

**P4 (I:50-62)**
*Ḫammurabi, rēʾûm, nibīt Ellil, anāku*
*mukammer nuḫšim u ṭuḫdim*
*mušaklil mimma šumšu ana Nippur, markas šamê erṣetim.*
*zāninum naʾdum ša Ekur.*

**P5 (I:63-II:12)**
*šarrum*[18] *lēʾûm, mutēr Eridu ana ašrišu,*
*mubbib šuluḫ Eabzu, tīb kibrāt*[19] *erbettim,*
*mušarbi*[20] *zikru Bābilim,*
*muṭīb libbi Marduk bēlišu,*
[21]*ša ūmīšu* izzazzu ana*[22] *Esagil.*

**P6 (II:13-21)**
*zēr šarrūtim, ša Sîn ibniušu*[23] *munaḫḫiš Urim,*
*wašrum*[24] *muštēmiqum, bābil ḫegallim ana Egišnugal.*

**P7 (II:22-31)**
*šar tašīmtim, šēmû Šamaš*
*dannum*[25]*, mukīn išdī Sippar*

14. B: *mīšariam*(!).
15. B: *ḫulluqiam*(!).
16. B: *waṣêm<ma>* (haplography).
17. B: *šumīam*(!).
18. B: ø.
19. B: *kibrātim.*
20. B: *mušarbiʾu.*
21. B: *ūmīšam.*
22. A: *ina.*
23. A: *ibnāšu.*
24. B: *wašrim.*
25. Stele: *da-núm* as IV:69 and V:3 (P:20); A: *da-a-ni*; B: *DI.KUD*(!), epithet of *Šamaš.*

to destroy evil and wickedness,
to stop the mighty exploiting the weak,
to rise like Shamash over the mass of humanity, illuminating the land;
they ordained me[2],
to improve the welfare of my people[3].

**(P4)** I am Hammurabi,
Enlil's chosen shepherd
who heaps up plenty and abundance
supplying Nippur, where earth and heaven meet, with whatever it needs,
the devoted provider for Ekur.

**(P5)** I am the powerful king, who restored the site of Eridu,
who purified worship in Eabzu,
who marched in every corner of the world,
who made the name Babylon famous,
who made the heart of Marduk his lord happy,
who attended Esagila at the proper time.

**(P6)** I am a descendant of the royal line,
one whom Sin created, who made Ur prosper,
the humble and clever one, who brought prosperity to Ekishnugal.

**(P7)** I am a prudent king, who listens obediently to Shamash,
who powerfully fixes the foundations of Sippar,

---

2. Literally (hereafter 'lit.') 'they named me by my name'.
3. The literal meaning of the verb phrase is 'to improve the flesh of the people', but it probably has more to do with social reform than medical science.

*mušalbiš warqim gigunē Aya,*
*muṣīr bīt Ebabbar*[26] *ša kî šubat šamā'i.*

**P8 (II:32-54)**

*qarrādum, gāmil Larsa*
*muddiš Ebabbar, ana Šamaš rēṣišu*
*bēlum, muballiṭ Uruk*[27]
*šākin mê nuḫšim*[28] *ana nišīšu*[29]
*mullî*[30] *rēš Eanna, mukammer ḫiṣbim ana Anim u Ištar*
*ṣulūl*[31] *mātim*
*mupaḫḫir nišī sapḫātim*[32] *ša Isin*
*muṭaḫḫid*[33] *nuḫšim bīt*[34] *Egalmaḫ.*

**P9 (II:55-67)**

*ušumgal šarrī, talīm Zababa*
*mušaršid šubat Kiš, muštasḫir*[35] *melemmē*[36] *Emeteursag*
*mušteṣbî*[37] *parṣī rabûtim ša Ištar, pāqid bītim*[38] *Ḫursagkalamma.*

**P10 (II:68–III:12)**

*sapar nakirī*[39], *ša Erra*[40] *rūšu, ušakšidu*[41] *nizmassu*[42]
*mušāter*[43] *Kutî, murappiš mimma šumšu ana Meslam*[44].

---

26. B: *É.bar$_6$-ra*, but *É.bab.bar* in P8; perhaps to be transcribed with previous word as *bīt Ebabbar* (so Roth).
27. Stele: *UNUG.KI*. E: + gloss *ú-ru-uk*.
28. B: *nuḫšu*.
29. E: + *bēlum*.
30. B: *mu-ul-la*(!).
31. E: *su*(!)-*lu-ul*.
32. E: *dapḫātim*(!).
33. E: *muṭeḫḫed*.
34. A: *ina*; B: ø. E: *ḫepi*, 'broken, missing'.
35. E: *muštaspiḫir*(!).
36. B: *melammū*(!). C: *melemmī*.
37. B: *muštēšir*.
38. Stele: *bi-tim*; A: *bi-ti É*; B: *É* (=? *bīt*).
39. B: *na-ki-du*(!).
40. B: *èr-ra*{-*ra*}.
41. A, B: *ušakšidušu*.
42. B: *nizmassu*(!).
43. B: *mu'āter*(!).
44. Roth: <*E*>-*meslam*.

who covers the chapels of Aya with greenery,
who exalts the shrine of Ebabbar to look like a home in heaven.

**(P8)** I am a hero, who shows favour to Larsa,
who makes Ebabbar anew for Shamash his helper,
the lord, who makes Uruk come alive,
and secures plentiful supplies of water for its people,
who raises up high the pinnacles of Eanna,
who heaps up luxury for Anu and Ishtar;
a shade for the land,
who gathers together the scattered people of Isin,
who spreads riches in the shrine of Egalmah.

**(P9)** I am the most fearsome[4] of kings,
the kinsman of Zababa,
who establishes Kish as a residence,
who makes Emeteursag shine on every side,
who organizes the magnificent rituals for Ishtar,
and the guardian of the temple of Hursagkalamma.

**(P10)** I am the net that traps the enemy,
the one with Erra as his friend,
who allowed him to achieve his ambition,
the one who extended Kutû, and enlarged E-Meslam in different ways.

---

4. Lit. 'the dragon of the kings'.

*rīmum kadrum, munakkip zā'irī*
*narām Tutu, murīš Barsippa*

**P11 (III:13-23)**
*na'dum, la mupparkûm ana Ezida*
*ilu*[45] *šarrī, mudē igigallim*
*mušaddil* [46]*mēreštim ša* Dilbat, mugarrin karê ana Uraš gašrim*

**P12 (III:24-35)**
*bēlum, simat ḫaṭṭim u agêm*
*ša ušaklilušu*[47] *erištum Mama*
*mukīn uṣurātim ša Keš*
*mudeššī mākalī ellūtim ana Nintu*[48]

**P13 (III:36-54)**
*muštālum gitmālum, šā'im*[49] *mirītim u mašqītim ana Lagaš u Giršîm*
*mukīl*[50] *nindabê rabûtim ana Eninnu,*
*mutammeḫ ayyābī, migir Telītim*[51]
*mušaklil* [52]*tērētim ša* Sugal*[53]
*muḫaddi libbi Ištar.*

**P14 (III:55-64)**
*rubûm ellum, ša nīš qātišu Adad idû*
*munēḫ libbi Adad*
*qurādim in*[54] *Bīt Karkara*[55]
*muštakkin simātim ina Eudgalgal.*

---

45. Stele: *i-lu*; A: *i-li*; B, E: *ì-lí;* Roth emends: <*šubat*> *ili*, the dwelling of the 'god of kings'; see p. 140 note 1 for a full discussion of the meaning of this difficult phrase.

46. E: *mīrišti.*

47. A: *ušaklilušum.*

48. Stele, A: *DINGIR nin-tu*; B: *DINGIR be-let ì-lí*; D: *DINGIR MAḪ* (= *bēlet ilī*).

49. A, D: *šākin.*

50. B, D(?): *mukīn.*

51. Perhaps to be read as a name *Telītu.*

52. A: *tērēt.*

53. Otherwise read *Zabalam*; Roth: *Zabala.*

54. A: + *a-lim* (instead of determinative *URU*).

55. Roth: *ina Karkara.*

I am a raging ox that tosses his opponent,
the one whom Tutu loves, and who makes Borsippa rejoice,

**(P11)** the devoted one who never neglects Ezida.
I am the god of the kings, possessing deep wisdom,
who develops land to be ploughed in Dilbat,
who fills up the granaries for mighty Urash;

**(P12)** the lord with symbolic crown and sceptre,
which Mama the wise goddess completed for him,
who brought the plans for Kesh to fulfilment,
who established the sacred food for Nintu;

**(P13)** the perfect arbitrator,
who designates pastures and the watering places for Lagash and Girsu,
who sends magnificent food offerings to Eninnu,
who grasps hold of the enemy;
the darling of Tellitum[5], who fulfils the oracles for Sugal,
the one who makes the heart of Ishtar rejoice.

**(P14)** I am the sacred prince,
whose raised hand[6] Adad acknowledges,
who quietens the heart of Adad as he fights in Bit Karkara,
who maintains the ceremonials properly in E-udgalgal.

---

5. The name means 'the capable lady', an epithet of Ishtar.
6. The raising of one's hand denotes an attitude of prayer.

**P15 (III:65–IV:6)**
*šarrum, nādin napištim ana Adab, āšer*[56] *bīt*[57] *Emaḫ*
*etel šarrī, qabal la maḫārim*
*šû*[58] *iqīšu napšatam*[59] *ana*[60] *Maškan-šāpir*
*mušešqi*[61] *nuḫšim ana Meslam*[62].

**P16**[63] **(IV:7-22)**
*emqum muttabbilum*[64]
*šû*[65] *ikšudu nagab uršim*
[66]*mušpazzir nišī Malgīm*[67] *in*[68] *karašîm*
*mušaršidu šubātišin*[69]* *in*[70] *nuḫšim*
*ana Ea u Damgalnunna*[71] *mušarbû*[72] *šarrūtišu*
*dāriš išīmu*[73] *zībī ellūtim*

**P17 (IV:23-37)**
*ašared šarrī, mukanniš*[74] *dadmē*[75] *nār Purattim*
[76]*ittum Dagan bānîšu*[77].

---

56. A: *wāšer.*
57. B: ø.
58. B: *ša.*
59. B: *napšatim.*
60. A: + *ālim* instead of *KI* determinative.
61. A: *mušašqi*; B: *mu-še-eš*[-*še*]-*qi.*
62. A, B: *É.mes-lam*, followed by Roth.
63. This passage omitted by A, C and F; see Introduction.
64. B: *muttabbilam.*
65. A, B: *ša.*
66. A, B, C: ø.
67. Roth: *Malgium.*
68. Roth: *ina.*
69. B: *šubātišina.*
70. A: *ina.*
71. Stele: *dam.gal.nun.na*; A: *dam.ki.na*; B: *dam.ki.en.na*; perhaps follow reading of Roth: *Enki u Damkina.*
72. A: *mušarbi.*
73. B: *ia-ši-im*(!).
74. A: *mukannišu.*
75. A: *āšib.*
76. Stele: *ì-tum*; A: *it-tu-um Dagan*; B: *DINGIR. ÍD*(!) *u Dagan.*
77. A: *bānu.*

**(P15)** I am the king who gives Adab its life,
the controller of the temple of Emah,
the most eminent of kings, unrivalled in the strife;
the gift he gives to Mashkan-shapir is life,
and for Meslam he provides an abundant water-supply.

**(P16)** He is the clever one who gets things done;
who reaches the depths of wisdom,
who protects the people of Malgium from catastrophe,
who secures their habitations with plentiful supplies,
who decrees that sacred offerings always be made to Ea and Damgal-nunna,
the ones who have made his kingship magnificent,

**(P17)** the leader of kings, who controls the Euphrates communities
under the guidance of Dagan his creator.

*šû*[78] *igmilu nišī Mera*[79] *u Tuttul*[80]
*rubûm na'dum*
*munawwer pani*[81] *Tišpak*[82]
*šākin*[83] *mākalī ellūtim*[84] *ana Ninazu*

**P18**[85] **(IV:38-52)**
[86]*šāṭip nišīšu in pušqim*
*mukinnu*[87] *išdīšin*[88] *qerbum*[89] *Bābilim šulmāniš*
*rē'î nišī, ša epšētušu eli Ištar ṭāba**
*mukinni*[90] *Ištar ina Eulmaš*[91], *qerbum*[92] *Akkadim*[93] *ribītim*

**P19 (IV:53-59)**
*mušēpī*[94] *kīnātim, mušūšer*[95] *ammi*[96]
*mutêr lamassišu*[97] *damiqtim ana*[98] *ālim Aššur, mušeppi*[99] *nābiḫī*[100]

78. B: *ša.*
79. A: *Mari*; B: *Meri.*
80. A: *Tutu.* B: *Tultul.*
81. B: *pan.*
82. B: usually has *DINGIR.INANNA* for *DINGIR.SUḪ* (= *Tišpak*).
83. A, B: *muštakin.*
84. B: *ellūtu.*
85. This passage omitted by A and F; see Introduction.
86. A, F: ø.
87. B: *mukīn.*
88. B: *išdīšina.*
89. B: *qereb.*
90. B: *mukīn.*
91. A: *Ulmaš.*
92. A, C: *qerbu,* followed by Roth.
93. Roth: *Akkade.*
94. B, C: *mušarbi*(?).
95. A, B: *mušešer.* C: *mušišer.*
96. A: *ḫammi.*
97. Stele: *DINGIR.LAMMA-šu*; A: *la-ma-sí-šu*; B: *DINGIR.LAMMA-su.*
98. A: + *ālim.*
99. B: *mušeb*(!).
100. A: *na-bi-i*; B: *na-bi-iḫ*(?).

He is the one who shows favour
to the inhabitants of Mari and Tuttul,
the devout prince,
who brightens the face of the god Tishpak,
and ensures that pure food is presented to the goddess Ninazu;

**(P18)** the deliverer of his people from affliction,
who provides secure foundations for them
in the midst of Babylon;
the shepherd of the people,
whose achievements bring pleasure to Ishtar,
who sets Ishtar in the E-ulmash within the centre of the city of Akkad;

**(P19)** the one who demonstrates justice,
who guides the population aright,
who brings back the protective statues to Asshur,
who silences the objectors;

**P20[101] (IV:60-66 )**
[102]*šarrum, ša ina Ninua*[103] *ina Emesmes ušūpi'u*[104] *mê*[105] *Ištar na'dum, muštēmiqum*[106] *ana ilī rabûtim*[107]*.

**P21 (IV:67–V:13)**
*liplippim ša Sumula'il*[108]
*aplum dannum*[109] *ša Sîn-muballiṭ*
*zērum dārium*[110] *ša šarrūtim*
*šarrum dannum*[111], *šamšu Bābilim*
*mušēṣi nūrim*[112] *ana māt Šumerim u Akkadîm*
*šarrum muštešmi kibrāt*[113] *arba'im*
*migir Ištar*[114] *anāku.*

**P22 (V:14-25)**
*inūma Marduk*[115] *ana šutēšur nišī mātim ūsim šūḫuzim*[116] *uwa'eranni, kittam u mīšaram ina pī mātim aškun, šīr nišī uṭīb, inūmišu*[117]...

## THE LAWS

**L1 (V:26-31)**
*šumma awīlum awīlam ubbirma nērtam elišu iddīma la uktīnšu, mubbiršu iddâk.*

---

101. This passage omitted by A and C; see Introduction.
102. A, C: ø.
103. B: unclear.
104. B: *ušēpu*; C: *ušīpu*.
105. B: *mēsu*(!).
106. B: *muštēmiq*.
107. B: *rabi'ūtim*.
108. B: *su<-mu>-la-il*.
109. F: *eṭlu*(!).
110. A, B, F: *dāru*.
111. E: *eṭlum*, see above *dannum/eṭlum ša Sinmuballiṭ*.
112. B: *nūrium*(!).
113. B: *kibrāti*.
114. B: *ÉN.LÍL*.
115. B: *ÉN.LÍL*.
116. B: *šūḫuzu*.
117. A: *ina ūmišu*.

**(P20)** the king who made famous the rites of Ishtar
in Nineveh and E-mesmes;
the devout one who holds intercourse with the mighty gods.

**(P21)** I am the descendant of Sumu-la-il,
the mighty heir of Sin-muballit,
with royal ancestors for generations; the mighty king,
the sun of Babylon who shines all over the lands of Sumer and Akkad;
the king who has made the four parts of the world listen;
the one beloved of Ishtar.

**(P22)** And so when Marduk urged me to direct the people of the land
to adopt correct behaviour,
I made the land speak with justice and truth,
and improved the welfare of the people.
Accordingly therefore:

## THE LAWS

## Unsubstantiated Allegations (L1–5)

### Homicide

**(1)** If a man has made allegations[7] against another man, and he has laid a charge of homicide[8] against him but is unable to substantiate his guilt[9], the one who made the allegations against him shall be killed.

---

7. The verb *ubburu,* which will be cited thus in *CAD* but in *AHw* occurs under *abāru* III, is used here in a special sense. Elsewhere in Akkadian it means 'to encompass, to embrace'; for references see *AHw*.

8. Lit. 'to throw murder'; another example of an idiomatic expression.

9. Since *kunnu* really means 'fix' the suffix would naturally refer to the 'charge of murder', i.e *nērtam*; but since this is a feminine noun the suffix must refer to 'another gentleman', i.e. *awīlam*. The idea of 'fixing someone' in the sense of 'demonstrating someone's guilt' also appears to be idiomatic.

**L2 (V:33-56)**

*šumma awīlum kišpī eli awīlim iddīma la uktīnšu, ša elišu kišpū nadû ana Id illak, Id išalliamma.*
*šumma Id iktašassu, mubbiršu bīssu itabbal.*
*šumma awīlam šuāti Id ūtebbibaššuma*[118] *, ištalmam*[119].
*ša elišu kišpī iddû, iddâk.*
*ša Id išliam, bīt mubbirišu itabbal.*

**L3–4 (V:57–VI:5)**

**(3)** *šumma awīlum ina dīnim ana šībūt*[120] *sarrātim ūṣiamma, awat iqbû la uktīn,*
*šumma dīnum šû dīn napištim, awīlum šû iddâk.*
**(4)** *šumma ana šībūt še'im u kaspim ūṣiam, aran*[121] *dīnim*[122] *šuāti ittanašši*[123].

**L5 (VI:6-30)**

*šumma dayyānum dīnam idīn, purussâm iprus, kunukkam ušēzib, warkānumma dīnšu ītene, dayyānam šuāti ina dīn idīnu enêm ukannūšuma, rugummâm ša ina dīnim šuāti ibaššû adi 12-šu inaddin. u ina puḫrim ina kussî dayyānūtišu ušetbûšuma, ul itârma, itti dayyānī ina dīnim ul uššab.*

---

118. r: *ūtabbibaššuma.*
119. r: *ištalma.*
120. F: *šebūt.*
121. r: *rugummānē*(?).
122. r: ø, broken, but perhaps restore [*dīnim*] with stele; see Roth.
123. r: *ippal.*

**Witchcraft**

**(2)** If a man has laid a charge of witchcraft against another man but cannot substantiate his guilt, the person against whom witchcraft has been alleged shall go to the River[10] and jump into the River.

And if the mighty river overpowers him, the one who laid the allegations against him shall take possession of his house.

But if the River cleanses that man from his guilt[11] he shall go away restored[12].

The one who laid a charge of witchcraft against him shall be put to death; the one who jumped into the River shall take possession of the house of the one who made the allegations against him.

**In a trial**

**(3)** If a man has appeared with false evidence in a trial, and he cannot substantiate the story he has told, that man shall be put to death if the trial carries the death penalty[13].

**(4)** If he has appeared with evidence involving grain or silver, he will always have to pay[14] the penalty in that trial.

**A vacillating judge**

**(5)** If a judge has conducted a trial, given a verdict, had a seal placed on the document, but some time later modifies his verdict, they can show that that judge is guilty of changing the verdict he has reached, and he shall pay 12 times the amount of the loss which had occasioned that trial.

Furthermore they shall have him removed from being a judge in the assembly and from his place on the legal bench[15]; he shall not go back and sit with the judges in any other trial.

---

10. The word is prefixed in this law with the ideogram for a deity; any special significance of this may be conveniently suggested by the use of a capital letter in English.

11. The emphatic repetition of the direct object by the resumptive pronoun can be expressed in English by introducing an associated indirect object.

12. The verb *šalāmu* is used elsewhere in CH to indicate a healed fracture.

13. Lit. 'a trial of life'; the Akkadian word is cognate with the Hebrew word for 'soul'.

14. The infix *-tan-* in verbs seems here to indicate 'normal practice' rather than 'repeated action'.

15. Lit. 'the seat of his judging'.

**L6 (VI:31-40)**
*šumma awīlum makkūr ilim u*[124] *ekallim išriq, awīlum šû iddâk, u ša šurqam ina qātišu imḫuru iddâk.*

**L7–8 (VI:41-69)**
**(7)** *šumma awīlum lu*[125] *kaspam lu ḫurāṣam lu wardam lu amtam lu alpam lu immeram lu imēram u lu mimma šumšu ina qāt*[126] *mār awīlim u lu warad awīlim balum šībī u riksātim ištām u lu ana maṣṣarūtim imḫur, awīlum šû šarrāq iddâk.*
**(8)** *šumma awīlum lu alpam lu immeram lu imēram lu šaḫâm u lu eleppam išriq,*
*šumma ša ilim šumma ša ekallim, adi 30-šu inaddin.*
*šumma ša muškēnim, adi 10-šu iriab.*
*šumma šarrāqānum ša nadānim la išu, iddâk.*

**L9–13 (VI:70–VIII:24)**
**(9)** *šumma awīlum ša mimmûšu ḫalqu mimmāšu ḫalqam ina qāti awīlim iṣṣabat,*
*awīlum ša ḫulqum ina qātišu ṣabtu 'nādinānummi iddinam, maḫar šībīmi ašām' iqtabi, u bēl ḫulqim 'šībī mudē ḫulqiyami lublam' iqtabi, šāyyimānum nādin iddinušum u šībī ša ina maḫrišunu išāmu itbalam u bēl ḫulqim šībī mudē ḫulqišu itbalam,*
*dayyānū awâtišunu immarūma.*
*šībū ša maḫrišunu šīmum iššāmu u šībū*[127] *mudē ḫulqim mudūssunu maḫar ilim iqabbûma.*

---

124. F: *ša.*
125. F: ø passim.
126. I: *qāti.*
127. r: *šibī*(!)

## Theft (L6–25)

### PROPERTY (L6–13)

**Official property**

**(L6)** If a man has stolen property from a god or from a temple[16] that man shall be killed.

Furthermore, anyone who has acquired stolen goods from him shall be killed.

**Undocumented sales of possessions**

**(L7)** If a man has bought silver, gold, a slave, a slave-girl, an ox, a sheep, a donkey or anything else from a man's son or a man's slave without properly witnessed receipts, even if he has accepted them just to look after them, that man is a thief, and shall be killed.

**(L8)** If a man has stolen an ox, or a sheep, or a donkey, or a pig, or a boat he shall pay thirty times its value if it belongs to a god or a temple[17] and repay ten times its value if it belongs to a workman. If that thief does not have enough to pay he shall be killed.

**An allegedly documented sale**

**(L9)** If, after he has lost something, a man has discovered what he has lost in the possession of another man, but the man in whose possession the goods are found has said, 'Someone gave it to me officially; I made the purchase with witnesses present,' and the owner of the property has said, 'But I could bring witnesses who know it is my property,' and the purchaser has brought the man who gave it to him and the witnesses who were present when he purchased it, and the owner of the property has brought the witnesses who know it is his property, then the judges shall investigate what they have to say.

The witnesses in whose presence the purchase was made and the

---

16. *ekallum* may refer to the temple or to the palace. Translators have been inclined to see here a distinction between 'church' and 'state' (see Meek) but it is equally possible that the distinction is made between property from the divine shrine and that from the temple precincts. In any event, the same penalty is due.

17. Alternatively, 'the palace'. The crimes alluded to in L6 and L7 are similar, but the death penalty is invoked only in the case of missing documentation (L6). Presumably it should not simply be concluded that an ox, sheep or donkey stolen from an *awīlum*, for which the death penalty is invoked (L6), is a less serious crime than the same object stolen from an *ilum*, for which restitution can be made (L7).

*nādinānum šarrāq iddâk*
*bēl ḫulqim ḫuluqšu ileqqe.*
*šāyyimānum ina bīt nādinānim kasap išqulu ileqqe.*
**(10)** *šumma šāyyimānum nādin*[128]*iddinušum u šībī ša ina maḫrišunu išāmu*[129] *la itbalam bēl ḫulqimma šībī mudē ḫulqišu itbalam, šāyyimānum šarrāq iddâk.*
*bēl ḫulqim ḫuluqšu ileqqe.*
**(11)** *šumma bēl ḫulqim šībī mudē ḫulqišu la itbalam, sār tuššamma iddī*(!)[130], *iddâk.*
**(12)** *šumma nādinānum ana šīmtim ittalak, šāyyimānum ina bīt nādinānim rugummē*[131] *dīnim šuāti adi ḫamšīšu ileqqe.*
**(13)** *šumma awīlum šû šībūšu la qerbu, dayyānū adannam ana šeššet warḫī išakkanūšumma, šumma ina šeššet warḫī šībīšu la irdeam, awīlum šû sār, aran dīnim šuāti ittanašši.*

**L14 (VIII:25-29)**
*šumma awīlum mār awīlim ṣeḫram ištariq, iddâk.*

**L15 (VIII:30-36)**
*šumma awīlum lu warad ekallim lu amat ekallim lu warad muškēnim lu amat muškēnim abullam uštēṣi, iddâk.*

**L16 (VIII:37-48)**
*šumma awīlum lu wardam lu amtam ḫalqam ša ekallim u lu muškēnim ina bītišu irtaqīma ana šisīt nāgirim la uštēṣiam, bēl bītim šû iddâk.*

---

128. r: *nādinān,* followed by Roth.
129. r: *šīmu iššamu*, i.e. passive.
130. Stele: *idkē*(!); r: *iqbī*; read *iddī*, following *BAL* and Roth.
131. r: (?)*rugummāne.*

witnesses who know the property shall state what they know in the presence of god.

Since the man who gave it to him was the thief he shall be killed.

The owner of the property shall take his property.

The purchaser shall take the silver he has paid from the house of the man who gave it to him.

**(10)** If the purchaser has not brought along the man who gave it to him or the witnesses in whose presence he made the purchase, but the owner of the property has brought along witnesses who know it is his, it is the purchaser who is the thief and he shall be killed.

The owner of the property shall take his property.

**(11)** If the owner of the property has not brought along the witnesses who know it is his, he is the liar.

He has perpetrated corruption and shall be killed.

**(12)** If the man who gave it has gone to his destiny, the purchaser shall take five times the value of the damages in this case from his house.

**(13)** If the witnesses for that man are not available the judges shall fix a date six months hence for him, and if he has not collected his witnesses within the six months that man will normally have to pay[18] the penalty in this case himself, for he is a liar.

## KIDNAP (L14–20)

### A child

**(14)** If a man has stolen another man's small child, he shall be killed.

### a slave

**(15)** If a man has taken a slave or a slave-girl from the palace or from a workman outside the city gate, he shall be killed.

### concealment

**(16)** If a man has hidden in his house a slave or slave-girl who has disappeared from the temple or from a workman and does not produce them when the alarm is raised, the owner of that house shall be killed.

---

18. The *-tan-* form of the verb is usually understood as indicating a repeated action. Clearly here the penalty has to be paid only once. A similar nuance may be intended, such as that this is the regularly occurring punishment for such a crime; using 'normally have to' in English to some extent conveys this idea.

**L17–20 (VIII:49–IX:13)**

**(17)** *šumma awīlum lu wardam lu amtam ḫalqam ina ṣērim iṣbatma ana bēlišu irtediaššu, 2 šiqil kaspam bēl wardim inaddiššum.*
**(18)** *šumma wardum šû bēlšu la izzakar, ana ekallim ireddīšu. warkassu ipparrasma ana bēlišu utarrūšu.*
**(19)** *šumma wardam šuāti ina bītišu iktalāšu, warka wardum ina qātišu ittaṣbat, awīlum šû iddâk.*
**(20)** *šumma wardum ina qāt ṣābitānišu iḫtaliq, awīlum šû ana bēl wardim nīš ilim izakkarma ūtaššar.*

**L21 (IX:14-21)**

*šumma awīlum bītam ipluš, ina pani pilšim šuāti idukkūšuma iḫallalūšu.*

**L22–24 (IX:22-50)**

**(22)** *šumma awīlum ḫubtam iḫbutma ittaṣbat, awīlum šû iddâk.*
**(23)** *šumma ḫabbātum la ittaṣbat awīlum ḫabtum mimmâšu*[132] *ḫalqam maḫar ilim ubârma ālum*[133] *u rabiānum, ša ina erṣetišunu u paṭṭišunu ḫubtum iḫḫabtu, mimmâšu ḫalqam iriabbūšum*[134].
**(24)** *šumma napištum*[135] *ālum u rabiānum 1 mana kaspam ana nišīšu išaqqalū*[136].

132. r: *mimmūšu*.
133. r: (?)*ālu*.
134. r: (?)*iriabbūšu*.
135. J: (?)*napištum*, but reading not completely certain.
136. J: (?)*išaqqalū*, but reading not completely certain.

**Discovering runaway slaves**

**(17)** If a man has found a lost slave or slave-girl in the open country and has brought them back to their owner, their owner shall give him two shekels of silver.

**(18)** If that slave will not declare the name of his owner, he shall bring him back to the temple authorities where his record can be examined, and they shall return him to his owner.

**(19)** If he has held that slave captive in his house and later the slave is found in his possession, that man shall be killed.

**(20)** If a slave has escaped from the possession of his captor, the man involved shall solemnly swear by the god to the slave's owner and shall be innocent.

## ROBBERY (L21–25)

**Breaking and entering**

**(21)** If a man has smashed a way into a house, they shall kill him by hanging him just where he broke in.

**Robbery detected and undetected**

**(22)** If a man has committed robbery and is caught, that man shall be killed.

**(23)** If a criminal has not been caught, the injured man shall declare in the presence of god what he has lost and the citizens of the state or the leader of the province[19] where the crime was committed shall repay to him anything he has lost.

**(24)** If someone is killed, the citizens or the leaders shall pay one mana of silver to his people[20].

---

19. Presumably if the criminal was caught within the bounds of another city the elders of that place would be responsible for satisfying the law. But if he were caught in the open country, provincial officials would be required to act, since no one city could be held responsible.

20. Since the word *nišū*, 'people' rather than *kinātu*, 'kin' is used it is possible that the leaders of one community would pay the money to the leaders of another, and that they in turn would distribute it to satisfy the immediate needs of the dependants of the murdered victim.

**L25 (IX:51-65)**

*šumma ina bīt awīlim išātum innapiḫma awīlum ša ana bullîm*[137] *illiku ana numāt bēl bītim īnšu iššīma numāt bēl bītim ilteqe*(!)[138] , *awīlum šû ana išātim šuāti innaddi.*

**L26 (IX:66–X:12)**

*šumma lu*[139] *rēdûm u*[140] *lu*[141] *bā'irum, ša ana ḫarrān šarrim*[142] *alākšu qabû*[143] *la illik*[144] *u*[145] *lu agram īgurma, pūḫšu iṭṭarad,*[146] *lu rēdûm u*[147] *lu bā'irum šû iddâk.*
*munaggiršu bīssu itabbal.*

**L27–29 (X:13-50)**

**(27)** *šumma lu*[148] *rēdûm u*[149] *lu*[150] *bā'irum ša ina dannat šarrim turru*[151] *warkišu*[152] *eqelšu u kirāšu*[153] *ana šanîm*[154] *iddinūma ilikšu ittalak. šumma ittūramma ālšu iktašdam*[155] *eqelšu u kirāšu utarrūšumma, šûma ilikšu illak.*
**(28)** *šumma lu rēdûm u lu bā'irum, ša ina dannat šarrim turru mārušu ilkam alākam ile'i, eqlum u kirûm innaddiššumma.*
*ilik abišu illak.*
**(29)** *šumma mārušu ṣeḫerma ilik abišu alākam la ile'i, šalušti eqlim u kirîm ana ummišu innaddinma, ummašu urabbāšu.*

---

137. r: *išāti bullī.*
138. Stele: *il-te-di*; *BAL*: for /*di*/ read /*qe*/, following J and r: *ilteqe*; followed also by Roth.
139. J, r: ø.
140. J: ø.
141. r: ø.
142. J: *šar-ri-a'*(!).
143. r: *qabûma.*
144. r: *illiku*(!).
145. r: ø.
146. J: *ittarad.*
147. J: ø.
148. J: ø.
149. J: ø.
150. r: ø.
151. r: *turruma.*
152. J: *arkišu.*
153. r: +*u bīssu.*
154. r: *šānîmma.*
155. r: *iktašda.*

**Looting**
**(25)** If there has been an outbreak of fire in a man's house and a man who has gone to put it out catches sight of the private possessions of the owner of the house and takes them, that man shall be thrown into that same fire.

## Agriculture

### OBLIGATIONS OF STATE OFFICIALS (L26–41)

**Impersonation**
**(26)** If a soldier or a trapper has not gone on a royal expedition after being commanded to do so but has hired a labourer and sent him as his substitute, that soldier or trapper shall be killed.

The one who was hired by him shall take over his house.

**Substitute labour**
**(27)** If they have assigned the field and orchard of a soldier or trapper who ought to have returned[21] with the royal fighting troops to someone else and that person takes over his duties, but then he does manage to return and reach his city, they shall give him back his field and his orchard, and he shall assume his own duties.
**(28)** If the son of a soldier or trapper who ought to have returned with the royal fighting troops is able to assume his duties, the field and the orchard shall be given to him and he shall assume his father's duties.
**(29)** If his son is too small and unable to assume his father's duties, one third part of the field or the orchard shall be given to his mother while she is rearing him.[22]

---

21. Usually the word *turru* has been translated here as 'he has been detained' (so Meek; see also *BL*, Finet, and Roth), while later in the sentence *utarrušumma* has been translated 'he has returned'. Both words clearly come from the same root and the same verbal theme. It is preferable to translate similar words similarly in such close contexts and I have therefore assumed that the stative verb is capable of including the nuance 'ought to'.

22. Perhaps this last clause expresses the purpose of the previous one, as Meek suggests, but then the question has to be raised why the single mother could not have the benefit of all her husband's land. There may well be a recognition here that a woman should not be expected to cope with the whole of a man's work at the same time as rearing a child.

**L30–31 (X:51–XI:12)**

**(30)** *šumma lu rēdûm u lu bā'irum eqelšu kirāšu u bīssu ina pani ilkim iddīma uddappir, šanûm warkišu eqelšu kirāšu u bīssu iṣbatma, šalaš šanātim ilikšu ittalak. šumma itūramma, eqelšu kirāšu u bīssu irriš. ul innaddiššum*[156].

*ša iṣṣabtuma*[157] *ilikšu ittalku*[158] *šûma illak.*

**(31)** *šumma šattam ištiatma*[159] *uddappirma ittūram, eqelšu*[160] *kirāšu u bīssu innaddiššumma*[161] *šûma*[162] *ilikšu illak.*

**L32 (XI:13-38)**

*šumma lu rēdûm u lu bā'irum, ša ina ḫarrān šarrim turru, tamkārum ipṭuraššuma ālšu uštakšidaššu,*

*šumma ina bītišu ša paṭārim*[163] *ibašši, šûma ramanšu ipaṭṭar.*

*šumma ina bītišu ša paṭārišu la ibašši, ina bīt il ālišu ippaṭṭar.*

*šumma ina bīt il ālišu ša paṭārišu la ibašši, ekallum ipaṭṭaršu*(!)[164] *eqelšu kirāšu u bīssu ana ipṭerišu*[165] *ul innaddin.*

**L33 (XI:39-50)**

*šumma lu*[166] *ša ḫaṭṭātim u*[167] *lu*[168] *laputtûm ṣāb nisḫātim*[169] *irtaši u lu ana ḫarrān šarrim agram pūḫam imḫurma irtede*[170] *lu ša ḫaṭṭātim u*[171] *lu laputtûm šû iddâk.*

---

156. J: *inaddinšum.*
157. J: *iṣṣabtušu*(!).
158. J: *ittalka.*
159. J: *išteatat*(!).
160. J: ø.
161. J: *innaddinšumma.*
162. J: *šumma*(!) .
163. J: *paṭārišu.*
164. Stele: *i-pa-aṭ-ṭa-ri-šu*; *BAL*: for /ri/ read /ar/, following r: *ipaṭṭaršu*, followed also by Roth; J: *ipaṭṭaršum*(!).
165. r: *ipṭirišu.*
166. J and r: ø.
167. J: ø.
168. r: ø.
169. r: *ana nisiḫtim.*
170. r: *irde.*
171. r: ø.

**Neglect of duty**

**(30)** If the soldier or the trapper has been lazy with regard to his duties concerning his field, his orchard or his house, and has been away and someone else has then decided to take possession of his field, his orchard or his house and has assumed his duties for three years, but then he returns and requires them back, neither his field, nor his orchard nor his house shall be given to him.

The one who has taken them over and assumed the duties shall continue to do so himself.

**(31)** If he has been away for one year only and has returned, his field, his orchard and his house shall be given to him.

He shall perform his own duties again.

**A ransomed servant**

**(32)** If a merchant has paid a ransom for one particular soldier or trapper who ought to have returned from a royal expedition and enabled him to get back to his city, he shall pay back the ransom himself provided there is silver for ransom in his house; if there is no silver for ransom in his house he shall be ransomed by the temple in his city; if the temple in his city has no silver for ransom the palace shall pay the ransom.

But neither his field, his orchard or his house should be given for his ransom price.

**Deportees**

**(33)** If a captain or inspector has taken a group of deportees[23] , or has hired a mercenary and sent him as a substitute on a royal expedition, such a captain or inspector shall be killed.

---

23. The etymology of these terms is not quite clear. The sign PA has been interpreted as *ḫaṭṭu*, 'sceptre' and understood as indicating some kind of officer. PA.PA. is usually translated 'captain'; Sumerian NU.BÀNDA becomes a loan word in Akkadian as *laputtû* , 'inspector'(see *CAD*, *laputtû* [L99b]); and *ṣāb nisḫatim*, from *nasāḫu*, ' to deport' could indicate 'prisoners of war', as suggested here, or 'deserters', as suggested by *CAD*, *nisiḫtu*, 3; Roth: 'If either a captain or a sergeant should recruit (!) deserters'.

**L34–39 (XI:51–XII:38)**

**(34)** *šumma lu ša ḫaṭṭātim u lu*[172] *laputtûm numāt rēdîm ilteqe, rēdiam iḫtabal rēdiam* [173]*ana igrim ittadin* rēdiam ina dīnim ana dannim ištarak qīšti šarrum ana rēdîm iddinu*[174] *ilteqe lu ša ḫaṭṭātim u*[175] *lu laputtûm šû iddâk.*

**(35)** *šumma awīlum liātim*[176] *u ṣēnī ša šarrum ana rēdîm iddinu ina qāti rēdîm ištām, ina kaspišu ītelli.*

**(36)** *eqlum kirûm u bītum ša rēdîm bā'irim u nāši biltim ana kaspim ul innaddin*(!)[177].

**(37)** *šumma awīlum eqlam kirâm u bītam ša rēdîm bā'irim u nāši biltim ištām ṭuppašu iḫḫeppe u*[178] *ina kaspišu*[179] *ītelli.*
*eqlum kirûm u bītum ana bēlišu itâr.*

**(38)** *rēdûm bā'irum u nāši biltim ina eqlim kirîm u bītim ša ilkišu ana aššatišu u mārtišu ul išaṭṭar u ana e'iltišu ul inaddin.*

**(39)** *ina eqlim, kirîm u bītim ša išammuma iraššû ana aššatišu u mārtišu išaṭṭar u ana e'iltišu inaddin.*

**L40 (XII:39-48)**

*nadītum tamkārum u ilkum aḫûm eqelšu kirāšu u bīssu ana kaspim inaddin. šāyyimānum ilik eqlim kirîm u bītim ša išammu illak.*

---

172. r: ø.
173. r: ø ...*.
174. r: + *ina qāti rēdîm.*
175. r: ø.
176. r: (?)*liātim.*
177. Stele: *i-na-ad-di-in = inaddin* , G prs. of *nadānu*; *BAL*: for /*i*/ read /*in*/ = *innaddin* N prs.; r: *innadin* = N prt.
178. r: ø.
179. r: *kaspī.*

**The property of a soldier**

**(34)** If a captain or an inspector has taken the private property of a soldier, has treated a soldier unfairly, has allowed a soldier to be hired, has offered a soldier to a powerful man in a court, or has taken from a soldier a presentation given by the king, such a captain or inspector shall be killed.[24]

**(35)** If a man has bought from a soldier cattle or sheep[25] which the king had given to the soldier, he shall surrender his silver.[26]

**The real estate of a soldier, trapper or official tenant**

**(36)** The field, orchard and house of a soldier, trapper or official tenant shall not be exchanged for silver.[27]

**(37)** If a man has purchased the field, orchard or house of a soldier, trapper or official tenant, the sale document shall be broken and he shall surrender his silver.

The field, orchard or house shall return to its owner.

**(38)** A soldier, trapper or official tenant shall not donate to his wife or to his daughter a field, orchard or house which is his official property, nor shall he exchange it for any debt.

**(39)** Any field, orchard or house which he may purchase and possess he may donate to his wife or daughter or give it in exchange for debt.

**The real estate of a temple-woman**

**(40)** A temple-woman, a merchant and a tenant with special duties may exchange their field, their orchard or their house for silver.

The purchaser shall perform the duties for the field, orchard or house which he buys.

---

24. It is usual to assume that *šû* is a demonstrative pronoun linked to both the alternative subjects, and as such is a variation on the simpler *awīlum šû iddāk*. Or it may be a pronoun in parenthesis to the alternative subjects of the passive verb, and could then be translated 'whether a captain or an inspector, he shall be killed'; in which case CH could be seen to apply the law (in certain cases) without regard to a culprit's social position.

25. *ṣēnû* means smaller animals in general, and would include goats as well as sheep; cf. Roth.

26. The subject of the protasis (*awīlum*) is not the same as the subject of the apodosis (*rēdûm*).

27. This sentence summarizes the principle behind the laws in this section. It has already been stated in slightly different words at the end of L32, but here the statement seems to introduce the next law rather than summarize the preceding one.

**L41 (XII:49-62)**

*šumma awīlum eqlam kirâm u bītam ša rēdîm bā'irim u nāši biltim upīḫ u niplātim iddin, rēdûm bā'irum u nāši biltim ana eqlišu kirîšu u bītišu itâr u niplātim ša innadnušum itabbal.*

**L42–44 (XII:63–XIII:34)**

**(42)** *šumma awīlum eqlam ana errēšūtim ušēṣīma ina eqlim še'am la uštabši, ina eqlim šiprim la epēšim ukannūšuma še'am kīma itēšu ana bēl eqlim inaddin.*

**(43)** *šumma eqlam la īrišma ittadi, še'am kīma itēšu ana bēl eqlim inaddin.*

*u eqlam ša iddû mayyārī imaḫḫaṣ*[180] *išakkakma ana bēl eqlim utâr.*

**(44)** *šumma awīlum kankallam ana šalaš šanātim ana teptītim*[181] *ušēṣīma aḫšu iddīma eqlam la iptete*[182] *ina rebûtim šattim eqlam mayyārī imaḫḫaṣ imarrar u išakkakma ana bēl eqlim utâr.*

*u ana 1 burum 10*[183] *kur še'am imaddad.*

---

180. r: + *imarrar u.*
181. r: *tiptīti.*
182. r: *ipti.*
183. r: (?)60.

**Bartering with real estate**

**(41)** If a man has taken in exchange a field, orchard or house of a soldier, a trapper or an official tenant and has paid compensation, the soldier, trapper or official tenant shall go back to his field, orchard or house and shall keep the compensation that was paid to him.

## AGRICULTURAL TENANTS (L42–56)

**A lazy tenant**

**(42)** If a man has rented a field to be cultivated but does not produce grain from the field, they shall charge him with not having worked the field, and he shall pay the same amount of grain to the owner of the field as his neighbour does.

**(43)** If he has abandoned the field without having cultivated it at all, he shall pay the same amount of grain to the owner of the field as his neighbour; moreover he shall break up the field that he has abandoned with mattocks and harrow it and return it to the owner of the field.

**(44)** If a man has rented an abandoned field to be developed over a period of three years but he drags his feet[28] and does not develop the field, he shall break up the field in the fourth year with mattocks, scuffle[29] and harrow it and return it to the owner of the field; furthermore he shall make an assessment of 70 bushels for 16 acres[30].

---

28. The idiomatic expression would be translated literally as 'he drops his arm'; the English idiom 'to drag one's feet' seems to have a similar meaning.

29. The word (*CAD marāru* B) is not common, but fairly clearly means a process between the initial rough digging of untouched ground and the final preparation of a tilth for sowing. This idea is confirmed by occurrence of the word in the N-theme in a letter from the Manchester collection (Fish, 10:9); there as here it is an operation that follows on from *mayyarī maḫāṣu*. The most appropriate specialized agricultural term in English seems to be 'to scuffle', rather than the commoner 'to hoe'.

30. This is a very general traditional English equivalent for the 10 kur-measures of corn for every 18 iku-measures of land in the text. It appears to set the standard for an average yield for corn.

**L45–48 (XIII:35–XIV:17)**

**(45)** *šumma awīlum eqelšu ana biltim ana errēšim*[184] *iddinma u bilat eqlišu imtaḫar, warka eqlam Adad irtaḫiṣ*[185] *u lu bibbulum itbal bitiqtum ša errēšimma.*

**(46)** *šumma bilat eqlišu la imtaḫar, u lu ana mišlāni u lu ana šaluš eqlam iddin še'am ša ina eqlim ibbaššû errēšum u bēl eqlim ana apšītêm izuzzū.*

**(47)** *šumma errēšum aššum ina šattim maḫrītim mānaḫātišu la ilqû eqlam erēšam iqtabi bēl eqlim ul uppas.*

*errēssuma eqelšu irrišma ina*[186] *ebūrim* kīma riksātišu še'am ileqqe.*

**(48)** *šumma awīlum ḫubullum*[187] *elišu ibaššīma eqelšu Adad irtaḫiṣ u lu bibbulum itbal u lu ina la mê še'um ina eqlim*[188] *la ittabši ina šattim šuāti še'am ana bēl ḫubullišu ul utâr.*

*ṭuppašu uraṭṭab u ṣibtam ša*[189] *šattim šuāti ul inaddin.*

**L49–52 (XIV:18–XV:6)**

**(49)** *šumma awīlum kaspam itti tamkārim ilqēma eqel epšētim ša še'im u lu šamaššammī ana tamkārim iddin, "eqlam erišma, še'am u lu šamaššammī ša ibbaššû esip, tabal" iqbīšum,*

*šumma errēšum ina eqlim še'am u lu šamaššammī uštabši, ina ebūrim še'am u šamaššammī ša ina eqlim ibbaššû bēl eqlimma ileqqēma še'am ša kaspišu u ṣibassu ša itti tamkārim ilqû, u mānaḫāt erēšim, ana tamkārim inaddin.*

---

184. O: *errēšūtim.*

185. O: + *u.*

186. O: ø ...*.

187. If this word is the subject of the sentence, as the inflection suggests, *awīlum* is left hanging until its function within the clause is defined by *elīšu* (with its resumptive pronoun). Alternatively, the verb *bāšû* may be deemed not to have an object as such but rather a complement, which is inflected with the subject marker. But since CVC signs are less precise about vowel quality than the other phonetic types of sign, the inflection /am/ may be intended.

188. L: *eqelšu.*

189. L: ø.

**Storm damage**

**(45)** If a man has let his field to be cultivated for a rent, and he has received the rental payment for the field, but some time later The Storm[31] has eroded away the land or a flood has overwhelmed it, it is the cultivator who has to bear the loss.

**(46)** If he has not received any rent for his field, or has rented only a half or a third of the field, the cultivator and the owner of the field shall share by agreement whatever grain is produced from the field.

**(47)** If the cultivator has asked to work the field again because he has not regained his investment for the first year, the owner of the field shall not object.

That same cultivator of his shall work the field and at the harvest he shall collect whatever was agreed.

**(48)** If a man has incurred a debt and The Storm has eroded away his field, or a flood has overwhelmed it, or if grain has not been produced from the field because of a lack of water, he need not repay grain to his creditor for that year.

He shall moisten[32] the tablet and pay no instalment for that year.

**Borrowing until harvest**

**(49)** If a man has taken silver from a merchant and has given to the merchant a field suitable for grain or sesame, and has told him[33] , 'Cultivate the field, harvest the grain or sesame which is produced, and take it away,' then, assuming that the cultivator has produced some grain or sesame from the field, it is the owner of the field who should collect whatever grain or sesame may have been produced in the field, and he shall give the merchant grain for the silver which he received from him, as well as for the interest on it, as well as for the effort of cultivating it.

---

31. Weather conditions personified by the god Adad.

32. Presumably it was possible to moisten a sun-dried tablet sufficiently to change the date that interest became payable. Alternatively it may be an idiomatic expression meaning 'to waive the terms of a contract'; Roth: 'he shall suspend performance of his contract'.

33. Akkadian tends to use direct speech where it is more natural in English to use indirect speech; direct speech is preserved here since the law seems to be concerned with interpreting the precise implications of an oral contract.

**(50)** *šumma eqel <še’im>*[190] *eršam u lu eqel šamaššammī eršam iddin, še’am u lu šamaššammī ša ina eqlim ibbaššû bēl eqlimma ileqqēma kaspam u ṣibassu ana tamkārim utâr.*
**(51)** *šumma kaspam ana turrim la išu <še’am u lu>*[191] *šamaššammī ana maḫīrātišunu ša kaspišu u ṣibtišu ša itti tamkārim ilqû ana pī ṣimdat šarrim ana tamkārim inaddin.*
**(52)** *šumma errēšum ina eqlim še’am u lu šamaššammī la uštabši, riksātišu ul inni.*

**L53–56 (XV:7-45)**

**(53)** *šumma awīlum ana kār eqlišu dunnunim aḫšu iddīma kāršu la udanninma ina kārišu pītum ittepte u ugāram mê uštābil, awīlum ša ina kārišu pītum ippetû še’am ša uḫalliqu iriab.*
**(54)** *šumma še’am riābam la ile’i, šuāti u bīšašu ana kaspim inaddinūma mārū ugārim ša še’šunu mû ublū izuzzū.*
**(55)** *šumma awīlum atappašu ana šiqītim ipte aḫšu iddīma eqel itēšu mê uštābil, še’am kīma itēšu imaddad.*
**(56)** *šumma awīlum mê iptēma epšētim ša eqel itēšu mê uštābil, ana 1 burum 10 kur še’am imaddad.*

190. Restored thus in *BAL* and Roth.
191. Restored thus in *BAL* and Roth.

**(50)** If he has given him a field already set <with grain>[34] or a field already set with sesame, it is the owner of the field who should collect whatever grain may be produced from the field and repay the merchant the silver and the interest.
**(51)** If he does not have the silver for the repayment he shall give the merchant <grain or>[35] sesame at their current prices for the silver which he received from the merchant and the interest on it, in accordance with the decision of the king.
**(52)** If a cultivator has not produced grain or sesame from a field, the contract shall not be changed.

**Careless drainage**

**(53)** If a man has been careless regarding the maintenance of his field dyke and he has not maintained the ditch and a breach has opened up in the dyke so that water has destroyed the cultivable area, the man in whose dyke the breach occurred shall restore any grain that may have been lost.
**(54)** If he is not able to recompense with grain they shall exchange him and his property for silver, and the men in the cultivable area whose grain the water destroyed shall share it.
**(55)** If a man has been careless in opening an irrigation channel and he lets the water surge over his neighbour's field, he shall calculate the amount of grain just as his neighbour.[36]
**(56)** If a man has opened up a watercourse and let it destroy the work on a neighbour's field he shall calculate 70 bushels for 16 acres[37].

---

34. The omission of the word corn seems to be a scribal error (see L51).

35. Only sesame is mentioned in the text, but presumably this is a scribal error (see L50).

36. If one neighbour has lost all his corn, presumably the calculation is based on another neighbour's yield; alternatively it may mean that whatever corn the man himself is able to grow should be shared equally with the neighbour to whom he caused the loss.

37. The rate is the same as in L44.

**L57–58 (XV:46–XVI:3)**

**(57)** *šumma rē'ûm ana šammī ṣēnim šūkulim itti bēl eqlim la imtagarma, balum bēl eqlim eqlam ṣēnam uštākil, bēl eqlim eqelšu iṣṣid.*
*rē'ûm ša ina balum bēl eqlim eqlam ṣēnam ušākilu, elēnumma*[192] *ana 1 burum 20 kur še'am ana bēl eqlim inaddin.*[193]
**(58)** *šumma, ištu ṣēnum ugārim ītelianim kannu gamartim ina abullim ittaḫlalū, rē'ûm ṣēnam ana eqlim iddīma eqlam ṣēnam uštākil, rē'ûm eqel ušākilu inaṣṣarma ina ebūrim ana 1 burum 60 kur še'am ana bēl eqlim imaddad.*

**L59 (XVI:4-9)**

**(59)** *šumma awīlum balum bēl kirîm ina kirī awīlim iṣam ikkis,* ½ *mana kaspam išaqqal.*

**L60–63 (XVI:10-57)**

**(60)** *šumma awīlum eqlam ana kirîm zaqāpim ana nukaribbim iddin, nukaribbum kiriam izqup, erbe šanātim kiriam urabba. ina ḫamuštim šattim bēl kirîm u nukaribbum mitḫāriš izuzzū. bēl kirîm zittašu inassaqma ileqqe.*
**(61)** *šumma nukaribbum eqlam ina zaqāpim la igmurma nidītam īzib, nidītam ana libbi zittišu išakkanūšum.*
**(62)** *šumma eqlam ša innadnušum ana kirîm la izqup šumma šer'um*[194] *bilat eqlim ša šanātim ša innadû nukaribbum ana bēl eqlim kīma itēšu imaddad.*
*u eqlam šipram ippešma ana bēl eqlim utâr.*

---

192. This word is an adverb, widely separated from its verb.

193. It is not usual to have so many clauses linked asyndetically, and the repetition of the phrase *bēl eqlim* is also particularly persistent. The second clause appears to explain *la imtagar*, and the third clause is a temporal one introducing the apodosis.

194. *ab.sín* can also be read as *abšinnum.*

## LIVESTOCK (L57–58)

### Careless pasturing

**(57)** If a shepherd has not agreed with the owner of a field to let his flock feed on the plants there, but he does let his flock feed on the field without the permission of the owner of the field, the owner of the field shall harvest it.

The shepherd who let his flock feed on the field without the permission of the owner of the field shall make a supplementary gift to the owner of the field of 140 bushels of grain for every 16 acres[38].

**(58)** If a shepherd has left his flock in a field and let the flock feed on the field after the flocks have come away from the meadows and the flags showing it is ended have been hung on the city gate, the shepherd shall take custody of the field on which he let them feed and calculate 420 bushels of grain for each 16 acres[39] for the owner of the field at harvest time.

## ORCHARDS (59–66+)

### Careless tree-felling

**(59)** If a man has cut down a tree in another man's orchard without the permission of the owner of the orchard he shall pay half a mana of silver.

### Planting out an orchard

**(60)** If a man has given a gardener a field to plant out as an orchard, when the gardener has planted out the orchard he shall look after it for four years.

In the fifth year the owner of the orchard and the gardener shall make an equal share.

The owner of the orchard shall choose his share and take it first.

**(61)** If the gardener has not completed the planting out of the field and has left an area abandoned, they shall reckon the abandoned area as a part of his share.

**(62)** If he has not planted out any of the field that was given to him as an orchard and if it was a cultivable field, the gardener shall calculate the same rent for the owner of the field as his neighbours for the number of years the field was abandoned.

Moreover he shall still do the work on the field before returning it to the owner of the field.

---

38. 20 measures of corn for every measure of land.

39. 60 measures of corn for every measure of land.

**(63)** *šumma kankallum eqlam šipram ippešma, ana bēl eqlim utâr. u ana 1 burum 10 kur še'am ša šattim ištiat imaddad.*

**L64–65 (XVI:58–XVII:1)**

**(64)** *šumma awīlum kirâšu ana nukaribbim ana rukkubim iddin, nukaribbum adi kirâm ṣabtu ina bilat kirîm šittīn ana bēl kirîm inaddin. šaluštam šû ileqqe.*

**(65)** *šumma nukaribbum kirâm la urakkibma biltam umtaṭṭi, nukaribbum bilat kirîm ana <bēl kirîm kīma> itēšu* [*imaddad*...].

**L66 (*BL* §A; MSS P, Q, l; Roth gap a)**

*šumma awīlum kaspam itti tamkārim ilqēma tamkāršu īsiršuma, mimma ša nadānim la ibaššīšum, kirâšu ištu tarkibtim ana tamkārim iddinma, 'suluppī mala ina kirîm*[195] *ibbaššû ana kaspika tabal', iqbīšum*[196] *tamkārum šû ul immaggar*[197].
*suluppī ša ina kirîm ibbaššû bēl kirîmma ileqqēma kaspam u ṣibassu ša pī ṭuppišu tamkāram ippalma suluppī watrūtim ša ina kirîm ibbaššû bēl kirîmma ileqqe*[198].

**L67–§5.1 (fragments b-k)**

**(67) (*BL* §B; MS P; Roth gap b)**

*šumma* [*awīlum*] *bītam* [*ippešma*] *ṭēḫušu*...*ša*...

---

195. P: *kirīya*(?).
196. P: *-šu*.
197. P: *imaggara*.
198. Q: + *-ma*.

**(63)** If it had been an abandoned field he shall still do the work on the field before returning it to the owner of the field, but calculate 70 bushels for 16 acres[40] for each year.

**Pollination**

**(64)** If a man has given a gardener his orchard to pollinate, the gardener shall pay to the owner of the orchard as rent for the orchard two-thirds of the produce for as long as the orchard was in his possession.

He shall keep a third himself.

**(65)** If the gardener did not pollinate the orchard and produced a lower yield, the gardener shall calculate the same rent as his neighbours for the orchard <for the owner of the orchard>.

> Damage to the stela prohibits a coherent translation of L66–99, but a partial translation of some of the Laws can be made from parallel fragmentary tablets; since it is not possible to number these restorations with certainty following the numeration of the Stela, letters are used to show their relative sequence; fragment a overlaps in content with L66.

**A merchant is paid with silver, not dates**

(Fragment a, L66) If a man has received silver from a merchant and the merchant has pressed him for payment and, having nothing with which to pay, he has given the merchant his orchard after the pollination, and has said to him, 'Have as many dates as are produced in the orchard instead of your silver,' that merchant may not agree.[41] The owner of the orchard shall himself collect the dates that are produced in the orchard but he shall repay the merchant the silver together with the interest according to the terms on the document; any surplus dates that may be produced in the orchard the owner of the orchard may keep.

**HOUSES AND LAND (fragment b-fragment)**

(Fragment b, L67) If a man is going to build a house, and his neighbour...who...

---

40. 10 measures of corn for every measure of land.

41. The N-theme of the verb can sometimes have an obligatory nuance, in which case 'should not' would be the translation.

**67+a (*BL* §C; MSS P, Q, Frag. Noug. JA 245; Roth gap c)** [*šumma*] *...ana šīmim...ul inaddiššum*
*šumma še'am kaspam u bīšam ana bīt ilkim ša bīt itēšu ša išāmu inaddin ina mimma ša iddinu ītelli bītum ana* [*bēlišu*] *itâr*
*šumma bītum šû ilkam la išu išâm ana bītim šuāti še'am kaspam u bīšam inaddin*

**68+a (*BL* §D; MS P, R; Roth gap d)** *šumma awīlum* [*nidītam*] *balum* [*itēšu ītepuš*] *ina bīt...*[*itēšu*]*...ana...*

**68+b (*BL* §H, §G; MSS P, R; Roth gap e)** [*šumma...*] '*nabalkattaka dunnin, ištu bītika ibbalakkatunim*' *ana bēl nidītim* '*nidītka epuš* [*ištu*] *nidītika* [*bītī*] *ipallašūnim*' *iqbi, šībī*[199] *iškun,* [*šumma*] *ina nabalkattim* [*šarrāqum...mimma ša ina*] *nabalkattim* [*ḫalqu*] *bēl...šumma...bēl... mimma...iriab.*
*šumma...*

**68+c (*BL* §J; MS R; Roth gap f)** [*šumma*] *ina...bītum*[200]

**69+c (*BL* §J, §E; MSS P, R, s; Roth gap g)**
[201][*šumma awīlum...ina...*] *awīlum* ašbumma*[202] *kasap kiṣrišu gamram ša šanat ana bēl* [*bītim*] *iddinma*[203] *bēl bītim ana waššābim ina ūmīšu la malûtim waṣâm iqtabi bēl bītim aššum waššābam ina ūmīšu la malûtim ina bītišu* [*ušēṣû*] *ina kaspim ša waššābum* [*iddinušum ītelli*].

**§4.12 (Roth gap h)**
[*šumma wašbum bīt muškēnim*] *išām...kiṣrim ša ippušu* [*ana*] *bīt muškēnim šâmim...ša išakkanu...išakkanšu...*
*šumma rūqim...ša muškēnim...*
*šumma ul išāmma* [*ina kaspim ša*] *ilqû* [*ītellīma bīt muškēnim ana bēlišu itār*].

---

199. Finet restores *ṭemam*.

200. *BAL* reads (with hesitation) $E_2$.$GAR_8$, which would be transcribed *ina... igārim*.

201. *BAL* restores these fragmentary lines rather differently: *šumma bēl bītim wašbam ina bītišu ušešibma awīlum.*

202. P thus, for Old Babylonian *wašbumma*.

203. *BAL id-di*[*-in*]; Roth: *iddinma*.

(Fragment c, L67+a)... for a price...he will not give to him.

If he would give grain, silver or property for a house with a service obligation attached which belongs to the house of his neighbour which he wishes to purchase, he shall forfeit whatever he paid.

It shall return to its owner.

If that house has no service obligation attached he may purchase it.

He may give grain, silver or property for that house.

**Neglected land**

(Fragment d, L68+a) If a man has worked the uncultivated land of his neighbour without the permission of his neighbour...in the house...his neighbour...

**Neglected buildings**

(Fragment e, L68+b) If...has said, 'Reinforce your wall that can be climbed over; people can climb from your house here over the wall,' or if he has said to the owner of land that is uncultivated, 'Work on your neglected land; people could break into my house from your uncultivated land,' and he has witnesses for his statement, and...a thief...over the wall...whatever [was lost] he shall restore.

(Fragment f, L68+c) ...house...

(Fragment g, L69+c) If...an occupier pays his annual rent in full in silver to the owner of the house, but the owner of the house then orders the tenant to quit before the full term of his contract has expired, because he has evicted the occupier before the expiry of the full term of his contract the owner of the house shall forfeit the silver that the tenant gave him.

(Fragment h, §4.12) [If] an occupier...is going to purchase [the house of a commoner] any obligation which has to be paid in order to purchase the house of a commoner...which he has placed...he shall place it...

If he is far away...of the commoner...

If he does not make the purchase...he shall forfeit [any silver] that he has taken...shall revert to its owner.

**§§4.13, 4.14, 5.1 (Roth gap i, j, k) not preserved.**

**§5.2-L76+f (fragments l-bb)**
**§5.2 (Roth gap l)** [*šumma awīlum*...] *ina ebūrim kasapšu u ṣibassu* [*išaqqal*], *šumma anadānim*(!)[204] *ul* [*išu*] *mimmûšu bīšam u še'am* [*inaddinšum*].
*šumma ana nadānim...išu...*

**§5.3a (Roth gap m)** *šumma tamkārum ša ana...ša ana...ana 5 šiqil kaspim...kunukkišu la išṭuršum...maḫar šu ma...mār awīlim la...šuāti idukkūšu.*

**§5.3b (Roth gap n)** *šumma warad awīlim...1/3 mana kaspam išaqqal u wardum šû...gamram...ša*[205] *idû iddâk.*

**§5.4 (Roth gap o)** [*šumma*] *awīlum awīlam...kaspum...*

**§5.5, 5.6 (Roth gap p, q) fragmentary.**
**§5.7 (Roth gap r)** [*šumma*...] *ana...idī...kaspam...*
*šumma awīlum šuāti ša...la...ina*[206] *kaspim ša iddinu*[207] *ītelli.*

**§5.8 (*BAL* L69+d; MS S; *BL* §K; Roth §5.8, gap s)** *šumma* [*lu*] *wardum lu* [*amtum*...] *ana bēlišu* [*utarrūšu*]
*šumma...itarrakaššu* [...*ana bēlišu*] *ul utarrūšum.*

**§5.9 (*BAL* L70+d; MS S; *BL* §L; Roth §5.9, gap t)** *šumma tamkārum še'am u kaspam ana ḫubullim iddin ana 1 kurrum 1 pān 4 sūt še'am ṣibtam ileqqe.*
*šumma kaspam ana hubullim iddin ana 1 šiqil kaspim 1/6 u 6 uṭṭet ṣibtam ileqqe.*

---

204. For *ana nadānim.*
205. Thus Roth hesitantly.
206. Thus Roth hesitantly.
207. Thus Roth hesitantly.

(fragments i, j, k, §§4.13, 4.14, 5.1)
[...]

## THE MERCHANT (Fragment l–L107)

**FRAGMENTS**

(Fragment l, §5.2) At the harvest [...he shall weigh out] his silver and the interest on it.

If he [has] nothing to give [...he shall give him] whatever property and grain he has.

If he has [something] to give...

(Fragment m, §5.3a) If a merchant who...for five shekels of silver...he did not write for him a sealed document...in his presence...the son of the man...they shall kill him.

(Fragment n, §5.3b) If the slave of a man...he shall weigh out a third of a mana of silver...and that slave...all of it...knowing...he shall be killed.

(Fragment o, §5.4)...a man another man...

(Fragment p, q, §5.5, 5.6) [...]

(Fragment r, §5.7)... fees...silver...

If that man who...does not...the silver he gave he shall forfeit.

(Fragment s, §5.8, L69+d) If [either] a male slave or [a female slave] to his master [they shall return him].

If...he has been beating him, they shall not return him [to his master].

(Fragment t, §5.9, L70+d) If a merchant has made a loan of grain or silver, for grain he shall take one panu and four sutu for every kur.[42]

If he has made a loan of silver he shall take a sixth of a shekel and six grains for every shekel[43].

---

42. Equivalent to a third more than the amount borrowed (see Roth).
43. Equivalent to a fifth more than the amount borrowed (see Roth).

**§5.10 (*BAL* L71+d; MS S; *BL* §M; Roth gap u)** *šumma awīlum ša ḫubullam iršû kaspam ana turrim la išu še'am u kaspam kīma ṣimdat šarrim u ṣibassu 1 kurrum še'am 1 pān ana šattim*(?) *ileqqe. šumma tamkārum ṣibat ḫubulli…ana 1 kur…1/6 u 6 uṭṭet…uwatterma ilqe ina* [*mimma*] *ša iddinu* [*ītelli*].

**§5.11 (*BAL* L72+d; MS S; *BL* §N; Roth gap v)** *šumma tamkārum še'am* [*u kaspam*] *ana ṣibtim* [*iddinma*] *ṣibtam mala* [*qaqqadišu*] *še'am kaspam…ilteqēma…še'um u kaspum* [*qaqqadašu*] *u ṣibassu…*] *tuppi rikistišu* [*iḫeppe*].

**§5.12 (*BAL* L72+e; MS S; *BL* §0; Roth gap w)** *šumma tamkārum… ana…ṣibtam…ilteqēma…u lu še'am* [*u lu kaspam*] *mala* [*imḫuru u lu*] *la uštaḫriṣma ṭuppam eššam* (?) *la išṭur u lu ṣibātim ana qaqqadim uṭṭeḫḫi tamkārum šû še'am mala ilqû uštašannāma utâr.*

**§5.13 (*BAL* L73+e; MS S; *BL* §P; Roth gap x)** *šumma tamkārum še'am u kaspam ana ḫubullim iddinma inūma ana ḫubullim iddinu kaspam ina abnim maṭītim u še'am ina sūtim maṭītim iddin u inūma imḫuru kaspam ina abnim* [*rabītim*] *še'am ina sūtim rabītim imḫur* [*tamkārum šû*] *ina* [*mimma ša iddinu ītelli*].

**§5.14 (*BAL* L74+e; MS S; *BL* §Q; Roth gap y)** *šumma* [*tamkārum…*] *ana ḫubullim…iddin ina mimma* [*ša*] *iddinu ītelli.*

**§5.15 (*BAL* L75+e; MSS P, S; *BL* §R; Roth gap z)** *summa awīlum še'am u kaspam itti tamkārim ilqēma še'am u kaspam ana turrim la išu bīšamma išu mimma ša ina*[208] *qātišu ibaššû maḫar šībī kīma ubbalu ana tamkārišu inaddin tamkārum*[209] *ul uppas imaḫḫar.*

---

208. P: ø.
209. P: *tamkārum šû.*

(Fragment u, §5.10, L:71+d) If a man who has taken out a loan does not have any silver to make the repayment, he shall take[44] grain and silver in accordance with the decision of the king with an annual rate of interest on it of one panu for every kur.[45]

If the merchant increases the interest on the loan and takes for every kur [of grain...or for every shekel of silver] a sixth of a shekel and six grains [46], he shall forfeit what he gave him.

(Fragment v, §5.11, L:72+d) If a merchant [has given] grain or silver on loan and takes as much grain or silver in interest as [the principal loan], the grain and silver, principal and interest...

The tablet for that contract [shall be broken].

(Fragment w, §5.12, L:72+e) If a merchant...as...interest...has taken... and he has not deducted as much...or grain [or silver as he received] and has not written out a new (?) document, or he adds the interest payments to the capital sum[47], that merchant shall return twice as much grain as he received.

(Fragment x, §5.13, L:73+e) If a merchant has given a loan of grain or silver, and when he gave the loan he used the smaller stone-weight for the silver or the smaller measuring pan for the grain, but when he receives it he uses the [larger] stone-weight for the silver and the larger measuring-pan for the grain...he shall [forfeit].

(Fragment y, §5.14, L74+e) If...he has given a loan, he shall forfeit anything he gave.

(Fragment z, §5.15, L:75+e) If a man has received grain or silver from a merchant and he does not have grain or silver for the repayment, but he does have possessions, he shall give the merchant whatever he has in his possession of equivalent value in the presence of witnesses.

The merchant shall not make an objection; he will accept.

---

44. While the subject of the protasis is the borrower, the subject of the apodosis is the merchant.

45. Equivalent to 60 silas per kur, or a fifth more than the amount borrowed (see Roth).

46. More than half as much interest again, for the imposed rate appears to be equivalent to an increase from 20 per cent to 33 per cent (see Roth).

47. The phrase appears to prohibit taking compound interest.

**§5.16 (*BAL* L'76+e'; MS T; *BL* §S; Roth gap aa; possibly the conclusion of §5.15)** [*šumma…awīlum…*] *kīma…*

**76+f (*BL* §T; ms. S)** [*šumma*]…*iddâk…*

**L77+f (fragment cc; *BL* §U; MS S)** *šumma awīlum ana awīlim kaspam ana tappûtim iddin nēmelam u butuqqâm ša ibbašû maḫar ilim mitḫāriš izuzzū.*

**L100–107 (*BL* §V; MS S:1-11, and 12-21 parallel to Stele XXIV [Rv. I]:1–XXV [Rv. II]:14)**
**(100)** *šumma tamkārum ana šamallêm kaspam ana* [*nadānim u maḫārim*] *iddinma ana ḫarrānim iṭrussu, šamallûm ina ḫarrānim* […] *šumma ašar illiku* [*nēmelam*] *ītamar,*[210] *ṣibāt kaspim mala ilqû isaddarma ūmīšu imannūma tamkāršu ippal.*
**(101)** *šumma ašar illiku nēmelam la ītamar, kasap ilqû uštašannāma šamallûm ana tamkārim inaddin.*
**(102)** *šumma tamkārum ana šamallîm kaspam ana tadmiqtim ittadinma ašar illiku bitiqtam ītamar, qaqqad kaspim ana tamkārim utâr.*
**(103)** *šumma ḫarrānam ina alākišu nakrum mimma ša našû uštaddīšu, šamallûm nīš ilim izakkarma ūtaššar.*
**(104)** *šumma tamkārum ana šamallîm še'am šipātim šamnam u mimma bīšam ana pašārim*[211] *iddin, šamallûm kaspam isaddarma ana tamkārim utâr.*
*šamallûm kanīk kaspim ša ana tamkārim inaddinu ileqqe*[212].
**(105)** *šumma šamallûm ītegīma*[213] *kanīk kaspim ša ana tamkārim iddinu la ilteqe, kasap la kanīkim ana nikkassim ul iššakkan.*

---

210. Stele text resumes here after break.
211. P: *pa-ša-ri-em*(!).
212. T: *i-le-eq*(!).
213. Stele: unusual writing, perhaps because of *KI* in next column.

(Fragment aa, §5.16, L:76+e) ...like...
(Fragment bb, L:76+f) ...he shall be killed.

**Partnership**
(Fragment cc, L:77+f) If a man gives silver to another man in a partnership arrangement they shall divide equally in the presence of the god any profit or loss which results.

**Using an agent**
**(100)** If a merchant has sent an agent on a journey to give or to receive silver, but on the journey the agent...if where he went he should have made a profit, he shall work out the interest for the amount of silver he took and count the number of days, and shall recompense the merchant.
**(101)** If he has not seen any profit where he went, the agent shall give the merchant twice the amount of silver he took.
**(102)** If a merchant has given silver to a salesman as a gratuity[48] and where he went he saw a loss, he shall repay the initial amount of silver to the merchant.
**(103)** If an enemy has made him drop all he was carrying as he travelled on the road, the salesman shall swear by the god and go free.
**(104)** If a merchant has given an agent grain or wool or oil or any other material to trade, the agent shall set out in order the silver and repay the merchant.[49].

The agent shall receive a sealed document for the silver he has given to the merchant.
**(105)** If an agent has neglected to obtain a sealed document for the silver he has given to the merchant, any silver without a sealed document may not be counted in the reckoning[50].

48. Roth prefers to understand the term as signifying a sum to be invested, but the etymology suggests it is an extra payment to help the agent on his way; cf. *AHw* (following Edzard): 'ein zinsloser Geschäftsreisevorschuss'.

49. *sadāru* really means 'set in order'. Here it appears to refer to the order of selling the items (see *CAD*, *šamallû* 1b.); Roth: 'the silver for each transaction'.

50. Presumably this sealed document counted as a receipt.

**(106)** *šumma šamallûm kaspam itti tamkārim ilqēma tamkāršu ittakir tamkārum šû ina*[214] *maḫar ilim u šībī ina kaspim leqêm šamallâm ukânma*
*šamallûm kaspam, mala ilqû, adi 3-šu ana tamkārim*[215] *inaddin.*
**(107)** *šumma tamkārum* [216]*kaspam šamallâm iqīpma* šamallûm mimma ša tamkārum iddinušum ana tamkārišu*[217] *uttēr, tamkārum mimmā ša šamallûm iddinušum ittakiršu šamallûm šû ina*[218] *maḫar ilim u šībī tamkāram ukânma, tamkārum, aššum šamallâšu ikkiru, mimma ša ilqû adi 6-šu ana šamallîm inaddin.*

**L108–11 (XXV [Rv. II]:15-49)**

**(108)** *šumma sābītum ana šīm šikarim še'am la imtaḫar, ina abnim rabītim kaspam imtaḫar u maḫīr šikarim ana maḫīr še'im umtaṭṭi, sābītam šuāti*[219] *ukannūšima*[220] *ana mê inaddûši.*
**(109)** *šumma sābītum sarrūtum ina bītiša ittarkasūma sarrūtim šunūti la iṣṣabtamma ana ekallim la irdeam, sābītum šî iddâk.*
**(110)** *šumma nadītum*[221] *ugbabtum ša ina gagîm la wašbat bīt sībim iptete u lu ana šikarim ana bīt sībim īterub, awīltam šuāti iqallûši.*
**(111)** *šumma sābītum ištēn pīḫam*[222] *ana qīptim iddin, ina ebūrim 5 sūt še'am ileqqe.*

---

214. t: ø.
215. S: *tamkāršu.*
216. S: *samallâm kaspam iqimma.*
217. t: *tamkārim.*
218. S: ø.
219. S: *šiāti.*
220. S: *ikassûšima*, 'they shall bind her and'.
221. S: + *u.*
222. Stele: *NI* for *GAG* in ideogram.

**(106)** If the agent has taken silver from a merchant and disagrees[51] with him, and that merchant can prove in the presence of god with witnesses that the agent took the silver, the agent shall give the merchant three times the value of whatever silver he took.
**(107)** If a merchant has entrusted silver to an agent and the agent has repaid him all that he gave him, but the merchant disagrees with him about what the agent had given him, yet that salesman can prove in the presence of god with witnesses that the merchant is wrong[52], the merchant shall give the agent six times the value of whatever he had taken because he has disagreed with the agent.

## Selling Alcohol (L108–11)

**(108)** If instead of grain a brewer has accepted silver weighed with a large weight-stone for the price of drink, thus making the price of the drink less than the price of the grain, they shall prove that brewer guilty and throw her into the water.
**(109)** If there is a brewer in whose house villains have congregated but she has not caught those villains and has not taken them to the palace, such a brewer shall be killed.
**(110)** If a temple-woman, a priestess who has not been living in the communal house, opens a drinking house[53] or enters a drinking house for a drink, they shall burn such a woman.
**(111)** If a brewer gives one keg of beer[54] on trust, she shall receive five measures of grain at harvest.

---

51. Lit. 'becomes his enemy'.
52. *kānu* is used here in the sense of 'to prove wrong' (as in L1) whereas in the previous law it meant simply ' to prove'.
53. Perhaps it means opening the door of such a house, or opening up the place as a business (see Meek; Roth).
54. The word may denote a jug, or a special kind of drink (see Meek).

**L112 (XXV [Rv. II]:50-74)**

*šumma awīlum ina ḫarrānim wašibma*[223] *kaspam*[224] *ḫurāṣam*[225] *abnam u*[226] *bīš*[227] *qātišu ana awīlim iddinma*[228] *ana šēbultim*[229] *ušābilšu*[230], *awīlum šû mimma ša*[231] *šūbulu*[232] *ašar šūbulu*[233] *la iddinma itbal, bēl šēbultim awīlam šuāti ina mimma ša šūbuluma la iddinu ukânšuma*[234], *awīlum šû adi 5-šu mimma ša innadnūšum ana bēl šēbultim*[235] *inaddin.*

**L113 (XXV [Rv. II]:75–XXVI [Rv. III]:16)**

*šumma awīlum eli awīlim še'am u kaspam išūma ina balum bēl še'im ina našpakim u lu ina maškanim še'am ilteqe, awīlam šuāti ina balum bēl še'im ina našpakim u lu ina*[236] *maškanim ina še'im leqêm ukannūšuma še'am mala* [237]*ilqû utâr*.*
*u ina*[238] *mimma šumšu mala iddinu ītelli.*

**L114–16 (XXVI [Rv. III]:17-53)**

**(114)** *šumma awīlum eli awīlim še'am u kaspam la išūma nipûssu ittepe, ana nipûtim ištiat 1/3 mana kaspam išaqqal.*
**(115)** *šumma awīlum eli awīlim še'am u kaspam išūma nipûssu ippēma*[239] *nipûtim ina bīt nēpīša ina šīmātiša imtūt, dīnum šû rugummâm ul išu.*
**(116)** *šumma nipûtim ina bīt nēpīša ina maḫāṣim u lu ina uššušim imtūt bēl nipûtim tamkāršu ukânma.*

---

223. P: *ašibma*; t: *ašimma lu.*
224. t: + *lu.*
225. t: + *lu.*
226. t: *lu.*
227. t: *bīši*(?).
228. t: *iddimma.*
229. t: *šubulti.*
230. P: *ušābilaššu*; t: *ušābil*; see Roth.
231. S: ø.
232. P: *šūbula*(?).
233. P: *šūbula*(?).
234. Stele: *ukannūšuma*(!); S: *-a*[*n-x*]*-šu.*
235. t: *šubultim.*
236. t: ø.
237. Stele: *il-qú-ú ú-ta-ar*; but S: *il-qú ú-ta-ar* (perhaps haplography).
238. S: ø.
239. t: *it-te*[...] .

## Other People's Property (112–26)

### Consignment of goods

**(112)** If a man is travelling on a journey and has given another man some silver, gold, a precious stone[55] or anything he owns and made him transport them, but that man did not give whatever he had to transport at the destination but took it away, the owner of the goods for transport shall prove that that man has not delivered whatever had to be transported, and that man shall give the owner of the goods for transport five times the value of whatever was given to him.

### Loans without security

**(113)** If a man has lent[56] another man some grain or silver and he takes some grain from a storehouse or from a heap without the owner's permission, they shall prove that that man has taken some grain from a storehouse or from a heap without the owner's permission and he shall bring back whatever grain he has taken.

Moreover he shall forfeit his right to anything at all that he has given.

### Loans with security

**(114)** If a man has not lent another man grain or silver but has seized someone as security, he shall pay a third of a mana of silver for each secured person.

**(115)** If a man has lent another man grain or silver and has seized someone as security but the secured person has died inexplicably while on the creditor's property, there is no basis for complaint in such a case.

**(116)** If the secured person has died on the property of the creditor after a beating or cruelty, the owner of the secured person shall prove the merchant involved guilty.

---

55. The singular noun could be translated by a plural; see Roth.

56. *awīlum eli awīlim še'am...īšū* literally means 'a man has corn against a man'.

*šumma mār awīlim mārašu idukkū.*
*šumma warad awīlim 1/3 mana kaspam išaqqal u ina mimma šumšu mala iddinu ītelli.*

**L117–19 (XXVI [Rv. III]:54–XXVII [Rv. IV]: 3)**

**(117)** *šumma awīlam e'iltum iṣbassuma aššassu mārašu u mārassu ana kaspim iddin u lu ana kiššātim ittandin, šalaš šanātim bīt šāyyimānišunu u kāšišišunu ippešū*[240] *ina rebûtim šattim andurāršunu iššakkan.*
**(118)** *šumma wardam*[241] *u lu amtam*[242] *ana kiššātim ittandin tamkārum ušetteq, ana kaspim inaddin ul ibbaqqar.*
**(119)** *šumma awīlam e'iltum iṣbassuma amassu ša mārī uldušum ana kaspim ittadin, kasap tamkārum išqulu bēl amtim išaqqalma amassu ipaṭṭar.*

**L120–26 (XXVII [Rv. IV]:4–XXVIII [Rv.V]:24)**

**(120)** *šumma awīlum še'ašu ana našpakūtim ina bīt awīlim išpukma ina qarītim ibbûm ittabši u lu bēl bītim našpakam iptēma še'am ilqe*[243]*, u lu še'am ša ina bītišu iššapku*[244] [245]*ana gamrim* ittakir, bēl še'im maḫar ilim še'ašu ubârma bēl bītim še'am ša ilqû uštašannāma*[246] *ana bēl še'im inaddin.*
**(121)** *šumma awīlum ina bīt awīlim še'am išpuk, ina šanat ana*[247] *1 kur še'im 5 qa še'am idī našpakim inaddin*[248].
**(122)** *šumma awīlum ana awīlim kaspam ḫurāṣam u mimma šumšu ana maṣṣarūtim inaddin*[249]*, mimma mala inaddinu šībī ukallam riksātim išakkanma ana maṣṣarūtim inaddin.*

240. t: *ippušuma*(?).
241. P: + determinative *SAG*.
242. P: + determintive *SAG*.
243. t: *ilteqe*.
244. t: *šapku*.
245. P: *ina gamriam*(!); S: *ana gamrišu*.
246. P: *uš-ta-aš-na-ma*, with *aš* written over an erasure.
247. t: *1 ŠE.GUR* for Stele: *1 ŠE.GUR.E*.
248. t: *ileqqe*.
249. t: *iddinma*(?).

If it was the man's son, they shall kill his son.
If it was the man's slave, he shall pay a third of a mana of silver.
Moreover he shall forfeit his right to anything at all that he has given.

**Bondage and redemption**

**(117)** If a man is gripped in poverty, and he has sold his wife, or his son, or his daughter for silver, or has put them into bound-service[57], they shall work in the house of their purchaser or of their bond-master for three years but in the fourth year their liberation shall be agreed.
**(118)** If he has given a slave or a slave-girl into bound-service, the merchant may pass them on[58] and sell them for silver.
The person cannot be reclaimed.
**(119)** If a man is gripped in poverty and has sold his slave-girl for silver after she has borne him sons, the slave-girl's owner may pay back the silver the merchant had loaned and redeem his slave-girl.

**Storage**

**(120)** If a man has put his grain into store in another man's storehouse and then some damage has occurred in the granary, or the owner has opened the storehouse and taken the grain, or he completely disagrees about the grain which had been deposited in his house, the owner of the grain shall declare in the presence of the god the amount of grain, and the owner of the house shall give the owner of the grain double the amount of grain he had accepted.
**(121)** If a man has stored his grain in another man's storehouse he shall give five qa-measures of grain for each kur of grain[59] as the storage charge for one year.
**(122)** If a man intends to give[60] silver, gold or anything else into another man's custody, he shall show to witnesses absolutely everything that he intends to give and draw up agreements and then put it into custody.

---

57. An alternative parsing of the verb gives a reflexive meaning, 'he has put himself into bondage' (see Meek), but this meaning of the infixed *-t-* is unusual in CH.

58. Meek makes the apodosis start later; Roth understands the verse to mean 'to extend the term'.

59. Since there were 300 qu-measures in 1 kur-measure the storage charge represents 1.7 per cent of value.

60. One of the few examples of a present tense verb in the protasis.

**(123)** *šumma balum šībī u riksātim ana maṣṣarūtim iddinma*[250] *ašar iddinu ittakrūšu, dīnum šû rugummâm ul išu.*
**(124)** *šumma awīlum ana awīlim kaspam ḫurāṣam u mimma šumšu maḫar šībī ana maṣṣarūtim iddinma ittakiršu, awīlam šuāti ukannūšuma mimma ša ikkiru uštašannāma inaddin.*
**(125)** *šumma awīlum mimmâšu ana maṣṣarūtim iddinma ašar iddinu u lu ina pilšim u lu ina nabalkattim mimmûšu itti mimmê bēl bītim iḫtaliq, bēl bītim ša īgūma mimma ša ana maṣṣarūtim iddinušumma uḫalliqu ušallamma ana bēl makkūrim iriab.*
*bēl bītim mimmâšu ḫalqam ištene'īma itti šarrāqānišu ileqqe.*
**(126)** *šumma awīlum mimmûšu la ḫaliqma 'mimmê ḫaliq' iqtabi, babtašu ūtebbir*[251]*, kīma mimmûšu la ḫalqu babtašu ina*[252] *maḫar ilim ubâršuma mimma ša*[253] *irgumu uštašannāma ana babtišu inaddin.*

**L127 (XXVIII [Rv. V]:25-34)**
*šumma awīlum eli ugbabtim u aššat awīlim ubānam ušatriṣma la uktīn awīlam šuāti maḫar dayyānī inaṭṭûšu.*
*u muttassu ugallabū.*

**L128 (XXVIII [Rv. V]:35-41)**
*šumma awīlum aššatam īḫuzma riksātiša la iškun, sinništum šî ul aššat.*

250. t: *iddimma.*
251. t: *ūtabbir.*
252. t: *u.*
253. t: *ø.*

**(123)** If he has given anything into custody without witnesses or agreements and they disagree with him at the place where he gave it, there is no cause for complaint in such circumstances.
**(124)** If a man has given silver, gold or anything else into another man's custody in the presence of witnesses but he disagrees with him, they shall prove that man guilty and he shall give double the amount of whatever was disputed.
**(125)** If a man has given something into custody and his belongings have disappeared together with those of the owner of the house because of a break-in or a burglary[61] at the place where he deposited it, the owner of the house, who has been careless and allowed the loss of something that was given into his custody, shall make amends by repaying the owner of the goods.

The owner of the house shall keep on searching for whatever was lost and take it back from the thief.
**(126)** If a man who has lost nothing says, 'Something of mine has been lost,' and deceives his community, his community shall make a declaration in the presence of the god that nothing was lost, and he shall give to his community twice the value of anything he had claimed.

## Women And Children

### WOMEN (L127–84)

### False accusations

**(127)** If a man has pointed his finger at a priestess or another man's wife but does not prove her guilty, they shall beat that man in front of the judges.

In addition they may half-shave[62] his hair.

### Cohabitation

**(128)** If a man has taken a wife but has not drawn up contracts with her, that woman is not married.

---

61. The word *pilšim* suggests breaking down an obstacle to gain entrance, and *nabalkattim* (see *CAD*) seems to imply climbing over a wall or through a gap.

62. To shave off half the hair seems to be a mark of humiliation. The clause is introduced with the conjunction *u* , rather than the commoner *-ma*, which is why it is treated as a separate sentence.

**L129 (XXVIII [Rv. V]:42-53)**
*šumma aššat awīlim itti zikarim šanîm ina itūlim ittaṣbat ikassûšunūtima ana mê inaddûšunūti.*
*šumma bēl aššatim aššassu uballaṭ, u šarrum warassu uballaṭ.*

**L130 (XXVIII [Rv. V]:54-67)**
*šumma awīlum aššat awīlim ša zikaram la idûma ina bīt abiša wašbat ukabbilšima ina sūniša ittatīlma iṣṣabtūšu, awīlum šû iddâk. sinništum šî ūtaššar.*

**L131–32 (XXVIII [Rv. V]:68–XXIX [Rv. VI]:6)**
**(131)** *šumma aššat awīlim mussa ubbiršima itti zikarim šanîm ina utūlim la iṣṣabit, nīš ilim izakkarma ana bītiša itâr.*
**(132)** *šumma aššat awīlim aššum zikarim šanîm ubānum eliša ittariṣma itti zikarim šanîm ina utūlim la ittaṣbat, ana mutiša Id išalli*

**L133a–36 (XXIX [Rv. VI]:7-73)**
**(133a)** *šumma awīlum iššalilma ina bītišu ša akālim ibašši, aššassu [adi mussa ṣabtu pagarša inaṣṣar]*[254]*, ana bīt šanîm ul irrub.*
**(133b)** *šumma sinništum šî pagarša la iṣṣurma ana bīt šanîm īterub, sinništam šuāti ukannūšima ana mê inaddûši.*
**(134)** *šumma awīlum iššalilma ina bītišu ša akālim la ibašši, aššassu ana bīt šanîm irrub.*
*sinništum šî arnam ul išu.*

254. Restoration according to *BAL*, but not followed by Roth.

**Adultery**

**(129)** If a man's wife has been caught copulating with another male, they shall tie them up and throw them into water.

If the woman's husband allows his wife to live, so similarly the king may allow his slave to live.[63]

**Rape of a virgin**

**(130)** If a man has restrained another man's wife, who has known no other male, and has actually copulated with her and they have caught him, that man shall be killed, but that woman shall be innocent.

**Suspected infidelity**

**(131)** If the wife of a husband has been accused by her husband but she has not been caught copulating with another male, she shall swear a solemn oath and return to her house.

**(132)** If a finger has been pointed at a man's wife because of some male but she has not been caught copulating with another male, she shall leap into the River[64] for the sake of her husband.

**Absent husband**

**(133a)** If a man has been taken away captive but there is a supply of food in his house, his wife [shall support herself while her husband is away; she shall not enter anyone else's house.]

**(133b)** If that woman has not kept herself to herself[65] but has entered someone else's house, they shall prove that woman guilty and throw her into the water.

**(134)** If a man has been taken captive but there is no supply of food in his house, his wife may enter someone else's house.

That woman has no guilt.

---

63. In the second conditional sentence the verb of the protasis is present tense (rather than the more common preterite), and the apodosis is introduced by *u* (rather than the more common *-ma*).

64. Because the noun is prefixed with the divine determinative a possible translation would be 'holy river'; Roth: she shall submit to the divine River Ordeal.

65. Lit. 'she has not guarded her body'.

**(135)** *šumma awīlum iššalilma ina bītišu ša akālim la ibašši ana panīšu aššassu ana bīt šanîm īterubma mārī ittalad, ina warka mussa ittūramma ālšu iktašdam, sinništum šî ana ḫāwiriša itâr. mārū warki abišunu illakū.*
**(136)** *šumma awīlum ālšu iddīma ittābit warkišu aššassu ana bīt šanîm īterub šumma awīlum šû ittūramma, aššassu iṣṣabat aššum ālšu izēruma innabitu, aššat munnabtim ana mutiša ul itâr.*

**L137–41 (XXIX [Rv. VI]:74–XXX [Rv. VII]:59)**

**(137)** *šumma awīlum ana šugītim ša mārī uldušum, u lu nadītim ša mārī ušaršûšu ezēbim panīšu ištakan, ana sinništim šuāti šeriktaša utarrūšim u muttat eqlim kirîm u bīšim inaddinūšimma mārīša urabba. ištu mārīša urtabbû ina mimma ša ana mārīša innadnu zittam kīma aplim ištēn inaddinūšimma mutu libbiša iḫḫassi.*
**(138)** *šumma awīlum ḫīrtašu ša mārī la uldušum izzib, kaspam mala terḫatiša inaddiššim. u šeriktam ša ištu bīt abiša ublam ušallamšimma izzibši.*
**(139)** *šumma terḫatum la ibašši, 1 mana kaspam ana uzubbêm inaddiššim.*
**(140)** *šumma muškēnum, 1/3 mana kaspam inaddiššim.*
**(141)** *šumma aššat awīlim ša ina bīt awīlim wašbat ana waṣêm panīša ištakanma, sikiltam isakkil, bīssa usappaḫ, mussa ušamṭa, ukannūšima. šumma mussa ezēbša iqtabi, izzibši. ḫarrānša uzubbūša mimma ul innaddiššim. šumma mussa la ezēbša iqtabi, mussa sinništam*[255] *šanītam iḫḫaz. sinništum šî kīma amtim ina bīt mutiša uššab.*

255. S: *sí-ni-in-iš-tam*; transpose *ni* and *in*.

**(135)** If a man has been taken captive but there is no supply of food in his house, and his wife has entered someone else's house until his return and has given birth to sons, but then later her husband comes back and rejoins his community, that woman shall go back to her first husband.

The sons shall go after their father.[66]

**(136)** If a man has abandoned his city and fled, and afterwards his wife has entered someone else's house, but then that man returns and would take his wife back, the wife of a fugitive shall not return to her husband because he has despised his city and fled.

**Separation and divorce**

**(137)** If a man who has fixed his ideas on leaving a priestess who has born him sons, or a temple-woman who provided him with sons, they shall give back her dowry to that woman. They shall give her half the field, the orchard or the goods and she shall bring up her sons.

After she has brought up her sons they shall give her the same share as one son from whatever was given to her for her sons.

She will choose a husband as she likes.

**(138)** If a man has left his first wife who has born him no children, he will give her as much silver as her bride-price.

He shall pay back the gift she brought from her father's house and leave her.

**(139)** If there is no bride-price, he shall give one mana of silver as a divorce claim.

**(140)** If he is a workman, he shall give a third of a mana of silver.

**(141)** If the wife of a man who has been living in the man's house has made a plan to go away, and has dealt deviously[67], dissipated her household and belittled her husband, they shall prove her guilty.

If her husband has said he will leave her, he shall leave her.

Nothing at all shall be given her for her journey or her divorce claim.

If her husband has said he will not leave her, her husband shall marry a different wife.

The other wife shall live in her husband's house like a slave-girl.

---

66. Roth prefers to translate the expression as 'they shall inherit from their father'.

67. Probably by misappropriating household property (see *CAD* and Roth).

**L142–43 (XXX [Rv. VII]:60–XXXI [Rv. VIII]:12)**
**(142)** *šumma sinništum mussa izērma 'ul taḫḫazanni' iqtabi, warkassa ina bābtiša ipparrasma*
*šumma naṣratma ḫiṭītam la išu u mussa waṣīma magal ušamṭāši, sinništum šî arnam ul išu*
*šeriktaša ileqqēma ana bīt abiša ittallak.*
**(143)** *šumma la naṣratma waṣiāt bīssa usappaḫ mussa ušamṭa, sinništam šuāti ana mê inaddûši.*

**L144–47 (XXXI [Rv. VIII]:13-64)**
**(144)** *šumma awīlum nadītam īḫuzma nadītum šî* [256]*amtam ana mutiša* iddinma, mārī uštabši awīlum šû ana šugītim aḫāzim panīšu ištakan, awīlam šuāti ul imaggarūšu.*
*šugītam ul iḫḫaz*
**(145)** *šumma awīlum nadītam īḫuzma mārī la ušaršīšuma*[257] *ana šugītim aḫāzim panīšu ištakan, awīlum šû šugītam iḫḫaz.*
*ana bītišu ušerrebši*[258].
*šugītum šî itti nadītim ul uštamaḫḫar.*
**(146)** *šumma awīlum nadītam īḫuzma amtam ana mutiša iddinma*[259] *mārī ittalad warkānum*[260] *amtum šî itti bēltiša uštatamḫir aššum mārī uldu, bēlessa ana kaspim ul inaddišši*[261].
*abuttam išakkanšimma itti amātim imannûši.*
**(147)** *šumma mārī la ūlid, bēlessa ana kaspim inaddišši.*

**L148–49 (XXXI [Rv. VIII]:65–XXXII [Rv. IX]:9)**
**(148)** *šumma awīlum aššatam īḫuzma la'bum iṣṣabassi ana šanītim aḫāzim panīšu ištakkan, iḫḫaz.*
*aššassu ša la'bum*[262] *iṣbatu ul izzibši.*
*ina bīt īpušu uššamma adi balṭat ittanaššīši.*
**(149)** *šumma sinništum šî ina bīt mutiša wašābam la imtagar, šeriktaša ša ištu bīt abiša ublam ušallamšimma ittallak.*

---

256. S: *ana mutiša amtam.*
257. V: *ušaršīšu.*
258. V: *ušerreb.*
259. V: *inaddinma.*
260. V: *arkānum.*
261. V: *inaddinši.*
262. S: *li-i'-bu-um.*

**Unwilling to marry**

**(142)** If a wife has despised her husband and has said, 'You shall not take me', her situation shall be assessed by her community.

If she has been looked after and there is no blame, but her husband has erred and greatly disparaged her, that woman has no guilt.

She shall take away her marriage gift and go to her father's house.

**(143)** If she has not been careful but has erred and dissipated her household and disparaged her husband, they shall throw that woman into the water.

**Temple women and priestesses**

**(144)** If a man has married a temple-woman and that temple-woman has given her husband a slave-girl and she has produced sons, but that man has made plans to marry a priestess, they shall not allow that man to marry the priestess.

**(145)** If a man has married a temple-woman but she has not given him sons and he has made plans to marry a priestess, that man may marry the priestess.

He shall let her come into his house.

That priestess shall not take over the position of the temple-woman.

**(146)** If a man has married a temple-woman and she has given a slave-girl to her husband and she has born sons, but afterwards that slave-girl takes over the position of her mistress because she has born sons, her mistress may not sell her for silver.

She shall put on her the mark of slavery and she shall be treated[68] as a slave-girl.

**(147)** If she has not had any sons, her mistress may sell her for silver.

**A wife with disease**

**(148)** If a man has married a wife and she falls ill with a serious disease,[69] and he has made plans to marry someone else, and does marry, he shall not leave the wife who has fallen ill with the serious disease.

She shall live in the house which he has built and he shall support her as long as she lives.

**(149)** If that wife does not agree to live in her husband's house, he shall pay back the gift she brought from her father's house and she shall depart.

---

68. The 3rd pl. verb with impersonal subject is translated as a passive.

69. Lit. 'she is gripped by' some unidentified serious illness.

**L150 (XXXII [Rv. IX]:10-25)**
*šumma awīlum ana aššatišu eqlam* [263]*kirâm bītam* u bīšam išrukšim, kunukkam īzibšim.*
*warki mutiša mārūša ul ipaqqarūši*
*ummum warkassa ana māriša ša irammu inaddin.*
*ana aḫîm*[264] *ul inaddin.*

**L151–52 (XXXII [Rv. IX]:26-60)**
**(151)** *šumma sinništum ša ina bīt awīlim wašbat*[265] *aššum bēl*[266] *ḫubullim ša mutiša la ṣabātiša mussa urtakkis, ṭuppam uštēzib.*
*šumma awīlum šû lāma sinništam šuāti*[267] *iḫḫazu ḫubullum elišu ibašši, bēl*[268] *ḫubullīšu aššassu ul iṣabbatu*[269].
*u šumma sinništum šî lāma ana bīt awīlim irrubu ḫubullum eliša ibašši, bēl ḫubullīša mussa ul iṣabbatu*[270].
**(152)** *šumma ištu sinništum šî ana bīt awīlim īrubu elišunu*[271] *ḫubullum ittabši, kilallāšunu*[272] *tamkāram ippalū.*

**L153 (XXXII [Rv. IX]:61-66)**
*šumma aššat awīlim aššum zikarim šanîm mussa ušdīk, sinništam šuāti ina gašīšim išakkanūši.*

**L154–56 (XXXII [Rv. IX]:67–XXXIII [Rv. X]:17)**
**(154)** *šumma awīlum mārassu iltamad, awīlam šuāti ālam ušeṣṣûšu.*
**(155)** *šumma awīlum ana mārišu kallatam iḫīrma mārušu ilmassi šû warkānumma ina sūniša ittatīlma, iṣṣabtūšu.*
*awīlam šuāti ikassûšuma ana mê inaddûšu*[273].

---

263. S: *bītam u kirâm.*
264. V: *aḫîtim.*
265. V: *ašbat.*
266. V: *bēli.*
267. S: *šiāti.*
268. V: *bēli.*
269. The reason for the subjunctive is not clear here or in the next sentence.
270. See previous note.
271. V: *eli mutiša.*
272. S: *kilallūšunu.*
273. Stele: *-ši*(!).

**Right of inheritance**

**(150)** If a man has bequeathed to his wife a field, an orchard, a house or other property[70], he shall leave an official document in her possession.

After the death of her husband her sons shall not dispute with her.

The mother shall give her inheritance to her beloved son.

She shall not give it to a stranger.

**A wife's responsibility for debt**

**(151)** Concerning[71] a woman who is residing in the house of a man and whose husband has left her a document saying that she may not be taken by someone with a claim against her husband:

If he had incurred the debt before he married that woman, his creditors may not take his wife.

Furthermore if that woman had incurred a debt before she went into the man's house, her creditors shall not take her husband[72].

**(152)** If the debt was incurred after that woman had entered the man's house, both of them shall be responsible to the merchant.

**A wife has her husband killed**

**(153)** If a woman has let her husband be killed because of another man they shall stick that woman on a stake.

**A father dallies with his daughter**

**(154)** If a man has got to know[73] his daughter, they shall make that man leave his city.

**(155)** If a man has chosen a bride for his son and his son has got to know her and afterwards he himself copulates with her, and they have caught him, they shall bind that man and throw him into water.

---

70. The apodosis could begin here or later.

71. It appears that the logical structure of this sentence has collapsed; the first protasis is left without a normal apodosis, but instead is completed by two related conditional sentences; in such a sentence it seems better not to translate the first *šumma* as 'if'.

72. The inflection of the verb with *-u* suggests that the subject is plural, but the mark of the plural is on the second element (*nomen regens*) instead of the logical first (*nomen rectum*) element of the construct phrase.

73. There can be little doubt that the verb *lamādu*, to learn about, has sexual connotations in this set of laws.

**(156)** *šumma awīlum* [274]*ana mārišu* kallatam iḫīrma mārušu la ilmassima šû ina sūniša ittatīl, ½ mana kaspam išaqqalšimma. u*[275] *mimma ša ištu bīt abiša ublam ušallamšimma mutu*[276] *libbiša iḫḫassi.*

**L157–58 (XXXIII [Rv. X]:18-32)**

**(157)** *šumma awīlum warki abišu ina sūn ummišu ittatīl, kilallīšunu iqallûšunūti.*

**(158)** *šumma awīlum warki abišu ina sūn rabītišu*[277] *ša mārī waldat*[278] *ittaṣbat, awīlum šû ina bīt abim*[279] *innassaḫ.*

**L159–61 (XXXIII [Rv. X]:33-77)**

**(159)** *šumma awīlum ša ana bīt emišu*[280] *biblam ušābilu terḫatam iddinu*[281] *ana sinništim šanītim uptallisma*[282] *ana emišu*[283] *'māratka ul aḫḫaz' iqtabi, abi mārtim mimma ša ibbablušum*[284] *itabbal.*

**(160)** *šumma awīlum ana bīt emim biblam ušābil*[285] *terḫatam iddinma abi mārtim, 'mārtī ul anaddikkum' iqtabi, mimma mala*[286] *ibbablušum uštašannāma utâr.*

**(161)** *šumma awīlum ana bīt emišu biblam ušābil terḫatam iddinma ibiršu uktarrissu emušu ana bēl*[287] *aššatim, 'mārtī ul taḫḫaz' iqtabi, mimma mala ibbablušum*[288] *uštašannāma utâr.*
*u aššassu ibiršu ul iḫḫaz.*

---

274. X: ø.
275. One of the rare occasions when the particle *u* is preceded by *-ma*.
276. V: *mūt.*
277. Meek (*ANET*) emended to *murabītišu*, but V corroborates Stele (see *CAD* M/2, 216b).
278. V: *aldat.*
279. S: *abišu.*
280. V: *ewišu.*
281. V: *iddinma.*
282. V: *uttalliṣ*(!).
283. V: *e-wi-šu,* but *wi* glossed as *mi.*
284. S: unclear.
285. S: *uštābil.*
286. S: *ša.*
287. S: *bēli.*
288. V: *-u.*

**(156)** If a man has chosen a bride for his son but his son has not got to know her and he himself copulates with her, he shall pay her half a mana of silver.

Furthermore he shall repay her all that she brought from her father's house and she shall choose the husband she wants.

**Other prohibited sexual relationships**

**(157)** If a man copulates with his mother after the death of his father,[74] they shall burn them both.

**(158)** If, after the death of his father, a man is caught copulating with his principal wife who has born sons, that man shall be disinherited by his father's household.

**Broken engagements**

**(159)** If, after having brought a wedding-gift to the house of his father-in-law and having given him the bride-price, a man hankers after another woman and has said to his father-in-law, 'I will not marry your daughter,' the father shall take away whatever he had given him for the daughter.

**(160)** If a man has brought a gift to his bride's father's house, and after he has given the bride-price the father of the girl has said, 'I shall not give you my girl,' he shall double the quantity of any gift he has brought to make recompense.

**(161)** If a man has brought a gift to his bride's father's house, and after he has given the bride-price one of his neighbours gossips about him and the father of his bride says to the bridegroom, 'You shall not take my girl,' he shall double the quantity of any gift he has brought to make recompense.

In no way shall the neighbour take that wife.

---

74. The preposition *warki* seems to imply that the father has died.

**L162–67 (XXXIII [Rv. X]:78–XXXV [Rv. XII]:8)**

**(162)** *šumma awīlum aššatam īḫuz mārī ūlissumma sinništum šî ana šīmtim ittalak, ana šeriktiša abuša ul iraggum šeriktaša ša mārīšama.*

**(163)** *šumma awīlum aššatam īḫuzma mārī la ušaršīšu sinništum šî ana šīmtim ittallak, šumma terḫatam ša awīlum šû ana bīt* [289]*emišu ublu* emušu uttēršum*[290]*, ana šerikti sinništim šuāti mussa ul iraggum šeriktaša ša bīt abišama.*

**(164)** *šumma emušu terḫatam la uttēršum, ina šeriktiša mala terḫatiša iḫarraṣma šeriktaša ana bīt abiša*[291] *utâr.*

**(165)** *šumma awīlum ana aplišu ša īnšu maḫru eqlam kirâm u bītam išruk*
*kunukkam išṭuršum, warka abum ana šīmtim ittalku inūma aḫḫū izuzzū, qīšti abum iddinušum ileqqēma.*
*elēnumma ina makkūr bīt abim mitḫāriš izuzzū.*

**(166)** *šumma awīlum ana mārī*[292] *ša iršû*[293] *aššātim īḫuz*[294] *ana mārišu ṣeḫrim aššatam la īḫuz*[295] *warka abum ana šīmtim ittalku, inūma aḫḫū izuzzū ina makkūr bīt abim* [296]*ana aḫḫišunu* ṣeḫrim ša aššatam*[297] *la aḫzu eliāt zittišu kasap terḫatim išakkanūšumma aššatam ušaḫḫazūšu.*

**(167)** *šumma awīlum aššatam īḫuzma mārī ūlissum sinništum šî ana šīmtim ittalak warkiša sinništam šanītam ītaḫazma mārī ittalad warkānum*[298] *abum ana šīmtim ittalku, mārū ana ummātim ul izuzzū. šerikti ummātišunu ileqqûma makkūr bīt abim mitḫāriš izuzzū.*

---

289. V: *ewišu ublam.*

290. V: *uttēršu.*

291. Stele: *a-ta*(!)*-ša*, perhaps under the influence of *še-ri-ik-ta-ša* at the end of the previous line.

292. Thus Stele; Roth: *mārī*<*šu*>, quoting *mārī* as a variant.

293. Roth prefers to emend, reading *irbû*, 'for his eligible sons', i.e. for the sons who have grown up.

294. The proposal to emend and read *iḫīr* (see *BAL*) is not supported by V, which agrees with Stele here.

295. See previous note.

296. m: unclear.

297. m: *-tum.*

298. *BAL* emends to read *warka*, i.e. *wa-ar-ka*{*-nu-um*}.

**The estate of a deceased parent**

**(162)** If a man has taken a wife and she has born him sons and that woman has passed to her destiny, her father shall have no claim on her dowry.

Her dowry belongs to her sons.

**(163)** If a man has taken a wife but she does not provide him with sons, when that woman passes to her destiny, her husband shall have no claim on the dowry of that woman, provided his father-in-law has returned to him the bride-price which that man had brought to his house.

Her dowry belongs to her father.

**(164)** If his father-in-law has not returned the bride-price, he shall subtract from the dowry the amount of the bride-price.

He shall return her dowry to her father's house.

**(165)** If a man has granted a field, an orchard or a house to his heir who is the apple of his eye[75] and has written an official document for him and afterwards the father passes to his destiny, he shall keep the gift his father gave him when the brothers share the estate.

Apart from that they shall make equal shares of the property in their father's house.

**(166)** If a man has chosen wives for all the sons he has raised but has not taken a wife for his small son before the father passes to his destiny, when the brothers make the allocation they shall reserve from the property in the father's house something in addition to the normal share to pay for the bride-price for their little brother who has not taken a wife, so allowing him to take a wife.

**(167)** If a man has taken a wife and she has borne him sons and that woman has passed to her fate, and after her death he has taken a second wife, and she has borne sons, and finally the father has passed to his fate, the sons shall not divide the property according to their mothers.

They shall take the dowries of their respective mothers, but the property of their father's house they shall divide equally.

75. Lit. 'the one who is accepted in his sight'.

**L168–69 (XXXV [Rv. XII]:9-36)**

**(168)** *šumma awīlum ana mārišu nasāḫim panam ištakan, ana dayyānī "mārī anassaḫ" iqtabi*[299] *dayyānū warkassu iparrasūma.*
*šumma mārum arnam kabtam ša ina aplūtim nasāḫim la ublam abum mārašu ina aplūtim ul inassaḫ.*
**(169)** *šumma arnam kabtam ša ina aplūtim nasāḫim ana abišu itbalam ana ištiššu panīšu ubbalū.*
*šumma arnam kabtam adi šinīšu itbalam abum mārašu ina aplūtim inassaḫ.*

**L170–76b (XXXV [Rv. XII]:37–XXXVII [Rv. XIV]:21)**

**(170)** *šumma awīlum ḫīrtašu mārī ūlissum u amassu mārī ūlissum abum ina bulṭišu ana mārī ša* [300]*amtum uldušum*, "mārūa" iqtabi, itti mārī ḫīrtim imtanûšunūti,*
*warka abum ana šīmtim ittalku ina makkūr bīt abim* [301]*mārū ḫīrtim u mārū amtim* mitḫāriš*[302] *izuzzū.*
[303]*aplum mār* ḫīrtim ina zittim inassaqma*[304] *ileqqe.*
**(171a)** *u*[305] *šumma abum* [306]*ina bulṭišu* ana mārī ša amtum uldušum, 'mārūa' la iqtabi*[307]*, warka*[308] *abum ana šīmtim ittalku ina makkūr bīt abim mārū amtim itti mārī ḫīrtim ul izuzzū.*
*andurār amtim u mārīša ištakan*(!)[309].
*mārū ḫīrtim ana mārī amtim ana wardūtim*[310] *ul iraggumū.*

---

299. This verb could be transcribed as a present tense, if it seems preferable to begin the apodosis here rather than later.

300. Y: *amatšu uldušu.*

301. Cf. Y: *DUMU. MEŠ GEMÉ u DUMU. MEŠ ḫīrtim.*

302. Y: *-ri<-iš>.*

303. V: *IBILA* for Stele: *IBILA DUMU.*

304. Y: *inassaqūma.*

305. Y: ø.

306. Y: ø.

307. Z: *iq-KA*(!)*-bi* for *iq-DUG4.-bi.*

308. Z: *wa-ar<-ka>.*

309. This word is normally emended to *iššakkan* (see *BAL*, followed by Roth) as an N-theme; as it stands the infixed *-t-* could convey the desired passive meaning.

310. V: *ardūtim.*

**Disinheritance**

**(168)** If a man has come to the decision to dispossess his son and he has stated before the judges, 'I will dispossess my son,' the judges shall make the decisions about his affairs and the father shall not dispossess his son from his inheritance unless the son has committed an offence serious enough to be disinherited.

**(169)** If he has committed an offence against his father serious enough to be disinherited, on the first occasion they will turn a blind eye.

If he has committed an offence for a second time the father shall disinherit his son.

**Rights over the child of a slave**

**(170)** If the first wife of a man has borne him sons and also his slave-girl has borne him sons, and during his lifetime the father has said to the sons the slave-girl bore him, 'My sons,' they shall reckon them together with the first wife's sons.

After the father has passed to his destiny the first wife's sons and the slave-girl's sons shall share out the treasures in the father's house equally.

An heir, the son of a first wife, shall have the choice of which share to take.

**(171a)** However, if the father has not stated while he was alive to the sons the slave-girl bore him, 'My sons,' the slave-girl's sons shall not share the treasures in the father's house with the first wife's sons after the father has passed to his destiny.

An emancipation shall be arranged for the slave-girl and her sons.

The first wife's sons shall have no rights of slavery over the slave-girl's sons.

**(171b)** *ḫīrtum šeriktaša u nudunnâm ša mussa iddinušim*[311] [312]*ina ṭuppim* išṭurušim ileqqēma ina šubat mutiša uššab.*
*adi balṭat ikkal.*
*ana kaspim ul inaddin.*
*warkassa ša mārīšama.*
**(172)** *šumma mussa nudunnâm la iddiššim, šeriktaša ušallamūšimma ina makkūr bīt mutiša zittam kīma aplim ištēn ileqqe.*
*šumma mārūša aššum ina bītim šūṣîm usaḫḫamūši, dayyānū warkassa*[313] *iparrasūma mārī arnam immidū.*
*sinništum šî ina bīt mutiša ul uṣṣi*
*šumma sinništum šî ana waṣêm panīša ištakan nudunnâm ša mussa iddinušim ana mārīša izzib.*
*šeriktam ša bīt abiša ileqqēma.*
*mut libbiša iḫḫassi.*
**(173)** *šumma sinništum šî ašar īrubu ana mutiša warkîm mārī ittalad warka sinništum šî imtūt, šeriktaša mārū maḫrûtum u warkûtum izuzzū.*
**(174)** *šumma ana mutiša warkîm mārī la ittalad, šeriktaša mārū ḫāwirišama*[314] *ileqqû.*
**(175)** *šumma lu warad ekallim u lu warad muškēnim mārat awīlim īḫuzma mārī ittalad, bēl wardim ana mārī*[315] *mārat awīlim ana wardūtim ul iraggum.*
**(176a)** *u šumma*[316] *warad ekallim u*[317] *lu warad muškēnim mārat awīlim īḫuzma inūma īḫuzuši qadum šeriktim ša bīt abiša*[318] *ana bīt warad ekallim u lu warad muškēnim īrubma ištu innemdū bītam īpušū bīšam iršû warkānumma*[319] *lu warad ekallim u lu warad muškēnim ana šīmtim*[320] *ittalak, mārat awīlim šeriktaša*[321] *ileqqe.*
*u mimma ša mussa u šî ištu innemdū iršû ana šinīšu izuzzūma mišlam bēl wardim ileqqe.*
*mišlam mārat awīlim ana mārīša ileqqe.*

---

311. a: *iddinuši.*
312. V: ø.
313. V: *arkassa.*
314. Y: *maḫ<-ru>-ú-tum.*
315. V: ø(!); perhaps haplography.
316. V: + *lu.*
317. V: ø.
318. A: *abuša*(!).
319. V: *warkānum.*
320. V: *šimātišu.*
321. V: + *elēnumma.*

**(171b)** The first wife shall take the dowry and the wedding gift which her husband presented to her and wrote on a document for her and she shall live in her husband's home.

She shall enjoy it as long as she lives. She shall not sell it for silver. Her property will certainly belong to her sons.

**(172)** If her husband did not give her a wedding gift, they shall restore to her a dowry and she shall take the same share as a single heir from the property in the house of her husband.

If her sons begin to pester her to make her leave the house, the judges shall make the decisions about her affairs and the sons shall bear the blame.

That woman does not have to leave her husband's house.

If that woman has made the decision to leave, she shall leave the gift her husband gave her for her sons.

She shall take the dowry from her father's house. She shall choose a husband she likes.

**(173)** If that woman has borne sons to her later husband after entering a new place and then that woman dies, the first sons and the last sons shall share her dowry.

**(174)** If she has not borne children to her later husband, it is the first husband's children who shall take the dowry.

**(175)** If a slave of the palace or the slave of a working man marries a man's daughter and she bears sons, the slave's owner shall have no right of slavery over any son of the daughter of the man.

**(176a)** Moreover if the slave of the temple or the slave of the working man has married the girl and after he has married her she entered the house of the slave of the temple or the slave of the working man with a dowry from her father's house, and after they have settled down, built a house and acquired property, subsequently the slave of the temple or the slave of the working man has passed to his destiny, the man's daughter shall keep her dowry.

Then they shall divide into two that which she and her husband acquired after they had settled down: the slave's owner shall take half, and the man's daughter shall take half for her sons.

**(176b)** *šumma mārat awīlim šeriktam la išu, mimma ša mussa u šî ištu innemdū iršû ana šinīšu izuzzūma mišlam bēl wardim ileqqe. mišlam mārat awīlim ana mārīša ileqqe.*

**L177 (XXXVII [Rv. XIV]:22-60)**

*šumma almattum ša mārūša ṣeḫḫeru ana bīt šanîm erēbim panīša ištakan balum dayyānī ul irrub.*
*inūma ana bīt šanîm irrubu dayyānū warkat bīt mutiša panîm iparrasūma bītam ša mutiša panîm ana mutiša warkîm*[322] *u sinništim šuāti ipaqqidūma*[323] *ṭuppam ušezzebūšunūti.*
*bītam inasssarū, u ṣeḫḫerūtim urabbû.*
*uniātim ana kaspim ul inaddinū.*
*šāyyimānum ša unūt mārī almattim išammu ina kaspišu ītelli.*
*makkūrum ana bēlišu itâr.*

**L178–84 (XXXVII [Rv. XIV]:61–XXXIX [Rv. XVI]:30)**

**(178)** *šumma ugbabtum nadītum u lu sekretum ša abuša šeriktam išrukušim ṭuppam išṭurušim ina ṭuppim ša išṭurušim warkassa ēma eliša ṭābu nadānam*[324] *la išṭuršimma mala libbiša la ušamṣīši warka abum ana šīmtim ittalku eqelša u kirāša aḫḫūša ileqqûma kīma emūq zittiša ipram piššatam u lubūšam inaddinūšimma libbaša uṭabbū.*
*šumma aḫḫūša kīma emūq zittiša ipram piššatam u lubūšam la ittadnūšimma libbaša la uṭṭibbū, eqelša u kirāša ana errēšim ša eliša ṭābu inaddinma errēssa ittanaššīši*[325]
*eqlam kirâm*[326] *u mimma ša abuša iddinušim*[327] *adi balṭat ikkal.*
*ana kaspim ul inaddin.*
*šaniam ul uppal.*
*aplūssa ša aḫḫīšama.*

---

322. V: *arkim.*
323. V: *ipaqqidū.*
324. Thus *BAL*; Roth: *nadānamma.*
325. V: *ittanašši.*
326. V: + *bītam.*
327. V: *išṭurušim.*

**(176b)** If the man's daughter had no dowry, they shall divide what she and her husband acquired after they had settled down into two: the slave's owner shall take half, and the man's daughter shall take half for her sons.

**A widow who remarries**

**(177)** If a widow with small children has come to a decision to enter the house of a second man, she shall not enter without legal authority.

Before she enters the house of another man the judges will make decisions about the affairs in her first husband's house and entrust her first husband's household to that woman and her second husband, and they shall make them deposit a written statement.

They shall take care of the house and bring up the children.

They shall not sell the furniture for silver.

Anyone who buys the belongings of a widow's sons shall forfeit his silver.

The property shall return to its owner.

**Support for temple-women from their brothers**

**(178)** If the father of a priestess or a temple-woman or a devotee has presented her with a dowry and written out a document for her but has not written on that document that she may dispose of her property in the way she thinks best or that he has empowered her to do what she likes, after he has passed to his destiny her brothers shall take the field or the orchard and make her comfortable by giving her food, oil and garments according to the size of her share.

If her brothers have not made her comfortable by giving her food, oil and clothing according to the size of her share, she shall give her field or her orchard to a farmer she favours and he shall do the cultivation, and he shall support her.

She shall enjoy the field, the orchard or anything else her father has given her as long as she lives.

She shall not sell it for silver or become responsible to anyone else.

Her inheritance belongs to her brothers.

**(179)** *šumma ugbabtum nadītum*[328] *u lu sekretum ša abuša šeriktam išrukušim kunukkam išṭurušim ina ṭuppim ša išṭurušim warkassa ēma eliša ṭābu nadānam išṭuršimma mala libbiša uštamṣīši.*
*warka abum ana šīmtim ittalku, warkassa ēma eliša ṭābu inaddin.*
*aḫḫūša ul ipaqqarūši.*
**(180)** *šumma abum ana mārtišu nadīt*[329] *gagîm u lu sekretim šeriktam la išrukšim(!)*[330] *warka abum ana šīmtim ittalku, ina makkūr bīt abim zittam kīma aplim ištēn izâzma adi balṭat ikkal.*
*warkassa ša aḫḫīšama.*
**(181)** *šumma abum nadītam qadištam u lu kulmašītam ana ilim iššīma šeriktam la išrukšim warka abum ana šīmtim ittalku, ina makkūr bīt abim šalušti aplūtiša izâzma adi balṭat ikkal.*
*warkassa ša aḫḫīšama.*
**(182)** *šumma abum ana mārtišu nadīt Marduk ša Bābilim šeriktam la išrukšim kunukkam la išṭuršim warka abum ana šīmtim ittalku, ina makkūr bīt abim šalušti aplūtiša itti aḫḫīša izâzma ilkam ul illak.*
*nadīt Marduk warkassa ēma eliša ṭābu inaddin.*
**(183)** *šumma abum ana mārtišu šugītim šeriktam išrukšim ana mutim iddišši kunukkam išṭuršim warka abum ana šīmtim ittalku, ina makkūr bīt abim ul izâz.*
**(184)** *šumma awīlum ana mārtišu šugītim šeriktam la išrukšim ana mutim la iddišši warka abum ana šīmtim ittalku, aḫḫūša kīma emūq bīt abim šeriktam išarrakūšimma ana mutim inaddinūši.*

## L185–90 (XXXIX [Rv. XVI]:31-74)

**(185)** *šumma awīlum ṣeḫram ina mêšu ana mārūtim ilqēma urtabbīšu, tarbītum šî ul ibbaqqar.*

---

328. Perhaps here read *kulmašitum* for *nadītum* (Finkelstein).
329. Perhaps here read *kallatum* for *nadītum* (Stol).
330. Reading Stele as *iš<-ru>-uk-ši-im*, see *BAL*.

**(179)** If the father of a priestess or a temple-woman or a devotee has presented her with a dowry and written out an official document for her and has written on that document before he passed to his destiny that she may dispose of her property in the way she thinks best and that he has empowered her to do what she likes, she shall dispose of her property in the way she thinks best.

Her brothers shall have no argument with her.

**(180)** If the father of a confined temple-woman or a devotee has not given a dowry to his daughter, after the father has passed to his destiny she shall be given the share of one heir from the wealth of her father's house, and she shall enjoy it as long as she lives.

Her affairs belong to her brothers.

**(181)** If the father has offered to the god a temple-woman, a holy-woman or a nun but has not given her a dowry, after the father has passed to his destiny she shall have one-third of an heir's share from the wealth of her father's house and she shall enjoy it as long as she lives.

Her affairs belong to her brothers.

**(182)** If a father has not presented a dowry to his daughter who is a temple-woman of Marduk in Babylon, and he has not written out any official document, after he has passed to his destiny she shall share with her brothers one-third of the wealth of her father's house as her inheritance, but she shall not perform any statutory duty.

A temple-woman of Marduk may dispose of her property in the way she thinks best.

**(183)** If a father has presented a dowry to his daughter who is a priestess and has given her to a husband, and has written out an official document, after the father passes to his destiny she will have no share of the wealth in the father's house.

**(184)** If a man has not presented a dowry to his daughter who is a priestess and has not given her to a husband, after the father has passed to his destiny her brothers shall present her with a dowry appropriate to the wealth in the father's house and they shall give her to a husband.

## CHILDREN (L184–95)

### Reclaiming an adopted a child

**(185)** If a man has taken in a tiny child at birth as a son and has brought him up, that ward shall not be reclaimed.

**(186)** *šumma awīlum ṣeḫram ana mārūtim ilqe inūma ilqûšu abašu u ummašu iḫiaṭ, tarbītum šî ana bīt abišu itâr.*
**(187)** *mār girseqîm muzzaz ekallim u mār sekretim*[331] *ul ibbaqqar.*
**(188)** *šumma mār ummānim ṣeḫram*[332] *ana tarbītim ilqēma šipir qātišu uštāḫissu, ul ibbaqqar.*
**(189)** *šumma šipir qātišu la uštāḫissu, tarbītum šî ana bīt abišu itâr.*
**(190)** *šumma awīlum ṣeḫram ša ana mārūtišu ilqûšuma urabbûšu itti mārīšu la imtanūšu, tarbītum šî ana bīt abišu itâr.*

**L191 (XXXIX [Rv. XVI]:75-95)**
*šumma awīlum ṣeḫram ša ana mārūtišu ilqûšuma urabbûšu bīssu*[333] *īpuš warka mārī irtašīma ana tarbītim nasāḫim panam ištakan, ṣeḫrum*[334] *šû rēqūssu*[335] *ul ittallak.*
*abum murabbīšu ina makkūrišu šalušti aplūtišu inaddiššumma ittallak.*
*ina eqlim kirîm u bītim ul inaddiššum.*

**L192–95 (XXXIX [Rv. XVI]:96–XL [Rv. VII]:44)**
**(192)** *šumma mār girseqîm u lu mār sekretim ana abim murabbīšu u ummim murabbītišu 'ul abī atta, ul ummī atti' iqtabi, lišānšu inakkisū.*
**(193)** *šumma mār girseqîm u lu mār sekretim bīt abišu uweddīma abam murabbīšu u ummam murabbīssu izērma ana bīt abišu ittalak īnšu inassaḫū.*
**(194)** *šumma awīlum mārašu ana mušēniqtim iddinma ṣiḫrum*[336] *šû ina qāt mušēniqtim imtūt, mušēniqtum balum abišu u ummišu ṣiḫram šaniamma irtakas.*
*ukannūšima, aššum balum abišu u ummišu ṣiḫram šaniam irkusu tulāša inakkisū.*
**(195)** *šumma mārum abašu imtaḫaṣ, rittašu inakkisū.*

331. Thus Roth; Stele: *MÍ.ZI.IK.RU.UM*, left without transcription in *BAL*.

332. Stele: *DUMU*, transcribed in *BAL* as *māram*, but by Roth as *ṣeḫram;* see also L191 and 194.

333. Stele: *É-ba*(!).

334. Following Roth for *DUMU*, as L188; *BAL*: *mārum*.

335. The word appears to be an unusual adverbial form, where the regular marker *-um* is followed by a suffixed pronoun.

336. Following Roth for *DUMU*, instead of *BAL mārûm*, as previously (L188; 191) and also twice later in this Law.

**(186)** If a man has taken in a tiny child as a son, and then soon after he has taken him in his father and mother search him out, that adopted child shall return to his father's house.
**(187)** The son of an official with a position in the palace and the son of a priestess shall not be reclaimed.
**(188)** If a professional craftsman has taken in a child as a ward and instructed him in manual skills, he shall not be reclaimed.
**(189)** If he has not instructed him in manual skills, that ward shall return to his father's house.
**(190)** If a man has not counted together with his own sons, the child whom he has taken in as a son and whom he has brought up, that ward shall return to his father's house.

**The rights of an adopted child**
**(191)** If a man has established his house after taking in a child as a son and bringing him up, and then has his own children and reaches a decision to expel the ward, that child shall not go away empty-handed.
The father who brought him up shall give him as his inheritance one-third of his wealth, and then he shall go away.
He shall not give him any field, orchard or house.

**Child-care problems resulting in physical punishment**
**(193)** If the son of an official or the son of a priestess has said to the father or the mother who has brought him up, 'You are not my father. You are not my mother,' they shall cut out his tongue.
**(193)** If the son of an official or the son of a priestess declares he knows his father's house, and he hates the father and the mother who have brought him up, and he has gone away to his father's house, they shall pull out his eye.
**(194)** If a man gives his son to a wet-nurse and that son dies in the hands of the wet-nurse, and the wet-nurse has made a contract for another child without the father or the mother knowing, they shall prove her guilty of having made a contract for another child without the father or mother knowing.
They shall cut off her breast.
**(195)** If a son has struck his father, they shall cut off his hand.

**L196–201 (XL [Rv. VII]:45-74)**

**(196)** *šumma awīlum īn mār awīlim uḫtappid, īnšu uḫappadū.*
**(197)** *šumma eṣemti awīlim ištebir, eṣemtašu išebbirū.*
**(198)** *šumma īn muškēnim uḫtappid u lu eṣemti*(!)[337] *muškēnim ištebir, 1 mana kaspam išaqqal.*
**(199)** *šumma īn warad awīlim uḫtappid u lu eṣemti warad awīlim ištebir, mišil šīmišu išaqqal.*
**(200)** *šumma awīlum šinni awīlim meḫrišu ittadi, šinnašu inaddû.*
**(201)** *šumma šinni*[338] *muškēnim ittadi 1/3 mana kaspam išaqqal.*

**L202–14 (XL [Rv. VII]:75–XLI [Rv. XVIII]:54)**

**(202)** *šumma awīlum lēt awīlim ša elišu rabû imtaḫaṣ, ina puḫrim ina qinnaz alpim 1 šūši immaḫḫaṣ.*
**(203)** *šumma mār awīlim lēt mār awīlim ša kīma šuāti imtaḫaṣ 1 mana kaspam išaqqal.*
**(204)** *šumma muškēnum lēt muškēnim imtaḫaṣ, 10 šiqil kaspam išaqqal.*
**(205)** *šumma warad awīlim lēt mār awīlim imtaḫaṣ, uzunšu inakkisū.*
**(206)** *šumma awīlum awīlam ina risbātim*[339] *imtaḫaṣma simmam ištakanšu, awīlum šû 'ina idû la amḫaṣu'*[340] *itamma u asâm ippal.*
**(207)** *šumma ina maḫāṣišu imtūt, itammāma:*
*šumma mār awīlim 1/2 mana kaspam išaqqal.*
**(208)** *šumma mār muškēnim, 1/3 mana kaspam išaqqal.*
**(209)** *šumma awīlum mārat awīlim imḫaṣma ša libbiša uštaddīši, 10 šiqil kaspam ana ša libbiša išaqqal.*
**(210)** *šumma sinništum šî imtūt, mārassu idukkū.*
**(211)** *šumma mārat muškēnim ina maḫāṣim ša libbiša uštaddīši, 5 šiqil kaspam išaqqal.*
**(212)** *šumma sinništum šî*[341] *imtūt, 1/2 mana kaspam išaqqal.*
**(213)** *šumma amat awīlim imḫaṣma ša libbiša uštaddīši, 2 šiqil kaspam išaqqal.*

---

337. Stele *GÌR.NÍG.DU* for *GÌR.PAD.DU*.

338. Stele *ši-in-gag*(!).

339. Roth prefers to read the word as a fem. sing. and transcribes *risbatim*.

340. Roth transcribes *am-ḫa-ṣú* thus, assuming a subjunctive form; it is possible that the expected affixed pronoun *-šu* has been assimilated, giving an alternative transcription *amḫaṣṣu* (< **amḫaṣšu*).

341. Stele *ši* for usual *ši-i*.

## Compensation and Fees

### Accidental Injury (L196–201)

**(196)** If a man has destroyed the sight of another similar person, they shall destroy his sight.
**(197)** If he has broken another man's bone, they shall break one of his bones.
**(198)** If he has destroyed the sight of a working man or broken a bone of a working man, he shall pay one mana of silver.
**(199)** If he has destroyed the sight of another man's slave or broken a bone of another man's slave, he shall pay half his value in silver.
**(200)** If a man has knocked out the tooth of a man who is his colleague, they shall knock out his tooth.
**(201)** If he has knocked out the tooth of a working man, he shall pay a third of a mana of silver.

### ASSAULT (L202–14)

**(202)** If a man has struck the cheek of a man who is more important than he, he shall be struck in the council 60 times with an ox-tail.
**(203)** If one man has struck the cheek of another such man of similar status, he shall pay one mana of silver.
**(204)** If a working man has struck the cheek of another working man, he shall pay ten shekels of silver.
**(205)** If a man's slave has struck the cheek of another man, they shall cut off his ear.
**(206)** If a man has struck another man in a brawl and has injured him, that man shall solemnly declare, 'I did not wound him intentionally.' It is he who shall be responsible for the physician.
**(207)** If someone has died in that brawl, he shall similarly make a solemn declaration; and if it was a man's son, he shall pay half a mana of silver.
**(208)** If he was a working man's son, he shall pay a third of a mana of silver.
**(209)** If a man has struck the daughter of a man and has made her lose her unborn child, he shall pay ten shekels of silver for the foetus.
**(210)** If that woman has died, they shall kill his daughter.
**(211)** If he has made a commoner's daughter lose her unborn child by the violence, he shall pay five shekels of silver.
**(212)** If that woman has died, he shall pay half a mana of silver.
**(213)** If he has struck a man's slave-girl and made her lose her unborn child, he shall pay two shekels of silver.

**(214)** *šumma amtum šī imtūt, 1/3 mana kaspam išaqqal.*

**L215–25 (XLI [Rv. XVIII]:55–XLII [Rv. XIX]:35)**

**(215)** *šumma asûm awīlam simmam kabtam ina karzilli siparrim īpušma awīlam ubtalliṭ u lu nakkapti awīlim ina karzilli siparrim iptēma īn awīlim ubtalliṭ, 10 šiqil kaspam ileqqe.*
**(216)** *šumma mār muškēnim, 5 šiqil kaspam ileqqe.*
**(217)** *šumma warad awīlim, bēl wardim ana asîm 2 šiqil kaspam inaddin.*
**(218)** *šumma asûm awīlam simmam kabtam ina karzilli siparrim īpušma awīlam uštamīt u lu nakkapti*[342] *awīlim ina karzilli siparrim iptēma īn awīlim uḫtappid, rittašu inakkisū.*
**(219)** *šumma asûm simmam kabtam warad muškēnim ina karzilli siparrim īpušma uštamīt, wardam kīma wardim iriab.*
**(220)** *šumma nakkaptašu ina karzilli siparrim iptēma īnšu uḫtapid(!)*[343], *kaspam mišil šīmišu išaqqal.*
**(221)** *šumma asûm eṣemti awīlim šebirtam uštallim u lu šerʾānam marṣam ubtalliṭ, bēl simmim ana asîm 5 šiqil kaspam inaddin.*
**(222)** *šumma mār muškēnim, 3 šiqil kaspam inaddin.*
**(223)** *šumma warad awīlim, bēl wardim ana asîm 2 šiqil kaspam inaddin.*
**(224)** *šumma asî alpim u lu imērim lu alpam u lu imēram simmam kabtam īpušma ubtalliṭ, bēl alpim u lu imērim 1/6 kaspam*[344] *ana asîm idīšu inaddin.*
**(225)** *šumma alpam u lu imēram simmam kabtam īpušma uštamīt, 1/4 šīmišu ana bēl alpim u lu imērim inaddin.*

**L226–27 (XLII [Rv. XIX]:36-55)**

**(226)** *šumma gallābum balum bēl wardim abbutti wardim la šêm ugallib ritti gallābim šuāti inakkisū.*
**(227)** *šumma awīlum gallābam idāṣma abbutti wardim la šêm ugdallib, awīlam šuāti idukkūšūma ina bābišu iḫallalūšu.*
*gallābum 'ina idû la ugallibu' itammāma utaššar.*

---

342. Stele: *na-id*(!)-*ti*.
343. Stele *uḫ-tap-da* for *uḫ-tap-pi-id*.
344. Stele: *IGI.6 GÁL*; here, and elsewhere (see L225), no ideogram for *šiqlu* is written when the numeral is a fraction.

**(214)** If that slave-girl has died, he shall pay a third of a mana of silver.

**Medical and Veterinary Help (L215–25)**

**(215)** If a physician has made a deep incision with a surgeon's knife on a man and has saved the man's life, or has opened out a man's eye-socket and saved the man's sight, he shall receive ten shekels of silver.

**(216)** If it was a working man's son, he shall receive five shekels of silver.

**(217)** If it was a slave, the slave's owner shall give the physician two shekels of silver.

**(218)** If a physician has made a deep incision with a surgeon's knife on a man and has caused the man's death, or has opened out a man's eye-socket and destroyed the man's sight, they shall cut off his hand.

**(219)** If a physician has made a deep incision with a surgeon's knife on a working man's slave and has caused his death, he shall make recompense with slave for slave.

**(220)** If he has opened up his eye-socket and destroyed his sight, he shall pay half of his value in silver.

**(221)** If the physician has mended a man's broken bone, or has freed a painful joint, the wounded person shall pay the physician five shekels of silver.

**(222)** If it was a working man's son he shall pay three shekels of silver.

**(223)** If it was a man's slave, the slave's owner shall pay the doctor two shekels of silver.

**(224)** If the vet for cattle or donkeys makes a deep incision on a cow or a sheep and saves its life, the owner of the cow or the donkey shall pay the physician his fee of a sixth of a shekel of silver.

**(225)** If he has made a deep incision on the cow or the donkey and has made it die, he shall pay a quarter of its value to the owner of the cow or donkey.

**Barbers (L226–27)**

**(226)** If a barber has shaved away the mark of a slave which is not his own without the slave's owner knowing, they shall cut off the hand of that barber.

**(227)** If a man has tricked the barber and he has shaved away the mark of a slave which is not his own, they shall kill that man by hanging him in his doorway.

The barber shall swear, 'I did the shaving without proper information,' and he shall go free.

**L228–33 (XLII [Rv. XIX]:56–XLIII [Rv.XX]:3)**

**(228)** *šumma itinnum bītam ana awīlim īpušma ušaklilšum ana 1 musar bītim 2 šiqil kaspam ana qīštišu inaddiššum.*

**(229)** *šumma itinnum ana awīlim bītam īpušma šipiršu la udanninma bīt īpušu imqutma bēl bītim uštamīt, itinnum šû iddâk.*

**(230)** *šumma mār bēl bītim uštamīt, mār itinnim šuāti idukkū.*

**(231)** *šumma warad bēl bītim uštamīt, wardam kīma wardim ana bēl bītim inaddin.*

**(232)** *šumma makkūram uḫtalliq mimma ša uḫalliqu iriab.*
*u, aššum bīt īpušu la udanninuma imqutu, ina makkūr ramanišu bīt imqutu ippeš.*

**(233)** *šumma itinnum bītam ana awīlim īpušma šipiršu la ušteṣbīma igārum iqtūp, itinnum šû ina kasap ramanišu igāram šuāti udannan.*

**L234–40 (XLIII [Rv. XX]:4-80)**

**(234)** *šumma malāḫum elep 60 kur ana awīlim ipḫe, 2 šiqil kaspam ana qīštišu inaddiššum.*

**(235)** *šumma malāḫum eleppam ana awīlim ipḫēma šipiršu la utakkilma ina šattimma šuāti eleppum šî iṣṣabar, ḫiṭītam irtaši.*
*malāḫum eleppam šuāti inaqqarma ina makkūr ramanišu udannanma eleppam dannatam ana bēl eleppim inaddin.*

**(236)** *šumma awīlum eleppašu ana malāḫim ana igrim iddinma malāḫum īgīma eleppam uṭṭebbi u lu uḫtalliq, malāḫum eleppam ana bēl eleppim iriab.*

**(237)** *šumma awīlum malāḫam u eleppam īgurma še'am šipātim šamnam suluppī u mimma šumšu ša ṣênim iṣēnši malāḫum šû īgīma eleppam uṭṭebbi u ša libbiša uḫtalliq, malāḫum eleppam ša uṭebbû u mimma ša ina libbiša uḫalliqu iriab.*

**(238)** *šumma malāḫum elep awīlim uṭṭebbīma uštēliašši, kaspam mišil šīmiša inaddin.*

**Houses and Builders (228–33)**

**(228)** If a builder has built a house for a man and has completed it for him, he shall pay as his fee[76] two shekels of silver for each sar in area.

**(229)** If a builder has built a house for a man and has not made his work strong enough and the house he has made has collapsed and caused the death of the owner of the house, that builder shall be killed.

**(230)** If it has caused the death of the son of the owner of the house, they shall kill that builder's son.

**(231)** If it has caused the death of a slave of the owner of the house, he shall give a slave for the slave to the owner of the house.

**(232)** If he has destroyed possessions, he shall make recompense for whatever he destroyed.

Moreover, since the house he had built collapsed because he had not made it strong enough, he shall rebuild the house which collapsed from his own resources.

**(233)** If a builder has made a house for a man and has not made his work solid enough and a wall has toppled, that builder shall strengthen that wall from his own resources.

**Boats and Boatmen (L234–40)**

**(234)** If a boat-builder has caulked a boat of 60 kur capacity for a man, he shall give him one shekel of silver as his fee.

**(235)** If a boat-builder has caulked a boat for a man but has not done it properly and in the same year the boat begins to leak[77] and shows a defect, the boat-builder shall repair that boat and reinforce it at his own expense, and give the reinforced boat to the owner of the boat.

**(236)** If a man has given his boat to a boatman for hire and the boatman is careless and sinks the boat or loses it altogether, the boatman shall repay the owner of the boat with another boat.

**(237)** If a man has hired a boatman or a boat and has stowed it with grain, wool, oil, dates or some other cargo, but that boatman has been careless and has sunk the boat and completely lost what was in it, the boatman shall make repayment for the boat that he sank and for whatever was in it that he lost.

**(238)** If a boatman has sunk a man's boat but brings it up again, he shall pay half its value in silver.

---

76. A similar expression occurs earlier when the physician's fee is mentioned, and later with regard to the boat-builder.

77. The N-form can sometimes have an ingressive nuance.

**(239)** *šumma awīlum malāḫam [īgur], 6 [kur šeʾam] ina šanat inaddiššum.*
**(240)** *šumma elep ša māḫirtim elep ša muqqelpītim imḫaṣma uṭṭebbi, bēl eleppim ša eleppašu ṭebiat mimma ša ina eleppišu ḫalqu ina maḫar ilim ubârma ša māḫirtim ša elep ša muqqelpītim uṭebbû eleppašu u mimmâšu ḫalqam iriabšum.*

**L241 (XLIII [Rv. XX]:81-84)**
*šumma awīlum alpam ana nipûtim ittepe 1/3 mana kaspam išaqqal.*

**L242–49 (XLIII [Rv. XX]:85-XLIV [Rv. XXI]:23)**
**(242/3)** *šumma awīlum <alpam>*[345] *ana šattim ištiat īgur, idī alpim ša warka 4 kur seʾam,*[346] *idī alpim ša qabla 3 kur šeʾam, ana bēlišu inaddin.*
**(244)** *šumma awīlum alpam imēram īgurma ina ṣērim nēšum iddūkšu, ana bēlišuma.*
**(245)** *šumma awīlum alpam īgurma ina mēgûtim u lu ina maḫāṣim uštamīt, alpam kīma alpim ana bēl alpim iriab.*
**(246)** *šumma awīlum alpam īgurma šēpšu ištebir u lu labiānšu ittakis alpam kīma alpim ana bēl alpim iriab.*
**(247)** *šumma awīlum alpam īgurma īnšu uḫtappid,* [347]*kaspam 1/2 šīmišu ana bēl alpim inaddin*.*
**(248)** *šumma awīlum alpam īgurma qaranšu išbir*[348] *zibbassu ittakis u lu šašallašu ittasak*[349]*, kaspam 1/4(?) sīmišu inaddin.*
**(249)** *šumma awīlum alpam īgurma ilum imḫassuma*[350] *imtūt, awīlum ša alpam īguru nīš ilim izakkarma ūtaššar.*

**L250–52 (XLIV [Rv. XXI]:24-68)**
**(250)** *šumma alpum sūqam ina alākišu awīlam ikkipma uštamīt dīnum šû rugummâm ul išu.*

---

345. Restoration according to *BAL*, but not in Roth.

346. L242 was thought to end here, but it is better to run on the text and treat L243 together with it.

347. p: *mišil šīmīšu kaspam išaqqal (Ì.LÁ[.E]).*

348. Roth restores *iš<te>bir*.

349. Following Stele *it-ta-sa-ag*; *BAL* prefers to read *ittasaḫ*(!), see *nasāḫu*.

350. b: *imtaḫassuma.*

**(239)** If a man has hired a boatman he shall pay him six kur of grain a year.

**(240)** If a boat being rowed strikes a boat under sail and it sinks, the boat owner whose boat was sunk shall declare in the presence of god whatever has been lost from the boat, and the oarsman who sank the boat under sail shall make a repayment for the boat and all the damage.

### THE VALUE OF ANIMALS (L241–52)

#### As security

**(241)** If a man has taken an ox as security, he shall pay a third of a mana of silver.

#### When hired

**(242/3)** If a man has hired <an ox> for one year, he shall pay to its owner the charges for a rear-ox of four kur of grain, and the charges for a lead-ox three kur of grain.

**(244)** If a man has hired an ox or a donkey and a lion has killed it in the open country, it is the owner's responsibility.

**(245)** If a man has hired an ox and has let it die through carelessness or violent treatment, he shall make a repayment to the owner of the ox of an ox for an ox.

**(246)** If a man has hired an ox and breaks its leg or cuts a tendon, he shall make a repayment to the owner of the ox of an ox for an ox.

**(247)** If a man has hired an ox and destroyed its sight he shall pay the owner of the ox half its value in silver.

**(248)** If a man has hired an ox and broken its horn, or cut off its tail, or torn its flesh, he shall pay a quarter of its value in silver.

**(249)** If a man has hired an ox and a god has struck it down and it has died, the man who hired the ox shall solemnly swear by a god and be innocent.

#### Causing damage

**(250)** If an ox has tossed a man while walking along the road and caused his death, there is no cause for complaint.

**(251)** *šumma alap awīlim nakkāpīma kīma nakkāpû bābtašu ušēdīšumma qarnīšu la ušarrim alapšu la usanniqma alpum šû mār awīlim ikkipma uštamīt,* ½ *mana kaspam inaddin.*
**(252)** *šumma warad awīlim,* ⅓ *mana kaspam inaddin.*

**L253–58 (XLIV [Rv. XXI]:69–XLV [Rv. XXII]:9)**
**(253)** *šumma awīlum awīlam ana panī eqlišu uzuzzim īgurma aldâm iqīpšu liātim*[351] *ipqissum* [*ana*] *eqlim erēšim urakkissu. šumma awīlum šû zēram u lu ukullâm išriqma ina qātišu ittaṣbat, rittašu inakkisū.*
**(254)** *šumma aldâm ilqēma liātim ūtenniš*[352]*, tašna še'am ša imḫuru*[353] *iriab.*
**(255)** *šumma liāt awīlim ana igrim ittadin u lu zēram išriqma ina eqlim la uštabši, awīlam šuāti ukannūšuma ina ebūrim ana 1 burum* 60 *kur še'am imaddad.*
**(256)** *šumma pīḫassu*[354] *apālam la ile'i, ina eqlim šuāti*[355] *ina liātim*[356] *imtanaššarūšu.*
**(257)** *šumma awīlum ikkaram*[357] *īgur, 8 kur še'am ina šattim ištiat inaddiššum.*
**(258)** *šumma awīlum kullizam īgur, 6 kur še'am ina* [358]*šattim ištiat* inaddiššum.*

**L259–60 (XLV [Rv. XXII]:10-20)**
**(259)** *šumma awīlum epinnam ina ugārim išriq, 5 šiqil kaspam ana bēl epinnim inaddin.*
**(260)** *šumma ḫarbam u lu maškakātim ištariq, 3 šiqil kaspam inaddin.*

**L261–67 (XLV [Rv. XXII]:21-89)**
**(261)** *šumma awīlum nāqidam ana liātim u ṣēnim re'îm īgur, 8 kur še'am ina šattim ištiat inaddiššum.*

---

351. BAL suggests *sugullum* as an alternative transcription for the Sumerogram *áb. gu*$_4$*.ḫá* here and in subsequent clauses.
352. Stele *ú-te-en-gag*(!)*-iš*.
353. Stele *im-ri*(!)*-ru*.
354. p: *IGI-ḫa-su* for *pi-ḫa-su*.
355. p: *šuātu*(!).
356. p: *GU*$_4$.
357. Stele: poorly written; see *BAL*.
358. p: [*ša-at*]*-ti-šu*.

**(251)** If a man has an ox which tosses and his council have informed him that it tosses and he has not covered its horns and has not tied the ox up and the ox tosses a man's son and causes his death, he shall pay half a shekel of silver.
**(252)** If it was a man's slave he shall give a third of a mana of silver.

## Casual Labour (L253–58 )

**(253)** If a man has hired another man to stand beside his field, and has lent him seed-grain, entrusted him with the oxen, and arranged with him to plough his field, and if that man has stolen the feeding grain or other fodder and it has been found in his possession, they shall cut off his hand.
**(254)** If he has taken the feeding grain and made the animals weak, he shall make a repayment of double the amount of grain he received.
**(255)** If he has hired out the man's oxen, or has stolen the seed-grain and has produced nothing in the field, they shall prove that man guilty and make an assessment of 60 kur of grain for 18 iku of land.
**(256)** If he was not able to respond to his obligations, they shall drag him all over that field with the animals.
**(257)** If a man hires a farmer, he shall give him eight kur of grain for one year.
**(258)** If a man has hired a cowman, he shall give him six kur of grain for one year.

## Fines for Stolen Implements (L259–60)

**(259)** If a man has stolen a plough from the fields, he shall give five shekels of silver to the owner of the plough.
**(260)** If he has stolen a harrow or a scuffle, he shall give three shekels of silver.

## Herdsmen and Shepherds (L261–67)

**(261)** If a man has hired a herdsman to feed the cattle or the sheep, he shall give him eight kur of grain for one year.

**(262)** mostly broken
*šumma awīlum alpam u lu immeram ana [nāqidim…*
**(263)** badly broken
*šumma [alpam] u lu [immeram] ša innadnušum uḫtalliq alpam kīma [alpim] immeram kīma [immerim] ana bēlišu*[359] *iriab.*
**(264)** *šumma [rē'ûm] ša liātum u lu ṣēnum ana re'îm innadnušum idīšu gamrātim maḫir libbašu ṭāb liātim uṣṣaḫḫir ṣēnam uṣṣaḫḫir tālittam umtaṭṭi, ana pī riksātišu tālittam u biltam inaddin.*
**(265)** *šumma rē'ûm ša liātum u lu ṣēnum ana re'îm innadnušum usarrirma šimtam uttakkir.*
*u ana kaspim ittadin, ukannūšuma adi 10-šu ša išriqu liātim u ṣēnam ana bēlišunu iriab.*
**(266)** *šumma ina tarbaṣim* [360]*lipit ilim* ittabši u lu nēšum iddūk, rē'ûm maḫar*[361] *ilim ubbamma*[362] *miqitti*[363] *tarbaṣim bēl tarbaṣim imaḫḫaršu.*
**(267)** *šumma rē'ûm īgūma*[364] *ina tarbaṣim pissatam uštabši rē'ûm ḫiṭīt pissatim ša ina tarbaṣim ušabšû liātim u ṣēnam ušallamma ana bēlišunu inaddin.*

**L268–73 (XLV [Rv. XXII]:90–XLVI [Rv. XXII]:19)**
**(268)** *šumma awīlum alpam ana diāšim īgur 2 sūt še'um idūšu.*
**(269)** *šumma imēram ana diāšim īgur 1 sūt še'um idūšu.*
**(270)** *šumma urīṣam ana diāšim īgur 1 qa še'um idūšu.*
**(271)** *šumma awīlum liātim ereqqam u murteddīša īgur, ina ūmim ištēn 3 parsikat še'am inaddin.*

---

359. The word is broken, and *BAL* prefers to restore a plural suffix *bēlišunu*.
360. c: *lipitti ilim* (perhaps through mishearing the text pronounced).
361. Stele: *ma-ḫi*(!).
362. c: *ubbabma.*
363. c: *miqit.*
364. Stele: *i-GEMÉ*(!)*-ma.* c: *e-gi-šu*(!).

**(262)** If a man...an ox or a sheep...
**(263)** If he loses [the cattle or the sheep] which have been given him, he shall make a repayment to their owner of an ox [for an ox] and a sheep [for a sheep].
**(264)** If a shepherd who has been given cattle and sheep to feed has received everything to make him satisfied, but he has diminished the herd and the flock and there are less births, he shall give some young animals or some produce according to the words of the agreement.
**(265)** If a shepherd who has been given cattle and sheep to feed has been deceitful and has changed the mark and sold them for silver, they shall prove him guilty and he shall make a repayment to their owner of cattle and sheep of ten times what he stole.
**(266)** If there has been an act of god[78] in a sheepfold or a lion has made a kill, the shepherd shall absolve himself in the presence of the god, and the owner of the sheepfold shall accept from him the damage in the sheepfold[79].
**(267)** If a shepherd has been careless and has let foot-rot[80] start in the sheepfold, the shepherd shall make good the loss of the cattle and the sheep from the foot-rot which he allowed to start in the sheepfold, and shall give it to their owner.

### Hire of Animals and Equipment (L268–73)

**(268)** If a man has hired an ox to do the threshing, the charge for it is two sa of grain.
**(269)** If he has hired a donkey to do the threshing the charge for it is one sa of grain.
**(270)** If he has hired a goat to do the threshing the charge for it is one qa of grain.
**(271)** If a man has hired cattle and a cart as well as a driver, for them he shall pay three parsikat of grain for one day.

---

78. Probably a periphrasis for inexplicable disease; Roth: 'epidemic'.

79. The verb *maḫāru* here may mean simply that the owner formally receives the sheepfold (and the animals), removing it from the control of the hired labourer; alternatively it may have legal significance, showing that the hired labourer does not have to make recompense, as suggested by Roth's 'to accept responsibility for the loss'.

80. Whether it means mange (Roth), or foot-rot, or any other disease which can spread in a herd or flock, cannot at present be determined.

**(272)** *šumma awīlum ereqqamma ana ramaniša īgur ina ūmim ištēn 4 sūt še'am inaddin.*
**(273)** *šumma awīlum agram īgur, ištu rēš šattim adi ḫamšim warḫim 6 uṭṭet kaspam ina ūmim ištēn inaddin, ištu šiššim warḫim adi taqtīt šattim 5 uṭṭet kaspam ina ūmim ištēn inaddin.*

**L274 (XLVI [Rv. XXII]:20-44): badly broken**
*šumma awīlum mār ummānim iggar,*

| | |
|---|---|
| *idī* [ ] | 5 *uṭṭet kaspam* |
| *idī kāmidim* | 5 *uṭṭet kaspam* |
| [*idī*] *ša kitîm* | [...*uṭṭet*] *kaspam* |
| [*idī*] *purkullim* | [...*uṭṭet*] *kaspam* |
| [*idī*] *sasinnim* | [...*uṭṭet*] *kaspam* |
| [*idī*] *nappāhim* | [...*uṭṭet*] *kaspam* |
| *idī naggārim* | 4(?) *uṭṭet kaspam* |
| *idī aškāpim* | [ ] *uṭṭet kaspam* |
| *idī atkuppim* | [ ] *uṭṭet kaspam* |
| [*idī*] *itinnim* | [...*uṭṭet*] *kaspam* |

[*ina ūmim*] *ištēn* [*inaddin*].

**L275–77 (XLVI [Rv. XXII]:45-57)**
**(275)** slightly broken
[*šumma*] *awīlum* [...] *īgur, ina ūmim ištēn 3 uṭṭet kaspum idūša.*
**(276)** *šumma māḫirtam īgur, 2½ uṭṭet kaspam idīša ina ūmim ištēn inaddin.*
**(277)** *šumma awīlum elep šūšim īgur, ina ūmim ištēn ⅙ kaspam idīša inaddin.*

**L278–82 (XLVI [Rv. XXIII]:58-102)**
**(278)** *šumma awīlum*[365] [366]*wardam amtam* išāmma waraḫšu*[367] *la imlāma benni elišu imtaqut ana nādinānišu*[368] *utârma*[369] *šāyyimānum kasap išqulu ileqqe*[370]

---

365. e: perhaps different.
366. d, q: *amtam wardam*; c, d: + determinative *SAG*.
367. d: *ištēn warḫu*.
368. e: *-ima*.
369. e: *utâr*.
370. e: *ilaqqe*.

**(272)** If a man has hired a cart on its own, he shall pay four sa of grain for one day.
**(273)** If a man has hired a labourer, he shall pay six grains of silver for one day from the beginning of the year until the fifth month, and five grains of silver for one day from the sixth month until the end of the year.

### Tradesmen's Rates (L274)

**(274: *badly broken*)** If a man intends to hire someone who is a craftsman, the fee for one day is:

| | |
|---|---|
| or … | five grains of silver; |
| or a textile worker | five grains of silver; |
| or a linen-weaver | ...silver; |
| or a seal cutter | ...silver; |
| or a maker of bows | ...silver |
| or a smith | ...silver; |
| or a carpenter | four (?) grains of silver; |
| or a leather-worker | ...grains of silver; |
| or a basket-maker | ...grains of silver; |
| or a builder | ...silver. |

### Rates for Boats (L275–77)

**(275 *broken*)** [If a man] has hired...the charge for it is three grains of silver for one day.
**(276)** If a man has hired a rowing boat, he shall pay a charge of two and a half grains of silver for it for one day.
**(277)** If a man has hired a boat of 60 kur, the charge for it is a sixth of a shekel for one day.

### Unworkable Slaves (L278–82)

**(278)** If a man has bought a slave or a slave-girl and, before they have finished the first month, sickness has struck them down, he shall return them to the seller and the purchaser shall take back any silver he has paid.

**(279)** *šumma awīlum* [371]*wardam amtam* išāmma baqrī irtaši nādin-ānšu baqrī*[372] *ippal*[373].
**(280)** *šumma awīlum ina māt nukurtim wardam amtam ša awīlim ištām inūma ina libbū mātim ittalkamma bēl wardim u lu amtim lu warassu u lu amassu ūteddi,*
*šumma wardum u amtum šunu mārū mātim, balum kaspimma andurāršunu iššakkan.*
**(281)** *šumma mārū mātim šanītim, šāyyimānumma*(!)[374] *ina maḫar ilim kasap išqulu*[375] *iqabbīma*[376], *bēl wardim u lu amtim kasap išqulu ana tamkārim inaddinma, lu warassu lu amassu ipaṭṭar*[377].
**(282)** *šumma wardum ana bēlišu 'ul bēlī atta' iqtabi, kīma warassu ukânšuma bēlšu uzunšu inakkis.*

## EPILOGUE

### E1 (= XLVII:1-8)

*dīnāt mīšarim, ša Ḫammurabi šarrum lēʾûm ukinnuma*
*mātam ussam kīnam u rīdam damqam ušaṣbitu.*

### E2 (= XLVII:9-14)

*Ḫammurabi šarrum gitmālum anāku*
*ana ṣalmāt qaqqadim, ša Ellil išrukam, rēʾûssina Marduk iddinam*
*ul ēgu, aḫi ul addī.*

### E3 (= XLVII:15-21)

*ašrī šulmim ešteʾīšināšim*[378]
*pušqī wašṭūtim upetti*
*nūram ušēṣišināšim.*

### E4 (= XLVII:22-31)

*ina kakkim dannim ša Zababa u Ištar ušatlimūnim*

---

371. e: + determinative *SAG*.
372. e: + *-šu*.
373. e: *i-ip-pa-il*(!).
374. *BAL* suggests emending text to read *šāyyimānum*, which is followed by Roth.
375. Stele: *išlulu*(!).
376. Stele: *bi* for *qa*.
377. Stele: *ag* for *ṭar*.
378. e: *-šināšinim*(!).

**(279)** If a man has bought a slave or a slave-girl and then claims are found to exist, the one who sold to him shall be responsible for the claims.
**(280)** If a man in a foreign country has bought a slave or a slave-girl from someone, and when he is travelling in the land the owner of the slave or the slave-girl has told him that it is his slave or his slave-girl, he shall arrange the emancipation of such slaves and slave-girls without payment provided they are citizens of the land[81].
**(281)** If they are citizens of a different land the purchaser shall state the amount of silver he paid in the presence of the god and the owner of the slave or the maid shall pay the silver and redeem his slave or his slave-girl.
**(282)** If the slave has stated to his master, 'You are not my master,' his master shall prove that it is his slave and cut off his ear.

## EPILOGUE

**(E1)** Proper laws established by Hammurabi, the able king,
who made the land adopt solid principles and good conduct.

**(E2)** I am Hammurabi, the efficient king.
I have not been careless with the mass of mankind,
which Enlil has entrusted to me and which Marduk has made my flock;
I have not been lazy.

**(E3)** I have searched for peaceful places for them.
I have solved impossible difficulties.
I have made the light shine for them.

**(E4)** With the fierce weapon that Zababa and Ishtar have presented to me,

81. The phrase is apparently used to mean a citizen of Babylonia.

*ina igigallim ša Ea išīmam*[379]
*ina lē'ûtim*[380] *ša Marduk iddinam*[381]
*nakrī*[382] *eliš u šapliš assuḫ.*

**E5 (= XLVII:32-39)**
*qablātim ubelli, šīr mātim uṭīb*
*nišī dadmī aburrī ušarbiṣ, mugallitam ul ušaršīšināti.*

**E6 (= XLVII:40-45)**
*ilū rabûtum ibbûninnima*
*anākuma rē'ûm mušallimum, ša ḫaṭṭašu išarat.*

**E7 (= XLVII:46-58)**
*ṣillī ṭābum ana āliya tariṣ*
*ina utliya nišī māt Šumerim u Akkadîm ukīl*
*ina lamassiya iḫḫiša*
*ina šulmim attabbalšināti*
*ina nēmeqiya uštapziršināti*[383].

**E8 (= XLVII:59-78)**
*dannum enšam ana la ḫabālim, ekūtam almattam šutēšurim*
*ina Bābilim*
*ālim ša Anum u Ellil rēšīšu ullû*
*ina Esagil*
*bītim ša kīma šamê u erṣetim išdāšu kīnā*
*dīn mātim ana diānim*[384]
*purussê mātim ana parāsim*[385]
[386]*ḫablim šutēšurim**
*awâtiya šūqurātim ina narîya ašṭurma*
*ina maḫar ṣalmiya šar mīšarim ukīn.*

---

379. e: *-a.*
380. e: *tu*(!)*-u-tim.*
381. e: *išrukam.*
382. e: *nakiri.*
383. See *BAL*; neither *pazāru* or *paṣāru* are known words.
384. f: *-u.*
385. f: *-u.*
386. f: ø ... *.

with the omniscience that Ea has assigned to me,
with the capability that Marduk has granted to me,
I have rooted out enemies that are above and those below[82].

**(E5)** I have made conflicts cease.
I have improved the wellbeing of the nation.
I have made the people lie down in well-watered pastures.
I have let no one disturb their prosperity.

**(E6)** It is the great gods that have nominated me
so that I am the shepherd who brings peace, with a staff that is straight.

**(E7)** My protective shadow has been spread over my city,
I have set the people of the land of Sumer and Akkad securely on my knees.
They have come to prosper under my protection;
I have always governed them in peace,
I have always guided[83] them by my wisdom.

**(E8)** So that the mighty might not exploit the weak,
and so that the orphan and the widow may be treated properly,
I have written these very special words of mine on this stone;
I have set them together with the image of me, the king of justice,
in Babylon, the city whose pinnacles Anu and Enlil have raised up,
in Esagila, the temple with foundations as firm as heaven and earth,
so that disputes may be settled in the land,
so that decisions may be made in the land,
so that the oppressed may be treated properly.

---

82. The expression probably refers to attacks into mountainous territory as well as into the plain; an alternative explanation is that up refers to the north, and down to the south.

83. A word of uncertain meaning.

**E9 (= XLVII:79-83)**
*šarrum ša in šarrī šūturu anāku*
*awâtūa nasqā*
*lē'ûtī šāninam ul išû*[387]

**E10 (= XLVII:84–XLVIII:2)**
*ina qibīt Šamaš*[388]
[389]*dayyānim rabîm ša šamê u erṣetim*
*mīšarī ina mātim* lištēpi*
*ina awat Marduk bēliya*
*uṣurātūa mušassikam ay iršia*
*ina Esagil ša arammu*[390]
*šumī ina damiqtim ana dār lizzakir.*

**E11 (= XLVIII:3-19)**
*awīlum ḫablum, ša awatam iraššû*
*ana maḫar ṣalmīya šar mīšarim lillikma,* [391]*narî šaṭram lištassīma*
*awâtiya šūqurātim lišmēma, narî awatam*[392] *likallimšu*
*dīnšu līmur, libbašu linappišma.*

**E12 (= XLVIII:20-47)**
*'Ḫammurabimi*[393] *bēlum*
*ša kīma abim wālidim ana nišī ibaššû*
*ana awat Marduk bēlišu uštaktitma*
*irnitti Marduk eliš u šapliš*[394] *ikšud*
*libbi Marduk bēlišu uṭīb*
*u šīram ṭābam ana nišī ana dār išīm*[395]
*u mātam uštēšer'*
*annītam liqbīma*
*ina maḫar Marduk bēliya Zarpānītum bēltiya*
*ina libbišu gamrim likrubam.*

---

387. f: *iši.*
388. f: + *u Adad.*
389. e: *dā'inu dênim pārisu purussê dêni**; f: *dā'in dêni* [...].
390. e: *-um.*
391. i: *u*(?) *narû šaṭru.*
392. h: *amātu.*
393. i: *Hammurabi.*
394. i: + *issuḫ.*

**(E9)** I am the king who is better than other kings.
What I say is special; what I do is never outdone.

**(E10)** By the command of Shamash, the almighty judge in heaven and earth,
let my justice shine over the land!
By the word of Marduk, my lord,
let no one bent on taking my engraved image ever remove it!
May my name be uttered as a blessing for evermore,
in Esagila, the place I love!

**(E11)** Let any man oppressed, anyone who has a complaint,
come before this statue of the king of justice
and let him have the message on the stone read aloud,
and let him listen to the treasured words I have written,
and may my stela resolve his complaint,
and may he understand his problem,
and may he be content in his heart.

**(E12)** And let him say these words:
'It is the lord Hammurabi,
who like a father gave his people their birth,
who has been obedient to the command of his lord Marduk
and who both above and below[84] has achieved success for Marduk,
who has brought pleasure to Marduk his lord,
by ensuring health and prosperity for his people for evermore,
and by maintaining justice in the land.'
Let him bless me with all his heart,
in the presence of my lord Marduk and of my lady Zarpanitu.

---

84. The phrase here probably refers to success in the eyes of god and man.

**E13 (= XLVIII:48-58)**
*šēdum, lamassum,*
*ilū ēribūt Esagil, libitti Esagil,*
*igirrê ūmišam ina maḫar Marduk bēliya Zarpānītum bēltiya lidammiqū.*

**E14 (= XLVIII:59-74)**
*ana warkiāt ūmī ana mātima*
*šarrum ša ina mātim ibbaššû*
*awât mīšarim ša ina narîya ašṭuru liṣṣur*
*dīn mātim ša adīnu, purussē mātim ša aprusu, ay unakkir,*
*uṣurātiya ay ušassik.*

**E15 (= XLVIII:75-85)**
*šumma awīlum šû tašīmtam išūma māssu šutēšuram ile'i,*
*ana* [396]*awâtim ša* ina narîya ašṭuru liqūlma* [397],
*kibsam rīdam dīn mātim ša adīnu, purussē mātim ša aprusu,*
*narûm šû likallimšuma.*

**E16 (= XLVIII:86-94)**
*ṣalmāt qaqqadišu lištēšer,*
*dīnšina lidīn, purussāšina liprus,*
*ina mātišu raggam u ṣēnam lissuḫ, šīr nišīšu liṭīb.*

**E17 (= XLVIII:95–XLIX:1)**
*Ḫammurabi šar mīšarim, ša Šamaš kīnātim išrukušum, anāku*
*awâtūa nasqā epšētūa šāninam ul išâ*
*ela ana la ḫassim rēqa*
*ana emqim ana tanādātim šūṣâ.*

**E18 (= XLIX:2-17)**
*šumma awīlum šû ana awâtiya ša ina narîya ašṭuru iqūlma*

---

396. h: *awāt**.
397. K19375: *li-ši-it-ma* (perhaps an error).

**(E13)** May the Guardian and the Protector,
the deities who go into Esagila, and the brickwork of Esagila,
look kindly on the daily petitions
made in the presence of my lord Marduk and my lady Zarpanitu.

**(E14)** May any king who appears in this land at any time at all in the future
heed the righteous commands that I have inscribed on this stone.
May no one change the justice for the land which I have ordained
and the verdicts for the land which I have rendered.
May no one remove my graven image.

**(E15)** If he is man of intelligence, who is able to direct his land aright,
let him adhere to the commands I have written on this stela,
and let this stela explain to him the customs and traditions,
the social problems I have encountered
and the decisions I have taken for the community.

**(E16)** So then may he direct the mass of humanity aright,
Let him consider their problems, let him take decisions for them.
Let him weed out evil and wickedness from his land,
let him improve the condition of his people.

**(E17)** I am Hammurabi the king of righteousness,
to whom Shamash has entrusted the truth.
My words are special.
My deeds cannot be surpassed.
It is only to the senseless they are meaningless;
To the wise they are a cause for praise.

**(E18)** If that man has paid attention
to the commandments that I have inscribed on this stone
and has not cast aside my rules,

*dīnī la ušassik, awâtiya la uštepēl, uṣurātiya la unakkir,*
*awīlum šû kīma īâti šar mīšarim Šamaš ḫaṭṭašu lirrik*
*nišīšu ina mīšarim lirē.*

**E19 (= XLIX:18-52)**

*šumma awīlum šû ana awâtiya ša ina narîya ašṭuru la iqūlma*
*errētiya imēšma, errēt ilī la īdurma,*
*dīn adīnu uptassis, awâtiya uštepēl*[398], *uṣurātiya*[399] *uttakkir*
*šumī šaṭram ipšiṭma, šumšu ištaṭar*[400]
*aššum errētim*(!)[401] *šināti šaniamma uštāḫiz*
*awīlum šû lu šarrum lu bēlum lu iššiakkum*
*u lu awīlūtum ša šumam nabiat*
*Anum rabûm abu ilī nābû palêya,*
*melemmī šarrūtim līṭeršu, ḫaṭṭašu lišbir, šīmātišu līrur.*

**E20 (= XLIX:53-80)**

*Ellil bēlum mušīm šīmātim*
*ša qibīssu la uttakkaru*
*mušarbû šarrūtiya,*
*tēšî la šubbîm, gabaraḫ ḫalāqišu, ina šubtišu lišappiḫaššum*[402]
*palê tānēḫim*
*ūmī īṣūtim, šanāt ḫušaḫḫim*
*iklet la nawārim, mūt niṭil īnim*
*ana šīmtim lišīmšum*
*ḫalāq ālišu, naspuḫ nišīšu*
*šarrūssu šupēlam*
*šumšu u zikiršu ina mātim la šubšâm*
*ina pīšu kabtim liqbi.*

---

398. o: *uštapāl.*

399. o: *usurātiya*(!).

400. o: *ištaṭra.*

401. For Stele *er-re-šum* read *er-re-tim*; cf. c and o: ]*ti;* accepted by *BAL* and Roth.

402. *BAL*: transcription uncertain; *CAD*: *lišappiḫaššum*, s.v. *šuppuḫu*, to incite rebellion (*tēšû*), but occurring only once; cf. *AHw*: *šapāḫu*, with one other occurrence in D-theme.

if he has not changed my commandments
or emended what I have written,
Shamash will surely make that man's rule last
for as long as he has made mine last,
the rule of the king of righteousness.
He shall feed his flock in pastures of righteousness.

**(E19)** If that man has not paid attention
to the commandments that I have inscribed on this stone
and if he has forgotten my threatened curses
and has shown no fear for the curses threatened by god,
and if he has destroyed the rules I ordained
and changed my commandments
and emended what I have written,
and if he has removed my name from the inscription
and inscribed his own
or has forced someone else to do it because of these threatened curses,
almighty Anu, the father of the gods,
the one who designated me to rule,
will surely remove from him the splendour of sovereignty,
whether that man is a king or a lord or a governor
or a person appointed to some other function,
and he will smash his staff and curse his destiny.

**(E20)** O Enlil, the lord who decides destinies,
whose commands cannot be altered,
who makes my sovereignty magnificent,
  bring into his home turmoil which cannot be suppressed,
  upheaval which will bring him to an end,
  make his destiny a reign of depression,
  not enough days, years of hunger,
  no light in the darkness, death in the flash of an eye;
  command with your grave tones the loss of his city,
  the exile of his people, the overthrow of his kingdom,
  the extinction of his name and reputation from the land.

**E21 (= XLIX:81-97)**
*Ninlil ummum rabītum, ša qibīssa ina Ekur kabtat,*
*bēltum mudammiqat igirrēya*
*ašar šipṭim u purussêm, ina maḫar Ellil awassu lilemmin*
*šulput mātišu, ḫalāq nišīšu, tabāk napištišu kīma mê*
*ina pī Ellil šarrim lišaškin.*

**E22 (= XLIX:98–L:13)**
*Ea rubûm rabium*
*ša šīmātušu ina maḫra illakā*
*apkal ilī mudē mimma šumšu*
*mušāriku ūm balāṭiya*
*uznam u nēmeqam līṭeršuma*
*ina mīšītim littarrušu*
*nārātišu ina nagbim liskir*
*ina erṣetišu ašnān*[403] *napišti nišī ay ušabši.*

**E23 (= L:14-40)**
*Šamaš dayyānum rabium*
*ša šamê u erṣetim*
*muštēšer šaknat napištim*
*bēlum tukultī*
*šarrūssu liskip, dīnšu ay idīn*
*uruḫšu līši, išdī ummānišu lišḫelṣi*
*ina bīrišu šīram lemnam*
*ša nasāḫ išdī šarrūtišu u ḫalāq mātišu*
*liškunšum*
*awatum maruštum*
*ša Šamaš arḫīš likšussu*
*eliš ina balṭūtim lissuḫšu*
*šapliš ina erṣetim eṭemmašu mê lišaṣmi.*

**E24 (= L:41-63)**
*Sîn bēl šamê*
*ilum bānî*
*ša têressu(!)*[404] *ina ilī šūpât*

---

403. i: *Nisaba.*

404. Stele: *še-re-su; CAD* (vol. A/2: p. 203b) emends to read *têressu* his oracular decision, see *apû* A 4 (= *šūpû*) b.

**(E21)** O Ninlil, almighty mother, whose voice is honoured in Ekur,
the lady who ensures acceptability for my requests,
make his words stink in the presence of Enlil
where judgment is to be decided;
make king Enlil decree that his land be plagued,
that his people be lost, that his life ebb away like a stream.

**(E22)** O Ea, almighty prince, whose opinions gain precedence,
the counsellor of the gods, who knows about everything,
who lengthens the days of my life,
take from him wisdom and understanding
and turn him into someone confused;
stop up the springs of his rivers,
banish from his land the grain to feed the people.

**(E23)** O Shamash, almighty judge of heaven and earth
who directs the lives of all living creatures, the lord in whom I trust,
overthrow his kingdom, do not judge his cause,
confuse him on his path,
cause the foundations of his military power to crumble,
when he seeks divination send an inauspicious portent,
so that the foundations of his kingdom will be torn up
and he will lose his land;
let the bitter words of Shamash quickly overpower him;
cut him off from those who live above,
in the land below make his shadow thirst for water.

**(E24)** O Sin, lord of heaven, creator god,
whose brilliance[85] outshines all other gods,

85. A small change to the text gives an alternative translation 'oracular decision'.

*agâm kussiam ša šarrūtim līṭeršu*
*arnam kabtam šēressu rabītam*
*ša ina zumrišu la iḫalliqu*
*līmussuma*
*ūmī warḫī šanāt palēšu ina tānēḫim*
*u dimmatim lišaqti*
*kammāl šarrūtim lišaṭṭilšu*
*balāṭam ša itti mūtim šitannu ana šīmtim lišīmšum.*

**E25 (= L:64-80)**
*Adad bēl ḫegallim*
*gugal šamê u erṣetim, rēṣūa*
*zunnī ina šamê mīlam ina nagbim līṭeršu*
*māssu ina ḫušaḫḫim u bubūtim liḫalliq*
*eli ālišu ezziš lissīma*
*māssu ana til abūbim litēr.*

**E26 (= L:81-91)**
*Zababa qarrādum rabium*
*mārum rēštûm ša Ekur*
*āliku imniya*
*ašar tamḫārim kakkašu lišbir*
*ūmam ana mūšim litēršumma*
*nakiršu elišu lišziz.*

**E27 (= L:92-LI:23)**
*Ištar bēlet tāḫazim u qablim, pātiat kakkiya*
*lamassī damiqtum, rā'imat palêya*
*ina libbiša aggim, ina uzzātiša rabiātim*
*šarrūssu līrur*
*damqātišu ana lemnētim litēr*
*ašar tāḫazim u qablim kakkašu lišbir*
*išītam saḫmaštam liškunšum*

remove his kingly crown and throne;
impose on him a harsh punishment
and severe condemnation from which his body will not recover;
bring each day, each month, each year of his rule to a close
with weeping and wailing;
bring him face to face with a rival of his kingdom,
make his destiny a life that vies all the time with death.

**(E25)** O Adad, lord of plenty,
who looks after the water channels in heaven and earth, my helper,
deprive him of showers from heaven
and spring water from the ground;
destroy his land by famine and pestilence;
thunder angrily over his city;
turn his land into the ruin left after the flood.

**(E26)** O Zababa, almighty warrior
the first son born in Ekur, the companion at my right hand
shatter his weapon on the battlefield;
turn his day into night;
let his enemy stand victorious over him.

**(E27)** O Ishtar, lady of war and conflict, the one who draws out my weapons,
my gracious Protecting Spirit, who loves me to rule,
curse his kingship with unsurpassable anger and rage in your heart;
turn his blessings into troubles;
shatter his weapons wherever he struggles and fights;
ensure that he has revolts and insurrections;

*qarrādīšu lišamqit*
*damīšunu erṣetam lišqi*
*gurun*[405] *šalmāt ummānātišu*[406] *ina ṣērim littaddi*[407]
*ummānšuma*(!)[408] *rēmam ay*[409] *ušarši*
*šuāti ana*[410] *qāt nakrīšu limallīšuma*
*ana māt nukurtišu kamîš līrûšu.*

**E28 (= LI:24-39)**
*Nergal dannum ina ilī*
[411]*qabal la maḫār**
*mušakšidu irnittiya*
*ina kašūšišu rabîm*
*kīma išātim*[412] *ezzetim ša*[413] *appim*
*nišīšu liqmi*
*in*[414] *kakkišu dannim lišaṭṭīšuma*
*biniātišu kīma ṣalam ṭiddim liḫbuš.*

**E29 (= LI:40-49)**
*Nintu*[415] *bēltum ṣīrtum ša mātātim*
*ummum bānītī*
*aplam līṭeršuma*
*šumam ay ušaršīšu*
*ina qerbīt nišīšu zēr awīlūtim ay ibni.*

**E30 (= LI:50-69)**
*Ninkarrak mārat Anim*
*qābiat dumqiya ina Ekur*
*murṣam kabtam, asakkam lemnam, simmam marṣam,*

---

405. e: *qurun.*
406. e: *ummānišu.*
407. e: *lištaddi.*
408. Thus Stele, but it is questioned by *BAL*, and Roth emends to read *ummānšu.*
409. e: *ā.*
410. e: *adi.*
411. e: *qabal la immaḫaru.*
412. e: *i-il*(!)*-ti.*
413. e: *iš*(!).
414. e: *ina*, the reading adopted by Roth.
415. e: *rubātum.*

bring down his heroes, let the earth drink their blood;
keep on piling up his soldiers on to the heap of corpses in the desert,
and show them no mercy;
hand over that man himself into the hand of his enemy;
they will take him off bound into a hostile land.

**(E28)** O Nergal, fighter for the gods, unrivalled in the battle,
who sees me through to victory,
you shall burn up his people with a massive holocaust,
like flames blazing through the reeds;
you shall beat him with a violent weapon,
you shall crush his limbs like those of a clay doll.

**(E29)** O Nintu, noble lady of the nations, the mother who has created me,
let him have no heir, deprive him of posterity,
let him not raise a family amidst his people.

**(E30)** Ninkarrak, daughter of Anu, interceding for my blessings in E-kur,
summon up a terrible illness in his body,
with demonic pain, and fever, and weeping sores,

*ša la ipaššeḫū*
*asûm qerebšu la ilammadu*
*ina ṣimdi la unaḫḫušu*
*kīma nišik mūtim la innassaḫu*
*ina biniātišu lišāṣiaššumma*
*adi napištašu ibellû*
*ana eṭlūtišu liddammam.*

**E31 (= LI:70-83)**
*ilū rabûtum ša šamê u erṣetim*
*Anunnakū ina napḫarišunu*
*šēd*[416] *bītim, libitti Ebabbara*
*šuāti zērašu māssu ṣābašu nišīšu u ummānšu*
*errētam maruštam līrurū.*

**E32 (= LI:84-91)**
*errētim*[417] *anniātim*(!)[418] *Ellil, ina pīšu ša la uttakkaru*[419]
*līruršuma*[420] *arḫiš likšudašu.*

---

416. e: *DINGIR.RA*[ (?).
417. e: *-um.*
418. For Stele *DA-ni-a-tim* read *á-ni-a-tim.*
419. e: *nakārim.*
420. e: *-ušuma.*

one which cannot be relieved,
one which no physician understands,
one which cannot be soothed by bandaging,
one which, like the sting of death, cannot be removed;
may he groan among his fellow men[86], until his spirit is exhausted.

(E31) O almighty gods of heaven and earth,
all you Anunnaku assembled together,
protectors of the shrine, brickwork of E-babbar,
curse him and his family and his land
and his army and his people and his workmen
with an appalling curse.

(E32) May Enlil, the word of whose mouth can never be changed,
curse him, and immediately come and overpower him.

---

86. Following *CAD* s.v. *damāmu* 1a, and also s.v. *eṭlu* 2b1´ (last citation), taking the word as the plural of *eṭlu*; Roth prefers to take it as the homonym *eṭlūtu*, an abstract singular noun meaning 'manhood' (see *CAD* E: 411b) and translates as 'may he bewail his lost virility!'

# GLOSSARY

Where a word occurs twice in a quotation the reference is repeated; where it occurs again in the same Law, but not in the actual quotation, the number of occurrences is specified. An occurrence of the word in another Law in a similar context has the reference to that Law prefixed with cf.

## A

*ā* > *ay*, not.

***abālu***, vb., to bring, bring away. < *ʾ-b-l.*

A: without infix.

1. to produce witnesses, bring goods before witnesses (see B8): *šībī mudē ḫulqiyami lublam,* 'I will bring witnesses who know my lost property' (L9).

2. to take away, remove crops by erosion or flood (see B9): *mārū ugārim ša šeʾšunu mû ublū,* the land workers whose grain the water has removed (L54).

3. to commit an offence (see B10): *arnam kabtam ša ina aplūtim nasāḫim la ublam,* he has not committed an offence serious enough for excluding from the inheritance (L168).

4. of a woman providing a dowry: *šeriktam ša ištu bīt abiša ublam,* the dowry she brought from her father's house (L138; cf. L149; 156).

5. of a man providing a dowry, bride-price, gift: *terḫatam ša awīlum šû ana bīt emišu ublu,* the marriage price which that gentleman had brought to his father-in-law's house (L163).

6. with *panû*, to excuse someone of an offence (see *CAD* A/1, 18b-19a): *ana ištiššu panīšu ubbalū,* they shall excuse him for the first time (L169).

7. to have a value, be worth (see *CAD* A/1, p. 20, s.v. 5b´). *maḫar šībī kīma ubbalu ana tamkārišu inaddin,* he shall give to his merchant before witnesses according to the value it has (§5.15).

B: with infixed *-t-* (sometimes indistinguishable in form from *tabālu*, to bring).

8. to produce witnesses (see A1): *šībī ša ina maḫrišunu išāmu itbalam,* he has brought witnesses in whose presence he made the purchase

(L9; cf. L10); *šībī mudē ḫulqišu itbalam*, he has brought witnesses who recognize his lost property (L9; cf. L10; 11).

9. to erode (see A2): *bibbulum itbal*, the flood has caused erosion (L45; cf. L48).

10. to commit an offence (see A3): *arnam kabtam ša ina aplūtim nasāḫim ana abišu itbalam*, he has committed an offence against his father serious enough for excluding from the inheritance (L169, twice).

C: with *-tan-*.

11. to guide a community: *ina šulmim attabbalšināti*, I have always led them in peace (E7).

*abāru* > ***ubburu***, to accuse.

*abātu* B, to flee > ***nābutu***, to become a fugitive. < *ʾ-b-d.*

***abbuttu***, sbst., slave's distinguishing mark.

*abbuttam išakkanšimma itti amātim imannûši*, she shall place the slave mark on her and count her as one of the slave-girls (L146); *gallābum balum bēl wardim abbutti wardim la šêm ugallib*, the barber has shaved off the mark of a slave not belonging to him without the knowledge of the slave's owner (L226; cf. L227).

***abnu***, sbst., stone.

1. precious stone: *kaspam ḫurāṣam abnam u bīš qātišu ana awīlim iddinma*, he has given a gentleman silver, gold, gems or any property in his charge (L112).

2. stone weight: *kaspam ina abnim maṭītim*, silver according to the light weight (§5.13); *ina abnim rabītim*, according to the heavy weight (§5.13 [partly restored]; L108).

***absinnu***, sbst., > ***šerʾu*** cultivable field.

***abu***, sbst., father.

1a. human father, in relationship to his sons: *abum ina bulṭišu ana mārī ša amtum uldušum mārūʾa iqtabi*, the father has said in his lifetime to the sons whom the slave-girl bore him, 'My sons' (L170; cf. L171a); *abum mārašu ina aplūtim ul inassaḫ*, the father shall not debar his son from the inheritance (L168; cf. L169); *qīšti abum iddinušum*, the gift which his father gave him (L165); *mārum abašu imtaḫaṣ*, a son has struck his father (L195); *arnam kabtam ša ina aplūtim nasāḫim ana abišu itbalam*, he has committed an offence against his father serious enough for exclusion from the inheritance (L169); *mārū warki abišunu illakū*, the sons shall follow their father (L135); *ilik abišu illak*, he shall perform his father's service (L28; cf. L29).

b. in relationship to his daughters: *abi mārtim*, the father of the girl (L159; 160); *abuša ul iraggum*, her father shall have no claim (L162); *ša abuša šeriktam išrukušim*, whose father provided her with a dowry

(L178; 179); *abum ana mārtišu...šeriktam la išrukšim*(!), a father gave no dowry to his daughter (L180; 182; cf. L183); *abum...ana ilim iššīma*, a father dedicated (her) to the god (L181); *mimma ša abuša iddinušim*, whatever her father gave to her (L178).

c. also in relationship to the mother of his children: *ṣeḫram ana mārūtim ilqe inūma ilqûšu abašu u ummašu iḫiaṭ*, he has taken a small child for adoption and after he has taken him he pines for his father and mother (L186); *balum abišu u ummišu*, without his father and mother knowing (L194+); *ana abim murabbīšu u ummim murabbītišu ul abī attā ul ummī atti iqtabi*, he has said to the father who has brought him up and to the mother who has brought him up, 'You are not my father. You are not my mother' (L192; cf. L191; 193).

2. a deceased father: *warka abum ana šīmtim ittalku*, afterwards the father has gone to his fate (L165; 166; 167; 170; 171a; 178; 179; 180; 181; 182; 183; 184); *awīlum warki abišu ina sūn ummišu ittatīl*, a man has had intercourse with his mother after his father (L157; cf. L158).

3. a god as father: *Anum rabûm abu ilī nābû palēya*, almighty Anum, the father of the gods, who designated me to rule (E19); *kīma abim wālidim*, like a father who produces a child (E12).

4. ***bīt abim***, father's house, a deceased father's estate:

a. and a father's children: *ina makkūr bīt abim mitḫāriš izuzzū*, they shall share the property of the father's house equally (L165; cf. L166; 167; cf. L170; 171a; 180; 181; 182; 183).

b. and a father's daughter: *ina bīt abiša wašbat*, she is living in her father's house (L130); *ana bīt abiša ittallak*, she goes away to her father's house (L142); *šeriktam ša ištu bīt abiša ublam*, the dowry she brought from her father's house (L138; cf. L149); *mimma ša ištu bīt abiša ublam*, whatever she brought from her father's house (L156); *šeriktam ša bīt abiša ileqqēma*, the dowry she took from her father's house (L172); *qadum šeriktim ša bīt abiša*, together with the dowry from her father's house (L176a, variant *abuša*); *šeriktaša ša bīt abišamma*, her dowry does indeed belong to her father's house (L163); *šeriktaša ana bīt abiša utâr*, her dowry shall return to her father's house (L164!); *kīma emūq bīt abim šeriktam išarrakūšimma*, they shall provide a dowry for her according to the wealth of her father's estate (L184).

c. and a father's son: *ana bīt abišu ittalak*, he goes away to his father's house (L193); *ana bīt abišu itâr*, he shall return to his father's house (L186; 189; 190); *bīt abišu uweddīma*, he discovers his father's house (L193); *ina bīt abim innassaḫ*, he shall be excluded from his father's estate (L158, variant *abišu*).

***abūbu***, sbst., deluge, primaeval flood.

*māssu ana til abūbim litēr*, let him turn his land into a deluge-ruined heap (E25).

***abullu***, sbst., main gate.

*abullam uštēṣi*, he has given permission to go outside the gate (L15); *kannū gamartim ina abullim ittaḫlalū*, the flags showing it is finished have been hung on the city gate (L58).

***aburru***, sbst., water meadow, pasture.

*nišī dadmī aburrī ušarbiṣ*, I let the people rest in settlements in the meadows (E5).

***adannu***, sbst., appointed time.

*adannam ana šeššet warḫī išakkanūšumma šumma ina šeššet warḫī šībīšu la irdeam*, they shall set him a time limit of six months, but if he has not obtained witnesses within six months… (L13).

***adāru***, vb., to fear. < *ʾ-d-r*.

*errēt ilī la īdurma*, he was not afraid of the divine curse (E19).

***adi***, particle, until.

1. until (= *CAD adi* A prep.; see A/1, 117b, s.v. 2b): *ištu rēš šattim adi ḫamšim warḫim*, from the beginning of the year to the fifth month (L273+); *adi napištašu ibellû*, until his life expires (E30, with present, see *AHw* s.v. B1).

2. times (before a numeral; see *CAD* A/1, 121, s.v. 4; *AHw* s.v. A3d): *adi 3-šu*, three times (L106); *adi ḫamšīšu* and *adi 5-šu*, five times (L12 and L112); *adi 6-šu*, six times (L107); *adi 10-šu*, ten times (L8; 265); *adi 12-šu*, twelve times (L5); *adi 30-šu*, thirty times (L8).

3. as long as, with stative (= *CAD* A/1 112, *adi* conj.; see *AHw* s.v. B3): *adi kirâm ṣabtu*, as long as the orchard is held (L64); *adi balṭat*, as long as she lives (L148; 171b; 178; 180; 181).

4. with (= *CAD* A/1, 121b, *adi* B prep.) > ***qadu***.

***agāru***, vb., to hire equipment, animals, or human labour. < *ʾ-g-r*.

to hire: *ana šattim ištiat īgur*, he hired for one year (L242); *agram īgurma pūḫšu iṭṭarad*, he hired a mercenary and sent him as his substitute (L26; also *īgur*, L273); *malāḫam u eleppam īgurma*, he hired a boatman and a boat (L237; cf. *īgur* (restored) L239); *ikkaram īgur*, he hired a farmer (L257); *kullizam īgur*, he hired a herdsman (L258); *nāqidam ana liātim u ṣēnim re'îm īgur*, he hired a herdsman to look after his herd and flock (L261); *ana panī eqlišu uzuzzim īgurma*, he hired him to attend to his field (L253); *šumma awīlum mār ummānim iggar*, if a gentleman would hire a craftsman (L274, fragmentary); *alpam imēram īgurma*, he hired an ox or a donkey (L244); *alpam īgurma*, he hired an ox (L245; 246; 247; 248; 249; and also *īguru*); *alpam ana diāšim īgur*, he hired an ox for threshing (L268); *imēram īgur*, he hired a donkey (L269), and *urīṣam īgur*, he hired a goat (L270), also for threshing; *liātim ereqqam u murteddīša īgur*, he hired cattle, a wagon and a driver (L271); *ereqqamma ana ramaniša īgur*, he hired a wagon on its own (L272); *māḫirtam īgur*, he hired a rowing boat (L276); *eleppam šūšim kurri īgur*, he hired a boat of 60 kur capacity (L277); broken context: *īgur* (L275).

***aggu***, sbst., rage.
*ina libbiša aggim ina uzzātiša rabiātim šarrūssu līrur*, may she curse his kingdom with unsurpassable anger and a raging heart (E27).

***agru***, sbst., labourer, mercenary. < *ʾ-g-r*.
*agram īgur*, he hired a labourer (L273); *agram īgurma pūḫšu iṭṭarad*, he hired a mercenary and sent him as his substitute (L26); *agram pūḫam imḫurma*, he acquired a mercenary as a substitute (L33).

***agû***, sbst., crown.
*sīmat ḫaṭṭim u agêm*, the sign of the crown and sceptre (P12); *agâm kussâm ša šarrūtim liṭeršu*, let him remove his kingly crown and throne from him (E24).

***aḫāzu***, vb., to take, choose a wife. < *ʾ-ḫ-z*.
1. to take as a wife for oneself, marry: *mārat awīlim īḫuzma*, he married a gentleman's daughter (L175; 176a; also *īḫuzuši*); *aššatam īḫuz mārī ūlissumma*, he married a wife and she bore him children (L162; also *īḫuzma* L163; 167; also *ītaḫazma*, L167); *mutu libbiša iḫḫassi*, the man she loves may marry her (L137; 156; cf. L172); *mussa sinništam šanītam iḫḫaz*, her husband shall marry another woman (L141; cf. L167); *ul taḫḫazanni iqtabī*, she has said, 'You shall not marry me' (L142); *māratka ul aḫḫaz iqtabi*, he has said, 'I shall not marry your daughter' (L159); *aššassu ibiršu ul iḫḫaz*, his neighbour shall not marry his wife (L161, and also *taḫḫaz*); *aššatam īḫuzma riksātiša la iškun*, he has married a wife but has not provided her with a contract (L128); *aššatam īḫuzma laʾbum iṣṣabassi*, he has married a wife but a disease has taken hold of her (L148); *ana šanītim aḫāzim panīšu ištakkan iḫḫaz*, he sets his mind on marrying another woman and marries her (L148; 148); *ana šugītim aḫāzim panīšu ištakan*, he has determined to marry a priestess (L144; 145); *lāma sinništam šuāti iḫḫazu ḫubullum elišu ibašši*, the debt against him existed before he married that woman (L151); *nadītam īḫuzma*, he has married a priestess (L144; 145; 146); *šugītam ul iḫḫaz*, he shall not marry a priestess (L144; cf. 145).
2. to choose a wife for one's son to marry: *ana mārī ša iršū aššātim īḫuz*, he found a wife for the sons he had obtained (L166); *ana mārīšu ṣeḫrim aššatam la īḫuz*, he did not find a wife for his youngest son (L166; perhaps read *iḫīr*, he chose, both for this and the previous

occurrence); *ša aššatam la aḫzu*, who has no wife (L 166).
> ***šūḫuzu*** to allow to marry.

***aḫu* 1**, sbst., brother; = *CAD aḫu* A.
*warka abum ana šīmtim ittalku inūma aḫḫū izuzzū*, when the brothers do the sharing after the father has gone to his destiny (L165; 166); *itti aḫḫīša izâzma*, she shall divide with her brothers (L182); *ana aḫišunu ṣeḫrim*, for their little brother (L166); *eqelša u kirāša aḫḫūša ileqqūma*, her brothers shall take her field and her orchard (L178); *aplūssa ša aḫḫīšama*, her inheritance belongs to her brothers (L178); *warkassa ša aḫḫīšama*, her affairs belong to her brothers (L180; 181); *aḫḫūša ul ipaqqarūši*, her brothers shall have no claim against her (L179); *aḫḫūša kīma emūq bīt abim šeriktam išarrakūšimma*, her brothers shall provide a dowry for her according to the substance of the father's estate (L184); *šumma aḫḫūša...la ittadnūšimma*, if her brothers...do not give her (L178).

***aḫu* 2**, sbst., side; = *CAD aḫu* B.
*aḫam nadû*, to be lazy: *aḫi ul addī*, I have not been lazy (E2); *aḫšu iddīma*, he has been lazy (L44; 53; 55).

***aḫû***, adj., other (see *CAD* A/1, 210).
*ana mārīša ša irammu inaddin ana aḫîm ul inaddin*, she may give it to the son she loves; she may not give to anyone else (L150); *nadītum tamkārum u ilkum aḫûm*, a priestess, a merchant, or some other duty-bound person (L40).

***akālu***, vb., to eat. < *ʾ-k-l*.
*ina bītīšu ša akālim ibašši*, there is something to eat in his house (L133a; cf. L134; 135); *adi balṭat ikkal*, she shall consume it as long as she lives (L171b; 178; 180; 181).

*aklu*, sbst., overseer, in the expression *wakil ḫaṭṭātim*, 'overseer of the sceptres' (see *CAD* A/1, 280, *aklu* A, s.v. e) is now read ***ša ḫaṭṭātim***, captain > ***ša*** C 11.

***alādu***, vb., to give birth. < *ʾ-l-d*.
*mārī ūlissumma*, she bore him sons (L162; *ūlissum* 167); *mārī ittalad*, she has then born sons (L135; 146; 167; 173; 175; cf. *la ittalad* L174; *uldu* L146; *ūlid* L147); *amassu ša mārī uldušum*, his slave-girl who bore him sons (L119); *ana mārī ša amtum uldušum*, to the sons the slave-girl bore him (L170; 171a); *šugītim ša mārī uldušum*, the priestess who bore him sons (L137); *ḫīrtašu ša mārī la uldušum*, the first wife who did not bear him sons (L138; also *ūlissum* L170); *ina sūn rabītišu ša mārī waldat ittaṣbat*, he has been caught having intercourse with his foster mother who has born sons (L158).

***alāku***, vb., to go, go away. < *ʾ-l-k*.
1. *ana šīmtim alāku*, to go to one's destiny: with *ittalak* (L12; 162;

163; 167; 176a); *ittalku*, L165; 166; 167; 170; 171a; 178; 179; 180; 181; 182; 183; 184.

2. *ilkam alāku*, to do a duty: with *illak*, L27; 28; 29; 30; 31; 40; 182; with *ittalku* (subjunctive) L30; with *ittalak*, L27, 30; *ilkam alākam ile'i*, he is able to do the duty (L28).

3. G-theme: *ana Id illak*, he shall go to the River (L2); *awīlum ša ana bullîm illiku*, the man who has gone to put out the fire (L25); *ašar illiku*, the place he went to (L100; 101; 102); *ina alākišu*, while he was going (L103; 250); *mārū warki abišunu illakū*, the sons shall follow their father (L135); *alākšu qabū la illik*, his despatch was ordered but he did not go (L26; 26); *ana maḫar ṣalmīya šar mīšarim lillikma*, let him approach the statue of me, the king of justice (E11); *Ea rubûm rabium ša šīmātušu ina maḫra illaka*, Ea, the almighty prince whose decisions come first (E22).

4. Gtn-theme, to go away: *ana bīt abiša ittallak*, she shall go off to her father's house (L142; cf. L149); *ana bīt abišu ittallak īnšu inassaḫū*, he shall go off to his father's house and they shall gouge out his eye (L193); *ṣiḫrum šû reqūssu ul ittallak*, that son shall not go away destitute (L191, twice);

5. Gtn-theme, to travel about: *ina libbū mātim ittalkamma*, he was travelling about in the land (L280).

***alālu***, vb., to execute by hanging. < *ḫ-l-l.*

*ina pani pilšim šuāti idukkūšuma iḫallalūšu*, they shall kill him by hanging him in front of that hole (L21); *awīlam šuāti idukkūšūma ina bābišu iḫallalūšu*, they shall kill that gentleman by hanging him before his doorway (L227).

> ***naḫlulu***, to be hung.

***aldû***, sbst., seed corn. < *'-l-d.*

*aldâm iqīpšu*, he lent him seed-corn (L253); *aldâm ilqēma*, he took the seed-corn (L254).

***ālidu***, adj., progenitor. < *'-l-d.*

*Ḫammurabimi bēlum ša kīma abim wālidim ana nišī ibaššû*, Hammurabi, the lord who is like a father with a child to the people (E12).

***āliku***, adj., walking < *'-l-k.*

*āliku imniya*, walking at my right hand (E26).

***almattu***, sbst., widow.

*almattum ša mārūša ṣeḫḫeru*, a widow whose sons are small (L177); *šāyyimānum ša unūt mārī almattim išammu ina kaspišu ītelli*, a buyer who buys the property of a widow's sons shall forfeit his silver (L177); *ekūtam almattam šutēšurim*, to show justice to the orphan and widow (E8).

***alpu***, sbst., ox.

1. working beast: *alpam ana diāšim īgur*, he hired an ox to thresh (L268); *alpam imēram īgurma*, he hired an ox or a sheep (L244; cf. L245; 246; 247; 248; 249+); *alpam u lu immeram*, an ox and a sheep (L262; [263]); *bēl alpim*, the owner of an ox (L224; 225; 247); *alpam kīma alpim ana bēl alpim iriab*, he shall restore an ox like the ox to the owner of the ox (L245; 245; 246; 246; cf. L263; [263]); *idī alpim ša warka 4 kur še'am idī alpim ša qabla 3 kur še'am*, four kur of grain as the fee for the rear ox, and three kur of grain for the fore ox (L242/3; 242/3; also < *alpam*> 242/3).

2. needing attention: *asî alpim u lu imērim lu alpam u lu imēram simmam kabtam īpušma*, a surgeon for an ox or a surgeon for a sheep made a dangerous incision upon the ox or the sheep (L224; 224; cf. *alpam* L225); *alpum sūqam ina alākišu awīlam ikkipma*, an ox gored a man as it walked in the street (L250; cf. *alpum šû*, L251); *alap awīlim nakkāpīma*, a man's ox is prone to gore (L251); *alapšu la usanniqma*, he has not tethered his ox (L251).

3. stolen: *lu alpam lu immeram lu imēram lu šaḫâm lu eleppam išriq*, he stole an ox, or a sheep, or a donkey, or a pig, or a boat (L8; cf. L7).

4. seized as security: *alpam ana nipûtim ittepe*, he has seized an ox as a pledge (L241).

5. flogging with an ox-tail: *ina puḫrim ina qinnaz alpim 1 šūši immaḫḫaṣ*, he shall be beaten 60 times with an ox-tail in the assembly (L202).

***ālu***, sbst., city.

1. as an administrative centre: *ālum u rabiānum*, the city and the governor (L23; 24).

2. as someone's residence: *ālšu iktašdam*, he has reached his city (L27; 135); *ālšu uštakšidaššu*, he has let him reach his city (L32); *ālšu iddīma*, he has deserted his city (L136); *aššum ālšu izēruma innabitu*, because he has hated his city and made off (L 136); *ālam ušeṣṣûšu*, they shall make him leave the city (L154); *ḫalāq ālišu*, the destruction of his city (E20); *eli ālišu ezziš lissīma*, let him shout angrily over his city (E25).

3. associated with a deity: *ṣillī ṭābum ana āliya tariṣ*, my beneficial shadow is stretched over my city (E7); *ina Bābilim ālim ša Anum u Ellil*, in Babylon, the city of Anu and Enlil (E8); *ina bīt il ālišu*, by the estate of his local god (L32+).

4. as a determinative before names of cities: > ***Aššur*, *Barsipa*, *Bīt Karkara*, *Eridu*, *Kiš*, *Kuta*, *Maškanšapir*, *Uru*.**

***amāru***, vb., to see. < *ʾ-m-r*.

1. to consider, examine judicially: *dayyānū awâtišunu immarūma*,

the judges shall consider their evidence (L9); *dīnšu līmur libbašu linappišma*, let it examine his complaint and let it relieve his heart (E11).

2. to see a result, see a profit or loss: *nēmelam la ītamar*, he has not seen any profit (L101; cf. L100); *bitiqtam ītamar*, he has seen a loss (L102).

***ammu***, sbst., people.

*mušēpī kīnātim mušūšer ammi*, who makes justice appear, who keeps my people straight (P19).

***amtu***, sbst., slave-girl.

1. a female servant: *amat ekallim*, a palace slave-girl (L15); *amat muškēnim*, the slave-girl of a working man (L15); *amatam ḫalqam ša ekallim u lu muškēnim*, a lost slave-girl of the palace or of a working man (L16); *itti amātim imannûši*, she shall count her among the slaves (L146); *amat awīlim imḫaṣma*, he has struck a man's slave-girl (L213); *amtum šî imtūt*, that slave-girl has died (L214); *nadītum šî amtam ana mutiša iddinma*, that priestess has given a slave-girl to her husband (L144; cf. L146); *amtum šî itti bēltiša uštatamḫir*, that slave-girl shall try to rival her mistress (L146); *sinništum šī kīma amtim ina bīt mutiša uššab*, that woman shall live like a slave-girl in her husband's house (L141).

2. a female-servant who has had a child by the owner of the house: *amassu ša mārī uldušum*, a slave-girl who has born him sons (L119); *amassu mārī ūlissum*, his slave-girl has born him sons (L170); *ana mārī ša amtum uldušum*, for the sons which the slave-girl bore him (L170; 171a); *bēl amtim išaqqalma amassu ipaṭṭar*, the owner of the slave-girl shall make the payment and redeem his slave-girl (who had been sold into service to satisfy the obligations of her master, L 119; 119).

3. compared with *ḫirtum*: *mārū ḫīrtim u mārū amtim mitḫāriš izuzzū*, the sons of the wife and the sons of the slave-girl shall share alike (L170; cf. L171a); *andurār amtim u mārīša ištakan*, they shall set a time for the slave-girl and her sons, *mārū ḫīrtim ana mārī amtim ana wardūtim ul iraggumū*, but the sons of the wife shall have no claim for service from the sons of the slave-girl (L171a; 171a).

4. for other instances > ***ardu***, slave.

***ana***, particle, to.

A. marking an infinitive to indicate the purpose of an action.

1a. in order to, with reference to: *ana šūpîm* (P3); *ana ḫulluqim* (P3); *ana ṣalmāt qaqqadim waṣêmma* (P3); *ana uzuzzim* (L253); see also P22; L25; 51; 53; 57; 60; 64; [§4.12]; 5.2(!); 5.10; 5.15; L100, partly

restored; 104; 141; 145; 148; 168; 172; 177; 191; 261; 268; 269; 270; E8; 8.
b. with ***la***: *ana la ḫabālim* (P3; E8).
B. with verbs used intransitively, marking the indirect object or adverbial phrase.
1. with verbs of motion: *alāku* L2; 26; 142; 193; also *ana šīmtim alāku* L12; 162; 163; 165; 166; 167; 167; 170; 171a; 176a; 178; 179; 180; 181; 182; 183; 184; *aṣû* (P3); *erēbu* (L133a; 134; 151; 152; 176a; 177); also *itērub* (L110; 133b; 135; 136); *ezēbu* (L172); *izzuzu* (P5); *redû* (L17); 18; *târu* L41; 67+a; [§4.12]; L131; 135; 136; 177; 186; 189; 190.
3. with verbs of speaking:
a. *qabû* L68+b; 69+c; 159; 161; 168; 170; 171a; 192; 282.
b. *zakāru* L20.
4. with other verbs: *damāmu* (E30); *egû* (E2); *muštēmiqum* (P20); *naparku* (P11); *palāsu* (L159); *paqādu* (L177); *qâlu* (E15; 18; 19); *ragāmu* (L162; 163; 171a; 175); *šūṣû*: *ana tanādātim šūṣâ* (E17); *šutaktutu* (E12); *zâzu* (L46; 167; 176a).
C. with transitive verbs (with a direct object expressed or implied) marking the indirect object or adverbial phrase:
5. with ***nadānu***.
a. to give silver (*kaspam*) to a person: L217; 221; 223; 259; 265; for *ana kaspim* see below, paragraph c.
b. to give other items: P15; L;27; 34; 34; 35; 36; 38; 39; 40; 42; 43; 45 (*ana errēšim*); 49; 49; 54; 57; 60; 64; 66; 69+c; §5.15; L77+f; 100; 101; 102; 104; 104; 105; 106; 107; 112; 112; 120; 122; 122; 124; 126; 137; 146; 150; 150; 178;183; 184; 184; 194; 224; 225; 231; 235; 236; 242/3; 247; 264; 265; 267; 281.
c. to indicate particular types of commercial payment: ***ana biltim*** (L45); ***ana ḫubullim*** (§5.9; 5.9; 5.13; 5.13; 5.14); ***ana igrim*** (L236; 255); ***ana kaspim*** (L117; 118; 119; 146; 147; 171b; 177); ***ana kiššātim*** (L117; 118); ***ana māḫirātišunu*** (L51); ***ana qīptim*** (L111); ***ana qīštišu*** (L228, 234); ***ana maṣṣarūtim*** (L122; 123; 124; 125; 125); ***ana ṣibtim*** (§5.11); ***ana šīmim*** (L67+a, partly restored); ***ana tadmiqtim*** (L102); ***ana tappûtim*** (L77+f); ***ana uzzubêm*** (L139).
d. to pay for an object: *ana bīt ilkim…inaddin* (L67+a).
6. with other verbs and participles:
a. indicating the person or deity for whom or in whose presence an action is performed: *abālu*: *arnam…ana abišu…itbalam*, he has committed an offence against his father (L169); *bašû*: *ša kīma abim wālidim ana nišī ibaššû*, who was like their own father to his people (E12); *ḫâru*, to choose a bride L155; *aḫāzu*, to secure a wife (L166;

166); *epēšu*: *bītam ana awīlim īpušma*, he built a house for a man (L228; 233; cf. 229); *leqû*, to receive (L176a; 176b); *madādu*, to measure out (L58; 62; 65, partly restored); *peḫû*, to repair (L234; 235); *râbu*, to make recompense (L125; 236; 245; 246; 263); *šakānu*, to set (L166); *šaqālu* to pay out (L24; L209); *šaṭāru*, to assign (L38; 39); *šarāku*, to hand over (L 34; 150; 165; 180; 182; 183; 184); *našû* to dedicate to a god (L181); also with *īnšu*, to look at someone (L25); *alādu*, to bear children (L173; 174); *ṭarādu*, to point a finger (L100); *mullû*, to hand over (E27); *muddišu*, renewing (P8); *mudeššû*, causing to flourish (P12); *mukammeru*, heaping up (P8); *mušaklilu*, providing (P13); *mušarbû*, extolling (P16); *ana Marduk...išīmūšum*, to him, to Marduk, they allotted (P1); *šākin*, placing (P8); *šalû*: *ana mutišsa Id išalli*, she shall leap into the River for her husband's sake (L132); *šūṣû*: i). to let out land to someone (L42; 44); ii). to be produced for: *ana emqim...šuṣâ*, produced for the wise (E17); *turru*, to give back to (L18; 43; 44; 48; 50; 62; 63; §5.8, partly restored; L102; 104; 107; 137; 164; 278; for *litēr*, 'may he change into', see below, paragraph e).

b. indicating the place where, or for the advantage of which, an action is performed: *arû*, to lead (E27); *bābil ḫegallim*, bringing prosperity (P6); *mugarrinu*, storing (P11); *mukillu*, holding (P13); *murappišu*, making extensions (P10); *mušēṣi*, bringing out (P21); *mušešqi*, bringing water (P15); *mutêr*, returning (P5; 19); *nadû* (1). to throw down L25; 108; 129; 133b; 155; (2) to abandon (L58); *šakānu*, to set (L61; also *šākin*, P17); *abālu*, to bring (L163); *šūbulu*, to have brought (L159; 160; 161); *šūrubu*, to cause to enter (L145); *ṣillī ṭābum ana āliya tariṣ*, my beneficent shadow is stretched over my city (E7); *mušaklilu*, providing (P4); *qâšu*, to grant life to a place (P15); *šā'im*, allotting (P13); *zaqāpu*, to plant out (L62).

c. as an expression of time: *ana šeššet warḫī išakkanūšumma* (L13); *ana dār* (E10; E12); *ana warkiāt umī ana mātima šarrum ša ina mātim ibaššû* (E14; 14); *ana šisīt nāgirim* (L16; see also L44; §5.10; L169; 242/3).

d. as an expression of measurement or price: *ana 1 burum* (L44; 56; 57; 58; 63; see also §5.3a; 5.9; 5.9; 5.10; L121; 255); *ana šīm šikarim* (L108); *ana maḫīr še'im* (L108); *ana 5 šiqil kaspim* (fragmentary, §5.3a); *ana šinīšu* (L176a; 176b); *ana 1 musar* (L228); *ana pī riksātišu* (L264).

e. indicating the purpose of an action: *aṣû*: *ana šibūt sarratim* (L3; cf. L4); *leqû*: *ana mārūtim ilqēma*, he received as an adoptee (L185; 186; cf. L188; 190; 191; 191); *maḫāru*, to obtain (L33); *petû*, to open a water channel (L55); *šaqālu*, 'to pay out for something' (L114); *turru*: *litēr*, may he change into (E25; 26; 27).

f. together with: *naškunu*, to be placed together with (L105); *ṭuḫḫû*, to aggregate together with (§5.12).

g. instead of: *ina kaspika tabal*, take away instead of your silver (L66).

h. belonging to, the responsibility of: *ana bēlišuma* (L244).

j. by itself: *ana ramāniša* (L272).

k. completetely: *ana gamrim* (L120).

m. with cognate noun and verb: *ana nipûtim ittepe*, he has taken in pledge (L241); also *ana šīmtim lišīmšum* (E24); *ana šēbultim šūbulu*, to send as a consignment (L112); *ana našpakūtim...išpukma*, he put into storage (L120).

n. compound preposition: *ana maḫar*, in front of (E11); *ana panišu* (L135).

7. fragmentary: L68+a; §5.3a; 5.3a; 5.3a; 5.7; 5.12; L262.

***anāku***, pronoun, I.

*Ḫammurabi šarrum gitmālum anāku*, I am Hammurabi, the perfect king (E2); *Ḫammurabi šar mīšarim ša Šamaš kīnātim išrukušum anāku*, I am Hammurabi, the king of justice to whom Shamash has given the law (E17); *Ḫammurabi re'ûm nibīt Ellil anāku*, I am Hammurabi, the shepherd named by Enlil (P4); *ilū rabûtim ibbûninnima anākuma rē'ûm mušallimum*, the great gods called me and so I am the shepherd who brings peace (E6); *šarrum ša in šarrī šūturu anāku*, I am the king who is the best of kings (E9); *migir Ištar anāku*, I am the favourite of Ishtar (P21).

***andurāru***, sbst., freedom.

*andurāršunu iššakkan*, their freedom shall be arranged (L117; 280; cf. L171a [!]).

***annû***, adj., this.

*annītam liqbīma*, let him say this (E12); *errētim anniātim* (!), these curses (E32).

***apālu***, vb., to be answerable for a debt, pay. < *'-p-l*.

*tamkāršu ippal*, he shall pay his merchant (L100; cf. *ippalū*, L152; *ippalma*, L66); *asâm ippal*, he shall pay the doctor (L206); *pīḫassu apālam la ile'i*, he was not able to pay his debt (L256); *nādinānšu baqrī ippal*, the one who gave it to him shall pay the claim (L279).

***apkallu***, sbst., expert.

*apkal ilī mudē mimma šumšu*, most skilled of the gods, who knows about everything (E22).

***aplu***, sbst., heir. < *'-p-l* 2.

1. heir to an inheritance: *aplišu ša īnšu maḫru*, the heir whom he favours (L165); *aplum mār ḫīrtim ina zittim inassaqma*, the heir, the son of the first wife, shall pick from the allocation (L170); *zittam kīma*

*aplim ištēn inaddinūšimma*, they shall give her a portion like that of an heir (L137; cf. L172; 180).

2. heir to a title: *liplippim ša Sumula'il aplum dannum ša Sinmuballiṭ zērum dāri'um ša šarrūtim*, the descendant of Shumula'il, the mighty heir of Sin-muballit, with royal ancestors in every generation (P21); *aplam līṭeršuma šumam ay ušaršīšu ina qerbīt nišīšu zēr awīlūtim ay ibni*, take away his eldest son before he has established his name, and stop him raising a family of men amidst his people (E29).

***aplūtu***, sbst., inheritance.

*aplūssa ša aḫḫīšama*, her inheritance belongs to her brothers (L178); *ina makkūr bīt abim šalušti aplūtiša izâzma*, from the property of her father's house she shall have a share of a third of an inheritance (L181; cf. L182; *aplūtišu*, 191); *šumma mārum arnam kabtam ša ina aplūtim nasāḫim la ublam abum mārašu ina aplūtim ul inassaḫ*, if the son has not committed an offence serious enough for excluding from the inheritance, the father shall not debar his son from the inheritance (L168; 168; cf. L169; 169).

***apšītû***, sbst., agreement

*errēšum u bēl eqlim ana apšītêm izuzzū*, the labourer and the owner of the field shall share it by agreement (L46).

***apu***, sbst., reedbed

*ina kašūšišu rabîm kīma išātim ezzetim ša apim nišīšu liqmi in kakkišu dannim lišaṭṭīšuma*, let him burn his people by his mighty power, raging like a fire through the reeds, with his powerful weapons may he strike him (E28).

*apû*, to become visible > ***šūpû***, to make resplendent.

*arāku*, to become long > ***mušāriku***, lengthening; > ***urruku***, to make long.

***arāru***, vb., to curse. < *'-r-r*.

*ḫaṭṭašu lišbir šīmātišu līrur*, let him break his weapon, let him curse his destiny (E19); *ina uzzātiša rabiātim šarrūssu līrur*, may she curse his kingdom with her tremendous fury (E27); *errētam maruštam līrurū*, let them curse him with an evil curse (E31); *errētim anniātim Ellil ina pīšu ša la uttakkaru līruršuma*, let Enlil invoke these curses against him by his word that will not be changed (E32).

*arba'u*, num., four; for *kibrāt arba'im*, the four regions > ***erbe***, four.

***ardu***, sbst., slave, royal subject.

1. often paired with ***amtu***: *wardum u amtum šunu mārū mātim*, the slave and the slave-girl were native to the land (L280); *wardam amtam išāmma*, he bought a slave or a slave-girl (L278; 279; cf. L280); *lu wardam lu amtam*, a slave or a slave-girl (L7; 16; 17; cf. L118); *bēl wardim u lu amtim lu warassu u lu amassu uteddī*, the owner of the slave or slave-girl recognizes his slave or his slave-girl

(L280; 280); *lu warad ekallim lu amat ekallim*, a palace slave or a palace slave-girl (L15); *lu warad muskēnim lu amat muskēnim*, a worker's slave or a worker's slave-girl (L15); *bēl wardim u lu amtim kasap išqulu ana tamkārim inaddinma*, the master of the slave or the slave-girl shall give back the money paid to the merchant (L281); *lu warassu lu amassu ipaṭṭar*, he shall ransom his slave or his slave-girl (L281); [*lu*] *wardum lu* [*amtum*...], fragmentary (§5.8).

2. other instances where the owner of the slave is specified: *warad awīlim*, a man's slave (L7; 116; 199; 199; 205; 217; 223; 252); *warad ekallim*, a palace slave (L175; 176a; 176a); *warad muškēnim*, a worker's slave (L175; 176a; 176a; 219); *warad bēl bītim*, the slave of the owner of the house (L231); *bēl wardim*, the slave's master (L17; 20; 175; 176; 176b; 217; 223; 226); *šarrum warassu uballaṭ*, the king may let his subject live (L129).

3. a slave behaving wrongly: *wardum šû bēlšu la izzakar*, that slave does not then declare the name of his master (L18); *wardum ina qāt ṣābitānišu iḫtaliq*, the slave has escaped from the control of his captors (L20); *wardum ana bēlišu ul bēlī atta iqtabi kīma warassu ukânšuma*, the slave has said to his master, 'You are not my master' but he has proved that he is his slave (L282).

4. a slave wrongfully detained: *wardam šuāti ina bītišu iktalāšu warka wardum ina qātišu iṭṭaṣbat*, he has kept that slave in his house and afterwards the slave is found in his possession (L19; 19).

5. a slave given in compensation: *wardam kīma wardim iriab*, he shall make recompense with a slave for the slave (L219; 219); *wardam kīma wardim ana bēl bītim inaddin*, he shall repay the master of the house with a slave for the slave (L231; 231).

6. the mark of a slave: *abbutti wardim*, a slave's tonsure (L226; 227).

7. the house of a slave: *ana bīt warad ekallim u lū warad muškēnim irrubma*, she has moved into the house of the palace slave or the worker's slave with the dowry from her father's house (L176).

8. fragmentary: *warad awīlim* (§5.3b); *wardum šû* (§5.3b).

***ardūtu***, sbst., slavery.

*mārū ḫīrtim ana mārī amtim ana wardūtim ul iraggumū*, the sons of the wife shall have no claim against the sons of the slave-girl for slavery (L171a; cf. L175).

***arḫiš***, adv., quickly. < *ʾ-r-ḫ*.

*awatum maruštum ša Šamaš arḫiš likšussu*, let the evil word of Shamash speedily overpower him (E23); *arḫiš likšudašu*, he is sure to do it for him quickly (E32).

***arḫu***, sbst., month. < *ʾ-r-ḫ*.

*ūmī warḫī šanāt*, days, months and years (E24); *ištu rēš šattim adi ḫamšim warḫim*, from the beginning of the year until the fifth month (L273); *ištu šiššim warḫim adi taqtīt šattim*, from the sixth month until the end of the year (L273); *adannam ana šeššet warḫī išakkanūšumma šumma ina šeššet warḫī šībīšu la irdeam*, they shall set him a time limit of six months, but if he has not obtained witnesses within six months (L13); *waraḫšu la imlāma*, his month has not expired (L278).

***arka***, adv., after, afterwards. < *ʾ-r-k*.

1. after, followed by subjunctive: *warka abum ana šīmtim ittalku*, after the father has gone to his destiny (L165; 166; 170; 171a; 178; 179; 180; 181; 182; 183; 184; for 167[!] > ***arkānum***).

2. afterwards, followed by indicative: *warka wardum ina qātišu ittaṣbat*, afterwards the slave was found in his possession (L19); *warka eqlam Adad irtaḫiṣ*, afterwards the field was inundated by the Storm (L45); *warka sinništum šî imtūt*, afterwards that woman died (L173); *warka mārī irtašīma*, afterwards he had children (L191).

***ina warka***, afterwards: *ina warka mussa itturamma*, afterwards her husband came back (L135).

***arkānu***, ***arkānum***, adv., afterwards. < *ʾ-r-k*.

1. *warkānum amtum šî itti bēltiša uštatamḫir*, afterwards that slave-girl has tried to rival her mistress (L146).

2. emendation: for *warkānum* (L167) Borger reads *warka*, i.e. *wa-ar-ka*{*-nu-um*}.

***arkānumma***, adv., afterwards. < *ʾ-r-k*.

*warkānumma dīnšu ītene*, and afterwards he changed his decision (L5); *šû warkānumma ina sūniša ittatīlma*, but afterwards he himself has had intercourse with her (L155); *warkānumma lu warad ekallim u lu warad muškēnim ana šīmtim ittalak*, and afterwards the palace slave or the workman's slave went to his fate (L176a).

***arkatu***, sbst., circumstances. possessions. < *ʾ-r-k*.

1. circumstances: *dayyānū warkat bīt mutiša panîm iparrasūma*, the judges shall investigate the conditions in her former husband's house (L177); *dayyānū warkassu iparrasūma*, the judges shall investigate his circumstances (L168; cf. L172: *warkassa*); *warkassa ina bābtiša ipparrasma*, her circumstances shall be investigated in her city gate (L142; cf. L18: *warkassu*).

2. possessions: *ummum warkassa ana māriša ša irammu inaddin*, the mother may give her possessions to the son she loves (L150); *warkassa ša mārīšama*, her possessions belong just to her sons (L171b); *warkassa ša aḫḫišama*, her possessions belong just to her brothers (L180; 181); *warkassa ēma eliša ṭābu nadānam la išṭuršimma*, he has not written that she may allocate her possessions how she likes (L178; cf. L179; 179; 182).

***arki***, preposition, after (local or temporal). < *ʾ-r-k.*

1. local: *mārū warki abišunu illakū*, the sons shall go after their father (L135).

2. temporal:

a. after a departure: *warkišu eqelšu u kirāšu ana šanîm iddinūma*, they have given his field and orchard to another after his departure (L27; cf. L30; 136).

b. after a death: *awīlum warki abišu ina sūn ummišu ittatīl*, a man has had intercourse with his mother after the death of his father (L157; cf. L158); *warki mutiša*, after the death of her husband (L150); *warkiša*, after her death (L167).

***arkītu***, sbst., future. < *ʾ-r-k.*

*ana warkiāt ūmī ana mātima šarrum ša ina mātim ibbaššû*, any king who is present in this land at any time at all in the future (E14).

***arkû***, adj., subsequent, rear. < *ʾ-r-k.*

1. subsequent (temporal, see *CAD* s.v. 1b2´): *ana mutiša warkîm*, by her second husband (L173; 174; 177); *mārū maḫrûtum u warkûtum*, the children of the earlier marriage and of the later marriage (L173).

2. rear (local, see *CAD* s.v. 1d2´c): *idī alpim ša warka 4 kur šeʾam*, four kur of grain as the fee for the rear ox (L242/3).

***arnu***, sbst., offence, blame, penalty.

1. offence: *arnam kabtam ša ina aplūtim nasāḫim la ublam*, he has not committed an offence serious enough for excluding from the inheritance (L168; cf. L169, twice).

2. blame: *mārī arnam immidū*, they shall lay the blame on the sons (L172).

3. penalty: *aran dīnim šuāti ittanašši*, he will always have to pay the penalty in that trial (L4; 13); *arnam ul išu*, there is no penalty (L134; 142); *arnam kabtam šēressu rabītam ša ina zumrišu la iḫalliqu līmussūma*, let him impose on him a harsh punishment and severe condemnation from which his body will not recover (E24).

***arqu***, sbst., verdure.

*mušalbiš warqim gigunē Aya*, decorating the shrine of Aya with greenery (P7).

*arratu* > ***erretu***, curse.

***arû***, vb., to lead away, take away (see *CAD arû* A; *AHw warûm* II). < *ʾ-r-ʾ.*

1. G-theme: *ana māt nukurtišu kamîš līrūšu*, let her remove him to a hostile land far away (E27; cf. *CAD* s.v. 1c [A/2, 314a]: may she lead him captive to the land of his enemy).

2. Gtn-theme (see in *CAD* s.v. 2): *ina mīšītim littarrūšu*, let him take him away into oblivion (E22; cf. *CAD* A/2, 315a s.v. 2 (*itarrû*) b: may they take him away into captivity unnoticed).

*âru*, to advance > ***u'uru***, to give an order.

***asakku***, sbst., demon.

*asakkam lemnam simmam marṣam ša la ipaššeḫū asūm qerebšu la ilammadu*, devilish pain and weeping sores which they cannot relieve and the cause of which no physician understands (E30).

***asû***, sbst., physician, treating people and also animals.

*asâm ippal*, he shall pay the physician (L206); *ana asîm 2 šiqil kaspam inaddin*, he shall give the physician two shekels of silver (L217; 223; cf. L221: *5 šiqil kaspam*); *1/6 kaspam ana asîm idīšu inaddin*, he shall pay a sixth in silver to the physician as his fee (L224); *asûm awīlam simmam kabtam ina karzilli siparrim īpušma*, a surgeon performed a serious operation with a knife (L215; 218; cf. L219); *asûm eṣemti awīlim šebirtam uštallim*, a physician has mended a man's broken bone (L221); *asûm qerebšu la ilammadu*, the cause of which no physician understands (E30); *asî alpim u lu imērim*, a vet for cattle or sheep (L224).

***aṣû***, vb., to leave, abandon, come out with evidence (in court), rise (of the sun). < *ʾ-ṣ-ʾ*.

1. to leave, abandon: *waṣâm iqtabi*, he has told him to leave (L69+c); *aššat awīlim ša ina bīt awīlim wašbat ana waṣêm panīša ištakanma*, the wife of a man, who has been living in the man's house, has determined to leave (L141; cf. L172); *u mussa waṣīma magal ušamṭāši*, although her husband has been greatly disparaging her as he went out (L142); *la naṣratma waṣiāt bīssa usappaḫ*, she has not been looked after, been going out and wasting her possessions (L143); *ina bīt mutiša ul uṣṣi*, she shall not leave her husband's house (L172).

2. to appear in court with evidence: *ina dīnim ana šībūt sarrātim ūṣiamma*, he has come out in court with evidence about lying (L3); *ana šībūt šeʾim u kaspim ūṣiām*, he has come out with evidence about silver or grain (L4).

3. to rise: *kīma Šamaš ana ṣalmāt qaqqadim waṣêmma mātim nuwwurim*, to rise like Shamash over the mass of humanity and to illuminate the land (P3).

> ***šūṣû***, bring out.

***ašābu***, vb., to live, stay, remain. < *ʾ-š-b*.

1. to live: *nadītum ugbabtum ša ina gagîm la wašbat*, a priestess, a lady who has not been living in a community (L110); *aššat awīlim ša ina bīt awīlim wašbat ana waṣêm panīša ištakanma*, the wife of a man, who has been living in the man's house, has determined to leave (L141; cf. L151); *ina bīt abiša wašbat*, she has been living in her father's house (L130); *ina bīt mutiša uššab*, she shall live in her husband's house (L141); *ina bīt mutiša wašābam la imtagar*, she has

not agreed to live in her husband's house (L149); *ina šubat mutiša uššab*, she shall live in her husband's home (L171b); *ina bīt īpušu uššamma*, she shall live in the house he has built (L148); *awīlum ašbumma*(!), the man who has been living there (L69+c: later ms. for Old Babylonian *wašbumma*).

2. to stay: *itti dayyānī ina dīnim ul uššab*, he shall not stay with the judges in the court (L5).

3. to be occupied with: *ina ḫarrānim wašibma*, he is involved in a journey (L112).

***ašaridu***, sbst., chief; compounded from *ašru*, place and *ēdu*, one.

*ašared šarrī mukanniš dadmē nār Purattim ittum Dagan bānîšu*, the chief of the kings, who controls the communities of the Euphrates under the guidance of his creator god Dagan (P17).

*ašāru* A, vb., to provide for > ***āširu***.

*ašāru* C, to hang loose > ***uššuru***, to release.

*ašāšu*, to be in distress > ***uššušu***, to misuse.

***ašbu***, resident in a house, tenant. < *w-š-b*.

*wašbum* [*bīt muškēnim*] *išām*, a tenant wishes to purchase the house of a commoner (§4.12).

***āširu***, participle, organizing. < *ʾ-š-r*

*šarrum nādin napištim ana Adab āšer bīt Emaḫ*, the king who gave Adab its life and made provision for the temple of Emah (P15).

***aškāpu***, sbst., leather worker.

*idī aškāpim*, the charge for a leather worker (L274).

***ašnan***, sbst., grain.

*ašnān napišti nišī*, grain to feed my people (E22).

***ašru*** sbst., sacred place, place. < *ʾ-š-r*

1. place: *ašar tamḫārim*, the place of battle (E26); *ašar tāḫazim u qablim*, the place of conflict and strife (E27).

2. sacred place: *mutēr Eridu ana ašrišu*, restoring Eridu as a holy place (P5); *ašrī šulmim*, peaceful places (E3); *ašar šipṭim*, a place for judgment (E21).

3. in construct state before subjunctive, the place where: *ašar illiku*, where he went (L100; 101; 102); *ašar šūbulu*, where it was to be delivered (L112); *ašar iddinu*, where he made the deposit (L123; 125); *ašar īrubu*, where she entered (L173).

> ***ašarīdu***, chief.

***ašru***, adj., humble. < *ʾ-š-r*

*wašrum muštēmiqum*, humble and prayerful (P6)

***aššābu***, occupant of a house, tenant. < *ʾ-š-b*.

*ana waššābim ina ūmīšu la malûtim waṣâm iqtabi*, he has told the occupant to leave before his time has expired (L69+c; also L69+c:

*waššābam*); *ina kaspim ša waššabum iddinušum*, some of the silver which the occupant paid him (L69+c); equivalent to *ašbu*, occupant, as the word is written in later ms.

***aššatu***, sbst., wife. < *'-n-š*.

1. a wife living with her husband: *aššat awīlim ša ina bīt awīlim wašbat*, a man's wife who lives in the man's house (L141); *aššat awīlim ša zikaram la idûma*, a man's wife who has not known any man (L130).

2. choosing a wife for one's sons: *ana mārī ša iršû aššātim īḫuz ana mārišu ṣeḫrim aššatam la īḫuz*, he has taken wives for the sons he has raised but he has not taken a wife for the smallest son (L166; 166).

3. bridal gifts for a wife: *eliāt zittišu kasap terḫatim išakkanūšumma aššatam ušaḫḫazūšu*, in addition to his share they shall set aside silver for him for a bridal gift and let him marry a wife (L166); *awīlum ana aššatišu eqlam kirâm bītam u bīšam išrukšim*, a man has donated to his wife a field, an orchard, a house or property (L150).

4. a marriage planned but not accomplished: *emušu ana bēl aššatim mārtī ul taḫḫaz iqtabi*, his father-in-law has said to the wife's intended husband, 'You shall not take my daughter' (L161); *aššassu ibiršu ul iḫḫaz*, his friend shall not take his wife (L161); *šumma awīlum aššatam īḫuzma riksātiša la iškun sinništum šî ul aššat*, if a man has taken a wife but not made the contract with her officially, that woman is not a wife (L128; 128).

5. a wife who has children: *aššatam īḫuz mārī ūlissuma*, he has taken a wife and she has born him sons (L162; cf. L167); *aššatam īḫuzma mārī la ušaršīšu*, he has taken a wife but she has not provided him with sons (L163).

6. a wife who becomes seriously ill: *awīlum aššatam īḫuzma la'bum iṣṣabassi*, a man has taken a wife but then she has been afflicted by disease (L148; cf. L148).

7. a wife guilty of misconduct: *aššassu ana bīt šanîm irrub*, his wife shall not enter another man's house (L134; cf. L135; 136; also L133, damaged); *aššat awīlim itti zikarim šanîm ina itūlim ittaṣbat*, a man's wife has been seized while lying with another man (L129); *aššat awīlim mussa ubbiršima itti zikarim šanîm ina utūlim la iṣṣabit*, a man's wife has been accused by her husband of sleeping with some other male but she has not been caught (L131); *aššat awīlim aššum zikarim šanîm mussa ušdīk*, a man's wife has had her husband killed because of another male (L153); *eli ugbabtim u aššat awīlim ubānam ušatriṣma*, he has pointed his finger at a priestess or a man's wife (L127; cf. L132).

8. reconciliation: *aššassu iṣṣabbat*, he wishes to take his wife back

(L136); *bēl aššatim aššassu uballaṭ*, the husband of the wife may allow his wife to live (L129; 129); *aššat munnabtim ana mutiša ul itâr*, the wife of a fugitive shall not return to her husband (L136).
9. selling a wife: *aššassu mārašu u mārassu ana kaspim iddin*, he has sold his wife, his son or his daughter for silver (L117); *bēl ḫubullīša aššassu ul iṣabbatū*, the ones to whom she is in debt shall not take his wife (L151); *ana aššatišu u mārtišu ul išaṭṭar*, he shall not sign over to his wife or his daughter (L38; cf. L39).

***aššum***, particle, because (with verb), because of (with noun), concerning.
1. with subjunctive verb, because: *aššum ina šattim maḫrītim mānaḫātišu la ilqû*, because he did not receive his investment for the previous year (L47); *aššum šamallâšu ikkiru*, because he has disputed with his trader (L107); *aššum ālšu izēruma innabitu*, because he has hated his city and fled (L136); *aššum mārī uldu*, because she has born sons (L146); *aššum balum abišu u ummišu ṣeḫram šaniam irkusu*, because she has made a contract for another son without the knowledge of the father or the mother (L194); *aššum bīt īpušu la udanninuma imqutu*, because he did not strengthen the house he built and it collapsed (L232); *aššum waššābam ina ūmīšu la malûtim ina bītišu [ušēṣu]*, because he has made the lodger leave his house before his time had expired (L69+c, subjunctive restored); *aššum ina bītim šūṣîm usaḫḫamūši*, they pester her to make her leave the house (L172, plural subjunctive).
2. with noun, because of: *aššum zikarim šanîm*, because of another male (L132; 153); *aššum errētim šināti*, because of those curses (E19).
3. introducing a dependent clause, so that: *aššum bēl ḫubullim ša mutiša la ṣabātiša mussa urtakkis*, she will then make her husband agree so that no creditor of her husband may seize her (L151).

***ašṭu***, adj., hard, difficult.
*pušqī wašṭūtim upetti*, I solved difficult problems (E3).

***atappu***, sbst., ditch.
*atappašu ana šiqītim ipte*, he has opened his dyke for irrigation (L55).

*atāru* > ***utturu***, to exceed; ***šūturu***, to make excellent.

***atkuppu***, sbst., basketmaker.
*idī atkuppim*, the wage of a basketmaker (L274).

***atru***, adj., extra, superfluous. *ʾ-t-r*.
*suluppī watrūtim ša ina kirîm ibbaššu*, the extra dates that are produced in the orchard (L66).

***atta***, pronoun, you (masc. sing.).
*ul abī attā*, you are not my father (L192); *ul bēlī attā*, you are not my master (L282).

***atti***, pronoun, you (fem. sing.).

*ul ummī attī*, you are not my mother (L192).

***awātu***, sbst., statement, the word of a god, the words of a person.

1. statement: *awat iqbû la uktīn*, he cannot substantiate the story he has told (L3); *dayyānū awâtišunu immarūma*, the judges shall examine their testimony (L9); *awīlum ḫablum ša awatam iraššû*, a man in trouble who has something to say (E11); *awatam likallimšu*, let him explain his problem (E11); *awassu lilemmin*, let her denigrate his statement (E21).

2. the word of a god: *ina awat Marduk*, according to the word of Marduk (E10); *ana awat Marduk bēlišu uštaktitma*, he submitted himself (?) to the word of his lord Marduk (E12); *awatum maruštum ša Šamaš arḫiš likšussu*, let the terrible word of Shamash quickly overpower him (E23).

3. the words of a person: *awât mīšarim*, words of justice (E14); *ana awâtim ša ina narîya ašṭuru liqūlma*, let him heed the words which I have written on my stele (E15; cf. *ana awâtiya* E18; 19); *awâtiya šūqurātim*, my words are precious (E8; 11); *awâtūa nasqā*, my words are treasured (E9; 17); *awâtiya la uštepēl*, let him not change my words (E18; cf. E19).

***awīltu***, sbst., woman.

*awīltam šuāti iqallūši*, they shall burn such a woman (L110).

***awīlu***, sbst., man, gentleman.

1. occurring immediately after *šumma* at the beginning of a new numbered law (according to conventional editing); sometimes there is specific emphasis on the person's social status, but clearly not above the law:

a. in the nominative (*awīlum*): *šumma awīlum lēt awīlim ša elišu rabû imtaḫaṣ*, if a gentleman has struck the cheek of a gentleman greater than himself (L202); *šumma awīlum šinni awīlim meḫrišu ittadi*, if a gentleman has knocked out the tooth of a gentleman like himself (L200); *šumma awīlum epinnam ina ugārim išriq 5 šiqil kaspam ana bēl epinnim inaddin*, if a man has stolen a plough from a field he shall give five shekels of silver to the owner of the plough (L259); for all such occurrences see ***šumma*** 1a.

b. in the accusative (*awīlam*): L117; 119.

2. other instances of *awīlum*:

a. L3; 6; 7; 9; 13; 19; 20; 22; 23; 25; 25; 53; 69+c; L112; 249; E11.

b. ***awīlum šû***: L130; 144; 145; 158; 163; 206; E18; 19.

c. ***šumma awīlum***: §5.7; 136; 151; 253; E15; 18; 19.

3. other instances of *awīlam*:
a. L1; 2; §5.4; L112; 113; 124; 127; 206; 215; 215; 218; 218; 250; 253.
b. ***awīlam šuāti***: L144; 154; 155; 227; 255.
5. instances of *awīlim*: —a. L2; 9; 59; §77+f; L112; 112; 113; 114; 115; 122; 124; 197; 200; 202; 215; 215; 218; 221; 228; 229; 233; 234; 235; 238; 251; 255; 280.
b. ***bīt awīlim***, a man's house or household: *ina bīt awīlim išātum innapiḫma*, fire has broken out in a man's house (L25); *še'ašu ana naspakūtim ina bīt awīlim išpukma*, he has set aside grain for storage in a man's house (L120; cf. L121); see also L110; 141; 151; 151; 151; 152.
c. persons in the household: ***amat awīlim***, a man's slave-girl: L213. ***aššat awīlim***, a man's wife: L127; 129; 130; 131; 132; 141; 153. ***mār awīlim*** someone of a certain social status, who will receive greater compensation for damages than someone of a lower status (such as the *muškēnu* or *ardu*): *mār awīlim lēt mār awīlim ša kīma šuāti imtaḫaṣ*, a gentleman has struck the cheek of another gentleman like himself (L203; 203, contrasting with the two following laws); see also L7; 14; §5.3a; L116; 196; 205; 207; 251. ***mārat awīlim***, a man's daughter: L175; 175; 176a; 176a; 176a; 176b; 176b; 209. ***warad awīlim***, a man's slave: L7; §5.3b; L117; 199; 199; 205; 217; 223; 252.

***awīlūtu***, sbst., human being, humanity.
*awīlūtum ša šumam nabiat*, a person who has been given a name (E19); *zēr awīlūtim ay ibni*, let him have no human descendant (E29).

***ay***, also ***ā***, particle with prohibitive nuance, followed by preterite: not.
*ay ušarši* (E27); *ay iršia* (E10); *ay unakkir* (E14); *ay ušassik* (E14); *ay ušabši* (E22); *dīnšu ay idīn* (E23); *ay ušaršīšu* (E29); *ay ibni* (E29).

***ayyābu***, sbst., enemy.
*mutammeḫ ayyābī*, who takes hold of the enemies (P13).

## B

*babālu*, vb., to bring (variant of *abālu*, see *AHw*), > *bābilu*.

***bābilu***, adj., bringing. < *w-b-l*.
*bābil ḫegallim ana Egišnugal*, bringing wealth to Egishnugal (P6).

***babtu***, sbst., area of the city, community.
*šumma awīlum mimmûšu la ḫaliqma mimme ḫaliq iqtabi babtašu ūtebbir*, if a man who has not lost anything says, 'I have lost something,' he makes an accusation against his community (L126); *kīma mimmûšu la ḫalqu babtašu ina maḫar ilim ubâršuma*, his community shall make him declare before the god that his property has not been

lost (L126); *ana babtišu inaddin*, he shall pay to his community (L126); *warkassa ina babtiša ipparrasma*, her circumstances shall be investigated by her community (L142); *kīma nakkāpû babtašu ušēdīšumma*, his community made him aware that it was an ox prone to gore (L251).

***bābu***, sbst., doorway.

*awīlam šuāti idukkūšuma ina bābišu iḫallalūšu*, they shall kill that man by hanging him in his doorway (L227).

***bā'iru***, sbst., hunter.

*lu rēdûm u lu bā'irum*, a soldier or a hunter (L26; 26; 27; 28; 30; 32; cf. *bitum ša rēdîm bā'irim* (L36, *bītam*, L37; 41); *rēdûm bā'irum*, a soldier or hunter (L38; 41).

*balāṣu*, to ogle > ***pullusu***, to covet.

***balāṭu***, vb., to live. < *b-l-ṭ*.

*adi balṭat*, as long as she lives (L148; 171b; 178; 180; 181).

> ***bulluṭu***, to grant life.

***balāṭu***, sbst., life. < *b-l-ṭ*.

*ūm balāṭiya*, the days of my life (E22); *balāṭam ša itti mūtim šitannu ana šīmtim lišīmšum*, let him ordain for him a life that is always vying with death as his destiny (E24).

***balṭu***, adj., alive. < *b-l-ṭ*.

*eliš ina balṭūtim lissuḫšu šapliš ina erṣetim eṭemmašu mê lišaṣmi*, may he cut him off from those living above and make his shadow thirst for water in the land below (E23).

***balu***, part., without, without someone knowing. < *b-l-'*.

1. without: *balum šībī u riksātim ištām*, he made a purchase without witnesses or contracts (L7; cf. L123); *balum kaspimma*, without any money (L280).

2. without someone knowing: *balum abišu u ummišu*, without the knowledge of his father and his mother (L194; 194); *balum bēl wardim*, without the knowledge of the slave's owner (L226); *balum bēl eqlim*, without the knowledge of the owner of the field (L57; 57); *ina balum bēl kirîm*, without the knowledge of the owner of the orchard (L59); *balum bēl še'im*, without the knowledge of the owner of the grain (L113, twice); *balum dayyānī*, without the knowledge of the judges (L177); *balum itēšu*, without informing his neighbour (L68+a).

***balû***, vb., to come to an end. < *b-l-'*.

*adi napištašu ibellû*, until his soul is exhausted (E30).

> ***bullû***, to terminate.

***bānītu***, adj., creatress (see *CAD banû* vb., A). < *b-n-ʾ*.

*Nintu bēltum ṣīrtum ša mātātim ummum bānītī*, O Nintu, noble lady of the nations, the mother who has raised me up (E29).

***banû***, vb., to beget. < *b-n-ʾ*.

*zēr šarrūtim ša Sîn ibniušu*, descendant of the royal line which Sin began (P6); *zēr awīlūtim ay ibni*, let him have no human descendants (E29).

***bānû***, adj., creator (see *CAD banû* vb., A). < *b-n-ʾ*.

*ittum Dagan bānîšu*, by decree of Dagan his creator (P17); *Sîn bēl šamê ilum bānî*, Sin the lord of the sky, the god who created me (E24).

*baqāru* > ***paqāru***, to claim.

***baqrū***, sbst., claim. < *b-q-r*.

*šumma awīlum wardam amtam išāmma baqrī irtaši nādinānšu baqrī ippal*, if a man has bought a slave or a slave-girl and then has received a claim, the one who sold him shall be responsible for the claim (L279; 279; see *AHw* s.v. 3).

*bâru*, to become certain (*CAD bāru* A), > ***burru***, to clarify.

***bašû***, vb., to exist. < *b-š-ʾ*.

*rugummâm ša ina dīnim šuāti ibaššû*, the loss that pertains in that trial (L5); *ḫubullum elišu ibašši*, he is in debt (L151; also *ibaššīma*, L48); *ḫubullum eliša ibašši*, she is in debt (L151); *mimma ša nadānim la ibaššīšum*, he does not have anything at all to give (L66); *ina bītišu ša paṭārim ibašši*, there is enough for redemption in his house (L32; cf. *la ibašši*, L32, twice); *ina bītišu ša akālim ibašši*, there is enough to eat in his house (L133a; cf. L134; 135); *terḫatum la ibašši*, there is no bridal gift (L139); *mimma ša ina qātišu ibaššû*, whatever he has in his possession (§5.15); *bēlum ša kīma abim wālidim ana nišī ibaššû*, the lord who is like a father with children for his people (E12).

> *nabšû*, to be produced; *šubšû*, to produce.

***bēltu***, sbst., mistress, lady. < *b-ʾ-l*.

1. the mistress of a household, in relation to her slave-girl: *amtum šî itti bēltiša uštamḫir*, that slave-girl has tried to rival her mistress (L146); *bēlessa ana kaspim ul inaddišši*, her mistress shall not sell her (L146; cf. L147).

2. the lady (as a divine epithet): *ina maḫar Marduk bēliya Zarpānītum bēltiya*, in the presence of my lord Marduk and my lady Sarpanitu (E12; 13); *bēltum mudammiqat igirrēya*, the lady who makes my petitions acceptable (E21); *Ištar bēlet tāḫazim u qablim*, Ishtar, the mistress of conflict and strife (E27); *Nintu bēltum ṣīrtum*, Nintu, noble lady of the nations (E29).

***bēlu***, sbst., lord, master, owner, possessor. < *b-ʾ-l*.

1. the ruler of a community: *awīlum šû lu šarrum lu bēlum lu*

*iššiakkum u lu awīlūtum ša šumam nabiat*, whether that man is a king, a lord, a governor, or a person with designated responsibility (E19); *Ḫammurabimi bēlum*, the lord Hammurabi (E12).
2. the lord (as a divine epithet): *bēlum sīmat ḫaṭṭim u agêm*, the lord with the sign of the crown and sceptre (P12); *Marduk bēlišu*, his lord Marduk (P5; E12; 12; cf. *bēliya*, E10; 12; 13); *Ellil bēl šamê*, Enlil, lord of the sky (P1; cf. *bēlum*, E20); *Sîn bēl šamê*, Sin, lord of the sky (E24); *ana Šamaš rēṣišu bēlum muballiṭ Uruk*, for Shamash his helper, the lord who revives Uruk (P8); *Adad bēl ḫegallim*, Adad lord of plenty (E25); *bēlum tukultī*, the lord in whom I put my trust. (E23).
3. the owner:
a. ***bēl bītim***, the owner of a house: *bēl bītim*, the owner of a house (L16; 25, twice; [69+c]; 120, twice; 125; 229; 230; 231, twice); *bītum ana bēlišu itâr*, the house shall return to its owner (L37; [67+a]); [*bīt muškēnim ana bēlišu itār*], the house of the commoner shall return to its owner [§4.12].
b. of other real estate: *bēl eqlim*, the owner of a field (L42; 43; 43; 44; 46; 47; 57, five times; 58; 62; 62; 63; cf. *bēl eqlimma* L49; 50); *bēl kirīm*, the owner of an orchard (L59; 60; 60; 64;<65>); *bēl tarbaṣim*, the owner of a sheepfold (L266).
4. the master of a slave or of another person: *ul bēlī atta*, 'You are not my master!' (L282); *bēl wardim*, the owner of a slave (L17; 20; 175; 176a; 176b; 217; 223; 226; 280; 281; cf. *bēlišu*, L18; 282; *ana bēlišu*, L18; 282); *bēl amtim*, the owner of a slave-girl (L119); *ana* [*bēlišu utarrūšu*], they shall return him (the slave) to his owner (§5.8; also with verb negated); *bēl aššatim*, husband (L129; 161).
5. the owner of an animal or chattel: *bēl alpim*, the owner of an ox (L224; 225; 245; 246; 247; cf. *ana bēlišu* L243; *ana bēlišuma* L244; *ana bēlišu* or *ana bēlišunu*, see *BAL*, L263; see also L265; 267 for cattle and sheep); *bēl še'im*, the owner of grain (L113, twice; 120, twice;); *bēl šēbultim*, the owner of a package (L112; 112); *bēl eleppim*, the owner of a boat (L235; 236; 240); *bēl epinnim*, the owner of a plough (L259); *bēl makkūrim*, the owner of possessions (L125); *bēl ḫulqim*, the owner of lost property (L9, three times; 10 and also *bēl ḫulqimma*; 11); *bēl nidītim*, the owner of the derelict property (L68+b, with two further occurrences, partly broken); *bēl nipûtim*, the owner of a pledge (L116).
6. an owner of capital: *bēl ḫubullim*, creditor (L151; cf. *bēl ḫubullišu* L48; 151; *bēl ḫubulliša*, L151).
7. the victim of an accident: *bēl simmim*, the one who sustained the injury (L221).

***bennu***, sbst., epilepsy.

*benni elišu imtaqut*, epilepsy has struck him (L278).

*bibbulu* > ***bubbulu*** floodwater.

***biblu***, sbst., marriage gift. < *ʾ-b-l.*

*awīlum ša ana bīt emišu biblam ušābilu*, a man who had a marriage gift brought to his father-in-law's house (L159; cf. L160; 161).

***biltu***, sbst., rent. < *ʾ-b-l.*

*eqelšu ana biltim ana errēšim iddinma u bilat eqlišu imtaḫar*, he has given his field for rent to a labourer and has received rental produce from his field (L45; cf. *bilat eqlišu la imtaḫar*, L46); *bilat eqlim ša šanātim ša innadû*, an estimated yield for the years it was left fallow (L62); *bilat kirīm*, rental produce from the orchard (L64; 65); *nāši biltim*, one who should pay rent (L36; 37; 38; 41; 41); *ana pī riksātišu tālittam u biltam inaddin*, he shall give the offspring and rent according to the terms of his contract (L264); *biltam umtaṭi*, he has diminished the yield (L65).

***binâtu***, sbst., pl., limbs, body. < *b-n-ʾ.*

*biniātišu kīma ṣalam ṭiddim liḫbuš*, may he shatter his limbs like a clay statue (E28); *murṣam kabtam...ina biniātišu lišāṣiaššuma*, let him cause a serious disease to break out in his body (E30).

***bīru***, sbst., divination. < *b-ʾ-r.*

*ina bīrišu šīram lemnam ša nasāḫ išdī šarrūtišu u ḫalāq mātišu liškunšum*, let him (Shamash) provide a bad omen during his divination for the uprooting of the foundations of his kingdom and for the destruction of his land (E23).

***bīšu***, sbst., tradeable product, possessions. < *b-š-ʾ.*

1. commodity, product: *ana bītim šuāti šeʾam kaspam u bīšam inaddin*, he may pay grain, silver or goods for that house (L67+e, and again, similarly); *šeʾam šīpātim šamnam u mimma bīšam ana pašārim iddin*, he gave grain, wool, oil or some other product for reselling (L104); *kaspam ḫurāṣam abnam u bīš qātišu ana awīlim iddinma*, he gave silver, gold, jewels or some small possessions to a man (L112).

2. possessions: *mimmûšu bīšam u šeʾam*, whatever property or grain he has (§5.2); *bīšama išu*, he does possess goods (§5.15); *bītam ipušū bīšam iršû*, they made a house and acquired possessions (L176); *muttat eqlim kirîm u bīšim*, a half of the field, the orchard and the goods (L137; cf. *bīšam*, L150); *šuāti u bīšašu ana kaspim inaddinūma*, they shall sell him and his possessions for silver (L54).

3. occurs frequently with > ***eqlu***, field.

***bitiqtu***, sbst., loss. < *b-t-q.*

*bitiqtum ša errēšimma*, the loss will be the labourer's (L45); *ašar illiku bitiqtam ītamar*, he makes a loss in the place where he went (L102).

***bītu***, sbst., house, household, shrine.

1. house, property, real estate:

a. with *epēšu*, to build a house, set up house: *šumma [awīlum] bītam [ippešma]*, if a man is going to build a house (L67); *ina bīt īpušu uššamma*, she shall dwell in the house that he has built (L148); *bītam ana awīilim īpušma*, he has built a house for a man (L228; 233; cf. L229); *bīt īpušu*, the house he built (L229; 232); *ištu innemdū bītam īpušū*, after they have lain together they have built a house (L176a); *bīssu*(!) *īpuš*, he has set up house (L191).

b. with other verbs: *bīssu itabbal*, he shall take away his house (L2); *bīt mubbirišu itabbal*, he shall take away the house of his accuser (L2); *wardam šuāti ina bītišu iktalāšu*, he has held that slave back in his house (L19); *ana bītim šuāti še'am kaspam u bīšam inaddin*, he may pay grain, silver or goods for that house (L67+a); *bītum ana [bēlišu] itâr*, the house shall return to its owner (L67+a); *bītum šû ilkam la išu*, that property has no levy (L67+a); *bīt ilkim ša bīt itēšu*, a property on which there is a levy which is the property of his neighbour (L67+a); *awīlum bītam ipluš*, the man burgled the house (L21); *[ištu] nidītika [bīti] ippalašūnim*, they may burgle my house from your neglected land (L68+b); *ištu bītika ibbalakkatūnim*, 'they will climb over here from your house' (L68+b); *šēšu ana našpākūtim ina bīt awīlim išpukma*, he has put his grain in another man's house for storage (L120); *še'am ša ina bītišu iššapku*, the grain that was stored in his house (L120); *bītam inaṣṣarū*, they shall protect the house (L177); *ana 1 musar bītim*, for one unit of measurement of the building (L228); *bīt imqutu*, the house which collapsed (L232); — fragmentary: *ina...bītum* (L68+c).

2. household, persons and contents: *šāyyimānum ina bīt nādinānim kasap išqulu ileqqe*, the purchaser shall take from the seller's house the silver he paid (L9; cf. L12); *ina bītišu ša paṭārim ibašši*, there is something in his house for making redemption (L32, twice); *ina bītišu [ušēṣû]*, because he has made him leave his house (L69+c); *ana bītiša itâr*, she shall return to her house (L131); *ina bītišu ša akālim ibašši*, there is something to eat in his house (L133a; cf. 134; 135); *bīssa usappaḫ*, she has squandered her household wealth (L141; 143); *ana bītišu ušerrebši*, they shall make her enter his house (L145); *ina bītim šūṣîm usaḫḫamūši*, they shall pressurize her to leave the house (L172); *ana bīt šanîm*, to someone else's house (L177, twice); *bīt mutiša panîm*, the house of her former husband (L177; also *bītam ša mutiša panîm*).

3. with the possessor of the house identified by a noun:
a. ***bīt abim*** > ***abu***, father.
b. ***bīt awīlim*** > ***awīlu***, man.
c. ***bīt ilim*** > ***ilu***, god.
d. ***bīt muškēnim*** > ***muškēnu***, working man.
e. ***bīt mutiša*** > ***mutu***, husband.
f. ***bīt šanîm*** > ***šanû***, someone else.
g. ***bīt šāyyimānim*** > ***šāyyimānu***, purchaser; ***bīt sībim*** > ***sību***, beer.
h. ***bīt wardim*** > ***ardu***, slave.
j. ***bēl bītim*** > ***bēlu***, master.
4. occurs frequently with > ***eqlu***, field.
5. occurs frequently with > ***epēšu***, to make.
6. shrine: *ina Esagil bītim ša kīma šamê u erṣetim išdāšu kīnā*, in Esagila, the shrine whose foundations are as secure as heaven and earth (E8); *bīt Ebabbar*, the shrine of Ebabbar (P7); *bīt Egalmaḫ*, the shrine of Egalmah (P8); *bītim Ḫursagkalamma*, the shrine of Hursagkalamma (P9); *bīt Emaḫ*, the shrine of Emah (P15); *bītim libitti Ebabbara*, the shrine and brickwork of Ebabbar (E31); *bīt il ālīšu*, the shrine of his local deity (L32, twice); *šēd bītim*, the demon of the temple (E31).

***bubbulu***, sbst., floodwater. < *w-b-l*.
*eqlam Adad irtaḫiṣ u lu bibbulum itbal*, the Storm has swept across the field or a flood has eroded it (L45; 48).

***bubūtu***, sbst., famine.
*māssu ina ḫušaḫḫim u bubūtim liḫalliq*, may he annihilate his land by hunger and famine (E25).

***bullû***, vb., to terminate. < *b-l-ʾ*.
*awīlum ša ana bullîm illiku*, the man who went to extinguish the fire (L25); *qablātim ubelli*, he has made the conflict cease (E5).

***bulluṭu***, vb., to let live, heal, enliven. < *b-l-ṭ*.
1. to allow to live: *aššassu uballaṭ u šarrum warassu uballaṭ*, he may allow his wife to live and the king may allow his subject to live (L129; 129);
2. to restore to life: *simmam kabtam īpušma ubtalliṭ*, he performed a serious operation and saved its life (L224); *awīlam ubtalliṭ*, he saved the man's life (L215).
3. to restore to health: *īn awīlim ubtalliṭ*, he saved the man's sight (L215); *šerʾānam marṣam ubtalliṭ*, he has eased a painful muscle (L221).

***bulṭu***, sbst., life. < *b-l-ṭ*.
*ina bulṭišu*, during his life (L170; 171a).

***burru***, vb., to make a declaration. < *b-ʾ-r*.

*mimmâšu ḫalqam maḫar ilim ubârma*, in the presence of the god he shall declare what has been lost (L23; cf. L240); *maḫar ilim šeʾašu ubârma*, in the presence of the god he shall declare what grain he had (L120); *babtašu ina maḫar ilim ubâršuma*, his community shall make a declaration about him in the presence of the god (L126, and also *ūtebbir*).

***buru***, sbst., measurement of area (6.48 hectares, 16-17 acres, see *CAD*).

*ana 1 burum 10 kur šeʾam imaddad*, he shall measure out ten kur of corn per bur (L44; 56; cf. L63); *ina ebūrim ana 1 burum 60 kur šeʾam ana bēl eqlim imaddad*, he shall make an assessment of 60 kur of corn for each bur of land for the owner of the field at harvest time (L58; cf. L255); *elēnumma ana 1 burum 20 kur šeʾam ana bēl eqlim inaddin*, he shall give in addition 20 kur of grain per bur to the owner of the field (L57).

***butuqqû***, loss. < *b-t-q*.

*nēmelam u butuqqâm ša ibbašû*, any profit or loss that arose (L77+f).

## D

***dadmū***, sbst., pl., settlements.

*nišī dadmī aburrī ušarbiṣ*, I let the people in the settlements rest in pastureland (E5); *mukanniš dadmē nār Purattim*, controlling the villages on the Euphrates (P17).

***dâku***, vb., to kill, execute. < *d-ʾ-k*.

1. to kill: *awīlum alpam imēram īgurma ina ṣērim nēšum iddūkšu*, a man has hired an ox or a sheep and a lion has killed it in the desert (L244; cf. *iddūk* L266).

2. to execute: *mārašu idukkū*, they shall kill his son (L116); *mār itinnim šuāti idukkū*, they shall kill the son of that builder (L230); *mārassu idukkū*, they shall kill his daughter (L210); *ina pani pilšim šuāti idukkūšuma iḫallalūšu*, they shall kill him by hanging him in front of the opening he made (L21); *awīlam šuāti idukkūšuma ina bābīšu iḫallalūšu*, they shall kill that man by hanging him before the doorway (L227).

3. fragmentary: *idukkūšu*, they shall kill him (§5.3a).

> ***nadāku***, to be killed; ***šudūku***, to arrange a murder.

***damāmu***, vb., to grieve. < *d-m-m*.

*ana eṭlūtišu liddammam*, let him grieve with his young men (E30).

*damāqu* > ***dummuqu***, to be kind.

***damiqtu***, sbst., blessing, favour. < *d-m-q*.

*ina Esagil ša arammu šumī ina damiqtim ana dār lizzakir*, may my name be uttered as a blessing for evermore in Esagila, the place I love! (E10); *damqātišu ana lemnētim litēr*, may he change his blessings into trouble (E27).

***damqu***, adj., good, beneficent. < *d-m-q*.

*mātam ussam kīnam u rīdam damqam ušaṣbitu*, he has made the land accept proper behaviour and good customs (E1); *mutêr lamassišu damiqtim ana ālim Aššur*, who has brought back the beneficent statue to Ashur (P19); *lamassī damiqtum rā'imat palêya*, my gracious protector, the one who loves me to reign (E27).

***damu***, sbst., blood.

*qarrādīšu lišamqit damīšunu erṣetam lišqi*, he shall let the blood of his warriors spill and let the earth drink their blood (E27).

*danānu* > ***dunnunu***, to strengthen.

***dannatu***, sbst., place of security. < *d-n-n*.

*ša ina dannat šarrim turru*, who has been taken back to one of the king's camps (L27; 28; see *CAD* s.v. 2b).

***dannu***, adj., strong. < *d-n-n*.

1. of a person: *šarrum dannum*, the mighty king (P21); *aplum dannum*, the mighty son (P21); *dannum enšam ana la ḫabālim*, so that the strong should not oppress the weak (P3; E8); *rēdiam ina dīnim ana dannim ištarak*, he has given a soldier to a strong man in a dispute (L34).

2. of a god: *Nergal dannum ina ilī*, Nergal, strongest of the gods (E28); *dannum mukīn išdī Sippar*, the strong one who fixed the foundation of Sippar (P7).

3. of an object: *ina kakkim dannim*, with a mighty weapon (E4; cf. E28); *eleppam dannatam*, a boat that has been repaired (L235).

***dânu***, vb., to conduct a trial, legislate. < *d-'-n*.

*dayyānum dīnam idīn*, a judge has conducted a trial (L5); *dīn idīnu*, the case he judged (L5); *dīn mātim ša adīnu*, the law of the land which I have administered (E14; 15; cf. E19; also *lidīn*, 16); *dīn mātim ana di'ānim*, to administer the law of the land (E8); *dīnšu ay idīn*, let him not administer justice (E23).

***dāriš***, adv., for ever. < *d-r-'*

*dāriš išīmū* , they have made an everlasting decree (P16).

***dāri'u*** > *dārû*.

***dāru***, sbst., generation. < *d-r-'*.

***ana dār***, for evermore: *šumī ina damiqtim ana dār lizzakir*, let my name be uttered as a blessing for evermore (E10); *šīram ṭābam ana nišī ana dār išīm*, he has secured good health for the people for all time (E12).

***dārû***, adj., everlasting. < *d-r-ʾ*.
*šarrūtam dārītam ša kīma šamê u erṣetim išdāša šuršudā*, an everlasting kingdom with foundations as secure as heaven and earth (P2); *zērum dārium ša šarrūtim*, everlasting royal descendants (P21).

***dâṣu***, vb., to trick. < *d-ʾ-ṣ*.
*awīlum gallābam idāṣma*, a gentleman has tricked the barber (L227).

***dâšu***, vb., to thresh. < *d-ʾ-š*.
*alpam ana diāšim īgur*, he has hired an ox to thresh (L268); *imēram ana diāšim īgur*, he has hired a donkey to thresh (L269); *urīṣam ana diāšim īgur*, he has hired a goat to thresh (L270).

***dayyānu***, sbst., judge (see *CAD dayānu*). < *d-ʾ-n*.
*dayyānū warkassu iparrasūma*, the judges will examine his circumstances (L168; 172; cf. L177); *dayyānum dīnam idīn purussâm iprus kunukkam ušēzib*, a judge has conducted a trial, reached a decision, had the seal placed on the document (L5); *dayyānam šuāti ina dīn idīnu enêm ukannūšūma*, they will prove that that judge is guilty of changing a decision he has made (L5); *itti dayyānī ina dīnim ul uššab*, he shall not sit with the judges in a case (L5); *dayyānū awātišunu immarūma*, judges shall investigate their testimony (L9); *dayyānū adannam ana šeššet warḫī išakkanūšumma*, the judges shall fix a date in six months' time for him (L13); *maḫar dayyānī inaṭṭûšu*, they shall flog him in front of the judges (L127); *ana dayyānī mārī anassaḫ iqtabi*, he has said in front of the judges, 'I will disinherit my son' (L168); *balum dayyānī*, without the knowledge of the judges (L177); *ina qibīt Šamaš dayyānim rabîm ša šamê u erṣetim*, by the will of Shamash, almighty judge of heaven and earth (E10; cf. E23).

***dayyānūtu***, sbst., judiciary (see *CAD dayānūtu*). < *d-ʾ-n*.
*u ina puḫrim ina kussî dayyānūtišu ušetbûšuma*, furthermore they shall have him removed from the council and from his place on the legal bench (L5).

***dekû***, vb., to move, start up. < *d-k-ʾ*.
*tuššamma idke*(!) *iddāk*, he has perpetrated corruption and he shall be killed (L11: but for *idkē* read *iddi* with Roth; see also *CAD*; variant *iqbi*).

*dešû* > ***mudeššû***, making abundant supplies.

***dimmatu***, sbst., moaning. < *d-m-m*.
*ina tānēḫim u dimmatim*, with moaning and wailing (E24).

***dīnu***, sbst., law, problem, decision, tribunal. < *d-ʾ-n*.
1. law: *dīnāt mīšarim ša Ḫammurabi šarrum lēʾûm ukinnuma*, just laws which the mighty king Hammurabi has established (E1); *dīn mātim ana diānim*, to formulate the law of the land (E8; cf. E14; 15); *dīnī la ušassik*, he has not rescinded my law (E18).

2. legal problem: *awatam likallimšu dīnšu līmur libbašu linappišma*, let him explain his allegation and understand his problem and be satisfied in his soul (E11); *rēdiam ina dīnim ana dannim ištarak*, he has given a soldier to a strong man in a dispute (L34).
3. verdict: *dīnšu ītene*, he has changed his decision (L5); *dīn idīnu*, the decision he made (L5; cf. *dīn adīnu*, E19; *dīnšu*, 23); *dīnšina lidīn*, let him reach verdicts for them (E16).
4. legal hearing: *dayyānum dīnam idīn*, a judge has conducted a trial (L5); *dīnum šû dīn napištim*, that trial is one involving death (L3; 3); *aran dīnim šuāti ittanašši*, he shall pay the penalty in that case (L4; 13); *rugummâm ša ina dīnim šuāti ibaššû*, the loss that occurred in that trial (L5; cf. L12; 115; 123; 250).
5. tribunal: *ina dīnim ana šībūt sarrātim ūṣiamma*, he has come into the tribunal with false evidence (L3); *itti dayyānī ina dīnim ul uššab*, he shall not sit with the judges in the tribunal (L5).

***dummuqu***, vb., to show kindness. < *d-m-q*.
*ūmišam ina maḫar Marduk bēlīya Zarpānītum bēltīya lidammiqū*, let them show kindness every day in the presence of my lord Marduk and my lady Zarpanitum (E13).
> ***mudammiqu***, benefactor.

***dumqu***, sbst., favour. < *d-m-q*.
*Ninkarrak mārat Anim qābiat dumqiya*, Ninkarrak the daughter of Sin who speaks in my favour (E30).

***dunnunu***, vb., to strengthen, reconstruct. < *d-n-n*.
1. to strengthen a dyke: *ana kār eqlišu dunnunim*, to strengthen the dyke in his field (L53); *kāršu la udanninma*, he has not strengthened his dyke (L53).
2. to strengthen a wall: *igāram šuāti udannan*, he shall strengthen the wall (L233).
3. to do reliable work: *šipiršu la udanninma*, he has not made his work strong enough (L229); *aššum bīt īpušu la udanninuma*, because he has not made the house he constructed strong enough (L232).
4. to repair: *nabalkattaka dunnin*, repair your damage (L68+b); *eleppam šuāti inaqqarma ina makkūr ramanišu udannanma*, he shall dismantle that boat and reconstruct it properly from his own resources (L235).

***duppuru***, vb., to absent onself. < *d-p-r*.
*ina pani ilkim iddīma uddappir*, he has been negligent about his duty and absented himself (L30; also *uddappirma*, L31).

*duššû* > ***mudeššû***, making abundant supplies.

## E

*ebēbu* > ***mubbibu***, making clean; ***ubbubu***, to purify.

***ebūru***, sbst., harvest.

*ina ebūrim kīma riksātišu še'am ileqqe*, he shall take the grain at harvest-time according to his contract (L47; cf. L49); *ina ebūrim kasapšu u ṣibassu [išaqqal]*, he shall pay the silver and the interest at harvest (§5.2); *ina ebūrim 5 sūt še'am ileqqe*, he shall take five sa of grain at harvest-time (L111); *ina ebūrim ana 1 burum 60 kur še'am ana bēl eqlim imaddad*, he shall make an assessment of 60 kur of corn for each bur of land for the owner of the field at harvest-time. (L58; cf. L255).

*edēšu* > ***muddišu***, renewing.

*edû*, to know > ***idû***.

*egirrû* > ***igirrû***, reputation.

***egû***, vb., to be negligent. < *'-g-'*.

1. to be negligent about procedure: *šamallûm ītegīma kanīk kaspim ša ana tamkārim iddinu la ilteqe*, the salesman has been careless and not taken the sealed receipt for the silver which he gave to the merchant (L105); *bēl bītim ša īgûma*, the owner of the house who has been negligent (L125).

2. to do work carelessly: *malāḫum īgīma*, the boatman has been negligent (L236; cf. L237); *rē'ûm īgūma*(!), the shepherd has been negligent (L267).

3. to be remiss: *ana ṣalmāt qaqqadim ša Ellil išrukam rē'ûssina Marduk iddinam ul ēgu*, I have not neglected the people whom Enlil gave me and whose shepherding Marduk entrusted to me (E2).

***e'iltu***, *īltu*, sbst., debt (see *CAD*).

*awīlam e'iltum iṣbassuma*, a man has fallen into debt (L117; 119); *ana e'iltišu inaddin*, he shall give them in exchange for his debt (L39); *ana e'iltišu ul inaddin*, he shall not give them in exchange for his debt (L38).

***ekallu***, sbst., palace, or temple (often either translation is appropriate).

*makkūr ilim u ekallim išriq*, he has stolen property from the god or from the palace (L6; cf. L8); *ana ekallim ireddīšu*, he shall escort him to the palace (L18; cf. L109); *ekallum ipaṭṭarišu*(!), the palace shall ransom him (L32); *lu warad ekallim lu amat ekallim*, a palace slave or a palace slave-girl (L15; 15; cf. L16; 175; 176a, three times); *muzzaz ekallim*, a palace attendant (L187).

***ekūtu***, sbst., orphan girl.

*ekūtam almattam šutēšurim*, to show justice to the waif and to the widow (E8).

***ela***, adv., only.

*ela ana la ḫassim rēqā ana emqim ana tanādātim šūṣâ*, they are useless only for the one who does not understand, they are brought as precious gifts to the wise (E17).

***elēnu***, conj., furthermore, in addition. < *ʾ-l-ʾ*.

*elēnumma ana 1 burum 20 kur šeʾam ana bēl eqlim inaddin*, in addition he shall give 20 kur of grain per bur to the owner of the field (L57); *elēnumma ina makkūr bīt abim mitḫāriš izuzzū*, moreover they shall share the goods from the father's house equally (L165).

***eleppu***, sbst., boat (see *CAD elippu*).

*awīlum eleppašu ana malāḫim ana igrim iddinma*, a man has given his boat for hire to a boatman (L236); *malāḫam u eleppam īgurma*, he has hired a boatman and a boat (L237); *eleppam išriq*, he has stolen a boat (L8); *elep 60 kur*(!), a boat of 60 kur capacity (L234; cf. *elep šūšim*, 277); *malāḫum eleppam ana awīlim ipḫēma*, a boatman caulked the boat for a man (L235); *eleppum šî iṣṣabar*, then that boat leaked (L235); *eleppam uṭṭebbi*, he then let the boat sink (L236; 237; cf. *eleppam ša uṭebbû*, L237; *elep awīlim uṭṭebbīma*, L238); *eleppam šuāti inaqqarma*, he shall pull that boat apart (L235); *eleppam dannatam ana bēl eleppim inaddin*, he shall give the boat that has been repaired to the owner of the boat (L235; 235); *malāḫum eleppam ana bēl eleppim iriab*, the boatman shall recompense the boat owner with a boat (L236; 236).

***elep ša muqqelpītim***, a boat moving with the current, and ***elep ša māḫirtim***, a boat moving against the current, mentioned only in L240: *elep ša māḫirtim elep ša muqqelpītim imḫaṣma*, a boat going upstream has struck a boat going downstream (L240); *ša māḫirtim ša elep ša muqqelpītim uṭebbû eleppašu u mimmašu ḫalqam iriʾabšum*, the man in the boat going upstream who made the boat going downstream sink shall recompense him for his boat and for whatever was lost (L240; see also *māḫirtum*); cf. also *bēl eleppim ša eleppušu ṭebiʾat*, the owner of the boat whose boat was sunk (L240; 240); *mimma ša ina eleppišu ḫalqu*, whatever was lost from that boat (L240).

***eli***, prep., against, on.

1. introducing an indirect object after a transitive verb: *awīlum eli ugbabtum u aššat awīlim ubānam ušatriṣma*, a man has pointed the finger at a priestess or a man's wife (L127; cf. L132); *nakiršu elišu lišziz*, let him allow his enemy to stand over him (E26).

2. introducing an indirect object after an intransitive verb:

a. with *ḫubullum…bašû*, to be in debt: *ḫubullum elišu ibaššīma*, he is in debt (L48; cf. L151, twice; *elišunu* L152).

b. with ***išu***, to have a claim against: *awīlum eli awīlim šeʾam u kaspam* *išûma*, a man has a claim against a man for grain or silver (L113; 115; cf. L114).

c. with ***maqātu***, to fall on: *benni elišu imtaqut*, he has been afflicted with epilepsy (L278).

d. with ***nadû***, to make an accusation against: *nērtam elišu iddīma*, he accused him of murder (L1; cf. *eli awīlim*, L2; also *elišu*, L2, twice).

e. with ***šasû***, to shout: *eli ālišu ezziš lissīma*, let him shout violently against his city (E25).

f. with ***ṭâbu***, to be pleasing to: *eli Ištar ṭāba*, pleasing to Ishtar (P18); *ēma eliša ṭābu*, wherever it pleases her (L178; 179, twice; 182); *ana errēšim ša eliša ṭābu*, to the cultivator who pleases her (L178).

3. comparative marker in adjectival expressions, more than: *awīlum lēt awīlim ša elišu rabû imtaḫaṣ*, a man has struck the cheek of a man who is more important than himself (L202).

*eli'atu* > ***ēlītu***, additional amount.

***eliš***, adv., above (as opposed to *šapliš*, below).

*nakrī eliš u šapliš assuḫ*, I eradicated my enemies above and below (E4); *irnitti Marduk eliš u šapliš ikšud*, he secured the triumph of Marduk above and below (E12); *eliš ina balṭūtim lissuḫšu šapliš ina erṣetim eṭemmašu mê lišaṣmi*, may he cut him off from the living on high and may he let his ghost thirst for water in the land down below (E23).

***elītu***, sbst., extra part. < *'-l-'*.

*eliāt zittišu kasap terḫatim išakkanūšumma aššatam ušaḫḫazūšu*, as additions to his share they shall set aside for him silver for a bridal gift and let him marry a wife (L166; see *AHw* 202b-203a s.v. *ēlītu*).

***ellilūtu***, sbst., leadership (an abstract noun derived from the name of the god Enlil, see *AHw Ellilūtu*).

*ellilūt kiššat nišī*, the leadership of the people of the world (P1).

***ellu***, adj., pure, holy.

*mākalī ellūtim*, pure food (P12; 17); *zībī ellūtim*, holy sacrifices (P16); *rubûm ellum*, holy prince (P14).

***elû***, vb., to go up, give up. < *'-l-'*.

1. to ascend to higher ground: *ištu ṣēnum ugārim ītelianim*, after the flocks have come away from the meadows (L58).

2. to hand over, forfeit: *ina kaspišu ītelli*, he shall give up his silver (L35; 37; 177); [*ina kaspim ša*] *ilqū* [*ītellīma*], he shall forfeit the silver that he took (§4.12); *ina*(?) *kaspim ša iddinu*(?) *ītelli*, he shall forfeit the silver that he gave (§5.7, fragmentary); *ina mimma ša iddinu ītelli*, he shall forfeit whatever he has paid (L67+a; [§5.10]; [5.13]; 5.14; cf. L113; 116).

> ***šūlû***, to bring to the surface; ***ullû***, to raise high.

***elû***, adj., upper. < *ʾ-l-ʾ*.

*ṭuppam eliʾam la išṭur*, he has not written an extra tablet (§5.12; thus *BAL* 72+e [*e*(?)-(*lil*[?])-*am*]; but for *eliʾam* Roth prefers to read *eššam* (i.e. *eš-ša-am*), > ***eššu***, new).

***ēma***, adv., wherever.

*warkassa ēma eliša ṭābu nadānam*, giving her possessions wherever she wants (L178; 179; 179; cf. L182).

***emēdu***, vb., to impose (a punishment). < *ʾ-m-d*.

*mārī arnam immidū*, they shall impose the penalty on the sons (L172); *arnam kabtam šēressu rabītam ša ina zumrišu la iḫalliqu līmussuma*, let him impose a heavy punishment with great condemnation that will not disappear from his body (E24).

> ***nenmudu***, to lie down together.

*emēqu* > ***muštēmiqu***, making wise.

***emqu***, adj., wise. < *ʾ-m-q*.

*emqum muttabbilum*, the clever one who gets things done (P16); *ela ana la ḫassim rēqa ana emqim ana tanādātim šūṣâ*, although they are useless to the one who has no sense, they are brought as precious gifts to the wise (E17).

***emu***, sbst., father-in-law.

1. *ana emišu māratka ul aḫḫaz iqtabi*, he has said to his prospective father-in-law, 'I will not take your daughter' (L159; cf. *emušu… iqtabi*, L161); *emušu uttēršum*, his father-in-law has given back to him (L163; cf. L164).

2. ***bīt emišu***, the house of his father-in-law: *awīlum ša ana bīt emišu biblam ušābilu*, a man who had the gift brought to his prospective father-in-law's house (L159; cf. L161; also *bīt emim*, L160) *terḫatam ša awīlum šû ana bīt emišu ublu*, the betrothal gift which that man had brought to his father-in-law's house (L163).

***emūqu***, sbst., value (of an inheritance). < *ʾ-m-q*.

*kīma emūq zittiša ipram piššatam u lubūšam inaddinūšimma*, they shall give her food, oil and garments according to the value of her share (L178; 178); *aḫḫūša kīma emuq bīt abim šeriktam išarrakū-šimma*, her brothers shall offer her a dowry proportionate to the size of the father's property (L184).

*enēšu* > ***unnušu***, to weaken.

***enšu***, sbst., weak. < *ʾ-n-š*.

*dannum enšam ana la ḫabālim*, so that the strong should not oppress the weak (P3; E8).

*ēntu* > ***ugbabtu***, sbst., priestess.

***enû***, vb., to change, modify a statement. < *ʾ-n-ʾ*.

*dīnsu ītene*, he has changed his judgment (L5); *ina dīn idīnu enêm ukannūšuma*, they shall convict him of having changed the judgment he made (L5); *riksātišu ul inni*, he shall not change the terms of his contract (L52).

*epēsu* > ***uppusu***, to make a problem.

***epēšu***, vb., to act, work, build. < *ʾ-p-š*.

1. to perform a task: *simmam kabtam ina karzilli siparrim īpušma*, he has performed a serious operation with a bronze knife (L215; 218; cf. L219; 224; 225); *awīlum* [*nidītam*] *balum* [*itešu ītēpuš*], a man has built on neglected land without informing his neighbour (L68+a); *eqlam šipram ippešma*, he shall do the work in the field (L62; 63; cf. *ina eqlim šiprim la epēšim*, L42); *nidītka epuš*, 'Work on your derelict property' (L68+b).

2. fragmentary: *kiṣrim ša ippušu*, the obligation for rent which he shall perform (§4.12).

3. with ***bītu***.

a. to construct a building: *šumma* [*awīlum*] *bītam* [*ippešma*], if a man constructs a house (L67); *itinnum bītam ana awīlim īpušma*, a builder has constructed a house for a man (L228; 233; cf. L229); *bīt īpušu imqutma*, the house he built collapsed (L229); *aššum bīt īpušu la udanninuma imqutu*, because he has not made the house he constructed strong enough and it collapsed (L232); *bīt imqutu ippeš*, he shall reconstruct the house that collapsed (L232).

b. to contribute to the formation of a household: *bīt šāyyimānišunu u kāšišišunu ippešū*, they shall work in the house of the one who has bought them or the one who controls them (L117); *ištu innemdū bītam īpušū bīšam iršû*, after they slept together they made a house and acquired property (L176a); *bīssu*(!) *īpuš*, he has made a house of his own (L191); *ina bīt īpušu uššamma*, she shall live in the house he has made (L148).

***epinnu***, sbst., plough.

*šumma awīlum epinnam ina ugārim išriq 5 šiqil kaspam ana bēl epinnim inaddin*, if a man has stolen a plough from a field he shall give five shekels of silver to the owner of the plough (L259; 259).

***epištu***, sbst., work, achievement. < *ʾ-p-š*.

1. results of manual labour: *mê iptēma epšētim ša eqel itēšu mê uštābil*, he has let out his water and allowed the water to destroy the work in his neighbour's field (L56); *eqel epšētim ša še'im u lu šamaššammī*, a field for the production of grain or sesame (L49).

2. accomplishments: *epšētušu eli Ištar ṭāba*, his deeds please Ishtar (P18); *epšētūa šāninam ul išâ*, my deeds have no rival (E17).

***eqlu***, field.

1. in general: *awīlum awīlam ana panī eqlišu uzuzzim īgurma*, a man has hired a man to stand in front of his field (L253).

2. irrigated land: *ana kār eqlišu dunnunim aḫšu iddīma*, he has been negligent about repairing the dyke on his field (L53); *eqel itēšu mê uštābil*, he has allowed the water to run over his neighbour's field (L55; 56).

3. arable land: *eqlam ana errēšūtim ušēṣīma*, he has let out the field for cultivation (L42); *ina eqlim še'am la uštabši*, he has not produced any grain in the field (L42; cf. L52); *ina eqlim šiprim la epēšim ukannūšuma*, they shall convict him of not doing working a field (L42); *eqlam la īrišma ittadi*, he has not cultivated the field but abandoned it (L43); *eqlam ša iddû*, the field he abandoned (L43); *eqlam la iptete*, he has not opened up the field (L44); *eqlam mayyārī imaḫḫaṣ*, he shall attack the field with mattocks (L44); *eqelšu ana biltim ana errēšim iddinma*, he has given his field to be cultivated for the produce (L45); *bilat eqlišu imtaḫar*, he has received the produce from his field (L45; cf. L46); *eqlam Adad irtaḫiṣ*, the Storm has eroded the field (L45; cf. L48); *u lu ana mišlāni u lu ana šaluš eqlam iddin*, whether he has given the field on the basis of a half a share or a one-third share (L46); *še'am ša ina eqlim ibaššû*, the grain that there is in the field (L46; cf. L48); *eqlam erēšam iqtabi*, he has declared that he will cultivate the field (L47); *errēssuma*(!) *eqelšu irrišma*, his ploughman shall plough his field (L47); *eqel epšētim ša še'im u lu šamaššammī*, a field for grain or sesame (L49); *eqlam erišma še'am u lu šamaššammī ša ibaššû esip*, cultivate the field and harvest the grain or sesame which is there (L49; cf. L50); *errēšum ina eqlim še'am u lu šamaššammī uštabši ina ebūrim še'am u šamaššammī ša ina eqlim ibaššû bēl eqlimma ileqqēma*, the cultivator has produced grain or sesame from the field and at the harvest the owner of the field shall take the grain or sesame which is in the field (L49; 49; for *bēl eqlimma* see *bēlu*); *eqel* < *še'im*> *eršam u lu eqel šamaššammī eršam*, a field being cultivated with grain or a field being cultivated with sesame (L50; 50); *eqelšu iṣṣid*, he shall harvest the field (L57); [*ana*] *eqlim erēšim urakkissu*, he formally agrees with him to cultivate the field (L253); *ina eqlim la uštabši*, he produces nothing from the field (L255); *ina eqlim šuāti ina liātim imtanaššarūšu*, they shall drag him all over that field with oxen (L256).

4. land used for grazing: *eqlam ṣēnam uštākil*, he has allowed the flock to graze the (cultivated) field (L57 [without permission], twice); *re'um ṣēnam ana eqlim iddīma eqlam ṣēnam uštākil*, the shepherd abandoned the flock in the field and let the flock graze the field (L58;

58); *re'ûm eqel ušākilu inaṣṣarma*, the shepherd shall look after the field he allowed to be grazed (L58).

5. land used as an orchard: *nukaribbum eqlam ina zaqāpim la igmurma*, the gardener did not complete the planting out of the land (L61); *eqlam ša innadnušum ana kirîm la izqup*, he did not plant out the land that was given to him as an orchard (L62); *bilat eqlim*, produce from the land (L62); *eqlam šipram ippešma*, he shall do the work in the field (L62; 63).

6. together with ***kirû***, orchard (see also paragraph 4): *eqelšu u kirāšu ana šanîm iddinūma*, they have given his field or his orchard to someone else (L27); *eqelšu u kirāšu utarrūšumma*, they shall give him his field or orchard back (L27); *eqlum u kirûm innaddiššumma*, the field and the orchard shall be given to him (L28); *šalušti eqlim u kirîm*, one-third of the field or orchard (L29); *eqlam ana kirîm zaqāpim*, a field to be planted out as an orchard (L60); *eqelša u kirāša aḫḫūša ileqqūma*, her brothers shall take possession of her field and orchard (L178); *eqlam kirâm u mimma ša abuša iddinušim*, the field, orchard and anything else which her father gave her (L178).

7. together with ***kirû*** and also ***bītu***, house: *eqlam kirâm u bītam ša rēdîm bā'irim u nāši biltim upīḫ u niplātim iddin*, he has acquired by exchange the field, orchard or house of a soldier, hunter or tribute bearer and paid a supplement (L41); *eqlum kirûm u bītum ša rēdîm bā'irim u nāši biltim ana kaspim ul innaddin*(!), the field, orchard or house of a soldier, hunter or tribute bearer shall not be sold for silver (L36; cf. *eqlam*, L37, twice); *rēdûm bā'irum u nāši biltim ina eqlim kirîm u bītim ša ilkišu ana aššatišu u mārtišu ul išaṭṭar u ana e'iltišu ul inaddin*, a soldier, hunter or tribute bearer shall not sign over to his wife or daughter a field or orchard or house pertaining to his duty nor shall it be given for debt (L38; cf. L39); *nadītum tamkārum u ilkum aḫûm eqelsu kirāšu u bīssu ana kaspim inaddin*, a priestess, a merchant or any other duty-bound person may sell a field, an orchard or a house for silver (L40); *ilik eqlim kirîm u bītim ša išammu illak*, he shall perform the duty for the field, orchard or house which he has bought (L40); *eqelšu kirāšu u bīssu irriš* he shall cultivate his field, orchard or house (L30); *ana eqlišu kirîšu u bītišu itâr*, he shall repossess his field, orchard or house (L41); *eqelšu kirāšu u bīssu ina pani ilkim iddīma*, he has abandoned his field, orchard or house because of the duty (L30); *šanûm warkišu eqelšu kirāšu u bīssu iṣbatma*, someone else has taken control of his field, orchard or house after his departure (L30); *eqlum kirûm u bītum ana bēlišu itâr*, his field, orchard or house shall return to its owner (L37); *eqelšu kirāšu u bīssu innaddiššumma*, his field, his orchard or his house shall be given to him (L31);

*eqelšu kirāšu u bīssu ana ipṭerišu ul inaddin*, his field orchard and house shall not be given as his ransom (L32); *ina eqlim kirîm u bītim ul inaddiššum*, he may not give him any of the field, orchard or house (L191); *eqlam kirâm u bītam išruk*, he has presented the field, the orchard and the house (L165).

8a. together with ***kirû***, ***bītu*** and with ***bīšū***, property: *ana aššatišu eqlam kirâm bītam u bīšam išrukšim kunukkam īzibšim*, he has presented his wife with a field, orchard, house or property and has deposited a sealed document (L150).

b. without ***bītu***: *muttat eqlim kirîm u bīšim inaddinūšimma mārīša urabba*, they shall give her half the field. orchard or property and she shall bring up her sons (L137).

9. ***bēl eqlim*** > ***bēlu***, master.

***erbe***, sbst., four.

*kibrāt erbettim*, the four parts of the earth (P5; cf. *kibrāt arbā'im*, the four parts of the earth, P21); *erbe šanātim kiriam urabba*, he shall make the orchard grow for four years (L60); *ana 1 kurrum 1 pān 4 sūt še'am ṣibtam ileqqe*, he shall receive one parshikah and four sa of grain in interest per kur (§5.9); *idī alpim ša warka 4 kur še'am*, the fee for the rear ox is four kur of grain (L242).

***erēbu***, vb., to enter, move into. < *'-r-b*.

1. to enter a building: *ana šikarim ana bīt sībim īterub*, she has entered a drinking house for a drink (L110).

2. to take up residence: *inūma iḫḫuzuši qadum šeriktim ša bīt abiša ana bīt warad ekallim u lu warad muškēnim īrubma*, after he has married her she has moved into the house of the palace slave or the worker's slave with the dowry from her father's house (L176); *ana bīt šanîm ul irrub*, she shall not move into someone else's house (L133a; cf. L134; also *īterub*, L133b; 136; *īterubma*, L135; *inūma …irrubu* and *ana…erēbim*, L177; 177); *balum dayyāni ul irrub*, she shall not move without the judge's knowledge (L177); *lāma ana bīt awīlim irrubu ḫubullum eliša ibašši*, she was in debt before she moved into the man's house (L151; also *ištu…īrubu*, L152); *ašar īrubu*, where she moved to (L173).

> ***ēribu***, entering; ***šūrubu***, bring into.

*ereqqu* > ***eriqqu*** waggon.

***erēšu* A**, vb., to demand. < *'-r-š* 1.

*eqelšu kirāšu u bīssu irriš*, he demanded his field, his orchard or his house (L30).

***erēšu* B**, vb., to cultivate. < *'-r-š* 2.

*errēssuma*(!) *eqelšu irrišma*, his cultivator shall cultivate his field (L47); *eqlam la īrišma ittadi*, he has not cultivated the field but abandoned it (L43); *eqlam erēšam iqtabi,* he has asked someone to cultivate the field (L47); [*ana*] *eqlim erēšim urakkissu*, he has made a contract with him to cultivate the field (L253); *eqlam erišma*, 'cultivate the field' (L49); *mānaḫāt erēšim*, the costs of cultivation (L49).

***ēribu***, adj., entering. < *ʾ-r-b.*
*ilū ēribūt Esagil,* the gods entering Esagila (E13).

***eriqqu***, sbst., waggon.
*liātim ereqqam u murteddīša īgur*, he has hired oxen, a waggon and a driver for it (L271); *ereqqam ana ramaniša īgur*, he has hired a waggon by itself (L272).

***errēšu***, sbst., cultivator. < *ʾ-r-š* 2.
*eqelša u kirāša ana errēšim ša eliša ṭābu inaddinma errēssa ittanaššīši*, she shall give her field and orchard to the cultivator she likes best and her cultivator shall always support her (L178; 178); *eqelšu ana biltim ana errēšim iddinma*, he has given his field to a cultivator for a rent (L45); *errēssuma eqelšu irrišma*, his cultivator shall plough his field (L47); *errēšum ina eqlim šeʾam u lu šamaššammī uštabši*, the cultivator has produced corn and sesame from the field (L49; cf. L52); *errēšum u bēl eqlim ana apšītêm izuzzū,* the labourer and the owner of the field shall share it by agreement (L46); *errēšum aššum ina šattim maḫrītim mānahātišu la ilqû eqlam erēšam iqtabi,* because he has not regained his costs from the previous year, the cultivator has asked someone to cultivate the field (L47); *bitiqtum ša errēšimma,* the loss is the cultivator's (L45).

***errēšūtu***, sbst., ploughing, cultivation. < *ʾ-r-š* 2.
*eqlam ana errēšūtim ušēṣīma*, he has let out the field for cultivation (L42).

***erretu***, sbst., curse. < *ʾ-r-r.*
*aššum errētim*(!) *šināti šaniamma uštāḫiz*, he has forced someone else to do it because of these curses (E19, for Stele: *errēšum*); *errētiya imēšma errēt ilī la īdurma*, he has forgotten my threats and has had no fear of the divine threats (E19; 19); *errētam maruštam līrurū*, let them curse him with an evil curse (E31); *errētim anniātim*(!) *Ellil ina pīšu ša la uttakkaru līruršuma*, let Enlil, whose word is one that will not be changed, invoke these curses against him (E32).

***erṣetu***, sbst., territory, earth, underworld.
1. territory: *rabiānum ša ina erṣetišunu u paṭṭišunu ḫubtum iḫḫabtu*, the governor in whose territory or province the robbery was committed (L23); *ina erṣetišu ašnān napišti nišī ay ušabši*, let there be no grain in his land to nourish the people (E22).
2. ground: *damīšunu erṣetam lišqi*, let the earth be given their blood to drink (E27).

3. underworld: *eliš ina balṭūtim lissuḫšu šapliš ina erṣetim eṭemmašu mê lišaṣmi*, may he cut him off from those living above, make his shadow thirst for water in the land below (E23).
4. often paired with ***šamû***, heaven: *ilū rabûtum ša šamê u erṣetim*, the great gods of heaven and earth (E31); *Adad bēl ḫegallim gugal šamê u erṣetim rēṣūa*, Adad lord of plenty, irrigator of heaven and earth, my helper (E25); *Ellil bēl šamê u erṣetim*, Ellil the lord of heaven and earth (P1); *ina qibīt Šamaš dayyānim rabîm ša šamê u erṣetim*, at the command of Shamash the great judge of heaven and earth (E10; cf. E23); *šarrūtam dārītam ša kīma šamê u erṣetim išdāša suršudā*, an everlasting kingdom the foundations of which are as sure as heaven and earth (P2); *bītim ša kīma šamê u erṣetim išdāšu kīnā*, a house with firm foundations like heaven and earth (E8); *mušaklil mimma šumšu ana Nippur markas šamê erṣetim*, providing every kind of thing for Nippur, the bond between heaven and earth (P4).

***eršu* A**, adj., wise. < *ʾ-r-š* 1.
*ša ušaklilušu erištum Mama*, whom the wise Mama brought to perfection (P12).

***eršu* B**, adj., cultivated. < *ʾ-r-š* 2.
*eqel < šeʾim> eršam u lu eqel šamaššammī eršam iddin*, he has given a field planted with grain or a field planted with sesame (L50; 50).

***esēpu***, vb., to gather. < *ʾ-s-p*.
*eqlam erišma šeʾam u lu šamaššammī ša ibbaššû esip tabal*, cultivate the field, gather the grain and the sesame which will be produced and take it away (L49).

***esēru* A**, vb., to press for payment. < *ʾ-s-r*.
*tamkāršu īsiršuma*, his merchant has pressed him for payment (L66).

***eṣēdu***, vb., harvest. < *ʾ-ṣ-d*.
*bēl eqlim eqelšu iṣṣid*, the owner of the field shall harvest his field (L57).

***eṣemtu***, sbst., bone.
*šumma eṣemti awīlim ištebir eṣemtašu ušebbirū*, if he has broken the bone of a gentleman they shall break his bone (L197; 197; cf. L198; 199); *eṣemti awīlim šebirtam uštallim*, he has healed a gentleman's broken bone (L221).

***ešēru***, vb., to be straight. < *y-š-r*.
*anākuma rēʾûm mušallimum ša ḫaṭṭašu išarat*, I am the shepherd whose staff is straight (i.e. who rules with righteousness; stative verb, see *AHw* 254b s.v. G 2b; E6).

***ešir*** (*AHw ešer*), numeral, ten.
*ana 1 burum 10 kur šeʾam imaddad*, he shall measure out ten kur of corn per bur (L44; 56; cf. L63); *10 šiqil kaspam išaqqal*, he shall pay

ten shekels of silver (L204; cf. L209); *10 šiqil kaspam ileqqe*, he shall take ten shekels of silver (L215); *adi 10-šu ešrīšu iri'ab*, he shall make a tenfold recompense (L8); *adi 10-šu ša išriqu*, ten times the amount he stole (L265).

***ešītu***, sbst., revolt.

*išītam saḫmaštam liškunšum*, may she instigate a revolt and an insurrection for him (E27).

***ešrā***, sbst., twenty.

*elēnumma ana 1 burum 20 kur še'am ana bēl eqlim inaddin*, he shall give in addition 20 kur of grain per bur to the owner of the field (L57).

***eššu***, adj., new

*ṭuppam eššam la išṭur*, he has not written a new tablet (§5.12; thus Roth; *BAL eliam*).

***ešû***, vb., to confuse. < '-š-'.

*šarrūssu liskip dīnšu ay idīn uruḫšu līši išdī ummānišu lišḫelṣi*, he will overthrow his kingdom, not judge his cause, confuse him on his path, make the foundations of his people crumble (E23).

***etellu***, sbst., eminent leader.

*etel šarrī qabal la maḫārim*, most eminent of kings, without a rival to compare (P15).

*etēqu*, to pass along > ***šūtuqu***, to avert, bring to an end.

***eṭemmu***, sbst., ghost.

*eliš ina balṭūtim lissuḫšu šapliš ina erṣetim eṭemmašu mê lišaṣmi*, cut him off from those living above, make his shadow thirst for water in the land below (E23).

***eṭēru***, vb., to remove. < '-ṭ-r.

1. to remove a garment: *agâm kussâm ša šarrūtim līṭeršu*, remove his kingly crown and throne (E24).

2. to remove a person: *aplam līṭeršuma šumam ay ušaršīšu*, let him take away his heir and stop him raising any name (E29).

3. to remove a personal asset: *uznam u nēmeqam līṭeršuma*, let him deprive him of wisdom and understanding (E22); *melemmī šarrūtim līṭeršu ḫaṭṭašu lišbir šīmātišu līrur*, he will take from him the splendour of his kingdom, break his sceptre and curse his destiny (E19).

4. to stop the rain falling: *zunnī ina šamê mīlam ina naqbim līṭeršu*, let him deprive him of showers from the sky and floods from the depths (E25).

***eṭlu***, sbst., youth, strong young man.

*adi napištašu ibellû ana eṭlūtišu liddammam*, let him moan to his young men until his soul is exhausted (E30).

***ezēbu***, sbst., to leave. < *ʾ-z-b*.

1. to leave unfinished: *nukaribbum eqlam ina zaqāpim la igmurma nidītam īzib*, the gardener has not completed the planting of the orchard but left a neglected area (L61).

2. to leave something for someone else: *nudunnâm ša mussa iddinušim ana mārīša izzib*, she shall leave for her sons the gift which her husband gave her (L172); *kunukkam īzibšim*, he left her with a sealed document (L150).

3. to abandon a wife: *ḫīrtašu ša mārī la uldušum izzib*, he would divorce a wife who does not bear him sons (L138, and also *izzibši*, L138); *ezēbim panīšu ištakan*, he has made up his mind to divorce (L137); *šumma mussa ezēbša iqtabi izzibši*, if her husband has said he will divorce her, he may divorce her (L141; 141); *la ezēbša iqtabi*, he said he would not divorce her (L141); *aššassu ša laʾbum iṣbatu ul izzibši*, he shall not divorce his wife because a disease has attacked her (L148).

> ***šūzubu***, to arrange to have deposited.

***ezziš***, adv., angrily.

*eli ālišu ezziš lissīma*, let him shout angrily over his city (E25).

***ezzu***, adj., angry, violent.

*ina kašūšišu rabîm kīma išātim ezzetim ša appim nišīšu liqmi in kakkišu dannim lišaṭṭīšuma*, let him burn his people by his mighty power, like a fire raging through the reeds, with his powerful weapons may he strike him (E28).

## G

***gabaraḫḫu***, sbst., trouble, upheaval.

*gabaraḫ ḫalāqišu ina šubtišu lišappiḫaššum*, in his dwelling place let him instigate against him a riot which will be the end of him (E20).

***gagû***, sbst., harem (special buildings reserved for the *nadītu* priestesses).

*nadītum ugbabtum ša ina gagîm la wašbat bīt sībim iptete*, a priestess, or a lady, who has not been living in the harem, has opened the door of a drinking house (L110); *abum ana mārtišu nadīt gagîm lu sekretim šeriktam la išrukšim* (!), the father of a confined sister or a priestess has not given a dowry to his daughter (L180).

*galātu*, to be restless > ***mugallitu***, villain.

***gallābu***, sbst., barber. < *g-l-b*.

*gallābum balum bēl wardim abbutti wardim la šêm ugallib*, the barber has shaved away the mark of a slave who is not his own without the slave's owner knowing (L226); *ritti gallābim šuāti inakkisū*, they shall cut off the hand of that barber (L226); *gallābam idāṣma*, he has tricked the barber (L227); *gallābum ina idû la ugallibu itammāma*, the barber shall swear, 'I shaved without the information' (L227).

***gamālu***, vb., to act kindly. < *g-m-l.*

*šû igmilu nišī Mera u Tuttul*, he is the one who treated the inhabitants of Mari and Tuttul kindly (P17).

***gamartu***, sbst., completion. < *g-m-r.*

*kannu gamartim ina abullim ittaḫlalū*, the flags have been hung on the city gate showing it is finished (L58).

***gamāru***, vb., to complete. < *g-m-r.*

*nukaribbum eqlam ina zaqāpim la igmurma*, the gardener has not completed the planting of the orchard (L61).

***gāmilu***, adj., showing kindness. < *g-m-l.*

*qarrādum gāmil Larsa*, the warrior who was kind to Larsa (P8).

***gamru***, adj., complete. < *g-m-r.*

*ina libbišu gamrim likrubam*, let him bless me with his whole heart (E12); *kasap kiṣrišu gamram ša šanat*, all the money for the rent for the year (L69+c); *idīšu gamrātim maḫir libbašu ṭāb*, having received the whole of his due he is glad in his heart (L264); *gamram*, fragmentary (§5.3b).

***ana gamrim***, completely: *ana gamrim ittakir*, then he has completely changed the facts (L120).

*garānu*, to store > ***mugarrinu***, heaping up.

***gašīšu***, sbst., stake.

*sinništam šuāti ina gašīšim išakkanūši*, they shall impale that woman on a stake (L153).

***gašru***, adj., strong, mighty. < *g-š-r.*

*mugarrin kārê ana Uraš gašrim*, who fills up the granaries in mighty Urash (P11).

***gigunû***, sbst., shrine.

*mušalbiš warqim gigunē Aya*, decorating the shrine of Aya in green (P7).

***girseqû***, sbst., attendant.

*mār girseqîm muzzaz ekallim u mār sekretim ul ibbaqqar*, the son of an attendant with a duty in the temple and the son of a priestess shall not be reclaimed (L187); *mār girseqîm u lu mār sekretim ana abim murabbīšu u ummim murabbītišu 'ul abī atta, ul ummī attī' iqtabi*, the son of a secretary or the son of a priestess has said to the father and the mother who has brought him up, 'You are not my father and you are not my mother' (L192; cf. L193).

***gitmālu***, adj., perfect. < *g-m-l.*

*Ḫammurabi šarrum gitmālum anāku*, I am Hammurabi, the perfect king (E2); *muštālum gitmālum*, reliable consultant (P13).

***gugallu***, sbst., chief irrigation officer.

*Adad bēl ḫegallim gugal šamê u erṣetim*, Adad, lord of plenty, in charge of the water in the sky and on the earth (E25).

***gullubu***, vb., to shave. < *g-l-b*.

*abbutti wardim la šêm ugallib*, he has shaved away the mark of a slave who is not his own (L226; cf. *ugdallib*, L227); *gallābum ina idū la ugallibu itammāma*, the barber shall swear, 'I shaved without that information' (L227); *muttassu ugallabū*, they shall shave off half his hair (L127).

*gurrunu*, to store > ***mugarrinu***, heaping up.

***gurunnu***, sbst., heap. < *q-r-n*.

*gurun šalmāt ummānātišu*, a heap of human bodies (E27).

## Ḫ

***ḫabālu***, vb., to exploit. < *ḫ-b-l*.

*numāt rēdîm ilteqe rēdiam iḫtabal*, he has taken a soldier's property or has exploited a soldier (L34); *dannum enšam ana la ḫabālim ekūtam almattam šutēšurim*, so that a mighty man might not exploit a weak man and a waif and a widow may be treated properly (E8; cf. P3).

***ḫabāšu***, vb., to shatter. < *ḫ-b-š*.

*biniātišu kīma ṣalam ṭiddim liḫbuš*, may he shatter his limbs like a clay doll (E28).

***ḫabātu***, vb., to rob. < *ḫ-b-t*.

*ḫubtam iḫbutma ittaṣbat*, he has committed a robbery and been caught (L22).

***ḫabbātu***, sbst., robber. < *ḫ-b-t*.

*ḫabbātum la ittaṣbat*, the robber was not caught (L23).

***ḫablu***, adj., exploited. *ḫ-b-l*.

*dīn mātim ana diānim purussê mātim ana parāsim ḫablim šūtēšurim* so that disputes in the land may be settled, so that decisions for the land may be made, so that the oppressed may be treated properly (E8); *awīlum ḫablum*, a wronged man (E11).

***ḫabtu***, adj., robbed. < *ḫ-b-t*.

*awīlum ḫabtum*, a man who has been robbed (L23, so *AHw*; *CAD*: prisoner, though this instance is not cited).

*ḫadû*, to be glad > ***muḫaddû***, gladdening.

*ḫāʾiru* > ***ḫāwiru***, first husband.

*ḫalālu* > ***alālu***, to hang.

***ḫalāqu***, vb., to disappear, come to an end. < *ḫ-l-q*.

1. of property, to be lost: *awīlum ša mimmûšu ḫalqu*, a man who has something missing (L9); *mimma ša ina eleppišu ḫalqu*, whatever he

had missing from the boat (L240); *mimmūšu itti mimme bēl bītim iḫtaliq*, his property as well as that of the owner has been lost (L125); [*mimma ša ina*] *nabalkattim* [*ḫalqu*], whatever was lost because of the damage [L68+b]; *šumma awīlum mimmûšu la ḫaliqma mimmê ḫaliq iqtabi babtašu utebbir*, if a gentleman who has not lost anything says, 'I have lost something,' he is bringing disrepute on his community (L126; 126); *kīma mimmûšu la ḫalqu babtašu ina maḫar ilim ubâr-šuma*, his community shall declare in the presence of the god that he had nothing missing (L126, possibly here to be regarded as adjectival, cf. *ḫalqu*).

2. of a person, to escape: *wardum ina qāt ṣābitānišu iḫtaliq*, a slave has slipped away from the control of his captors (L20).

3. to disappear for ever: *gabaraḫ ḫalāqišu ina šubtišu lišappiḫaššum*, in his dwelling place let him instigate against him a riot which will be the end of him (E20); *ḫalāq ālišu naspuḫ nišīšu šarrūssu šupēlam*, the loss of his city, the overthrow of his people, the disappearance of his kingdom (E20); *ḫalāq nišīšu tabāk napištišu kīma mê*, the loss of his people and the pouring out of his life like water (E21); *nasāḫ išdī šarrūtišu u ḫalāq mātišu liškunšum*, the destruction of the foundations of his kingdom and the loss of his land (E23); *arnam kabtam šēressu rabītam ša ina zumrišu la iḫalliqu līmussuma*, let him impose on him a heavy penalty as his great condemnation which will not disappear from his body (E24).

> **ḫulluqu**, to lose.

**ḫalqu**, adj., lost, missing. < *ḫ-l-q*.

1. property: *šumma awīlum ša mimmāšu ḫalqu mimmûšu ḫalqam ina qātī awīlim iṣṣabat*, if a man has something missing and the missing object is found in another man's possession (L9); *mimmâšu ḫalqam maḫar ilim ubârma*, he shall declare anything he has missing in the presence of the god (L23); *mimmâšu ḫalqam iriabbūšum*, they shall restore anything he has missing (L23; cf. L240); *mimmâšu ḫalqam ištene'īma*, he shall keep on looking for whatever he has missing (L125).

2. a person: *lu wardam lu amtam ḫalqam*, a lost slave or slave-girl (L16).

**ḫamiš**, numeral, five.

*5 šiqil kaspam išaqqal*, he shall pay five shekels of silver (L211; cf. L216; 221; 259); *5 uṭṭet kaspam*, five grains of silver (L274, twice, or perhaps more in this broken passage); *adi ḫamšīšu* and *adi 5-šu*, five times (L12; 112); *ina šanat ana 1 kur še'am 5 qa še'am idī našpakim inaddin*, he shall pay the storage charge of five qa of grain for one kur of grain per year (L121).

**ḫamšu**, adj., fifth.
*ištu rēš šattim adi ḫamšim warḫim*, from the beginning of the year to the fifth month (L273); *ina ḫamuštim šattim*, in the fifth year (L60).

**ḫamuštu**, sbst., a fifth.
1/5 *šīmīšu*, a fifth of its price (L225; 248; so *BAL* for numeral written indistinctly; Roth prefers to read 1/4).

**ḫarāṣu**, vb., to deduct. < *ḫ-r-ṣ*.
*ina šeriktiša mala terḫatiša iḫarraṣma*, he shall subtract from the dowry the amount of the bridal gift (L164).

**ḫarbu**, sbst., plough. < *ḫ-r-b*.
*ḫarbam u lu maškakātim ištariq*, he has stolen a plough or a harrow (L260).

**ḫarrānu**, sbst., expedition.
1. a royal expedition: *ana ḫarrān šarrim alākšu qabû*, he is told to go on a royal expedition (L26); *ina ḫarran šarrim turru*, he is detained on a royal expedition (L32); *ana ḫarran šarrim agram pūḫam imḫurma*, he has accepted a hired man as a substiture for a royal expedition (L33).
2 a trading expedition: *ana ḫarrānim iṭrussu*, he sent him on the expedition (L100; also *ina ḫarrānim* [...], L100); *ḫarrānam ina alākišu*, while he was travelling on an expedition (L103); *ina ḫarrānim wašibma*, he was staying away on a visit (L112).
3. a journey: *ḫarrānša uzzubūša mimma ul innaddiššim*, nothing at all shall be given to her for her journey or as her divorce settlement (L141).

**ḫâru**, vb., to choose. < *ḫ-ʾ-r*.
*ana mārišu kallatam iḫīrma*, he has chosen a bride for his son (L155; 156).

**ḫassu**, adj., intelligent.
*ana la ḫassim*, for the unintelligent (E17).

**ḫaṭṭu**, sbst., sceptre.
*simat ḫaṭṭim u agêm*, the sign of the crown and sceptre (P12); *ša ḫaṭṭašu išarat*, the one whose sceptre is straight (E6); *melemmī šarrūtim līṭeršu ḫaṭṭašu lišbir šimātišu līrur*, he will take from him the splendour of his kingdom, break his sceptre and curse his destiny (E19); *Šamaš ḫaṭṭašu lirrik*, may Shamash 'lengthen his sceptre' (= extend his rule, E18).
***wākil ḫaṭṭim*** (*ḫaṭṭātim*), sceptre-bearer > ***aklu***, overseer.

**ḫâṭu**, vb., to find out. < *ḫ-ʾ-ṭ*.
*inūma ilqûšu abašu u ummašu iḫiaṭ tarbītum šî ana bīt abišu itâr*, when he has taken him he finds out about his father and mother, then that adopted child shall return to his father's house (L186).

***ḫāwiru***, sbst., first husband. < *ḫ-ʾ-r*.
*sinništum šî ana ḫāwiriša itâr*, that woman shall go back to her husband (L135); *šeriktaša mārū ḫāwirišama ileqqû*, the children of the first husband shall take her dowry (L174).

***ḫegallu***, sbst., wealth.
*bābil ḫegallim ana Egišnugal*, bringing wealth to Egishnugal (P6); *Adad bēl ḫegallim gugal šamê u erṣetim*, Adad, lord of plenty, in charge of the water in the sky and on the earth (E25).

***ḫepû***, vb., to break. < *ḫ-p-ʾ*.
*ṭuppi rikistišu* [*iḫeppe*], he breaks the contract tablet (§5.11).
> ***neḫepû***, to be broken.

***ḫīrtu***, sbst., first wife. < *ḫ-ʾ-r*.
*ḫīrtum šeriktaša u nudunnām ša mussa iddinušim ina ṭuppim išṭurušim ileqqēma*, the first wife shall take the dowry and the gift, which her husband gave her by writing on a tablet for her (L171b); *ḫīrtašu ša mārī la uldušum*, his first wife who has not born him any sons (L138; cf. L170); *mārū ḫīrtim u mārū amtim mitḫāriš izuzzū*, the sons of the first wife and the sons of the slave-girl shall share equally (L170; cf. L171a); *itti mārī ḫīrtim imtanûšunūti*, they shall reckon them together with the sons of the first wife (L170); *aplum mār ḫīrtim ina zittim inassaqma ileqqe*, the son of the first wife, the heir, shall select from the portion and take it (L170); *ana mārī amtim ana wardūtim ul iraggumū*, the sons of the first wife shall have no right against the sons of the slave-girl for slavery (L171a).

***ḫiṣbu***, sbst., produce, abundance.
*mukammer ḫiṣbim ana Anim u Ištar*, heaping up produce for Anum and Ishtar (P8).

***ḫiṭītu***, sbst., fault. < *ḫ-ṭ-ʾ*.
1. defect in construction: *eleppum šî iṣṣabar ḫiṭītam irtaši*, the boat has begun to leak because it has become defective (L235).
2. symptom of disease: *ḫiṭīt pissatim*(!) *ša ina tarbaṣim ušabšû*, the damage from the disease which he has allowed to develop in the pen (L267).
3. guilt: *naṣratma ḫiṭītam la išu*, she has controlled herself and there is no blame (L142).

***ḫubtu***, sbst., robbery. < *ḫ-b-t*.
*ḫubtum iḫḫabtu*, a robbery was committed (L23); *ḫubtam iḫbutma*, he committed a robbery (L22).

***ḫubullu***, sbst., debt.
*ḫubullum elišu ibaššīma*, he is in debt (L48; cf. L151; 151; 152); *awīlum ša ḫubullam iršû*, a man who has a debt (§5.10); *ṣibat ḫubulli*, the interest on the debt (§5.10); *šeʾam u kaspam ana ḫubullim iddin*,

he has given grain or silver for discharging his debt (§5.9, twice; cf. §5.13, twice; 5.14).

> ***bēl ḫubullim***, creditor.

*ḫuddû*, to gladden > ***muḫaddû***, gladdening.

***ḫulluqu***, vb., to lose, destroy. < *ḫ-l-q*.

1. to lose: *mimma ša ana maṣṣarūtim iddinušumma uḫalliqu ušallamma*, whatever had been given him to look after and he lost he shall repay (L125); *še'am ša uḫalliqu iriab*, he shall make recompense for the grain he lost (L53); [*alpam*] *u lu* [*immeram*] *ša innadnušum uḫtalliq*, he has lost the ox or sheep that was given to him (L263).

2. to destroy an object: *šumma makkūram uḫtalliq mimma ša uḫalliqu iriab*, if it has destroyed property he shall make recompense for whatever it destroyed (L232; 232); *eleppam uṭṭebbi u lu uḫtalliq*, he has then sunk the boat or destroyed it (L236; cf. L237; also *uḫalliqu*, L237).

3. to bring to an end: *raggam u ṣēnam ana ḫulluqim*, to destroy wickedness and persecution (P3); *mâssu ina ḫušaḫḫim u būbutim liḫalliq*, may he annihilate his land by hunger and famine (E25).

***ḫulqu***, sbst., lost property. < *ḫ-l-q*.

*awīlum ša ḫulqum ina qātišu ṣabtu*, the man in whose possession the lost property was found (L9); *šībū mudē ḫulqim*, witnesses who know the property (L9; cf. *šībī mudē ḫulqiyami*, L9; *šībī mudē ḫulqišu*, L9; 10; 11); *ḫuluqšu ileqqe*, he shall take his property (L9; 10).

> ***bēl ḫulqim***, owner of lost property.

***ḫuppudu***, vb., to poke out an eye. < *ḫ-p-d*.

*šumma awīlum īn mār awīlim uḫtappid īnšu uḫappadū*, if a man has destroyed the sight of another man's son, they shall poke out his eye (L196; 196; cf. *uḫtappid*, L198; 199); *īn awīlim uḫtappid*, he has destroyed the man's sight (L218; cf. L220(!), written *uḫtapda* in error); *alpam īgurma īnšu uḫtappid*, he has hired an ox and poked out its eye (L247).

***ḫurāṣu***, sbst., gold.

*lu kaspam lu ḫurāṣam lu wardam lu amtam lu alpam lu immeram lu imēram u lu mimma šumšu ina qāt mār awīlim u lu warad awīlim balum šībī u riksātim ištām*, he has bought silver, gold, a slave, a slave-girl, a sheep, a donkey or anything else from a man's son or a man's slave without properly witnessed receipts (L7); *kaspam ḫurāṣam abnam u bīš qātišu*, silver, gold, gems or personal property (L112, variant with *lu*); *kaspam ḫurāṣam u mimma šumšu*, silver, gold, or anything else (L122; 124).

***ḫušaḫḫu***, sbst., famine.

*mässu ina ḫušaḫḫim u bubūtim liḫalliq*, may he annihilate his land by hunger and famine (E25); *šanāt ḫušaḫḫim*, years of famine (E20).

## I

***iâti***, pronoun, me.

*Ḫammurabi…iâti… Anum u Ellil…šumī ibbû*, Anum and Enlil ordained me, Hammurabi (P3); *awīlum šû kīma iâti*, that man is like me (E18).

***ibbû***, sbst., loss. *CAD*: *imbû* B.

*ina qarītim ibbûm ittabši*, a loss has occurred in the granary (L120).

***ibru***, sbst., friend, neighbour.

*ibiršu uktarrissu*, his friend has maligned him (L161); *aššassu ibiršu ul iḫḫaz*, his neighbour shall not marry the man's wife (L161).

*idu*, sbst., strength (so Szlechter, P17) > ***ittu***, omen; for *AHw idu*, fee (s.v. 9) > ***idū***, fees.

***idû***, vb., to know. < *ʾ-d-ʾ*.

1. to be aware: *ina idû la amḫaṣu itamma*, he said, 'I did not mean to do an injury' (L206); *ina idû la ugallibu*, I did not know it when I did the shaving (L227).

2. to recognize: *rubûm ellum ša nīš qātišu Adad idû*, the sacred prince, whose raised hand Adad recognizes (P14).

3. to have a sexual realtionship: *aššat awīlim ša zikaram la idûma*, a man's wife who has not known a man (L130).

4. fragmentary: *ša (?) idû* (§5.3b); *idī* (§5.7).

> ***uddû***, to find out; ***šūdû***, to make known.

***idū***, sbst., pl., charges, fees, wages; cf. *AHw* 365b–366a, s.v. *idu*, arm, paragraph 9.

*idī alpim ša warka 4 kur šeʾam idī alpim ša qabla 3 kur šeʾam ana bēlišu inaddin*, he shall give to its owner four kur of grain as the fees for the rear ox, and three kur of grain as the fees for the fore ox (L242/3, twice); *2½ uṭṭet kaspam idīša ina ūmim ištēn inaddin*, he shall pay two and a half grains of silver in charges for one day (L276); *⅙ kaspam ana asîm idīšu inaddin*, he shall pay the surgeon his fee, a sixth of a shekel of silver (L224; the same charge as for hiring *elep šūšim*, cf. L277); *2 sūt šeʾum idūšu*, the charge for it (i.e. *alpum ana diāšim*) is two sa of grain (L268; cf. *1 sūt šeʾum* for *imērum ana diāšim*, L269; *1 qa šeʾum* for *urīṣum ana diāšim*, L270; *3 uṭṭet kaspum* for something else [fragmentary], L275); *idī našpakim*, storage costs (L121); *idīšu gamrātim maḫir libbašu ṭāb*, he has received all his wages and his heart is happy (L264); the word (*idī*) occurs ten times (some of which are restored) to stipulate the wage for various types of craftsman (*ummānu*) in L274.

***igāru***, sbst., wall.

*igārum iqtūp*, the wall has collapsed (L233); *ina kasap ramanišu igāram šuāti udannan*, he shall repair that wall with his own money (L233); *ina...igārim*, on a wall (?) (Law 68+c, following the reading in *BAL É.GAR*$_8$; Roth reads *ina...bītim*).

***igigallu***, sbst., omniscience.

*ina igigallim ša Ea išīmam*, with the omniscience that Ea has assigned to me (E4); *ilu šarri mudē igigallim*, the divine king who knows all there is to know (P11).

***igirrû***, sbst., reputation.

*bēltum mudammiqat igirrēya*, the lady who makes my reputation acceptable (E21); *igirrî ūmišam ina maḫar Marduk bēliya Zarpānītum bēltīya lidammiqū*, may they grant me every day a good reputation in the presence of my lord Marduk and my lady Sarpanitum (E13; see *CAD* s.v. *egirrû* 1b).

***igru***, sbst., hire.

*eleppašu ana malāḫim ana igrim iddinma*, he has given his boat for hire to a boatman (L236); *liāt awīlim ana igrim ittadin*, he has given a man's oxen for hire (L255); *rēdiam ana igrim ittadin*, he has given a soldier for hire (L34).

*iḫiltu* > ***e'iltu***, debt.

***ikkaru***, sbst., labourer.

*awīlum ikkaram īgur*, a gentleman has hired a labourer (L257).

***ikletu***, sbst., darkness.

*eklet la nawārim*, darkness without any light (E20).

*ikû* > ***buru***, surface measure.

***ilku***, sbst., duty, duty-bound person.

1. duty:

a. with ***alāku***: *ilik eqlim kirûm u bītim ša išammu illak*, he shall perform the duty of the field, orchard or house which he purchases (L40); *eqelšu u kirāšu ana šanîm iddinūma ilikšu ittalak*, they gave his field or orchard to someone else and he performed his duty (L27); *šûma ilikšu illak*, he shall perform the duty himself (L27; 31); *mārušu ilkam alākam ile'i*, his son is able to perform the duty (L28); *ilik abišu illak*, he shall perform his father's duty (L28; cf. L29); *šalaš šanātim ilikšu ittalak*, he has performed the duty for three years (L30); *ša iṣṣabtuma ilikšu ittalku šûma illak*, the one who has then taken over and performed his duty shall continue to do it himself (L30); *ilkam ul illak*, he shall not perform the duty (L182).

b. with ***šaṭāru***: *ina eqlim kirîm u bītim ša ilkišu ana aššatišu u mārtišu ul išaṭṭar*, he shall not sign over to his wife or daughter a field, orchard and house on which he has a duty (L38).

2. levy on a property: *bīt ilkim ša bīt itēšu ša išāmu*, a property on which there is a levy which belongs to his neighbour and which he would purchase (L67+a); *bītum šû ilkam la išu*, that property has no levy (L67+a); *eqelšu kirāšu u bīssu ina pani ilkim iddīma*, he has abandoned his field, his orchard or his house because of the levy (L30).

3. duty-bound person: *nadītum tamkārum u ilkum aḫûm*, a priestess, a merchant, or some other duty-bound person (L40).

***ilu***, sbst., god.

1. particular named gods: *Anum rabûm abu ilī nābû palêya*, great Anu, the father of the gods who nominated me to reign (E19); *Sîn bēl šamê ilum bānî*, Sin the lord of the sky, my divine creator (E24); *Ea...apkal ilī*, Ea...the wisest of the gods (E22); *Nergal dannum ina ilī*, Nergal the strongest of the gods (E28).

2. the gods: *rubâm na'dam pāliḫ ilī*, the obedient prince who feared the gods (P3); *na'dum muštēmiqum ana ilī rabûtim*, the kindest and wisest of the great gods (P20); *ilū rabûtum ibbûninnima*, the great gods nominated me (E6); *ilū rabûtum ša šamê u erṣetim Anunnakū ina napḫarišunu*, the great gods of heaven and earth, the Anunnaki in their assembly (E31); *lamassum ilū ēribūt Esagil*, the divine images at the entrance to Esagila (E13); *apkal ilī mudē mimma šumšu*, most skilled of the gods, who knows about everything (E22); *errēt ilī la īdurma*, he did not fear the curse of the gods (E19); *ša têressu(!) ina ilī šūpât*, whose oracular decision shines out among the gods (E24).

3. a god (unnamed): *šumma ša ilim šumma ša ekallim adi 30-šu inaddin*, he shall pay 30 times its value if it belongs to a god or a temple (L8); *ana ilim iššīma*, he dedicated to the god (L181); *awīlum alpam īgurma ilum imḫassuma*, a man has hired an ox but a god has struck it (L249); *ina tarbaṣim lipit ilim ittabši*, an affliction of the god has occurred in the fold (L266).

4. with a god present: *šībū mudē ḫulqim mudūssunu maḫar ilim iqabbûma*, witnesses who know about the lost property shall state what they know in the presence of the god (L9); *ina maḫar ilim kasap išqulu iqabbīma*, they shall state the silver they paid in the presence of a god (L281); *maḫar ilim mitḫāriš izuzzu*, they shall share equally in the presence of the god (L77+f); *rē'ûm maḫar ilim ubbamma*, the shepherd shall make himself clean before the god (L266); *ḫalqam maḫar ilim ubârma*, he shall declare what is lost in the presence of the god (L23); *bēl še'im maḫar ilim še'ašu ubârma*, the owner of the grain

shall declare in the god's presence the amount of the grain (L120); *babtašu ina maḫar ilim ubâršuma*, his community shall make him clarify in the presence of a god (L126; cf. 240); *maḫar ilim u šībī*, in the presence of the god and witnesses (L106; 107).

5. the king as god: *ilu šarrī mudē igigallim*, the god among kings, who knows great wisdom (P11; Roth reads < *šubat*> *ili šarrī*, the dwelling of the god of kings).

6. ***bīt ili***, the house of the god: *ina bīt il ālišu ippaṭṭar*, he shall be redeemed by the house of the god of his city (L32); *ina bīt il ālišu ša paṭārišu la ibašši*, there is no possibility of redeeming him in the house of the god of his city (L32).

> ***bītu***, house.

7. ***makkūr ilim***, sacred property > ***makkūru***, goods.

8. ***nīš ilim***, an oath by god > ***nīšu*** **A**, life, oath.

*imbû* B > ***ibbû***, loss.

***imēru***, sbst., donkey.

*lu alpam lu immeram lu imēram lu šaḫam lu eleppam*, an ox, or a sheep, or a donkey, or a pig, or a boat (L8; cf. L7); *imēram ana diāšim īgur*, he has hired an ass to thresh (L269); *alpam imēram īgurma*, he has hired an ox or an ass (L244); *bēl alpim u lu imērim*, the owner of the ox or ass (L224; 225); *asî alpim u lu imērim lu alpam u lu imēram simmam*(!) *kabtam īpušma*, a surgeon for oxen or asses has performed a serious operation on an ox or an ass (L224; 224; cf. L225).

***immeru***, sbst., sheep.

*lu alpam lu immeram lu imēram lu šaḫam lu eleppam*, an ox, or a sheep, or a donkey, or a pig, or a boat (L8; cf. L7); *alpam u lu immeram*, an ox or a sheep (L262); *alpam kīma* [*alpim*] *immeram kīma* [*immerim*] *ana bēlišunu iriab*, he shall restore an ox for an ox and a sheep for a sheep to their owner (L263; *263; also [*immeram*] *L263).

***imnu***, sbst., right side.

*āliku imniya*, walking on my right (E26).

***in***, prep., in; variant of *ina*.

1. before proper names: *in Bīt Karkara* (P14); *in Igigī ušarbiūšu* (P2).

2. before other nouns: *in kibrātim* (P2); *in karašîm* (P16, but Roth: *ina*); *in nuḫšim* (P16, but Roth: *ina*); *in pušqim* (P18); *in šarri* (E9).

***ina***, prep., at, in, from.

1. at a time, for a time:

a. *ina ūmim ištēn* (L271; 272; 273; 273; [274]; 275; 276; 277); *ina ūmīšu la malûtim* (L69+e, twice); *ina šeššet warḫī* (L13); *ina šanat* (L121; 239); *ina šattim šuāti* (L48; cf. L235); *ina šattim ištiat* (L257; 258; 261); *ina rebūtim šattim* (L44; 117; cf. L47; 60); *ina ebūrim*

(L47; 49; 58; §5.2; L111; 255); *ina bulṭišu* (L170; 171a); *ina balṭūtim* (E23).
b. during a process: *ina dīnim* (L 3; 5; 5; 5; 34); *ina ḫarran* (L32; 100; 112).
2. at a place, in a place:
a. *ina bābīšu* (L227); *ina bābtiša* (L142); *ina biniātišu* (E30); *ina bīt* (L12; 16; 19; 25; 32; 32; 32; 68+a; 69+e; 109; 115; 116; 120; 120; 121; 130; 133a; 134; 135; 141; 141; 149; 151; 158; 172); *ina dannat* (L27; 28); *ina eqlim*, in the field (L38; 39; 42; 42; 46; 48; 49; 49; 50; 52; 191; 255; 256); *ina erṣetišunu* (L23; cf. E22; 23); *ina gagîm* (L110); *ina kārišu* (L53; 53); *ina kirī* (L59; 66; 66); *ina liātim* (L256); *ina mātim* (P3; L280; E10; 14; 16; 20); *ina mêšu* (L185); *ina nagbim* (E22; 25); *ina qarītim* (L120); *ina sūniša* (L130; 155; 156; 157; 158); *ina ṣerim* (L17; 244; E27); *ina šamê* (E25); *ina šubat* (L171b; cf. *ina šubtišu*, E20); *ina tarbaṣim* (L266; 267; 267).
b. a named place: *ina Emešmeš* (P20); *ina Eudgalgal* (P14); *ina Eulmaš* (P18); *ina Ninua* (P20); see also E8; 8; 10; 21; 30.
c. ***ina qāti***, in the possession of (L6; 7; 9; 9; 19; 20; §5.15; L194; 253).
3. on: *ina abullim* (L58); *ina gašīšim* (L153); *ina ṭuppim* (L171b; 178; 179); *ina narîya* (E8; 14; 15; 18).
4. from: *ina bilat kirīm* (L64); *ina kaspišu itelli* (L35; 37; 177; cf. L67; 69+c; §5.7; 5.10; 5.13; 5.14; L113; 116); *ina bīt nādinānim kasap išqulu ileqqe*, he shall take the silver he has paid from the seller's house (L9); *ina kussî dayyānūtišu ušetbûšuma*, they shall make him leave the judicial seat (L5); *ina maškanim* (L113; 113); *ina našpakim* (L113; 113); *ina qāti rēdim ištâm* (L35); *ina šeriktaša...iḫarraṣma* (L164); *ina mimma ša ana mārīša innadnu zittam kīma aplim ištēn inaddinūšimma* (L137); *ina makkūr...izuzzū* (L165; 166; 170; 171a; 180; 181; 182; 183); *ina makkūr bīt mutiša zittam...ileqqe* (L172); *ina aplūtim ul inassaḫ* (L168; 169; 169); *ina zittim inassaqma* (L170); *ina makkūrišu šalušti aplūtišu inaddiššumma* (L191); *epinnam ina ugārim išriq* (L259); *ina zumrišu la iḫalliqu* (E24).
5. among people or deities: *ina napḫarišunu* (E31); *ina puḫrim* (L5; 202); *ina igigallim* (E4); *ina ilī* (E24; 28).
6. with, by means of, accompanied by: *ina abnim maṭītim* (§5.13); *ina abnim rabītim* (§5.13; L108); *ina awat* (E10); *ina ḫušaḫḫim* (E25); *ina kakkim* (E4); *ina karzilli siparrim* (L215; 215; 218; 218; 219); *ina kašūšišu rabîm* (E28); *ina lamassu* (E7); *ina lē'ûtim* (E4); *ina maḫāṣim* (L116); *ina megûtim* (L245); *ina mīšarim* (E18); *ina mīšītim* (E22); *ina nabalkattim* (L68+b; [68+b]; 125); *ine nēmeqiya* (E7); *ina pī mātim* (P22); *ina pīšu* (E20; 21; 32); *ina pilšim* (L125); *ina qibīt*

(E10); *ina qinnaz* (L202); *ina risbātim* (L206); *ina sūtim maṭītim* (§5.13); *ina ṣimdi* (E30); *ina šīmātiša imtūt* (L115); *ina sūtim rabītim* (§5.13); *ina makkūr ramānišu* (L232; 233; 235); *ina šulmim* (E7); *ina tānēḫim u dimmatim* (E24); *ina uššušim* (L116); *ina utliya* (E7); *ina uzzātiša* (E27).

7. before an infinitive: *ina alākišu* (L103; 250); *ina idû* (L206; 227); *ina ītulim* (L129); *ina kaspim leqêm* (L106; cf. L113); *ina maḫāṣim* (L245; cf. *ina maḫaṣišu imtūt*, L207; 211); *ina utūlim* (L131;132); *ina eqlam zaqāpim la igmurma* (L61); *dayyānam šuāti ina dīn idīnu ēnem ukannūšuma*, they shall convict that judge of changing the decision he made (L5); cf. also *ina mimma ša šūbuluma la iddinu ukânšuma* (L112).

9. compound prepositions:

a. ***ina balum***: *ina balum bēl eqlim* (L57; 113; 113).

b. ***ina bīrišu***, in the midst of it (E23).

c. ***ina libbi***, within: *ina libbišu šarrūtam dāritam…ukinnūšum*, they decreed for him an everlasting dynasty in the midst of it (P2); *inūma ina libbū mātim ittalkamma*, when he has come back into the homeland (L280); cf. also *mimma ša ina libbiša uḫalliqu*, whatever he lost from within it (L237); *ina libbišu gamrim*, with his whole heart (E12); *ina libbiša aggim*, with anger in her heart (E27).

d. ***ina maḫar***, in the presence of (L 106; 107; 126; 281; E8; 12; 13; 21; cf. L9; 10; *ina maḫrā*, E22).

e. ***ina pani***, in front of (L21; 30).

f. ***ina qerbit***, in the middle of (E29).

10. compounded with other particles: *ina la mê*, without water (L48); *ina warka* (L135).

11. fragmentary (L68+c).

***īnu***, sbst., eye.

1. eye, sight: *īnšu inassaḫū*, they shall gouge out his eye (L193); *šumma awīlum īn mār awīlim uḫtappid īnšu uḫappadū*, if a man has destroyed the sight of a man's son they shall destroy his sight (L196; 196; cf. L198; 199); *īn awīlim ubtalliṭ*, he has saved a man's sight (L215); *īn awīlim uḫtappid*, he has destroyed a man's sight (L218; cf. *īnšu*, L220; 247).

2. with ***niṭlu***, passing moment: *mūt niṭil īnim ana šīmtim lišīmšum*, let him ordain for him the destiny of death in the twinkling of an eye (E20).

3. with ***našû***, to covet: *ana numāt bēl bītim īnšu iššīma numāt bēl bītim ilteqe*(!), he has viewed the property of the owner of the house with greed and has taken the property of the owner of the house (L25).

4. with ***maḫāru***, to favour: *ana aplišu ša īnšu maḫru eqlam kirâm u bītam išruk*, he has presented a field, an orchard or a house to the son whom 'his eye has accepted' (= he likes, L165).

***īnu***, adv., when.

*īnu Anum...Ellil...ana Marduk...ellilūt kiššat nišī išīmūšum*, it was when Anum...and Enlil...determined that Marduk...should govern as Enlil (P1).

***inūma***, adv., when.

1. followed by a verb marked as subjunctive: *inūma ana ḫubullim iddinu*, when he made the interest bearing loan (§5.13); *u inūma imḫuru*, but at the time of receipt (§5.13); *warka abum ana šīmtim ittalku inūma aḫḫū izuzzū*, when the brothers do the sharing after the father has gone to his destiny (L165; 166); *inūma īḫuzuši*, when he married her (L176); *inūma ana bīt šanîm irrubu*, when she wishes to move into the house of someone else (L177); *inūma ilqûšu*, when he has taken him (L186).

2. followed by verb marked otherwise: *inūma ina libbū mātim ittalkamma*, when he has come back into the homeland (L280); *inūma Marduk ana šutēšur nišī mātim ūsim šūḫuzim uwaʾerranni*, when Marduk directed me to keep the people of the land straight and to take over control (P22).

***inūmišu***, adv., at that time.

*īnu Anu... Ellil... Bābilam...ukinnūšum inūmišu Ḫammurabi... Anum u Ellil...šumī ibbû*, it was when Anu...and Enlil...established... Babylon...that Anum and Enlil ordained Hammurabi (P3); *inūmišu*, at that time (P22, concluding the Prologue and formally introducing the Laws).

***ipru***, sbst., barley ration.

*kīma emūq zittiša ipram piššatam u lubūšam inaddinūšimma*, they shall give her food, oil and garments according to the size of her share (L178, twice).

***ipṭirū***, sbst., tantum pl., ransom. < *p-ṭ-r*.

*eqelšu kirāšu u bīssu ana ipṭerišu ul innaddin*, his field, orchard and house shall not be given as his ransom (L32).

***irnittu***, sbst., war cry, triumph.

*Nergal dannum ina ilī qabal la maḫār mušakšidu irnittiya*, Nergal, fighter for the gods, unrivalled in the battle, who lets me achieve my victory (E28); *irnitti Marduk eliš u šapliš ikšud*, he has secured the triumph of Marduk above and below (E12).

***iṣu***, sbst., tree.

*iṣam ikkis*, he felled a tree (L59).

***īṣu***, adj., insufficient.

*ūmī īṣūtim šanāt ḫušaḫḫim...ana šīmtim lišīmšum*, days of need and years of famine...may he grant as his destiny (E20).

***išātu***, sbst., fire

1. accidental blaze: *ina bīt awīlim išātum innapiḫma*, fire has broken out in a man's house (L25).

2. fire as punishment: *ana išātim šuāti innaddi*, he shall be thrown into that fire (L25); *kīma išātim ezzetim ša appim nišīšu liqmi*, let him burn his people like a fierce fire in the reeds (E28).

***išdu***, sbst., foundation.

1. the foundations of a building or a city: *ina Bābilim ālim ša Anum u Ellil rēšīšu ullû ina Esagil bītim ša kīma šamê u erṣetim išdāšu kīnā*, in Babylon, the city whose pinnacles Anum and Enlil have raised up, in Esagil, the temple whose foundations are as firm as heaven and earth (E8); *šar tašīmtim šēmû Šamaš dannum mukīn išdī Sippar*, the king who listens obediently to Shamash, the mighty one who fixed the foundations of Sippar (P7).

2. the foundations of a community or a kingdom: *mukinnu išdīšin qerbum Bābilim šulmāniš*, establishing their foundations within Babylon securely (P18); *nasāḫ išdī šarrūtišu*, tearing up the foundations of his kingdom (E23); *ina libbišu šarrūtam dārītam ša kīma šamê u erṣetim išdāša šuršudā ukinnūšum*, they established there an everlasting kingdom with foundations as sure as those of heaven and earth (P2); *išdī*(!) *ummānišu lišḫelṣi*, let the foundations of his workforce crumble (E23).

*išītu* > ***ešītu***, confusion.

***iššakku***, sbst., governor, holder of an official position.

*awīlum šû lu šarrum lu bēlum lu iššiakkum u lu awīlūtum ša šumam nabīat*, whether that gentleman is a king or a lord or a governor or holds another titled position (E19).

***ištēn*** (masc.), ***ištiat*** (fem.), numeral, one.

1. with masc. sbst: *ina makkūr bīt abim zittam kīma aplim ištēn izâzma*, she shall have the share of one heir from the treasures of her father's house (L180; cf. L137; 172); *ištēn pīḫam*, one jug of beer (L111); *ina ūmim ištēn*, for one day (L271; 272; 273, twice; 274, partly broken; 275; 276; 277); *ana 1 šiqil kaspim 1/6 u 6 uṭṭet ṣibtam ileqqe*, for one shekel of silver he shall receive one-sixth of a shekel and six grains in interest (§5.9; cf. §5.10); *ana 1 kurrum 1 pān 4 sūt še'am ṣibtam ileqqe*, he shall receive one parshikah and four sa of grain in interest per kur (§5.9; cf. §5.10).

2. with fem. sbst. (especially *šattu*, year): *šattam ištiatma*, for one year (L31, variant *išteatat*); *ša šattim ištiat*, for one year (L63); *ana nipûtim*

*ištiat*, for one restrained item (L114); <*alpam*> *ana šattim ištiat īgur*, he hired an ox for one year (L242/3); *še'am ina šattim ištiat inaddiššum*, he shall pay back the corn in one year (L257; cf. L258; 261).

***ištīššu***, adv., for the first time.

*ana ištiššu panīšu ubbalū*, they shall excuse him for the first time (L169).

***ištu***, prep., from, because of (*CAD* I, 286; = *AHw* s.v. B); conjunction, since (*CAD* I, 284; = *AHw* s.v. C, subjunction).

1. preposition:

a. from a place: *šeriktam ša ištu bīt abiša ublam*, the dowry she brought from her father's house (L138; cf. L149; 156).

b. because of: *ištu bītika ibballakatūnim*, they will cause me damage because of your house (L68+b); [*ištu*] *nidītika* [*bītī*] *ippalašūnim*, 'they may rob my house because of your mess' (L68+b).

2. conjunction, since, after: *ištu ṣēnum ugārim ītelianim*, after the flocks have come away from the meadows (L58); *ištu mārīša urtabbû*, after she has brought up her children (L137); *ištu sinništum šî ana bīt awīlim īrubu*, after that woman has moved into the man's house (L152); *ištu innemdū bītam ipušū*, after they had come together they made a house (L176a, twice; also L176b); *kirâšu ištu tarkibtim ana tamkārim iddinma*, he gave his orchard to the merchant after the pollination (L66); *ištu rēš šattim adi ḫamšim warḫim*, from the beginning of the year until the fifth month (L273); *ištu šiššim warqim adi taqtīt šattim*, from the sixth month until the end of the year (L273).

*išû* > ***ešû***, to confuse.

***išû***, vb. (defective), to have.

1. to possess (personal subject): *šarrāqānum ša nadānim la išu*, the thief does not have enough to pay (L8); *kaspam ana turrim la išu*, he does not have enough silver to give back (L51); *še'am u kaspam ana turrim la išu bīšamma išu*, he does not have enough grain or silver to repay but he has goods (§5.15; 5.15); *kaspam ana turrim la išu šeamma išu*, he does not have any silver but he does have grain for repaying (§5.10, following the reading in *BAL*, but Roth differently); *šeriktam la išu*, she has no dowry (L176b).

2. to be endowed with: *šumma awīlum šû tašīmtam išūma māssu šutēšuram ile'i*, if that gentleman has authority he will be empowered to direct his land (E15); *le'ûtī šāninam ul išû*, my power has no rival (E9); *epšētūa šāninam ul išâ*, my deeds are incomparable (E17).

3. to be associated with: *sinništum šî arnam ul išu*, that woman incurs no blame (L134); *ḫiṭītam la išu*, she has no sin (L142); *arnam ul išu*, there is no associated penalty (L142).

4. to be involved with (impersonal subject): *bītum šū ilkam la išu*, that property has no levy (L67+a); *dīnum šû rugummâm ul išu*, that judgment does not involve a claim (L115; 123; 250).
5. with ***eli***, to lend: *eli awīlim še'am u kaspam išūma*, he 'has against' (= has lent) a man grain or silver (L113; 115; cf. L114).
6. fragmentary: *išu* (§5.2).

***itinnu***, sbst., builder.
*itinnum bītam ana awīlim īpušma*, a builder has built a house for a man (L228; 233; cf. L229); *itinnum šû ina kasap ramanišu igāram šuāti udannan*, that builder shall repair that wall with his own money (L233); *itinnum šû iddâk*, that builder shall be killed (L229; cf. *mār itinnim šuāti idukkū* L230); [*idī*] *itinnim*, a builder's wages (L274).

***itti***, prep., with.
1. together with: *itti dayyānī ina dīnim ul uššab*, he shall not sit with the judges in a trial (L5); *itti bēl eqlim la imtagarma*, he has not made an agreement with the owner of the field (L57); *aššat awīlim itti zikarim šanîm*, a man's wife together with another male (L129; cf. L131; 132); *šugītum šî itti nadītim ul uštamaḫḫar*, that priestess shall not be treated the same as the lay-sister (L145); *amtum šî itti bēltiša uštamḫir*, that slave-girl tried to be the equal of her mistress (L146); *itti amātim imannūši*, they shall count her together with the slave-girls (L146); *itti mārī ḫīrtim imtanūšunūti*, he reckons them together with the sons of the first-ranking wife (L170; cf. L171a; 190); *itti aḫḫīšama izâzma*, she shall share together with her brothers (L182).
2. as well as: *mimmûšu itti mimmê bēl bitim*, his property as well as the property of the owner of the house (L125).
3. involving: *balāṭam ša itti mūtim šitannu*, a life which is continually striving with death (E24).
4. with *leqû*, to take away from: *kaspam itti tamkārim ilqēma*, he has borrowed silver from a merchant (L49, twice; 66; cf. L51; 106); *itti tamkārim ilqema*, he has borrowed from the merchant (§5.15); *itti šarrāqānišu ileqqe*, he shall take away from the person who stole it from him (L125).

***ittu***, subst., omen.
*ittum Dagan bānîšu*, in accordance with the omen of his creator, Dagan (P17, used adverbially); but perhaps to be read *idu*, strength (Szlechter) or *nāru*, river (Finet).

***itû***, sbst., neighbour.
*še'am kīma itēšu ana bēl eqlim inaddin*, he shall give as much grain as his neighbour to the owner of the field (L42; 43; cf. L55; 62; 65, partly restored); *eqel itēšu mê uštābil*, he has allowed the water to erode his neighbour's land (L55; 56); *awīlum* [*nidītam*] *balum* [*itēšu*

*ītepuš*], a man has built on neglected land without informing his neighbour [L68+a, twice]; *bīt ilkim ša bīt itēšu*, a property on which there is a levy which belongs to his neighbour (L67+a).

***itūlu***, vb., to copulate. < *ʾ-t-l.*

*aššat awīlim itti zikarim šanîm ina itūlim ittaṣbat*, a woman has been seized while lying with another man (L129; also *utūlim*, L131; 132); *ukabbilšima ina sūniša ittatīlma*, he raped her and had intercourse with her (L130); *mārušu ilmassi šû warkānumma ina sūniša ittatīlma*, his son 'learns about her' (i.e. consummates the marriage) but later he himself has intercourse with her (L155; also *ittatīl*, L156); *warki abišu ina sūn ummišu ittatīl*, he has intercourse with his mother after his father has gone (L157).

***izuzzu***, vb., to stand. < *n-z-z* / *ʾ-z-z* (mixed root).

1. to stand formally in position: *ša ūmīšu izzazzu ana Esagil*, who took his position in Esagil at his proper time (P5).

2. to take charge of: *awīlum awīlam ana panī eqlišu uzuzzim īgurma*, he has hired a man 'to stand in front of' (i.e. to oversee the management of) his field (L253).

> ***šūzuzzu***, to erect.

## K

*kabālu*, to be paralyzed > ***kubbulu***, to rape.

***kabātu***, vb., to be important. < *k-b-t.*

*Ninlil ummum rabītum ša qibīssa ina Ekur kabtat*, Ninlil, the great mother, whose utterance is important in Ekur (E21).

***kabtu***, sbst., serious. < *k-b-t.*

*ina pīšu kabtim*, with his grave words (E20); *arnam kabtam*, serious offence (L168; 169, twice); serious affliction (E24); *murṣam kabtam*, serious illness (E30); *simmam kabtam*, deep incision (L215; 218; 219; 224[!]; 225).

***kadru***, sbst., wild. < *k-d-r.*

*rīmum kadrum munakkip zāʾiri*, a wild ox that tosses its foe (P10).

***kakku***, sbst., weapon.

*ina kakkim dannim ša Zababa u Ištar ušatlimūnim*, with the fierce weapon that Zababa and Ishtar have presented to me (E4); *Ištar bēlet tāḫazim u qablim pātiat kakkiya lamassī damiqtum rāʾimat palêya*, Ishtar, lady of war and conflict who draws out my weapons, my gracious Protector who loves me to rule (E27); *in kakkišu dannim lišaṭṭīšuma biniātišu kīma ṣalam ṭiddim liḫbuš*, may he destroy him with his powerful weapons and shatter his body like a clay figurine (E28); *ašar tamḫārim kakkašu lišbir*, shatter his weapons on the battlefield

(E26); *ašar tāhazim u qablim kakkašu lišbir*, on the battlefield and in the conflict may he break his weapons (E27).

***kallatu***, sbst., bride, daughter-in-law.

*ana mārišu kallatam iḫīrma*, he has chosen a bride for his son (L155; 156).

***kalû***, vb., to retain. < *k-l-ʾ*.

*wardam šuāti ina bītišu iktalāšu*, he has held the slave in his house (L19).

> ***mukillu***, holding.

*kamāru*, to heap up > ***mukammeru***, heaping up.

***kāmidu***, sbst., weaver (of a special cloth, see *CAD*), or beetler (see *AHw*: *Stoffklopfer*), or rope-maker (see Finet: *cordier*, following *CAD* A/2, 442b). < *k-m-d*.

*idī kāmidim*, the wages of a weaver (L274).

***kamîš***, adv., in bonds (*CAD*: *kamîš* A); outside, far away (*CAD*: *kamîš* B).

*ana māt nukurtišu kamîš līrūšu*, let him remove him to a hostile land in bonds (E27); so *ANET*; *AHw*; *CAD*; alternatively 'may they lead him captive to a foreign country' (i.e. *kamîš* B, see *CAD* s.v. *nukurtu*, b4′).

***kammālu***, sbst., rival. < *k-m-l*.

*kammāl šarrūtim lišaṭṭilšu balāṭam ša itti mūtim šitannu ana šīmtim lišīmšum*, may he see the rival for his kingdom, make his destiny a life that all the time vies with death (E24).

*kanāšu*, to submit > ***mukannišu***, controlling.

***kanīku***, sbst., sealed document. < *k-n-k*.

*kanīk kaspim ša ana tamkārim inaddinu ileqqe*, he shall take a sealed document for the silver which he gives to the merchant (L104; cf. L105); *kasap la kanīkim ana nikkassim ul iššakkan*, silver without a sealed document may not be set in the account (L105).

***kankallu***, sbst., *CAD*: a type of hard soil; formerly read (see *BAL*) *eqel nidûtim*, neglected land.

*kankallam ana šalaš šanātim ana teptītim ušēṣīma*, he has taken over a neglected field to develop over three years (L44); *šumma kankallum eqlam šipram ippešma*, if it is neglected land he shall do the work (L63).

***kannu***, sbst., signal (= *CAD kannu* B, *AHw kannu*; II, to be distinguished from *AHw kannu* I, pot stand, = *CAD kannu* A).

*kannu gamartim ina abullim ittaḫlalū*, the flags have been hung on the city gate showing it is finished (L58); *AHw* refers to a pot-stand for the drinking vessel used by all the animals, s.v. *kannu* I, 3e.

*kânu*, to be firm > ***kunnu***, to establish, convict.

[*kapālu*] > ***kubbulu***, to rape.

***karābu***, vb., to pray. < *k-r-b.*

*ina libbišu gamrim likrubam*, let him pray with his whole heart (E12).

*karāṣu*, to snap off > ***kurruṣu***, to malign.

***karašû***, sbst., catastrophe.

*mušpazzir nišī Malgīm in karašîm mušaršidu šubātišin in nuḫšim*, who protected the people of Malgim from catastrophe, who made their homes completely secure (P16).

*karṣillu* > ***karzillu***, scalpel.

***kāru***, sbst., dyke.

*ana kār eqlišu dunnunim aḫšu iddīma kāršu la udanninma*, he has been careless about keeping the dyke in his field strong and has not repaired his dyke (L53; 53); *ina kārišu pītum ittepte u ugāram mê uštābil*, a break has been opened in his dyke so that the water destroys the meadow (L53); *awīlum ša ina kārišu pītum ippetû*, the man in whose dyke the break occurred (L53).

***karû***, sbst., heap of grain.

*mugarrin karê ana Uraš gašrim*, heaping up the stores of grain for mighty Urash (P11).

***karzillu***, sbst., scalpel (made from *siparru*, bronze).

*asûm awīlam simmam kabtam ina karzilli siparrim īpušma*, a surgeon has made a dangerous incision on a man with a bronze knife (L215; cf L218; 219); *nakkapti awīlim ina karzilli siparrim iptēma*, he has opened a man's eye-socket with a bronze knife (L215; cf. L218; 220).

***kaspu***, sbst., silver.

1. in general: *itinnum šû ina kasap ramanišu igāram šuāti udannan*, that builder shall repair that wall at his own expense (L233); *šumma wardum u amtum šunu mārū mātim balum kaspimma andurāršunu iššakkan*, their emancipation shall be arranged without any payment if the slave or the slave girl are natives to the country (L280).

2. a specified quantity:

a. expressed in terms of a *mana*: *1/3 mana kaspam inaddiššim*, he shall give her a third of a mana of silver (L140; cf. L252; with *šaqālu*, §5.3b; L201; 208; 214; 241); *1/2 mana kaspam išaqqal*, he shall pay half a mana of silver (L59; 207; 212; cf. L156; with *nadānu*, L251); *1 mana kaspam ana nišīšu išaqqalū*, they shall pay one mana of silver to his people (L24; cf. L198; 203).

b. expressed in terms of a *šiqlu*, although not expressed for fractional units: *1/6 kaspam ana asîm idīšu inaddin*, he shall pay a sixth (of a shekel) of silver to the physician as his fee (L224; cf. L277); for *1 šiqil kaspim* (§5.9) > ***ṣibtu***; *2 šiqil kaspam bēl wardim inaddiššum*, the owner of the field shall give him two shekels of silver (L17; cf. L213; 217; 223; 228; 234); *3 šiqil kaspam inaddin*, he shall pay three shekels of silver (L222; 260); *5 šiqil kaspam išaqqal*, he shall pay five shekels of silver (L211; cf. with *leqû*, L216; with *nadānu*, L221; 259; *ana 5 šiqil kaspim*, §5.3a, fragmentary); *10 šiqil kaspam išaqqal*, he shall pay ten shekels of silver (L204; cf. L209; with *leqû*, L215).

c. otherwise: [...] *uṭṭet kaspam*, [x] grains of silver (L274, seven times); *2½ uṭṭet kaspam idīša ina ūmim ištēn inaddin*, he shall pay two and a half grains of silver for one day as the charge for it (L276); *ina ūmim ištēn 3 uṭṭet kaspum idūša*, the hire charge for it is three grains of silver for one day (L275); [*4*(?)] *uṭṭet kaspam*, four (?) grains of silver (L274); *5 uṭṭet kaspam*, five grains of silver (L273; 274, twice); *6 uṭṭet kaspam*, six grains of silver (L273); *kaspam mišil šīmišu išaqqal*, he shall pay half his price in silver (L220, an injured slave); *kaspam mišil šīmiša inaddin*, he shall give half its price in silver (L238, a damaged boat); *kaspam ½ šīmišu ana bēl alpim inaddin*, he shall pay half its price in silver to the owner of the ox (L247, an ox that has been injured; cf. *kaspam ¼*(?) *šīmišu*, L248).

3. object of ***leqû***: *kaspam itti tamkārim ilqēma*, he has borrowed silver from a merchant (L49); *še'am ša kaspišu u ṣibassu ša itti tamkārim ilqû*, grain for the silver and its interest which he has borrowed from the merchant (L49; cf. L51); *kaspam itti tamkārim ilqēma*, he borrowed money from a merchant (L66); *šamallûm kaspam itti tamkārim ilqēma*, an agent has received silver from a merchant (L106); *kasap ilqû*, the silver he received (L101); *ina kaspim leqêm*, concerning the silver he received (L106); *kaspam mala ilqû*, as much silver as he received (L106).

4. object of ***nadānu***: *ana kaspim inaddin*, she shall sell (L40); *šuāti u bīšašu ana kaspim inaddinūma*, they shall sell that man and his goods (L54); *kaspam ana tappûtim iddin*, he has given silver in partnership (L77+f); *ina kaspim ša waššābum* [*iddinušum*], some of the silver which the occupant paid him (L69+c); *tamkārum ana šamallêm kaspam ana* [*nadānim u maḫārim*] *iddinma*, a merchant has given silver to an agent for buying and selling (L100); *tamkārum ana šamallîm kaspam ana tadmiqtim ittadinma*, a merchant has given silver to an agent as good-natured investment (L102); *ana kaspim ul inaddin šaniam ul uppal aplūssa ša aḫḫīšama*, she shall not sell or allow another to inherit; her portion definitely belongs to her brothers (L178); *bēlessa ana kaspim ul inaddišši*, her mistress shall not sell her (L146; cf. L147); *uniātim ana kaspim ul inaddinū*, they shall not sell the household effects (L 177).

5. object of ***šaqālu***: *ina maḫar ilim kasap išqulu*(!) *iqabbīma*, in the presence of a god he shall take the amount of silver he paid (L281); *kasap išqulu ana tamkārim inaddinma*, he shall give the silver he has

weighed out to the merchant (L281); *kasap išqulu ileqqe*, he shall take the silver he paid (L9; 278); *ina ebūrim kasapšu u ṣibassu [išaqqal]*, he shall pay the silver and the interest at harvest (§5.2).

6. object of ***turru***: *kaspam u ṣibassu ana tamkārim utâr*, he shall return the silver and its interest to the merchant (L50); *kaspam ana turrim la išu*, he does not have any silver to repay (L51); *qaqqad kaspim ana tamkārim utâr*, he shall return to the merchant the original amount of silver (L102).

7. object of ***elû***: *ina kaspišu ītelli*, he shall forfeit his silver (L35; 37); [*ina kaspim ša*] *ilqû* [*ītellīma*], he shall forfeit the silver that he took (§4.12).

8. bought, borrowed and sold: *lu kaspam lu ḫurāṣam lu wardam lu amtam lu alpam lu immeram lu imēram u lu mimma šumšu ina qāt mār awīlim u lu warad awīlim balum šībī u riksātim ištām*, he has bought silver, gold, a slave, a maid, a sheep, a donkey or something else without witnesses or contracts from a man's son or a man's slave (L7); *kaspam isaddarma*, he shall set out the various amounts of silver (L104); *tamkārum kaspam šamallâm iqīpma*, a merchant entrusted silver to an agent (L107); *kanīk kaspim*, a sealed tablet for the silver (L104; 105); *kasap la kanīkim*, silver with no sealed document (L105); *ana šībūt še'im u kaspim ūṣiam*, he has come forward with evidence about grain or silver (L4).

9. given or received as payment for goods or service: *ana kaspika tabal*, take instead of your silver (L66); *kaspam ana turrim la išu*, he has no silver to repay (§5.10); *kasap kiṣrišu gamram ša šanat*, all the agreed money for the year (L69+c); *kaspam ina abnim maṭītim*, silver according to the light weight (§5.13); *kaspam ina abnim* [*rabītim*], silver according to the heavy weight (§5.13); *ina abnim rabītim kaspam imtaḫar*, he has received the silver according to the heavier weight (L108); *usarrirma šimtam ittakir u ana kaspim ittaddin*, he has acted deceitfully and changed the marking or even sold them (L265).

10. given at a marriage: *kaspam mala terḫatiša inaddiššim*, he shall give her silver to the value of her bridal gift (L138); *eliāt zittišu kasap terḫatim išakkanūšumma aššatam ušaḫḫazūšu*, in addition to his share they shall set aside silver for a bridal gift and let him marry a wife (L166); *ana kaspim ul inaddin*, she may not sell it (L171b).

11. fragmentary: *kaspum* (§5.4);...*kaspam*...(§5.7); *ina*(!) *kaspim ša iddinu*(!) (§5.7).

12. also occurring with > ***še'u***, grain.

13. also occurring with > ***ṣibtu***, interest.

***kasû***, vb., to bind. < *k-s-'*.

*ikassûšunūtima ana mê inaddûšunūti*, they shall bind them together and throw them into the waters (L129; also *ikassûšuma*, L155).

***kašādu***, vb., to conquer, reach, achieve. < *k-š-d*.

1. to overpower: *šumma Id iktašassu mubbiršu bīssu itabbal*, if the River overcomes him the one who was accusing him shall take away his house (L2); *awatum maruštum ša Šamaš arḫīš likšussu*, let the devastating power of Shamash quickly overpower him (E23); *Ellil ina pīšu ša la uttakkaru līruršuma arḫiš likšudašu*, may Enlil curse him with one of his utterances that cannot be changed and may he quickly overpower him (E32).

2. to achieve: *irnitti Marduk eliš u šapliš ikšud*, he secured the triumph of Marduk above and below (E12).

3. to reach: *ittūramma ālšu iktašdam*, he has then returned and reached his own town (L27; 135); *šû ikšudu nagab uršim*, he is the one who has reached the source of wisdom (P16).

> ***mušakšidu***, granting victory; ***šukšudu***, to enable to reach, enable to achieve.

*kašāšu*, to enforce the payment of a debt > ***kāšišu***, creditor.

***kāšišu***, sbst., creditor. < *k-š-š*.

*šalaš šanātim bīt šāyyimānišunu u kāšišišunu ippešu*, she shall do the work at the house of the purchaser or the creditor for three years (L117).

***kašūšu***, sbst., supernatural power.

*ina kašūšišu rabîm kīma išātim ezzetim ša apim nišīšu liqmi in kakkišu dannim lišaṭṭīšuma*, let him burn his people by his mighty power, raging like a fire through the reeds, with his powerful weapons may he strike him (E28).

*katātu*, to be low (*AHw*: to tremble) > ***šutaktutu***, to be submissive(?), *AHw*: to be worried.

***kî***, adv., like.

*muṣīr bīt Ebabbar ša kî šubat šamā'i*, like the mantle of the sky he protects the house of Ebabbar (P7).

cf. ***kīma***, like.

***kibrātu***, sbst., pl., areas of the world.

*šarrum muštešmi kibrāt arba'im migir Ištar anāku*, I am the king who is obeyed in the four parts of the world (P21, variant *kibrāti*); *mubbib šuluḫ Eabzu tīb kibrāt erbettim*, showing purity through lustrating in Eabzu, striding through all four regions of the world (P5); *Bābilam šumšu ṣīram ibbiū in kibrātim ušāterūšu*, they gave Babylon its important name and made it the best in the world (P2).

***kibsu***, sbst., path, way of life. < *k-b-s*.

*kibsam rīdam dīn mātim ša adīnu*, and let this stone explain to him the traditional customs and rules of the land which I have decreed (E15).

**kilallān**, sbst., both.

*šumma...elišunu ḫubullum ittabši kilallāšunu tamkāram ippalū*, if they are in debt they shall both have to repay the merchant (L152); *kilallīšunu iqallûšunūti*, they shall burn both of them (L157).

**kīma**, conjunction, introducing dependent statement; preposition, like; *CAD* keeps the two words separate, while *AHw* attributes separate meanings to the one word.

1. conjunction: *kīma mimmûšu la ḫalqu babtašu ina maḫar ilim ubâršuma*, his community shall make him declare before the god that nothing of his was lost (L126); *kīma nakkāpû bābtašu ušēdīšumma*, he has informed his community about it, that it is likely to gore (L251); *kīma warassu ukânšuma*, he proves that he is his slave (L282).

2. preposition: in the same way as:

a. of people: *kīma Šamaš ana ṣalmāt qaqqadim waṣêmma*, rising like Shamash over the mass of humanity (P3); *bēlum ša kīma abim wālidim ana nišī ibaššû*, a ruler who is like their own father to my people (E12); *sinništum šî kīma amtim ina bīt mutiša uššab*, that woman shall dwell in the house of her husband like a slave-girl (L141).

b. of things: *bītim ša kīma šamê u erṣetim išdašu kīnā*, a temple whose foundations are established like those of heaven and earth (E8); *šarrūtam dārītam ša kīma šamê u erṣetim išdāša šuršudā*, an everlasting kingdom whose foundations are as well-established as heaven and earth (P2); *awīlum šû kīma iâti šar mīšarim Šamaš ḫaṭṭašu lirrik*, Shamash will surely make that man's rule last as long as he has made mine, the king of righteousness (E18); *ḫalāq nišīšu tabāk napištišu kīma mê*, the loss of his people and the pouring out of his life like water (E21); *kīma išātim ezzetim ša appim*, like a raging fire in the reed-bed (E28); *biniātišu kīma ṣalam ṭiddim liḫbuš*, let him shatter his limbs like an image of clay (E28); *kīma nišik mūtim la innassaḫu*, which, like the bite of death, cannot be taken away (E30).

3. people of the same quality: *lēt mār awīlim ša kīma šuati imtaḫaṣ*, he has struck the cheek of a man who is of the same status as himself (L203); *wardam kīma wardim iriab*, he shall make recompense with a slave of the same quality as the slave (L219; cf. L231).

4. of the same amount, value: *maḫar šībī kīma ubbalu ana tamkārišu inaddin*, before witnesses he shall give his merchant the same as it is worth (§5.15); *še'am kīma itēšu ana bēl eqlim inaddin*, he shall give to the owner of the field the same amount of grain as his neighbour (L42; 43); *še'am kīma itēšu imaddad*, he shall measure out the same amount of grain as his neighbour (L55); *ana bēl eqlim kīma itēšu imaddad*, he shall measure out for the owner of the field the same amount as his neighbour (L62; <L65>); *kīma ṣimdat šarrim*, according to the official

rate (§5.10); *ina ebūrim kīma riksātišu še'am ileqqe*, at the harvest he shall take grain according to the contract (L47); *alpam kīma alpim ana bēl alpim iriab*, he shall restore an ox like the ox to the owner of the ox (L245; 246); *alpam kīma* [*alpim*] *immeram kīma* [*immerim*] *ana bēlišu iriab*, he shall make recompense to his master with an ox like the ox and with a sheep like the sheep (L263; 263); *ina makkūr bīt abim zittam kīma aplim ištēn izâzma*, she shall be given a share from the goods of her father's house the same as the heir (L180; cf. L137; 172); *aḫḫūša kīma emūq bīt abim šeriktam išarrakūšimma*, her brothers shall grant her a dowry in proportion to the wealth of her father's house (L184).

5. fragmentary: *kīma* (§5.16).

***kīnātu***, sbst., pl., justice (see ***kittu***). < *k-'-n*.

*mušēpī kinātim mušūšer ammi*, making justice appear and keeping the people straight (P19; see *AHw* s.v. *kittu* I, 4b); *Ḫammurabi šar mīšarim ša Šamaš kīnātim išrukušum anāku*, I am Hammurabi, the king of justice, to whom Shamash has given the law (E17; see *AHw* s.v. *kittu* I, 4c).

***kīnu***, adj., firm, proper. < *k-'-n*.

1. secure: *ina Bābilim ālim ša Anum u Ellil rēšīšu ullû ina Esagila bītim ša kīma šamê u erṣetim išdāšu kīnā*, in Babylon, the city whose pinnacles Anum and Enlil have raised up, in Esagila, the temple whose foundations are as firm as heaven and earth (E8).

2. established: *ussam kīnam u rīdam damqam*, secure government and good tradition (E1).

***kirû***, sbst., orchard.

1. *balum bēl kirîm ina kirī awīlim iṣam ikkis*, he has felled a tree in a man's orchard without the owner of the orchard knowing (L59; 59); *šumma awīlum eqlam ana kirîm zaqāpim ana nukaribbim iddin nukaribbum kiriam izqup erbe šanātim kiriam urabba*, if a man gave a field to a gardener to plant out as an orchard and the gardener planted out the orchard, he shall make the orchard grow for four years (L60; 60; 60; cf. *ana kirîm la izqup*, L62); *bēl kirîm u nukaribbum mitḫāriš izuzzū bēl kirîm zittašu inassaqma*, the owner of the orchard and the cultivator shall share equally, but the owner of the orchard shall choose his part (L60; 60); *awīlum kirāšu ana nukaribbim ana rukkubim iddin*, a man gave his orchard to a gardener to pollinate (L64); *nukaribbum adi kirâm ṣabtu ina bilat kirîm šittīn ana bēl kirîm inaddin šaluštam šû ileqqe*, the gardener shall give the owner of the orchard two-thirds as rent for the orchard for as long as the orchard is held; he shall keep a third himself (L64; 64; 64); *kirâm la urakkibma*, he did not pollinate the orchard (L65); *bilat kirîm*, the produce from the orchard (L65);

*kirâšu ištu tarkibtim ana tamkārim iddinma*, he gave his orchard to the merchant after pollination (L66); *suluppī mala ina kirîm*, as many dates as there are in the orchard (L66, three times); *eqelša u kirâša aḫḫūša ileqqūma*, her brothers shall take her field and orchard (L178); *eqelša u kirāša ana errēšim ša eliša ṭābu inaddinma errēssa ittanaššīši*, she shall give her field or orchard to a cultivator who pleases her and her cultivator shall support her (L178).
2. occurring also with > ***eqlu***, field (with and without *bītu).*

***kiṣru***, sbst., agreed payment (alternatively read as *riksu*); see *CAD* s.v. 3 a 1′. < *k-ṣ-r*.
*kasap kiṣrišu gamram ša šanat*, all the money agreed for the year (L69+c); *kiṣrim ša ippušu*, of the rent obligation which he shall perform (§4.12).

***kišpū***, sbst., tantum pl., sorcery.
*šumma awīlum kišpī eli awīlim iddīma la uktīnšu*, if a man has laid a charge of witchcraft against another man but cannot substantiate his guilt (L2); *ša elišu kišpū nadû ana Id illak Id išalliamma*, the one who has been accused of sorcery shall go to the River and leap into the River (L2); *ša elišu kišpī iddû iddâk*, the one who laid a charge of witchcraft against him shall be put to death (L2).

***kiššatu***, sbst., mass.
*ellilūt kiššat nišī išīmūšum*, they have ordained him to the leadership of the mass of people (P1).

***kiššātu***, sbst., pl., pledge, security. < *k-š-š*.
*aššassu mārašu u mārassu ana kaspim iddin u lu ana kiššātim ittandin*, he has sold his wife, son or daughter, or has handed them over as pledges (L117; cf. *wardam u lu amtam ana kiššātim ittandin*, L118).

***kittu***, sbst., justice. < *k-'-n*.
*kittam u mīšaram ina pī mātim aškun*, I made the land speak with justice and truth (P22).

***kitû***, sbst., flax.
[*idi*] *ša kitîm*, the hire for someone working with flax (L274).

***kubbulu,*** vb., to rape (*AHw*: to gag). < *k-b-l*.
*ukabbilšima ina sūniša ittatīlma*, he raped her and had intercourse with her (L130).

***kullizu***, sbst., ox-driver.
*kullizam īgur*, he has hired a cattle herder (L258).

***kullu***, vb., to hold. < *k-'-l*.
*ina utliya nišī māt Šumerim u Akkadîm ukīl*, I held the people of Sumer and Akkad in my arms (E7).
> ***mukillu***, holding.

**kullumu**, vb., to explain. < *k-l-m*.

*mimma mala inaddinu šībī ukallam*, he shall show to witnesses however much he gives (L122); *narî awatam likallimšu*, let my stela explain the meaning to him (E11; also *likallimšuma*, E15).

**kulmašītu**, sbst., priestess.

*abum nadītam qadištam u lu kulmašītam ana ilim iššīma*, a father has offered to the god a priestess, a prostitute or a hierodule (L181).

*kummuru*, to heap up > ***mukammeru***, heaping up.

**kunnu**, vb., to provide legal proof, convict, fix, establish. < *k-ʾ-n*.

1. to prove: *awat iqbû la uktīn*, he did not prove the statement he made (L3); *ubānam ušatrišma la uktīn*, he has pointed his finger without any proof (L127); *awīlum awīlam ubbirma nērtam elišu iddīma la uktīnšu*, a man accused a man and charged him with murder but has not proved it (L1); *kišpī eli awīlim iddīma la uktīnšu*, he has made allegations of sorcery against a man but has not proved it (L2); *tamkārum šû ina maḫar ilim u šībī ina kaspim leqêm šamallâm ukânma*, that merchant shall prove in the presence of the god and witnesses that the trader borrowed the money (L106; cf. *tamkāram ukânma*, L107); *kīma warassu ukânšuma*, he shall prove that it is his slave (L282); *ina mimma ša šūbuluma la iddinu ukânšūma*(!), he (Stele: they) shall prove that he did not deliver what had to be transported (L112); *ina šeʾim leqêm ukannūšuma*, they shall prove that he took the grain (L113).

2. to convict: *bēl nipûtim tamkāršu ukânma*, the owner of the security shall convict that merchant (L116); *awīlam šuāti ukannūšuma*, they shall convict that man (L124; 255); *šiprim la epēšim ukannūšuma*, they shall convict him of not doing the work (L42); *dayyānam šuāti ina dīn idīnu enêm ukannūšuma*, they shall convict that judge of having changed his decision (L5); *šumma...šimtam uttakir u ana kaspim ittadin ukannūšuma*, if...he has changed the marking or sold them for silver, they shall convict him (L265); *šumma...mussa ušamṭa ukannūšima*, if...she has deprecated her husband, they shall convict her (L141); *ukannūšima ana mê inaddûši*, they shall convict her and throw her into the water (L108; 133b); *ukannūšima aššum balum abišu u ummišu ṣiḫram šaniam irkusu*, they shall convict her of making an agreement about another child without the knowledge of the father and mother (L194).

3. to fix securely: *awatiya šūqurātim ina narīya ašṭurma ina maḫar ṣalmiya šar mīšarim ukīn*, I have written my precious words on my stela and placed them on the picture of me, the king of justice (E8);

4. to establish securely: *šarrūtam dārītam ša kīma šamê u erṣetim išdāša šuršudā ukinnūšum*, they established an everlasting kingdom for him, the foundations of which are as secure as heaven and earth

(P2); *dīnāt mīšarim ša Ḫammurabi šarrum lēûm ukinnuma mātam ussam kīnam u rīdam damqam ušaṣbitu*, just laws which the mighty king Hammurabi has established, who made the land adopt solid leadership and good discipline (E1).

> ***mukīnu***, founder.

*kunnušu* > ***mukannišu***, forcing to submit.

***kunukku***, sbst., sealed document. < *k-n-k*.

*dayyānum dīnam idīn purussâm iprus kunukkam ušēzib*, a judge has formed a judgment, made his decision and has had a sealed document deposited (L5); *ana aššatišu eqlam kirâm bītam u bīšam išrukšim kunukkam īzibšim*, he has presented his wife with a field, orchard, house or property and has deposited a sealed document (L150); *kunukkam išṭuršum*, he has written out a sealed document for him (L165); *ša abuša šeriktam išrukušim kunukkam išṭurušim*, to whom her father has presented a dowry and has written out a sealed document for her (L179; cf. *išturšim*, L183); with negative: *kunukkam la išṭuršim*, he did not write out an official document for her (L182); *kunukkišu la išṭuršum*, he did not write out an official document for him (§5.3a).

*kuppulu* > ***kubbulu***, to rape.

***kurru***, sbst., measure for grain.

*ana 1 kurrum 1 pān 4 sūt še'am ṣibtam ileqqe*, he shall receive one pan and four sa of grain in interest per kur (§5.9; cf. §5.10); *ina šanat ana 1 kur še'im 5 qa še'am idī našpakim inaddin*, he shall pay the storage charge of five qa of grain for one kur of grain per year (L121); *idī alpim ša qabla 3 kur šeam*, three kur of grain as the fee for the fore ox (L242/3); *idī alpim ša warka 4 kur še'am*, four kur of grain as the fee for the rear ox (L242/3); *6* [*kur še'am*] *ina šanat inaddiššum*, he shall pay him six kur of grain for one year (L239); *8 kur še'am ina šattim ištiat inaddiššum*, he shall pay him eight kur of grain for one year (L257; 261; cf. *6 kur*, L258); *ana 1 burum 10 kur še'am imaddad*, he shall measure out ten kur of corn per bur (L44; 56); *10 kur še'am ša šattim ištiat imaddad*, he shall measure out ten kur of grain for one year (L63); *elēnumma ana 1 burum 20 kur še'am*, 20 kur of grain per bur in addition (L57); *ana 1 burum 60 kur še'am*, 60 kur of corn for each bur of land (L58; 255); *elep 60 kur ana awīlim ipḫe*, he has caulked a boat of 60 kur capacity for a man (L234); by implication: *elep šūšim īgur*, he hired a boat of 60, i.e. of 60 kur capacity (L277).

***kurruṣu***, to malign. < *k-r-ṣ*.

*ana bīt emišu biblam ušābil terḫatam iddinma ibiršu uktarrissu*, he has taken a present to the house of his father-in-law but his friend has maligned him (L161).

**kussû**, sbst., official seat, throne.
*u ina puḫrim ina kussî dayyānūtišu ušetbûšuma*, in the assembly they shall remove him from his judicial bench (L5); *agâm kussâm ša šarrūtim līṭeršu*, remove his kingly crown and throne (E24).

## L

**la** (*AHw*: *lā* ), part., not.
1. with a verb in the present or preterite: L1; 2; 3; 10; 11; 13; 16; 18; 23; 26; 29; 32; 32; 42; 43; 44; 46; 47; 48; 52; 53; 54; 57; 61; 62; 65; 66; §5.3a; 5.12; 5.12; L101; 105; 108; 109; 109; 112; 112; 127; 128; 130; 131; 132; 133b; 134; 135; 138; 139; 145; 147; 149; 156; 163; 164; 166; 166; 168; 171a; 172; 174; 178; 178; 178; 178; 180; 181; 182; 182; 184; 184; 189; 190; 206; 227; 229; 232; 233; 235; 255; 256; 278; E18; 18; 18; 19; 19; 20; 24; 30; 30; 30; 30; 32.
2. with a stative: *la ḫaliqma* (L126); *la ḫalqu* (L126); *la maḫar* (E28); *la naṣratma* (L143); *la qerbu* (L13); *la wašbat* (L110).
3. with ***išu***: L8; 51; 67+a; §5.10; 5.15; L114; 142; 176b.
4. with infinitive and other nominal forms: *la epēšim* (L42); *la ezēbša* (L141); *la ḫabālim* (E5); *ana la ḫassim* (E17); *la kanīkim* (L105); *la maḫārim* (P15); *la malûtim* (L69+c); *la mê* (L48); *la mupparkum* (P11); *la nawārim* (E20); *la ṣabātiša* (L151); *la šêm* (L226; 227); *la šubbîm* (E20); *la šubšam* (E20).
5. fragmentary: §5.3a; §5.7.

**labânu**, sbst., neck muscle.
*alpam īgurma šēpšu ištebir u lu labiānšu ittakis*, he has hired an ox and broken its foot or cut its neck muscle (L246).

*labāšu*, to put on clothing > ***mušalbišu***, decorating.

**la'bu**, sbst., disease.
*aššatam īḫuzma la'bum iṣṣabassi*, he has taken a wife but a disease has then struck her (L148); *aššassu ša la'bum iṣbatu*, the wife whom a disease has struck (L148).

**lāma**, conj., before.
*lāma sinništam šuāti iḫḫazu ḫubullum elišu ibašši*, the debt against him existed before he took that woman (L151); *lāma ana bīt awīlim irrubu*, before she moved into the man's house (L151).

**lamādu**, vb., to understand, have a sexual relationship. < *l-m-d*.
1. to understand: *asûm qerebšu la ilammadu*, a doctor will not understand its nature (E30).
2. to have a sexual relationship: *mārassu iltamad*, he has had sex with his daughter (L154); *ana mārišu kallatam iḫīrma mārušu ilmassi šû warkānumma ina sūniša ittatīlma*, he has chosen a bride for his son

and his son has had sex with her but he himself has intercourse with her later (L155; also *ilmassima*, L156).

***lamassu***, sbst., large protective statue, guardian spirit.

1. protective statue: *šēdum lamassum ilū ēribūt Esagil libitti Esagil*, the Demon, the Guardian, the deities going into Esagila and the brickwork of Esagila (E13); *Ištar bēlet tāḫazim u qablim pātiat kakkiya lamassī damiqtum rā'imat palêya*, O Ishtar, lady of war and conflict, who draws out my weapons; my gracious guardian spirit, who loves me to rule (E27); *mutêr lamassīšu damiqtim ana ālim Aššur*, taking back his beneficent guardian to Asshur (P19).

2. protection: *ina lamassiya iḫḫišā*, they come and go under my protection (E7).

*lapātu*, to touch (*AHw* to lay hold of) > ***šulputu***, to defile.

***laputtû***, officer.

*lu ša ḫaṭṭātim u lu laputtûm ṣāb nisḫātim irtaši*, a captain or officer has acquired a soldier who is a deserter (L33+); *lu ša ḫaṭṭātim u lu laputtûm numāt rēdîm ilteqe*, a captain or an officer has taken the property of a soldier (L34+).

*lemēnu*, to fall into misfortune > ***lummunu***, to spoil.

[*lemnētu*] > ***lemuttu***, calamity.

***lemnu***, adj., bad.

*šīram lemnam*, evil omen (E23); *asakkam lemnam*, a terrible curse (E30).

***lemuttu***, sbst., misfortune, calamity.

*damqātišu ana lemnētim litēr*, turn his blessings into a calamity (E27).

***leqû***, vb., to take. < *l-q-'*.

1. to take away illicitly, forcibly or oppressively: *šāyyimānum ina bīt nādinānim kasap išqulu ileqqe*, the purchaser shall take the silver he has paid from the house of the seller (L9); *numāt rēdîm ilteqe*, he has taken away the property of a soldier (L34); *qīšti šarrum ana rēdîm iddinu ilteqe*, he has taken away the gift the king gave the soldier (L34); *mimma ša ilqû*, whatever he took (L107); cf. *ina balum bēl še'im ina našpakim u lu ina maškanim še'am ilteqe*, he has taken grain from the threshing floor or from the granary without the knowledge of the owner of the grain (L113); *ina še'im leqêm ukannūšuma*, they shall convict him of taking the grain (L113); cf. *ina kaspim leqêm* (L106); *bēl bītim našpakam iptēma še'am ilqe*, the owner has opened the storehouse and taken the grain (L120); *še'am ša ilqû*, the grain which he took (L120); *še'am mala ilqû*, all the grain he took (§5.12; L113; also *ilteqēma*, §5.12); *itti šarrāqānišu ileqqe*, he shall take it away from the person who stole it from him (L125); *aldâm ilqēma liātim ūtenniš*, he has removed the stored grain and weakened the cattle (L254).

2. to receive as one's due, according to one's expectations: *bēl ḫulqim ḫuluqšu ileqqe*, the owner of the missing property shall take his property (L9; 10); *bēl eqlimma ileqqēma*, the owner of the field shall take (L49; 50); *zittašu inassaqma ileqqe*, he shall subtract his share and take it (L60; cf. L64; 66; also *ileqqēma*, L66); *še'am ileqqe*, he shall take the grain (L47); *mala ilqû*, as much as he received (L100); *ina ebūrim 5 sut še'am ileqqe*, she shall take five sutu-measures of grain at harvest (L111); *ṣibassu ša itti tamkārim ilqû*, the interest which he received from the merchant (L49; cf. L51); *adi ḫamšīšu ileqqe*, he shall take five times the amount (L12); *ana 1 šiqil kaspim 1/6 u 6 uṭṭet ṣibtam ileqqe*, for each shekel of silver he shall receive a sixth of a shekel and six grains in interest (§5.9, twice); *ileqqe*, he shall take (§5.10); *10 šiqil kaspam ileqqe*, he shall take ten shekels of silver (L215); *5 šiqil kaspam ileqqe*, he shall take five shekels of silver (L216); *ilteqēma*, he has received (§5.11); *kasap išqulu ileqqe*, he shall take the silver he weighed out (L278); *kasap ilqû*, the silver he took (L101); *mala ilqû*, as much as he took (L106; 113); [*ina kaspim ša*] *ilqû* [*ītellīma*], he shall forfeit the silver that he took (§4.12); *mārat awīlim šeriktaša ileqqe*, the daughter of the man shall take her wedding-gift (L176a, where the verb occurs three times, and twice more in 176b; cf. L170; 172; also *ileqqēma*, L142; 171b; 172; also *ileqqû*, 174; also *ileqqûma*, L167; 178;); *qīšti abum iddinušum ileqqēma*, he shall take the gift the father gave him (L165); *mānaḫātišu la ilqû*, he has not regained his investment (L47); *kanīk kaspim ša ana tamkārim inaddinu ileqqe*, he shall take a sealed document for the silver he gives to the merchant (L104; also *ilteqe*, L105).

3. to borrow: *kaspam itti tamkārim ilqēma*, he borrowed silver from a merchant (L49; 66; 106); *itti tamkārim ilqēma*, he borrowed from the merchant (§5.15).

4. to take control of a person: *ṣeḫram ina mêšu ana mārūtim ilqēma*, he adopted a small child at birth as a son (L185; also *ilqe*, L186; *ilqûšu*, L186; *ilqēma*, L188; *ilqûšuma*, L190; 191).

5. fragmentary: *ilqe* (§5.10).

***lētu***, sbst., cheek.

*awīlum lēt awīlim ša elišu rabû imtaḫaṣ*, a gentleman has struck the cheek of a gentleman greater than himself (L202); *mār awīlim lēt mār awīlim ša kīma šuāti imtaḫaṣ*, a gentleman's son has struck the cheek of another gentleman's son like himself (L203); *muškēnum lēt muškēnim imtaḫaṣ*, a working man has struck the cheek of another working man (L204); *warad awīlim lēt mār awīlim imtaḫaṣ*, a gentleman's slave has struck the cheek of a gentleman's son (L205).

***le'û***, vb., to be able. < *l-'-'*.

1. to have the necessary mental and physical resources: *mārušu ilkam alākam ile'i*, his son is capable of performing the duty (L28; cf. L29); *pīḫassu apālam la ile'i*, he is not able to discharge his responsibility (L256); *šumma awīlum šû tašīmtam išūma māssu šutēšuram ile'i*, if that man has intelligence and is capable of guiding his land aright (E15).

2. to have the necessary financial resources: *še'am riābam la ile'i*, he is not able to make recompense for the grain (L54).

***lē'u***, sbst., capable, masterly. < *l-'-'*.

*šarrum lē'ûm mutēr Eridu ana ašrišu*, the capable king who restored Eridu to its proper status (P5); *dīnāt mīšarim ša Ḫammurabi šarrum lē'ûm ukinnuma*, the laws of justice which the capable king Hammurabi established (E1).

***lē'ūtu***, sbst., supreme power. < *l-'-'*.

*ina lē'ûtim ša Marduk iddinam*, by the power that Marduk has given me (E4); *awâtūa nasqā lē'ûti šāninam ul išû*, my words are precious, my power is unequalled (E9).

*li'ātu*, Akk. equivalent of Sumerian collective *ÁB.GUD.ḪI.A*, instead of *sukullu*, > ***littu***, cow.

***libbu***, sbst., heart, desire, midst.

1. with ***ṭubbu***, to bring pleasure: *libbi Marduk bēlišu uṭīb u šiʾram ṭābam ana nišī ana dār išīm u mātam uštēšer*, he has brought pleasure to his lord Marduk so that he has decreed health and prosperity for his people for evermore (E12); *muṭīb libbi Marduk*, who made the heart of Marduk happy (P5); *libbaša uṭabbū*, they make her content (L178); *libbaša la uṭṭibbū*, they have not made her content (L178); also with ***ṭâbu***: *idīšu gamrātim maḫir libbašu ṭāb*, having received all his wages he is content in his heart (L264).

2. with other verbs: *muḫaddi libbi Ištar*, who made the heart of Ishtar rejoice (P13); *munēḫ libbi Adad*, who made the heart of Adad quiet (P14); *narî awatam likallimšu dīnšu līmur libbašu linappišma*, may my stele explain his problem, may he understand his rights and may he let his heart relax (E11).

3. symbolizing emotion: *mutu libbiša iḫḫassi*, the man of her heart shall take her (L137; 156; cf. *mut libbiša*, L172); *ina libbišu gamrim likrubam*, let him pray for me with his whole heart (E12); *ina libbiša aggim ina uzzātiša rabiātim*, with an angry heart and terrible rage (E27).

4. ***mala libbiša***, all she wants: *mala libbiša la ušamṣīši*, he did not allow her 'to find her heart completely' (= to do all she wants, L178; cf. L179).

5. ***ina libbi***, within > ***ina***.

6. ***ša libbiša***, cargo, foetus > ***ša***.

***libittu***, sbst., brickwork.

*šēdum lamassum ilū ēribūt Esagil libitti Esagil*, the Demon, the Guardian, the deities going into Esagila and the brickwork of Esagila (E13); *šēd bītim libitti Ebabbara*, Guardian of the shrine, brickwork of Ebabbar (E31).

***liblibbu***, sbst. (*AHw* s.v. *libbu*), descendant.

*liplippim ša Sumula'il aplum dannum ša Sīnmuballiṭ zērum dārium ša šarrūtim*, the descendant of Shumu-la'il, the mighty heir of Sin-muballit, with royal ancestors in every generation (P21).

*liplippu* > ***liblibbu***, descendant.

***liptu***, sbst., affliction. < *l-p-t.*

*ina tarbaṣim lipit ilim ittabši*, an inexplicable disaster has occurred in the pen (L266).

***lišānu***, sbst., tongue.

*lišanšu inakkisū*, they shall cut out his tongue (L192).

***littu***, sbst., cow; collective ***li'ātu***, formerly read *sugullu* or *sukullu*, herd, cattle.

*aldâm ilqēma liātim ūtenniš*, he has removed the stored grain and weakened the cattle (L254); *liāt awīlim ana igrim ittadin*, a man's cattle have been given for hire (L255); *ina eqlim šuāti ina liātim imtanaššarūšu*, they shall drag him all over that field with oxen (L256); *nāqidam ana liātim u ṣēnim re'îm īgur*, he has hired a herdsman to look after the herds and flocks (L261); [*rē'ūm*] *ša liātum u lu ṣēnum ana re'îm innadnušum*, a shepherd who has been given cattle or sheep to look after (L264; 265); *liātim uṣṣaḫḫir ṣēnam uṣṣaḫḫir*, he has diminished the herd and the flock (L264); *liātim u ṣēnam ana bēlišunu iriab*, he shall make recompense with cattle or small animals to their owner (L265); *liātim u ṣēnam ušallama*, he shall repay with cattle or small animals (L267); *liātim ereqqam u murteddīša īgur*, he hired cattle, a wagon and its driver (L271).

***lu*** (*AHw*: *lū*), part., or, either...or, whether...or.

1. ***lu...lu,*** introducing all elements in a series of nouns or noun phrases:

a. a series of two: L16; 281.

b. a series of four: L15.

2. ***lu...u lu***, with *u lu* before the last element:

a. a series of two: L26; 26; 27; 28; 30; 32; 33; 33; 34; 34; 176a; 224; 280.

b. a series of four: E19.

c. a series of five: L8.
d. a series of eight: L7.
3. ***u lu...u lu***, introducing both elements of a pair of phrases:
a. of noun phrases: L46; 125.
b. of complex verb phrases: L120.
4. ***u lu*** linking nouns or noun phrases:
a. a series of two: L7; 16; 49; 49; 49; 50; 50; 51; 52; 113; 113; 176a; 176a; 180; 192; 193; 224; 224; 225; 225; 245; 253; 260; 262; 263, partly restored; 264; 265; 280; 281.
b. the last in a series of three: L178; 179; 181.
5. ***u lu*** linking verbs or verb phrases:
a. a series of two: L7; 26; 33; 45; 110; 116; 117; 198; 199; 215; 218; 221; 236; 246; 255; 266.
b. linking all elements in a series of three: L48.
c. the last in a series of three: L248.

***lubūšu***, sbst., clothing.
*kīma emūq zittiša ipram piššatam u lubūšam inaddinūšimma*, they shall give her food, oil and clothing according to the size of her share (L178+).

***lummunu***, defame. < *l-m-n*.
*awassu lilemmin*, may she denigrate his statement (E21).

## M

***madādu***, vb., to measure. < *m-d-d*.
*ana 1 burum 10 kur še'am imaddad*, he shall calculate ten kur of corn per bur (L44; 56; cf. L63); *ina ebūrim ana 1 burum 60 kur še'am ana bēl eqlim imaddad*, he shall measure out of 60 kur of corn for each bur for the owner of the field at harvest time (L58; cf. L255); *še'am kīma itēšu imaddad*, he shall assess the grain like his neighbour (L55; cf. L62; [65]).

***magal***, adv., greatly.
*mussa waṣīma magal ušamṭāši*, her husband has greatly disparaged her when he left (L142).

***magāru***, vb., to agree, allow. < *m-g-r*.
1. to come to an agreement: *itti bēl eqlim la imtagarma*, he has not come to an agreement with the owner of the field (L57); *tamkārum šû ul immaggar*, that merchant shall not agree (L66); *ina bīt mutiša wašābam la imtagar*, she has not agreed to live in her husband's house (L149).
2. to permit: *awīlam šuāti ul imaggarūšu*, they shall not permit that man (L144).

*maḫar*, prep., in front > ***maḫar***, sbst., front.

***maḫāru***, vb., to receive, acquire, be comparable. < *m-ḫ-r*.

1. to receive into one's possession: *u ša šurqam ina qātišu imḫuru iddâk*, the one who accepted the stolen property into his possession shall be killed (L6); *ana maṣṣarūtim imḫur*, he has received it for safe keeping (L7); *bilat eqlišu imtaḫar*, he has received the rent for the field (L45; cf. L46); *kaspam ina abnim* [*rabītim*] *še'am ina sūtim rabītim imḫur*, he received silver according to the heavy weight and grain according to the large measure (§5.13); *u inūma imḫuru*, and when he receives (§5.13); *ana šīm šikarim še'am la imtaḫar ina abnim rabītim kaspam imtaḫar*, she has not received grain for the price of the drink but she has received a large amount of silver (L108; 108); *tašna še'am ša imḫuru*(!) *iriab*, he shall repay twice the grain he received (L254); *miqitti tarbaṣim bēl tarbaṣim imaḫḫaršu*, the owner of the enclosure shall receive the dead animals from the enclosure (L266); *idīšu gamrātim maḫir libbašu ṭāb*, having received all his due his heart is happy (L264).

2. to acquire: *ana ḫarrān šarrim agram pūḫam imḫurma*, he acquired a hired substitute for the king's expedition (L33).

3. to be comparable: *etel šarrī qabal la maḫārim*, the most eminent of kings with whom there is none to compare in battle (P15); *dannum ina ilī qabal la maḫār*, the mighty one among the gods, incomparable in battle (E28).

4. to find acceptable: *tamkārum ul uppas imaḫḫar*, the merchant shall not argue but accept (§5.15); *ša īnšu maḫru*, who is acceptable in his eyes (L165).

> ***šumḫuru***, to show rivalry.

***maḫāṣu***, vb., to strike, fight. < *m-ḫ-ṣ*.

1. to collide: *elep ša māḫirtim elep ša muqqelpītim imḫaṣma*, a rowing boat has struck a sailing boat (L240).

2. to treat violently: *mārat awīlim imḫaṣma*, he struck a man's daughter (L209); *mārum abašu imtaḫaṣ*, a son has beaten his father (L195); *lēt awīlim ša elišu rabû imtaḫaṣ*, he has struck the cheek of someone greater than himself (L202; cf. L203; 204; 205); *awīlum awīlam ina risbātim imtaḫaṣma*, a man has struck another in a brawl (L206); *ina idû la amḫaṣu*, I did not mean to injure (L206); *ina maḫāṣišu imtūt*, he has died in his fight (L207); *ina maḫāṣim u lu ina uššušim imtūt*, it has died from beating or abuse (L116); *ina mēgûtim u lu ina maḫāṣim uštamīt*, he has let it die through neglect or violence (L245); *ina maḫāṣim ša libbiša uštaddīši*, by violence he makes her lose her unborn child (L211; also *imḫaṣma*, L213).

3. of a god, to afflict: *ilum imḫassuma*, the god has struck it (L249).

4. to break up ground for planting: *eqlam ša iddû mayyāri imaḫḫaṣ*, he shall turn over the field he has neglected with mattocks (L43; cf. L44).
\> ***namḫaṣu***, to be beaten.

***māḫirtu***, adj. fem. (masc. *māḫiru*, see *CAD* s.v. 2), confronting, moving upstream against the current (describing a boat). < *m-ḫ-r*.
1. *māḫirtam īgur*, he has hired a boat to go upstream (L276).
2. *ša māḫirtim* the man in the boat: *ša māḫirtim ša elep ša muqqelpītim uṭebbû eleppašu u mimmašu ḫalqam iriabšum*, the man in the boat going upstream who made the boat going downstrean sink shall recompense him for his boat and for whatever was lost (L240).
3. with *eleppu* expressed: *elep ša māḫirtim elep ša muqqelpītim imḫaṣma*, a boat of someone going upstream has struck a boat of someone going downstream (L240).

***maḫīru***, sbst., tariff, value. < *m-ḫ-r*.
< *še'am u lu*> *šamaššammī ana maḫīrātišunu*, grain and sesame at their market rate (L51); *maḫīr šikarim ana maḫīr še'im umtaṭṭi*, she has diminished the value of the drink compared with the value of the grain (L108; 108).

***maḫra***, adv., in front. < *m-ḫ-r*.
***ina maḫra***: *Ea rubûm rabium ša šīmātušu ina maḫra illakā*, Ea, the almighty prince whose decisions come first (E22; *CAD* s.v. 2).

***maḫru***, sbst., front, used as preposition, ***maḫar***, in front of. < *m-ḫ-r*.
1. in the presence of people: *maḫar šībīmi ašām*, 'I made the purchase in the presence of witnesses' (L9); *šībū ša maḫrišunu šīmum iššāmu*, witnesses before whom the purchase was made (L9); *maḫar šībī*, before witnesses (§5.15; L124); *maḫar dayyānī inaṭṭûšu*, they shall drag him before the judges (L127).
2. in the presence of a deity: *mudūssunu maḫar ilim iqabbûma*, they shall declare in the god's presence what they know (L9); *maḫar ilim ubârma*, he shall make clear in the god's presence (L23); *bēl še'im maḫar ilim še'ašu ubârma*, the owner of the grain shall declare in god's presence the amount of grain (L120); *maḫar*(!) *ilim ubbamma*, he shall declare himself innocent in the presence of the god (L266); *maḫar ilim*(!) *mitḫāriš izuzzū*, they shall share equally in the presence of the god (L77+f).
3. with ***ina***: *šībī ša ina maḫrišunu išāmu*, witnesses in whose presence he made the purchase (L9; 10); *ina maḫar ilim*, in the presence of a god (L126; 240).
4. fragmentary: *maḫaršuma* (§5.3a).
***ana maḫar***, in front of: *ana maḫar ṣalmiya šar mīšarim lillikma*, let him come before this statue of me, the king of justice (E11).

***ina maḫar***, in front of: *ina maḫar ilim u šībī*, in the presence of the god and witnesses (L106; 107: variant *maḫar* on both occasions); *babtašu ina maḫar ilim ubâršuma*, his community shall make clear his position in the presence of the god (L126: variant *u maḫar*; cf. L240; 281: with *qabû*); *ina maḫar ṣalmiya šar mīšarim ukīn*, I, the king of justice, have fixed them on my image (E8); *ina maḫar Marduk*, in the presence of Marduk (E12; 13); *ina maḫar Ellil*, in the presence of Enlil (E21).

**maḫrû**, adj., former. < *m-ḫ-r*.

*ina šattim maḫrītim*, in the earlier year (L47); *mārū maḫrûtum u warkûtum izuzzū*, the children of the earlier wife and of the later wife shall share (L173).

*majāru* > ***mayyāru***, plough.

**mākālu**, sbst., food.

*mudeššī mākalī ellūtim ana Nintu*, providing in abundance the pure offerings for Nintu (P12); *šākin mākalī ellūtim ana Ninazu*, arranging pure feasts for Ninazu (P17).

**makkūru**, sbst., goods.

*makkūr ilim u ekallim išriq*, he has stolen property from the god or from the temple (L6); *ana bēl makkūrim iriab*, he shall recompense the owner of the goods (L125); *makkūrum ana bēlišu itâr*, the property shall return its owner (L177); *ina makkūr bīt abim mitḫāriš izuzzū*, they shall make equal shares from the goods of the father's house (L165; cf. L166; 167; 170; 171a; with *leqû*, 172; with *zâzu*, 180; 181; 182; 183); *ina makkūrišu šalušti aplūtišu inaddiššumma*, he shall give him a third of his inheritance from his property (L191); *makkūram uḫtalliq*, it has destroyed property (L232); *ina makkūr ramanišu bīt imqutu ippeš*, he shall reconstruct the house that has collapsed from his own property (L232; cf. L235, with *dunnunu*, to repair a boat).

**mala**, adv., as much as.

*suluppī mala ina kirîm*, as many dates as there are in the orchard (L66); *ṣibtam mala [qaqqadišu]*, as much interest as the principal borrowing (§5.11); *mala [imḫuru]*, as much as he received (§5.12); *mala ilqû*, as much as he has taken (§5.12; 100; 106; 113); *mala iddinu*, as much as he has given (L113; 116); *mimma mala inaddinu*, whatever and however much he is going to give (L122; cf. with *nābālu*, L160; 161); *kaspam mala terḫatiša inaddiššim*, he shall give her enough silver for her marriage gift (L138; cf. with *ḫarāṣu*, to deduct from a dowry, L164); *mala libbiša la ušamṣīši*, he has not allowed her to distribute as much as she likes (L178; cf. L179).

**malāḫu**, sbst., boatman.

*malāḫum elep awīlim uṭṭebbīma uštēlliašši*, a boatman has sunk a man's boat but then refloats it (L238); *malāḫum elep 60 kur ana awīlim ipḫe*, the boatman has caulked a boat of 60 gur capacity for a man (L234; cf. L235); *malāḫum eleppam šuāti inaqqarma*, the boatman shall pull that boat apart (L235); *eleppašu ana malāḫim ana igrim iddinma malāḫum īgīma*, he has given his boat on hire to a boatman but the boatman was careless (L236; 236; cf. L237); *malāḫam u eleppam īgurma*, he has hired a boat and a boatman (L237; cf. L239); *malāḫum eleppam ana bēl eleppim iriab*, the boatman shall give the boat back to its owner (L236; cf. L237).

***malû***, vb., to be full, expire (*AHw*: *malû* IV). < *m-l-ʾ*.

*awīlum wardam amtam išāmma waraḫšu la imlāma benni elišu imtaqut*, a man has purchased a slave or a slave-girl but epilepsy has struck him before one month has expired (L278).

> ***mullû***, betray.

***malû***, adj., expired (of time), literally: full (*AHw*: *malû* I). < *m-l-ʾ*.

*ina ūmīšu la malûtim*, before his time has expired (L69+c, twice).

***mānaḫtu***, sbst., expenses. < *ʾ-n-ḫ*.

*aššum ina šattim maḫrītim mānaḫātišu la ilqû*, because he has not recovered his outlay from the previous year (L47); *mānaḫāt erēšim ana tamkārim inaddin*, he shall give the costs of cultivation to the merchant (L49).

***manû***, vb., to count. < *m-n-ʾ*.

1. to count: *ūmišu imannûma*, he shall count up the time he spent (L100).

2. to reckon together with: *itti mārīšu la imtanûšu*, he has not reckoned him in with his own sons (L190); *itti mārī ḫīrtim imtanûšunūti*, they shall count them with the sons of the first wife (L170).

***manû***, sbst., mana (*AHw*: *manû* II).

a third: *1/3 mana kaspam išaqqal*, he shall weigh out a third of a mana of silver (L114; 116; 201; 208; 214; 241; §5.3b, fragmentary); *1/3 mana kaspam inaddin*, he shall pay a third of a mana of silver (L252; cf. L140).

a half: *1/2 mana kaspam išaqqal*, he shall pay a half of a mana of silver (L59; 207; 212; cf. L156); *1/2 mana kaspam inaddin*, he shall pay a half of a mana of silver (L251).

one mana: *1 mana kaspam išaqqal*, he shall pay a mana of silver (L198; 203; cf. L24); *1 mana kaspam ana uzubbêm inaddiššim*, he shall give her one mana of silver as a divorce payment (L139).

***maqātu***, vb., to fall. < *m-q-t*.

1. to collapse: *bīt īpušu imqutma*, the house he built collapsed (L229; also *imqutu*, L232); *bīt imqutu ippeš*, he shall rebuild the house that collapsed (L232).

2. of a disease, to afflict: *benni elišu imtaqut*, epilepsy has struck him (L278).

> ***šumqutu***, to bring down.

***marāru* B**, vb., to harrow.

*eqlam mayyārī imaḫḫaṣ imarrar u išakkakma*, he shall break up the field with mattocks, he shall scuffle and harrow it (L44).

***markasu***, sbst., link, metaphysical bond (see *CAD* s.v. 4). < *r-k-s*.

*Nippur markas šāmē u erṣētim*, Nippur, the bond between heaven and earth (P4, alternatively read as *rikis*, see ***riksu***, bond).

***marṣu***, adj., fem. *maruštu*, diseased, painful, evil. < *m-r-ṣ*.

1. painful: *šerḫanam marṣam ubṭalliṭ*, he has eased a painful muscle (L221); *simmam marṣam ša la ipaššeḫū*, a wound that they cannot soothe (E30).

2. evil: *errētam maruštam līrurū*, let them curse him with an evil curse (E31); *awatum maruštum*, a harmful message (E23; *CAD* s.v. 2b2′).

***mārtu***, sbst., daughter.

1. in general: *mārat awīlim*, a gentleman's daughter (L175, twice; 176a, three times; 176b, twice); *mārat muškēnim*, a tradesman's daughter (L211); *abi martim*, the father of the daughter (L159; 160).

2. as the recipient of an inheritance or marriage gift: *ana aššatišu u mārtišu ul išaṭṭar*, he shall not assign to his wife or daughter (L38; cf. L39); *abum ana mārtišu nadīt gagîm lu sekretim šeriktam la išrukšim*, the father of a confined sister or a priestess has not given a dowry to his daughter (L180; cf. L182; 183; 184).

3. given or refused in marriage: *māratka ul aḫḫaz*, I shall not take your daughter (L159); *mārtī ul anaddikkum*, I shall not give you my daughter (L160); *mārtī ul taḫḫaz*, you shall not have my daughter (L161).

4. given as a pledge: *aššassu mārašu u mārassu ana kaspim iddin*, he has given his wife, son or daughter in exchange for silver (L117).

5. victim of violence and sexual abuse: *mārat awīlim imḫaṣma*, he has struck a gentleman's daughter (L209); *mārassu iltamad*, he had sex with his daughter (L154).

6. put to death: *mārassu idukkū*, they shall put his daughter to death (L210).

7. the daughter of a god: *Ninkarrak mārat Anim*, Ninkarrak, Anu's daughter (E30).

***māru***, sbst., son, member of group; when plural often children (male and female).

1. male child: *mārušu ilkam alākam ile'i*, his son is able to perform the duty (L28); *mārušu ṣeḫerma ilik abišu alākam la ile'i*, his son is small and unable to do the duty of his father (L29); *aššassu mārašu u*

*mārassu ana kaspim iddin*, he has sold his wife, his son or his daughter for silver (L117); *mimma ša ana mārīša innadnu*, whatever was given to her sons (L137); *mārīša urabba*, she shall raise her own sons (L137); *ištu mārīša urtabbu*, after she has raised her sons (L137); *itti mārīšu la imtanūšu*, they shall not reckon him together with his own sons (L190).

2. a son's various rights to an inheritance or a share of a dowry: *warki mutīša mārūša ul ipaqqarūši ummum warkassa ana mārīša ša irammû inaddin*, after her husband has gone her sons shall not claim against her, but the mother shall give her affairs to the one of her sons she loves (L150; 150); *šeriktaša ša mārīšama*, her dowry belongs to her sons (L162); *mārū maḫrûtum u warkûtum izuzzū*, the children of the previous and of the subsequent wife shall share (L173); *mārū ana ummātim ul izuzzū*, the sons shall not share according to their mothers (L167); *ana mārīšu nasāḫim panam ištakan*, he has made up his mind to disinherit his son (L168); *mārī anassaḫ*, I will disinherit my son (L168); *mārum arnam kabtam ša ina aplūtim nasāḫim la ublam abum mārašu ina aplūtim ul inassaḫ*, the son has not committed a serious offence for which he should be removed from the inheritance and the father shall not disinherit the son (L168; 168; cf. L169); *mārū ḫirtim u mārū amtim mitḫāriš izuzzū*, the sons of the first wife and the sons of the slave-girl shall share equally (L170; 170; cf. L171a; 171a); *aplum mār ḫīrtim*, the main heir is the son of the first wife (L170); *warkassa ša mārīšama*, her affairs belong to her sons (L171b); *nudunnâm ša mussa iddinušim ana mārīša izzib*, she shall leave the wedding gift her husband gave her for her sons (L172); *šeriktaša mārū ḫāwirišama ileqqû*, the sons of her first husband shall receive her dowry (L174); *mišlam mārat awīlim ana mārīša ileqqe*, the daughter of the free man shall take half for her sons (L176a; cf. L176b).

3. the birth of a son, or failure to give birth: *ḫīrtašu ša mārī la uldušum*, his chosen wife who has not borne him sons (L138); *mārī ūlissumma*, she bore him sons (L162; cf. *ūlissum*, L167; 170); *rabītišu ša mārī waldat*, his principal wife who had given birth to sons (L158); *mārī la ušaršīšu*, she has not provided him with sons (L163); *warka mārī irtašīma*, afterwards he has sons of his own (L191).

4. a son with a wet-nurse: *mārašu ana mušēniqtim iddinma*, he gave his son to a nurse (L194).

5. sons of another partner: *mārī ittalad*, she has given birth to sons (L135; 167); *mārū warki abišunu illakū*, the sons shall follow their father (L135); *ana mutiša warkîm mārī ittalad*, she has borne sons to her later husband (L173; cf. L174).

6. sons of a slave or slave-girl: *lu warad ekallim u lu warad muškēnim mārat awīlim īḫuzma mārī ittalad*, the slave of the palace or the slave of a workman has married the daughter of a free man and she has given birth to sons (L175); *bēl wardim ana mārī mārat awīlim ana wardūtim ul iraggum*, the master of the slave shall have no claim for slavery on the sons of the daughter of the free man (L175); *amassu ša mārī uldušum*, his slave-girl who has born him sons (L119); *amassu mārī ulissum*, his slave-girl bore him sons (L170); *abum ina bulṭišu ana mārī ša amtum uldušum mārūa iqtabi*, the father has said in his lifetime to the sons whom the slave-girl bore him, 'My sons' (L170; 170; cf. 171a; 171a); *itti mārī ḫīrtim imtanūšunūti*, they have reckoned them together with the sons of the chosen wife (L170); *andurār amtim u mārīša ištakan*, he shall arrange the emancipation of the slave-girl and her sons (L171a); *mārū ḫīrtim ana mārī amtim ana wardūtim ul iraggumū*, the children of the first wife shall make no claims about slavery against the sons of the slave-girl (L171a).

7. the son(s) of a priestess or court official: *mār girseqîm*, the son of a court attendant (L187; 192; 193); *mār sekretim*, the son of a confined priestess (L187; 192; 193); *šugītim ša mārī uldušum*, a priestess who has borne him sons (L137); *nadītim ša mārī ušaršûšu*, a sister who has provided him with sons (L137; cf. *mārī la ušaršīšuma*, L145); *mārī uštabši*, she produces sons (L144); *mārī ittalad*, she has given birth to sons (L146); *aššum mārī uldu*, because she gave birth to sons (L146); *mārī la ūlid*, she did not give birth to sons (L147).

8. sons of a widow: *almattum ša mārūša ṣeḫḫerū ana bīt šanîm erēbim panīša ištakan*, a widow whose sons are small has made up her mind to enter the house of another man (L177); *šāyyimānum ša unūt mārī almattim išammu ina kaspišu ītelli*, anyone who purchases the property of the sons of a widow shall forfeit his silver (L177).

9. a son's bride: *awīlum ana mārišu kallatam iḫīrma mārušu ilmassi*, a man chose a bride for his son and his son consummates the relationship (L155; 155; cf. L156; 156); *ana mārī ša iršû aššātim īḫuz ana mārišu ṣeḫrim aššatam la īḫuz*, he chose wives for the sons he had acquired but did not choose a wife for the youngest son (L166; 166).

10. guilty sons, and those involved in an accident: *mārūša aššum ina bītim šūṣîm usaḫḫamūši*, her sons pester her about leaving the house (L172); *mārī arnam immidū*, they shall impose a penalty on the sons (L172); *mārum abašu imtaḫaṣ*, a son has struck his father (L195); *šumma mār bēl bītim uštamīt mār itinnim šuāti idukkū*, if he has caused the death of the son of the owner of the house they shall kill the son of that builder (L230; 230).

11. ***māru reštû***, oldest son: *ana Marduk mārim reštîm ša Ea*, to Marduk the eldest son of Ea (P1); *Zababa qarrādum rabium mārum rēštûm ša Ekur*, the great warrior Zababa, the first son of Ekur (E26).
12. members of particular groups:
a. ***mār awīlim***, someone belonging to the more privileged class, or the son of such a person: *ina qāt mār awīlim u lu warad awīlim balum šībī u riksātim ištām*, he has made a purchase from a man's son or a man's slave without witnesses or contracts (L7); *mār awīlim ṣeḫram*, a man's small child (L14); *šumma mār awīlim mārašu idukkū*, if it is the son of a gentleman they shall kill his son (L116; 116); *awīlum īn mār awīlim uḫtappid*, a gentleman has destroyed the sight of a gentleman's son (L196); *mār awīlim lēt mār awīlim ša kīma šuāti imtaḫaṣ*, a gentleman's son has struck the cheek of a gentleman's son like himself (L203; 203; cf. L205; 207); *alpum šû mār awīlim ikkipma*, that ox has gored a gentleman's son (L251); *mār awīlim*, fragmentary (§5.3a).
b. ***mārū mātim***, native inhabitants: *wardum u amtum šunu mārū mātim*, the slave and slave-girl are children of the land (L280; cf. L281).
c. ***mār muškēnim***, someone belonging to the class of working men, or the son of such a person: *mār muškēnim*, a workman's son (L208; 216; 222).
d. ***mārū ugārim***, the people who are working the arable land: *mārū ugārim ša še'šunu mû ublū*, the farm labourers whose grain the waters have destroyed (L54).
e. ***mār ummānim***, someone belonging to the class of skilled men, or the son of such a person: *mār ummānim ṣeḫram ana tarbītim ilqēma šipir qātišu uštāḫissu*, one of the tradesmen has taken a child in adoption and has made him skilled in the job he does (L188); *awīlum mār ummānim iggar*, a man has hired some craftsman (L274).

*maruštu* > ***marṣu***, diseased.

***mārūtu***, sbst., adoption.

*ṣeḫram ina mêšu ana mārūtim ilqēma urtabbīšu*, he has taken a child at birth for adoption and has brought him up (L185; cf. L186; cf. *mārūtišu*, 190; 191).

***maṣṣarūtu***, sbst., custody.

*ina qāt mār awīlim lū warad awīlim balum šībī u riksātim ištām u lū ana maṣṣarūtim imḫur*, he has made a purchase from a gentleman's son or a gentleman's slave or accepted for deposit without witnesses or contracts (L7); *ana maṣṣarūtim inaddin*, he would give on deposit (L122, twice; cf. L123; 124; 125, twice).

*maṣû*, to be equal > ***šumṣû***, to grant discretion.

***mašāru***, vb., to drag. < *m-š-r*.
*ina eqlim šuāti ina liātim imtanaššarūšu*, they shall drag him all over that field with oxen (L256).

***maškakātu***, sbst., pl., harrow. < *š-k-k*.
*ḫarbam u lu maškakātim ištariq*, he has stolen a plough or a harrow (L260).

***maškanu***, sbst., threshing place. < *š-k-n*.
*ina našpakim u lu ina maškanim še'am ilteqe*, he has taken grain from the granary or the threshing place (L113, twice).

***mašqītu***, sbst., watering place. < *š-q-'*.
*šā'im mirītim u mašqītim ana Lagaš u Girsim*, providing Lagash and Girsu with pastureland and water supplies (P13).

***matima***, part., whenever.
*ana warkiāt ūmī ana matima*, for ever until the end of time (E14).

***mātu***, sbst., land, country, nation.
1. a well-administered and blessed land: *šā'im šīmāt mātim*, fixing the destiny of the land (P1); *ṣulūl mātim*, a shade for the land (P8); *šīr mātim uṭīb*, I improved the health of the nation (E5); *kittam u mīšaram ina pī mātim aškun*, I put justice and righteousness in the mouth of the land (P22); *dīn mātim ana diānim purussê mātim ana parāsim*, to judge the cases in the land and to take the decisions for the land (E8; 8); *mātam uštēšer*, I put the land straight (E12); *dīn mātim ša adīnu purussē mātim ša aprusu*, the law of the land which I enacted, the decisions of national importance which I took (E14; 14; 15; 15); *mīšaram ina mātim ana šūpîm*, to make justice evident in the land (P3); *mīšarī ina mātim lištēpi*, may he display justice in the land (E10); *māssu šutēšuram ile'i*, he will be able to keep his land straight (E15); *mātam ussam kīnam u rīdam damqam ušaṣbitu*, I who made the land adopt proper customs and good traditions (E1); *šarrum ša ina mātim ibbaššû*, any king who will be in the country (E14); *ina mātišu raggam u ṣēnam lissuḫ šīr nišīšu liṭīb*, let him weed out evil and wickedness from the land and let him bring prosperity into the lives of his people (E16).
2. a cursed land: *šumšu u zikiršu ina mātim la šubšâm*, stopping him from producing a reputation or fame in the land (E20); *šulput mātišu ḫalāq nišīšu*, the plague on his land and the destruction of his people (E21); *ša nasāḫ išdī šarrūtišu u ḫalāq mātišu liškunšum*, let him arrange that his land be destroyed and the foundations of his kingdom be torn up (E23); *massu ina ḫušaḫḫim u bubūtim liḫalliq eli ālišu ezziš lissīma*, may he destroy his land by famine and pestilence, may he shout with rage over his city (E25); *māssu ana til abūbim litēr*, turn his land into a flooded rubbish tip (E25); *šuāti zērāšu massu ṣābāšu nišīšu u ummānšu errētam maruštam līrurū*, let them curse him, his

descendants, his land, his soldiers, his people and his army with a terrible curse (E31).

3. a foreign land: *ina māt nukurtim wardam amtam ša awīlim ištām inūma ina libbū mātim ittalkamma bēl wardim u lu amtim lu warassu u lu amassu ūteddi*, he has purchased a man's slave or slave-girl in a foreign land but, when he has come to his own country, the owner of the slave or slave-girl recognises his slave or slave-girl (L280; 280); *wardum u amtum šunu mārū mātim*, the slave and slave-girl were born in the land (L280); *mārū mātim šanītim*, natives of a different country (L281); *ana māt nukurtišu kamîš līrûšu*, let her remove him to a hostile land in bonds (E27).

4. the land of Sumer and Akkad: *mušēṣi nūrim ana māt Šumerim u Akkadîm*, who sheds light over the land of Sumer and Akkad (P21); *ina utliya nišī māt Šumerim u Akkadîm ukīl*, I protected the people of Sumer and Akkad with my own body (E7).

5. the whole world; pl., nations: *kīma Šamaš ana ṣalmāt qaqqadim waṣêmma mātim nuwwurim*, to illuminate the land like Shamash rising over the mass of humanity (P3); *Nintu bēltum ṣīrtum ša mātātim*, Nintu, the noble lady of the nations (E29).

***mâtu***, vb., to die. < *m-ʾ-t*.

1. of a human being: *sinništum šî imtūt*, that woman has died (L173; 210; 212); *amtum šî imtūt*, that slave-girl has died (L214); *ṣiḫrum šû ina qāt mušēniqtim imtūt*, that boy has died in the hands of the nurse (L194).

2. of an animal: *alpam īgurma ilum imḫassuma imtūt*, a man has hired an ox but it has died because of an act of a god (L249); *ina bīt nēpīša ina šīmātiša imtūt*, it has died naturally in the house of the creditor (L115); *ina maḫāṣim u lu ina uššušim imtūt*, it has died from beating or abuse (L116; cf. L207).

> ***šumūtu***, cause death.

*maṭû*, to be short > ***muṭṭu***, to lessen; ***šumṭû***, to treat badly.

***maṭû***, adj., small, light. < *m-ṭ-ʾ*.

*kaspam ina abnim maṭītim*, silver according to the light weight (§5.13); *šeʾam ina sūtim maṭītim iddin*, he gave the grain according to the little measure (§5.13).

***mayyāru***, sbst., plough, mattock.

*eqlam ša iddû mayyārī imaḫḫaṣ*, he shall break up the field he has neglected with mattocks (L43; cf. L44).

***mēgûtu***, sbst., neglect. < *ʾ-g-ʾ*.

*alpam īgurma ina mēgûtim u lu ina maḫāṣim uštamīt*, he has hired an ox and let it die through neglect or through rough treatment (L245).

***melammu***, sbst., radiance.

*muštasḫir melemmē Emeteursag*, putting a radiance all around Emeteursag (P9); *melemmī šarrūtim līṭeršu ḫaṭṭašu lišbir šīmātišu līrur*, may he take from him the splendour of his kingdom, break his sceptre and curse his destiny (E19).

***mēreštu* B**, sbst., arable land. < *ʾ-r-š*.

*mušaddil mēreštim ša Dilbat*, who develops the ploughland in Dilbat (P11).

*merētu* > ***mirītu***, pasture.

***mêšu***, vb., to disdain. < *m-ʾ-š*.

*errētiya imēšma*, he has disdained my threats (E19).

***migru***, sbst., favourite. < *m-g-r*.

*migir telītim*, favourite of the capable lady (P13); *migir Ištar*, favourite of Ishtar (P21).

***miḫru***, sbst., equal. < *m-ḫ-r*.

*šumma awīlum šinni awīlim meḫrišu ittadi šinnašu innaddû*, if a gentleman has knocked out the tooth of a gentleman like himself they shall knock out his own tooth (L200).

***mīlu***, sbst., flood. < *m-l-ʾ*.

*zunnī ina šamê mīlam ina naqbim līṭeršu*, let him deprive him of the rain from the sky and the flood from the wadi (E25).

***mimma***, pronoun, something.

1. non-negated: *mimma bīšam ana pašārim iddin*, whatever goods he gave for resale (L104).

2. with associated negative, nothing: *ḫarrānša uzzubūša mimma ul innaddiššim*, nothing at all shall be given her for her journey or her divorce settlement (L141).

3. ***mimma mala***, whatever and however much: *mimma mala inaddinu*, whatever and however much he gives (L122); *mimma mala ibbablušum*, whatever and however much he brought to him (L160; 161).

4. ***mimma ša***, whatever: *mimma ša nadānim la ibaššišum*, there is nothing at all in his possession for paying (L66); *mimma ša ina qātišu ibaššû*, whatever he has in his possession (§5.15); [*mimma ša ina*] *nabalkattim* [*ḫalqu*], whatever was lost because of the damage [L68+b, but not restored thus by Finet]; *ina mimma ša iddinu ītelli*, he shall forfeit some of whatever he has paid (L67+a; §5.10, partly restored; [5.13]; 5.14); *nakrum mimma ša našû uštaddīšu*, an enemy makes him throw down whatever he was carrying (L103); *mimma ša tamkārum iddinušum*, whatever the merchant gave him (L107); *mimma ša ilqû*, whatever he received (L107); *mimma ša šūbulu*, whatever had been brought (L112, twice); *mimma ša ikkiru*, whatever he denied (L124); *mimma ša irgumu*, whatever he claimed (L126); *mimma ša ana mārīša*

*innadnu*, whatever was given to her sons (L137); *mimma ša ibbablušum*, whatever had been brought to him (L159); *mimma ša mussa u šî ištu innemdū iršû*, whatever she and her husband have acquired after they have come together (L176a; cf. L176b); *mimma ša abuša iddinušim*, whatever her father gave to her (L178); *mimma ša uḫalliqu*, whatever he lost (L232); *mimma ša ina libbiša uḫalliqu*, whatever he lost from inside it (L237, a vessel that has sunk); *mimma ša ina eleppišu halqu*, whatever is missing from the vessel (L240); *apkal ilī mudē mimma šumšu*, the wisest of the gods who knows all kinds of things (E22).

5. ***mimma šumšu***, something else, anything at all; in a sequence: —a. in a series of items: *lu kaspam lu ḫurāṣam lu wardam lu amtam lu alpam lu immeram lu imēram u lu mimma šumšu*, silver, gold, a slave, a slave-girl, an ox, a sheep, an ass or something else (L7); *kaspam ḫurāṣam u mimma šumšu ana maṣṣarūtim inaddin*, he gives silver, gold or something else for safe-keeping (L122; cf. L124); *u ina mimma šumšu mala iddinu ītelli*, and he shall forfeit whatever and however much he gave (L113); *še'am šipātim šamnam sulippī u mimma šumšu*, grain, wool, oil, dates or anything else (L237).

b. as the principal object of a verb: *mušaklil mimma šumšu ana Nippur*, gathering together everything for Nippur (P4); *murappiš mimma šumšu ana Emeslam*(!), widening Emeslam in every way (P10); *apkal ilī mudē mimma šumšu*, wisest of the gods who knows all kinds of things (E22).

6. fragmentary: *bēl...mimma...iriab* (L68+b).

***mimmû***, sbst., property.

*mimmûšu bīšam u še'am*, whatever property or grain he has (§5.2); *awīlum mimmâšu ana maṣṣarūtim iddinma*, the man has delivered his property for safe-keeping (L125); *šumma awīlum ša mimmûšu ḫalqu mimmâšu ḫalqam ina qāti awīlim iṣṣabat*, if a man who has some property missing has discovered the missing property in the possession of another man (L9; 9); *mimmâšu ḫalqam*, the missing property (L23, twice); *mimmûšu itti mimmê bēl bītim iḫtaliq*, his property has been lost as well as the property of the owner of the house (L125; 125; cf. L126, twice); *mimmê ḫaliq iqtabi*, he said, 'Something of mine is lost' (L126); *bēl bītim mimmâšu ḫalqam ištene'ima*, the owner of the house shall continue to search for the lost property (L125); *eleppašu u mimmâšu ḫalqam iriabšum*, he shall recompense him for the vessel and whatever was missing (L240).

***miqittu***, sbst., damage. < *m-q-t*.

*miqitti tarbaṣim bēl tarbaṣim imaḫḫaršu*, the owner of the enclosure shall receive the debris from the enclosure (L266).

***mirītu***, sbst., pasture. < *r-ʾ-ʾ*.

*mirītim u mašqītim*, pastureland and water sources (P13).

*mīru* (Szlechter, cf. *CAD mīru* A, young bull) > ***alpum ša qabla***, leading ox.

***mīšaru***, sbst., justice. < *ʾ-š-r*.

1. acts of justice: *dīnāt mīšarim ša Ḫammurabi šarrum le'ûm ukinnuma*, just decisions which Hammurabi the all-powerful king enforced (E1); *mīšaram ina mātim ana šūpîm*, to make justice evident in the land (P3); *kittam u mīšaram ina pī mātim aškun*, I set justice and righteousness in the mouths of the people (P22); *ina qibīt Šamaš dayyānim rabîm ša šamê u erṣetim mīšarī ina mātim lištēpi*, may Shamash, the almighty judge in heaven and earth, let my justice shine over the land! (E10); *nišīšu ina mīšarim lirē*, he will surely feed his people in righteousness (E18); *awât mīšarim ša ina narîya ašṭuru*, the statement of justice that I have inscribed on my stele (E14).

2. king of justice: *Ḫammurabi šar mīšarim*, Hammurabi the king of justice (E17; cf. E18); *awâtiya šūqurātim ina narîya ašṭurma ina maḫar ṣalmiya šar mīšarim ukīn*, I have written my precious words on the stela and placed them on the picture of me, the king of justice (E8; cf. E11).

***mīšītu***, sbst., confusion. < *ʾ-š-ʾ*.

*uznam u nēmeqam līṭeršuma ina mīšītim littarūšu*, let him deprive him of wisdom and understanding and may they lead him away in confusion (E22).

***mišlānū***, sbst. pl., halves: *u lu ana mišlāni u lu ana šaluš eqlam iddin*, whether he has divided the field in halves or in thirds (L46).

***mišlu***, sbst., half.

*1/2 mana kaspam išaqqal*, he shall pay half a mana of silver (L59; 207; 212; cf. L156; with *nadānu*, L251); *kaspam mišil šīmišu išaqqal*, he shall pay half his value in silver (L220; cf. L199; with *nadānu*, L238; 247); *mišlam bēl wardim ileqqe mišlam mārat awīlim ana mārīša ileqqe*, the owner of the slave shall take a half and the man's daughter shall take a half for her children (L176a; 176a; 176b; 176b); *2 1/2 uṭṭet kaspam idīša ina ūmim ištēn inaddin*, he shall pay two and a half grains of silver as the charge for it for one day (L276).

***mitḫāriš***, *adv*., equally. < *m-ḫ-r*.

*bēl kirîm u nukaribbum mitḫāriš izuzzū bēl kirîm zittašu inassaqma*, the owner of the orchard and the cultivator shall share equally but the owner of the orchard shall choose his part (L60); *maḫar ilim mitḫāriš izuzzū*, they shall share equally in the presence of the god (L77+f; cf. L165; 167; 170).

***mû* A**, sbst., pl., water.

1. water supply, or lack of it: *šākin mê nuḫšim ana nišīšu*, ensuring

abundant water for its people (P8); *ina la mê še'um ina eqlim la ittabši*, there has not been any grain in the field because of a lack of water (L48); *eliš ina balṭūtim lissuḫšu šapliš ina erṣetim eṭemmašu mê lišaṣmi*, may he cut him off from those living above and make his shadow thirst for water in the land below (E23).

2. water that destroys crops: *ugāram mê uštābil*, he has allowed the water to cascade over the land (L53; cf. L56); *mārū ugārim ša še'šunu mû ublū*, the workers in the fields whose grain the water has destroyed (L54); *eqel itēšu mê uštābil*, he has allowed the water to erode his neighbour's land (L55); *awīlum mê iptēma*, a man has let out water (L56).

3. water used for trial and punishment: *ikassûšunūtima ana mê inaddû-šunūti*, they shall bind them together and throw them into the water (L129; cf. L155); *sinništam šuāti ukannûšima ana mê inaddûši*, they shall prove that woman guilty and throw her into the water (cf. L133b; 143); *sābītam šuāti ukannūšima ana mê inaddûši*, they shall prove that beer-seller guilty and throw her into the water (L108).

4. in simile: *ḫalāq nišīšu tabāk napištišu kīma mê*, the loss of his people and the pouring out of his life like water (E21).

5. ***ṣeḫrum ina mêšu***, a newborn baby: *awīlum ṣeḫram ina mêšu ana mārūtim ilqēma urtabbīšu*, a man has taken a newborn baby into adoption and has brought him up (L185).

***mû* B**, sbst., pl., ritual.

*šarrum ša ina Ninua ina Emesmes ušūpi'u mê Ištar*, the king who performs the ritual for Ishtar in Emesmes in Nineveh (P20).

***muballiṭu***, sbst., reviving. < *b-l-ṭ*.

*bēlum muballiṭ Uruk*, the lord who revives Uruk (P8).

***mubbibu***, sbst., purifying. < *'-b-b*.

*mubbib šuluḫ Eabzu tīb kibrāt erbettim*, ensuring the purity of the lustrations in Eabzu, striding through all four regions of the world (P5).

***mubbiru***, sbst., accuser. < *'-b-r*.

*mubbiršu iddâk*, his accuser shall be killed (L1); *mubbiršu bīssu itabbal*, the one who made the allegations against him shall take possession of his house (L2); *bīt mubbirišu itabbal*, he shall take away the house of his accuser (L2).

***mudammiqu***, sbst., benefitting. < *d-m-q*.

*mudammiqat igirrēya*, making my reputation good (E21).

***muddišu***, sbst., making new. < *'-d-š*.

*qarrādum gāmil Larsa muddiš Ebabbar ana Šamaš rēṣišu*, the hero who showed favour to Larsa, who made Ebabbar anew for Shamash his helper (P8).

***mudeššû***, sbst., making abundant. < *d-š-ʾ*.
*mukīn uṣurātim ša Keš muddeššī mākalī ellūtim ana Nintu*, who established the design of Kesh, who made abundant supplies of sacred food for Nintu (P12).

***mudû***, sbst., acquainted with. < *ʾ-d-ʾ*.
*šībī mudē ḫulqišu itbalam*, he has brought the witnesses who know it is his property (L9, three times; 10; cf. L11); *ilu šarrī mudē igigallim*, the divine king who knows great wisdom (P11); *apkal ilī mudē mimma šumšu*, the wisest of the gods, knowing about everything (E22).

***mudûtu***, sbst., knowledge. < *ʾ-d-ʾ*.
*šībū mudē ḫulqim mudūssunu maḫar ilim iqabbûma*, the witnesses who recognize the missing property shall say before the god what they know (L9).

***mugallitu***, sbst., villain. < *g-l-t*.
*nišī dadmī aburrī ušarbiṣ mugallitam ul ušaršīšināti*, I let the people lie down in well-watered pastures, I let no villain possess them (E5).

***mugarrinu***, sbst., heaping up. < *q-r-n*.
*mugarrin karê ana Uraš gašrim*, who fills up the granaries in mighty Urash (P11).

***muḫaddû***, sbst., gladdening. < *ḫ-d-ʾ*.
*muḫaddi libbi Ištar*, who makes the heart of Ishtar rejoice (P13).

***mukammiru***, sbst., heaping up. < *k-m-r*.
*mukammer nuḫšim u ṭuḫdim*, the plentiful and abundant provider (P4); *mukammer ḫiṣbim ana Anim u Ištar*, who heaped up luxury for Anum and Ishtar (P8).

***mukannišu***, sbst., controlling. < *k-n-š*.
*mukanniš dadmē nār Purattim ittum Dagan bānîšu*, who controls the River Euphrates communities under the guidance of his creator god Dagan (P17).

***mukillu***, sbst., holding. < *k-ʾ-l*.
*mukīl nindabê rabûtim ana Eninnu*, the one who holds the magnificent offerings in Eninnu (P13).

***mukīnu***, sbst., founder, one who makes secure. < *k-ʾ-n*.
*mukīn uṣurātim ša Keš*, who established the design of Kish (P12); *mukīn išdī Sipparim*, who fixed the foundations of Sippar (P7); *mukinnu išdīšin qerbum Bābilim šulmāniš*, who fixed their foundations in the midst of Babylon safely (P18); *mukinni Ištar ina Eulmaš*, who set Ishtar securely in the Eulmash (P18).

***mullû*** **1**, vb., to fill, hand over. < *m-l-ʾ*.
*ana qāt nakrīšu limallīšuma*, let him hand him over to his enemy (E27).

***mullû*** **2**, sbst., raising. < *'-l-'*.

*mullî rēš Eanna mukammer ḫiṣbim ana Anim u Ištar*, who raised up high the pinnacles of Eanna, who heaped up luxury for Anum and Ishtar (P8).

***munaggiru***, sbst., informer. < *n-g-r*.

*munaggiršu bīssu itabbal*, the one who has informed about him shall take away his house (L26).

***munaḫḫišu***, sbst., giving prosperity, munificent. < *n-ḫ-š*.

*munahhiš Urim*, who made Ur prosper (P6).

***munakkipu***, sbst., tossing. < *n-k-p*.

*rīmum kadrum munakkip zā'irī*, the raging ox that tosses its opponents (P10).

***munammiru***, sbst., shedding light. < *n-w-r*.

*rubûm na'adum munawwer pani Tišpak*, the obedient prince, who sheds his light on the faces of Tishpak (P17).

*munawwiru* > ***munammiru***, shedding light.

***munēḫu***, sbst., quietening. < *n-'-ḫ*.

*munēḫ libbi Adad qurādim in Bīt Karkara*, who quietens the heart of Adad the hero at Bitkarkara (P14).

***munnabtu***, sbst., fugitive. < *'-b-t*.

*aššum ālšu izēruma innabitu aššat munnabtim ana mutiša ul itâr*, because he has hated his city and fled, the wife of the fugitive shall not return to her husband (L136).

***mupaḫḫiru***, sbst., assembling. < *p-ḫ-r*.

*ṣulūl mātim mupaḫḫir nišī sapḫātim ša Isin muṭaḫḫid nuḫšim bīt Egalmaḫ*, a shade for the land, who massed together the people from everywhere in Isin, who spreads around vast riches in the shrine of Egalmah (P8).

***mupparkû***, sbst., abandoning, neglecting. < *p-r-k*.

*narām Tutu murīš Barsippa na'dum la mupparkûm ana Ezida*, loved by Tutu, making Barsippa exult, the devoted one who never neglects Ezida (P11).

***muqqelpītu***, sbst., drifting. < *q-l-p-'*.

> ***ša muqqelpītim***, the one in charge of a ship drifting downstream.

***murabbītu***, sbst., foster mother. < *r-b-'*.

*ana abim murabbīšu u ummim murabbītišu ul abī atta ul ummī atti iqtabi*, he has said to the father who has brought him up and to the mother who has brought him up, 'You are not my father. You are not my mother' (L192; cf. *ummam murabbīssu*, L193).

***murabbû***, sbst., foster father. < *r-b-'*.

*ana abim murabbīšu*, to the father who has brought him up (L 192; cf. *abum*, L191; *abam*, L193).

***murappišu***, sbst., extending. < *r-p-š*.
*mušāter Kutî murappiš mimma šumšu ana Meslam*, who made Kuta excellent, who expanded Meslam in every way (P10).

***murīšu***, sbst., bringing pleasure. < *r-ʾ-š*.
*narām Tutu murīš Barsippa*, whom Tutu loves and who makes Borsippa rejoice (P10).

***murṣu***, sbst., disease. < *m-r-ṣ*.
*murṣam kabtam asakkam lemnam simmam marṣam ša la ipaššeḫū asûm qerebšu la ilammadu*, a terrible illness, with pain and fever and weeping sores, which they cannot relieve, which no physician understands (E30).

***murteddû***, sbst., driver. < *r-d-ʾ*.
*ereqqam u murteddīša īgur*, he hired a wagon and a driver for it (L271).

*musaru* > ***mušaru***, surface area measure.

***muṣīru***, sbst., designing. < *ṣ-ʾ-r*.
*mušalbiš warqim gigunē Aya muṣīr bīt Ebabbar ša kî šubat šamāʾi*, who covered the chapels of Aya with greenery, who made famous the Ebabbar shrine, which is like a heavenly home (P7).

***mušaddilu***, sbst., developing.
*mušaddil mēreštim ša Dilbat mugarrin karê ana Uraš gašrim*, who develops the land to be ploughed in Dilbat, who fills up the huge granaries in Urash (P11).

***mušaklil***, sbst., providing, fulfilling. < *k-l-l*.
*mušaklil mimma šumšu ana Nippur*, supplying Nippur with whatever it needs (P4); *mušaklil tērētim ša Sugal*, who fulfils the oracles for Sugal (P13).

***mušakšidu***, sbst., granting victory. < *k-š-d*.
*mušakšidu irnittiya*, granting me the victory (E28).

***mušalbišu***, sbst., decorating. < *l-b-š*.
*mušalbiš warqim gigunē Aya muṣīr bīt Ebabbar ša kî šubat šamāʾi*, who covered the chapels of Aya with greenery, who designed the shrine of Ebabbar like a home in heaven (P7; see *CAD labāšu*, 5.c.1, line 22a).

***mušallimu***, sbst., bringing peace. < *š-l-m*.
*ilū rabûtim ibbûninnima anākuma rēʾûm mušallimum*, the great gods called me and so I am the shepherd who brings peace (E6).

***mušarbû***, sbst., extolling. < *r-b-ʾ*.
*mušarbi zikru Bābilim muṭīb libbi Marduk bēlišu*, who made the name of Babylon famous, who made the name of Marduk his lord happy (P5); *mušarbû šarrūtišu*, those who have made his kingdom magnificent (P16; cf. E20).

***mušāriku***, sbst., lengthening. < *ʾ-r-k.*

*apkal ilī mudē mimma šumšu mušāriku ūm balāṭiya*, counsellor of the gods, who knows about everything, who lengthens the days of my life (E22).

***mušaršidu***, sbst., protecting. < *r-š-d.*

*mušaršid šubat Kiš*, who made Kish a secure abode (P9); *mušaršidu šubātišin in nuḫšim*, who made their homes secure in every way (P16).

***mušaru***, sbst., measure of surface area, corresponding to 12 square cubits.

*ana 1 musar bītim 2 šiqil kaspam ana qīštišu inaddišum*, for one mushar-area of building he shall pay him two shekels of silver in compensation (L228).

***mušassiku***, sbst., disposing. < *n-s-k.*

*ina awat Marduk bēliya uṣurātūa mušassikam ay iršia*, may Marduk, my lord, forbid anyone to throw out my plans (E10).

***mušātiru***, sbst., making excellent. < *w-t-r.*

*mušāter Kutî murappiš mimma šumšu ana Meslam*, who made Kuta excellent, who expanded Meslam in every way (P10).

***mušēniqtu***, sbst., nurse. < *ʾ-n-q.*

*mārašu ana mušēniqtim iddinma ṣiḫrum šû ina qāt mušēniqtim imtūt mušēniqtum balum abišu u ummišu ṣiḫram šaniamma irtakas*, he has given his son to a nurse but that child has died in the care of the nurse and the nurse has then made an agreement about another child without the knowledge of the father and the mother (L194; 194; 194).

***mušeppû***, sbst., silencing. < *š-p-ʾ.*

*mutêr lamassišu damiqtim ana ālim Aššur mušeppi nābiḫī*, who has brought back the protective statues to the city of Asshur, who silences the objectors (P19).

***mušēpû***, sbst., making visible. < *ʾ-p-ʾ.*

*mušēpī kīnātim mušūšer ammi*, who makes justice appear, who keeps the people straight (P19).

***mušēṣû***, sbst., bringing out. < *ʾ-ṣ-ʾ.*

*šarrum dannum šamšu Bābilim mušēṣi nūrim ana māt Šumerim u Akkadîm*, the mighty king, the sun of Babylon, who brings out the light all over the lands of Sumer and Akkad (P21).

***mušešqû***, sbst., giving to drink. < *š-q-ʾ.*

*mušešqi nuḫšim ana Meslam*, who supplies water to Meslam abundantly (P15; variant *mušašqi*).

***mušīmu***, sbst., deciding fate. < *š-ʾ-m.*

*mušīm šīmātim*, controller of destiny (E20).

***muškēnu***, sbst., working citizen, commoner, craftsman.

1. owning property: [*bīt muškēnim*] *išām*, he has purchased the house of a commoner (§4.12); [*ana*] *bīt muškēnim šāmim*, in order to pur-

chase the house of a commoner (§4.12); [*bīt muškēnim ana*] *bēlišu itār*, the house of the commoner shall return to its owner (§4.12); fragmentary: *ša muškēnim*, of the commoner (§4.12).
2. owning a slave: *lu warad muškēnim lu amat muškēnim*, a slave of a working man or a slave-girl of a working-man (L15; 15); *warad ekallim u lu warad muškēnim*, a palace slave or a worker's slave (L175; 176a; 176a; 176a).
3. with a son or daughter who has the same social status: *mār muškēnim*, a working man's son (L208; 216; 222); *mārat muškēnim*, a working man's daughter (L211).
4. victim of an accident or of a violent incident: *muškēnum lēt muškēnim imtaḫaṣ*, a working man has struck the cheek of another working man (L204; 204); *šinni*(!) *muškēnim*, a working man's tooth (L201); *īn muškēnim uḫtappid*, he has poked out the eye of a working man (L198); *eṣemti*(!) *muškēnim ištebir*, he has broken the bone of a working man (L198); *asûm simmam kabtam warad muškēnim ina karzilli siparrim īpušma uštamīt*, a doctor has inflicted a serious wound on the slave of a commoner with the surgical knife (L219).
5. considered to be worth less than someone of the *awīlu* class:
a. awarded less compensation for damages: *šumma ša muškēnim adi 10-šu iriāb*, if it belongs to a workman, he shall repay ten times its value (L8; see also paragraph 4, L198; 201; 204).
b. pays less compensation for divorcing his childless wife: *šumma muškēnum 1/3 man kaspam inaddiššim*, if he is a commoner he shall give her a third of a shekel of silver (L140).
c. pays less for medical help (see above paragraph 3, L222).

***mušpazzir***, sbst., protecting. < *p-z-r*.
*mušpazzir nišī Malgīm in karašîm*, who protected the people of Malgim from catastrophe (P16).

***muštālu***, sbst., arbitrator. < *š-ʾ-l*.
*muštālum gitmālum*, the perfect arbitrator (P13).

***muštakīn***, sbst., arranging. < *k-ʾ-n*.
*munēḫ libbi Adad qurādim in Bīt Karkara muštakkin simātim in Eudgalgal*, quietening the heart of Adad, the hero in Bit Karkara, arranging the destinies in Eudgalgal (P14).

***muštasḫiru***, sbst., surrounding. < *s-ḫ-r*.
*muštasḫir melemmē Emeteursag*, who made Emeteursag shine on every side (P9).

***muštēmiqu***, sbst., making supplication. < *ʾ-m-q*.
*wašrum muštēmiqum bābil ḫegallim ana Egišnugal*, who by his devotion and by his intercession gathered in the wealth to Egishnugal

(P6); *na'dum muštēmiqum ana ilī rabûtim*, the obedient one who displays his wisdom to the mighty gods (P20).

***mušteṣbû***, sbst., arranging. < *ṣ-b-'*.

*mušteṣbî parṣī rabûtim ša Ištar*, who arranged the performance of the magnificent ceremonies for Ishtar (P9).

***muštēširu***, sbst., keeping straight. < *'-š-r*.

*muštēšer šaknat napištim*, who keeps straight the certainties of life (E23).

***muštešmû***, sbst., one who is obeyed. < *š-m-'*.

*šarrum muštešmi kibrāt arba'im*, I am the king who is obeyed in the four parts of the world (P21).

***mūšu***, sbst., night.

*ūmam ana mūšim litēršumma*, let him turn his day into night (E26).

***mušūšeru***, sbst., keeping straight. < *w-š-r*.

*mušūšer ammi*, keeping the people straight (P19).

***mutammiḫu***, sbst., grasping. < *t-m-ḫ*.

*mutammeḫ ayyābī*, who takes hold of the enemy (P13).

***mutēru***, sbst., returning. < *t-'-r*.

*mutêr Eridu ana ašrišu*, bringing back Eridu to its position (P5); *mutêr lamassišu damiqtim ana ālim Aššur*, who has brought back the protective statues to the city of Asshur (P19).

***muttabbilu***, sbst., leader. < *w-b-l*.

*emqum muttabbilum*, the wise one, the organizer (P16; see *CAD* M, 302, s.v. a).

***muttatu***, sbst., half, part, section.

*muttassu ugallabū*, they shall shave off half his hair (L127); *muttat eqlim kirîm u bīšim inaddinūšimma mārīša urabba*, they shall give her a section of the field, orchard or property, and she shall bring up her sons (L137).

***mutu***, sbst., husband.

1. a father gives away his daughter to be married: *ana mutim iddišši*, he has given her to a husband (L183; cf. L184, also *inaddinūši*, L184).
2. a husband chosen by his wife: *mutu libbiša iḫḫassi*, she shall choose the husband she prefers (L137; 156, vnt. *mut*; *mut libbiša* L172).
3. one living together with his wife: *ina bīt mutiša uššab*, she shall dwell in the house of her husband (L141; cf. L149); *ina šubat mutiša uššab*, she shall dwell in the home of her husband (L171b); *sinništum šî ina bīt mutiša ul uṣṣi*, that woman shall not leave her husband's house (L172); *mussa ušamṭa*, she made little of her husband (L141); *mussa waṣīma magal ušamṭāši*, her husband disparaged her greatly when he was out (L142); *sinništum mussa izērma ul taḫḫazanni iqtabi*, a woman has hated her husband and said, 'You shall not hold me'

(L142); *bīssa usappaḫ mussa ušamṭa*, she wasted away her household and disparaged her husband (L143).
4. one separated from his wife: [*adi mussa ṣabtu*], when her husband has been captured (L133a); *ina warka mussa ittūramma*, after a time her husband has come back (L135); *ana mutiša ul itâr*, she shall not return to her husband (L136).
5. one who has children by a slave-girl: *amtam ana mutiša iddinma*, she gave a slave-girl to her husband (L144; 146).
6. one who is cuckolded, or suspects his wife of infidelity: *aššat awīlim mussa ubbiršima itti zikarim šanîm ina utūlim la iṣṣabit*, a man's wife is accused by her husband of lying with another man but has not been caught (L131); *ana mutiša Id išalli*, she shall jump into the River for the sake of her husband (L132).
7. a husband (or his wife) with a debt: *aššum bēl ḫubullim ša mutiša la ṣabātiša mussa irtakkis*, her husband has agreed that the one to whom her husband is in debt may not seize her (L151; 151); *bēl ḫubulliša mussa ul iṣabbatu*, the one to whom she is in debt may not seize her husband (L151).
8. one who divorces or is divorced: *mussa ezēbša iqtabi*, her husband has said he will leave her (L141, twice); *mussa sinništam šanītam iḫḫaz*, her husband may take another woman (L141).
9. one who is murdered: *aššat awīlim aššum zikarim šanîm mussa ušdīk*, a woman has let her husband be killed because of another man (L153).
10. a deceased husband's estate, or that of his deceased wife: *warki mutiša mārūša ul ipaqqarūši*, after her husband's death her sons shall have no grounds for complaint against her (L150); *ana šerikti sinništim šuāti mussa ul iraggum*, her husband shall not lay claim to the dowry of that woman (L163); *šeriktaša u nudunnâm ša mussa iddinušim*, the dowry and wedding gift which her husband gave her (L171b); *mussa nudunnâm la iddiššim*, her husband did not give her any wedding gift (L172); *nudunnâm ša mussa iddinušim*, the wedding gift her husband gave her (L172); *makkūr bīt mutiša*, the property in her husband's house (L172); *mimma ša mussa u šî ištu innemdū iršû*, whatever she and her husband have acquired after they have come together (L176a; 176b); *warkat bīt mutiša panîm iparrasūma*, they shall investigate the affairs of the household of her former husband (L177).
11. a second husband: *ana mutiša warkîm mārī ittalad*, she has given birth to sons for her later husband (L173; cf. L174); *bītam ša mutiša panîm ana mutiša warkîm u sinništim šuāti ipaqqidūma*, they shall entrust the house of her former husband to that woman and her later husband (L177; 177).

***mūtu***, sbst., death. < *m-ʾ-t*.

*mūt niṭil īnim*, instant death (E20); *balāṭam ša itti mūtim šitannu*, a life which is continually striving with death (E24); *ina ṣimdi la unaḫḫušu kīma nišik mūtim la innassaḫu*, which he cannot soothe with a dressing, and which, like the sting of death, cannot be removed (E30).

***muṭaḫḫidu***, sbst., showing generosity. < *ṭ-ḫ-d*.

*muṭaḫḫid nuḫšim bīt Egalmaḫ*, spreading abundance in the shrine of Egalmah (P8).

***muṭību***, sbst., making happy. < *ṭ-ʾ-b*.

*muṭīb libbi Marduk bēlišu*, pleasing the heart of his lord Marduk (P5).

***muṭṭû***, vb., to lessen. < *m-ṭ-ʾ*.

*kirâm la urakkibma biltam umtaṭṭi*, he has not pollinated the orchard and has therefore reduced the yield (L65); *maḫīr šikarim ana maḫīr šeʾim umtaṭṭi*, she has diminished the value of the drink compared with the value of the grain (L108); *liātim uṣṣaḫḫir ṣēnam uṣṣaḫḫir tālittam umtaṭṭi*, he has decreased the number of cattle and sheep and thus diminished the birth rate (L264).

***muzzazu***, sbst., attending, attendant. < *ʾ-z-z*.

*mār girseqîm muzzaz ekallim u mār sekretim ul ibbaqqar*, the son of an attendant with a position in the temple and the son of a priestess shall not be reclaimed (L187).

## N

*naʾādu* > ***naʾdu***, pious.

*nabāḫu* > ***nābiḫu***, objector.

***nabalkattu***, sbst., damage, burglary, climbing in. < *n-b-l-k-t*.

*lu ina pilšim u lu ina nabalkattim mimmûšu itti mimmê bēl bītim iḫtaliq*, whether through breaking in or climbing over his property has been lost together with that of the owner of the house (L125); [*mimma ša ina*] *nabalkattim* [*ḫalqu*], whatever was lost because of the intrusion (L68+b); *ina nabalkattim* [*šarrāqum…*], because of the intrusion a thief… (L68+b; also *nabalkattaka dunnin*, repair your damage, L68+b).

***nabalkutu***, vb., to intrude, destroy. < *n-b-l-k-t*.

*ištu bītika ibbalakkatūnim*, from your house they will intrude into mine (L68+b).

***nābālu***, vb., to be brought. < *ʾ-b-l*.

*mimma ša ibbablušum*, whatever had been brought to him (L159); *mimma mala ibbablušum*, just as much as had been brought to him (L160).

***nābiḫu***, sbst., rebel.
*mušeppi nābiḫī*, who muzzles the rebels (P19).

*nabquru* > ***napquru***, to be reclaimed.

***nabšû***, vb., to be produced, exist. < *b-š-'*; sometimes it is difficult to separate G-theme from N-theme forms, see *CAD* B 161a, last paragraph of general discussion on *bašû*.
1. to exist: *elišunu ḫubullum ittabši*, they got into debt (L152); *ana warkiāt ūmī ana mātima šarrum ša ina mātim ibbaššû*, a king who shall be in the land for ever, until the end of time (E14).
2. to be cultivated to maturity: *še'am ša ina eqlim ibbaššû*, the grain that was produced from the field (L46; cf. L49; 49; 50; also *ittabši*, L48); *suluppī ša ina kirîm ibbaššû*, dates that were produced in the orchard (L66, three times; for *ibaššīšum* see *bašû*).
3. to occur: *ina qarītim ibbûm ittabši*, damage has occurred in the granary (L120); *ina tarbaṣim lipit ilim ittabši*, an inexplicable disaster has occurred in the enclosure (L266); *nēmelam u butuqqâm ša ibbaššû*, any profit or loss that shall arise (L77+f).

***nabû***, vb., to nominate, designate. < *n-b-'*.
*Bābilam šumšu ṣīram ibbiū*, they gave Babylon its exalted name (P2); *ilū rabûtim ibbûninnima anākuma re'ûm mušallimum*, the great gods called me and so I am the shepherd who brings peace (E6); *iâti… Anum u Ellil ana šīr nišī ṭubbim šumī ibbû*, Anum and Enlil ordained me to bring health to the bodies of my people (P3); *awīlūtum ša šumam nabiat*, someone who has been designated to a position (E19).

***nābû***, sbst., one who nominates. < *n-b-'*.
*Anum rabûm abu ilī nābû palêya*, the father of the gods, who has designated my reign (E19).

***nābutu***, vb., to flee. < *'-b-d*.
*ālšu iddīma ittābit*, he has abandoned his city and become a fugitive (L136); *aššum ālšu izēruma innabitu*, because he has hated his city and made off (L 136).

***nadānu***, vb., to give, entrust. < *n-d-n*.
1. to give:
a. in general, give as a gift, hand on inherited property: *qīšti šarrum ana rēdîm iddinu*, the gift that the king had given the soldier (L34; cf. L35); *qīšti abum iddinušum*, the gift that his father had given him (L165); *eqelšu u kirāšu ana šānîm iddinūma*, they have given his field or his orchard to someone else (L27); *warkassa ēma eliša ṭābu nadānam*, to give her property to whomsoever she prefers (L178); *eqelša u kirāša ana errēšim ša eliša ṭābu inaddinma*, she shall give her field or orchard to a cultivator who pleases her (L178); *eqlam kirâm u mimma ša abuša iddinušim*, the field, the orchard or whatever

else her father gave her (L178, vnt. *išṭurušim*); *inaddinūšimma libbaša uṭabbū*, they shall give to her and make her happy (L178; also *ittadnūšimma* L178); *šalušti aplūtišu inaddiššumma*, he shall give him a third of his inheritance (L191); *ina eqlim kirîm u bītim ul inaddiššum*, he may not give him any of the field, orchard or house (L191); *ana māriša ša irammu inaddin ana aḫîm ul inaddin*, she shall pass it on to the son she loves; she shall not pass it on to an outsider (L150; 150); *warkassa ēma eliša ṭābu nadānam išṭuršimma*, he has given her written authority to entrust her affairs to whomsover she likes (L179); *ēma eliša ṭābu inaddin*, she shall pass it on as she pleases (L179; 182).
b. to give property to meet a debt: *ana e'iltišu ul inaddin*, he shall not give it to meet a debt (L38; cf. L39).
2. to pay:
a. in general: *ša nadānim la išu*, he does not have anything to give (L8); *uštašanāma ana bēl še'im inaddin*, he shall pay the owner of the grain double the amount (L120); *adi 12-šu inaddin*, he shall pay 12 times the amount (L5); *adi 30-šu inaddin*, he shall pay 30 times the amount (L8); *ana bītim šuāti še'am kaspam u bīšam inaddin*, he may pay grain, silver or goods for that house (L67+a, twice); *ina mimma ša iddinu ītelli*, he shall forfeit whatever he has paid (L67+a; §5.10; [5.13]; 5.14); *ana tamkārišu inaddin*, he shall give the merchant (§5.15).
b. to pay rent: *še'am kīma itēšu ana bēl eqlim inaddin*, he shall give grain to the owner of the field just like his neighbour (L42; 43); *ina bilat kirîm šittīn ana bēl kirîm inaddin*, he shall give the owner of the orchard two-thirds of the yield of the orchard (L64); *ana pī riksātišu tālittam u biltam inaddin*, he shall pay the rent as offspring according to the terms of his contract (L264).
c. to pay for storage: *idī našpakim inaddin*, he shall pay the fee for storage (L121).
d. to pay with silver: *ana kaspim inaddin*, he shall pay with silver (L40); *kasap kiṣrišu gamram ša šanat ana bēl* [*bītim*] *iddinma*, he paid all the silver for the year to the owner of the house according to the contract (L69+c); *ina kaspim ša waššābum* [*iddinušum*], some of the silver which the lodger paid [L69+c]; *ina*(?) *kaspim ša iddinu*(?), fragmentary (§5.7); *kasap ilqû uštašannāma šamallûm ana tamkārim inaddin*, he shall pay the merchant twice the amount of the silver he took (L101; cf. L106; 107); *ana kaspim ul inaddin*, she may not sell (L171b); *2 šiqil kaspam ana qīštišu inaddiššum*, he shall pay him two shekels of silver as his fee (L228; 234); *kaspam mišil šīmiša inaddin*, he shall pay half its value in silver (L238).

e. to pay as a reward for the recovery of a lost slave: *2 šiqil kaspam bēl wardim inaddiššum*, the owner of the slave shall pay him two shekels of silver (L17).
f. to pay a fee for the health-care of people or livestock: *ana asîm 2 šiqil kaspam inaddin*, he shall pay the physician two shekels of silver (L217; cf. L221; 222; 223; 224).
g. to pay as a hire charge: *8 kur še'am ina šattim istiat inaddiššum*, he shall pay eight kur-measures of grain for each year (L257, for a farm-hand; L261, for a herdsman; cf. L239, partially restored, for a boatman; 258, for a driver of oxen); see also *inaddin*, for the hire of oxen (L242/3); for the hire of a wagon (L271; 272); for the hire of a labourer (L273; 273); for the hire of particular craftsman (L274, partially restored, and any other possible occurrence in this law is now completely lost); for the hire of a boat (L276; 277).
h. to pay the price of redemption: *bēl wardim u lu amtim kasap išqulu ana tamkārim inaddinma lu warassu lu amassu ipaṭṭar*, the owner of the slave or the slave-girl shall repay to the merchant the silver that he had weighed out, and he shall redeem the slave or the slave-girl (L281).
3a. to give in order to settle, or attempt to settle, a business arrangement: *kirâšu ištu tarkibtim ana tamkārim iddinma*, after the pollination he has given over his orchard to the merchant (L66); *kanīk kaspim ša ana tamkārim inaddinu*, a sealed document for any silver which he gives to the merchant (L104; also *iddinu*, L105); *ana bēl šēbultim inaddin*, he shall give to the owner of the goods to be transported (L112); *tamkārum mimmā ša šamallûm iddinušum ittakiršu*, the merchant denies anything about the agent giving it to him (L107); for further business transactions see paragraph 10 below.
b. to give and then to forfeit: *mala iddinu ītelli*, he shall forfeit whatever he had given (L113; 116).
4a. to give a person: *mārtī ul anaddikkum*, I shall not give you my daughter (L160); *amtam ana mutiša iddinma*, she has given a slave-girl to her husband (L144; 146); *ana mutim iddišši*, he has given her to her husband (L183; cf. L184); also *inaddinūši* (L184); *awīlum mārašu ana mušēniqtim iddinma*, a man has given his son to a wet-nurse (L194).
b. to hire out a person: *rēdiam ana igrim ittadin*, he has then given a soldier for hire (L34).
c. to hire out something: *awīlum eleppašu ana malāḫim ana igrim iddinma*, a man has give his boat on hire to a boatman (L236); *liāt awīlim ana igrim ittadin*, he has given out on hire a man's cattle (L255).

5a. to sell something: *uniātim ana kaspim ul inaddinū*, they shall not sell the household goods (L177); *ana kaspim ul inaddin*, she may not sell it (L178); *ana šīmim* [...] *ul inaddiššum*, he shall not sell it to him (L67+a).
b. to 'sell' without proper documentation: *nādinānummi iddinam*, someone gave it to me officially (L9); *nādin iddinušum*, the one who is supposed to have sold to him (L9); *nādinān iddinušum*, the salesman who sold to him (L10).
c. to sell livestock: *šimtam uttakir u ana kaspim ittadin*, he has changed the brand-mark (of the animals) and has then made a sale (L265).
6a. to sell a person: *šuāti u bīšašu ana kaspim inaddinūma*, they shall sell him and his possessions (L54); *amassu ša mārī uldušum ana kaspim ittaddin*, he then sells the slave-girl who has borne him children (L119); *bēlessa ana kaspim inaddišši*, her master may sell her for silver (L147; cf. L146).
b. to give a person as a pledge for debt: *aššassu mārašu u mārassu ana kaspim iddin u lu ana kiššātim ittandin*, he has sold his wife, his son, or his daughter or given them as a pledge for a debt (L117; 117, with *-tan-*); *wardam u lu amtam ana kiššātim ittandin*, he may have given a slave or slave-girl as a pledge for a debt (L118, with *-tan-*); *ana kaspim inaddin*, he may sell (L118, after the terms of the pledge have expired, see *šūtuqu*).
7. to pledge a field for debt: *eqel epšētim ša še'im u lu šamaššammī ana tamkārim iddin*, he has pledged a field planted with grain or sesame to the merchant (L49; cf. L50).
8a. to give in connection with marriage: *terḫatam iddinu*, he has paid the bridal gift (L159; also *iddinma*, L160; 161); *kaspam mala terḫatiša inaddiššim*, he shall give her silver to the value of her bridal gift (L138); *mussa nudunnâm la iddiššim*, her husband has not given her a marriage gift (L172); *šeriktaša u nudunnâm ša mussa iddinušim*, the bride-price and marriage gift that her husband had given her (L171b, vnt. *iddinuši*; cf. L172).
b. to give as a divorce settlement: *1 mana kaspam ana uzzubêm inaddiššim*, he shall give her one mana of silver as a divorce payment (L139; cf. L140); *šeriktaša utarrūšim u muttat eqlim kirîm u bīšim inaddinūšimma*, they shall return her dowry and give her half of the field, the orchard and the property (L137, twice).
9. to give in compensation for a loss, pay a fine: *niplātim iddin*, he has given compensation (L41); *elēnumma ana 1 burum 20 kur še'am ana bēl eqlim inaddin*, he shall pay in addition to the owner of the field 20 kur-measures of grain for 1 bur-measure of land (L57, for unautho-

rized grazing); 1/4 *šīmišu ana bēl alpim u lu bēl imērim inaddin*, he shall pay a quarter of its price to the owner of the ox or of the donkey (L225); *wardam kīma wardim ana bēl bītim inaddin*, he shall recompense the owner of the house with a slave like the slave (L231, for the death of a slave; cf. *inaddin*, for damage to hired oxen, L247; 248); for death caused by a goring ox (L251; 252); *šumma awīlum epinnam ina ugārim išriq 5 šiqil kaspam ana bēl epinnam inaddin*, if a man has stolen a plough from the arable land he shall pay the owner of the plough five shekels of silver (L259; cf. L260); *mimma ša ikkiru uštašannāma inaddin*, he shall pay twice the amount of whatever he disputed (L124); *ana babtišu inaddin*, he shall compensate his community (L126); *liātim u ṣēnam ušallamma ana bēlišunu inaddin*, he shall pay back cattle or small animals to their owner in compensation (L267).

10. to return something that has been repaired: *elippam dannatam ana bēl eleppim inaddin*, he shall give back the repaired boat to the owner of the boat (L235).

11. to give silver as an investment: *tamkārum ana šamallîm kaspam ana tadmiqtim ittadinma*, the merchant has then given silver to the agent as an investment (L102; cf. L100, twice, [*ana nadānim*] L100; and *iddinma*, L109); *šamallûm mimma ša tamkārum iddinušum ana tamkārišu uttēr*, the agent has returned to his merchant everything that the merchant had given him (L107).

12a. to lend on interest: *tamkārum še'am u kaspam ana ḫubullim iddinma*, a merchant has given grain or silver on interest (§5.13; also *iddinu*, §5.13; also *iddin*, §5.9; 5.9; 5.14, fragmentary); *kaspam ana tappûtim iddin*, he has given silver in partnership (L77+f); *še'am ina sūtim maṭītim iddin*, he gave the grain in a little measure (§5.13).

b. to pay interest: *ṣibtam ša šattim šuāti ul inaddin*, he shall pay no interest for that year (L48); *mānaḫāt erēšim ana tamkārim inaddin*, the interest and cultivation expenses he shall pay to the merchant (L49); *ana pī ṣimdat šarrim ana tamkārim inaddin*, he shall pay to the merchant in accordance with the royal decree (L 51).

c. to lend on credit: *ištēn pīḫam ana qīptim iddin*, she has given one measure of beer on credit (L111).

13. to lease land to a tenant farmer: *awīlum eqelšu ana biltim ana errēšim iddinma*, a man has given his field for rent to a cultivator (L45); *u lu ana mišlāni u lu ana šaluš eqlam iddin*, he has leased a half or a third of the field (L46); *ana nukaribbim iddin*, he has entrusted it to a planter (L60); *kirāšu ana nukaribbim ana rukkubim iddin*, he has entrusted his orchard to a gardener for pollination (L64).

14. to give objects for trading: *ana pašārim iddin*, he gave for the purpose of trading (L104).
15a. to entrust to someone to transport: *ana awīlim iddinma ana šēbultim ušābilšu*, he has given to a man and made him make the delivery (L112; and also N-theme, *innadnušum*).
b. to deliver: *ašar šūbulu la iddinma*, he did not get it to the delivery point (L112); *mimma ša šūbuluma la iddinu*, whatever he failed to get delivered (L112).
16a. to entrust for safe-keeping: *ana maṣṣarūtim inaddin*, he intends to place for safe-keeping (L122, twice; cf. *iddinma*, L123; 124; 125; also *iddinušumma*, L125); *mimma mala inaddinu*, the full amount of what he has given (L122); for *ašar iddinu*, see below.
b. to entrust (of a deity): *ṣalmāt qaqqadim ša Ellil išrukam rē'ûssina Marduk iddinam*, the mass of mankind, which Enlil has entrusted to me and which Marduk has made my flock (E2); *ina lē'ûtim ša Marduk iddinam*, by the power that Marduk has given me (E4).
17. ***ašar iddinu***, the place where he gave it (L123; 125).
18. ***ana nadānim***: *mimma ša nadānim la ibaššīšum*, there is nothing at all for him to give (L66); *šumma ana <na>dānim ul* [*išu*], if he does not have anything to give (§5.2; and also *ana nadānim*, §5.2).
> *naddunu*, to be given.

***naddû***, vb., to be thrown, be abandoned. < *n-d-'*.
1. to be thrown: *awīlum šû ana išātim šuāti innaddi*, that man shall be thrown into that fire (L25).
2. to be neglected: *bilat eqlim ša šanātim ša innadû*, rent for the field for the years when it was abandoned (L62).

***naddunu***, vb., to be given. < *n-d-n*.
1. to be given into one's possession: *ana ummišu innaddinma*, it shall be given to his mother (L29); *eqelšu kirâšu u bīssu innaddiššumma*, his field, his orchard or his house shall be given to him (L31, variant *innaddinšumma*; cf. *innaddiššum*, L30, variant *innaddinšum*; *innaddiššumma*, L28); *niplātim ša innadnušum*, the amount of compensation that was given to him (L41); *eqlam ša innadnušum*, the field that was given to him (L62); *mimma ša ana mārīša innadnu*, whatever had been given to her sons (L137); *adi 5-šu mimma ša innadnušum*, five times the amount of whatever was given to him (L112).
2. to be given to look after: *rē'ûm ša liātum u lu ṣēnum ana re'îm innadnušum*, a shepherd who has been given a herd or a flock to feed (L264; 265; cf. L263).
3. not to be given: *eqelšu kirâšu u bīssu ana ipṭerišu ul innaddin*, his field orchard and house shall not be given as his ransom (L32); *ana kaspim ul innaddin*(!), he shall not be sold (L36, with variants

G-present and N-preterite); *mimma ul innaddiššim*, nothing at all shall be given to her (L141).

***nādinānu***, sbst., seller. < *n-d-n*.

*nādinānummi iddinam maḫar šībīmi ašām iqtabi*, he has said, 'Someone sold it to me, I bought it in front of witnesses' (L9); *šāyyimānum ina bīt nādinānim rugummē dīnim šuāti adi ḫamšīšu ileqqe*, the purchaser shall take five times the value of the damages in this case from the house of the seller (L12; cf. L9); *nādinānum šarrāq iddāk*, the seller is a thief and he shall be killed (L9); *nādinānum ana šīmtim ittalak*, the seller has gone to his destiny (L12); *nādinān iddinušum*, the seller who sold to him (L10, so Roth following variant, but Stele: *nādin*); *ana nādinānišu utârma*, he shall take back (the sick slave) to to the person who sold him (L278, variant *nādinānimma utâr*); *nādinānšu baqrī ippal*, the person who sold him shall be responsible for the claims (L279).

***nādinu***, adj., giving. < *n-d-n*.

*šarrum nādin napištim ana Adab*, the king who gave Adab its life (P15); *nādin* (variant *nādinān*) *iddinušum*, the man who gave it to him (L10).

***nadītu***, sbst., devotee, priestess. < *n-d-ʾ*.

1. one given a gift by her father: *ugbabtum nadītum u lu sekretum ša abuša šeriktam išrukšim*, a priestess, a lay-sister or a confined woman whose father makes her a presentation (L178; 179).

2. one who sells property: *nadītum tamkārum u ilkum aḫûm eqelsu kirāšu u bīssu ana kaspim inaddin*, a priestess, a merchant or any other duty-bound person may sell a field, an orchard or a house for silver (L40).

3. one who marries: *nadītim ša mārī ušaršušu*, a priestess who provides him with children (L137); *awīlum nadītam iḫuzma*, a man has married a priestess (L144; 145; 146); *nadītum šî amtam ana mutiša iddinma*, that priestess gave a slave-girl to her husband (L144); *abum ana mārtišu nadīt gagîm lu sekretim šeriktam la išrukšim*(!), the father of a confined priestess or a sister has not given a dowry to his daughter (L180); *abum nadītam qadištam u lu kulmašītam ana ilim iššīma šeriktam la išrukšim*, a father has offered to the god a priestess, a holy girl or a hierodule and has not given her a marriage gift (L181); *šugītum šî itti nadītim ul uštamaḫḫar*, that holy woman shall not make herself equal with the confined sister (L145).

4. one who opens a drinking house: *nadītum ugbabtum ša ina gagîm la wašbat*, a priestess, a lady who has not been living in a community (L110).

***na'du***, adj., devout. < *n-'-d*.

*na'dum la mupparkûm ana Ezida*, the devoted one who never neglects Ezida (P11); *zāninum na'dum ša Ekur*, the passionate supporter of Ekur (P4); *rubâm na'dam pāliḫ ilī*, the pious prince who fears the gods (P3); *rubûm na'dum munawwer pani Tišpak*, the pious prince who brings light to the face of Tishpak (P17); *na'dum muštēmiqum ana ilī rabûtim*, devout, making supplication to the great gods (P20).

***nadû***, vb., to throw down. < *n-d-'*.

1a. to knock down, knock out: *šumma awīlum šinni awīlim meḫrišu ittadi šinnašu inaddû*, if a man has knocked out the tooth of a man comparable to him, they shall knock out his own tooth (L200; 200; cf. *ittadi* L201).

1b. to throw down to the ground: *gurun šalmāt ummānātišu ina ṣērim littaddi*, let him keep on throwing human bodies on to the heap in the desert (E27).

2. to throw into the river as a punishment: *sābītam šuāti ukannūšima ana mê inaddûši*, they shall prove that beer-seller guilty and throw her into the water (L108; cf. L133b and 143, with *sinništam*); *ikassūšunūtima ana mê inaddûšunūti*, they shall tie them up and throw them into the water (L129, with *aššat awīlim itti zikarim šanîm*); *ana mê inaddûšu*, they shall throw him into the water (L155, with *awīlam*).

3. to abandon property, leave land fallow: *eqelšu kirāšu u bitīšu ina pani ilkim iddīma*, he has abandoned his field, orchard or house because of the duty (L30); *eqlam la īrišma ittadi*, he did not cultivate the field but left it fallow (L43); *eqlam ša iddû*, the field which he left fallow (L43); *rē'ûm ṣēnam ana eqlim iddīma*, a shepherd has left his flock in a field (L58); *ālšu iddīma ittābit*, he has abandoned his city and fled (L136).

4. with *eli*, to charge with an offence: *awīlum awīlam ubbirma nērtam elišu iddīma la uktīnšu*, a gentleman has accused a gentleman and charged him with (= 'thrown against him') murder but has not proved it (L1; cf. L2); *ša elišu kišpī iddû*, the one who charged him with sorcery (= 'who threw sorcery against him') (L2); *ša elišu kišpū nadû*, the one who has been charged with sorcery (= 'against whom sorcery has been thrown') (L2).

5. with *aḫū*, to be lazy (literally: to throw down one's arms): *aḫšu iddīma*, he has been lazy (L44; 53; 55); *aḫi ul addī*, I have not been lazy (E2).

> ***šuddû***, to cause to lose; ***naddû***, to be thrown down.

***nadūku***, vb., to be executed for a criminal offence. < *d-'-k*.

*awīlum šû iddâk*, that man should be killed (L3; 6; 19; 22; 130; cf. L14; 15); *bēl bītim šû iddâk*, the owner of that house should be killed

(L16); *lu rēdûm u lu bā'irum šû iddâk*, that soldier or that hunter should be killed (L26); *lu ša ḫaṭṭātim u lu laputtûm šû iddâk*, that captain or that officer should be killed (L33; 34); *itinnum šû iddâk*, that builder should be killed (L229); *sābītum šî iddâk*, that drink-seller should be killed (L109); *mubbiršu iddâk*, the one who has accused him should be killed (L1); *ša elišu kišpī iddû iddâk*, the one who has accused him of sorcery should be killed (L2); *ša šurqam ina qātišu imḫuru iddâk*, the one who received the stolen property into his possession should be killed (L6); *awīlum šû šarrāq iddâk*, that man is a thief and should be killed (L7); *šarrāqānum ša nadānim la išu iddâk*, the thief who does not have enough to pay back should be killed (L8); *nādinānum šarrāq iddâk*, the one who gave it is a thief and should be killed (L9); *šāyyimānum šarrāq iddâk*, it is the purchaser who is the thief and he should be killed (L10); *sār tuššamma idkē*(!) *iddâk*, he is the liar; he has perpetrated corruption and shall be killed (L11).

2. fragmentary: *iddâk* (§5.3b; 76+f).

*nagāru*, vb., to be disloyal (?) (meaning uncertain, see *CAD*), > ***munaggiru***, informer.

***nagbu***, sbst., source.

*nagab uršim*, the fount of wisdom (P16); *nārātišu ina nagbim liskir* let him stop up his rivers at the source (E22); *zunnī ina šamê mīlam ina nagbim līṭeršu*, let him deprive him of showers from the sky and floods from the depths (E25).

***naggāru***, sbst., carpenter.

*idī naggārim*, the wages of a carpenter (L274).

***nāgiru***, sbst., crier.

*ana šisīt nāgirim la uštēṣiam*, he has not brought him out when the crier shouts (L16).

***naḫāšu***, vb., to prosper. < *n-ḫ-š*.

*ṣillī ṭābum ana ālīya tariṣ ina utliya nišī māt Šumerim u Akkadîm ukîl ina lamassiya iḫḫiša ina šulmim attabbalšināti*, with my kind shadow stretched over my city I held the people of Sumer and Akkad in my arms; there was prosperity under my protection, for I always led them in peace (E7).

> ***munaḫḫišu***, making prosperous.

***naḫbutu***, vb., to be robbed. < *ḫ-b-t*.

*ālum u rabiānum ša ina erṣetišunu u paṭṭišunu ḫubtum iḫḫabtu*, the city and governor in whose territory and district the robbery occurred (L23).

**naḫlulu**, vb., to be hung. < *ḫ-l-l*.

*kannu gamartim ina abullim ittaḫlalū*, the flags have been hung on the city gate showing it is finished (L58).

*nâḫu*, to be still > ***nuḫḫu***, soothe; ***munēḫu***, quietening.

**nakāpu**, vb., to toss, butt. < *n-k-p*.

*alpum sūqam ina alākišu awīlam ikkipma uštamīt*, an ox gored a man while it was walking in the street and caused his death (L250; cf. L251).

> *munakkipu*, tossing.

**nakāru**, vb., to change one's mind, argue. < *n-k-r*.

*samallûm kaspam itti tamkārim ilqēma tamkāršu ittakir*, a salesman has received silver from a merchant but has then argued with the merchant (L106); *tamkārum mimma ša samallûm iddinušum ittakiršu*, the merchant has argued with him about what the salesman gave him (L107; cf. L124); *aššum samallâšu ikkiru*, because he had an argument with the salesman (L107); *ana gamrim ittakir*, he disagreed completely (L120); *ašar iddinu ittakrūšu*, they argued with him where he put it (L123); *mimma ša ikkiru uštašannāma inaddin*, he shall pay double the amount he disputed (L124).

> **nukkuru**, alter.

**nakāsu**, vb., to cut off, cut down. < *n-k-s*.

1. to cut down a tree: *balum bēl kirîm ina kirī awīlim iṣam ikkis*, he has felled a tree in a man's orchard without the owner of the orchard knowing (L59).

2. to sever a part of a body: *lišānšu inakkisū*, they shall cut out his tongue (L192); *tulāša inakkisū*, they shall cut off her breast (L194); *rittašu inakkisū*, they shall cut off his hand (L195; 218; 253; cf. *ritti gallābim šuāti inakkisū*, L226); *uzunšu inakkisū*, they shall cut off his ear (L205; also *inakkis*, L282); *qaranšu išbir zibbassu ittakis*, he has broken off its horn or cut off its tail (L248).

3. to cut into: *alpam īgurma šēpšu ištebir u lu labiānšu ittakis*, he has hired an ox and broken its foot or cut its neck muscle (L246).

**nakkaptu**, sbst., forehead, temple, eye-socket.

*nakkapti awīlim ina karzilli siparrim iptēma*, he has opened a man's eye-socket with a scalpel (L215; 218(!); cf. *nakkaptašu*, L220).

**nakkāpû**, sbst., an ox in the habit of goring. < *n-k-p*.

*alap awīlim nakkāpīma kīma nakkāpû bābtašu ušēdīšumma*, a man's ox was prone to gore and his community had let him know that it was prone to gore (L251; 251).

**nakru**, sbst., enemy.

*ḫarrānam ina alākišu nakrum mimma ša našû uštaddīšu*, while he was on a journey an aggressor made him surrender what was being carried

(L103); *nakrī eliš u šapliš assuḫ*, I have rooted out my enemies from above and down below (E4); *šuāti ana qāt nakrīšu limallīšuma*, hand over the man himself into the hands of his enemies (E27); *nakiršu elišu lišzīz*, let him allow his enemy to stand over him (E26); *sapar nakirī*, the scourge of the enemies (P10).

***namāru***, vb., to shine, brighten up. < *n-w-r*.
*iklet la nawārim*, unbrightening darkness (E20).
> ***nummuru***, to shed light; ***munammir***, brightening.

***namḫuṣu***, vb., to be beaten. < *m-ḫ-ṣ*.
*ina puḫrim ina qinnaz alpim 1 šūši immaḫḫaṣ*, he shall be beaten 60 times with an ox-tail in the assembly (L202).

*namkūru* > ***makkūru***, property.

*napāḫu*, to blow, kindle a fire > ***nappuḫu***, to flare up.

*naparkû*, to abandon (= *AHw naparkû* II) > ***mupparkum***, abandoning.

*napāšu*, to breathe freely > ***nuppušu***, to relax.

***napḫaru***, sbst., group. < *p-ḫ-r*.
*ilū rabûtum ša šamê u erṣetim Anunnakū ina napḫarišunu*, the almighty gods of heaven and earth, the Anunnaki in their assembly (E31).

***napištu***, sbst., life. < *n-p-š*.
1. life sustained: *šarrum nādin napištim ana Adab*, the king who gave life to Adab (P15); *šû iqīšu napšatam ana Maškanšāpir*, it was he who gave life to Mashkanshapar (P15); *ašnān napišti nišī ay ušabši*, let him have no grain for the people to live on (E22).
2. life brought to an end: *adi napištašu ibellû ana eṭlūtišu liddammam*, until his spirit is exhausted and his strength is silenced (E30); *ḫalāq nišīšu tabāk napištišu kīma mê*, the loss of his people and the pouring out of his life like water (E21); *šumma napištum ālum u rabiānum 1 mana kaspam ana nišīšu išaqqalū*, if life was lost the city and the governor shall pay his people one mana of silver (L24); *šumma dīnum šû dīn napištim awīlum šû iddâk*, that gentleman shall be put to death if the trial is one of murder (L3).
3. all living creatures: *muštēšer šaknat napištim*, allowing all life on earth to have justice (= 'keeping the fixtures of life straight', E23).

***nappāḫu***, sbst., smith. < *n-p-ḫ*.
[*idī*] *nappāḫim*, the wages for a smith (L274).

***nappuḫu***, vb., to become ablaze. < *n-p-ḫ*.
*ina bīt awīlim išātum innapiḫma*, a fire has broken out in a man's house (L25).

***napquru***, vb., to be reclaimed. < *p-q-r*.
*ul ippaqqar*, he shall not be reclaimed (L118; 185; 187; 188).

**naprusu**, vb., to be decided. < *p-r-s*.

*warkassu ipparrasma*, a decision will be made about his circumstances (L18); *warkassa ina bābtiša ipparrasma*, a decision will be made in her community about her circumstances (L142).

**naptû**, vb., to be opened. < *p-t-ʾ*.

*ina kārišu pītum ittepte u ugāram mê uštābil*, a break has been opened in the dyke and he has let the water destroy the meadow (L53); *awīlum ša ina kārišu pītum ippetû*, the man in whose dyke the opening was made (L53).

**napṭuru**, vb., to be redeemed. < *p-ṭ-r*.

*ina bīt il ālišu ippaṭṭar*, he shall be redeemed in the shrine of his local god (L32).

**naqāru**, vb., to pull apart. < *n-q-r*.

*malāḫum eleppam šuāti inaqqarma*, the boatman shall take that boat to pieces (L235).

*naqbu* > *nagbu*, source.

**nāqidu**, sbst., herdsman, shepherd.

*nāqidam ana liātim u ṣēnim reʾîm īgur*, he hired a herdsman to pasture the cattle and sheep (L261).

**narāmu**, sbst., beloved. < *r-ʾ-m*.

*narām Tutu murīš Barsippa*, beloved of Tutu, the one who makes Borsippa rejoice (P10).

**narkusu**, vb., to meet by agreement. < *r-k-s*.

*sābītum sarrūtum ina bītiša ittarkasūma*, deceivers have arranged to meet in the house of a drink-seller (L109).

**narû**, sbst., stele.

*awâtia šūqurātim ina narîya ašṭurma*, I have inscribed these precious words of mine on my stela (E8; cf. E14; 15; 18; 19); *narî šaṭram lištassīma awâtiya šūqurātim lišmēma*, and let him then shout out the inscription on the stone, and let him listen to the very precious words I have written (E11); *narî awatam likallimšu*, my stele shall explain the message for him (E11); *purussē mātim ša aprusu narûm šû likallimšuma*, this stela shall explain to him the decisions I have taken for the nation (E15).

**nāru**, sbst., river.

1. the Euphrates: *mukanniš dadmē nār Purattim ittum Dagan bānîšu*, who controls the communities beside the River Euphrates under the guidance of his creator god Dagan (P17: *ittum* may perhaps be read as *nārum*, see Finet).

2. the river as a source of water: *nārātišu ina nagbim liskir ina erṣetišu ašnān napišti nišī ay ušabši*, stop up the springs of his rivers and banish from his land the grain to feed the people (E22).

3. the river represented as the god Id, as the arbiter: *ša elišu kišpū nadû ana Id illak Id išalli'amma*, the person against whom witchcraft has been alleged shall go to the River and jump into the River (L2; 2); *ša Id išliam*, the one who jumped into the River (L2); *awīlam šuāti Id ūtebbibaššuma*, the River has cleansed that man (L2); *Id iktašassu*, the River has overwhelmed him (L2); *itti zikarim šanîm ina utūlim la ittaṣbat ana mutiša Id išalli*, she has not been caught while copulating with another man, but she shall leap into the river for her husband's sake (L132).

***nasāḫu***, vb., to remove, tear out, disinherit. < *n-s-ḫ*.

1. to gouge out an eye: *īnšu inassaḫū*, they shall gouge out his eye (L193); for *šašallašu ittasak*, he has wounded its rump (L248), > *nasāku* B, to wound.

2. to rip up foundations: *nasāḫ išdī šarrūtišu*, the tearing out of the foundations of his kingdom (E23).

3. to destroy wickedness: *nakrī eliš u šapliš assuḫ*, I have rooted out the enemies from above and down below (E4); *ina mātišu raggam u ṣēnam lissuḫ*, let him root out evil and wickedness from his land (E16).

4. to separate: *eliš ina balṭūtim lissuḫšu šapliš ina erṣetim eṭemmašu mê lišaṣmi*, may he cut him off from those living up above and may he let his ghost thirst for water in the land down below (E23).

5. to disinherit: *šumma mārum arnam kabtam ša ina aplūtim nasāḫim la ublam abum mārašu ina aplūtim ul inassaḫ*, if the son has not committed an offence serious enough to be debarred from the inheritance, the father shall not debar his son from the inheritance (L168; 168; cf. L169); *mārī anassaḫ iqtabi*, he has said, 'I will disinherit my son' (L168); *arnam kabtam ša ana aplūtim nasāḫim*, a serious offence which results in disinheritance (L169); *ana mārišu nasāḫim panam ištakan*, he has decided to disinherit his son (L168); *ana tarbītim nasāḫim panam ištakan*, he has decided to disinherit his foster son (L191).

> ***nasuḫu***, to be removed.

*nasāku* A, to throw away > *šussuku*, to throw out; *mušassiku*, disposing.

***nasāku* B**, vb., to wound (*CAD*: possibly by-form of *nasāḫu*, to tear out). < *n-s-k*.

*alpam īgurma qaranšu išbir zibbassu ittakis u lu šašallašu ittasak*(!), he has hired an ox and broken its horn, cut off its tail or wounded its rump (L248); *BAL* reads *ittasaḫ*, > *nasāḫu*, to tear out.

***nasāqu***, vb., to choose. < *n-s-q*.

*bēl kirîm zittašu inassaqma ileqqe*, the owner of the orchard shall choose his share and take it (L60); *aplum mār ḫīrtim ina zittim inassaqma ileqqe*, the son of the first wife, the heir, shall select from the portion and take it (L170).

**naspuḫu**, vb., to be scattered. < *s-p-ḫ*.

*ḫalāq ālišu naspuḫ nišīšu šarrūssu šupēlam šumšu u zikiršu ina mātim la šubšâm ina pīšu kabtim liqbi*, may he command with his grave tones the loss of his city, the dispersion of his people, the overthrow of his kingdom, the extinction of his name and reputation from the land (E20).

**nasqu**, sbst., selected. < *n-s-q*.

*awâtūa nasqā epšētūa šāninam ul išâ*, my words are special, my deeds cannot be surpassed (E17; cf. E9)

**nassuḫu**, vb., to be removed, be disinherited. < *n-s-ḫ*.

*awīlum šû ina bīt abim innassaḫ*, that man shall be disinherited from his father's estate (L158); *kīma nišik mūtim la innassaḫu*, like the sting of death there is no taking it away (E30).

**naṣāru**, vb., to keep, observe. < *n-ṣ-r*.

1. to take charge of: *rē'ûm eqel ušākilu inaṣṣarma*, the shepherd shall take custody of the field on which he let them feed (L58); *bītam inaṣṣarū u ṣeḫḫerūtim urabbû*, they shall keep charge of the house and bring up the children (L177).

2. to observe instructions: *awât mīšarim ša ina narîya ašṭuru liṣṣur*, let him observe the righteous words that I have written on my stela (E14).

3. to maintain sexual integrity: *pagarša la iṣṣurma*, she has not looked after her body (L133b; cf. *inaṣṣar* [L133a], so Borger but not Roth); *naṣratma ḫiṭītam la išu*, her integrity is preserved and there is no blame (L142; cf. L143).

**naṣbutu**, vb., to get caught. < *ṣ-b-t*.

1. to get caught in a sexual act: *aššat awīlim itti zikarim šanîm ina itūlim ittaṣbat*, a man's wife has been caught lying with another man (L129); *aššat awīlim mussa ubbiršima itti zikarim šanîm ina utūlim la iṣṣabit*, a man's wife is accused by her husband of lying with another man but she has not been caught (L131; cf. *ittaṣbat*, L132); *awīlum warki abišu ina sūn rabītišu ša mārī waldat ittaṣbat*, a man has been caught after his father's death copulating with his principal wife (L158).

2. to be caught after an offence: *awīlum ḫubtam iḫbutma ittaṣbat*, a man has committed a robbery and been caught (L22; cf. L23)

3. to be seized in someone's possession: *wardum ina qātišu ittaṣbat*, the slave is caught in his possession (L19); *awīlum šû zēram u lu ukullâm išriqma ina qātišu ittaṣbat*, that man has stolen seed or foodstuff and it is then found in his possession (L253).

***naškunu***, vb., to be arranged. < *š-k-n.*
*andurāršunu iššakkan*, their freedom shall be arranged (L117; 280; cf. L171a, where Stele reads *ištakan* [Gt-theme], but emendation suggested: *iššakkan*, i.e. N-theme); *kasap la kanīkim ana nikkassim ul iššakkan*, silver without a sealed document may not be set in the account (L105).

***našlulu***, vb., to be taken into captivity. < *š-l-l.*
*awīlum iššalilma ina bītišu ša akālim ibaššī*, a man has been taken into captivity but there is enough to eat in his house (L133a; cf. L134; 135).

***našpaku***, sbst., granary. < *š-p-k.*
*bēl bītim našpakam iptēma še'am ilqe*, the owner has opened the storehouse and taken the grain (L120); *ina našpakim u lu ina maškanim še'am ilteqe*, he has taken grain from the granary or the threshing place (L113, twice); *idī našpakim inaddin*, he shall pay the charge for storage (L121).

***našpakūtu***, sbst., storage. < *š-p-k.*
*še'ašu ana našpakūtim ina bīt awīlim išpukma*, he has put his grain in storage in another man's house (L120).

***našpuku***, vb., to be stored. < *š-p-k.*
*še'am ša ina bītīšu iššapku ana gamrim ittakir*, he has changed the facts completely about the grain which had been deposited in his house (L120).

***našû***, vb., to carry, support, pay, lift. < *n-š-'.*
1. to carry: *ḫarrānam ina alākišu nakrum mimma ša našû uštaddīšu*, while he was on a journey an aggressor made him surrender what was being carried (L103).
2. to bring as a gift: *abum nadītam qadištam u lu kulmašītam ana ilim iššīma šeriktam la išrukšim*, a father has offered to the god a priestess, a holy girl or a hierodule and has not given her a marriage gift (L181).
3. to pay a penalty: *aran dīnim šuāti ittanašši*, he will always have to pay the penalty in this case (L4; 13).
4. to maintain someone: *adi balṭat ittanaššīši*, he will continue to support her while she lives (L148); *errēssa ittanaššīši*, her cultivator shall continue to support her (L178).
5. with ***īnu***, to covet: *ana numāt bēl bītim īnšu iššīma*, he has become envious of (= 'lifted his eye towards') the property of the owner of the house (L25).

***nāšû***, sbst., carrying. < *n-š-'.*
***nāši biltim***, tribute bearer: *eqlam kirâm u bītam ša rēdîm bā'irim u nāši biltim upīḫ u niplātim iddin*, he has acquired by exchange the field, orchard or house of a soldier, hunter or tribute bearer and paid a

supplement (L41, twice); *eqlum kirûm u bītum ša rēdîm bāʾirim u nāši biltim ana kaspim ul innaddin*(!), the field, orchard or house of a soldier, hunter or tribute bearer shall not be sold for silver (L36; cf. L37); *rēdûm bāʾirum u nāši biltim ina eqlim kirîm u bītim ša ilkišu ana aššatišu u mārtišu ul išaṭṭar u ana eʾiltišu ul inaddin*, a soldier hunter or tribute bearer shall not sign over to his wife or daughter a field or orchard or house pertaining to his duty nor shall it be given for debt (L38).

**našūmu**, vb., to be sold. < *š-ʾ-m*.

*šībī ša ina maḫrīšunu iššāmu*, the witnesses in whose presence the sale was conducted (L9).

**natruṣu**, vb., to be stretched out towards. < *t-r-ṣ*.

*aššat awīlim aššum zikarim šanîm ubānum elîša ittarişma*, a gentleman's wife has had the finger pointed at her because of another man (L132).

**naṭālu**, to see > **šuṭṭulu**, to make visible.

**naṭû**, vb., to hit. < *n-ṭ-ʾ*.

*awīlam šuāti maḫar dayyānī inaṭṭûšu*, they shall flog that man in the presence of the judges (L127).

> **šuṭṭu**, to strike.

**nawāru** > **namāru**, to shine.

**nazkuru**, vb., to be spoken. < *z-k-r*.

*šumī ina damiqtim ana dār lizzakir*, my name shall always be uttered as a blessing (E10).

**neḫelṣû**, to slip > **šuḫulṣû**, to allow to crumble.

**neḫpû**, vb., to be broken. < *ḫ-p-ʾ*.

*ṭuppašu iḫḫepe*, his document has been destroyed (L37).

**nēmelu**, sbst., profit.

*nēmelam u butuqqâm ša ibbaššû*, any profit or loss that shall arise (L77+f); *ašar illiku nēmelam la ītamar*, he has not seen any profit where he went (L101).

**nēmequ**, sbst., wisdom.

*ina šulmim attabbalšināti ina nēmeqiya uštapziršināti*, I have led them in peace, I have protected them by my wisdom (E7); *uznam u nēmeqam līteršuma ina mīšītim littarūšu*, let him deprive him of wisdom and understanding and let him take him away to be lost for ever (E22).

**nenmudu**, vb., to join, cohabit. < *ʾ-m-d*.

*ištu innemdū bītam īpušū bīšam iršû*, after they were joined together they established a household and acquired property (L176a, twice; cf. L176b).

***nepû***, vb., to seize. < *n-p-ʾ*.
*šeʾam u kaspam la išūma nipûssu ittepe*, he had no grain or silver and a security has been seized from him (L114); *nipûssu ippēma*, a security has been seized from him (L115); *alpam ana nipûtim ittepe*, he has seized an ox as a pledge (L241).

***nēpû***, adj., taking into custody. < *n-p-ʾ*.
*nipûtum ina bīt nēpīša ina šīmātiša imtūt*, the pledge has died naturally in the house of the creditor (L115; cf. L116).

***nērtu***, murder. < *n-ʾ-r*.
*awīlum awīlam ubbirma nērtam elišu iddīma la uktīnšu*, a man has accused another man and charged him with murder but has not proved it (L1).

***nēšu***, sbst., lion.
*alpam imēram īgurma ina ṣērim nēšum iddūkšu*, he has hired an ox or an ass and a lion has killed it in the desert (L244); *ina tarbaṣim lipit ilim ittabši u lu nēšum iddūk*, an inexplicable disease has occurred in the fold or a lion has made a kill (L266).

***nibītu***, sbst., nominee. < *n-b-ʾ*.
*nibīt Ellil anāku*, I am Enlil's nominee (P4; *CAD* s.v. 4).

***nidītu***, sbst., neglected land. < *n-d-ʾ*.
*nidītam īzib*, and has left an abandoned area (L61); *nidītam ana libbi zittišu išakkanūšum*, they shall put the abandoned area in the middle of his share (L61); *awīlum [nidītam] balum [itēšu ītepuš]*, a man has built on neglected land without informing his neighbour (L68+a: cf. *CAD* 'house in ruins' s.v. *epēšu* 2b p. 198a); *bēl nidītim*, the owner of the derelict property (L68+b); [*ištu*] *nidītika bītī ipallašūnim*, they may rob my house because of your mess (L68+b); *nidītka epuš*, work on your derelict property (L68+b).

***nidûtu***, sbst., neglected land (so Borger, but Roth: *kankallu*). < *n-d-ʾ*.
*eqel nidûtim* (Roth: *kankallam*) *ana šalaš šanātim ana teptītim ušēṣīma*, he has taken over a neglected field to develop over three years (L44); *šumma eqel nidûtim* (Roth: *kankallum*) *eqlam šipram ippešma*, if it is neglected land, he shall do the work (L63).

***nikkassu***, sbst., account.
*kasap la kanīkim ana nikkassim ul iššakkan*, silver without a sealed document may not be set in the account (L105).

***nindabû***, sbst., offering.
*nindabê rabûtim ana Eninnu*, the splendid offerings for Eninnu (P13).

***nipiltu***, sbst., supplementary payment, compensation. < *ʾ-p-l*.
*eqlam kirâm u bītam ša rēdîm bāʾirim u nāši biltim upīḫ u niplātim iddin*, he has acquired by exchange the field, orchard or house of a soldier, hunter or tribute bearer and made supplementary payments

(L41); *niplātim ša innadnušum itabbal*, he shall take away the supplementary payments that were given to him (L41).

***nipûtu***, sbst., pledge, security. < *n-p-ʾ*.

*eli awīlim šeʾam u kaspam la išūma nipûssu ittepe*, he had no grain or silver owing from the man but has seized a security from him (L114; cf. L115); *alpam ana nipûtim ittepe*, he has then seized an ox as a pledge (L241); *ana nipûtim ištiat 1/3 mana kaspam išaqqal*, he shall pay one-third of a mana of silver for one security (L114); *nipûtum ina bīt nēpīša ina šīmātiša imtūt*, the pledge has died naturally in the house of the creditor (L115; cf. L116); *bēl nipûtim tamkāršu ukânma*, the owner of the security shall convict his merchant (L116).

***nisiḫtu***, sbst., deserter. < *n-s-ḫ*.

*lu ša ḫaṭṭātim u lu laputtûm ṣāb nisḫātim irtaši*, a captain or officer has acquired one of the deserting soldiers (L33, *CAD* s.v. 3).

*nismatu* > ***nizmatu***, wish.

***nišku***, sbst., bite. < *n-š-k*.

*ina ṣimdi la unaḫḫušu kīma nišik mūtim la innassaḫu*, which he cannot soothe with a dressing and which, like the sting of death, cannot be removed (E30).

***nišū***, sbst. pl., people.

1. the people of a named place: *ina utliya nišī māt Šumerim u Akkadîm ukīl*, I held the people of Sumer and Akkad in my arms (E7); *nišī saphātim ša Isin*, the scattered people of Isin (P8); *nišī Malgim*, the people of Malgu (P16); *nišī Mera u Tuttul*, the people of Mera and Tuttul (P17).

2. a community of people:

a. in general: *1 mana kaspam ana nišīšu išaqqalū*, they shall pay one mana of silver to his folk (L24).

b. blessed: *ša kīma abim wālidim ana nišī ibaššû*, who became like a real father to the people (E12); *šīram ṭābam ana nišī ana dār išīm*, he decreed good health for the people for evermore (E12); *rēʾî nišī*, the shepherd of the people (P18); *šāṭip nišīšu in pušqim*, saving his people in distress (P18); *ana šutēšur nišī mātim*, to set the people in the land straight (P22); *nišī dadmī aburrī ušarbiṣ*, I let my people lie down in well-watered pastures (E5); *nišīšu ina mīšarim lirē*, let him shepherd his people with justice (E18); *ašnān napišti nišī*, grain to sustain the people (E22); *šākin mê nuḫšim ana nišīšu*, spreading abundant supplies of water for his people (P8).

c. cursed: *ḫalāq ālišu naspuḫ nišīšu*, the loss of his city and the scattering of his people (E20); *ḫalāq nišīšu*, the loss of his people (E21); *kīma išātim ezzetim ša appim nišīšu liqmi*, let him burn his people with a fierce fire in the reed-bed (E28); *šuāti zērašu māssu ṣābašu nišīšu u ummānšu errētam maruštam līrurū*, let them curse him, his family his land, his army, his people and his workmen with an appalling curse (E31).

3. humanity: *kiššat nišī*, the mass of the people (P1); *ina qerbīt nišīšu zēr awīlūtim ay ibni*, let him raise no human descendant among his people (E29).

4. ***šir niši***, the health ('flesh') of the nation > ***širu***, flesh.

***nīšu* A**, sbst., life, oath.

*nīš ilim izakkarma*, he shall swear an oath by god (literally 'he shall utter the life of the god', L20; 103; 131; 249).

***nīšu* B**, sbst., raising. < *n-š-ʾ*.

*rubûm ellum ša nīš qātišu Adad idû*, the sacred prince, the raising of whose hand Adad recognizes (P14).

***niṭlu***, sbst., glance.

*mūt niṭil īnim*, sudden death (literally 'death in the flash of an eye', E20).

***nizmatu***, sbst., wish.

*ušakšidu nizmassu*, who allowed him to achieve his ambition (P10).

***nuddunu***, vb. to be given. < *n-d-n*.

*mimma ul innaddiššim*, nothing at all shall be given to her (L141).

***nudunnû***, marriage gift from a husband to a wife. < *n-d-n*.

*šeriktaša u nudunnâm ša mussa iddinušim*, the dowry and gift which her husband gave her (L171b; cf. L172); *mussa nudunnâm la iddiššim*, her husband has not given her any present (L172).

*nugguru*, to denounce > ***munaggiru***, informer.

***nuḫḫu***, vb., to soothe. < *n-ʾ-ḫ*.

*ina ṣimdi la unaḫḫušu kīma nišik mūtim la innassaḫu*, which he cannot soothe with a dressing and, like the sting of death, it cannot be removed (E30).

> ***munēḫu***, quietening.

***nuḫšu***, sbst., plenty; adj. abundant. < *n-ḫ-š*.

1. plenty: *mukammer nuḫšim u ṭuḫdim*, supplying abundance and plenty (P4); *muṭaḫḫid nuḫšim bīt Egalmaḫ*, spreading vast riches around the temple of Egalmah (P8); *mušaršidu šubātišin in nuḫšim*, making their homes secure in every way (P16).

2. abundant supplies of water: *šākin mê nuḫšim ana nišīšu*, establishing abundant water supplies for his people (P8); *mušešqi nuḫšim ana Meslam*, who gives abundant drink to Meslam (P15).

***nukaribbu***, sbst., gardener.

*eqlam ana kirîm zaqāpim ana nukaribbim iddin*, he gave a field to a gardener to plant out as an orchard (L60); *nukarribum kiriam izqup erbe sanātim kirâm urabba*, the gardener has planted out the orchard, and he shall make the orchard grow for four years (L60); *nukaribbum eqlam ina zaqāpim la igmurma*, the gardener has not completed the planting of the orchard (L61); *kirāšu ana nukaribbim ana rukkubim iddin*, he gave his orchard to a gardener to pollinate (L64); *nukaribbum kirâm la urakkibma*, the gardener has not completed the pollination of the orchard (L65); *bēl kirîm u nukaribbum mitḫāriš izuzzū*, the owner of the orchard and the cultivator shall share equally (L60); *nukarribum...ana bēl kirîṃ inaddin*, the gardener shall pay the owner of the orchard...(L64); *nukaribbum ana bēl eqlim kīma itēšu imaddad*, the gardener shall make the same assessment as his neighbour for the owner of the field (L62; cf. L65).

***nukkuru***, vb., to alter. < *n-k-r*.

1. to change an order: *dīn mātim ša adīnu purussē mātim ša aprusu ay unakkir*, let him not change the law which I have made for the land and the decisions I have taken for the land (E14); *awâtiya la uštepēl uṣurātiya la unakkir*, he should not emend my commandments or change my purposes (E18); *dīn adīnu uptassis awâtiya uštepēl uṣurātia uttakir*, if he has destroyed the rules I ordained and emended my commandments and changed what I have written (E19); *ša qibīssu la uttakkaru*, whose word cannot be altered (E20); *ina pīšu ša la uttakkaru*, according to what he said, which cannot be altered (E32).

2. to alter a mark: *šimtam uttakkir*, he has then altered the marking (L265).

***nukurtu***, sbst., hostility. < *n-k-r*.

*ina māt nukurtim wardam amtam ša awīlim ištām*, he has purchased a gentleman's slave or slave-girl in a foreign land (L280); *ana māt nukurtišu kamîš līrûšu*, let him remove him to a hostile land far away (E27).

***numātu***, sbst. pl., property.

*ana numāt bēl bītim īnšu iššīma*, he has coveted the property of the owner of the house (L25); *numāt bēl bītim ilteqe*(!), he has taken the property of the owner of the house (L25); *numāt rēdîm ilteqe*, he has taken the property of a soldier (L34).

***nummuru***, vb., to shed light. < *n-ʾ-r*.

*kīma Šamaš ana ṣalmāt qaqqadim waṣêmma mātim nuwwurim*, to rise like Shamash over the dark headed ones and shed light on the land (P3).

> ***munawwir***, brightening.

***nuppušu***, vb., to relax. < *n-p-š*.

*dīnšu līmur libbašu linappišma*, let him understand his problem and let him feel at ease (= 'he will make his heart relax'; E11).

***nūru***, sbst., light.

*mušēṣi nūrim* [vnt. *nūrium*] *ana māt Šumerim u Akkadîm*, bringing out the light in the land of Sumer and Akkad (P21); *nūram ušēṣišināšim*, he brought out the light for them (E3).

*nuwwuru* > ***nummuru***, to shed light.

## P

***pagru***, sbst., body.

[*adi mussa ṣabtu pagarša inaṣṣar*], while her husband was captured she kept her sexual modesty (L133a); *sinništum šû pagarša la iṣṣurma ana bīt šanîm īterub*, that woman did not maintain her sexual modesty but entered the house of another man (L133b).

*paḫāru*, to assemble > ***mupaḫḫiru***, assembling.

*palāhu*, to worship > ***pāliḫu***, worshipping.

*palāsu*, to look at > ***pullusu***, to covet.

***palāšu***, vb., to break into. < *p-l-š*.

*šumma awīlum bītam ipluš ina pani pilšim šuāti idukkūšuma*, if a man has broken into a house they shall kill him in front of the hole (L21); [*ištu*] *nidītika* [*bīti*] *ipallašūnim*, 'they may rob my house because of your mess' (L68+b).

***pālihu***, ptcp., worshipping. < *p-l-ḫ*.

*rubâm na'dam pāliḫ ilī*, the attentive prince who fears the gods (P3).

***palû***, sbst., reign.

*Anum rabûm abu ilī nābû palêya*, almighty Anum, father of the gods, who supports my rule (E19); *lamassī damiqtum rā'imat palêya*, the gracious protector who loves my rule (E27); *palê tānēḫim ūmī īṣūtim šanāt ḫušaḫḫim iklet la nawārim mūt niṭil īnim ana šīmtim lišīmšum*, make his destiny a reign of depression, not enough days, years of hunger, no light in the darkness, death in the flash of an eye (E20); *ūmī warḫī šanāt palēšu ina tānēḫim u dimmatim lišaqti*, let him conclude the days, the months and the years of his reign with weeping and wailing (E24).

***pānu* A**, sbst., face (*AHw pānu* I).

1. as a verbal object:

a. face: *munawwer pani Tišpak*, bringing light to the face of Tishpak (P17).

b. with ***abālu***, to excuse: *ana ištiššu panīšu ubbalū*, for his first offence they shall excuse him (literally 'they shall move his face', L169).

c. with ***šakānu***, to decide: *ezēbim pānīšu ištakan*, he has made up his mind ('he has fixed his face') to leave (L137; elsewhere with *ana* and infinitive: cf. L144, 145 and 148; *panam ištakan*, L168 and 191; *panīša ištakan*, L172 and 177; *panīša ištakanma*, L141).

2. as a prepositional auxiliary:

a. ***ina pāni***, because of, in front of: *bīssu ina panī ilkim iddīma*, he has neglected the estate because of the duty (L30); *ina panī pilšim šuāti idukkūšuma*, they shall kill him in front of (or 'because of') the hole (L21).

b. ***ana pāni***, previously, in front of: *ana panīšu aššassu ana bīt šanîm īterubma*, before that his wife had moved to another man's house (L135); *ana panī eqlišu uzzuzim īgurma*, he has hired him to stand in front of his field (L253).

***pānu* B**, sbst., basket, measure of capacity (*AHw pānu* II; 50 litres, one-fifth of a *kurru*; cf. *BAL* I:117, commentary on L44: *parsiktu*, 60 litres).

*ana 1 kurrum 1 pān 4 sūt še'am ṣibtam ileqqe*, he shall receive one pan and four sa of grain in interest per kur (§5.9); *ṣibassu 1 kurrum še'am 1 pān ana šattim*(?), as annual interest on 1 pan per kur of grain (§5.10).

***pānû***, adj., previous.

*warkat bīt mutiša panîm iparrasūma*, they shall examine the condition of her former husband's house (L177, twice).

***paqādu***, vb., to entrust, care for. < *p-q-d*.

1. to entrust an animal: *aldâm iqīpšu liātim ipqissum* [*ana*] *eqlim erēšim urakkisū*, he has lent him seed and entrusted him with oxen and they have made a contract to cultivate the field (L253).

2. to entrust property: *bītam ša mutiša panîm ana mutiša warkîm u sinništim šuāti ipaqqidūma ṭuppam ušezzebūšunuti*, they shall entrust her former husband's house to her later husband and the woman herself and make them deposit a tablet (L177).

***paqāru***, vb., to claim. < *p-q-r*.

*mārūša ul ipaqqarūši*, her sons shall have no claim against her (L150); *aḫḫūša ul ipaqqarūši*, her brothers shall have no claim against her (L179).

> ***napqaru***, to be reclaimed.

***pāqidu***, ptcp., caring for. < *p-q-d*.

*pāqid bītim Ḫursagkalamma*, caring for the temple of Hursagkalamma (P9).

[*parāku*] > ***naparkû***, to be negligent.

***parāsu***, vb., to reach a decision. < *p-r-s*.

*dayyānum dīnam idīn purussâm iprus kunukkam ušēzib*, the judge has heard the trial, reached his decision and had a sealed document deposited (L5); *dayyānū warkassu iparrasūma*, the judges shall make a decision about his circumstances (L168; 172; cf. L177); *purussē mātim ana parāsim*, to make decisions of national importance (E8); *dīnšina lidīn purussāšina liprus*, let him make judgments for them, let him take decisions for them (E16); *dīn mātim ša adīnu purussē mātim ša aprusu ay unakkir*, let him not change the law which I have made for the land and the decisions I have taken for the land (E14; cf. E15).

> ***naprusu***, to be decided.

***parkullu***, sbst., seal-cutter, lapicide.

[*idī*] *purkullim*, the wages of a lapicide (L274).

***parsiktu*** (cf. *BAL* I:117, commentary on L44).

*ina ūmim ištēn 3 parsikat še'am inaddin*, he shall give three parsiktu of grain for one day (L271).

> ***pānu* B**, measure of capacity.

***parṣu***, sbst., rite.

*parṣī rabûtim ša Ištar*, the magnificent ceremonies for Ishtar (P9).

*pasāsu*, to annul > ***pussusu***, to annul.

***pašāḫu***, vb., to soothe. < *p-š-ḫ*.

*simmam marṣam ša la ipaššeḫū*, a painful wound which they cannot soothe (E30).

***pašāru***, vb., to loosen, trade freely. < *p-š-r*.

*tamkārum ana šamallîm še'am šīpātim šamnam u mimma bīšam ana pašārim iddin*, a merchant has given a trader grain, wool, oil or some other product for resale (L104).

***pašāṭu***, vb., to remove. < *p-š-ṭ*.

*šumī šaṭram ipšiṭma*, he has removed my inscribed name (E19).

***paṭāru***, vb., to repurchase, redeem. < *p-ṭ-r*.

*bēl amtim išaqqalma amassu ipaṭṭar*, the owner of the maid shall pay and repurchase his maid (L119; cf. L281(!)); *tamkārum ipṭuraššuma*, the merchant shall buy him back (L32); *ekallum ipaṭṭaršu*(!), the temple shall redeem him (L32, for Stele: *ipaṭṭarišu*, vnt. *ipaṭṭaršum*); *šûma ramanšu ipaṭṭar*, he shall redeem himself (L32); *ina bītišu ša paṭārim ibašši*, there is enough in his house for redemption (L32; also *paṭārišu*, twice).

> ***napṭuru***, to be redeemed.

***pātiu***, ptcp., of weapons, 'opening out', making effective. < *p-t-'*.

*Ištar bēlet tāḫazim u qablim pātiat kakkiya lamassī damiqtum rā'imat palêya*, O Ishtar, lady of war and conflict, who draws out my weapons; my gracious Protector, who loves me to rule (E27; see *AHw* s.v. *petû* II, G 8).

***pāṭu***, sbst., district.

*ālum u rabiānum ša ina erṣetišunu u pāṭṭišunu ḫubtum iḫḫabtu*, the city and governor in whose territory and district the robbery occurred (L23).

*pazāru*, to hide, protect > ***muštazzir***, protecting.

***peḫû***, vb., to seal up, caulk. < *p-ḫ-ʾ*.

*malāḫum elep 60 kur ana awīlim ipḫe*, the boatman has caulked a boat of 60 gur capacity for a man (L234; cf. *ipḫēma*, L235; see *AHw* s.v. 4c).

***petû***, vb., to open, develop. < *p-t-ʾ*.

1. to open a watercourse: *atappašu ana šiqītim ipte*, he has opened his dyke for irrigation (L55); *mê iptēma epšētim ša eqel itēšu mê uštābil*, he lets out water and allows the water to erode his neighbour's land (L56).

2. to open a building: *bēl bītim našpakam iptēma še'am ilqe*, the owner has opened the storehouse and taken the grain (L120); *bīt sībim iptete u lu ana šikarim ana bīt sībim īterub*, she has opened the door of a drinking house or has entered a drinking house for a drink (L110).

3. to make a surgical incision: *nakkapti awīlim ina karzilli siparrim iptēma*, he has opened a man's eye-socket with the bronze knife (L215; cf. L218; 220).

4. to develop land: *aḫsu iddīma eqlam la iptete*, he has been lazy and not developed the field (L44, variant *ipti*).

> ***puttû***, to solve.

***pīḫātu***, sbst., debt.

*pīḫassu apālam la ile'i*, he was not able to pay his debt (L256).

***pīḫu***, sbst., jug of beer (see *AHw*); vat of beer (see Roth).

*sābītum ištēn pīḫam*(!) *ana qīptim iddin*, the drink-seller has sold a jug of beer on credit (L111).

***pilšu***, sbst., burglary, break-in. < *p-l-š*.

*šumma awīlum bītam ipluš ina pani pilšim šuāti idukkūšuma*, if a man has broken into a house, they shall kill him because of the burglary (L21); *u lu ina pilšim u lu ina nabalkattim*, whether by breaking in or by scaling over (L125).

***pissātu***, sbst., disease.

*ina tarbaṣim pissātam uštabšī*, he has allowed disease to develop in the pen (L267); *ḫiṭīt pissatim ša ina tarbaṣim ušabšû*, the damage from the disease that he has allowed to develop in the pen (L267).

***piššatu***, sbst., oil.

*kīma emūq zittiša ipram piššatam u lubūšam inaddinūšimma*, they shall give her food, oil and clothing according to the size of her share (L178, twice).

***pītu***, sbst., opening. < *p-t-ʾ*.

*ina kārišu pītum ittepte*, a break has been opened in his dyke (L53); *awīlum ša ina kārišu pītum ippetû*, the man in whose dyke the opening was made (L53).

***pû***, sbst., mouth, message.

1. mouth: *kittam u mīšaram ina pī mātim aškun*, I have put rules and justice in the mouth of the nation (P22); *ina pī Ellil šarrim lišaškin*, let her have it decreed by the command of the sovereign Enlil (E21).

2. message: *ina pīšu kabtim liqbi*, let him speak with his grave words (E20); *ana pī riksātišu*, according to the words of his agreement (L264); *errētim anniātim*(!) *Ellil ina pīšu ša la uttakkaru līruršuma arḫiš likšudašu*, these are the curses which Enlil will certainly invoke —what he says is never changed—and which he will certainly bring on him quickly (E32).

3. terms: *ana pī ṣimdat šarrim ana tamkārim inaddin*, he shall pay the merchant according to the rate agreed by the king (L51); *kaspam u ṣibassu ša pī ṭuppišu*, silver and the interest on it according to the terms of the document (L66).

***puḫḫu***, vb., to exchange. < *p-ʾ-ḫ*.

*eqlam kirâm u bītam ša rēdîm bāʾirim u nāši biltim upīḫ u niplātim iddin*, he has acquired by exchange the field, orchard or house of a soldier, hunter or tribute bearer and paid a supplement (L41).

***puḫru***, sbst., assembly, council. < *p-ḫ-r*.

*ina puḫrim ina qinnaz alpim 1 šūši immaḫḫaṣ*, he shall be beaten 60 times with an ox-tail in the assembly (L202); *u ina puḫrim ina kussî dayyānūtišu ušetbûšuma*, furthermore they shall have him removed from the Assembly and from his place on the legal bench (L5).

***pūḫu***, sbst., substitute. < *p-ʾ-ḫ*.

*agram īgurma pūḫšu iṭṭarad*, he has hired a mercenary and sent him as his substitute (L26); *agram pūḫam imḫurma*, he acquired a mercenary as a substitute (L33).

***pullusu***, vb., to covet (formerly read *balāṣu*, to ogle). < *p-l-s*.

*ana sinništim šanītim uptallisma ana emišu māratka ul aḫḫaz iqtabi*, he has coveted another woman and has said to his intended father-in-law, 'I will not have your daughter' (L159).

***purussu***, sbst., decision. < *p-r-s*.

*dayyānum dīnam idīn purussâm iprus kunukkam ušēzib*, the judge has heard the trial, reached his decision and had a sealed document deposited (L5); *dīnšina lidīn purussāšina liprus*, let him make judgments for them, let him take decisions for them (E16); *purussē mātim ana parāsim*, to make decisions of national importance (E8); *purusse mātim ša aprusu*, the decisions I have made for the nation (E14; 15); *ašar šipṭim u purussêm ina maḫar Ellil awassu lilemmin*, may she demonstrate the wickedness of his word in the presence of Enlil in the place of judgment and decision (E21).

***pussusu***, vb., to annul. < *p-s-s*.

*dīn adīnu uptassis awâtiya uštepēl uṣurātiya uttakir*, he has annulled the rules I ordained and emended my commandments and changed what I have written (E19).

***pušqu***, sbst., distress.

*šāṭip nišīšu in pušqim*, saving his people in distress (P18); *pušqī waštūtim upetti*, I solved impossibly distressing situations (E3).

***puttû***, vb., to solve. < *p-t-ʾ*.

*pušqī waštūtim upetti*, I have solved impossibly distressing situations (E3).

## Q

*qa* > ***qû***, grain measure.

***qablu*** (= *CAD qablu* B), sbst., conflict.

*Ištar bēlet tāhazim u qablim*, Ishtar the lady of conflict and strife (E27); *Nergal dannum ina ilī qabal la maḫār mušakšidu irnittiya*, Nergal, strongest of the gods unrivalled in the battle, who sees me through to victory (E28); *etel šarrī qabal la maḫārim*, most eminent of kings, unequalled in the strife (P15); *ašar tāhazim u qablim*, the place of conflict and strife (E27); *qablātim ubelli šīr mātim uṭīb*, I made conflicts cease, I improved the health of the nation (E5).

***qablû***, sbst./adj., middle, referring to an ox positioned in the middle of the ploughing team (see *CAD* Q: 16b-17a s.v. 1a).

*idī alpim ša warka 4 kur šeʾam idī alpim ša qabla 3 kur šeʾam ana bēlišu inaddin*, he shall give to its owner four kur of grain as the fee for the rear-ox, and three kur of grain for the middle-ox (L242/3).

***qabû***, vb., to speak. < *q-b-ʾ*.

1. of a deity: *annītam liqbīma ina maḫar Marduk bēliya Zarpānītum bēltiya ina libbišu gamrim likrubam*, let him speak in this way and let him bless me with all his heart in the presence of my lord Marduk and of my lady Zarpanitum (E12); *ina pīšu kabtim liqbi*, let him speak with his grave words (E20).

2. to utter a formal statement: *awat iqbû la uktīn*, he did not prove the statement he made (L3); *mudūssunu maḫar ilim iqabbûma*, they shall state what they know in the presence of the god (L9); *ina maḫar ilim kasap išqulu*(!) *iqabbīma*(!), he shall state the amount of silver he paid in the presence of the god (L281); *ša ana ḫarrān šarrim alākšu qabû*, who has said that he would go on a royal expedition (L26, variant *qabûma*).

3. to make a request: *ana waššābim ina ūmīšu la malûtim waṣâm iqtabi*, he has told the lodger to leave before his time has expired

(L69+c); *eqlam erēšam iqtabi*, he has asked for the field to be cultivated (L47); *ezēbša iqtabi*, he has said he will divorce her (L141, twice).

4. following direct speech: *awīlum mimmûšu la ḫaliqma mimmê ḫaliq iqtabi*, a man who has not lost anything said, 'I have lost something' (L126); *šībī mudē ḫulqiyami lublam iqtabi*, he has said, 'I could bring witnesses who know it is my property' (L9, twice); *esip tabal iqbīšum*, he has commanded him, 'Harvest it and take it away...' (L49); *ana kaspika tabal iqbīšum*, he said, 'Take away as payment for your silver' (L66); *ana bēl nidītim nidītka ēpuš* [*ištu*] *nidītika* [*bīti*] *ippalašūnim iqbi*, he said to the owner of the derelict property, 'Clear up your mess in case they rob my house because of your mess' (L68+b); *sinništum mussa izērma ul taḫḫazanni iqtabi*, a woman has hated her husband and said, 'You shall not have me' (L142); *māratka ul aḫḫaz iqtabi*, he has said, 'I shall not take your daughter' (L159); *mārti ul anaddikkum iqtabi*, he has said, 'I will not give you my daughter' (L160); *mārti ul taḫḫaz iqtabi*, he has said, 'You shall not take my daughter' (L161); *mārī anassaḫ iqtabi*, he has said, 'I will disinherit my son' (L168); *ana mārī ša amtum uldušum mārūa iqtabi*, he has said to the sons the slave-girl bore him, 'My sons' (L170; cf. *la iqtabi*, L171a); *ul abī atta ul ummī atti iqtabi*, he has said, 'You are not my father, you are not my mother' (L192); *ul bēlī atta iqtabi*, he has said, 'You are not my master' (L282).

**qābû**, ptcp., speaking. < *q-b-ʾ*.
*Ninkarrak mārat Anim qābiat dumqiya*, Ninkarrak the daughter of Sin who speaks in my favour (E30).

**qadištu**, sbst., temple prostitute. < *q-d-š*.
*abum nadītam qadištam u lu kulmašītam ana ilim iššīma šeriktam la išrukšim*, a father has offered to the god a priestess, a temple prostitute or a hierodule and has not given her a marriage gift (L181).

**qadu**, with (see *CAD adi* B).
*qadum šeriktim ša bīt abiša ana bīt warad ekallim u lu warad muškēnim īrubma*, she has gone into the house of a palace slave or a workman's slave together with the dowry from her father's house (L176).

**qalû**, vb., to execute by burning. < *q-l-ʾ*.
*awīltam šuāti iqallūši*, they shall burn such a woman (L110); *kilallīšunu iqallūšunūti*, they shall burn both of them (L157).

**qâlu**, vb., to heed. < *q-ʾ-l*.
*ana awâtim ša ina narîya ašṭuru liqūlma*, let him heed the message which I have inscribed on my stela (E15; cf. *iqūlma*, E18; *la iqūlma*, E19).

***qamû***, vb., to burn in rage. < *q-m-ʾ*.

*ina kašūšišu rabîm kīma išātim ezzetim ša appim nišīšu liqmi*, let him burn his people by his mighty power, raging like a fire in the reeds (E28).

***qâpu* A**, vb., to entrust. < *q-ʾ-p*.

*tamkārum kaspam šamallâm iqīpma*, a merchant has entrusted silver to a salesman (L107); *aldâm iqīpšu liātim ipqissu* [*ana*] *eqlim erēšim urakkisū*, he has lent him seed and entrusted him with oxen and they have made a contract to cultivate the field (L253).

***qâpu* B**, vb., to crumble. < *q-ʾ-p*.

*itinnum bītam ana awīlim īpušma šipiršu la uštesbīma igārum iqtūp*, a builder has built a house for a man but has not made his work strong enough and the wall has collapsed (L233).

***qaqqadu***, sbst., head, principal sum.

*ṣibtam mala* [*qaqqadišu*], as much interest as the principal loan (§5.11); *u lu ṣibātim ana qaqqādim uṭṭeḫḫi*, or he has put the interest together with the principal (§5.12); *qaqqad kaspim ana tamkārim utâr*, he shall repay the principal to the merchant (L102).

for ***ṣalmāt qaqqadim***, mankind, > ***ṣalmu* 1**, black.

***qarītu***, sbst., granary.

*ina qarītim ibbûm ittabši*, a loss has occurred in the granary (L120).

***qarnu***, sbst., horn.

*qaranšu išbir zibbassu ittakis*, he has broken off its horn or cut off its tail (L248); *qarnīšu la ušarrim*, he has not padded its horns (L251).

***qarrādu***, sbst., hero.

*qarrādišu lišamqit damīšunu erṣetam lišqi gurun šalmāt ummānātišu ina ṣērim littaddi ummānšuma rēmam ay ušarši*, bring down his heroes, let the land drink their blood, keep on throwing men's bodies on to the heap in the desert and show them no mercy (E27); *Zababa qarrādum rabium mārum rēštûm ša Ekur āliku imniya*, O Zababa, almighty warrior, the first son born in Ekur, companion at my right hand (E26); *qarrādum gāmil Larsa*, the hero who restored Larsa (P8).

***qâšu***, vb., to give. < *q-ʾ-š*.

*šû iqīšu napšatam ana Maškan-šāpir*, he was the one who granted the gift of life to Mashkan-shapar (P15).

*qatû*, to come to an end > ***šuqtû***, to terminate.

***qātu***, sbst., hand, skill, possession.

1. hand raised in prayer: *rubûm ellum ša nīš qātišu Adad idû*, the sacred prince, whose raised hand Adad recognizes (P14).

2. manual skill: *mār ummānim ṣeḫram ana tarbītim ilqēma šipir qātišu uštāḫissu*, a professional person has taken a son to adopt and has taught him his own craft (L188; cf. L189).

3. possession: *bīš qātišu*, his personal possessions (L112).
4. with ***ana***, into the possession of someone: *šuāti ana qāt nakrīšu limallīšuma*, let him hand him over into the hands of his enemies (E27).
5. with ***ina***, in (or from) the possession of someone: *ina qāt mār awīlim u lu warad awīlim balum šībī u riksātim ištām*, he has made a purchase from a gentleman's son or a gentleman's slave without witnesses or contracts (L7); *ina qāti rēdîm ištām*, he has made a purchase from a soldier (L35); *ḫalqam ina qāti awīlim iṣṣabat*, he then found the missing property in the possession of another man (L9); *awīlum ša ḫulqum ina qātišu ṣabtu*, the man in whose possession the lost property was found (L9); *wardum ina qātišu ittaṣbat*, the slave was found in his possession (L19; cf. L253); *ša šurqam ina qātišu imḫuru iddâk*, the one who received the stolen property from his possession shall be killed (L6); *wardum ina qāt ṣābitānišu iḫtaliq*, the slave has slipped out of the hands of his captor (L20); *ina qāt mušēniqtim imtūt*, he has died in the custody of the nurse (L194); *mimma ša ina qātišu ibaššû*, whatever there was in his possession (§5.15).

***qerbītu***, sbst., midst, interior. < *q-r-b*.
*ina qerbīt nišīšu zēr awīlūtim ay ibni*, may he not raise a human family amidst the people (E29).

***qerbu***, sbst., inside. < *q-r-b*.
1. inner nature: *asakkam lemnam simmam marṣam ša la ipaššeḫū asûm qerebšu la ilammadu*, devilish pain and weeping sores which they cannot relieve and the nature [= 'inside'] of which no physician understands (E30).
2. ***qerbum***, used adverbially: *mukinni Ištar ina Eulmaš qerbum Akkadim ribītim*, establishing Ishtar in Eulmash within the enclosure at Akkad (P18); *mukinnu išdīšin qerbum Bābilim šulmāniš*, establishing their foundations within Babylon securely (P18).

***qerēbu***, vb., to be near at hand. < *q-r-b*.
*šumma awīlum šû šībūšu la qerbu*, if the witnesses for that man are not available (L13).

***qibītu***, sbst., command. < *q-b-ʾ*.
*ina qibīt Šamaš dayyānim rabîm ša šamê u erṣetim*, at the command of Shamash, the almighty judge in heaven and earth (E10); *Ellil bēlum mušīm šīmātim ša qibīssu la uttakkaru*, Enlil the lord who fixes destinies, whose decrees cannot be altered (E20); *Ninlil ummum rabītum ša qibīssa ina Ekur kabtat*, Ninlil, the great mother, whose decree is revered in Ekur (E21).

***qinnazu***, sbst., whip.

*ina puḫrim ina qinnaz alpim 1 šūši immaḫḫaṣ*, he shall be beaten 60 times with a whip in the assembly (L202).

***qīptu***, sbst., trust. < *q-ʾ-p*.

*sābītum ištēn pīham ana qīptim iddin*, the drink-seller has sold a jug of beer on trust (L111).

***qīštu***, sbst., gift, fee.< *q-ʾ-š*.

*qīšti šarrum ana rēdîm iddinu ilteqe*, he has taken away a presentation the king gave the soldier (L34); *qīšti abum iddinušum ileqqēma*, he shall keep the presentation the father gave him (L165); *2 šiqil kaspam ana qīštišu inaddiššum*, he shall pay him two shekels of silver as his fee (L228; 234).

***qû***, sbst., grain measure.

*1 qa šeʾum idūšu*, the fee for it is one qu of grain (L270); *ina šanat ana 1 kur šeʾim 5 qa šeʾam idī našpakim inaddin*, he shall pay the storage charge of five qu of grain for one kur of grain per year (L121).

***qurādu***, hero.

*munēḫ libbi Adad quradim in Bīt Karkara*, quietening the heart of Adad, the hero at Bit Karkara (P14).

## R

*rabāṣu*, to lie down > ***šurbuṣu***, pasture.

***rabiānu***, sbst., headman, governor. < *r-b-ʾ*.

*ālum u rabiānum ša ina erṣetišūnu u pāṭišunu ḫubtum iḫḫabtu*, the city and governor in whose territory and district the robbery occurred (L23); *ālum u rabiānum 1 mana kaspam ana nišīšu išaqqalū*, the city and the governor shall pay his people one mana of silver (L24).

***rabītu***, sbst., principal wife (= 'great lady') cf. *CAD* s.v. *rabû*, adj. < *r-b-ʾ*.

*warki abišu ina sūn rabītišu ša mārī waldat ittaṣbat*, he has been caught after the departure of his father in the bosom of his principal wife (L158; cf. *ANET*: *murabbītišu*(!), foster mother).

***rabû* A**, vb., to be great. < *r-b-ʾ*.

1. to be great in importance: *awīlum lēt awīlim ša elišu rabû imtaḫaṣ*, a man has struck the cheek of a man more important than himself (L202).

2. to be grown up: *ana mārī ša irbû aššātim īḫuz*, he has taken wives for the sons who have grown up (L166, following Roth's emendation of Stele: *iršû*; Roth translates: for his eligible sons; see *rašû*, 3).

> ***rubbû***, to grow; ***šurbû***, to extol.

***rabû* B**, adj., large, important, mighty. < *r-b-ʾ*.

1. large: *kaspam ina abnim [rabītim] šeʾam ina sūtim rabītim imḫur*, he received silver according to the heavy weight and grain according to the large measure ([§5.13]; 5.13); *ina abnim rabītim kaspam imtaḫar*, she has received a large weight of silver (L108).

2. severe, excessive: *arnam kabtam šēressu rabītam ša ina zumrišu la iḫalliqu līmussuma*, let him lay upon him a serious punishment and great condemnation which will not disappear from his body (E24); *ina libbiša aggim ina uzzātiša rabiātim šarrūssu līrur*, let her curse his kingdom with unsurpassable anger and rage in her heart (E27); *ina kašūšišu rabîm*, by his mighty power (E28).

3. important: *parṣī rabûtim ša Ištar*, important rituals for Ishtar (P9); *nindabê rabûtim ana Eninnu*, important offerings for Eninnu (P13);

4. mighty (of deities): *naʾdum muštēmiqum ana ilī rabûtim*, pious and devout towards the almighty gods (P20, variant *rabiʾūtim*); *ilū rabûtim ša šamê u erṣetim*, the almighty gods of heaven and earth (E31); *ilū rabûtim ibbûninnima*, the almighty gods have named me (E6); *Anum rabûm abu ilī*, mighty Anu, father of the gods (E19); *Ea rubûm rabiʾum*, Ea the mighty prince (E22); *Ninlil ummum rabītum*, Ninlil the great mother (E21); *ina qibīt Šamaš dayyānim rabîm ša šamê u erṣetim*, at the command of Shamash the mighty judge of heaven and earth (E10; cf. *dayyānum rabium*, E23); *Zababa qarrādum rabium*, Zababa the mighty hero (E26).

***râbu***, vb., to replace, recompense. < *r-ʾ-b*.

1. to compensate for lost property: *šeʾam riabam la ileʾi*, he is not able to make recompense for the grain (L54); *mimmâšu ḫalqam iriabbūšum*, they shall recompense him for whatever was lost (L23, variant *iriabbūšu*; also *iriabšum*, L240); *ana bēl makkūrim iriab*, he shall make recompense to the owner of the goods (L125); *šeʾam ša uḫalliqu iriab*, he shall make recompense for the grain that he lost (L53); *mimma ša uḫalliqu iriab*, he shall make recompense for whatever he allowed to get lost (L232; cf. L237); *eleppam ana bēl eleppim iriab*, he shall recompense the owner of the boat with another boat (L236); *iriab*, he shall repay (L68+b, fragmentary).

2. to compensate for the loss of a person: *wardam kīma wardim iriab*, he shall recompense a slave with a slave (L219).

3. to compensate for the loss of an animal: *alpam kīma alpim ana bēl alpim iriab*, he shall recompense an ox with an ox to the owner of the ox (L245; 246); *immeram kīma [immerim] ana bēlišu iriab*, he shall recompense a sheep with a sheep (L263, but *BAL*: *ana bēli[šunu]*);

4. to make increased compensation: *tašna šeʾam ša imḫuru*(!) *iriab*, he shall make recompense with twice the amount of grain he received

(L254); *adi 10-šu iriab*, he shall make a ten-fold recompense (L8); *adi 10-šu ša išriqu liātim u ṣēnam ana bēlišunu iriab*, he shall make a ten-fold recompense in cattle or sheep for what he has stolen (L265).

***ragāmu***, vb., to call, claim. < *r-g-m.*

*mimma ša irgumu uštašanāma ana babtišu inaddin*, he shall give to his community double whatever he had laid claim to (L126); *ana šeriktiša abuša ul iraggum šeriktaša ša mārīšama*, her father has no claim on her dowry; her dowry belongs to her sons (L162; cf. L163); *mārū ḫīrtim ana mārī amtim ana wardūtim ul iraggumū*, the sons of the first wife shall have no claim for service from the sons of the slave-girl (L171a; cf. *ul iraggum*, L175).

***raggu***, adj., wicked.

*raggam u ṣēnam ana ḫulluqim*, to destroy evil and wickedness (P3); *ina mātišu raggam u ṣēnam lissuḫ šīr nišīšu liṭīb*, let him weed out evil and wickedness and let him bring prosperity into the lives of his people (E16).

***raḫāṣu***, vb., to devastate. < *r-ḫ-ṣ.*

*eqlam Adad irtaḫiṣ u lu bibbulum itbal*, Adad has inundated the field and has devastated the produce (L45; cf. L48).

***rā'imu***, ptcp., loving. < *r-ʾ-m.*

*Ištar bēlet tāḫazim u qablim pātiat kakkiya lamassī damiqtum rā'imat palêya*, Ishtar, lady of war and conflict, who draws out my weapons; my gracious Protector, who loves me to rule (E27).

*rakābu*, to ride > *rukkubu*, to pollinate.

***rakāsu***, vb., to agree formally. < *r-k-s.*

*mušēniqtum balum abišu u ummišu ṣiḫram šaniamma irtakas*, the nurse has made an agreement about another child without the knowledge of the father and the mother (L194; also *irkusu*, subjunctive, L194).

> ***rukkusu***, to demand a contract; ***narkusu***, to congregate.

***ramanu***, sbst., oneself, single item.

1. oneself: *šûma ramanšu ipaṭṭar*, he shall redeem himself (L32); *ina makkūr ramanišu bīt imqutu ippeš*, he shall reconstruct the house that has collapsed from his own resources (L232; cf. L235); *ina kasap ramanišu igāram šuāti udannan*, he shall repair that wall at his own expense (L233).

2. one single item: *ereqqamma ana ramaniša īgur*, he has hired a wagon by itself (L272).

***râmu***, vb., to love. < *r-ʾ-m.*

1. to love a person: *warkassa ana māriša ša irammu inaddin*, she may give her property to the son she loves (L150).

2. to love a place: *ina Esagil ša arammu šumī ina damiqtim ana dār lizzakir*, may my name be uttered as a blessing for evermore in Esagila, the place I love! (E10).

*rapāšu*, to be wide > ***murappišu***, widen.

***raqû***, vb., to hide. < *r-q-ʾ*.

*ina bītišu irtaqīma ana šisīt nāgirim la uštēṣiam*, he hid him in his house and did not produce him at the crier's announcement (L16).

*rašādu*, to be grounded > ***šuršudu***, to provide foundations; ***mušaršidu***, protecting.

***rašû***, vb., to possess, permit. < *r-š-ʾ*.

1. to possess, acquire concrete objects: *ina eqlim kirîm u bītim ša išammuma iraššû*, as for a field, orchard or house which he may acquire by purchase (L39); *mimma ša mussa u šî ištu innemdū iršû*, whatever she and her husband have acquired after they have come together (L176a; 176b); *bīšam iršû*, they have acquired possessions (L176a).

2. with an abstract object: *awīlum ša ḫubullam iršû*, a man who has a debt (§5.10); *wardam amtam išāmma baqrī irtaši*, he has bought a slave or a slave-girl but has also taken on a claim (L279); *awīlum ḫablum ša awatam iraššû*, a wronged man who has a matter of concern (E11).

3. to take people into one's possession: *ṣāb nisḫātim irtaši*, he has taken possession of deserting troops (L33, Roth, hesitantly, suggests 'to recruit').

4. to have children: *warka mārī irtašīma*, afterwards he has children of his own (L191); *ana mārī ša iršû aššātim īḫuz*, he found wives for the sons he has had (L166; but Roth emends to *ana mārī ša iršû*, for the sons who have grown up, see *rabû*).

5. to permit: *uṣurātūa mušassikam ay iršia*, may he not permit him to throw out my plans (E10).

6. to show, exhibit a fault (*CAD* s.v. 4c): *eleppum šî iṣṣabar ḫiṭītam irtaši*, that boat has sprung a leak and shown it was faulty (L235).

> ***šuršû***, allow to have.

*râšu* (= *riāšu*, to be glad) > ***murīšu***, bringing joy.

*raṭābu*, to be moist > ***ruṭṭubu***, to moisten.

***rebītu*** (*CAD*: *ribītu*), sbst., city-square. < *r-b-ʾ*.

*mukinni Ištar ina Eulmaš qerbum Akkadim ribītim*, who set Ishtar in the Eulmash in the midst of the great square of Asshur (P18; see *AHw* s.v. 1b).

***rebû***, adj., fourth.

*ina rebûtim šattim*, in the fourth year (L44; 117).

***redû***, vb., to pursue, catch, send. < *r-d-ʾ*.

1. to obtain for oneself: *šumma ina šeššet warḫī šībīšu la irdeam awīlum šû sār*, and if he has not collected his witnesses within the six months, that man is a liar (L13).

2. to obtain for someone else: *lu wardam lu amtam ḫalqam ina ṣērim iṣbatma ana bēlišu irtediaššu*, he has caught a slave or a maid in the desert and brought him back to his master (L17); *ana ekallim ireddīšu*, he shall take him to the palace (L18; also *la irdeam*, L109).

3. to send: *agram pūḫam imḫurma irtede*, he acquired and sent a mercenary as a substitute (L33).

> ***murtedū***, wagon-driver.

***rēdû***, sbst., soldier. < *r-d-ʾ*.

*lu rēdûm u lu bāʾirum ša ana ḫarrān šarrim alākšu qabû*, a soldier or a hunter who is asked to go on an royal expedition (L26); *lu rēdûm u lu bāʾirum šû iddâk*, that soldier or hunter shall be killed (L26); *lu rēdûm u lu bāʾirum ša ina dannat šarrim turru*, a soldier or a hunter who is taken back to a royal fortress (L27; 28; 32); *lu rēdûm u lu bāʾirum eqelšu kirāšu u bīssu ina pani ilkim iddīma*, a soldier or a hunter neglected his field, his orchard or his house because of a duty (L30); *numāt rēdîm ilteqe rēdiam iḫtabal rēdiam ana igrim ittadin rēdiam ina dīnim ana dannim ištarak qīšti šarrum ana rēdîm iddinu ilteqe*, he has taken the property of a soldier, has exploited a soldier, has given a soldier out for hire, offered a soldier to a strong person in a legal dispute or has taken a present which the king had given to the soldier (L34; 34; 34; 34; 34); *liātim*(!) *u ṣēnī ša šarrum ana rēdîm iddinu ina qāti rēdîm ištām*, he has bought from the hand of soldier cattle or sheep which the king gave the soldier (L35; 35); *eqlam kirâm u bītam ša rēdîm bāʾirim u nāši biltim upīḫ u niplātim iddin*, he has acquired by exchange the field, orchard or house of a soldier, hunter or tribute bearer and paid a supplement (L41); *rēdûm bāʾirum u nāši biltim ana eqlišu kirîšu u bītišu itâr*, the soldier, hunter or tribute bearer shall return to his field, orchard or house (L41); *eqlum kirûm u bītum ša rēdîm bāʾirim u nāši biltim ana kaspim ul innaddin*(!), the field, orchard or house of a soldier, hunter or tribute bearer shall not be sold for silver (L36; cf. L37); *rēdûm bāʾirum u nāši biltim ina eqlim kirîm u bītim ša ilkišu ana aššatišu u mārtišu ul išaṭṭar u ana eʾiltišu ul inaddin*, a soldier hunter or tribute bearer shall not sign over to his wife or daughter a field or orchard or house pertaining to his duty, nor shall it be given for debt (L38).

***rēmu***, sbst., pity, love. < *r-ʾ-m*.

*rēmam ay ušarši*, let him not offer any love (E27).

***rēṣu***, sbst., helper. < *r-ʾ-ṣ*.

*muddiš Ebabbar ana Šamaš rēṣišu*, renewing Ebabbar for Shamash his helper (P8); *Adad bēl ḫegallim gugal šamê u erṣetim rēṣūʾa*, O Adad lord of plenty, bringing water to heaven and earth, my helper (E25).

***rēštû***, adj., oldest.

***māru rēštû***, oldest son: *ana Marduk mārim rēštîm ša Ea*, for Marduk, the first born son son of Ea (P1); *Zababa qarrādum rabium mārum rēštûm ša Ekur*, Zababa the mighty hero, first son in Ekur (E26).

***rēšu***, sbst., head, height, beginning.

1. top: *mullî rēš Eanna mukammer ḫiṣbim ana Anim u Ištar*, who raised up high the pinnacles of Eanna, who heaped up luxury for Anum and Ishtar (P8); *ina Bābilim ālim ša Anum u Ellil rēšīšu ullû*, in Babylon, the city whose skyline Anu and Enlil raised high (E8).

2. beginning: *ištu rēš šattim*, from the beginning of the year (L273).

***reʾû***, vb., to tend small animals. < *r-ʾ-ʾ*.

1. to look after animals: *nāqidam ana liātim u ṣēnim reʾîm īgur*, he has hired a herdsman to care for the cattle and sheep (L261); [*rēʾūm*] *ša liātum u lu ṣēnum ana reʾîm innadnušum*, a shepherd who has been given cattle and sheep to feed (L264; 265).

2. to tend to the needs of people: *nišīšu in mīšarim lirē*, he will surely feed his people with righteousness (E18).

***rēʾû***, sbst., shepherd. < *r-ʾ-ʾ*.

1. one who tends to the needs of animals: *rēʾûm ana šammī ṣēnim šūkulim itti bēl eqlim la imtagarma*, a shepherd has not made an agreement with the owner of the field to pasture his flock in a meadow (L57, twice); *rēʾûm ṣēnam ana eqlim iddīma*, a shepherd has left his flock in a field (L58); *rēʾûm eqel ušākilu inaṣṣarma*, the shepherd shall take custody of the field on which he let them feed (L58); [*rēʾūm*] *ša liātum u lu ṣēnum ana reʾîm innadnušum*, a shepherd who has been given cattle and sheep to feed ([L264]; 265); *rēʾûm maḫar*(!) *ilim ubbamma*, the shepherd shall acquit himself in the presence of the god (L266); *šumma reʾûm īgūma ina tarbaṣim pissatam uštabši reʾûm ḫiṭit pissatim ša ina tarbaṣim ušabšû liātim u ṣēnamušallamma*, if a shepherd has been negligent and allowed disease to occur in the fold the shepherd shall make good the damage from the disease that he has allowed to develop in the fold with cattle and sheep (L267; 267).

2. one who tends to the needs of people: *Ḫammurabi rēʾûm nibīt Ellil anāku*, I am Hammurabi, Enlil's chosen shepherd (P4); *rēʾî nišī ša epšētušu eli Ištar ṭāba*, the shepherd of the people, whose achievements bring pleasure to Ishtar (P18); *ilū rabûtum ibbûninnima*

*anākuma rē'ûm mušallimum*, the great gods called me and I am the shepherd who brings peace (E6).

***rē'ûtu***, sbst., shepherdship, governance. < *r-'-'*.

*šarrum gitmālum anāku ana ṣalmāt qaqqadim ša Ellil išrukam rē'ûssina Marduk iddinam*, I am the perfect king for the mass of humanity whom Enlil has entrusted to me and whose leadership Marduk has given me (E2).

*riāšu*, to be glad > ***murīšu***, bringing joy.

*ribītu* > ***rebītu***, square.

***rīdu***, sbst., behaviour; adj. sensible.

*mātam ussam kīnam u rīdam damqam ušaṣbitu*, he made the land adopt proper conduct and a good behaviour (E1); *kibsam rīdam dīn mātim ša adīnu*, the sensible customs and rules of the land which I have decreed (E15).

***rikistu***, sbst., contract. < *r-k-s*.

*ṭuppi rikistišu* [*iḫeppe*], he shall break the tablet for the contract (§5.11).

***riksu***, sbst., contract, bond. < *r-k-s*; see also ***kiṣru***, agreed payment.

1. a contract between persons: *ina ebūrim kīma riksātišu še'am ileqqe*, he shall pay the grain at harvest according to the contracts (L47); *ana pī riksātišu tālittam u biltam inaddin*, he shall pay the rent as offspring according to the terms of his contract (L264); *mimma mala innadinu šībī ukallam riksātim išakkanma*, he shall show to witnesses everything that is to be given and make a contract (L122); *riksātišu ul inni*, he shall not change his contracts (L52); *balum šībī u riksātim ištām*, he bought without witnessed contracts (L7; cf. L123); *awīlum aššatam īḫuzma riksātiša la iškun*, he has taken a wife but not made contracts for her (L128).

see also ***markasu***, link and ***kiṣru***, agreed payment.

***rīmu***, sbst., ox.

*rīmum kadrum munakkip zā'irī*, the raging ox that tosses opponents (P10).

***rīqu***, adj., empty. < *r-'-q*.

*ela ana la ḫassim rēqa ana emqim ana tanādātim šūṣâ*, although empty to the one without understanding, from the wise they bring out praise (E17).

***rīqūtu***, sbst., emptiness. < *r-'-q*.

*ṣeḫrum šû reqūssu ul ittallak*, that son shall not go away with nothing (L191).

***risbatu***, sbst., fight. < *r-s-b*.

*ina risbatim imtaḫaṣma simmam ištakanšu*, he has struck him in a fight and wounded him (L206).

***rittu***, sbst., hand.

*rittašu inakkisū*, they shall cut off his hand (L195; 218; 253); *ritti gallābim šuāti inakkisū*, they shall cut off the hand of that barber. (L226).

*rubātu*, lady > ***bēltu***, lady.

***rubbû***, vb., to grow crops, bring up children. < *r-b-ʾ*.

1. to grow crops: *kiriam urabba*, he shall make the orchard grow (L60).

2. to rear children: *ummašu urabbāšu*, his mother shall bring him up (L29; also *urabba* and *urtabbû*, L137; 137); *ṣeḫḫerūtim urabbû*, they shall rear the little ones (L177); *ṣeḫram ina mêšu ana mārutim ilqēma urtabbīšu*, he has adopted a new-born child as his son and has brought him up (L185; also *urabbûšu*, L190; 191).

> ***murabbū***, foster father, ***murabbītu***, foster mother; ***šurbû***, to glorify.

***rubû***, sbst., prince.

*rubâm naʾdam pāliḫ ilī*, the favoured prince who fears the gods (P3); *rubûm ellum ša nīš qātišu Adad idû*, the sacred prince, whose raised hand Adad recognizes (P14); *rubûm naʾdum munawwer pani Tišpak*, the obedient prince, who sheds his light on the faces of the men of Tishpak (P17); *Ea rubûm rabium*, Ea the chief prince (E22).

***rugummû***, sbst., loss. < *r-g-m*.

*šāyyimānum ina bīt nādinānim rugummē dīnim šuāti adi ḫamšišu ileqqe*, the purchaser shall take five times the value of the damages in this case from his house (L12); *rugummâm ša ina dīnim šuāti ibaššû adi 12-šu inaddin*, whatever the loss that had occasioned that trial he shall pay 12 times over (L5); *dīnum šû rugummâm ul išu*, there shall be no damages in that case (L115; 123; 250).

***rukkubu***, vb., to pollinate. < *r-k-b*.

*kirāšu ana nukaribbim ana rukkubim iddin*, he gave his orchard to a gardener to pollinate (L64); *nukaribbum kirâm la urakkibma*, the gardener has not completed the pollination of the orchard (L65).

***rukkusu***, vb., to demand a contract. < *r-k-s*.

*aššum bēl ḫubullim ša mutiša la ṣabātiša mussa urtakkis*, she has made her husband make a contract that no creditor of her husband may seize her (L151); *aldâm iqīpšu liātim ipqissum* [*ana*] *eqlim erēšim urakkissu*, he has lent him seed and entrusted him with oxen and made him contract to cultivate the field (L253).

> ***narkusu***, congregate.

***rūqu***, adj., distant. < *r-ʾ-q*.

*šumma rūqim*, if he is far away (§4.12, fragmentary).

***ruṭṭubu***, vb., to moisten. < *r-ṭ-b*.

*ṭuppašu uraṭṭab u ṣibtam ša šattim šuāti ul inaddin*, he shall ignore the contract (literally 'wet the tablet') and not pay interest for that year (L48).

***rū'u***, sbst., comrade.

*sapar nakirī ša Erra rūšu ušakšidu nizmassu*, the scourge of the enemies and the friend of Erra, who allowed him to achieve his ambition (P10).

## S

***sābītu***, sbst., barmaid, beer-seller; cf. *CAD sābû*, beer merchant. < *s-b-'*.

*ṣābītum ana šīm šikarim še'am la imtaḫar*, the drink-seller has not received grain as the price of the drink (L108); *ṣābītam šuāti ukannūšima ana mê inaddûši*, they shall convict that drink-seller and throw her into the water (L108); *ṣābītum sarrūtum ina bītiša ittarkasūma*, a drink-seller in whose house deceivers have assembled together (L109); *sābītum šû iddâk*, that drink-seller shall be killed (L109); *sābītum ištēn pīḫam ana qīptim iddin*, a drink-seller has sold a jug of beer on trust (L 111).

*sābû*, beer-seller > ***sību***, beer.

***sadāru***, vb., to arrange. < *s-d-r*.

*ṣibāt kaspim mala ilqû isaddarma*, he shall set out the value of whatever he has taken (L100); *samallûm kaspam isaddarma ana tamkārim utâr*, the trader shall set out the value and pay it back to the merchant (L104).

*saḫāmu*, to be under pressure > ***suḫḫumu***, pester.

*saḫāru*, to go around > ***muštasḫer***, surrounding.

***saḫmaštu***, sbst., anarchy.

*išītam saḫmaštam liškunšum*, let him grant him revolts and insurrections (E27).

***sakālu*** (*AHw sakālu* I), vb., to appropriate by fraud (see *CAD*, *sakālu* A). < *s-k-l*.

*sikiltam isakkil bīssa usappaḫ mussa ušamṭa*, she engages in fraudulent practice, spoils her house and deprecates her husband (L141).

***sakāpu***, vb., to overturn. < *s-k-p*.

*šarrūssu liskip*, let him overturn his kingdom (E23).

*sanāqu*, to supervise > ***sunnuqu***, to control.

*sapāḫu*, to disrupt > ***suppuḫu***, to disturb; ***naspaḫu***, to be scattered.

***saparru***, sbst., net.

*sapar nakirī ša Erra rūšu ušakšidu nizmassu*, the scourge of the enemies but the friend of Erra, who grants him his ambition (P10).

***saphu***, sbst., widespread. < *s-p-ḫ*.
*mupaḫḫir nišī sapḫātim* [variant *dapḫātim*, error] *ša Isin*, gathering the scattered people of Isin (P8).

***sarāru***, vb., to deceive. < *s-r-r*.
*awīlum šû sār*, that man is a deceiver (L 13).
> ***surruru***, to deceive.

***sarru***, adj., criminal, reprobate. < *s-r-r*.
*sarrūtum ina bītiša ittarkasūma sarrūtim šunūti la iṣṣabtamma*, criminal men have assembled together in her house but she has not arrested those criminals (L109; 109).

***sartu***, sbst., deception, false evidence. < *s-r-r*.
*awīlum ina dīnim ana šībūt sarrātim ūṣiamma*, a gentleman has come out in a trial with false evidence (L3).

***sasinnu***, sbst., maker of bows and arrows (cf. *CAD* S, 192); previously read > ***zadimmu***, stonemason.
[*idī*] *sasinnim*, the fee for a bowmaker (L274).

***sekēru***, vb., to shut off, clog up. < *s-k-r*.
*nārātišu ina nagbim liskir*, let him clog up his rivers at their source (E22).

***sekretu***, sbst., cloistered woman, priestess (also read as *zikru*). < *s-k-r*.
*sekretum ša abuša šeriktam išrukušim ṭuppam išṭurušim*, a priestess whose father gave her a dowry and wrote out a tablet for her (L178; cf. L179); *abum ana mārtišu nadīt gagîm lu sekretam šeriktaša la išrukšim*(!), the father of a confined sister or a priestess has not given a dowry to his daughter (L180); *mār sekretim*, the son of a priestess (L187; 192; 193).

***sību***, sbst., beer. < *s-b-ʾ*.
***bīt sībim***, 'beer-house' (formerly read *bīt sābī*, house of a beer-seller, or *bīt šikarim*, house of strong drink).
*bīt sībim iptete u lu ana šikarim ana bīt sībim īterub*, she has opened a drinking house or she has entered a drinking house for a drink (L110; 110).

***sikiltu***, sbst., fraudulent practice, acquisition (see *CAD*, s.v. *sakālu*). < *s-k-l*.
*sikiltam isakkil*, she gets hold of goods illegally (L141).

***simmu***, sbst., injury.
*ina risbātim imtaḫaṣma simmam ištakanšu*, he has wrestled with him in a brawl and inflicted an injury on him (L206); *simmam marṣam ša la ipaššeḫū*, a terrible injury they cannot cure (E30); *bēl simmim*, an injured man (L221); *simmam kabtam*, a dangerous incision (L215; 218; 219; 224; 225).

***simtu***, sbst., symbol. < *w-s-m*.
*bēlum simat ḫaṭṭim u agêm*, the lord with the crown and sceptre for a

symbol (P12); *muštakīn simātim ina Eudgalgal*, who maintains the symbols in E-udgalgal (P14).

***sinništu***, sbst., woman. < *ʾ-n-š*.

1. one who is married: *sinništum ša ina bīt awīlim wašbat*, the woman is resident in a man's house (L151); *sinništum šî ul aššat*, that woman is not a wife (L128).

2. one who receives attention from a betrothed man: *ana sinništim šanītim uptallisma*, he begins to give his attention to another woman (L159).

3. one who has committed a crime: *sinništum šî pagarša la iṣṣurma*, that woman has not protected her body (L133b); *mussa sinništam*(!) *šanītam iḫḫaz*, her husband may take another woman (L141); *sinništum šî kīma amtim ina bīt mutiša uššab*, that woman shall dwell in her husband's house like a slave-girl (L141).

4. one who is punished: *sinništam šuāti ukannūšima ana mê inaddûši*, they shall convict that woman and cast her into the water (L133b; cf. L143); *sinništam šuāti ina gašīšim išakkanūši*, they shall impale that woman on a stake (L153).

5. one who is acquitted: *sinništum šî ūtaššar*, that woman shall be released (L130); *sinništum šî arnam ul išu*, that woman has committed no crime (L134; 142).

6. one who is impoverished: *sinništum šî ana ḫāwiriša itâr*, that woman shall return to her first husband (L135); *awīlum šû lāma sinništam šuāti*(!) *iḫḫazu ḫubullum elišu ibašši*, that man has incurred a debt before he married that woman (L151); *sinništum šî lāma ana bīt awīlim irrubu ḫubullum eliša ibašši*, that woman has incurred a debt before she entered the man's house (L151); *ištu sinništum šî ana bīt awīlim īrubu elišunu ḫubullum ittabši*, they have incurred a debt after that woman has entered the man's house (L152).

7. one who divorces or is divorced: *sinništum mussa izērma ul taḫḫazanni iqtabi*, the woman has hated her husband and declared, 'You shall not have me' (L142); *sinništum šî ina bīt mutiša wašābam la imtagar*, that woman shall not agree to dwell in her husband's house (L149); *ana sinništim šuāti šeriktaša utarrūšim*, they shall return her dowry to that woman (L137).

8. one who marries a widower: *warkiša sinništam šanītam ītaḫazma*, he has married another woman after her death (L167).

9. one who is a widow: *sinništum šî ina bīt mutiša ul uṣṣi*, that woman shall not depart from her husband's house (L172); *sinništum šî ana waṣêm panīša ištakan*, that woman has made up her mind to leave (L172).

10. one who remarries: *sinništum šî ašar īrubu ana mutiša warkîm mārī ittalad*, that woman has born children to her subsequent husband in the place she went to (L173); *bītam ša mutiša panîm ana mutiša warkîm u sinništim šuāti ipaqqidūma ṭuppam ušezzebūšunūti*, they shall entrust the property of her former husband to her subsequent husband and that woman, and they shall have a document issued for them (L177).

11. a woman and her dowry: *ana šerikti sinništim šuāti mussa ul iraggum*, her husband shall have no claim to that woman's dowry (L163).

12. one who dies: *sinništum šî ana šīmtim ittalak*, that woman has gone to her fate (L162; 163; 167); *sinništum šî imtūt*, that woman died (L173; 210; 212).

> ***šî, šuāti*** for all examples with demonstrative adjective.

*siparru*, bronze > ***karzillu***, a surgeon's bronze knife.

*sugullu* > ***littu***, cow.

***suḫḫumu***, vb., to maltreat, pester. < *s-ḫ-m*.

*mārūša aššum ina bītim šūṣîm usaḫḫamūši*, her sons pester her to make her get out of the house (L172).

*sukullu*, by-form of *sugullu* > ***littu***, cow.

***suluppū***, sbst. pl., dates.

*suluppī mala ina kirîm*, however many dates there are in the orchard (L66); *suluppī ša ina kirîm ibbaššû*, the dates that are to be found in the orchard (L66); *suluppī watrūtim ša ina kirîm ibbaššû*, the extra dates that are to be found in the orchard (L66); *še'am šipātim šamnam suluppī*, grain, wool, oil and dates (L237).

***sunnuqu***, vb., to keep in tight control. < *s-n-q*.

*alapšu la usanniqma*, he has not kept a tight control over his ox (L251).

***sūnu***, sbst., womb.

*ukabbilšima ina sūniša ittatīlma*, he overpowered her and had intercourse with her (L130); *mārušu la ilmassima šû ina sūniša ittatīl*, his son has not known her but he himself had intercourse with her (L156; cf. L155); *ina sūn ummišu ittatīl*, he had intercourse with his mother (L157); *ina sūn rabītišu ša mārī waldat ittaṣbat*, he has been caught in intercourse with his foster mother who has her own children (L158).

***suppuḫu***, vb., to disrupt. < *s-p-ḫ*.

*sikiltam isakkil bīssa usappaḫ mussa ušamṭa*, she engages in deception, disrupts her house and deprecates her husband (L141; cf. L143).

> ***naspuḫu***, to be scattered.

***sūqu***, sbst., street.

*alpum sūqam ina alākišu awīlam ikkipma*, an ox gored a man while walking in the street (L250).

***surruru***, vb., to deceive. < *s-r-r*.

*usarrirma šimtam uttakkir*, he has cheated and changed the mark. (L265).

***sūtu***, sbst., measure for grain.

*še'am ina sūtim maṭītim iddin*, he gave the grain in a smaller measure (§5.13); *še'am ina sūtim rabītim imḫur*, he received the grain in a larger measure (§5.13); *4 sūt še'am inaddin*, he shall pay four sutu of grain (L272); *4 sūt še'am ṣibtam ileqqe*, he shall receive four sutu of grain in interest (§5.9; cf. *5 sūt*, L111); *2 sūt še'am idūšu*, the fee for it is two sutu of grain (L268; cf. *1 sūt*, L269).

## Ṣ

***ṣabāru***, vb., of a new boat, to list, become unstable. < *ṣ-b-r*.

*ina šattimma šuāti eleppum šî iṣṣabar*, within that very year that boat has then become unstable (L235).

***ṣabātu***, vb., to seize, find. < *ṣ-b-t*

1. to be seized, be detained (stative): *awīlum ša ḫulqum ina qātišu ṣabtu*, the man from whose possession the lost property was seized (L9); [*adi mussa ṣabtu*], as long as her husband is detained [L133a].

2. to seize possession of persons or property: *ḫalqam ina qāti awīlim iṣṣabat*, he has then seized a man in possession of the lost property (L9; literally, the lost property in the possession of a man); *awīlum lu wardam lu amtam ḫalqam ina ṣērim iṣbatma*, a man has seized a lost slave or slave-girl in the open-country (L17); *sarrūtim šunūti la iṣṣabtamma*, she does not then seize those ne'er-do-wells (L109); *awīlum šû ittūramma aššassu iṣṣabat*, he has then returned and retaken possession of his wife (L136); *aššum bēl ḫubullim ša mutiša la ṣabātiša mussa urtakkis*, he has made a contract that no creditor of her husband may seize her (L151); *bēl ḫubullīšu aššassu ul iṣabbatū*, his creditors shall not seize his wife (L151); *bēl ḫubullīša mussa ul iṣabbatū*, her creditors shall not seize her husband (L151).

3. to catch in the act: *ina sūniša ittatīlma iṣṣabtūšu*, he has had sexual intercourse with her and then they have caught him (L130; 155).

4. to take possession of land as a tenant: *šanûm warkišu eqelšu kirāšu u bīssu iṣbatma*, someone else takes over his field, his orchard and his house after him (L30); *ša iṣṣabtuma*, the one who has then taken over (L30); *adi kirâm ṣabtu*, as long as the orchard is leased (L64).

5. to catch a disease: *la'bum iṣṣabassi*, she has then caught a disease (L148); *aššassu ša la'bum iṣbatu*, his wife who has caught a disease (L148); on both occasions, lit., 'a disease has caught'.

6. of a financial obligation forcing a man to dispose of his assets: *awīlam e'iltum iṣbassuma*, the financial obligation has overtaken a man (L117; 119).
> ***naṣbutu***, to be found; ***šuṣbutu***, to oblige to accept.

***ṣābitānu***, sbst., captor. < *ṣ-b-t*.
*wardum ina qāt ṣābitānišu iḫtaliq*, a slave has slipped out of the hand of his captor (L20).

*ṣabû* (*AHw ṣabû* IV; see also *CAD ṣubbu* 4) > ***šuteṣbû***, to make careful arrangements.

***ṣābu***, sbst., soldier.
*šuāti zērašu māssu ṣābašu nišīšu u ummānšu errētam maruštam līrurū*, let them curse him, his descendants, his land, his soldiers, his people and his army with a terrible curse (E31); *ṣāb nisḫātim*, conscripted soldier (L33).
> ***ummānu***, army.

***ṣalmu* 1**, adj. (AHw: *ṣalmu* I; *CAD* Ṣ p. 77: *ṣalmu*, adj.), black. < *ṣ-l-m*.
***ṣalmāt qaqqadim***, 'black on the head', a figurative expression for mankind: *kīma Šamaš ana ṣalmāt qaqqadim waṣêmma*, rising like Shamash over mankind (P3); *ana ṣalmāt qaqqadim ša Ellil išrukam rē'ûssina Marduk iddinam ul ēgu*, I have not been careless with the mass of mankind, which Enlil has entrusted to me and whose governance Marduk has given me (E2); *ṣalmāt qaqqadi lištēšer*, let him keep mankind going straight (E16).

***ṣalmu* 2**, sbst. (AHw: *ṣalmu* II; *CAD* Ṣ p. 78: *ṣalmu*, subst.) statue, figurine. < *ṣ-l-m* (?).
*awīlum ḫablum ša awatam iraššû ana maḫar ṣalmīya šar mīšarim lillikma*, let any oppressed man who wants to speak come before this my statue of the king of justice (E11); *awâtiya šūqurātim ina narîya ašṭurma ina maḫar ṣalmiya šar mīšarim ukīn*, I have written these very special words of mine on this stone and I have placed them beneath the picture of me, the king of justice (E8); *kīma ṣalam ṭīddim liḫbuš*, may he shatter his body like a clay figurine (E28).

*ṣamû* > ***šuṣmû***, make thirsty.

*ṣebû*, to wish (so *CAD*; see *BAL*; *AHw ṣabû* IV) > ***ṣubbu***, to get a comprehensive view; ***šuteṣbû***, to make careful arrangements.

***ṣeḫēru***, vb., to be small, be young. < *ṣ-ḫ-r*.
*mārušu ṣeḫerma ilik abišu alākam la ile'i*, his son is young and is not able to perform the duty of his father (L29).
> ***ṣuḫḫuru***, lessen.

***ṣeḫḫeru***, adj./sbst., very young. < *ṣ-ḫ-r*.
*almattum ša mārūša ṣeḫḫerū*, a widow whose sons are very young (L177); *ṣeḫḫerūtim urabbū*, they shall raise the youngsters (L177).

***ṣeḫru***, sbst., youngster; sometimes also read as *māru*. < *ṣ-ḫ-r*.

*ṣeḫram istariq*, he has kidnapped a youngster (L14); *ana mārišu ṣeḫrim aššatam la īḫuz*, he has not taken a wife for the youngest son (L166); *ana aḫišunu ṣeḫrim ša aššatam la aḫzu*, for their little brother who does not have a wife (L166); *ṣeḫram ina mêšu ana mārūtim ilqēma urtabbīšu*, he has adopted a small child as his own and has brought him up (L185; cf L186; 190; 191); *mār ummānim ṣeḫram ana tarbītim ilqēma*, he has accepted the small son of a tradesman for education (L188); *ṣeḫrum šû rēqūssu ul ittallak*, that youngster shall not go away empty-handed (L191); *ṣeḫrum šû ina qāt mušēniqtim imtūt*, that youngster died while in the care of the working man (L194); *ṣeḫram šaniamma irtakas*, she has entered into a contract for a different youngster (L194, twice).

***ṣēnu* 1**, sbst., flock; *CAD* Ṣ p. 128b.

1. flock: *rē'ûm ana šammī ṣēnim šūkulim itti bēl eqlim la imtagarma*, the shepherd has not agreed with the owner of a field to pasture his flock on the grassland (L57); *balum bēl eqlim eqlam ṣēnam uštākil*, he let the flock feed without the knowledge of the owner of the field (L57; also *ṣēnam ušākilu* L57; cf. L58); *ištu ṣēnum ugārim ītelianim*, after the flocks have come away from the meadows (L58); *rē'ûm ṣēnam ana eqlim iddīma*, a shepherd has left his flock in a field (L58).
2. together with ***liātum***, cattle: *liātim u ṣēnī ša šarrum ana rēdîm iddinu*, the cattle or sheep which the king has given into the charge of a soldier (L35); *nāqidam ana liātim u ṣēnim re'îm īgur*, he has hired a herdsman to look after his cattle and sheep (L261); *[rē'ûm] ša liātum u lu ṣēnum ana re'îm innadnušum*, a shepherd who has been given cattle and sheep to feed (L264; 265); *liātim uṣṣaḫḫir ṣēnam uṣṣaḫḫir*, he has diminished the herd and the flock (L264); *liātim u ṣēnam ana bēlišunu iriab*, he shall return the cattle and sheep to their owner (L265); *liātim u ṣēnam ušallamma ana bēlišunu inaddin*, he shall replace the cattle and sheep and give them to their owner (L267).

***ṣēnu* 2**, adj., wicked; *CAD* Ṣ, 127b, *ṣēnu* A adj.,

*raggam u ṣēnam ana ḫulluqim*, to make evil and wicked people disappear (P3); *ina mātišu raggam u ṣēnam lissuḫ šīr nišīšu liṭīb*, may he root out evil and wicked people and benefit the life of his people (E16).

***ṣênu***, vb., to load as cargo. < *ṣ-'-n*.

*mimma šumšu ša ṣênim iṣēnši*, any other cargo he has loaded on it (L237; 237).

***ṣēru***, sbst., open country. < *ṣ-'-r*.

*lu wardam lu amtam ḫalqam ina ṣērim iṣbatma*, he has caught a lost slave or slave-girl in the desert (L17); *alpam imēram īgurma ina ṣērim nēšum iddūkšu*, he has hired an ox or an ass and a lion has killed it in the desert (L244); *gurun šalmāt ummānātišu ina ṣērim littaddi*, let the pile of the bodies of his soldiers be thrown down in the desert (E27).

***ṣibtu***, sbst., interest. < *ṣ-b-t*.

1. in general: *ṣibtam ša šattim šuāti ul inaddin*, he shall pay no interest for that year (L48); *ṣibat ḫubulli*, interest on the debt (§5.10); *ṣibassu 1 kurrum še'am 1 pān ana šattim*(?) *ileqqe*, he shall take interest of one pan for one kur of grain for a year (§5.10); *ṣibtam mala [qaqqadišu]*, as much interest as capital (§5.11); *[qaqqadašu] u ṣibassu*, his capital and his interest (§5.11); *1 pān 4 sūt še'am ṣibtam ileqqe*, he shall receive one pan and four sut of grain in interest (§5.9); *u lu ṣibātim ana qaqqādim uṭṭeḫḫi*, or he has put the interest together with the principal (§5.12; also *ṣibtam*, §5.12).

2. together with ***kaspu***, silver: *ina ebūrim kasapšu u ṣibassu [išaqqal]*, he shall pay the silver and the interest at harvest (§5.2); *[še'am u kaspam] ana ṣibtim [iddinma]*, he has given grain or silver on interest (§5.11); *ana 1 šiqil kaspim 1/6 u 6 uṭṭet ṣibtam ileqqe*, for each shekel of silver he shall receive one-sixth of a shekel and six grains in interest (§5.9); *ṣibāt kaspim mala ilqû isaddarma*, he shall set out the interest on all the silver he has taken (L100); *še'am ša kaspišu u ṣibassu*, grain for the silver and the interest (L49; cf. *kaspam u ṣibassu*, L50; *kaspīšu u ṣibtišu*, L51); *kaspam u ṣibassu ša pī ṭuppišu*, the silver and the interest according to the terms on the tablet (L66).

***ṣillu***, sbst., shadow. < *ṣ-l-l*.

*ṣillī ṭābum ana āliya tariṣ ina utliya nišī māt Šumerim u Akkadîm ukîl*, with my shadow of safety cast over my city I hold the people of the land of Sumer and Akkad to my breast (E7).

***ṣimdatu***, sbst., regulation, official rate of interest. < *ṣ-m-d*.

*ana pī ṣimdat šarrim ana tamkārim inaddin*, he shall pay the merchant according to the rate agreed by the king (L51); *kīma ṣimdat šarrim*, according to the official rate (§5.10).

***ṣimdu***, sbst., bandaging. < *ṣ-m-d*.

*ina ṣimdi la unaḫḫušu*, which he cannot soothe with a dressing (E30).

***ṣīru***, sbst., exalted. < *ṣ-'-r*.

*Anum ṣīrum*, Anum the exalted one (P1); *Bābilam šumšu ṣīram ibbiū*, he gave Babylon its illustrious name (P2); *Nintu bēltum ṣīrtum ša mātātim ummum bānītī*, Nintu, the exalted lady lady of the lands, the mother of creation (E29).

*ṣubbû*, to observe from afar, look at comprehensively, > ***šuteṣbû***, to make careful arrangements; ***mušteṣbī***, making a proper job.

**ṣuḫḫuru**, vb., to diminish. < *ṣ-ḫ-r*.

*liātim uṣṣaḫḫir ṣēnam uṣṣaḫḫir*, he has diminished the herd and the flock (L264; 264).

**ṣulūlu**, sbst., shade. < *ṣ-l-l*.

*ṣulūl mātim mupaḫḫir nišī sapḫātim ša Isin muṭaḫḫid nuḫšim bīt Egalmaḫ*, a shade for the land, who massed together the people from everywhere in Isin, who spreads around vast riches in the shrine of Egalmah (P8).

## Š

**ša**, possessive and relative pronominal particle:

I. nominalized expressions, with antecedent implied.

1. before a noun, 'something belonging to': *ša ilim* (L8); *ša ekallim* (L8); *ša muškēnim* (L8).

2. before an infinitive, 'something to be used for': *ša akālim* (L133a; 134; 135); *ša nadānim* (L8; 66); *ša ina la aplūtim nasāḫim* (L168; 169); *ša patārim* (L31; 31; 31); *ša ṣēnim* (L237).

3. forming the predicate of nominal sentence: *aplussa ša aḫḫīšama* (L178); *bitiqtum ša errēšima* (L45); *šeriktaša ša bīt abišama* (L163); *warkassa ša aḫḫīšama* (L180; 181); *warkassa ša mārīšama* (L171b).

4. before a verb:

a. 'the person who': *ša Id išliam* (L2); *ša šurqam ina qātišu imḫuru iddâk* (L6); *ša iṣṣabtuma* (L30).

b. the thing which: *ša išriqu* (L265).

II. qualifying antecedent with a noun or noun phrase.

5. relative particle, sometimes with more than one antecedent and more than one referent:

a. 'belonging to': *na'dum ša Ekur* (P4); *aplum dannum ša Sîn-muballiṭ* (P21, three times); *dayyānum rabium ša šamê u erṣetim* (E23); *epšētim ša eqel itēšu* (L56); *lu wardam lu amtam ḫalqam ša ekallim u lu muškēnim* (L16); for other examples see P1; 8; 9; 12; 13; L36; 38; 41; 48; 49; 49; 62; 66; 67+a; 151; 176a; 177; 182; 280; E10; 24; 26; 28; 29; 31.

b. for a period of (cf. *ina*): *še'am ša šattim ištiat*, grain for one year (L63).

c. separated from antecedent: < *še'am u lu* > *šamaššammī ana maḫīrātišunu ša kaspišu u ṣibtišu* (L51).

6. followed by adverb or adverbial expression: *alpim ša warka* (L242/3); *alpim ša qabla* (L242/3); *ša ina maḫrišunu* (L9; 10); *ša maḫrišunu* (L9); *bīti Ebabbar ša kî šubat šamā'i* (P7); *awīlim ša kīma*

*šuāti* (L203); *bītim ša kīma šamê u erṣetim* (E8); *bēlum ša kīma abum wālidim* (E12).

III. introducing a relative clause.

7. followed by stative verb: *ša elišu kišpū nadū* (L2); *ša in šarrī šūturu* (E9); *ša qibīssa ina Ekur kabtat* (E21); *ša itti mūtim šitannu* (E24; for other examples see P2; 18; L25; 27; 28; 32; 110; 119; 141; 151; 158; 165 (*ša īnšu maḫru*); 166; 177; 178 (*ša eliša ṭābu*); 202 (*ša elišu rabû*); E6; 19; 21.

8. followed by preterite or present:

a. as subject, with active verb: *ša in Ninua ina Emešmeš ušūpi'u* (P20); see also P5; L53; 57; §5.10; L104; 105; 125; 130; 137; 138; 159; 177; 249; E11; 30.

b. with passive verb: *ina pīšu ša la uttakkaru* (E32); see also L23; 263; 264; 265; E32.

c. as direct object, sometimes serving more than one dependent clause: *ša Sîn ibni'ušu* (P6); *ina Esagila ša arammu* (E10); *dīnāt mīšarim ša Ḫammurabi šarrum lē'ûm ukinnuma mātam ussam kīnam u rīdam damqam ušaṣbitu* (E1); *ṣalmāt qaqqadim ša Ellil išrukam rē'ûssina Marduk iddinam* (E2); see also P10; 12; L35; 39; 40; 40; 43; 49; 51; 53; 62; 62; 67+a; 69+c; §5.7; L120; 120; 138; 148; 149; 150; 163; 166; 170; 171a; 171b; 172; 178; 178; 179; 190; 191; 254; 267; E4; 4; 4; 14; 14; 14; 15; 15; 15; 18; 19; 23.

d. as indirect object: *ša elišu kišpī iddū* (L2); *ša Šamaš kīnātim išrukušum* (E17).

e. with anticipated possessive pronominal suffix: *ša niš qātišu Adad īdū* (P14); *ša še'šunu mû ublū* (L54); *ša ina zumrišu la iḫalliqu* (E24); see also L9; 9; 26; 178; 179; E8; 20; 22; 23; 24.

9. followed by *bašû*: L5; 49; 49; 50; 66; 66; 77+f; E14.

10. ***mimma ša*** > ***mimma***, whatever.

11. ***ša ḫaṭṭātim***, captain, formerly read *wakil ḫaṭṭātim*, 'overseer of the sceptres': *lu ša ḫaṭṭātim u lu laputtûm ṣāb nisḫātim irtaši*, a captain or officer has acquired one of the deserting soldiers (L33); *lu ša ḫaṭṭātim u lu laputtûm numāt rēdîm ilteqē*, a captain or an officer took the possessions of a soldier (L34); on the different readings of this term, see *CAD* A/1, 280b, para. 2; Roth: *ša ḫaṭṭātim*; cf. *dēkū*, officer.

12. ***ša libbiša***, cargo, foetus: *ša libbiša uḫtalliq*, he has made her lose her cargo (L237; also *mimma ša ina libbiša uḫalliqu*, L237); *mārat awīlim imḫaṣma ša libbiša uštaddīši*, he has struck a gentleman's daughter and 'made her drop what was in her heart', that is, caused her to have a miscarriage (L209; cf. *ana ša libbiša*, L209; cf. L211; 213).

13. ***ša māḫirtim***, rower, 'the one in a boat moving against the current': *elep ša māḫirtim elep ša muqqelpītim imḫaṣma*, the boat of a rower

has struck the boat of a sailor (L240); *ša māḫirtim ša elep ša muqqelpītim uṭebbu eleppašu u mimmašu ḫalqam iriabšum*, the rower who has sunk the vessel of a sailor shall repay him for his vessel and for whatever else was lost (L240).

14. ***ša muqqelpītim***, sailor, 'the one in a boat that is moving with the stream': *elep ša māḫirtim elep ša muqqelpītim imḫaṣma*, the boat of a rower has struck the boat of a sailor (L240); *ša māḫirtim ša elep ša muqqelpītim uṭebbu eleppašu u mimmašu ḫalqam iriabšum*, the rower who has sunk the vessel of a sailor shall repay him for his vessel and for whatever else was lost (L240).

15. fragmentary: L67; §4.12; 4.12; 4.12; 5.3a; 5.3b; 5.7.

*šabāḫu* > ***šapāḫu***, to scatter.

*šadālu*, to be broad > ***mušaddil***, enlarging.

***šaḫû***, sbst., pig.

*lu alpam lu immeram lu imēram lu šaḫâm lu eleppam išriq*, he has stolen an ox or an ass or a sheep or a pig or a boat (L8).

***šā'imu***, ptcp., determining. < *š-'-m* 2.

*Ellil bēl šamê u erṣetim šā'im šīmāt mātim*, Enlil, the lord of heaven and earth, who determines the destiny of the nation (P1); *šā'im* [vnt. *šākin*] *mirītim u mašqītim ana Lagaš u Girsîm*, who decides the feeding and the watering places in Lagash and Girsu (P13).

***šakāku***, sbst., harrow. < *š-k-k*.

*eqlam ša iddû mayyārī imaḫḫaṣ išakkakma*, he shall break up the field he has neglected with mattocks and harrow it (L43); *imaḫḫaṣ imarrar u išakkakma*, he shall break up, plough and harrow (L44).

***šakānu***, vb., to set, arrange, provide, set aside. < *š-k-n*.

1. to set a time: *dayyānu adannam ana šeššet warḫī išakkanūšumma*, the judges shall set a time limit of six months for him (L13).

2. to make arrangements: *riksātim išakkanma*, he shall arrange contracts (L122; also *riksātiša la iškun*, L128); *kasap terḫatim išakkanūšumma*, they shall arrange for him the silver for the bride-price (L166); *šībī iškun*, he arranged witnesses (L68+b; see below paragraph 7 for alternative reading *ṭemam iškun).*

3. to fix the future: *išītam saḫmaštam liškunšum*, may he fix for him revolt and insurrection (E27); *nasāḫ išdī šarrūtišu u ḫalāq mātišu liškunšum*, may he grant that the foundations of his kingdom be destroyed and that his land be lost (E23).

4. to place: *kittam u mīšaram ina pī mātim aškun*, I have set justice and righteousness in the mouth of the people (P22); *sinništam šuāti ina gašīšim išakkanūši*, they shall impale that woman on a stake. (L153); *nidītam ana libbi zittišu išakkanūšum*, they shall put the abandoned area in the middle of his share (L61).

5. to make a mark: *abbuttam išakkanšimma*, she may put a slave-mark on her (L146); *simmam ištakanšu*, he has inflicted an injury on him (L206).
6. with ***panû***, to make up one's mind: *panīšu ištakan*, he has set his mind (L137; 144; 145; cf. *panīšu ištakkan*, L148; *panīša ištakan*, L172; 177; *panīša ištakanma*, L141; *panam ištakan*, L168; 191).
7. with ***ṭemû***, to make a declaration: *ṭemam iškun*, he made a declaration (alternative reading for *šībī iškun*, L68+b, see Finet; see also paragraph 2 above).
8. fragmentary: *ša išakkanu*, which he shall place (§4.12); *išakkanšu*, he shall place him (§4.12).
> ***našakanu***, be fixed.

*šakintu*, adj. fem. > *šaknu*.

***šākinu***, ptcp., providing. < *š-k-n*.
*bēlum muballiṭ Uruk šākin mê nuḫšim ana nišīšu*, the lord who made Uruk come alive, arranging plentiful supplies of water for its people (P8); *šākin* [vnt. *muštakin*] *mākallī ellūtim ana Ninazu*, who provides the pure food for Ninazu (P17); *šākin*, vnt. for *šā'im* (P13, > *šā'imu*).

***šaknu***, adj., fem. ***šakintu***, as sbst., provided with. < *š-k-n*.
***šaknat napištim***, the living world (see *CAD*, s.v., 2b): *muštēšer šaknat napištim bēlum tukultī*, who regulates what has been provided with life, the lord in whom I trust (E23).

*šalālu* A, to take into captivity > ***našlalu***, to be taken into captivity.

***šalamtu***, sbst., corpse. < *š-l-m*.
*gurun šalmāt ummānātišu ina ṣērim littaddi*, let the pile of the bodies of his soldiers be thrown down in the desert (E27).

***šalāmu***, vb., to be free, be safe. < *š-l-m*.
*awīlam šuāti Id ūtebbibaššuma ištalmam* [vnt. *ištalma*], the river has cleansed that man and he shall be free (L2).

***šalaš***, num., three. < *š-l-š*.
1. with *šattu*: *kankallam ana šalaš šanātim ana teptītim ušēṣīma*, he has taken over a neglected field to develop over three years (L44); *šalaš šanātim bīt šāyyimānišunu u kāšišišunu ippešū ina rebûtim šattim andurāršunu iššakkan*, they shall work for three years in the house of their purchaser or creditor; in the fourth year their freedom shall be granted (L117).
2. other expressions: *3 šiqil kaspam inaddin*, he shall give three shekels of silver (L222; 260); *3 uṭṭet kaspum idūša*, the charge for it is three grains of silver (L275); *3 kur še'am ana bēlišu inaddin*, he shall give three kur of grain to its owner (L243); *šalaš šanātim ilikšu ittalak*, he has performed the duty for three years (L30); *adi 3-šu ana*

*tamkārim inaddin*, he shall give three times its value to the merchant (L106).

**šalāšā**, thirty. < *š-l-š*.

*adi 30-šu inaddin*, he shall pay at the rate of 30 times (L8).

**šalšu**, one-third. < *š-l-š*.

*šalušti eqlim u kirîm ana ummišu innaddinma*, one-third of the field or the orchard shall be given to his mother (L29); *u lu ana mišlāni u lu ana šaluš eqlam iddin*, whether he has given the field for a half-share or a third-share (L46); *nukaribbum adi kirâm ṣabtu ina bilat kirîm šittīn ana bēl kirîm inaddin šaluštam šû ileqqe*, as rent for the orchard the gardener shall give the owner of the orchard two-thirds according to the produce in the orchard; he shall take one-third himself (L64); *ina makkūr bīt abim šalušti aplūtiša izâzma*, from the property of her father's house she shall have a share of one-third of an inheritance (L181; cf. L182; *šalušti aplūtišu*, L191).

**šalû**, vb., to immerse oneself, submerge. < *š-l-ʾ*.

*ša elišu kišpū nadû ana Id illak Id išalliamma*, the one who has been accused of witchcraft shall go to the River and sink into the River (L2); *ša Id išliam bīt mubbirišu itabbal*, the one who has sunk into the River shall take the house of his accuser (L2); *ana mutiša Id išalli*, she shall sink into the River for the sake of her husband (L132).

**šamallû**, sbst., trader.

*tamkārum ana šamallêm kaspam ana [nadānim u maḫārim] iddinma*, the merchant gave the agent silver for buying and selling (L100); *šamallûm ina ḫarrānim*, the agent on an expedition (L100, fragmentary); *šamallûm nīš ilim izakkarma*, the trader shall swear a sacred oath (L103); *šamallûm šû ina maḫar ilim u šībī tamkāram ukânma*, that trader shall accuse the merchant in the presence of the god and witnesses (L107); *šamallûm ana tamkārim inaddin*, the trader shall pay the merchant (L101; cf. L106); *šamallûm kanīk kaspim ša ana tamkārim inaddinu ileqqe*, the trader shall take the sealed document which he gave to the merchant (L104); *šamallûm kaspam itti tamkārim ilqēma*, a trader has received silver from a merchant (L106); *šamallûm kaspam isaddarma*, the trader shall set aside the silver (L104); *šamallûm mimma ša tamkārum iddinušum ana tamkārišu utter*, the trader shall give back to his merchant whatever the merchant had given to him (L107); *mimma ša šamallûm iddinušum*, whatever the trader had given him (L107); *šamallûm ītegīma*, the trader has been negligent (L105); *tamkārum kaspam šamallûm iqīpma*, the merchant has entrusted money to a trader (L107); *tamkārum ana šamallîm kaspam ana tadmiqtim ittadinma*, a merchant has given silver to a trader as a kindness (L102); *tamkārum ana šamallîm šeʾam šīpātim šamnam u mimma bīšam ana pašārim iddin*, a merchant has given a trader grain, wool, oil or some other product for resale (L104); *ana šamallîm inaddin*, he shall give to the trader (L107); *aššum šamallâšu ikkiru*, because he has wronged his trader (L107); *ina kaspim leqêm šamallâm ukânma*, he shall assert that the trader took the money (L106).

***šamaššammū***, sbst., sesame.

*eqel epšētim ša še'im u lu šamaššammī ana tamkārim iddin*, he has given to the merchant a field that has been worked for grain or sesame (L49); *še'am u lu šamaššammī ša ibbaššû esip tabal*, collect and remove the grain and the sesame that is there (L49, twice; cf. L50); *še'am u lu šamaššammī uštabši*, he has then produced grain and sesame (L49; cf. L52); *eqel šamaššammī eršam*, a field planted with sesame (L50); < *še'am u lu*> *šamaššammī ana maḫīrātišunu*, grain and sesame according to the market value (L51).

***šammu***, sbst., grass.

*rē'ûm ana šammī ṣēnim šūkulim itti bēl eqlim la imtagarma*, a shepherd has not agreed with the owner of a field to let his flock feed on the grass (L57).

***šamnu***, sbst., oil.

*tamkārum ana šamallîm še'am šipātim šamnam u mimma bīšam ana pašārim iddin*, a merchant has given a trader grain, wool, oil or some other product for resale (L104); *še'am šipātim šamnam suluppī u mimma šumšu ša ṣênim iṣēnši*, grain, wool, oil, dates or any other cargo he has loaded on it (L 237).

***šamšu***, sbst., sun.

*šarrum dannum šamšu Bābilim mušēṣi nūrim ana māt Šumerim u Akkadîm*, the mighty king, the sun of Babylon who shines all over the lands of Sumer and Akkad (P21).

***šamû***, sbst., sky, heaven.

1. sky: *muṣīr bīt Ebabbar ša kî šubat šamā'i*, designing the shrine of Ebabbar like a heavenly abode (P7); *Sîn bēl šamê ilum bānî*, Sin lord of the sky, divine creator (E24); *zunnī ina šamê mīlam ina nagbim līṭeršu*, let him deprive him of showers from the sky and floods from the depths (E25).

2. often paired with *erṣetu*, earth: *ilū rabûtum ša šamê u erṣetim*, the great gods of heaven and earth (E31); *Adad bēl ḫegallim gugal šamê u erṣetim rēṣūa*, Adad lord of plenty, irrigator of heaven and earth, my helper (E25); *Ellil bēl šamê u erṣetim*, Ellil the lord of heaven and earth (P1); *ina qibīt Šamaš dayyānim rabîm ša šamê u erṣetim*, at the command of Shamash the great judge of heaven and earth (E10; cf. E23); *šarrūtam dārītam ša kīma šamê u erṣetim išdāša suršudā*, an everlasting kingdom the foundations of which are as sure as heaven

and earth (P2); *bītim ša kīma šamê u erṣetim išdāšu kīnā*, a house with firm foundations like heaven and earth (E8); *mušaklil mimma šumšu ana Nippur markas šamê erṣetim*, providing every kind of thing for Nippur, the bond between heaven and earth (P4).

***šâmu*** **A**, vb., to purchase. < *š-ʾ-m* 1.

*ina qāt mār awīlim lu warad awīlim balum šībī u riksātim ištām*, he has made a purchase from a gentleman's son or a gentleman's slave without witnesses or contracts (L7); *maḫar šībīmi ašām iqtabi*, he has said, 'I purchased it in front of witnesses' (L9); *šībī ša ina maḫrišunu išāmu itbalam*, the witnesses in whose presence he made the purchase (L9; cf. L10); *šāyyimānum ša unūt mārī almattim išammu ina kaspišu ītelli makkūrum ana bēlišu itâr*, the person who buys the household goods of a widow's sons shall be parted from his silver and the property shall return to its owner (L177); *ina qāti rēdîm ištām*, he has purchased from the hand of a soldier (L35); *eqlam kirâm u bītam ša rēdîm bāʾirim u nāši biltim ištām*, he has purchased a field an orchard or a house from a soldier, a hunter or a tax-payer (L37); *wardam amtam išāmma*, he has purchased a slave or a slave-girl (L278; 279; cf. *ištām*, L280); *ina eqlim kirîm u bītim ša išammuma*, for the field, the orchard or the house which he may purchase (L39; cf. *išammu*, L40); *ana bīt ilkim ša bīt itēšu ša išâmu*, a property on which there is a levy which belongs to his neighbour and which he intends to purchase (L67+a); *šumma bītum šû ilkam la išû išâm*, if that property is free from any obligation he may make the purchase (L67+a); [*ana*] *bīt muškēnim šâmim*, in order to purchase the house of a worker (§4.12); [*wašbum bīt muškēnim*] *išām*, a tenant wishes to purchase the house of a worker (§4.12); *šumma ul išāmma*, if he does not complete the purchase (§4.12).

> ***našāmu***, to be sold.

***šâmu*** **B**, vb., to establish, determine, assign. < *š-ʾ-m* 2.

*šīram ṭābam ana nišī ana dār išīm*, he has ordained health and prosperity for the people for ever (E12); *ana Marduk mārim rēštîm ša Ea ellilūt kiššat nišī išīmūšum*, for Marduk, the first son born to Ea they determined that he should govern as Enlil all the peoples of the world (P1); *ana Ea u Damgalnunna mušarbû šarrūtišu dāriš išīmu zībī ellūtim*, who has decreed that sacred offerings always be made to Ea and Damgalnunna, who have made his kingdom magnificent (P16); *ina igigallim ša Ea išīmam*, with the omniscience that Ea has assigned to me (E4).

2. with ***ana šimtim***, to decide a destiny: *ana šīmtim lišīmšum*, let him fix as his destiny (E20); *balāṭam ša itti mūtim šitannu ana šīmtim*

*lišīmšum*, let him ordain for him a life that is always striving with death as his destiny (E24).

> ***mušīmu*** (*mušimmu*), fixing.

***šanānu***, vb., to strive. < *š-n-n*.

*balāṭam ša itti mūtim šitannu ana šīmtim lišīmšum*, let him ordain for him a life that is always vying with death as his destiny (E24).

***šāninu***, sbst., rival. < *š-n-n*.

*lē'ûtī šāninam ul išû*, there is no rival to my power (E9); *epšētūa šāninam ul išâ*, no rival to my deeds has come (E17).

***šanû***, sbst./adj., someone else, another.

1. sbst. masc., another man: *šanûm warkišu eqelšu kirāšu u bīssu iṣbatma*, another man has taken his field or orchard after his departure (L30); *šaniam ul uppal*, she shall not bequeath it to someone else (L178); *aššum errētim šināti šaniamma uštāḫiz*, he shall make another man do it because of these curses (E19); *warkišu eqelšu u kirāšu ana šanîm iddinūma*, after his departure they gave his field or orchard to another man (L27); *ana bīt šanîm erēbim panîša ištakan*, she has set her mind on entering the house of another man (L177); *ana bīt šanîm irrubu*, she enters the house of another man (L177); *ana bīt šanîm ul irrub*, she shall not return to someone else's house (L133a; cf. L133b; 134; 135; 136).

2. sbst. fem., another woman: *ana šanītim aḫāzim panīšu ištakkan*, he then sets his mind on taking another woman (L148).

3. adj., another: *balum abišu u ummišu ṣiḫram šaniamma irtakas*, she has agreed to have another child without the knowledge of the father and the mother (L194; also *šaniam irkusu*); *itti zikarim šanîm ina itūlim la iṣṣabit*, she has not been caught lying with another man (L131; cf. L129; 132, twice; 153).

4. adj. fem., another: *mussa sinništam šanītam iḫḫaz*, her husband shall take another woman (L141; cf. L167); *ana sinništim šanītim uptallisma*, he has coveted another woman (L159); *mārū mātim šanītim*, people from another country (L281).

*šanû* A, to do again > ***šušnû***, to double.

*šapāḫu*, to scatter, sprinkle (*AHw*) > ***šuppuḫu***, to incite (see *CAD*).

***šapāku***, vb., to store. < *š-p-k*.

*awīlum še'ašu ana našpakūtim ina bīt awīlim išpukma*, a man has put his grain in another man's storehouse (L120; cf. *išpuk* L121).

> ***našpuku***, to be stored.

***šapliš***, adv., below.

*nakrī eliš u šapliš assuḫ*, I have torn out my enemies above and below (E4); *irnitti Marduk eliš u šapliš ikšud*, he has accomplished the victory of Marduk on high and down below (E12; variant *issuḫ*);

*šapliš ina erṣetim eṭemmašu mê lišaṣmi*, in the land down below may he let his ghost thirst for water (E23).

*šapû* C, to be silent > ***šuppu***, to silence.

***šaqālu***, vb., to weigh out, pay. < *š-q-l*.

*šāyyimānum ina bīt nādinānim kasap išqulu ileqqe*, the purchaser shall take the silver he has paid from the house of the seller (L9); *kasap tamkārum išqulu bēl amtim išaqqalma*, the owner of the slave-girl shall weigh out the silver which the merchant weighed out (L119; 119); *kasap išqulu ileqqe*, he shall take the silver he weighed out (L278); *kasap išqulu ana tamkārim inaddinma*, he shall pay the silver he has weighed out to the merchant (L281); *ina maḫar ilim kasap išqulu*(!) *iqabbīma*(!), he shall state the silver he paid in the presence of the god (L281); *kaspam mišil šīmišu išaqqal*, he shall pay half its price in silver (L220); *1/3 mana kaspam išaqqal*, he shall pay a third-mana of silver (§5.3b; L114; 116; 201; 208; 214; 241); *1/2 mana kaspam išaqqal*, he shall pay a half-mana of silver (L59; 207; 212; cf. *mišil šīmišu išaqqal* (L199; also *išaqqalšimma*, L156); *1 mana kaspam ana nišīšu išaqqalū*, they shall pay a mana of silver to his people (L24; cf. *išaqqal*, L198; 203); *2 šiqil kaspam išaqqal*, he shall pay two shekels of silver (L213); *5 šiqil kaspam išaqqal*, he shall pay five shekels of silver (L211); *10 šiqil kaspam išaqqal*, he shall pay ten shekels of silver (L204; cf. L209).

***šaqû***, vb., to give to drink. < *š-q-ʾ*.

*qarrādīšu lišamqit damīšunu erṣetam lišqi*, let him bring down his heroes and let him give the earth their blood to drink (E27).

> ***mušešqū***, give to drink.

***šarāku***, vb., to hand over, grant, give a dowry. < *š-r-k*.

1. to hand over: *rēdiam ina dīnim ana dannim ištarak*, he handed over a soldier to a powerful man in a trial (L34).

2. to grant: *ana ṣalmāt qaqqadim ša Ellil išrukam reʾûssina Marduk iddinam ul ēgu*, I have not been lazy towards the mass of humanity which Ellil granted to me and which Marduk gave me to shepherd (E2); *šar mīšarim ša Šamaš kīnātim išrukušu*, the king of righteousness, to whom Shamash has granted justice (E17); *ana aššatišu eqlam kirâm bītam u bīšam išrukšim*, he has granted to his wife a field, an orchard, a house or goods (L150); *ana aplišu ša īnšu maḫru eqlam kirâm u bītam išruk*, he presented a field, and orchard or a house to the heir who pleases him (L165).

3. to give a dowry to one's daughter: *abum ana mārtišu nadīt gagîm u lu sekretim šeriktam la išrukšim*(!), the father of a confined sister or a priestess has not given a dowry to his daughter (L180; cf. L181; 182; 183; 184; also *išrukušim*, L178; 179; also *išarrakūšimma*, L184).

*šarāmu*, to cut to size > ***šurrumu***, to trim (or cover) the horns of an ox.

***šarāqu***, vb., to steal. < *š-r-q*.

*makkūr ilim u ekallim išriq*, he has stolen the property of a god or of the temple (L6); *lu alpam lu immeram lu imēram lu šaḫâm u lu eleppam išriq*, he has stolen an ox or an ass or a sheep or a pig or a boat (L8); *mār awīlim ṣehram ištariq*, he has stolen a gentleman's small son (L14); *zēram u lu ukullâm išriqma*, he has stolen the seed or the foodstuff (L253; cf. L255); *epinnam ina ugārim išriq*, he has stolen a plough from the field (L259); *ḫarbam u lu maškakātim ištariq*, he has stolen a plough or a harrow (L260); *adi 10-šu ša išriqu*, ten times the value of what he stole (L265).

***šarrāqānum***, sbst., thief. < *š-r-q*.

*šumma šarrāqānum ša nadānim la išu iddâk*, if that thief does not have enough to pay he shall be killed (L8); *itti šarrāqānišu ileqqe*, they shall take it from the one who stole it (L125).

***šarrāqu***, sbst., thief. < *š-r-q*.

*awīlum šû šarrāq iddâk*, the man is a thief, he shall be killed (L7); *nādinānum šarrāq iddâk*, the seller is a thief, he shall be killed (L9); *šāyyimānum šarrāq iddâk*, the buyer is a thief, he shall be killed (L10); *ina nabalkattim šarrāqum*, because of the damage a thief... (L68+b, fragmentary).

***šarru***, sbst., king.

1. king: *šarrum lē'ûm mutēr Eridu ana ašrišu*, the powerful king who restored Eridu as a shrine (P5, vnt. without *šarrum*); *šar tašīmtim šēmû Šamaš*, king of destiny, listening to Shamash (P7); *šarrum nādin napištim ana Adab*, the king who gave life to Adab (P15); *šarrum ša ina Ninua ina Emešmeš ušūpi'u mê Ištar*, the king who demonstrated the rites of Ishtar in Nineveh and Emeshmesh (P20); *šarrum dannum šamšu Bābilim*, the mighty king, the Sun of Babylon (P21); *šarrum muštešmi*, the attentive king (P21); *ana warkiāt ūmī ana mātima šarrum ša ina mātim ibaššû*, in later days in any place any king who exists in the land (E14); *awīlum šû kīma iāti šar mīšarim Šamaš ḫaṭṭašu lirrik*, Shamash will surely make that man's rule last as long as he has made mine, the king of righteousness (E18); *šar mīšarim*, the king of righteousness (E8; 11); *qīšti šarrum ana rēdîm iddinu*, a gift which the king gave to a soldier (L34); *liātim u ṣēnī ša šarrum ana rēdîm iddinu*, cattle or sheep which the king gave to a soldier (L35); *šarrum warassu uballaṭ*, the king shall let his servant live (L129).

2. genitive used adjectivally: *lu rēdûm u lu bā'irum ša ana ḫarrān šarrim alākšu qabû*, a soldier or a hunter who has been ordered on a royal expedition (L26); *ḫarran šarrim*, a royal expedition (L32; 33);

*ina dannat šarrim turru*, detained in a royal stronghold (L27; 28); *kīma ṣimdat šarrim*, according to the official rate (§5.10); *ana pī ṣimdat šarrim*, according to the agreed royal rate (L51).

3. compared with other kings: *ušumgal šarrī talīm Zababa*, the leader of kings the brother of Zababa (P9); *ilu šarrī mudē igigallim*, the god of kings who knows great wisdom (P11); *etel šarrī qabal la maḫārim*, most eminent of kings, unrivalled in battle (P15); *ašared šarri*, the foremost of kings (P17); *šarrum ša in šarrī šūturu anāku*, I am the king who is better than the other kings (E9; 9); *awīlum šû lu šarrum lu bēlum lu iššiakkum u lu awīlūtum ša šumam nabiat*, whether that man is a king or a governor or a man with a designated duty (E19).

4a. explicitly identified as Hammurabi: *dīnāt mīšarim ša Ḫammurabi šarrum lēʾûm ukinnuma*, righteous laws which Hammurabi the almighty king established (E1); *Ḫammurabi šarrum gitmālum anāku*, I am Hammurabi the most accomplished king (E2); *Ḫammurabi šar mīšarim ša Šamaš kīnātim išrukušum*, I am Hammurabi the king of righteousness, to whom Shamash has entrusted the truth (E17).

b. explicitly identified as a divine king: *ina pī Ellil šarrim lišaškin*, let him cause to happen according to the word of Enlil the king (E21); *Anum ṣīrum šar Anunnakī*, exalted Anum, king of the Anunnaki (P1).

***šarrūtu***, sbst., kingship, dynasty.

1. blessed: *šarrūtam dārītam ša kīma šamê u erṣetim išdāša šuršudā ukinnūšum*, they established an everlasting kingdom the foundations of which were established like those of heaven and earth (P2, variant *šarrūtim dāriti*); *mušarbû šarrūtišu*, making his kingdom magnificent (P16; cf. *mušarbû šarrūtiya*, E20); *zēr šarrūtim ša Sîn ibniušu*, he created him the royal descendant of Sin (P6); *zērum dārium ša šarrūtim*, royal descendants for ever (P21).

2. cursed: *melemmī šarrūtim līṭeršu*, let him take from him the splendour of his kingdom (E19); *naspuḫ nišīšu šarrūssu šupēlam*, the scattering of his people, the downfall of his kingdom (E20); *šarrūssu liskip dīnšu ay idīn*, may he overthrow his kingdom and not judge his cause (E23); *šīram lemnam ša nasāḫ išdī šarrūtišu u ḫalāq mātišu liškunšum*, let him ordain for him a bad omen that will overthrow the foundations of his kingdom and destroy his land (E23); *agâm kussiam ša šarrūtim līṭeršu*, remove the kingly crown and throne (E24); *kammāl šarrūtim lišaṭṭilšu*, let him see a rival for the kingdom (E24); *ina libbiša aggim ina uzzātiša rabiātim šarrūssu līrur*, let her curse his kingdom with unsurpassable anger and rage in her heart (E27).

*šašallašu ittasak*, he has injured its hoof (L248).

***šasû***, vb., to shout. < *š-s-ʾ*.

*eli ālišu ezziš lissīma*, let him shout out against his city angrily (E25); *narî šaṭram lištassīma awâtiya šūqurātim lišmēma*, let him keep shouting out the inscription on my stela and heed my precious words (E11).

***šašallu***, sbst., tendon of the hoof (see *CAD*); otherwise translated pelt (see *AHw* s.v. 3a, 'Rückenfell').

***šattu***, sbst., year.

1. a part of a year: *ištu rēš šattim adi ḫamšim warḫim*, from the beginning of the year to the fifth month (L273); *ištu šiššim warḫim adi taqtīt šattim*, from the sixth month to the end of the year (L273); *ina šattim šuāti*, within that year (L48; cf. *šattimma*, L235).

2. a specific period of one year: *šattam ištiatma udappirma*, he has been absent for one year (L31, variant *šattam išteatat*); *10 kur šeʾam ša šattim ištiat imaddad*, he shall measure out 10 kur of grain for one year (L63); *ana šattim ištiat īgur*, he has hired for one year (L242); *6 [kur šeʾam] ina šanat inaddiššum*, he shall pay him six kur of grain for a year (L239); *8 kur šeʾam ina šattim ištiat inaddiššum*, he shall pay him eight kur of grain for one year (L257; 261; cf. L258, variant *šattišu*); *kasap kiṣrišu gamram ša šanat*, all the money for the year (L69+c); *ina šattim maḫrītim*, in the previous year (L47); *ṣibtam ša šattim šuāti*, interest for that year (L48); *ina šanat ana 1 kur šeʾim 5 qa šeʾam idī našpakim inaddin*, he shall pay the storage charge of five qa of grain for one kur of grain per year (L121); *1 kurrum šeʾam 1 pān ana šattim*(?) *ileqqe*, he shall receive one kurru of grain and one pan for a year (§5.10).

3. a specific period of more than one year: *šalaš šanātim ilikšu ittalak*, he has performed the duty for three years (L30); *kankallam ana šalaš šanātim ana teptītim ušēṣīma*, he has taken over a neglected field to develop over three years (L44); *šalaš šanātim bīt šāyyimānišu u kāšišišunu ippešū*, they shall work for three years in the house of their purchaser or creditor (L117); *ina rebûtim šattim*, in the fourth year (L44; 117); *erbe šanātim kiriam urabba ina ḫamuštim šattim bēl kirîm u nukaribbum mitḫāriš izuzzū*, for four years they shall develop the orchard and in the fifth year the owner of the orchard and the gardener shall share equally (L60; 60).

4. a long period of time: *bilat eqlim ša šanātim ša innadû*, rent for the field for the years when it was neglected (L62); *ūmī iṣûtim šanāt ḫušaḫḫim*, days of need and years of famine (E20); *ūmī warḫī šanāt palēšu ina tānēḫim u dimmatim lišaqti*, let him end the days and months and years of his reign with grief and tears (E24).

*šatû*, to strike (cf. *CAD* N/2 133b, *naṭû* 3), see ***šuṭṭû***, to strike.

*šaṭāpu*, to preserve life > ***šāṭipu***, carer.

***šaṭāru***, vb., to inscribe, assign. < *š-ṭ-r*.

1. to write on a clay tablet: *ṭuppam eššam la išṭur*, he has not written a new tablet (§5.12); *ina tuppim išṭurušim*, which he had written out for her on a tablet (L171b; cf. L178; *kunukkam išṭurušim* L179); *ina ṭuppim ša išṭurušim*, on the tablet which he wrote for her (L178; 179; also *išṭuršimma* L178; 179).

2. to write on a sealed document: *kunukkam išṭuršum*, he has written out a sealed document for him (L165; cf. *išṭuršim*, L182; 183); *kunukkišu la išṭuršum*, he did not write out an official document for him (§5.3a).

3. to inscribe on a stela: *awâtiya šūqurātim ina narîya ašṭurma*, I have written out my precious words on my stela (E8); *awât mīšarim ša ina narîya ašṭuru liṣṣur*, let him observe the words of righteousness which I have written out on my stela (E14); *ana awâtim ša ina narîya ašṭuru liqūlma*, let him pay attention to the words which I have written out on my stela (E15; cf. E18; 19); *šumī šaṭram ipšiṭma šumšu ištaṭar*, he has removed my inscribed name and written in his own name (E19).

4. to make a statement in writing: *ana aššatišu u mārtišu ul išaṭṭar*, he shall not assign them to his wife of his sons (L38; cf. L39).

***šāṭipu***, ptcp., saving, preserving life. < *š-ṭ-p*.

*šāṭip nišīšu in pušqim mukinnu išdīšin qerbum Bābilim šulmāniš*, the saviour of his afflicted people, who fixes their foundations peacefully in the midst of Babylon (P18).

***šaṭru***, sbst., inscribed. < *š-ṭ-r*.

*narî šaṭram lištassīma awâtiya šūqurātim lišmēma*, and let him shout out the inscription on my stela and listen to my precious words (E11); *šumī šaṭram ipšiṭma*, he has removed my inscribed name (E19).

***šāyyimānum***, sbst., purchaser. < *š-ʾ-m*.

*šāyyimānum nādin iddinušum u šībī ša ina maḫrišunu išāmu itbalam*, the purchaser shall bring the person who gave it to him together with witnesses in whose presence it was purchased (L9; cf. L10); *šāyyimānum ina bīt nādinānim kasap išqulu ileqqe*, the purchaser shall take the money he has paid away from the house of the seller (L9); *šāyyimānum šarrāq iddâk*, the buyer is a thief, he shall be killed (L10); *šāyyimānum ina bīt nādinānim rugummē dīnim šuāti adi ḫamšīšu ileqqe*, the buyer shall take from the house of the seller five times the claim in that case (L12); *šāyyimānum ilik eqlim kirîm u bītim ša išammu illak*, the buyer shall perform the duty of the field or the orchard or the house which he is buying (L40); *šalaš šanātim bīt šāyyimānišunu u kāšišišunu ippešū*, they shall work for three years in the house of their purchaser or creditor (L117); *šāyyimānum ša unūt mārī almattim išammu ina kaspišu ītelli makkūrum ana bēlišu itâr*, the person who buys the household goods of a widow's sons shall be parted from his silver and the property shall return to its owner (L177); *šāyyimānum kasap išqulu ileqqe*, the buyer shall take the silver he weighed out (L278); *šāyyimānumma ina maḫar ilim kasap išqulu*(!) *iqabbīma*(!), the buyer shall state the silver he paid in the presence of the god (L281).

***šebēru***, vb., to break. < *š-b-r*.

1. to break a part of the body: *šumma eṣemti awīlim ištebir eṣemta išebbirū*, if he has broken the bone of a gentleman, they shall break his bone (L197; 197; cf. *ištebir*, L198; 199); *alpam īgurma šēpšu ištebir*, he has hired an ox and broken its foot (L246); *qaranšu išbir zibbassu ittakis*, he has broken off its horn or cut off its tail (L248, but Roth: *iš<te>bir*).

2. to 'break someone's weapon', render ineffective: *ḫaṭṭašu lišbir*, let him break his weapon (E19); *ašar tāhazim u qablim kakkašu lišbir*, let him break his weapons where there is battle and conflict (E27; cf. E26).

***šebru***, adj., fem. *šebirtu*, broken. < *š-b-r*.

*asûm eṣemti awīlim šebirtam uštallim*, a physician has healed a man's broken bone (L221).

*šēbultu* > ***šūbulltu***, consignment.

***šēdu***, sbst., protecting spirit.

*šēdum lamassum ilū ēribūt Esagil libitti Esagil igirrê ūmišam ina maḫar Marduk bēliya Zarpānītum bēltiya lidammiqū*, may the guardian and protector, the deities going into Esagila, and the brickwork of Esagila look kindly on the daily petitions in the presence of my lord Marduk and of my lady Zarpanitum (E13); *šēd bītim libitti Ebabbara*, guardian of the shrine, brickwork of E-babbar (E31, vnt.: *DINGIR* [...]).

*šēm* > ***šû***, his.

***šemû***, vb., to hear, obey. < *š-m-ʾ*.

*narî šaṭram ligtassīma awâtiya šūqurātim lišmēma*, let him shout out the writing on my stele and listen to my precious words (E11).

> ***muštešmī***, making obedient.

***šēmû***, ptcp., listening. < *š-m-ʾ*.

*šar tašīmtim šēmû Šamaš dannum mukīn išdī Sippar*, the king who listens obediently to Shamash, who firmly fixed the foundations of Sippar (P7).

***šēpu***, sbst., foot.

*alpam īgurma šēpšu ištebir*, he has hired an ox and broken its foot (L246).

***šer'ānu***, sbst., sinew, muscle.

*asûm eṣemti awīlim šebirtam uštallim u lu šer'ānam marṣam ubṭalliṭ*, a physician has made a man's broken leg better or has eased a painful muscle (L221).

***šeriktu***, sbst., dowry; *CAD širiktu. < š-r-k.*

*šeriktaša u nudunnâm ša mussa iddinušim ina ṭuppim išṭurušim ileqqēma*, she shall take her dowry and the gift which her husband gave her with the document he wrote out for her (L171b); *qadum šeriktim ša bīt abiša ana bīt warad ekallim u lu warad muškēnim īrubma*, she shall enter the house of the palace slave or the workman's slave with the dowry from her father's house (L176a); *mārat awīlim šeriktaša ileqqe*, the man's daughter shall take her dowry (L176a); *šeriktaša utarrūšim*, they shall return her dowry to her (L137); *šeriktam ša ištu bīt abiša ublam ušallamšimma izzibši*, he shall completely reinstate for her the dowry which she brought from her father's house before divorcing her (L138; cf. *šeriktaša*, L149; 172); *šeriktaša ileqqēma*, she shall take her dowry (L142); *šeriktam ša bīt abiša ileqqēma*, she shall take her dowry from her father's house (L172); *ana šeriktiša abuša ul iraggum šeriktaša ša mārīšama*, her father shall have no claim to her dowry; her dowry belongs only to her sons (L162; 162; cf. L163, also *šerikti*); *šeriktaša mārū maḫrûtum u warkûtum izuzzū*, the earlier and later sons shall share her dowry (L173); *šeriktaša mārū ḫāwirišama ileqqû*, the sons of the first husband shall take her dowry (L174); *šeriktaša ana bīt abiša*(!) *utâr*, he shall return her dowry to her father's house (L164); *abum ana mārtišu nadīt gagîm u lu sekretim šeriktam la išrukšim*(!), the father of a confined sister or a priestess has not given a dowry to his daughter (L180; cf. L181; 182); *ša abuša šeriktam išrukušim*, whose father has presented her with a dowry (L178; 179; cf. L183; 184, also *šeriktam išarrakūšimma*); *ina šeriktiša mala terḫatiša iḫarraṣma*, he shall subtract from the dowry the amount of the bridal gift (L164); *šerikti ummātišunu ileqqûma*, they shall take the dowries of their mothers (L167); *šumma mārat awīlim šeriktam la išu*, if a man's daughter has no dowry (L176b).

***šērtu* B**, sbst., condemnation.

*arnam kabtam šēressu rabītam ša ina zumrišu la iḫalliqu līmussuma*, let him lay on him a heavy penalty as his great condemnation which will not disappear from his body (E24).

***šērtu* D**, sbst., brilliance (?).

*Sîn bēl šamê ilum bānî ša šēressu ina ilī šūpât*, O Sin, lord of heaven, creator god, whose brilliance outshines all other gods (E24, thus Stele, but preferred reading: *têressu*, 'whose oracular decision'; > ***tērtu***, oracle; see also *CAD*; Roth p. 142 note 53).

***šer'u***, sbst., cultivated field (formerly read as *absinnu*).

*šumma eqlam ša innadnušum ana kirîm la izqup šumma šer'um*, as for the field that had been given to him and that he had not planted as an orchard, if it was a cultivated field (L62).

***šeššet***, num. (cardinal), six.

*adannam ana šeššet warḫī išakkanūšumma šumma ina šeššet warḫī šībīšu la irdeam*, he shall set him a time limit of six months, but if he has not obtained witnesses within six months (L13; 13); *aššum šamallâšu ikkiru mimma ša ilqû adi 6-šu ana šamallîm inaddin*, he shall pay the trader six times as much as he took because he has wronged his trader (L107); *6 [kur še'am] ina šanat inaddiššum*, he shall pay him six kur of grain per year (L239); *6 kur še'am ina šattim ištiat inaddiššum*, he shall pay him six kur of grain for one year (L258); *6 uṭṭet kaspam ina ūmim ištēn inaddin*, he shall pay six grains of silver for one day (L273); *ana 1 šiqil kaspim 1/6 u 6 uṭṭet ṣibtam ileqqe*, for each shekel of silver he shall receive a sixth of a shekel and six grains in interest (L70+d; cf. L71+d).

***šeššu***, num. (ordinal), sixth.

1. *ištu šiššim warḫim adi taqtīt šattim*, from the sixth month to the end of the year (L273).

2. *šeššu*, a sixth, is always written ideographically in this text (a list of all ideographically written numerals is appended to this Glossary).

***še'u***, sbst., grain (barley).

1. grain in general: *še'am kīma itēšu ana bēl eqlim inaddin*, he shall give grain according to that given by his neighbour to the owner of the field (L42; 43; cf. L55); *kīma riksātišu še'am ileqqe*, he shall receive grain according to the terms of the contract (L47); *še'am ana bēl ḫubullišu ul utâr*, he shall not return the grain to his creditor (L48); *še'am ša uḫalliqu iriab*, he shall restore the grain he destroyed (L53); *še'am riābam la ile'i*, he is not able to repay the grain (L54); *mārū ugārim ša še'šunu mû ublū*, the agricultural workers whose grain the flood destoyed (L54); *sābītum ana šīm šikarim še'am la imtaḫar*, the woman who sells drink has not received grain for the price of the drink (L108); *u maḫīr šikarim ana maḫīr še'im umtaṭṭi*, she has reduced the price of the drink in comparison to the price of the grain (L108); *še'am šipātim šamnam u mimma bīšam*, grain, wool, oil or some other item (L104; cf. L237).

2. occurring with *šamaššammū*: *eqel epšētim ša še'im u lu šamaššammī*, a field for grain or sesame (L49); *errēšum ina eqlim še'am u lu*

*šamaššammī uštabši ina ebūrim še'am u šamaššammī ša ina eqlim ibbaššû bēl eqlimma ileqqēma*, the cultivator has produced grain or sesame from the field and at the harvest the owner of the field shall take the grain or sesame which is in the field (L49; 49); *eqlam erišma še'am u lu šamaššammī ša ibbaššû esip*, cultivate the field and harvest the grain or sesame which is there (L49; cf. L50); *eqel <še'im> eršam u lu eqel šamaššammī eršam*, a field being cultivated with grain or a field being cultivated with sesame (< L50> ; cf. *še'am* < L51> ).
3. elsewhere with *bašû*, *nabšû* or *šubšû*: *še'am ša ina eqlim ibbaššû*, the grain that there is in the field (L46); *še'um ina eqlim la ittabši*, there has been no grain in the field (L48); *ina eqlim še'am la uštabši*, he has not produced any grain in the field (L42; cf. L52).
4. stored grain: *ina našpakim u lu ina maškanim še'am ilteqe*, he has removed grain from the granary or the threshing floor (L113); *ina še'im leqêm ukannūšuma*, they shall convict him of removing the grain (L113); *še'am mala ilqû*, all the grain he took (§5.12; L113); *bēl bītim našpakam iptēma še'am ilqe*, the owner of the house opens the granary and removes the grain (L120); *še'am ša ilqû*, the grain he took (L120); *awīlum še'ašu ana našpakūtim ina bīt awīlim išpukma*, a man puts his grain into storage in a man's house (L120); *še'am ša ina bītišu iššapku*, the grain which was stored in his house (L120); *še'am išpuk*, he stored grain (L121).
5. a measured quantity:
a. in general: *še'am ina sūtim maṭitim iddin*, he gave the grain in the little measure (§5.13); *še'am ina sūtim rabītim*, grain in the large measure (§5.13); *tašna še'am ša imḫuru*, twice the amount of grain which he received (L254).
b. expressed in *parsikatu*: *ina ūmim ištēn 3 parsikat še'am inaddin*, he shall pay three parsikat of grain for one day (L271).
c. expressed in *qa*: *1 qa še'um idūšu*, the charge for it is one qa of grain (L270).
d. expressed in *sutu*: *1 sūt še'um idūšu*, the charge for it is one sutu of grain (L269); *2 sūt še'um idūšu*, the charge for it is two sutu of grain (L268); *ina ūmim ištēn 4 sūt še'am inaddin*, he shall pay four sutu of grain for one day (L272); *ina ebūrim 5 sūt še'am ileqqe*, she shall take five sutu of grain at the harvest (L111).
e. expressed in *kurru*: *3 kur še'am*, 3 kur of grain (L242/3); *4 kur še'am*, 4 kur of grain (L242/3); *6 kur še'am*, 6 kur of grain (L258); *8 kur še'am*, 8 kur of grain (L257; 261); *10 kur še'am*, 10 kur of grain (L44; 56; 63); *20 kur še'am*, 20 kur of grain (L57); *60 kur še'am*, 60 kur of grain (L58; 255).
f. expressed in more than one unit: *ana 1 kurrum 1 pān 4 sūt še'am*

*ṣibtam ileqqe*, for one kur he shall take one pan and four sut of grain as interest (§5.9); *u ṣibassu 1 kurrum še'am 1 pān ana šattim*(?), and the interest on it is one pan for one kur of grain per year (§5.10); *ina šanat ana 1 kur še'im 5 qa še'am idī našpakim inaddin*, he shall pay the storage charge of five qa of grain for one kur of grain per year (L121; 121).

6. together with ***kaspu***, silver: *še'am ša kaspišu u ṣibassu ša itti tamkārim ilqû*, grain for the silver and its interest which he has borrowed from the merchant (L49); *ana šībūt še'im u kaspim ūṣiam*, he came out with evidence about grain or silver (L4); *tamkārum še'am u kaspam ana ḫubullim iddin*, a merchant has given grain or silver on loan (§5.9); *tamkārum še'am u kaspam ana ḫubullim iddinma*, a merchant has given grain or silver on loan (§5.13); *še'am kaspam u bīšam ana bīt ilkim*, grain, silver or goods for a house with a duty (L67+a, twice); *še'am u kaspam kīma ṣimdat šarrim*, grain or silver according to the royal decree (§5.10); *u lu še'am* [*u lu kaspam*] *mala* [*imḫuru*], as much grain and silver as he received [§5.12]; *tamkārum še'am* [*u kaspam*] *ana ṣibtim* [*iddinma*], a merchant has given grain or silver on interest (§5.11, twice; also *še'um u kaspum* §5.11); *še'am u kaspam itti tamkārim ilqēma*, he shall take from the merchant grain or silver (§5.15); *še'am u kaspam ana turrim la išu*, he does not have grain or silver to give back (§5.15); *mimmûšu bīšam u še'am*, whatever property or grain he has (§5.2); *awīlum eli awīlim se'am u kaspam išūma*, a man has a claim against a man for grain or silver (L113).

7. ***bēl še'im***, the owner of the grain: *balum bēl še'im*, without the knowledge of the owner of the grain (L113, twice); *bēl še'im maḫar ilim še'ašu ubârma*, the owner of the grain shall declare how much grain he had before the god (L120; 120); *ana bēl še'im inaddin*, he shall give to the owner of the grain (L120).

***še'û***, vb., to search. < *š-'-'*.

*bēl bītim mimmâšu ḫalqam ištene'īma itti šarrāqānišu ileqqe*, the owner of the house shall thoroughly search for whatever he had lost and take it from the thief (L125); *ašrī šulmim ešte'īšināšim*, I have searched for peaceful places for them (E3).

***šî***, pron., she; adj., that.

1. pronoun: *mimma ša mussa u šî ištu innemdū iršû*, whatever she and her husband have acquired after they have come together (L176a; 176b).

2. demonstrative adjective:

a. with personal fem. sbst. (nominative): *sābītum šî* (L109); *sinništum šî*, (L128; 130; 133b; 134; 135; 141; 142; 149; 151; 152; 162; 163;

167; 172; 172; 173; 173; 210; 212); *nadītum šî* (L144); *šugītum šî* (L145); *amtum šî* (L146; 214); *tarbītum šî* (L185; 186; 189; 190).

b. with non-personal fem, sbst.: *eleppum šî* (L235).

*šiāmu* (*AHw*) > ***šâmu*** B, to establish, determine.

*šiāti*, vnt. for > ***šuāti*** (L108; 151).

***šību***, sbst., witness. < *š-b-ʾ*.

1. transaction with witnesses: *šībī mudē ḫulqišu itbalam*, he shall bring witnesses who recognize his lost property (L9; 10; cf. L11); *šībī ša ina maḫrīšunu išāmu itbalam*, he has produced witnesses in whose presence he made the purchase (L9); *šībū ša maḫrišunu šīmum iššamū u šibū mudē ḫulqim*, witnesses in whose presence the sale was conducted and witnesses who know the lost property (L9; 9); *maḫar šībīmi ašām iqtabi*, he has said, 'I bought it in the presence of witnesses, (L9); *šībī mudē ḫulqiyami lublam*, 'I will bring witnesses who know the lost property' (L9); *ina maḫar ilim u šībī*, in the presence of god and witnesses (L106; 107); *maḫar šībī kīma ubbalu ana tamkārīšu inaddin*, he shall give the merchant whatever he has brought before witnesses (§5.15); *šībī iškun*, he has established witnesses (L68+b, but Finet: *ṭemam*, he has made a declaration); *mimma mala inaddinu šībī ukallam*, he shall show the witnesses all that he is going to give (L122); *maḫar šībī ana maṣṣarūtim iddinma*, he has put into safe-keeping in the presence of witnesses (L124); *šībūšu la qerbu*, his witnesses were unavailable (L13); *šībīšu la irdeʾam*, he has not secured his witnesses (L13).

2. transaction without witnesses: *ina qāt mār awīlim u lu warad awīlim balum šībī u riksātim ištām*, he has made a purchase from the hands of a man's son or a man's slave without witnesses or contracts (L7); *balum šībī u riksātim*, without witnesses or contracts (L123).

*šībultu* > ***šūbultu***, load of goods.

***šībūtu***, sbst., evidence. < *š-b-ʾ*.

*ana šībūt sarrātim ūṣiamma*, he has come forward with evidence of theft (L3, vnt. *šēbūt*); *ana šībūt šeʾim u kaspim*, he has come forward with evidence about grain or silver (L4).

***šikaru***, sbst., beer.

*ana šīm šikarim šeʾam la imtaḫar*, she has not received grain for the price of the drink (L108); *maḫīr šikarim ana maḫīr šeʾim umtaṭṭi*, she has diminished the value of the drink compared with the value of the grain (L108); *bīt sībim ipteṭe lu ana šikarim ana bīt sībim īterub*, she has opened the door of a drinking house or has entered a drinking house for a drink (L110).

*bīt šikarim* is now to be read as *bīt sībim* > ***sībum***, beer.

***šimtu***, sbst., cattle mark, mark placed on a beast as a sign of ownership (*CAD* s.v. 2b′). < *w-š-m*.

*usarrirma šimtam uttakkir*, he has cheated and changed the mark (L265).

***šīmtu***, sbst., decision, destiny. < *š-ʾ-m*.

1. destiny: *Ellil bēl šamê u erṣetim šāʾim šīmāt mātim*, Enlil, the lord of heaven and earth, who determines the destiny of the nation (P1); *Ellil bēlum mušīm šīmātim ša qibīssu la uttakkaru*, Enlil the lord who fixes destinies, whose decrees cannot be altered (E20); *Ea rubûm rabium ša šīmātušu ina maḫra illakā*, Ea, the almighty prince whose decisions come first (E22); *ḫaṭṭašu lišbir šīmātišu līrur*, let him break his weapon, let him curse his destiny (E19); *ana šīmtim lišīmšum*, let him fix a destiny for him (E20; 24).

2. with ***alāku***, to die: *ana šīmtim ittalak*, he has gone to his fate (L12; 162; 163; 167; 176a, variant *šimātišu*; cf. with *ittalku*, L165; 166; 167; 170; 171a; 178; 179; 180; 181; 182; 183; 184).

3. with ***mâtu***, of an animal: *ina šimātiša imtūt*, it has died according to its fate (L115).

***šīmu***, sbst., sale, price. < *š-ʾ-m* A.

*šībū ša maḫrišunu šīmum iššāmu*, witnesses in whose presence the sale was conducted (L9); *ana šīmim*, in a sale (L67+a, fragmentary); *ana šīm šikarim šeʾam la imtaḫar*, she has not received grain for the price of the drink (L108); *mišil šīmišu išaqqal*, he shall pay half its price (L199; 220; cf. *mišil šīmišu inaddin*, L238; 1/2 *šīmišu*, L247); 1/4 *šīmīšu ana bēl alpim u lu imērim inaddin*, he shall pay a quarter of its price to the owner of the ox or the ass (L225; cf. L248).

***šina***, num., two.

*2 šiqil kaspam bēl wardim inaddiššum*, the owner of the slave shall pay two shekels of silver (L17; cf. *2 šiqil išaqqal*, L 213; 217; *inaddin*, L223); *2 šiqil kaspam ana qīštišu inaddišum*, he shall give him two shekels of silver in compensation (L228; 234); *ana šinīšu izuzzūma*, they shall divide into two (L176a; 176b); *arnam kabtam adi šinīšu itbalam*, he has incurred serious punishment for a second time (L169).

***šināti***, adj., these (fem. pl.); also pron., they (fem. pl.).

*aššum errētim*(!) *šināti*, because of these curses (E19).

***šinnu***, sbst., tooth.

*šumma awīlum šinni awīlim meḫrišu ittadi šinnašu innaddû*, if a gentleman has knocked out the tooth of a gentleman like himself they shall knock out his own tooth (L200; 200); *šinni*(!) *muškēnim*, a working-man's tooth (L201).

***šipātu***, sbst. pl., wool (*AHw*: *šīpātu*).

*šeʾam šipātim šamnam u mimma bīšam ana pašārim iddin*, he has given grain, wool, oil or something else for onward sale (L104); *še'am šipātim šamnam suluppī u mimma šumšu ša ṣênim iṣēnši*, grain, wool, oil, dates or any other cargo he has loaded on it (L237).

***šipru***, sbst., task, skill.

*ina eqlim šiprim la epēšim ukannūšumma*, they shall convict him of not doing the work in the field (L42); *eqlam šipram ippešma*, he shall do the work in the field (L62; 63); *šipiršu la udanninma*, he has not done a strong job (L229); *šipiršu la ušteṣbīma*, he has not done a proper job (L233); *šipiršu la utakkilma*, he has not done a reliable job (L235); *mār ummānim ṣeḫram ana tarbītim ilqēma šipir qātišu uštāḫissu*, a professional person has taken a son to adopt and has taught him his own craft (L188; cf. L189).

***šipṭu***, sbst., decision. < *š-p-ṭ*.

*ašar šipṭim u purussêm ina maḫar Ellil awassu lilemmin*, may he deprecate his words in the place of judgement and decision before Ellil (E21).

***šiqītu***, sbst., irrigation. < *š-q-'*.

*atappašu ana šiqītim ipte*, he has opened his canal for irrigation (L55).

***šiqlu***, sbst., shekel. < *š-q-l*.

1. paid in interest: *ana 1 šiqil kaspim 1/6 u 6 uṭṭet ṣibtam ileqqe*, for each shekel of silver he shall receive one-sixth of a shekel and six grains in interest (§5.9).

2. paid for the recovery of a slave: *2 šiqil kaspam bēl wardim inaddiššum*, the owner of the slave shall pay him two shekels of silver (L17).

3. paid for medical treatment: *ana asîm 2 šiqil kaspam inaddin*, he shall give the physician two shekels of silver (L217; 223); *3 šiqil kaspam* (L222); *5 šiqil kaspim* (L221).

4. paid for building work on a house or on a boat: *2 šiqil kaspam ana qīštišu inaddiššum*, he shall pay him two shekels of silver as his fee (L228; 234).

5. paid as a fine for theft: *5 šiqil kaspam ana bēl epinnim inaddin*, he shall give five shekels of silver to the owner of the plough (L260); *3 šiqil kaspam inaddin*, he shall give three shekels of silver (L260).

6. paid as a fine for assault: *2 šiqil kaspam išaqqal*, he shall pay two shekels of silver (L213);*5 šiqil kaspam išaqqal*, he shall pay five shekels of silver (L211); *10 šiqil kaspam išaqqal*, he shall pay ten shekels of silver (L204; cf. L209).

7. fragmentary: *ana 5 šiqil kaspim*, (§5.3a).

***šīru***, sbst., flesh, health.

1. good health, quality of life: *Anum u Ellil ana šīr nišī ṭubbim šumī ibbû*, Anum and Enlil have nominated me to improve the health of the people (P3; cf. P22); *šīr mātim uṭīb*, he has improved the health of the

nation (E5); *libbi Marduk bēlišu uṭīb u šīram ṭābam ana nišī ana dār išīm*, he has made Marduk's heart happy and ensured health and prosperity for the people for ever (E12); *ina mātišu raggam u ṣēnam lissuḫ šīr nišīšu liṭīb*, let him weed out evil and wickedness and let him make his people healthy (E16).

2. bad health: *ina bīrišu šīram lemnam ša nasāḫ išdī šarrūtišu u ḫalāq mātišu liškunšum*, when he seeks divination let him ordain bad health so that the foundations of his kingdom will be torn up and his people lost (E23).

***šisītu***, sbst., call. < *š-s-ʾ*.

*ana šisīt nāgirim la uštēṣiam*, he has not sent him out when the herald shouts (L16).

*šiššu* > ***šeššu***, six, sixth.

*šitannu* > ***šanānu***, strive.

***šittān***, num., two-thirds.

*ina bilāt kirîm šittīn ana bēl kirîm inaddin*, he shall give two-thirds of the produce of the orchard to the owner of the orchard (L64).

***šu***, pron., he of (see *CAD* Š/3, 152b; *AHw*, p. 1254a-b).

as the subject of a verb in the subjunctive, he is the one who: *šû iqīšu napšatam ana Maškan-šāpir mušesqi nuḫšim ana Meslam*, he is the one who granted life to Mashkan-shapar and he gives abundantly to Meslam (P15, variant *ša*; cited by *AHw* s.v. 2b); *šû ikšudu nagab uršim*, he is the one who delved into the spring of wisdom (P16, variant *ša*); *šû igmilu nišī Mera u Tuttul*, he is the one who cares for the people of Mera and Tuttul (P17, variant *ša*).

***šû* 1**, adj., his (see *CAD* Š/3, 153b, *šû*; *AHw*, p. 1254b, *šû*[*m*] I).

*abbutti wardim la šêm ugdallib*, he has shaved off the mark of a slave that was not his (L227; see also L226; see *CAD* s.v. b2′: Š/3, p.154 lines 16-21; *AHw* s.v. *šû* I, 2a: p. 1255a, line 5f.)

***šû* 2**, pron., he (see *CAD* Š/3, 155); 2. adj., this, that (see *CAD* Š/3, 160); cf. *AHw* 1254b s.v. *šū*.

1. as the subject of verb in the indicative (see *AHw šū*, s.v. 1): *šûma illikšu illak*, he himself shall perform the duty (L27; *CAD* s.v. 1b2′); *ša iṣṣabtuma ilikšu ittalku šûma illak*, the one who has taken possession of it and who has been performing the duty, he is the one to continue to do it (L30; cf. L31); *šaluštam šû ileqqe*, he himself shall take one-third (L64); *šû warkānumma ina sūniša ittatīlma*, at some later time he has sexual intercourse with her (L155; cf. L156).

2. demonstrative adj., this, that (see *AHw šū*, s.v. 2):

a. with personal substantive: *awīlum šû*, that man (L3; 19; 20; 130; 136; 144; 145; 151; 158; 163; 206; E15; 18, twice; 19, twice); *itinnum šû*, that builder (L229; 233); *laputtûm šû*, that officer (L33; 34);

*malāḫum šû*, that boatman (L237); *ṣeḫrum šû*, that young person (L191; 194); [*tamkārum šû*], that merchant (§5.13); *wardum šû*, fragmentary (§5.3b).

b. with non-personal substantive: *dīnum šû*, that law (L3; 123); *bītum šû*, that property (L67+a); *narûm šû*, this stela (E15).

***šuāti***, pron., him; adj. that.

1. pron., him: *šuāti idukkūšu*, they shall put him to death (§5.3a, fragmentary); *mār awīlim lēt mār awīlim ša kīma šuāti imtaḫaṣ*, the son of a gentleman has struck the son of another gentleman who is like himself (L203); *šuāti ana qāt nakrīšu limallīšuma*, let him betray him into the hands of his enemy (E27); *šuāti...līrurū*, let them curse him (E31).

2. demonstrative adj., that:

a. with personal substantive: *awīlam šu'āti*, that man (L2; 124; 127; 144; 154; 155; 227; cf. *awīlum šuāti*, fragmentary §5.7); *dayyānam šuāti*, that judge (L5); *ritti gallābim šuāti inakkisū*, they shall cut off the hand of that barber (L226); *mār itinnim šuāti*, the son of that builder (L230); *sinništam šuāti*, that woman (L133b; 143; 151 (vnt. *šiāti*); 153; cf. *ana sinništim šuāti*, L137; *ana šerikti sinništim šuāti*, L163; *sinništim šuāti*, L177); *wardam šuāti*, that slave (L19).

b. with non-personal substantive: *ana bītim šuāti še'am kaspam u bīšam inaddin*, he may pay grain, silver or goods for that house (L67+a); *aran dīnim šuāti*, the penalty in that case (L4); *rugummâm ša ina dīnim šuāti ibaššû*, the damages that occur in that case (L5); *eleppam šuāti*, that ship (L235); *igāram šuāti*, that wall (L233); *ina šattim šuāti*, in that year (L48, twice; cf. *ina šattimma šuāti*, L235).

c. with feminine substantive: *awīltam šuāti iqallûši*, they shall burn such a woman (L110); *sābītam šuāti*, that drink-seller (L108, vnt. *šiāti*); *sinništam šuāti ina gašīšim išakkanūši*, they shall impale that woman on a stake (L153).

*šubbû*, to suppress > ***šuppû***, to silence.

*šubbuḫu* > ***šuppuḫu***, to incite.

***šubšû***, vb., to produce, create. < *b-š-'*.

1. to produce crops: *ina eqlim še'am la uštabši*, he has not produced grain from the field (L42; cf. L49; 52; 255); *nārātišu ina nagbim liskir ina erṣetišu ašnān napišti nišī ay ušabši*, let him block up his rivers at their source, let him stop the production of sustenance for the the people to survive (E22).

2. to produce children: *mārī uštabši*, she has produced sons (L144); *šumšu u zikiršu ina mātim la šubšâm*, stopping him from producing a reputation or descendants in the land (E20).

3. to allow a disease to develop: *rē'ûm īgūma ina tarbaṣim pissatam*

*uštabši*, he has hired a shepherd and he has allowed disease to develop in the pen (L267); *ḫiṭīt pissatim ša ina tarbaṣim ušabšû*, the damage from the disease which he has allowed to develop in the pen (L267).

***šubtu***, sbst., dwelling, home. < *ʾ-š-b*.
*ina šubat mutiša uššab*, she shall dwell in the home of her husband (L171b); *mušaršid šubat Kiš muštasḫir melemmê Emeteursag*, establishing Kish as a dwelling place, surrounding Emeteursag with splendour (P9); *mušaršidu šubātišin in nuḫšim*, establishing dwelling places for them in peace (P16, variant *šubātišina*); *muṣīr bīt Ebabbar ša kî šubat šamāʾi*, designing the shrine of Ebabbar just like a heavenly home (P7); *gabaraḫ ḫalāqišu ina šubtišu lišappiḫaššum*, let him kindle for him in his dwelling place a riot which will destroy him (E20).

***šūbultu***, sbst., load of goods, consignment. < *ʾ-b-l*.
*awīlum ina ḫarrānim wašibma kaspam ḫuraṣam abnam u bīš qātišu ana awīlim iddinma ana šēbultim ušābilšu*, a man starting a journey has given silver, gold, stones or personal property to another man and made him transport it as a load (L112); *bēl šēbultim*, the owner of the load (L112).

***šūbulu***, vb., to bring, remove from use. < *w-b-l*.
1. to have transported: *ana šēbultim ušābilšu*, he has arranged for him to transport it (L112, vnt. *ušābilaššu*, and *ušābil*); *mimma ša šūbulu ašar ša šūbulu la iddinma*, he has not delivered what had to be transported to the destination (L112, variant *šūbula*(?); 112, vnt. *šūbula*(?); *mimma ša šūbuluma*, whatever was to be transported (L112).
2. to bring a wedding gift: *awīlum ana bīt emim biblam ušābil*, a man has brought a wedding gift to the house of his father-in-law (L160, vnt. *uštābil*; L161; cf. *ušābilu*, L159).
3. Št-theme, to cause to flow over and destroy: *ina kārišu pītum ittepte u ugāram mê uštābil*, a break opens up in the dyke and allows water to flow over the land (L53; cf. L55; 56).

***šuddû***, vb., to cause to drop. < *n-d-ʾ*.
*ḫarrānam ina alākišu nakrum mimma ša našû uštaddīšu*, while he was on a journey an aggressor made him surrender what was being carried (L103); *mārat awīlim imḫaṣma ša libbiša uštaddīši*, he has struck a man's daughter and made her lose her unborn child (L209; cf. L211; 213).

***šūdû***, vb., to make known. < *ʾ-d-ʾ*.
*kīma nakkāpû bābtašu ušēdīšumma*, his community has made known that it was one that gored (L251).

***šudūku***, vb., to arrange a murder. < *d-ʾ-k*.
*aššat awīlim aššum zikarim šanîm mussa ušdīk*, a woman has had her husband murdered because of another man (L153).

***šugītu***, sbst., priestess.

*ana šugītim ša mārī uldušum*, concerning a priestess who has born him sons (L137); *ana šugītim aḫāzim panīšu ištakan*, he has determined to marry a priestess (L144; 145); *šugītam ul iḫḫaz*, he shall not marry the priestess (L144; cf. L145); *šugītum šî itti nadītim ul uštamaḫḫar*, that priestess shall not rival the prostitute (L145); *ana mārtīšu šugītim šeriktam išrukšim*, he has given the marriage gift to his daughter, a priestess (L183; cf. L184).

***šuḫluṣû***, vb., to allow to crumble. < *ḫ-l-ṣ-ʾ*.

*šarrussu liskip dīnšu ā idīn uruḫšu līši išdī ummānišu lišḫelṣi*, he will overthrow his kingdom, not judge his cause, confuse him on his path, make the foundations of his people crumble (E23).

***šuḫruṣu*** (*šutaḫruṣu*), vb., to deduct. < *ḫ-r-ṣ*.

*u lu šeʾam* [*u lu kaspam*] *mala* [*imḫuru u lu*] *la uštaḫriṣma*, either as much grain or silver as he has received or he has not made the deduction (§5.12).

***šūḫuzu***, vb., to let marry, teach, enforce to do. < *ʾ-ḫ-z*.

1. to arrange a marriage: *aššatam ušaḫḫazūšu*, they shall enable him to take a wife (L166).

2. to teach: *mār ummānim ṣeḫram ana tarbītim ilqēma šipir qātišu uštāḫissu*, a professional person has taken a son to adopt and has taught him his own craft (L188; cf. L189).

3. to instruct someone else to do something: *aššum errētim šināti šaniamma uštāḫiz*, he makes someone else do it because of these curses (E19).

4. to adopt a certain pattern of behaviour: *ana šutēšur nišī mātim ūsim šūḫuzim uwaʾeranni*, he has commissioned me to make the people of the land righteous and adopt proper customs (P22, vnt. *šūḫuzu*).

***šuklulu***, vb., to make complete. < *k-l-l*.

1. to complete a building: *itinnum bītam ana awīlim īpušma ušaklilšum*, a builder made a house for a man and completed it for him (L228).

2. to endow a person with all attributes: *bēlum simat ḫaṭṭim u agêm ša ušaklilušu erištum Mama*, the lord with the crown and sceptre for a symbol, whom the wisest Mama made complete (P12, vnt. *ušaklilušum*).

> ***mušaklil***, providing.

***šukšudu***, vb., to enable to reach, enable to achieve. < *k-š-d*.

1. to enable to reach a destination: *tamkārum ipṭuraššuma ālšu ustakšidaššu*, the merchant has ransomed him and enabled him to reach his home town (L32).

2. to enable to achieve an ambition: *sapar nakirī ša Erra rūšu ušakšidu nizmassu*, the enemy's scourge and the friend of Erra, who allowed him to achieve his ambition (P10, variant *ušakšidušu*).
> ***mušakšidu***, granting victory.

***šūkulu***, vb., to allow to feed. < *ʾ-k-l*.
*ana šammī ṣēnim šūkulim itti bēl eqlim la imtagarma*, he has not agreed with the owner of the field to let the sheep feed on the grass (L57); *eqlam ṣēnam uštākil*, he has allowed them to feed on the grass (L57; 58; also *ušākilu*, L57; 58).

***šullumu***, vb., to reinstate to the original value, heal. < *š-l-m*.
1. to reinstate: *ušallamma ana bēl namkurim iriab*, he shall make a complete recompense and reimburse the owner of the property (L125); *liātim u ṣēnam ušallamma*, he shall reinstate the cattle and the sheep (L267); *šeriktam ša ištu bīt abiša ublam ušallamšimma izzibši*, he shall completely reinstate for her the dowry which she brought from her father's house and divorce her (L138; cf. L149; 156; also *ušallamūšimma*, L172).
2. to heal an injury: *asûm eṣemti awīlim šebirtam uštallim*, a physician has healed a man's broken bone (L221).

***šulmāniš***, securely. < *š-l-m*.
*mukinnu išdīšin qerbum Bābilim šulmāniš*, establishing its foundations in Babylon securely (P18).

***šulmu***, sbst., well-being, peace. < *š-l-m*.
*ašrī šulmim ešteʾīšināšim*, I have searched for peaceful places for them (E3); *ina šulmim attabbalšināti ina nēmeqia uštapziršināti*, I have always led them in peace, I have always guided them by my wisdom (E7).

***šulputu***, vb., to defile. < *l-p-t*.
*šulput mātišu ḫalāq nišīšu tabāk napištišu kīma mê ina pī Ellil šarrim lišaškin*, make Enlil the king decree that his land be defiled, that his people be lost, that his life flow away like a stream (E21).

***šūlû***, vb., to bring to the surface. < *ʾ-l-ʾ*.
*malāḫum elep awīlim uṭṭebbīma uštēlliašši*, a boatman made a man's boat sink but brought it back to the surface (L238).

***šuluḫḫu***, sbst., purification ritual, lustration.
*mubbib šuluḫ Eabzu*, ensuring the purity of the lustrations in Eabzu (P5).

***šumḫuru***, vb., to show rivalry. < *m-ḫ-r*.
*šugītum šî itti nadītim ul uštamaḫḫar*, that priestess shall never rival the devotee (L145); *amtum šî itti bēltiša uštatamḫir*, that maid has shown rivalry with her mistress (L146).

**šumma**, particle, if.

1. in the Laws, to introduce a new numbered law (according to conventional editing):

a. with *awīlum* as the subject: L1; 2; 3; 6; 7; 8; 9; 13; 14; 15; 16; 17; 21; 22; 35; 37; 41; 42; 44; 45; 48; 49; 53; 55; 56; 59; 60; 64; 66; 67, partly restored; 68+a; 69+c; §5.10; 5.15; L77+f; 112; 113; 114; 115; 117; 119; 120; 121; 122; 124; 125; 126; 127; 128; 130; 133a; 134; 135; 136; 137; 138; 144; 145; 146; 148; 150; 154; 155; 156; 157; 158; 159; 160; 161; 162; 163; 165; 166; 167; 168; 170; 184; 185; 186; 190; 191; 194; 196; 200; 202; 206; 209; 227; 236; 237; 239; 241; 242/3; 244; 245; 246; 247; 248; 249; 253; 257; 258; 259; 261; 262; 268; 271; 272; 273; 274; 275, partly restored; 277; 278; 279; 280.

b. with some other subject: L4; 5; 10; 11; 12; 18; 19; 20; 23; 24; 25; 26; 27; 28; 29; 30; 31; 32; 33; 34; 43; 46; 47; 50; 51; 52; 54; 57; 58; 61; 62; 63; 65; §5.3a; 5.3b; 5.8; 5.9; 5.11; 5.12; 5.13; 5.14, partly restored; L100; 101; 102; 103; 104; 105; 106; 107; 108; 109; 110; 111; 116; 118; 123; 129; 131; 132; 133b; 139; 140; 141; 142; 143; 147; 149; 151; 152; 153; 164; 169; 171a; 172; 173; 174; 175; 176b; 177; 178; 179; 180; 181; 182; 183; 188; 189; 192; 193; 195; 197; 198; 199; 201; 203; 204; 205; 207; 208; 210; 211; 212; 213; 214; 215; 216; 217; 218; 219; 220; 221; 222; 223; 224; 225; 226; 228; 229; 230; 231; 232; 233; 234; 235; 238; 240; 250; 251; 252; 254; 255; 256; 260; 263, partly restored; 264, partly restored; 265; 266; 267; 269; 270; 276; 281; 282; cf. *u šumma*, L176a.

c. occurring within a law: L2; 2; 3; 8; 8; 8; 8; 13; 27; 30; 32; 32; 32; 49; 62; 67+a; 67+a; 68+b; 68+b, fragmentary; §4.12; 4.12; 5.2; 5.2; 5.7; 5.8; 5.9; 5.10; L100; 116; 116; 129; 136; 141; 141; 142; 151; 151; 163; 168; 169; 172; 172; 178; 207; 253 (*šumma awīlum*); 280.

2. in the Epilogue, to introduce a clause (always with *awīlum* as the subject): E15; 18; 19.

**šumqutu**, vb., to bring down. < *m-q-t*.

*qarrādīšu lišamqit damīšunu erṣetam lišqi*, let her bring down his heroes and feed the earth with their blood (E27).

**šumṣû**, vb., to allow to dispose. < *m-ṣ-ʾ*.

*mala libbiša la ušamṣīši*, he has not allowed her to distribute as much as she likes (L178; cf. *uštamṣīši*, L179).

**šumṭû**, vb., to denigrate. < *m-ṭ-ʾ*.

*sikiltam isakkil bīssa usappaḫ mussa ušamṭa*, she engages in fraudulent practice, spoils her house and deprecates her husband (L141); *mussa waṣīma magal ušamṭāši*, her husband has seriously denigrated her as he went out (L142; cf. *ušamṭa*, L143).

***šumu***, sbst., name.

1. name of person, place or deity: *šumšu ṣīram ibbiū*, he gave Babylon its illustrious name (P2); *Anum u Ellil ana šīr nišī ṭubbim šumī ibbû*, Anum and Enlil have named me to benefit the health of the people (P3); *šumī ina damiqtim ana dār lizzakir*, let my name be uttered as a blessing for evermore (E10); *šumī šaṭram ipšiṭma šumšu ištaṭar*, he has removed my inscribed name and written in his own name (E19; 19).

2. reputation: *šumšu u zikiršu ina mātim la šubšâm*, stopping him from producing a reputation or fame in the land (E20); *aplam līṭeršuma šumam ay ušaršīšu ina qerbīt nišīšu zēr awīlūtim ay ibni*, let him remove his heir and stop him having a reputation, let him not create human descendants amidst his people (E29).

3. used idiomatically: *awīlūtum ša šumam nabiat*, lit. 'a human being who has been given a name', anyone at all (E19).

4. ***mimma šumšu***, anything else > ***mimma***, something.

***šumūtu***, vb., to cause death. < *m-ʾ-t*.

*simmam kabtam ina karzilli siparrim īpušma awīlam uštamīt*, he has made a deep incision with the scalpel and caused the death of the man (L218; cf. L219; 225); *bīt īpušu imqutma bēl bītim uštamīt*, the house he made has collapsed and he has caused the death of the owner of the house (L229; cf. L230; 231); *alpam īgurma ina mēgûtim u lu ina maḫāṣim uštamīt*, he has hired an ox and let it die through neglect or through rough treatment (L245); *alpum sūqam ina alākišu awīlam ikkipma uštamīt*, an ox gores a man while it is walking in the street and causes his death (L250; cf. L251).

***šunu***, pron., they.

*wardum u amtum šunu mārū mātim*, the slave and the slave-girl are native to the land (L280).

***šupêlu***, vb., to exchange. < *š-p-ʾ-l*.

*naspuḫ nišīšu šarrūssu šupēlam*, the scattering of his people, the overthrow of his kingdom (E20); *awâtiya la uštepēl uṣurātiya la unakkir*, he should not emend my commandments or change my purposes (E18; cf. E19, variant *uštapāl*).

***šuppû***, vb., to silence. < *š-p-ʾ*.

*tēšî la šubbîm gabaraḫ ḫalāqišu ina šubtišu lišappiḫaššum*, let him stir up for him in his dwelling place a revolt which cannot be silenced, a riot which will destroy him (E20, see *CAD šapû* C, s.v. 2).

> ***mušebbū***, muzzling.

***šuppuḫu***, vb., to scatter about, stir up (see *AHw šapāḫu*, D-theme; *CAD šuppuḫu*). < *š-p-ḫ*.

*gabaraḫ ḫalāqišu ina šubtišu lišappiḫaššum*, may he stir up trouble in his home which will destroy him (E20).

**šūpû**, vb., to display. < *ʾ-p-ʾ*.

*mīšaram ina mātim ana šūpîm*, to show justice to the nation (P3); *šarrum ša ina Ninua ina Emešmeš ušūpiʾu mê Ištar*, the king who made the power of Ishtar shine in Nineveh in Emeshmesh (P20, variants *ušēpu* and *ušīpu*); *ina qibīt Šamaš dayyānim rābîm ša šamê u erṣetim mīšarī ina mātim lištēpi*, may Shamash, the almighty judge in heaven and earth, let my justice shine over the land! (E10); *Sîn bēl šamê ilum bānî ša têressu ina ilī šūpât*, O Sin, lord of heaven, creator god, whose judgment outshines all other gods (E24).

> **mušēpīu**, displaying.

**šupuzzuru**, vb., to protect; < *p-z-r*.

*ina šulmim attabbalšināti ina nēmeqia uštapziršināti*, I have led them in peace, I have protected them by my wisdom (E7).

> **mušpazziru**, protecting.

**šuqtû**, vb., to terminate. < *q-t-ʾ*.

*ūmī warḫī šanāt palēšu ina tānēḫim u dimmatim lišaqti*, bring each day, each month each year of his rule to a close with weeping and wailing (E24).

**šūquru**, sbst., very precious. < *ʾ-q-r*.

*awâtiya šūqurātim ina narîya ašṭurma*, I have inscribed my precious words on my stela (E8); *awâtiya šūqurātim lišmēma*, let him hear my precious words (E11).

**šurbû**, vb., to extol. < *r-b-ʾ*.

*in Igigī ušarbiūšu*, they proclaimed him great among the Igigi (P2).

> **mušarbū**, proclaiming.

**šurbuṣu**, vb., to pasture. < *r-b-ṣ*.

*nišī dadmī aburrī ušarbiṣ*, I made the people feed in quiet pastures (E5).

**šurqu**, sbst., stolen property. < *š-r-q*.

*u ša šurqam ina qātišu imḫuru iddāk*, furthermore anyone who has acquired stolen goods from him shall be killed (L6).

**šurrumu**, vb., to trim (or cover) the horns of an ox. < *š-r-m*.

*kīma nakkāpû bābtašu ušēdīšumma qarnīšu la ušarrim*, his community informed him that it was a gorer but he did not cover its horns (L251).

**šuršû**, vb., to provide. < *r-š-ʾ*.

1. to provide children: *ana šugītim ša mārī uldušum u lu nadītim ša mārī ušaršûšu*, concerning a priestess who has born him sons or a hierodule who has provided him with sons (L137); *awīlum nadītam īḫuzma mārī la ušaršīšuma*, he has taken a priestess but she has not

provided him with sons (L145, variant *ušaršīšu*); *aššatam īhuzma mārī la ušaršīšu*, he has taken a wife but she has not provided him with sons (L163).

2. to provide a reputation: *šumam ay ušaršīšu*, may he not let him possess a name (E29).

3. to show mercy, or hostility: *gurun šalmāt ummānātišu ina ṣērim littaddi ummānšuma rēmam ay ušarši*, let the heap of bodies of their soldiers be piled in the desert and let him not allow him mercy (E27); *mugallitam ul ušaršīšināti*, I did not offer them any opposition (E5).

***šuršudu***, vb., to fix firmly. < *r-š-d*; *AHw* (s.v. *rašādu*) suggests possibly denominative from *išdu*, foundation.

*ina libbišu šarrūtam dārītam ša kīma šamê u erṣetim išdāša suršudā ukinnūšum*, they have established within it his everlasting kingdom whose foundations are as firm as those of heaven and earth (P2).

> ***mušaršidu***, protecting.

***šūrubu***, vb., to bring in. < *ʾ-r-b*.

*ana bītišu ušerrebši*, he shall make her move into his house (L145, variant *ušerreb*).

***šussuku***, vb., to throw out. < *n-s-k*.

*uṣurātiya ay ušassik*, let no one throw out my plans (E14); *dīnī la ušassik*, let no one throw out my law (E18).

> ***mušassiku***, disposing.

***šuṣbutu***, vb., to enforce. < *ṣ-b-t*.

*dīnāt mīšarim ša Hammurabi šarrum lēʾûm ukinnuma mātam ussam kīnam u rīdam damqam ušaṣbitu*, just laws which the mighty king Hammurabi has established, who made the land adopt solid leadership and good discipline (E1).

***šuṣmû***, vb., to make thirsty. < *ṣ-m-ʾ*.

*šapliš ina erṣetim eṭemmašu mê lišaṣmi*, in the land down below may he let his ghost thirst for water (E23).

***šūṣû***, vb., to expel, bring out, let out. < *ʾ-ṣ-ʾ*.

1. to expel: *ālam ušeṣṣûšu*, they shall make him leave the town (L154); *aššum ina bītim šūṣîm usahhamūši*, because they put pressure on her to leave the house (L172); *aššum...ina bītišu* [*ušēṣu*], because...he has made him leave his house (L69+c).

2. to allow to leave: *ana šisīt nāgirim la uštēṣiam*, when the crier shouts out he does not bring him out (L16); *abullam uštēṣi*, he has let out of the gate (L15).

3. to lease: *eqlam ana errēšūtim ušēṣīma*, he has leased out a field to be cultivated (L42); *ana teptītim ušēṣīma*, he has leased out to be developed (L44).

4. to let light shine: *pušqī waštūtim upetti nūram ušēṣišināšim*, I have solved impossible difficulties, I have made the light shine for them (E3).

5. to appear (stative): *ela ana la ḫassim rēqa ana emqim ana tanādātim šuṣâ*, although to the senseless they are empty to the wise they appear as treasures (E17).

6. to cause a disease to break out: *murṣam kabtam…ina biniātišu lišāṣiaššuma*, let him cause a serious disease to break out over his body (E30).

> ***mušēṣû***, bringing out.

***šūši***, num., sixty.

*ina puḫrim ina qinnaz alpim 1 šūši immaḫḫaṣ*, he shall be beaten sixty times with an ox-tail in the assembly (L202); *60 kur še'am ana bēl eqlim imaddad*, he shall measure out 60 kur of grain for the owner of the field (L58; cf. L255); *elep 60 kur ana awīlim ipḫe*, he has caulked a boat of 60 kur capacity for a man (L234); *elep šūšim īgur*, he hired a 60 kur boat (L277).

***šuškunu***, vb., to have arranged. < *š-k-n*.

*ina pī Ellil šarrim lišaškin*, may she have decreed by the word of Enlil the king (E21).

***šušnû***, vb., to make double. < *š-n-'*.

*kasap ilqû uštašannāma*, he shall double the silver he took (L101); *še'am ša ilqū uštašannāma*, he shall double the amount of grain he received (L120, vnt. *uštašnama*); *mimma ša ikkiru uštašannāma*, he shall double the amount of the error (L124); *mimma ša irgumu ustašannāma*, he shall double the amount of the complaint (L126); *mimma mala ibbablušum uštašannāma*, he shall double the full value of the gift (L160; cf. L161); *uštašannāma utār*, he shall doubly repay (§5.12).

***šuššān***, num., a third (i.e. two-sixths, dual of *šuššu*, see *AHw*).

*1/3 mana kaspam išaqqal*, he shall weigh out a third of a mana of silver (L114; 116; 201; 208; 214; 241); *1/3 mana kaspam inaddin*, he shall pay a third of a mana of silver (L252; cf. *inaddiššim*, L140).

***šuššu***, num., a sixth.

*ana 1 šiqil kaspim 1/6 u 6 uṭṭet ṣibtam ileqqe*, for each shekel of silver he shall receive a sixth of a shekel and six grains in interest (§5.9; cf. §5.10); *1/6 kaspam ana asîm idīšu inaddin*, he shall pay a sixth in silver to the doctor as his fee (L224); *ina ūmim 1/6 kaspam idīša inaddin*, he shall pay a sixth in silver for one day (L277); see also *šuššān* (dual), two-sixths, i.e. a third.

***šūšubu***, vb., to allow to dwell. < *ʾ-š-b*.

[*ina bītišu ušešibma*], he has allowed him to live in his house (L69+c; text so restored in *BAL*, but Roth significantly different).

***šūšuru***, vb., to show justice, keep in order. < *ʾ-š-r*.

1. to demonstrate justice to people: *Marduk ana šutēšur nišī mātim ūsim šūḫuzim uwaʾeranni*, Marduk urged me to show justice to the people in the land to take charge of the law (P22); *ekūtam almattam šutēšurim*, to show justice to the orphan and widow (E8); *purussē mātim ana parāsim ḫablim šutēšurim*, to make decisions of national importance and grant justice to anyone wronged (E8); *ṣalmāt qaqqadišu lištēšer dīnšina lidīn purussāšina liprus*, let him show justice to the mass of humanity and judge their disputes (E16).

2. to regulate the affairs of the nation: *libbi Marduk bēlišu uṭīb u šīram ṭābam ana nišī ana dār išīm u mātam uštēšer*, he has pleased the heart of his lord Marduk, and has also ordained health and prosperity for the people for ever and has regulated the land (E12); *tašīmtam išūma māssu šutēšuram ileʾi*, he has authority and he has the ability to regulate his land (E15).

*šutablu* (Št-theme of *abālu*) > ***šūbulu***, to bring.

***šutaktutu***, vb., to be submissive (*CAD*); to be eager (*AHw*). < *k-t-t*.

*ana awat Marduk bēlišu uštaktitma*, he submitted himself(?) to the word of his lord Marduk (E12).

***šutbû***, vb., to remove. < *t-b-ʾ*.

*ina puḫrim ina kussî dayyānūtišu ušetbûšuma*, they shall remove him from his seat of judgment in the assembly (L5).

*šutbulu* (Š-theme of *tabālu*) > *šūbulu* (cf. *šutablu*, Št-theme of *abālu*).

*šutēmuqu*, to plead > ***muštēmiqu***, supplicant.

***šuteṣbû***, vb., to work to plan, make careful arrangements (see *CAD ṣubbû* 4, *AHw ṣabû* IV). < *ṣ-b-ʾ*.

*šipiršu la ušteṣbīma*, he has not done a proper job (L233).

> ***mušteṣbu***, reinforcing.

***šutlumu***, vb., to bestow. < *t-l-m*.

*ina kakkim dannim ša Zababa u Ištar ušatlimūnim*, with the fierce weapon that Zababa and Ishtar have presented to me (E4).

***šutruṣu***, vb., to stretch. < *t-r-ṣ*.

*eli ugbabtim u aššat awīlim ubānam ušatriṣma*, he has pointed his finger at a priestess or a man's wife (L127).

***šūtuqu***, vb., to allow time to expire, or to take away overland. < *ʾ-t-q*.

*šumma wardam u lu amtam ana kiššātim ittandin tamkārum ušetteq ana kaspim inaddin*, if he has handed over a slave or a slave-girl as a security and the merchant has let the time expire he may sell (L118, so Roth; cf. *CAD etēqu* 4 [*šūtuqu*], f; but see citation in *CAD* E, p. 391, s.v. *etēqu* 4a: the merchant may take him [or her] overland [i.e. out of town] and sell him [or her]).

***šūturu***, vb., to proclaim as excellent. < *w-t-r*.

*Bābilam šumšu ṣīram ibbiū in kibrātim ušāterūšu*, they gave Babylon an exalted name and throughout the earth proclaimed it great (P2); *šarrum ša in šarrī šūturu anāku*, I am the king who is proclaimed great among the kings (E9; either the infinitive followed by personal pronoun, or to be taken as an adjective).

***šuṭṭû***, vb., to have someone beaten. < *n-ṭ-ʾ*.

*ina kašūšišu rabîm kīma išātim ezzetim ša appim nišīšu liqmi in kakkišu dannim lišaṭṭīšuma*, let him burn his people by his mighty power, raging like a fire through the reeds, with his powerful weapons may he have him beaten (E29; but possibly from a verb *šatû*, to strike, see *CAD* N/2, 133b, s.v. *naṭû* 3).

***šuṭṭulu***, vb., to make visible. < *n-ṭ-l*.

*kammāl šarrūtim lišaṭṭilšu balāṭam ša itti mūtim šitannu ana šīmtim lišīmšum*, let him make him see the rival for his kingdom, let him ordain as his destiny a life that is always vying with death (E24).

***šūzubu***, vb., to have deposited. < *ʾ-z-b*.

*kunukkam ušēzib*, he has had a sealed document deposited (L5); *ṭuppam uštēzib*, he has had a document deposited (L151); *ṭuppam ušezzebūšunūti*, they shall make them deposit a document (L177).

***šūzuzzu***, vb., to erect, cause to dominate. < *ʾ-z-z*(!).

*nakiršu elišu lišzīz*, let him allow his enemy to stand over him (E26).

## T

***tabāku***, vb., to pour out. < *t-b-k*.

*tabāk napištišu kīma mê*, the pouring out of his life like water (E21).

***tabālu***, vb., to remove (often indistinguishable from *abālu* with *-t-*). < *t-b-l*.

1. to confiscate, assume formal legal possession of something: *mimma ša ibbablušum itabbal*, whatever has been brought to him he shall confiscate (L159); *mubbiršu bīssu itabbal*, his accuser shall take possession of his house (L2); *bīt mubbiršu itabbal*, he shall remove the house of his accuser (L2); *munaggiršu bīssu itabbal*, the one who informed on him shall take away his house (L26); *niplātim ša innadnušum itabbal*, he shall take away the extra payment that was given to him (L41);

2. to take away, remove crops at harvest time: *šamaššammī ša ibaššû esip tabal*, collect and remove the sesame that is there (L49); *suluppī mala ina kirîm ibbaššû ana kaspika tabal iqbīšum*, he has said to him,

'Take away instead of your silver as many dates as will be produced in the orchard' (L66).

3. to remove, take away illegally: *mimma ša šūbulu ašar šūbulu la iddinma itbal*, he has not taken to its destination whatever had to be transported but has removed it (L112).

4. to take into safety: *ina šulmim attabbalšināti*, I have removed them for safe-keeping (E7).

***tadmiqtu***, sbst., kindness, recompense, interest free investment (see *AHw*). < *d-m-q*.

*tamkārum ana šamallîm kaspam ana tadmiqtim ittadinma*, a merchant has given silver to a merchant for an investment opportunity (L102).

***tāḫazu***, sbst., conflict. < *ʾ-ḫ-z*.

*Ištar bēlet tāhazim u qablim*, Ishtar the lady of conflict and strife (E27); *ašar tāḫazim u qablim*, the place of conflict and strife (E27).

*takālu*, to trust > ***tukkulu***, to inspire confidence.

***talīmu***, sbst., devoted follower.

*ušumgal šarrī talîm Zababa*, the leader of kings, the follower of Zababa (P9).

***tālittu***, sbst., young animal. < *ʾ-l-d*.

*tālittam u biltam inaddin*, he shall give a young animal for an offering (L264); *tālittam umtaṭṭi*, he has made the birth rate less (L264).

*tamāḫu*, to hold > ***mutammiḫu***, supporting.

***tamḫāru***, sbst., conflict

*ašar tamḫārim*, the place of battle (E26).

***tamkāru***, sbst., merchant. < *m-k-r*.

1. as subject:

a. with *nadānu*: *tamkārum šeʾam u kaspam ana ḫubullim iddin*, the merchant has given grain or silver on loan (§5.9); *tamkārum šeʾam* [*u kaspam*] *ana ṣibtim* [*iddinma*], the merchant has given grain or silver for interest (§5.11; cf. 5.13; [5.14]); *tamkārum...ana šamallîm inaddin*, the merchant shall give to the trader (L107); *tamkārum ana šamallîm kaspam ana tadmiqtim ittadinma*, a merchant has given silver to a trader as a kindness (L102; cf. L100; 104); *mimma ša tamkārum iddinušum*, whatever the merchant gave him (L107); *nadītum tamkārum u ilkum aḫum*, a priestess, a merchant or a contracted labourer (L40).

b. with other verbs: *tamkārum šû šeʾam mala ilqû uštašannāma utâr*, that merchant shall return twice as much grain as he received (§5.12; [§5.13]); *kasap tamkārum išqulu*, the silver which the merchant weighed out (L119); *tamkārum kaspam šamallâm iqīpma*, a merchant has entrusted silver to a trader (L107); *tamkārum ul uppas imaḫḫar*, the merchant shall not argue—he shall agree (§5.15, variant *tamkārum*

*šû*); *tamkārum šû ul imaggar*, that merchant shall not agree (L66); *tamkārum šû ina maḫar ilim u šībī ina kaspim leqêm šamallâm ukânma*, that merchant shall affirm in the presence of the god and witnesses that the tradesman took the money (L106); *tamkārum ipṭuraššuma*, the merchant has bought him free (L32); *tamkārum ušēteq*, the merchant has taken him away (L118: meaning uncertain; see *šūtuqu*); *tamkāršu ittakir*, he has become angry with his merchant (L106); *tamkārum mimma ša šamallûm iddinšum ittakiršu*, the merchant has disagreed about what the trader gave him (L107).
c. fragmentary: *tamkārum* (§5.3a; 5.10).
2. as direct object: *kaspam u ṣibassu ša pī ṭuppišu tamkāram ippalma*, he shall repay the merchant the silver plus the interest that the tablet states (L66; cf. L100; 152); *tamkāršu īsiršuma*, the merchant is pressing him (L66) *tamkāram ukânma*, he shall bring charges against the merchant (L107; cf. *tamkāršu ukânma*, L116).
3. as indirect object:
a. with *ana*: *eqel epšētim ša še'im u lu šamaššammī ana tamkārim iddin*, he has given a field for the production of grain or sesame to the merchant (L49); *u mānaḫāt erēšim ana tamkārim inaddin*, he shall give to the merchant as well as the costs of cultivation (L49); *maḫar šībī kīma ubbalu ana tamkārišu inaddin*, he shall give his merchant whatever he has brought before witnesses (§5.15); *ana tamkārim utâr*, he shall give back to the merchant (L50; cf. 102; 104); *ana tamkārim inaddin*, he shall give to the merchant (L51; 101; 106; cf. *iddinma*, L66; *inaddinma*, L281; *ana tamkārišu uttēr*, L107, vnt. *tamkārim*); *šamallûm kanīk kaspim ša ana tamkārim inaddinu ileqqe*, the trader shall take the sealed tablet about the silver which he has given to the merchant (L104; cf. L105).
b. with *itti*: *awīlum kaspam itti tamkārim ilqēma*, a man has received money from a merchant (L49); *še'am ša kaspišu u ṣibassu ša itti tamkārim ilqû*, the grain for the silver plus interest which he has received from the merchant (L49; cf. L51); *itti tamkārim ilqēma*, he has borrowed from the merchant (§5.15); *awīlum kaspam itti tamkārim ilqēma*, a man has received silver from a merchant (L66); *šamallûm kaspam itti tamkārim ilqēma*, a trader has received silver from a merchant (L106).

***tamû***, vb., to swear. < *'-m-'*.
*šumma awīlum awīlam in risbātim imtaḫaṣma simmam ištakanšu awīlum šû ina idû la amḫaṣu itamma*, if a man has struck another man in a fight and has inflicted an injury on him, that man shall declare, 'I did not strike intentionally' (L206; cf. *itammāma*, L207); *gallābum*

*ina idû la ugallibu itammāma*, the barber shall declare that he did the shaving without the information (L227).

*tanādātu* > ***tanattu***, praise (see *AHw*).

***tanattu***, sbst., praise. < *n-ʾ-d*.

*ela ana la ḫassim rēqa ana emqim ana tanādātim šūṣâ*, although they are empty to the one without understanding, from the wise they bring out praise (E17).

***tānēḫu***, sbst., weariness. < *ʾ-n-ḫ*.

*palēšu ina tānēḫim u dimmatim lišaqti*, may he bring his reign to an end with weariness and sadness (E24); *palê tānēḫim*, a reign of trouble (E20).

***tappûtu***, sbst., partnership.

*kaspam ana tappûtim iddin*, he has given silver in partnership (L77+f).

***taqtītu***, sbst., end. < *q-t-ʾ*.

*ištu šiššim warḫim adi taqtīt šattim*, from the sixth month to the end of the year (L 273).

***tarāku***, vb., to beat. < *t-r-k*.

*itarrakaššu*, fragmentary (§5.8).

***tarāṣu***, vb., to stretch out. < *t-r-ṣ*.

*ṣillī ṭābum ana āliya tariṣ*, my beneficent shadow is spread over my city (E7).

> *šutruṣu*; *natruṣu*.

***tarbaṣu***, sbst., animal pen. < *r-b-ṣ*.

*ina tarbaṣim lipit ilim ittabšī*, an inexplicable disaster has occurred in the pen (L266); *miqitti tarbaṣim bēl tarbaṣim imaḫḫaršu*, the owner of the pen shall receive the dead animals from the pen (L266; 266); *ina tarbaṣim pissatam uštabši*, he has allowed disease to develop in the pen (L267, twice); *ḫiṭīt pissatim ša ina tarbaṣim ušabšu*, the damage from the disease he allowed to develop in the pen (L267).

***tarbītu***, sbst., adopted child. < *r-b-ʾ*.

*šumma awīlum ṣeḫram ina mêšu ana mārūtim ilqēma urtabbīšu tarbītum šî ul ibbaqqar*, if a man has adopted a newborn child as his own and has brought him up that adopted child shall not be reclaimed (L185); *tarbītum šî ana bīt abišu itâr*, that adopted child shall return to his father's house (L186; 189; 190); *mār ummānim ṣeḫram ana tarbītim ilqēma šipir qātišu uštāḫissu*, a professional person has taken a son to adopt and has taught him his own craft (L188); *ana tarbītim nasāḫim panam ištakan*, he has made up his mind to rid himself of the adopted child (L191).

***tarkibtu***, sbst., pollination. < *r-k-b*.

*kirâšu ištu tarkibtim ana tamkārim iddinma*, he has given his orchard after pollination to a merchant (L66).

***tarû***, to lead off (see *AHw tarû* I). < *t-r-'*.

*uznam u nēmeqam līṭeršuma ina mīšītim littarušu*, let him deprive him of hearing and understanding and lead him off into confusion (E22).

***târu***, vb., to return. < *t-ʾ-r*.

1. of a woman, to return to her husband: *sinništum šî ana ḫāwiriša itâr*, that woman shall return to her house, and to her husband (L135); *nīš ilim izakkarma ana bītiša itâr*, she shall swear on oath and return to her house (L131); *aššat munnabtim ana mutiša ul itâr*, the wife of a deserter shall not return to her husband (L136).

2. of a man, to return to work at home: *itūramma eqelšu kirāšu u bīssu irriš*, he has returned and has taken possession of his field, his orchard and his house (L30; cf. *ittūram*, L31; *itâr*, L41); *ina warka mussa ittūramma ālšu iktašdam*, afterwards her husband has then returned and reached his city (L135; cf. L27; 136).

3. of a child, to return to his father: *tarbītum šî ana bīt abišu itâr*, that foster child shall return to his father's house (L186; 189; 190).

4. to return to an official position: *ina puḫrim ina kussî dayyānūtišu ušetbûšuma ul itârma*, they shall remove him from the seat of judgment in the assembly and he shall not return (L5).

5. of property, to return to its owner: *eqlum kirûm u bītum ana bēlišu itâr*, the field, the orchard and the house shall return to the owner (L37); *bītum ana* [*bēlišu*] *itâr*, the house shall return to its owner (L67+a); [*bīt muškēnim ana bēlišu itār*], the house of the commoner shall return to its owner (§4.12); *makkūrum ana bēlišu itâr*, the property shall return to its owner (L177).

***tašīmtu***, sbst., authority. < *š-ʾ-m*.

*šar tašīmtim*, the king in authority (P7); *šumma awīlum šû tašīmtam išūma māssu šutēšuram ileʾi*, if that man has authority, he will be empowered to regulate his land (E15).

***tašna***, num., twice as much. < *s-n-ʾ*.

*tašna šeʾam ša imḫuru iriab*, he shall repay double the grain that he has received (L254).

*tebû*, to attack > ***šutbû*** to remove.

***telītu***, adj., epithet of Ishtar; 'the uplifted one'; perhaps a proper name. < *ʾ-l-ʾ*.

*migir telītim*, loved by the uplifted one (P13).

***teptītu***, sbst., development. < *p-t-ʾ*.

*kankallam ana šalaš šanātim ana teptītim ušēṣīma*, he has taken over a neglected field to develop for three years (L44).

***terḫatu***, sbst., bridal gift.

*kaspam mala terḫatiša inaddiššim*, he shall give her silver to the value of her bridal gift (L138); *terḫatum la ibaššī*, there is no bridal gift (L139); *terḫatam iddinu*, who has paid the bridal gift (L159; cf. L160;

161); *terḫatam ša awīlum šû ana bīt emišu ublu*, the bridal gift which that man had brought to his father-in-law's house (L163); *emušu terḫatam la uttēršum*, his father-in-law has not returned to him the bridal gift (L164); *ina šeriktiša mala terḫatiša iḫarraṣma*, he shall subtract from her dowry the amount of the bridal gift (L164); *eliāt zittišu kasap terḫatim išakkanušumma*, in addition to his share they shall set aside silver for a bridal gift (L166).

***têrtu***, sbst., oracle.

*mušaklil tērētim ša Sugal*, fulfilling the oracles of Sugal (P13); *Sîn bēl šamê ilum bānî ša têressu ina ilī šūpât*, Sin, the lord of heaven, the god who created me, whose oracular decision is clear (E24, following emendation [*têressu* for Stele *šêressu* < *šērtu* D, brilliance, see Roth).

***tēšû***, sbst., turmoil. < *ʾ-š-ʾ*.

*tēšî la šubbîm*, turmoil which cannot be suppressed (E20).

***tību***, sbst., attacking. < *t-b-ʾ*.

*tīb kibrāt erbettim*, attacking the four regions (P5).

***tīlu***, sbst., desolate site.

*māssu ana til abūbim litēr*, may he turn his land into a flooded rubbish tip (E25).

***tukkulu***, vb., to show reliability. < *t-k-l*.

*šipiršu la utakkilma*, he has not done his work well (L 235).

***tukultu***, sbst., faith.

*bēlum tukultī*, the lord of my faith (E23).

***tulû***, sbst., breast.

*tulāša inakkisū*, they shall cut off her breast (L194).

***turru***, vb., to repay. < *t-ʾ-r*.

1. to repay grain or other goods: *ina šattim šuāti šeʾam ana bēl ḫubullišu ul utâr*, he shall not repay the grain to his creditor in that year (L48); *šeʾam u kaspam ana turrim la išu*, he does not have enough grain or silver to repay (§5.15 cf. L51; §5.10); *šeʾam mala ilqû utâr*, he shall repay as much grain as he took (L113).

2. to repay silver: *kaspam u ṣibassu ana tamkārim utâr*, he shall repay the silver and the interest (L50); *qaqqad kaspim ana tamkārim utâr*, he shall repay the principal amount of silver to the merchant (L102; cf. L104; also *uttēr*, L107).

3. to repay at a punitive rate: *tamkārum šû šeʾam mala ilqû uštašannāma utâr*, that merchant shall repay double the amount he received (§5.12, after fraudulent calculations; cf. L160; also L161, after aborted marriage arrangements).

4. to return property to its owner: *eqelšu u kirāšu utarrūšumma šûma ilikšu illak*, they shall give him back his field and his orchard and he

shall discharge his duty (L27); *ana bēl eqlim utâr*, he shall return the field to its owner (L43; 44; 62; 63).

5. to return a dowry or bride-price: *ana sinništim šuāti šeriktaša utarrūšim*, they shall return her dowry to that woman (L137); *terḫatam ša awīlum šû ana bīt emišu ublu emušu uttēršum*, his father-in-law returns to him the bride-price which he had taken to the house of his father-in-law (L163, variant *uttēršu*; cf. L164); *terḫatiša iḫarraṣma šeriktaša ana bīt abiša utâr*, he shall subtract the bride-price before returning her dowry to her father's house (L164).

6. to return a slave: *ana bēlišu utarrūšu*, they shall return him to his master (L18; cf. [§5.8], and also *utarrūšum*, §5.8, but both badly broken); *ana nādinānišu utârma*, he shall return him to the one who sold him (L278, vnt. *utâr*).

7. to be held back, be prevented from getting home: *ša ina dannat šarrim turru*, someone who has been held back in a stronghold of the king (L27, vnt. *turruma*; L28, cf. L32).

8. to change (see *AHw* s.v. *târu*, 21: p. 1335f.): *māssu ana til abūbim litēr*, let him change his land into a desolation (E25); *ūmam ana mūšim litēršumma*, let him change the day into night for him (E26); *damqātišu ana lemnētim litēr*, let him change his benefits into troubles (E27).

***tuššu***, sbst., deception. < *ʾ-š-ʾ*.

*sār tuššamma iddī*(!), he is a liar; he has planned deception (L11).

## Ṭ

***ṭâbu*** (*AHw*: *ṭiābu*), vb., to be good. < *ṭ-ʾ-b*.

1. with *eli*, to take pleasure in, be preferable to someone: *warkassa ēma eliša ṭābu nadānam la išturšimma*, he has not written that she may give her possessions to whomsoever she likes (L178; 179, twice; cf. L182); *ša eliša ṭābu inaddinma*, she may give to whomsover she likes, L178); *rēʾî nišī ša epšētušu eli Ištar ṭāba*, the shepherd of the people whose achievements are gratifying to Ishtar (P18).

2. with *libbu*, to be glad: *idīšu gamrātim maḫir libbašu ṭāb*, having received all his wages he is glad (L264).

> ***ṭubbu*** **1**, to improve.

***ṭābu***, adj., good, beneficial. < *ṭ-ʾ-b*.

*ṣilli ṭābum ana āliya tariṣ*, my beneficial shadow is stretched over my city (E7); *libbi Marduk bēlišu uṭīb u šīram ṭābam ana nišī ana dār išīm*, he has brought pleasure to Marduk his lord by ensuring health and prosperity for his people for evermore (E12).

*ṭaḫādu*, to be plentiful > ***muṭaḫḫidu***, making plentiful.

**ṭarādu**, vb., to send. < *ṭ-r-d*.

*agram īgurma pūḫšu iṭṭarad*, he has hired a mercenary and sent him in his place (L26, vnt. *ittarad*); *ana ḫarrānim iṭrussu*, he sent him off on an expedition (L100).

**ṭebû**, vb., to sink. < *ṭ-b-ʾ*.

*bēl eleppim ša eleppašu ṭebiat*, the boat owner whose boat sank (L240).

> **ṭubbu 2**, to sink (transitive).

**ṭeḫḫû**, sbst., neighbour. < *t-ḫ-ʾ*.

*ṭēḫušu* [...], his neighbour (L67).

*ṭeḫû*, to be near > **ṭuḫḫu**, to aggregate.

**ṭēmu**, sbst., report.

*ṭemam iškun*, he made a declaration (L68+b, following Finet; Roth: *šībī iškun*, he has secured witnesses).

*ṭiābu* > **ṭâbu**, to be good.

**ṭīdu**, sbst., clay figurine.

*kīma ṣalam ṭiddim liḫbuš*, may he shatter his body like a clay figurine (E28).

**ṭubbu 1**, vb., to improve. < *ṭ-ʾ-b*.

1. to improve the quality of life: *Anum u Ellil ana šīr nišī ṭubbim šumī ibbû*, Anum and Enlil have named me to benefit the health of the people (P3); *kittam u mīšaram ina pī mātim aškun šīr nišī uṭīb*, I made the land speak with justice and improved the health of my people (P22); *qablātim ubelli šīr mātim uṭīb*, I made conflicts cease, I improved the health of the nation (E5); *šīr nišīšu liṭīb*, let him benefit the health of his people (E16).

2. with ***libbu***, to bring pleasure to: *libbi Marduk bēlišu uṭīb u šīram ṭābam ana nišī ana dār išīm u mātam uštēšer*, he has brought pleasure to Marduk his lord by ensuring health and prosperity for his people for evermore and by keeping the land straight (E12); *libbaša uṭabbū*, they shall make her happy (L178); *libbaša la uṭṭibbū*, they have not made her happy (L178).

**ṭubbû 2**, vb., to sink. < *ṭ-b-ʾ*.

1. D-theme: *eleppam ša uṭebbû*, the boat which he sank (L237); *ša māḫirtim ša elep ša muqqelpītim uṭebbû*, the man in the rowing boat who sank the sailing boat (L240).

2. Dt-theme: *malāḫum šû īgīma eleppam uṭṭebbi*, that sailor has been negligent and sunk the boat (L236; cf. L237); *malāḫum elep awīlim uṭṭebbīma*, a sailor has sunk a man's boat (L238); *elep ša māḫirtim elep ša muqqelpītim imḫaṣma uṭṭebbi*, the rowing boat struck the sailing boat and sunk it (L240).

***ṭuḫdu***, sbst., plenty.

*mukammer nuḫšim u tuḫdim*, provider of abundance and plenty (P4).

***ṭuḫḫû***, vb., to aggregate. < *ṭ-ḫ-ʾ*.

*u lu ṣibātim ana qaqqādim uṭṭeḫḫi*, or he has aggregated the interest together with the principal (§5.12).

***ṭuppu***, sbst., tablet, document.

*ṭuppašu iḫḫeppe*, the tablet shall be broken (L37); *ṭuppi rikistišu* [*iḫeppe*], he broke the contract-tablet (§5.11); *ṭuppašu uraṭṭab*, he shall moisten the tablet (L48); *kaspam u ṣibassu ša pī ṭuppišu*, silver and its interest according to the terms on his tablet (L66); *mussa urtakkis ṭuppam uštēzib*, she has made a contract with her husband and made him deposit a tablet (L151); *ṭuppam ušezzebūšunūti*, they shall make them deposit a tablet (L177); *ina ṭuppim išṭurušim*, which he wrote on a tablet for her (L171b; cf. *ina ṭuppim ša išṭurušim*, L178; 179); *ṭuppam išṭurušim*, who wrote out a tablet for her (L178); *ṭuppam eššam*(?) *la išṭur*, he has not written an extra tablet (§5.12).

## U

***u***, particle, and, or.

1. linking two proper names: P3; 8; 13; 16; 17; 21; E4; 7; 8.
2. linking two nouns in the same or similar semantic fields:

a. *abašu u ummašu* (L186); *abim u ummim* (L192; 193; 193; 194); *alim u rabiānum* (L23; 24); *amtim u mārīša* (L171a); *ana mutiša warkîm u sinništim šuāti* (L177); *aššatišu u martišu* (L38; 39); *bēl kirîm u nukaribbum* (L60); *bīt šāyyimānišunu u kāšišunu* (L117); *bīšam u šeʾam* (§5.2); *eliš u šapliš* (E4; 12); *eqelšu u kirāšu* (L27; 28; 29; 178; 178); *ereqqam u murteddīša* (L271); *errēšūm u bēl eqlim* (L46); *erṣetišunu u paṭīšunu* (L23); *ḫaṭṭim u agêm* (P12); *ḫušaḫḫim u bubtim* (E25); *ilim u šībī* (L106; 107); *kaspam u ṣibassu* (L50; 51; 66); *kittam u mīšaram* (P22); *kīnam u rīdam* (E1); *liātim u ṣēnam* (L35; 261; 265; 267); *makkur ilim u ekallim* (L6); *malāḫam u eleppam* (L237); *mārū maḫrūtim u warkûtim* (L173); *mārū ḫīrtim u mārū amtim* (L170); *mārū maḫrûtum u warkûtum* (L173); *mirītim u mašqītim* (P13); [*nadānim u maḫārim*] (L100); *nišīšu u ummānšu* (E31); *nēmelam u butuqqâm* (L77+f); *nuḫšim u tuḫdim* (P4); [*qaqqadašu*] *u ṣibassu* (§5.11); *raggam u ṣenam* (P3; E16); *šamê u erṣetim* (P1; 2; E8; 10; 23; 25; 31); *šeʾim u kaspim* (L4; §5.9; 5.10; [5.11]; 5.11; 5.13; 5.15; 5.15; L114; 115); *šeʾam u šamššammī* (L49); *šeriktaša u nudunnâm* (L171b); *šiptim u purussêm* (E21); *šumšu u zikiršu* (E20); *šībī u rik-sātim* (L7; 123); *tālittam u biltam* (L264); *tānēḫim u dimmatim* (E24);

*tāḫazim u qablim* (E27; 27); *ugbabtim u aššat awīlim* (L127); *uznam u nēmeqam* (E22); *wardum u amtum* (L280).

b. with the linked terms expanded: *nādinān iddinušum u šībī ša ina maḫrišunu išāmu* (L10); *ḫīrtašu mārī ūlissum u amassu mārī ūlissum* (L170, or joining two clauses); *eleppam ša uṭebbû u mimma ša ina libbiša uḫalliqu* (L237).

3. linking a series of more than two words:

a. *eqlam kirâm bīšam u bītam* (L150; cf. L178); *eqlim kirîm u bītim* (L40; 165; cf. L30; 30; 30; 31; 36; 37; 37; 38; 39; 40; 40; 41; 41; 191); *eqlim kirîm u bīšim* (L137); *ipram piššatam u lubūšam* (L178; 178); *kaspam ḫuraṣam u mimma šumšu* (L122; 124); *mār girseqîm muzzaz ekallim u mār sekretim* (L187); *nadītum tamkārum u ilkum aḫûm* (L40); *rēdim bā'irim u nāši biltim* (L36; 37; 38; 41; 41); *še'am šipātim šamnam suluppī u mimma šumšu* (L237); *še'am šipātim šamnam u mimma bīšam* (L104).

b. with one or more of the terms expanded: *nasaḫ išdī šarrūtišu u ḫalaq mātišu* (E23); *še'am kaspam u bīšam* (L67+a; 67+a); *še'am ša kaspišu u ṣibassu ša itti tamkārim ilqû u mānaḫāt erēšim* (L49); *še'am u kaspam kīma ṣimdat šarrim u ṣibassu* (§5.10).

4. linking a particular noun with a more general word: *eleppašu u mimmašu ḫalqam* (L240); *mussa u šî* (L176a; 176b); *šuāti u bīšašu* (L54).

5. linking clauses with the same subject, which may often be understood as an expansion of the apodosis: —a. two clauses: *iddinma u…imtaḫar* (L45); *iddinušim u…itbalam* (L9); *imaddad u…utâr* (L62); *imtaḫar u…iumtaṭṭi* (L108); *inaddin u…inaḫḫaṣ* (L43); *inaddiššim u…ušallamšimma* (L138); *inaṭṭûšu u…ugallabu* (L127); *inaṣṣarū u…urabbū* (L177); *inūma ana ḫubillim iddinu…u inūma imḫuru* (§5.13); *iriab u aššum bīt īpušu la udanninuma imqutu ina makkūr ramanišu bīt imqutu ippeš* (L232); *itamma u asâm ippal* (L206); *itâr u…itabbal* (L41); *ittepte u…uštābil* (L53); *iḫḫepe u… ītelli* (L37); *išaṭṭar u…inaddin* (L39); *išaqqal u…ītelli* (L116); *iššamu u…iqabbûma* (L9); *uṭṭebbi u…uḫtalliq* (L237); *upīḫ u…iddin* (L41); *uraṭṭab u…ul inaddin* (L48); *utâr u…imaddad* (L44; 63) *utâr u…ītelli* (L113); *utarrūšim u…inaddinūšimma* (L137); *uttakkir u…ittadin* (L265); cf. also *ḫīrtašu mārī ūlissum u amassu mārī ūlissum* (L170, or to be taken with paragraph 2b above as linking two expanded nouns); such linking may also be done with ***u lu***, > ***lu***; e.g. *Adad irtaḫiṣ u lu bibbulum itbal* (L45).

b. linking all in a series of three clauses: *uṭīb u…išīm u…uštēšer* (E12).

c. linking the final pair in a series three verbs: *imaḫḫaṣ imarrar u išakkakma* (L44).

6. linking clauses with different subjects, or introducing a new sentence:

a. *inaddin u...ušetbūšuma* (L5); *awīlum...iqtabi u bēl ḫulqim...iqtabi* (L9); *šāyyimānum...u šībī...itbalam u bēl ḫulqim...itbalam* (L9, with reference to the second occurrence of the word); *naṣratma ḫiṭītam la išu u mussa waṣīma magal ušamṭāši* (L142); *išaqqalšimma u mimma ša ištu bīt abiša ublam* (L156); *utâr u aššassu ibiršu ul iḫḫaz* (L161); *ileqqe u mimma ša mussa u šî ištu innemdū iršû* (L176a, with reference to the first occurrence of the word).

b. with different grammatical subjects of passive verbs: *awīlum šû iddâk u ša šurqam ina qātišu imḫuru iddâk* (L6).

c. introducing a supplementary protasis, when subject matter is sustained from a previous clause: *u šumma* (L151; 171a; 176a).

d. introducing the main apodosis: *šumma bēl aššatim aššassu uballaṭ u šarrum warassu uballaṭ* (L129).

7. fragmentary: §5.3.

8. ***u lu*** > ***lu***, or.

***ubānu***, sbst., finger.

*eli ugbabtim u aššat awīlim ubānam ušatriṣma*, he has pointed his finger at a priestess or a man's wife (L127); *aššum zikarim šanîm ubānum eliša ittariṣma*, the finger has been pointed at her because of another man (L132).

***ubbubu***, vb., to cleanse, become clean. < *ʾ-b-b*.

1. to cleanse (see *CAD*, s.v. *ebēbu*, 2.b.2′): *awīlam šuāti Id ūtebbibaššuma*, the River has cleansed that man (L2, variant *ūtabbibaššuma*).

2. to clear oneself of an accusation (see *CAD*, s.v. *ebēbu*, 2d): *rēʾûm maḫar*(!) *ilim ubbamma*, the shepherd shall become clean before the god (L266, variant *ubbabma*).

> ***mubbibu***, making clean.

***ubburu***, vb., to bring disrepute, accuse; see *AHw abāru* III. < *ʾ-b-r*.

1. to bring disrepute: *šumma awīlum mimmûšu la ḫaliqma mimmê ḫaliq iqtabi babtašu ūtebbir*, if a gentleman who has not lost anything says, 'I have lost something', he is bringing disrepute on his community (L126, variant *ūtabbir*).

2. to accuse: *awīlum awīlam ubbirma nērtam elišu iddīma la uktīnšu*, a gentleman has accused a gentleman and charged him with murder but has not proved it (L1); *aššat awīlim mussa ubbiršima itti zikarim šanîm ina utūlim la iṣṣabit*, a man's wife is accused by her husband of sleeping with another man but she has not been caught (L131).

***uddû***, vb., to find out. < *ʾ-d-ʾ*.

*bīt abišu uweddīma*, he has found out his natural father's family (L193); *bēl wardim u lu amtim lu warassu u lu amassu ūteddi*, the owner of the slave or the slave-girl has found out about his slave or his slave-girl (L280).

***ugāru***, sbst., meadow.

*ina kārišu pītum ittepte u ugāram mê uštābil*, a break has been opened in the dyke and allows the water to flow over the meadow (L53); *ištu ṣēnum ugārim ītelianim*, after the flocks have come away from the meadows (L58); *awīlum epinnam ina ugārim išriq*, a man has stolen a plough from the meadow (L259); *mārū ugārim ša šeʾšunu mû ublu*, the workers in the fields whose grain the water has destroyed (L54).

***ugbabtum***, priestess; formerly read *entu*, priestess.

*nadītum ugbabtum ša ina gagîm la wašbat*, a sister or a priestess who is not resident in the cloister (L110); *ugbabtum nadītum u lu sekretum ša abuša šeriktam išrukušim*, a priestess or a sister or a confined woman whose father has presented her with a dowry (L178; 179); *eli ugbabtim u aššat awīlim ubānam ušatriṣma*, he has stretched out his finger towards a priestess or a man's wife (L127).

***ukullû***, sbst., foodstuff.

*zēram u lu ukullâm išriqma*, he has stolen the seed or the foodstuff (L253).

***ul***, part., not.

1. negating a verb in the present or preterite: L5; 5; 30; 32; 36; 38; 38; 47; 48; 48; 52; 66; 67+a; §4.12; 5.8; 5.15; L105; 118; 133a; 134; 136; 141; 142; 144; 144; 145; 146; 148; 150; 150; 151; 151; 159; 160; 161; 161; 162; 163; 167; 168; 171a; 171a; 171b; 172; 175; 177; 177; 178; 178; 179; 183; 185; 187; 188; 191; 191; E2; 2; 5.

2. with a verb in the stative or nominal sentence: *ul aššat* (L128); *ul abī atta ul ummī attī* (L192; 192); *ul bēlī atta* (L282).

3. with ***išu***: §5.2, partly restored; L115; 123; 142; 250; E9; 17.

***ullû***, vb., to raise. < *ʾ-l-ʾ*.

*ina Bābilim ālim ša Anum u Ellil rēšīšu ullû*, in Babylon, the city whose skyline Anu and Enlil raised high (E8).

*ulu* (*AHw ūlū*; but here read as two words, *u lu*) > ***lu*** 3, 4 and 5.

***ūmišam***, adv., daily.

*igirrê ūmišam ina maḫar Marduk bēliya Zarpānītum bēltiya lidammiqū*, let them show kindness to the daily prayers in the presence of my lord Marduk and my lady Zarpanitum (E13).

***ummānu***, sbst., craftsman, workforce, army.

1. craftsman: *mār ummānim ṣeḫram ana tarbītim ilqēma šipir qātīšu uštāḫissu*, a professional person has adopted a child and has taught

him his own craft (L188); *šumma awīlum mār ummānim iggar*, if a man would hire a craftsman (L274).

2. workforce, army: *išdī ummānišu lišḫelṣi*, let the foundations of his workforce crumble (E23); *gurun šalmāt ummānātišu ina ṣērim littaddi*, let the pile of the bodies of his soldiers be thrown down in the desert (E27, variant *ummānišu*); *ummānšuma*(!) *rēmam ay ušarši*, may she show his forces no mercy (E27); *šuāti zērašu māssu ṣābašu nišīšu u ummānšu errētam maruštam līrurū*, let them curse him, his descendants, his land, his soldiers, his people and his army with a terrible curse (E31).

***ummu***, sbst., mother.

1. human mother: *šalušti eqlim u kirîm ana ummišu innaddinma ummašu urabbāšu*, a third of the field or the orchard shall be given to his mother and his mother shall bring him up (L29; 29); *ummum warkassa ana māriša ša irammu inaddin*, the mother may give her inheritance to the son she loves (L150); *mārū ana ummātim ul izuzzū šerikti ummātišunu ileqqûma*, the sons shall not share according to the mothers but shall take the dowries of their mothers (L167; 167); *ana abim murabbīšu u ummim murabbītišu ul abī atta ul ummī atti iqtabi*, he has said to the father who has brought him up and to the mother who has brought him up, 'You are not my father. You are not my mother' (L192; 192); *abam murabbišu u ummam murabbissu izērma*, he has hated the father who raised him and the mother who raised him (L193); *inūma ilqûšu abašu u ummašu iḫiaṭ tarbītum šî ana bīt abišu itâr*, (if), after he has taken him, he longs for his father and mother, then that adopted child shall return to his father's house (L186); *awīlum warki abišu ina sūn ummišu ittatīl*, when his father has gone a man has had intercourse with his mother (L157); *balum abišu u ummišu*, without the knowledge of his father and his mother (L194, twice).

2. mother among the gods: *Ninlil ummum rabītum ša qibīssa ina Ekur kabtat*, Ninlil, the great mother, whose word is revered in Ekur (E21); *Nintu bēltum ṣīrtum ša mātātim ummum bānītī*, O Nintu, noble lady of the nations, the mother who has raised me up (E29).

***ūmu***, sbst., day, occasion.

1. day: *ina ūmim ištēn*, for one day (L271; 272; 273, twice; [274]; 275; 276; 277); *ūmī warḫī šanāt palēšu ina tānēḫim u dimmatim lišaqti*, bring the days, the months and the years of his rule to a close with weeping and wailing (E24); *ūmī īṣūtim šanāt ḫušaḫḫim*, days of need and years of famine (E20); *ūmam ana mūšim litēršumma*, let turn the day into the night for him (E26).

2. time: *ūmīšu imannûma*, he shall count up the time he has spent (L100); *ana warkiāt ūmī ana matima*, until time in the future and for ever (E14).

3. prescribed time: *ša ūmīšu izzazzu ana Esagil*, who took his position in Esagil at his proper time (P5); *mušārikuūm balāṭiya*, lengthening the duration of my life (E22); *ina ūmīšu la malûtim*, before his time has expired (L69+c, twice).

***unnušu***, vb., to weaken. < *ʾ-n-š*.

*aldâm ilqēma liātim ūtenniš*(!), he has taken the feed and weakened the cattle (L254).

***unūtu***, sbst., household goods.

*uniātim ana kaspim ul inaddinū*, they shall not sell the household effects (L177); *šāyyimānum ša unūt mārī almattim išammu ina kaspišu ītelli makkūrum ana bēlišu itâr*, the person who buys the household goods of a widow's sons shall be parted from his silver and the property shall return to its owner (L177).

***uppulu***, vb., to become answerable, pay a debt; see *CAD apālu* A, to satisfy a demand, answer, D-theme; *AHw apālu* II, D-theme: to make someone an heir, i.e. denominative verb. < *ʾ-p-l*.

*ana kaspim ul inaddin šaniam ul uppal aplussa ša aḫḫīšama*, she shall not exchange it for silver, or become answerable to someone else for it (cf. *AHw*: make someone else the heir); her portion definitely belongs to her brothers (L178).

***uppusu***, vb., to make a problem. < *ʾ-p-s*.

*bēl eqlim ul uppas*, the owner of the field shall not make difficulties (L47); *tamkārum ul uppas imaḫḫar*, the merchant shall not make difficulties, he shall agree (§5.15).

***urḫu***, sbst., way.

*dīnšu ay idīn uruḫšu līši*, let him not judge his case, let him confuse his path (E23).

***urīṣu***, sbst., goat.

*urīṣam ana diāšim īgur*, he has hired a goat to thresh (L270).

***urruku***, vb., to lengthen. < *ʾ-r-k*.

*Šamaš ḫaṭṭašu lirrik*, may Shamash extend his rule (E18).

> ***šūruku***, to make long.

***uršu***, sbst., desire, wisdom.

*šû ikšudu nagab uršim*, he is the one who reached the source of desire (P16).

***ūsu***, sbst., rule, order.

*inūma Marduk ana šutēšur nišī mātim ūsim šūḫuzim uwaʾeranni*, and when Marduk urged me to set the people in the land straight and to take control of the law (P22); *ussam kīnam u rīdam damqam*, proper government and good behaviour (E1); see *AHw ūsu* I, s.v. 2, with cross-reference to *aḫāzu*, Š-theme, 3a.

***uṣurtu***, sbst., plan.

*mukīn uṣurātim ša Keš*, establishing the design of Kish (P12); *awâtiya la uštepēl uṣurātiya la unakkir*, he should not emend my commandments or change my purposes (E18; cf. E19, variant *usurātiya*); *ina awat Marduk bēliya uṣurātūa mušassikam ay iršia*, may Marduk, my lord, forbid anyone to throw out my plans (E10); *uṣurātiya ay ušassik*, let no one throw out my plans (E14).

***uššuru***, vb., to prove innocent (*CAD* s.v. *ešēru* refers to *uššuru*; see *AHw wašārum*, to hang loose, s.v. Dt, 2b). < *w-š-r*.

with *-t-*, to be proved innocent, be allowed to go free: *nīš ilim izakkarma ūtaššar*, he shall make a sworn statement and go free (L20; 103; 249); *sinništum šî ūtaššar*, that woman shall go free (L130); *itammāma ūtaššar*, he shall swear and be proved innocent (L227).

> ***mušūšeru***, keeping straight.

***uššušu***, vb., to misuse. < *ʾ-š-š*.

*ina maḫāṣim u lu ina uššušim imtūt*, it has died from beating or abuse (L116).

***ušumgallu***, sbst., dragon.

*ušumgal šarrī talīm Zababa*, the leader of kings, the supporter of Zababa (P9).

***utlu***, sbst., bosom, breast.

*ina utliya nišī māt Šumerim u Akkadîm ukīl*, I clasped the people of Sumer and Akkad to my breast (E7).

***utturu***, vb., to exceed. < *ʾ-t-r*.

*uwatterma*, he shall exceed the official rate of interest (§5.10, fragmentary).

*utūlu* > ***itūlu***, to lie (so *AHw*, but not *CAD*).

***uṭṭatu***, sbst., grain (as a measure of silver), barleycorn.

*ana 1 šiqil kaspim* 1/6 *u 6 uṭṭet ṣibtam ileqqe*, for each shekel of silver he shall receive one-sixth of a shekel and six grains in interest (§5.9; cf. §5.10; L273, also *5 uṭṭet kaspam*; L274, five [plus five] times; *3 uṭṭet kaspum idûša*, L275; *2 1/2 uṭṭet kaspam idīša*, L276).

***uʾuru***, vb., to direct (see *AHw wâru*, D-theme). < *ʾ-ʾ-r*.

*inūma Marduk ana šutēšur nišī mātim ūsim šūḫuzim uwaʾeranni*, and when Marduk urged me to set the people in the land straight and to take hold of the land (P22).

***uznu***, sbst., ear, understanding.

*uzunšu inakkisū*, they shall cut off his ear (L205; cf. *inakkis*, L282); *uznam u nēmeqam līṭeršuma ina mīšītim littarušu*, let him deprive him of wisdom and understanding and let him remove him into oblivion (E22).

***uzubbû***, sbst., divorce settlement. < *ʾ-z-b*.

*1 mana kaspam ana uzubbêm inaddiššim*, he shall give her one mana of silver as a divorce payment (L140); *ḫarrānša uzubbūša mimma ul innaddiššim*, nothing at all shall be given her for her journey or her divorce settlement (L141).

***uzzatu***, sbst., anger. < *ʾ-z-z*.

*ina uzzātiša rabiātim šarrūssu līrur*, may she curse his kingdom with her tremendous fury (E27).

## W

*wabālu* > ***abālu***, to bring.
*wakil ḫaṭṭim* > ***ša ḫaṭṭātim*** (*ša* C 7).
*walādu* > ***alādu***, to give birth.
*wapû* > ***apû***, to be certain.
*wardu* > ***ardu***, slave.
*warḫu* > ***arḫu***, month.
*warka* > ***arka***, afterwards.
*warkānum* > ***arkānu***, afterwards.
*warkītu* > ***arkītu***, future.
*warku* > ***arkû***, rear.
*warqu* > ***arqu***, verdure.
*wašābu* > ***ašābu***, to dwell.
*watru* > ***atru***, extra.

## Z

*zadimmu*, older alternative for > ***sasinnu***, stone cutter, lapidary (see *CAD*).

***zāʾiru***, sbst., foe. < *z-ʾ-r*.

*rīmum kadrum munakkip zāʾirī*, a wild ox tossing the opponents (P10).

***zakāru***, vb., to utter a statement. < *z-k-r*.

*wardum šû bēlšu la izakkar*, that slave will not state the name of his master (L18); *nīš ilim izakkarma*, he shall utter a divine oath (L20; 103; 131; 249).

> ***nazkuru***, to be spoken.

*zanānu*, to care for > ***zāninu***, caretaker.

***zāninu***, sbst., caring for. < *z-n-n*

*zāninum naʾdum ša Ekur*, the one who takes devoted care of Ekur (P4).

*zapāru*, to leak > ***ṣabāru***, to become unstable (of a boat).

***zaqāpu***, vb., to plant. < *z-q-p*.

*eqlam ana kirîm zaqāpim ana nukaribbim iddin nukaribbum kiriam izqup*, he has given the field to a gardener to plant an orchard and the gardener has planted the orchard (L60; 60); *nukaribbum eqlam ina zaqāpim la igmurma*, the gardener has not completed the planting of the orchard (L61); *eqlam ša innadnušum ana kirîm la izqup*, he has not planted the field which was given him as an orchard (L62).

***zâzu***, vb., to share produce at harvest, divide an estate at death. < *z-ʾ-z*.

1. to share produce: *ana apšītêm izuzzū*, they shall share by agreement (L46); *mārū ugārim ša šeʾšunu mû ublu izuzzū*, those involved in the irrigated land whose grain the water has destroyed shall share out (L54); *mitḫāriš izuzzū*, they shall share out equally (L60).

2. to divide an estate:

a. in general: *warka abum ana šīmtim ittalku inūma aḫḫū izuzzū*, when the brothers do the sharing after the father has gone to his destiny (L165; 166); *mārū ana ummātim ul izuzzū*, the sons shall not share out among the mothers (L167); *mārū amtim itti mārī ḫīrtim ul izuzzū*, the sons of the slave-girl shall not share with the sons of the chosen wife (L171a); *mārū maḫrûtum u warkûtum izuzzū*, the children of the earlier marriage and of the later marriage shall share (L173); *itti aḫḫīša izâzma*, she shall share with her brothers (L182).

b. a specific allocation: *ina makkūr bīt abim zittam kīma aplim ištēn izâzma*, she shall have the share like that of one heir from the treasures of her father's house (L180; cf. *ul izâz*, she shall not share, L183); *šalušti aplūtiša izâzma*, she shall have a one-third share as her inheritance (L181); *ana šinīšu izuzzūma*, they shall divide into two (L176a; 176b); *mitḫāriš izuzzū*, they shall make the shares equal (L165; 167; 170).

3. to divide a profit: *mitḫāriš izuzzū*, they shall divide equally (L77+f).

***zēru***, sbst., seed, descendant, ancestry. < *z-r-ʾ*.

1. seed-corn: *zēram u lu ukullâm išriqma*, he has stolen the seed or the fodder (L253; cf. L255).

2. descendants: *zēr šarrūtim ša Sîn ibniušu*, royal descendants which Sin has created for him (P6); *liplippim ša Sumulaʾil aplum dannum ša Sîn-muballiṭ zērum dāriʾum ša šarrūtim…anāku*, I am the descendant of Shumula'il, the mighty heir of Sin-muballit, with royal ancestors in every generation (P21); *ina qerbīt nišīšu zēr awilūtim ay ibni*, let him not create any human descendants among his people (E29); *šuāti zērašu māssu ṣābašu nišīšu u ummanšu errētam maruštam līrurū*, let them curse that man, his descendants, his land, his soldiers, his people and his army with a terrible curse (E31).

***zêru*** , vb., to hate. < *z-ʾ-r*.

1. to hate a place: *aššum ālšu izēruma innabitu*, because he has hated his city and made off (L 136).

2. to hate a person: *sinništum mussa izērma ul taḫḫazanni iqtabi*, a woman has hated her husband and said, 'You shall not hold me' (L142); *abam murabbīšu u ummam murabbīssu izērma*, he has hated the father who raised him and the mother who raised him (L193).

***zibbatu***, sbst., tail.

*qaranšu išbir zibbassu ittakis*, he has broken off its horn or cut off its tail (L248).

***zību***, sbst., sacrifice. < *z-b-ʾ*.

*dāriš išīmu zībī ellūtim*, he has instigated holy sacrifices for evermore (P16).

***zikaru***, sbst., man.

*aššat awīlim itti zikarim šanîm ina itūlim ittaṣbat*, a woman has been seized while lying with another man (L129; cf. L131; 132); *aššat awīlim ša zikaram la idûma*, a man's wife who has not known another male (L130); *aššum zikarim šanîm ubānum eliša ittariṣma*, the finger was pointed at her because of another man (L132); *aššat awīlim aššum zikarim šanîm mussa ušdīk*, a man's wife has had her husband killed because of another man (L153).

***zikru***, sbst., name, reputation. < *z-k-r*.

1. name: *mušarbi zikru Bābilim*, making the name of Babylon great (P5).

2. reputation: *šumšu u zikiršu ina mātim la šubšâm*, stopping him from producing a reputation or fame in the land (E20).

***zittu***, sbst., share of an estate. < *z-ʾ-z*.

*bēl kirîm zittašu inassaqma ileqqe*, the owner of the orchard shall choose his share and take it (L60); *aplum mār ḫīrtim ina zittim inassaqma*, the heir as son of the preferred wife shall select from the share and take it (L170); *zittam kīma aplim ištēn inaddinūšimma*, they shall give her the share of one heir (L137; cf. L172; 180); *kīma emūq zittiša*, according to the value of her share (L178, twice); *eliāt zittišu kasap terḫatim išakkanūšumma*, they shall allocate for him some silver for the marriage over as additional to his share (L166); *nidītam ina libbi zittišu išakkanūšum*, they shall arrange for him to have the rough ground in the middle of his share (L61).

***zumru***, sbst., body.

*arnam kabtam šēressu rabītam ša ina zumrišu la iḫalliqu*, heavy affliction and serious disease which will not disappear from his body (E24).

***zunnu***, sbst., rain.

*zunnī ina šamê mīlam ina nagbim līṭeršu*, let him deprive him of the rain from the sky and the flood-water from the wadi (E25).

# PROPER NAMES, NUMERALS AND UNITS OF MEASUREMENT

## PROPER NAMES

***Adab***, modern Bismaya in central Mesopotamia; cult-centre for Nin-maḫ, goddess of motherhood.
*šarrum nādin napištim ana Adab*, the king who gives life to Adab (P15).

***Adad***, god of storms, whose temple E-ud-gal-gal was in Karkara.
*Adad bēl ḫegallim gugal šamê u erṣetim*, Adad the lord of abundance, controlling the water in the sky and on the earth (E25); *eqlam Adad irtaḫiṣ*, Adad eroded the field (L45; cf. L48); *munēḫ libbi Adad*, quietening the heart of Adad (P14); *rubûm ellum ša nīš qātišu Adad īdû*, the holy prince whose raised hand Adad recognizes (P14).

***Akkadum***, city of Agade, precise location unidentified but near Sippar, founded by Sargon I in the latter part of the third millennium; site of E-ul-maš, the temple of Ishtar; it also means the nation of Akkad, and when paired with Sumer, the whole of Babylonia.
*mukinni Ištar ina Eulmaš qerbūm Akkadim ribītim*, establishing Ishtar in E-ul-maš within the capital city of Agade (P18); *šamšu Bābilim mušēṣi nūrim ana māt Šumerim u Akkadim*, the sun of Babylon who sheds light on the land of Sumer and Akkad (P21); *ṣillī ṭābum ana āliya tariṣ ina utliya nišī māt Šumerim u Akkadim ukīl*, with my protective shadow spread over my city I held the people of Sumer and Akkad in my arms (E7).

***Anum***, god of the sky, identical to An the father of the gods in the Sumerian pantheon.
*Anum ṣīrum šar Anunnakī*, most exalted Anu, king of the Anunnaki (P1); *Anum rabûm abu ilī*, mighty Anum, father of the gods (E19); *Anum u Ellil ana šīr nišī ṭubbim šumī ibbû*, Anum and Enlil nominated me to improve the health of the people (P3); *ina Bābilim ālim ša Anum u Ellil rēšīšu ullū*, in Babylon, the city which Anum and Enlil elevated to greatness (E8); *mukammer ḫiṣbim ana Anim u Ištar*, piling up riches for Anum and Ishtar (P8); *Ninkarrak mārat Anim*, Ninkarrak the daughter of Anum (E30).

***Anunnakū***, all the main gods of the earth, above the earth and under the earth. *Anum ṣīrum šar Anunnakī*, most exalted Anu, king of the Anunnaki (P1); *ilū rabûtum ša šamê u erṣetim Anunnakū ina napḫarišunu*, the mighty gods of heaven and earth, the Anunnaki in their assembly (E31).

>***Igigū***.

***Aššur***, city of Asshur; modern Qalʿat Sherqāṭ; also the name of the patron deity of that city.

*mutêr lamassīšu damiqtim ana ālim Aššur*, returning the beneficent statues to Asshur (P19).

***Aya***, goddess of light, whose temple E-babbar was in Sippar; the consort of the sun-god Shamash.

*mušalbiš warqim gigunê Aya*, dressing the shrine of Aya with greenery (P7).

***Babilum***, Babylon, near modern Al-Ḥillah, 32°33' N, 44°26' E, cult-centre of Marduk; Hammurabi belonged to the First Babylonian Dynasty.

*Bābilam šumšu ṣīram ibbiʾū*, they gave Babylon its exalted name (P2); *mušarbi zikru Bābilim*, extolling the fame of Babylon (P5); *mukinnu išdīšin qerbum Bābilim šulmāniš*, establishing their foundation within Babylon securely (P18); *ina Bābilim ālim ša Anum u Ellil rēšīšu ullū*, in Babylon the city whose importance Anum and Enlil raised (E8); *šarrum dannum šamšu Bābilim*, the mighty king, the sun of Babylon (P21); *nadīt Marduk ša Bābilim*, a priestess of Marduk of Babylon (L182, and also *nadīt Marduk*).

***Barsippa***, city of Borsippa; modern Birs Nimrud; 32°04' N, 44°04' E; the site of E-zi-da, temple of Nabû, and in earlier times of Tutu.

*mūrīš Barsippa*, who makes Borsippa rejoice (P10)

*Bīt Karkara* > ***Karkara***.

***Dagan***, perhaps a fish deity, but particularly associated with grain and venerated especially in the west, as at Mari and Tuttul.

*mukanniš dadmē nār Purattim ittum Dagan bānîšu*, who controls the communities of the Euphrates under the guidance of Dagan, who created him (P17)

***Damgalnunna***, also known as Damkina, queen of the Apsu, consort of Ea (= Enki).

*ana Ea u Damgalnunna mušarbû šarrūtišu*, with Ea and Dam-gal-nunna, who have made his kingdom magnificent (P16).

***Dilbat***, perhaps to be identified with modern Tell Dulaihim, linked with Uraš.

*mušaddil mēreštim ša Dilbat mugarrin karê ana Uraš gašrim*, who develops the land to be ploughed in Dilbat, who fills up the huge granaries of Urash (P11).

***E-abzu***, 'house of fresh subterranean water', the temple of Ea in Eridu.

*mubbib šuluḫ Eabzu*, becoming purified through lustrating in E-abzu (P5).

***E-anna***, 'house of heaven (or of Anu)', the temple of Anu and Ishtar in Uruk.
*mullî rēš Eanna*, elevating the importance of E-anna (P8).

***E-babbar***, 'house of brightness', the temple of Shamash and Aya in Sippar and Larsa.
*muddiš Ebabbar ana Šamaš rēṣišu*, who renewed E-babbar with the help of Shamash (P8); *muṣīr bīt E-babbar ša kî šubat šamā'i*, designing the chapel of E-babbar just like a heavenly home (P7); *libitti Ebabbara*, the brickwork of E-babbar (E31).

***E-galmaḫ***, 'great house of splendour', the temple of Ninurta in Isin.
*muṭaḫḫid nuḫšim bītam Egalmaḫ*, spreading vast riches around the temple of E-gal-mah (P8).

***E-gišnugal***, 'house filled with moonlight', temple of the moon-god Sin in Ur.
*bābil ḫegallim ana Egišnugal*, bringing plenty to E-gishnugal (P6).

***E-kur***, 'house of the mountain', the temple of Enlil and Ninlil in Nippur.
*zāninum na'dum ša Ekur*, the one who takes devoted care of E-kur (P4); *Ninlil ummum rabītum ša qibīssa ina Ekur kabtat*, Ninlil the great mother, whose words are revered in E-kur (E21); *Zababa qarrādum rabium mārum rēštûm ša Ekur*, the great hero Zababa, first son of E-kur (E26); *Ninkarrak mārat Anim qābiat dumqiya ina Ekur*, Ninkarrak the daughter of Anum, who speaks in my favour in E-kur (E30).

***E-maḫ***, 'house of splendour', the temple of the goddess Nin-mah in Babylon.
*āšer bīt Emaḫ*, providing for the shrine of Emah (P15).

*E-meslam* > ***Meslam***.

***E-mesmes***, the temple of Ishtar at Nineveh.
*šarrum ša in Ninua in Emesmes ušūpi'u mē Ištar*, the king who made the power of Ishtar shine in E-mesmes in Nineveh (P20).

***E-meteursag***, 'house which befits the champion', the temple of Zababa and Ishtar at Kish.
*mušaršid šubat Kiš muštasḫir melemmē Emeteursag*, who made Kish a secure abode, who made E-meteursag shine on every side (P9).

***E-ninnu***, temple of Ningirsu at Girsu; 'house of fifty' (referring to 50 mythological birds, the *anzû*, which were like eagles).
*mukīl nindabê rabûtim ana Eninnu*, the one who holds the magnificent offerings in E-ninnu (P13).

***E-sagila***, temple of Marduk at Babylon; meaning 'house of the uplifted head, the house which is extremely high'.
*ina Esagil bītim ša kīma šamê u erṣetim išdāšu kinā*, in E-sagil, the shrine with foundations as solid as heaven and earth (E8); *ša ūmīšu izzazzu ana Esagil*, who takes his position in E-sagil at the proper time (P5); *ina Esagil ša arammu šumī ina damiqtim ana dār lizzakir*, may

my name be spoken as a blessing in E-sagil, which I love for ever (E10); *ilū ēribūt Esagil libitti Esagil*, the gods at the entrance to E-sagil and the brickwork of E-sagil (E13).

***E-udgalgal***, temple of Adad at Karkara; 'house of great storms'.
*muštakkin simātim ina Eudgalgal*, fixing destinies in E-udgalgal (P14).

***E-ulmaš***, temple of Ishtar in Akkad; 'house of Ulmash'.
*mukinni Ištar ina Eulmaš qerbūm Akkadim ribītim*, establishing Ishtar in E-ulmash within the capital city of Agade (P18).

***E-zida***, temple of Nabu (and earlier of Tutu) at Borsippa; 'house of righteousness'.
*la mupparkûm ana Ezida*, the one who never neglects E-zida (P11).

***Ea***, god of the subterranean sweet water; god of magic and wisdom, venerated at Eridu in the temple Eabzu; in Sumerian *En.ki*, 'lord of the earth'.
*Marduk mārim rēštîm ša Ea*, Marduk, firstborn son of Ea (P1); *Ea u Damgalnunna mušarbû šarrūtišu*, Ea and Damgalnunna, who have made his kingdom magnificent (P16); *ina igigallim ša Ea išīmam*, with the omniscience that Ea has ordained for him (E4); *Ea rubûm rabium ša šīmātušu ina maḫra illaka*, Ea the almighty prince whose decisions come first (E22).

**Ellil** < *Enlil*, 'lord of the wind', one of the most important gods of the Sumerian pantheon, consort of Ninlil; head of the pantheon at Nippur where he was vernerated in the temple Ekur.
*Ellil bēl šamê u erṣetim*, Enlil lord of heaven and earth (P1); *Ellil bēlum mušīm šīmātīm*, Enlil the lord who ordains the destiny (E20); *Ḫammurabi rē'ûm nibīt Ellil anāku*, I am Hammurabi, the shepherd appointed by Enlil (P4); *ṣalmāt qaqqadim ša Ellil išrukam*, the mass of humanity which Enlil entrusted to me (E2); *ina maḫar Ellil awassu lilemmin*, may she denigrate his statement in the presence of Enlil (E21); *ina pī Ellil šarrim lišaškin*, let him hake it happen according to the word of Enlil the king (E21); *errētim anniātim Ellil ina pīšu ša la uttakkaru līruršuma*, let Enlil curse him with these curses according to his words which cannot be changed (E32).
>***Anu***. cf. ***ellilūtu***, leadership like Enlil.

*Enki* > ***Ea***.

*Enlil* > **Ellil**.

***Eridu***, in southern Iraq, south of Ur; by tradition the place where the institution of kingship first descended from heaven to earth; centre for the worship of Ea in the temple Eabzu; modern Tell Abū Shahrain.
*šarrum lē'ûm mutēr Eridu ana ašrišu*, the clever king who restored Eridu to its proper state (P5).

***Erra***, god of war and disaster; venerated at Kutû.

*ša Erra rūšu ušakšidu nizmassu*, the one whom his friend Erra allows to achieve his ambitions (P10).

***Girsu***, a town dependent on Lagash to the south-east; centre of worship of Ningirsu in the temple Eninnu; modern Tello.

*šā'im mirītim u mašqītim ana Lagaš u Girsîm*, providing pasture and a water supply for Lagash and Girsu (P13).

***Ḫammurabi*** (1792–1750), sixth king of the First Dynasty of Babylon; the name as such means 'the god Hammu is great', but is sometimes transcribed as *Hammurāpi*, 'Hammu heals'.

*Ḫammurabi rubâm na'adam pāliḫ ilī*, Hammurabi, the devoted prince who fears god (P3); *Ḫammurapi rē'ûm nibīt Ellil anāku*, I am Hammurabi, the shepherd appointed by Enlil (P4); *Ḫammurabimi bēlum ša kīma abim wālidim ana niši ibaššû*, Hammurabi is the lord who rules his people like the father who begat them (E12); *Hammurabi šar mīšarim ša Šamaš kīnātim išrukušum anāku*, I am Hammurabi, the king of justice, whom Shamash has presented with the law (E17); *dīnāt mīšarim ša Ḫammurabi šarrum lē'ûm ukinnuma*, laws of righteousness which Hammurabi the skilful king established (E1); *Ḫammurabi šarrum gitmalum anāku*, I am Hammurabi the perfect king (E2).

***Ḫursagkalamma***, 'the mountain of the world'; sacred temple in Kish devoted to Ishtar.

*pāqid bītim Ḫursagkalamma*, caring for the temple of Hursagkallamma (P9).

***Idu***, the god of the rivers, called upon to decide cases where the evidence was not clear in the so-called river ordeal.

>***nāru***, river.

***Igigi***, the chief gods of the pantheon.

*in Igigi ušarbiūšu*, they made him one of the greatest of the Igigi (P2).

*Illil > Ellil.*

***Isin***, in southern Iraq, south-east of Nippur; centre of the worship of Ištar in the temple Egalmaḫ; administrative centre in the Early Old Babylonian period (the Isin Dynasty and the Isin-Larsa Period), 2000–1800 BCE; modern Išān al-Baḥriyāt.

*mupaḫḫir nišī sapḫātim ša Isin*, gathering the scattered people of Isin (P8).

***Ištar***, chief goddess of love and war; Inanna in Sumerian; venerated especially at Uruk in the temple Eanna.

*Ištar bēlet tāḫazim u qablim*, Ishtar lady of conflict and strife (E27); *šarrum ša ina Ninua in Emesmes ušūpi'u mê Ištar*, the king who made the power of Ishtar shine in E-meshmesh in Nineveh (P20); *migir Ištar anāku*, I am the one whom Ishtar loves (P21); *muḫaddi libbi Ištar*, bringing joy to the heart of Ishtar (P13); *rē'î nišī ša epšētušu eli Ištar ṭāba*, the shepherd of the people whose deeds benefit Ishtar (P18); *mušteṣbî parṣī rabûtim ša Ištar*, who arranged the performance of the magnificent ceremonies for Ishtar (P9); *mukammer ḫiṣbim ana Anim u Ištar*, heaping up luxury for Anum and Ishtar (P8); *ina kakkim dannim ša Zababa u Ištar ušatlimūnim*, with the powerful weapons which Zababa and Ishtar entrusted to me (E4).

***Karkara***, centre of worship for the storm-god Adad.

*qurādim in Bīt Karkara*, the hero at Bit Karkara (P14).

***Kešu***, in central Iraq but site unidentified; linked with Adab and Lagash; centre of worship for the mother goddess Mama (Nintu).

*mukīn uṣurātim ša Keš muddešī mākalī ellūtim ana Nintu*, establishing the design of Kesh, who kept on supplying the holy food offerings for Mama (P12).

***Kiš***, in southern Iraq, east of Babylon; centre of the worship of Zababa; modern Tell Uḥaimir.

*mušaršid šubat Kiš*, who made Kish a secure abode (P9).

***Kutû***, in central Iraq, north-east of Babylon; centre of the worship of Erra (Nergal) and the gods of the underworld in the temple E-meslam; modern Imām Ibrahīm.

*mušāter Kutî murappiš mimma šumšu ana Meslam*, who made Kutha the best and enlarged absolutely everything in the Meslam (P10).

***Lagaš***, capital of the city-state of Larsa, which also included Girsu; modern Tell el Hibā.

*šā'im mirītim u mašqītim ana Lagaš u Girsîm*, providing pasture and a water supply for Lagash and Girsu (P13).

*Lamassu* > ***lamassu***, protective statue.

***Larsa***, in southern Iraq, south-east of Uruk; devoted to Shamash; modern Senkara.

*qarrādum gāmil Larsa*, the hero who restored Larsa (P8).

***Malgium***, site unidentified; on the eastern bank of the Tigris, south-east of Eshnunna; ancient cult centre for Enki and Damkina; after some resistance eventually taken by Hammurabi on two occasions (in the tenth and thirty-third years of his reign).

*mušpazzir nišī Malgīm in karašîm*, who protected the people of Malgum from catastrophe (P16).

***Mama***, mother goddess; also known as Nintu.

*bēlum sīmat ḫaṭṭim u agêm ša ušaklilušu erištum Mama*, the lord with the crown and the sceptre, whom the most wise Mama brought to perfection (P12).

***Marduk***, chief god of Babylon, where he was venerated in the temple Esagil; the son of Ea.

*Marduk mārim rēštîm ša Ea ellilūt kiššat nišī išīmûšum*, Marduk, first-born son of Ea, to whom Ea has entrusted the leadership of the nations of the world (P1); *ana ṣalmāt qaqqadim ša Ellil išrukam rē'ûssina Marduk iddinam ul ēgu*, I have not been negligent about the mass of humanity which Enlil entrusted to me and to whose leadership Marduk appointed me (E2); *ina lē'ûtim ša Marduk iddinam*, with the power that Marduk has given him (E4); *Marduk ana šūtēšur nišī mātim ūsim šūḫuzim uwa'eranni*, Marduk has urged me to set the people in the land straight and to control behaviour (P22); *libbi Marduk bēlišu uṭīb*, he has made the heart of his lord Marduk happy (E12; also *muṭīb libbi Marduk*, P5); *irnitti Marduk eliš u šapliš ikšud*, he secured the triumph of Marduk above and below (E12); *ana awat Marduk bēlišu uštaktitma*, he allowed himself to be subject to the word of Marduk his lord (E12); *ina awat Marduk bēliya uṣurātūa mušassikam ay iršia*, let no one be allowed to throw out my plans according to the word of Marduk my lord (E10); *ina maḫar Marduk bēliya Zarpānītum bēltiya ina libbišu gamrim likrubam*, may he pray with his whole heart in the presence of my lord Marduk and my lady Zarpanitu (E12); *igirrê ūmišam ina maḫar Marduk bēliya Zarpanitum bēltiya lidammiqu*, may they grant the daily prayer made in the presence of my lord Marduk and my lady Sarpanitu (E13); *nadīt Marduk*, a priestess of Marduk (L182); *nadīt Marduk ša Bābilim*, a priestess of Marduk of Babylon (L182).

***Mari***, in eastern Syria, on the border with Iraq; centre for the worship of Dagan; modern Tell Ḥarīrī.

*šû igmilu nišī Mera u Tuttul*, he is the one who showed favour to the inhabitants of Mari and Tuttul (P17).

***Maškanšaprim***, a town bordering Malgum and dependent on Larsa; now identified with Tell Abu Duwari on the Tigris.

*šû iqīšu napšatam ana Maškanšāpir mušešqi nuḫšim ana Meslam*, he is the one who gave life in Mashkanshaprim, and provides abundant water for the Meslam (P15).

*Mera* > ***Mari***.

***Meslam***, temple in Kutû for the veneration of Erra (Nergal), who was also worshipped in Mashkan-shapir.

*mušāter Kutî murappiš mimma šumšu ana <E->meslam*, who made Kutha best of all and enlarged everything in the Meslam (P10); *muš-ešqi nuḫšim ana Meslam*, he provides abundant water for the Meslam (P15).

***Nergal***, great god of the underworld, closely identified with Erra; venerated especially at Kutû in the E-meslam.

*Nergal dannum ina ilī*, Nergal, the strongest of the gods (E28).

***Ninazu***, an ancient god of medicine, son of Enlil; venerated at Eshnunna before it became associated with Tishpak.
*šākin mākalī ellūtim ana Ninazu*, the one who ensures holy food for Ninasu (P17).

***Ninkarrak***, goddess of medicine and healing; daughter of Anu, spouse of Ninurta, equated with Gula.
*Ninkarrak mārat Anim qābiat dumqiya ina Ekur*, Ninkarrak the daughter of Anu, who speaks in my favour in E-kur (E30).

***Ninlil***, consort of Enlil.
*Ninlil ummum rabītum ša qibīssa ina Ekur kabtat*, Ninlil, the greatest mother, whose utterance is revered in Ekur (E21).

***Nintu***, epithet of Mama, the mother goddess.
*Nintu bēltum ṣīrtum ša mātātim ummum bānītī*, Nintu, exalted lady, she is the mother who created the nations (E29); *mākalī ellūtim ana Nintu*, who kept on supplying the sacred food for Nintu (P12).

***Ninua***, Nineveh, in Northern Iraq; centre for the worship of Ishtar in the temple E-mesmes; modern Kouynjik, across the river from Mosul.
*šarrum ša in Ninua in Emesmes ušūpi'u mê Ištar*, the king who made the power of Ishtar shine in E-mesmes in Nineveh (P20).

***Nippur***, centre for the worship of Enlil in the E-kur; modern Niffar in central Iraq.
*mušaklil mimma šumšu ana Nippur markas šamê u erṣetim*, providing all that is needed for Nippur, the bond between heaven and earth (P4).

***Purattum***, the river Euphrates.
*mukanniš dadmē Purattim ittum Dagan bānîšu*, controlling the settlements on the Euphrates at the behest of Dagan his creator (P17).

***Sīn***, god of the moon; venerated at Ur in the temple Egišnugal; Nanna in Sumerian.
*zēr šarrūtim ša Sîn ibniušu*, descendant of the royal line which Sin began (P6); *Sîn bēl šamê ilum bānî ša têressu*(!) *ina ilī šūpât*, Sin, lord of heaven, creator god, whose judgment outshines other gods (E24).

***Sīn-muballiṭ***, fifth king of the First Dynasty of Babylon, father of Hammurabi; reigned 1812–1793 BCE.
*liplippim ša Sumula'il aplum dannum ša Sinmuballiṭ zērum dārium ša šarrūtim*, the descendant of Sumula'il, the powerful son of Sin-muballit, of royal descent for generations (P21).

***Sipparum***, Sippar, cult centre for Shamash and Aya; modern Abu Ḥibba in southern Iraq.
*mukīn išdī Sippar*, fixing the foundations of Sippar (P7).

***Sugal***, south-east of Nippur; centre for the worship of Ishtar; modern Ibzaiḥ.
*mušaklil tērētim ša Sugal muḫaddi libbi Ištar*, fulfilling the oracles of Zabalam, bringing joy to the heart of Ishtar (P13).

***Sumula'il***, second king of First Dynasty of Babylon.
*liplippim ša Sumula'il*, the descendant of Sumula'il (P21).

*Ṣarpānītu* > ***Zarpānītu.***

***Šamaš***, god of the sun, god of justice; venerated at Larsa and Sippar; Utu in Sumerian.
*kīma Šamaš ana ṣalmāt qaqqadim waṣêmma*, rising like Shamash over the mass of humanity (P3); *šēmû Šamaš*, obedient to Shamash (P7); *ina qibīt Šamaš dayyānim rabîm ša šamê u erṣetim*, by the command of Shamash the great judge of heaven and earth (E10); *Šamaš dayyānum rabi'um ša šamê u erṣetim*, Shamash the great judge of heaven and earth (E23); *Šamaš ḫaṭṭa lirrik*, let Shamash prolong his rule (E18); *ša Šamaš kīnātim išrukušum*, whom Shamash has presented with the law (E17); *muddiš Ebabbar ana Šamaš rēṣišu*, who renewed E-babbar with the help of Shamash (P8); *awatum maruštum ša Šamaš arḫiš likšussu*, let the terrifying word of Shamash quickly overpower him (E23).

***Šumeru***, southern Mesopotamia; used together with Akkad to mean Mesopotamia as a whole .
*šamšu Bābilim mušēṣi nūrim ana māt Šumerim u Akkadim*, the sun of Babylon who sheds light on the land of Sumer and Akkad (P21); *ṣillī ṭābum ana āliya tariṣ ina utliya nišī māt Šumerim u Akkadim ukīl*, stretching out my protective shadow over my city, I held the people of Sumer and Akkad in my arms (E7).

*Tēlitum* > ***tēlitum***, epithet of Ishtar.

***Tišpak***, god of war; venerated at Eshnunna; equated with Ninurta.
*munawwer pani Tišpak šākin mākalī ellūtim ana Ninazu*, the one who brings light to the face of Tishpak, who ensures holy food for Ninazu (P17).

***Tuttul***, town on the Middle Euphrates on the road to Mari; cult centre for Dagan; identified with Ḥit.
*šû igmilu nišī Mera u Tuttul*, he is the one who showed favour to the inhabitants of Mari and Tuttul (P17).

***Tutu***, epithet for Nabu, and also for Marduk.
*narām Tutu mūrîš Barsippa*, whom Tutu loves and who makes Borsippa rejoice (P10).

***Uraš***, epithet of Ninurta at Dilbat.
*mušaddil mēreštim ša Dilbat mugarrin karê ana Uraš gašrim*, who develops the land to be ploughed in Dilbat, who fills up the huge granaries of Urash (P11).

***Uruk***, modern Warka; north-west of Larsa; centre of worship for Anu and Ishtar.
*bēlum muballiṭ Uruk*, the lord who brings life to Uruk (P8).

***Urum***, Ur, on the west bank of the Euphrates; centre for worship of Sin; administrative centre of the Neo-Sumerian period (the Third Dynasty of Ur), 2100–2000 BCE; modern Tell el-Muqayyar.
*munahhiš Urim wašrum muštēmiqum bābil ḫegallim ana Egišnugal*, who made Ur prosper, carefully and wisely bringing plenty to E-gishnugal (P6).

***Zababa***, venerated at Kish in Emeteursag; hypostasis of Ninurta.
*ušumgal šarri talîm Zababa*, the leader of kings, the supporter of Zababa (P9); *ina kakkim dannim ša Zababa u Ištar ušatlimūnim... nakri eliš u šapliš assuḫ*, with the powerful weapons which Zababa and Ishtar entrusted to me...I rooted out my enemies above and below (E4); *Zababa qarrādum rabium mārum rēštûm ša Ekur*, the great hero Zababa, first son of E-kur (E26).

*Zabalam* > ***Sugal***.

***Zarpānītu***, consort of Marduk.
*ina maḫar Marduk bēliya Zarpānītum bēltiya ina libbišu gamrim likrubam*, may he pray with his whole heart in the presence of my Lord Marduk and my lady Zarpanitu (E12); *igirrê ūmišam ina maḫar Marduk bēliya Zarpānītum bēltiya lidammiqū*, may they grant the daily prayer made in the presence of my Lord Marduk and my lady Zarpanitu (E13).

## NUMERALS WRITTEN IDEOGRAPHICALLY

a. fractions: *1/60* (L224); *1/6* (L224; 277); *1/4* (L225; 248[?]); *1/3* (§5.3b; L114; 116; 140; 201; 208; 214; 241; 252); *1/2* (L59; 156; 207; 212; 247; 251).

b. whole numbers: ***1*** (L24; 44; 57; 58; 63; 121; 139; 198; 202 [=60, see below]; 203; 228; 255; 269; 270); **2** (L17; 213; 217; 223; 228; 234; 268); ***3*** (L222; 242/3; 260; 271; 275); ***4*** (L242/3; 272; 274[?]); ***5*** (L111; 112; 121; 211; 216; 221; 259; 273; 274; 274); ***6*** (L239; 258; 273); ***8*** (L257; 261); ***10*** (L8; 44; 63; 204; 209; 215; 265); ***12*** (L5); ***20*** (L57); ***30*** (L8); ***60*** (L58; 202, written as *1 šūši*, see above; 234; 255).

c. compound numbers: ***2 1/2*** (L276).

## UNITS OF MEASUREMENT

| *Akkadian* | *Sumerian* | *Translation* | *Approximation* | *Multiplier* |
|---|---|---|---|---|
| **Area** | | | | |
| *mušaru* | SAR | sar | 36 sq. metres | |
| | | | | 100 |
| *iku* | IKU | iku | 3600 sq. metres | |
| | | | | 18 |
| *bur* | BUR | bur | 6.5 hectares | |
| **Length** | | | | |
| *uṭṭete* | ŠE | barley-corn | 0.25 centimetres | |
| | | | | 6 |
| *ubānu* | ŠU.SI | finger | 1.6 centimetres | |
| | | | | 24 |
| *ammatu* | KUŠ | cubit | 50 centimetres | |
| | | | | 6 |
| *qanû* | GI | reed | 3 metres | |
| | | | | 2 |
| *nindānu* | NINDA | ninda | 6 metres | |
| **Volume** | | | | |
| *qû* | SILA | sila | 1 litre | |
| | | | | 10 |
| *sūtu* | BÁN | seah | 10 litres | |
| | | | | 6 |
| *pānu* | BARIGA | bariga | 60 litres | |
| | | | | 5 |
| *kurru* | GUR | kur | 300 litres | |
| **Weight** | | | | |
| *uṭṭete* | ŠE | barley-corn | 0.05 grams | |
| | | | | 180 |
| *šiqlu* | GIN | shekel | 8.3 grams | |
| | | | | 60 |
| *manû* | MA.NA | mina | 0.5 kilograms | |
| | | | | 60 |
| *biltu* | GÚN | talent | 30 kilograms | |

# Roots and Stems

Roots that can be inferred from verbal forms (including participles) that are attested in CH are listed here; also included are the roots of verbs that are attested only elsewhere in Akkadian, but with which some of the nominal forms in CH are obviously to be associated. *AHw* mentions a number of roots that are restricted to nouns (like *y-r-ḫ* for *arḫu*, month), but such roots have here been omitted.

Where some uncertainty about the derivation of a word has been expressed in *CAD* or *AHw* those doubts are noted, principally because this list is restricted to roots that are used in verbal forms; such roots are marked with an asterisk.

This leaves unlisted here the words that either cannot be easily identified with a verbal root, or clearly have no verbal equivalent. Many such words are loan-words (especially from Sumerian), while others seem to be Semitic.

Bold font is used for the words attested in CH; other words are not emboldened. Verbs (with associated participles) are listed before any similarly derived nouns. Cross-references are marked with the sign >.

| | |
|---|---|
| *ʾ-b-b* | *ebēbu*, to become clean; ***ubbubu***, to purify; ***mubbibu***, purifying. |
| *ʾ-b-d* | ***nābutu*** to flee (cf. *AHw nābutu* II (p. 700b), referring to Western Semitic root *ʾ-b-d*); ***munnabtu***, fugitive. |
| *ʾ-b-l* | see *AHw abālu* I, corresponding to *CAD abālu* B, to dry up. for which the root is *ʾ-b-l* (so *AHw*); for ***abālu*** A, to bring, corresponding to *AHw wabālu*, and also ***babālu***, to bring > *w-b-l*; for ***tabālu*** to remove (a by-form of *abālu* to bring) > *t-b-l*. |
| *ʾ-b-r* | *abāru*, to encompass; see *AHw abāru* III, where it is also suggested that the verb may be denominative from *abāru* II, a kind of hammer (corresponding to *CAD abāru* B); ***ubburu***, to accuse, bring into disrepute; ***mubbiru*** accuser. |

| | |
|---|---|
| *ʾ-b-t* 1 | *abātu*,to destroy; *nābutu* (*AHw nābutu* [*abātu* N], p. 5), to be destroyed. |
| *ʾ-b-t* 2 | > *ʾ-b-d.* |
| *ʾ-d-ʾ* | > *y-d-ʾ.* |
| *ʾ-d-r* | ***adāru***, to fear. |
| *ʾ-d-š* | *edēšu*, to be new; *uddušu* to renew; ***muddišu***, renewing. |
| *ʾ-ḫ-z* | ***aḫāzu***, to take; ***šūḫuzu***, to let marry; ***tāḫazu***, conflict. |
| *ʾ-g-ʾ* | ***egû***, to be negligent; ***mēgûtu***, neglect. |
| *ʾ-g-r* | ***agāru***, to hire; ***agru***, labourer; ***igru***, hire. |
| *ʾ-k-l* | ***akālu***, to eat; ***šūkulu***, to allow to feed; ***mākālu***, food. |
| *ʾ-l-ʾ* (*ʾlī*) | ***elû* 1**, to go up; ***ullû***, to raise; ***mullû* 2**, raising; ***šūlû***, to bring up; ***elēnu***, in addition; ***elītu***, extra portion; ***elû* 2**, upper; ***telītu***, exalted lady. |
| *ʾ-l-d* | > *w-l-d.* |
| *ʾ-l-k* | ***alāku***, to go; ***āliku***, walking. |
| *ʾ-l-l* | > *ḫ-l-l.* |
| *ʾ-m-ʾ* | > *t-m-ʾ.* |
| *ʾ-m-d* | ***emēdu*** to impose; ***nenmudu*** to join. |
| *ʾ-m-q* | *emēqu* to beseech; *šutēmuqu*, to plead; ***muštēmiqu***, supplicating; ***emqu***, wise; ***nēmequ***, wisdom. |
| *ʾ-m-r* | ***amāru***, to see. |
| *ʾ-n-ʾ* | ***enû***, to change. |
| *ʾ-n-ḫ* | *anāḫu*, to become exhausted; ***mānaḫtu***, expenses; ***tānēḫu***, weariness. |
| *ʾ-n-q* | > *y-n-q.* |
| *ʾ-n-š* | *enēšu*, to be weak; ***unnušu***, to weaken; ***aššatu***, wife; ***enšu***, weak; ***sinništu***, woman. |
| *ʾ-p-ʾ* | > *w-p-ʾ.* |
| *ʾ-p-l* 1 | ***apālu* A** (*AHw apālu* I), to answer; D ***uppulu***, to make responsible (see *CAD*, s.v. 7). |
| *ʾ-p-l* 2 | *AHw apālu* II, to be late; D ***uppulu*** 1. to occur afterwards; 2. denominative from ***aplu***, heir (see *AHw* s.v. *apālu* II, D 2), to make someone else the heir. |
| *ʾ-p-s* | *epēsu*, to be difficult; ***uppusu***, to make a problem. |
| *ʾ-p-š* | ***epēšu***, to work; ***epištu***, work. |
| *ʾ-q-r* | > *w-q-r.* |
| *ʾ-r-ʾ* | ***arû***, to take away. |
| *ʾ-r-b* | ***erēbu***, to enter; ***ēribu***, entering; ***šūrubu***, to bring in. |
| *ʾ-r-ḫ* | *arāḫu* to be in haste; ***arḫiš***, quickly. |
| *ʾ-r-k* | *arāku* to become long; ***urruku***, to lengthen; *šūruku*, to lengthen; ***mušāriku***, lengthening; ***arkû***, subsequent; ***arki***, |

| | |
|---|---|
| | after; ***arka***, ***arkānu***, ***arkānumma***, afterwards; ***arkatu*** circumstances; ***arkītu***, future. |
| *ʾ-r-r* | ***arāru***, to curse; ***erretu***, curse. |
| *ʾ-r-š* 1 | ***erēšu* 1**, to demand; ***uršu***, wisdom (see *AHw*, s.v., for reference to verb). |
| *ʾ-r-š* 2 | ***erēšu* 2**, to cultivate; ***errēšu***, cultivator; ***errēšūtu***, cultivation; ***eršu***, cultivated; ***mēreštu***, arable land. |
| *ʾ-s-m* | > *w-s-m*. |
| *ʾ-s-p* | ***esēpu*** to gather. |
| *ʾ-s-r* | ***esēru*** to press. |
| *ʾ-ṣ-ʾ* | > *w-ṣ-ʾ*. |
| *ʾ-ṣ-b* | > *w-ṣ-b*. |
| *ʾ-ṣ-d* | ***eṣēdu*** to harvest. |
| *ʾ-ṣ-r* | *eṣēru* to draw; *uṣṣuru* to draw; ***uṣurtu*** plan. |
| *ʾ-š-ʾ* | > *ʾ-š-y* 1 and 2. |
| *ʾ-š-b* | > *w-š-b*. |
| *ʾ-š-m* | > *w-š-m*. |
| *ʾ-š-r* 1 | ***ašāru* 1**, to organize; ***āširu***, organizing; (?) ***ašru* 1**, shrine. |
| *ʾ-š-r* 2 | > *w-š-r*. |
| *ʾ-š-š* | *ašāšu*, to be in distress; ***uššušu***, to cause distress. |
| *ʾ-š-y* 1 | ***ešû***, to confuse; ***ēšītu***, disturbance; ***mīšītu***, confusion; ***tēšû***, turmoil; ***tuššu***, deception. |
| *ʾ-š-y* 2 (?) | ***išû***, to have |
| *ʾ-t-l* | ***itūlu***, to copulate. |
| *ʾ-t-q* | *etēqu*, to pass along; ***šūtuqu***, to avert. |
| *ʾ-t-r* | > *w-t-r*. |
| *ʾ-ṭ-r* | ***eṭēru***, to remove. |
| *ʾ-z-b* | ***ezēbu***, to leave; ***šūzubu***, to have deposited. |
| *ʾ-z-z* 1 | *ezēzu*, to be angry; ***ezziš***, angrily; ***ezzu***, angry; ***uzzatu***, anger. |
| *ʾ-z-z* 2 | > *n-z-z*. |
| *b-ʾ-l* | ***bēlu***, lord; ***bēltu***, lady. |
| *b-ʾ-r* 1 | *baʾāru* to trap animals (= *AHw bâru* I); ***bāʾiru***, hunter. |
| *b-ʾ-r* 2 | *bâru*, A to be certain (= *AHw bâru* III); ***burru***, to make certain, clarify a legal position; ***bīru***, divination. |
| *b-l-ʾ* (*blī*) | ***balû***, to come to an end; ***bullu***, to terminate; (?) ***balu*** without. |
| *b-l-ṣ* | *balāṣu*, to stare; *bulluṣu*, to stare; > *p-l-s*. |
| *b-l-ṭ* | ***balāṭu* 1**, to live; ***bulluṭu***, to save a life; ***muballiṭu***, reviving; ***balāṭu* 2**, life; ***balṭu***, alive; ***bulṭu***, life. |
| *b-n-ʾ* | ***banû***, to procreate; *binītu* creature; ***binâtu*** (tantum pl., see *CAD*) limbs; ***bānû***, creator; ***bānītu***, creatress. |

| | |
|---|---|
| *b-q-r* | ***baqāru***, to claim; ***nabquru***, to be reclaimed; ***baqru***, claim; > *p-q-r*. |
| *b-t-q* | *batāqu*, to cut off, deduct; ***bitiqtu***, loss; ***butuqqû***, loss. |
| *b-š-ʾ* | ***bašû***, to exist; ***šubšû***, to produce; ***nabšû***, to be produced; ***bīšu***, property. |
| *d-ʾ-k* | ***dâku***, to kill; ***šudūku***, to arrange a murder; ***nadūku***, to be killed. |
| *d-ʾ-n* (*dīn*) | ***dânu***, to legislate; ***dayyānu***, judge; ***dayyānūtu***, judiciary; ***dīnu***, verdict. |
| *d-ʾ-ṣ* | ***dâṣu***, to trick. |
| *d-ʾ-š* (*dīš*) | ***diāšu***, threshing (verbal noun). |
| *d-k-ʾ* | ***dekû***, to arrange. |
| *d-m-m* | ***damāmu***, to mourn; ***dimmatu***, weeping. |
| *d-m-q* | *damāqu*, to be kind; ***dummuqu***, to show kindness; ***mudammiqu***, benefiting; ***damqu***, good; ***damiqtu***, favour; ***dumqu***, favour; ***tadmiqtu***, kindness. |
| *d-n-n* | *danānu*, to be strong; ***dunnunu***, to strengthen; ***dannu***, strong; ***dannatu***, fortress. |
| *d-p-r* | ***duppuru***, to absent oneself. |
| *d-r-y* (?) | *darû*, to endure (but *AHw*: denominative from *dāru*, generation; > *d-w-r*). |
| *d-w-r* | ***dāru***, generation (*CAD dāru* A); ***dār***, for ever (so *CAD*; cf. *AHw* s.v. *dāru*(*m*) I, eternity, *ana dār*, for ever, which is distinguished from *dārum* II generation); ***dāriš***, for ever; ***dārû***, everlasting; for *darû*, to endure > *d-r-y*. |
| *d-š-ʾ* | *dešû*, to become abundant; *duššû*, to make abundant; ***mudeššû***, making abundant. |
| *g-l-b* | ***gullubu***, to shave; ***gallābu***, barber. |
| *g-l-t* | *galātu*, to be restless; *gullutu*, to cause trouble; ***mugallitu***, trouble-maker. |
| *g-m-l* | ***gamālu***, to care for; ***gāmilu***, showing kindness; ***gitmālu***, perfect. |
| *g-m-r* | ***gamāru***, to complete; ***gamartu***, completion; ***gamru***, complete. |
| *g-r-n* | > *q-r-n*. |
| *g-š-r* | *gašāru*, to become powerful; ***gašru***, mighty. |
| *ḫ-ʾ-r* (*ḫīr*) | ***ḫāru***, to choose; ***ḫāwiru***, husband; ***ḫīrtu***, wife. |
| *ḫ-ʾ-ṭ* | ***ḫâṭu***, to find out. |
| *ḫ-b-l* | ***ḫabālu***, to exploit; ***ḫablu***, exploited; ***ḫubullu***, debt. |
| *ḫ-b-š* | ***ḫabāšu***, to shatter. |
| *ḫ-b-t* | ***ḫabātu***, to rob; ***naḫbutu***, to be robbed; ***ḫabbātu***, robber; ***ḫabtu***, robbed; ***ḫubtu***, robbery. |

*ḫ-d-ʾ* — *ḫadû*, to be happy; *ḫuddû*, to make happy; ***muḫaddû***, gladdening.

*ḫ-l-l* — ***alālu*** (*ḫalālu*) to hang; ***naḫlulu***, to be hung.

*ḫ-l-q* — ***ḫalāqu*** to disappear; ***ḫulluqu*** to destroy; ***ḫalqu*** missing; ***ḫulqu*** lost property.

*ḫ-l-ṣ-ʾ* (*ḫlṣī*) — *neḫelṣû* to slip; ***šuḫluṣû*** to allow to crumble away.

*ḫ-p-ʾ* — *ḫepû* to smash; ***neḫpû*** to be broken.

*ḫ-p-d* — ***ḫuppudu*** to poke out an eye.

*ḫ-r-b* — *ḫarābu* to lie waste; ***ḫarbu*** plough.

*ḫ-r-ṣ* — ***ḫarāṣu*** to subtract; ***šuḫruṣu*** to deduct.

*ḫ-s-s* — *ḫasāsu* to be intelligent; ***ḫassu*** intelligent.

*ḫ-ṣ-b* — *ḫaṣābu* B to be thick, dense (= *AHw ḫaṣābu* II, to be green, cognate with Arabic *ḫ-ḍ-b*); *šuḫṣubu* to make pasture green (*AHw*), to make pasture rich (*CAD*: possibly denominative from *ḫiṣbu*); ***ḫiṣbu*** riches.

*ḫ-ṭ-ʾ* — *ḫaṭû* to be at fault; ***ḫiṭītu***, fault.

*k-ʾ-l* (*kūl*) — ***kullu***, to hold; ***mukillû***, holding.

*k-ʾ-n* (*kūn*) — *kânu*, to be firm (= CAD *kânu* A); ***kunnu***, to establish as true; ***kīnātu***, justice; ***kīnu***, secure; ***kittu***, justice; ***mukīnu***, founder; ***muštakīnu***, arranging.

*k-b-d* — > *k-b-t*.

*k-b-l* — *kabālu*, to be paralysed; ***kubbulu***, to rape.

*k-b-s* — *kabāsu*, to step upon; ***kibsu***, pathway.

*k-b-t* — ***kabātu***, to be important; ***kabtu***, serious.

*k-d-r* — *kadāru*, to be arrogant (= *CAD kadāru* A); ***kadru***, wild.

*k-l-ʾ* — ***kalû***, to withhold (= *AHw kalû* V); for ***kullu*** > *k-ʾ-l*.

*k-l-l* — ***šuklulu***, to make complete; ***mušaklil***, fulfilling; ***kilallān***, both

*k-l-m* — ***kullumu***, to explain.

*k-m-ʾ* (*kmī*) — *kamû* to bind (= *AHw kamû* III); ***kamîš***, in bonds (*CAD*: *kamîš* A).

*k-m-d* — *kamādu*, to weave cloth; ***kāmidu***, weaver, rope-maker.

*k-m-l* — *kamālu*, to become angry; ***kammālu***, rival.

*k-m-r* — *kamāru*, to heap up (= *AHw kamāru* III); *kummuru*, to heap up; ***mukammiru*** heaping up.

*k-n-k* — *kanāku* to seal; ***kanīku***, sealed document; ***kunukku***, sealed document.

*k-n-š* — *kanāšu*, to submit; *kunnušu*, to subjugate; ***mukannišu***, controlling.

*k-p-l* — > *k-b-l*.

*k-r-b* — ***karābu,*** to pray.

*k-r-ṣ* — *karāṣu*, to snap off; ***kurruṣu***, to malign.

*k-s-ʾ* — ***kasû***, to bind.

| | |
|---|---|
| *k-ṣ-r* | *kaṣāru*, to bind together; ***kiṣru***, agreed rent (alternatively read as *riksu*, > *r-k-s*). |
| *k-š-d* | ***kašādu***, to conquer; *kuššudu* to conquer; ***šukšudu***, to enable to attain; ***mušakšidu***, granting victory. |
| *k-š-š* | *kašāšu*, to enforce payment; ***kāšišu***, creditor; ***kašūšu***, supernatural power; ***kiššātu***, security. |
| *k-t-t* | *katātu*, to be low; ***šutaktutu***, to be submissive (*CAD*); to be worried (AHw). |
| *l-ʾ-ʾ* | ***leʾû***, to be able; ***lēʾu***, superhumanly strong; ***lēʾūtu***, supreme power. |
| *l-ʾ-b* | *laʾābu* to infect; ***laʾbu***, disease. |
| *l-b-n* | *labānu* to make bricks; ***libittu***, brickwork. |
| *l-b-š* | *labāšu*, to dress oneself; *lubbušu*, to clothe; *šulbušu*, to decorate; ***mušalbišu***, decorating; *lubūšu*, clothing. |
| *l-m-d* | ***lamādu***, to learn. |
| *l-m-n* | *lemēnu* to be unfortunate; ***lummunu***, to denigrate; *lemnu*, bad; *lemnētu*, ***lemuttu***, misfortune. |
| *l-p-t* | *lapātu* to lay hold on; ***šulputu*** to overthrow; ***liptu*** affliction. |
| *l-q-ʾ* | ***leqû***, to take. |
| *m-ʾ-t* (*mūt*) | ***mâtu***, to die; ***šumūtu***, to cause death; ***mūtu***, death. |
| *m-ʾ-š* | ***mêšu***, to disdain. |
| *m-d-d* | ***madādu***, to measure. |
| *m-g-r* | ***magāru***, to agree; ***migru***, favoured friend. |
| *m-ḫ-r* | ***maḫāru***, to receive; ***māḫiru***, confronting; ***šumḫuru***, to show rivalry; ***maḫru***, front; ***maḫrû***, former; ***maḫar***, in front of; ***māḫirtu***, moving upstream; ***maḫīru***, tariff; ***maḫra***, in front; ***miḫru***, equivalent; ***mitḫariš***, equally; ***tamḫāru***, conflict. |
| *m-ḫ-ṣ* | ***maḫāṣu***, to strike; ***namḫuṣu***, to be beaten. |
| *m-k-r* | *makāru* B, to do business; ***makkūru*** (*namkūru*) goods; ***tamkāru***, merchant. |
| *m-l-ʾ* | ***malû* 1**, to be full (= *AHw malû* IV); ***mullû* 1**, to fill; ***malû* 2**, full; ***mīlu***, flood. |
| *m-n-ʾ* | ***manû* 1**, to count; ***manû* 2**, mina (*AHw manû* II). |
| *m-q-t* | ***maqātu***, to fall; ***šumqutu***, to bring down; ***miqittu***, damage. |
| *m-r-r* | ***marāru***, to harrow. |
| *m-r-ṣ* | *maraṣu*, to be ill; ***marṣu*** (fem. ***maruštu***) diseased; ***murṣu***, disease. |
| *m-ṣ-ʾ* | *maṣû*, to be equal to; ***šumṣû***, to allow to dispose. |
| *m-š-ʾ* (*mšī*) | *mašû* A, to forget; ***mišītu***, confusion. |
| *m-š-r* | ***mašāru***, to drag. |
| *m-ṭ-ʾ* | *maṭû* 1, to be little; ***muṭṭû***, to lessen; ***šumṭû***, to denigrate; ***maṭû* 2** (fem. ***maṭītu***), small. |

| | |
|---|---|
| *n-ʾ-d (nād)* | *nâdu*, to praise; ***naʾdu***, devout; ***tanattu***, praise. |
| *n-ʾ-r (nār)* | *nêru*, to kill; ***nērtu***, murder; ***mayyāru***, mattock (root suggested hesitantly in *AHw*). |
| *n-ʾ-ḫ (nūḫ)* | *nâḫu*, to be still; ***nuḫḫu***, to soothe; ***munēḫu***, quietening. |
| *n-ʾ-š* | *nêšu*, to live; ***nīšu* A**, oath. |
| *n-b-ʾ 1 (nbī)* | ***nabû***, to nominate, designate; ***nābū***, nominating; ***nibītu***, nominee. |
| *n-b-ʾ 2* | *nabāʾu* A (= *AHw nabāʾu* I) to rise in flood; ***nābiḫu*** rebel (so *AHw* s.v. *nābiʾu* I); cf. *CAD*: *nabʾāu* B, to plunder. |
| *n-b-l-k-t* | ***nabalkutu***, to overwhelm, destroy; ***nabalkattu***, damage. |
| *n-d-ʾ* | ***nadû***, to throw down; ***šuddû***, to cause to drop; ***naddû***, to be thrown down; ***nadītu***, priestess; ***nidītu***, neglected land; ***nidûtu***, neglected land. |
| *n-d-n* | ***nadānu***, to give; ***nādinu***, giving; ***naddunu***, to be given; ***nādinānu***, giver; ***nudunnu***, marriage-gift. |
| *n-g-r 1* | *nagāru* (*CAD*; see *AHw nagāru* II), to speak; ***nāgiru***, crier. |
| *n-g-r 2* | *nugguru* (*CAD*), to denounce; ***munaggiru***, informer. |
| *n-ḫ-š* | ***naḫāšu***, to prosper; *nuḫḫušu*, to make prosperous; ***munaḫḫišu***, munificent; ***nuḫšu***, plenty. |
| *n-k-p* | ***nakāpu***, to butt; *nukkupu* to gore; ***munakkipu***, tossing; ***nakkāpû***, goring. |
| *n-k-r* | ***nakāru***, to argue; ***nukkuru***, to change; ***nakru***, enemy; ***nukurtu***, hostility.. |
| *n-k-s* | ***nakāsu*** to cut. |
| *n-p-ʾ* | ***nepû***, to seize; ***nēpû***, seizing; ***nipûtu***, pledge. |
| *n-p-l* | *napālu* B, to make a supplementary payment; ***nipiltu***, supplementary payment. |
| *n-p-ḫ* | *napāḫu*, to kindle; ***nappuḫu***, to become ablaze; ***nappāḫu***, smith. |
| *n-p-š* | *napāšu*, to breathe freely; ***nuppušu***, to relax; ***napištu***, life. |
| *n-q-r* | ***naqāru***, to pull apart. |
| *n-s-ḫ* | ***nasāḫu***, to remove (see also *n-s-k* 2); ***nassuḫu***, to be disinherited; ***nisiḫtu***, deserter. |
| *n-s-q* | ***nasāqu*** to choose; ***nasqu*** selected. |
| *n-s-k 1* | *nasāku* 1, to pull out; ***šussuku***, to throw out; ***mušassiku***, disposing. |
| *n-s-k 2* | ***nasāku* 2**, to wound (*CAD*: perhaps by-form of *nasāḫu*). |
| *n-ṣ-r* | ***naṣāru***, to keep; ***maṣṣarūtu***, custody |
| *n-š-ʾ* | ***našû***, to carry; ***nāšû***, carrying; ***nīšu* 1**, life, oath; ***nīšu* 2**, raising. |
| *n-š-k* | *našāku*, to bite; ***nišku***, bite. |
| *n-ṭ-ʾ* | *naṭû*, to hit; ***šuṭṭû***, to strike. |

| | |
|---|---|
| *n-ṭ-l* | *naṭālu*, to look at; ***šuṭṭulu***, to make visible; ***niṭlu***, glance. |
| *n-w-r* | ***namāru*** (*AHw nawāru*), to shine; ***nummuru***, to shed light; ***munammiru***, brightening; ***nūru***, light. |
| *n-z-m* | *nazāmu* to complain; ***nizmatu*** wish. |
| *n-z-z* (*ʾ-z-z* 2) | ***izuzzu***, to stand; ***šūzzuzu***, to erect; ***muzzazu***, serving. |
| *p-ʾ-l* | > *š-p-ʾ-l.* |
| *p-ʾ-ḫ* (*pūḫ*) | ***puḫḫu***, to exchange; ***pīḫātu***, debt; ***pūḫu***, substitute. |
| *p-ḫ-ʾ* | ***peḫû***, to seal up. |
| *p-ḫ-r* | *paḫāru*, to assemble (intransitive); *puḫḫuru*, to assemble (transitive); ***mupaḫḫiru***, assembling; ***napḫaru***, group; ***puḫru***, assembly. |
| *p-l-ḫ* | *palāhu* to worship; ***pāliḫu***, worshipping. |
| *p-l-s* | *palāsu*, to look at; ***pullusu***, to covet. |
| *p-l-š* | ***palāšu***, to break into; ***pilšu***, burglary. |
| *p-q-d* | ***paqādu***, to entrust; ***pāqidu***, caring for. |
| *p-q-r* | for *CAD paqāru*, to claim, and derivatives; *AHw*: *baqāru*; > *b-q-r*. |
| *p-r-k-ʾ* (*prkū*) | *naparkû*, to abandon; ***mupparkû***, neglecting. |
| *p-r-s* | ***parāsu***, to decide; ***naprusu***, to be decided; ***purussû***, decision. |
| *p-r-ṣ* | *paraṣu*, to conduct a ritual (*AHw*: denominative); ***parṣu*** ritual. |
| *p-s-s* | *pasāsu*, to annul; ***pussusu***, to annul. |
| *p-š-ḫ* | ***pašāḫu***, to soothe. |
| *p-š-q* | *pašāqu*, to be difficult; ***pušqu***, distress. |
| *p-š-r* | ***pašāru***, to trade. |
| *p-š-ṭ* | ***pašāṭu***, to remove. |
| *p-t-ʾ* | ***petû***, to open; ***pātiʾu***, opening out; ***puttû***, to solve; ***naptû***, to be opened; ***pītu***, opening; ***teptītu***, development. |
| *p-ṭ-r* | ***paṭāru***, to repurchase; ***napṭuru***, to be redeemed; ***ipṭiru***, ransom. |
| *p-z-r* | *pazaru*, to hide; ***šupuzzuru***, to protect; ***mušpazzir***, protecting. |
| *q-ʾ-l* | ***qâlu***, to heed. |
| *q-ʾ-p* 1 | ***qâpu* 1**, to entrust; ***qiptu***, trust. |
| *q-ʾ-p* 2 | ***qâpu* 2**, to crumble. |
| *q-ʾ-š* | ***qâšu***, to give; ***qīštu***, gift. |
| *q-b-ʾ* | ***qabû***, to speak; ***qābû***, speaking; ***qibītu***, command |
| *q-d-š* | *qadašu*, to be free of claims; *quddušu*, to make ritually clean; ***qadištu***, temple prostitute. |
| *q-l-ʾ* | ***qalû***, to burn. |
| *q-l-p-ʾ* | *neqelpû*, to drift; ***muqqelpītu***, drifting. |
| *q-m-ʾ* | ***qamû***, to burn. |

| | |
|---|---|
| *q-r-b* | ***qerēbu***, to be near; ***qerbītu***, interior; ***qerbu***, inside; ***qerbum***, within. |
| *q-r-d* | *qaradu*, to be heroic (*AHw*); *qurrudu*, to turn into a hero (*CAD*); ***qarrādu***, hero. |
| *q-t-ʾ* | *qatû*, to come to an end; ***šuqtû***, to terminate; ***taqtītu***, end. |
| *r-ʾ-ʾ* | ***reʾû***, to tend small animals; ***merētu***, (*mirītu*) pasture; ***rēʾû***, shepherd; ***rēʾûtu***, governance. |
| *r-ʾ-b* (*rīb*) | ***râbu***, to recompense. |
| *r-ʾ-m* | ***râmu***, to love; ***rāʾimu***, loving; ***rēmu***, love; ***narāmu***, beloved. |
| *r-ʾ-q* 1 (*rīq*) | *râqu* (*AHw riāqu*), to be empty; ***rīqu***, empty; ***rīqūtu***, emptiness. |
| *r-ʾ-q* 2 (*r*ʾ$_3$*q*) | *rêqu*, to be distant; ***rūqu***, distant. |
| *r-ʾ-ṣ* | *rêṣu*, to help; ***rēṣu***, helper. |
| *r-ʾ-š* | *râšu* (*AHw riāšu*), to be glad; *ruššu* to bring joy; ***murīšu***, bringing pleasure. |
| *r-b-ʾ* | ***rabû***, to be grand; ***rubbû***, to grow crops, bring up children; ***murabbû***, foster father; ***murabbītu***, foster mother; ***šurbû***, to extol; ***mušarbû***, extolling; ***rabiānu***, governor; ***rabītu***, principal wife; ***rabû***, grand; ***rebītu***, city square; *rubātu* lady; ***rubû***, prince; ***tarbītu***, adopted child. |
| *r-b-ṣ* | *rabāṣu*, to lie down; ***šurbuṣu***, to pasture; ***tarbaṣu***, animal pen. |
| *r-d-ʾ* | ***redû***, to catch; ***rēdû***, arresting officer; ***murteddû***, waggon-driver; ***rīdu***, tradition. |
| *r-g-m* | ***ragāmu***, to claim; ***rugummû***, loss. |
| *r-ḫ-ṣ* | ***raḫāṣu***, to devastate. |
| *r-k-b* | *rakābu*, to ride; ***rukkubu***, to pollinate; ***tarkibtu***, pollination. |
| *r-k-s* | ***rakāsu***, formally to agree; ***rukkusu***, to demand a contract; ***narkusu***, to meet by agreement; ***markasu***, link; ***rikistu***, contract; ***riksu***, contract. |
| *r-p-š* | *rapāšu*, to be wide; *ruppušu*, to widen; ***murappišu***, extending. |
| *r-q-ʾ* | ***raqû*** to hide. |
| *r-s-b* | *rasābu* to engage in conflict; ***risbatu*** fight. |
| *r-š-ʾ* | ***rašû*** to possess, permit; ***šuršû*** to provide. |
| *r-š-d* | *rašādu*, to have foundations; ***šuršudu***, to fix firmly; ***mušaršidu***, protecting. |
| *r-ṭ-b* | *raṭābu*, to be moist; ***ruṭṭubu*** to moisten. |
| *s-b-ʾ* | *sabû*, to draw beer (*CAD*); *sābû*, drink-seller; ***sābītu***, barmaid; ***sību***, beer. |
| *s-d-r* | ***sadāru***, arrange. |
| *s-ḫ-m* | *saḫāmu*, to be under pressure; ***suḫḫumu***, to pester. |

| | |
|---|---|
| *s-ḫ-r* | *saḫāru*, to go around; *šusḫuru*, to place around; ***muštasḫiru***, surrounding. |
| *s-k-l* | ***sakālu***, to acquire by fraud; ***sikiltu***, fraudulent acquisition. |
| *s-k-p* | ***sakāpu***, to overturn. |
| *s-k-r* | ***sekēru***, to shut off; ***sekretu***, cloistered woman. |
| *s-n-q* | *sanāqu*, to supervise; ***sunnuqu***, to keep in tight control. |
| *s-p-ḫ* | *sapāḫu*, to scatter; ***suppuḫu***, to disturb; ***naspuḫu***, to be scattered; ***sapḫu***, widespread. |
| *s-r-r* | ***sarāru***, to deceive; ***surruru***, to deceive; ***sarru***, reprobate; ***sartu***, deception. |
| *ṣ-ʾ-n* (*ṣʾ*$_4$*n*) | ***ṣênu***, to load as cargo; *AHw* also lists *ṣʾ*$_1$*n* for *ṣēnu* III (i.e. ***ṣēnu* 1**, flock), and *ṣʾ*$_5$*n* for *ṣēnu* I (i.e. ***ṣēnu* 2**, wicked). |
| *ṣ-ʾ-r* | *ṣiāru*, to be outstanding (*AHw*); *ṣurru*, to make famous (perhaps denominative, cf. *CAD*); ***muṣīru***, making famous; ***ṣīru***, exalted. |
| *ṣ-b-ʾ* | *ṣebû* = *AHw ṣabû* IV (*ṣebû*) to wish; cited in *BAL* for ***šuteṣbû*** (Št-theme, to execute work according to plan); cf. *CAD*: *ṣubbû* to look from a distance, obtain a comprehensive view; *šuṣbu* > ***šuteṣbû*** (Št-theme), to execute work according to plan; ***mušteṣbû***, arranging. |
| *ṣ-b-r* | ***ṣabaru***, to list to one side (*CAD*) = *zapāru*, to become rotten (*AHw*); > *z-p-r*. |
| *ṣ-b-ṭ* | ***ṣabātu***, to seize, find; ***šuṣbutu***, to enforce; ***naṣbutu***, to get caught; ***ṣābitānu***, captor. |
| *ṣ-ḫ-r* | ***ṣeḫēru***, to be small; ***ṣuḫḫuru***, to diminish; ***ṣeḫḫeru***, very young; ***ṣeḫru***, young. |
| *ṣ-l-l* | *ṣullulu* A, to put a roof over, provide shade (*AHw*: denominative); ***ṣulūlu***, shade; ***ṣillu***, shadow. |
| *ṣ-l-m* | *ṣalāmu*, to be black; ***ṣalmu* 1**, black; it is very uncertain if it is also the root of ***ṣalmu* 2**, statue. |
| *ṣ-m-ʾ* | *ṣamû*, to be thirsty; ***šuṣmû***, to allow to go thirsty. |
| *ṣ-m-d* | *ṣamādu*, to harness; ***ṣimdu***, bandaging; ***ṣimdatu***, regulation. |
| *š-ʾ-l* | *šâlu*, to ask; ***muštālu***, arbitrator. |
| *š-ʾ-ʾ* | ***šeʾû***, to search. |
| *š-ʾ-b* | *šâbu* B (*AHw šiābu*), to be old; ***šību***, old, witness (see *CAD* meaning 3; *AHw* meaning D). |
| *š-ʾ-m* 1 | ***šâmu* 1** (*AHw šâmu* I), to purchase; ***našūmu***, to be bought; ***šāyyimānu***, purchaser; ***šīmu***, sale. |
| *š-ʾ-m* 2 (*šīm*) | ***šâmu* 2** (*AHw šiāmu*) to determine; ***šāʾimu***, determining; ***mušīmu***, determining fate; ***šimtu***, destiny; ***tašīmtu***, authority. |
| *š-b-ʾ* | > *š-p-ʾ*. |
| *š-b-ḫ* | > *š-p-ḫ*. |

*š-b-r* — ***šebēru***, to break.
*š-d-l* — *šadālu*, to be broad; *šuddulu*, to enlarge; ***mušaddilu***, developing.
*š-k-k* — ***šakāku***, to harrow; ***maškakātu***, harrow.
*š-k-n* — ***šakānu***, to set; ***šākinu***, providing; ***šuškunu***, to have arranged; ***naškunu***, to be arranged; ***maškanu***, threshing place; ***šaknu***, provided with.
*š-l-ʾ* — ***šalû***, to submerge.
*š-l-l* — *šalālu*, to take into captivity; ***našlulu***, to be taken into captivity.
*š-l-m* — ***šalāmu***, to be safe; ***šullumu***, to reinstate; ***mušallimu***, bringing peace; ***šalamtu***, corpse; ***šulmāniš***, securely; ***šulmu***, well-being.
*š-m-ʾ* — ***šemû***, to hear; ***šēmû***, obeying; ***muštešmû***, one who is obeyed.
*š-n-ʾ* (*šnī*) — *šanû* 1, to repeat; ***šušnû***, to double; ***šanû*** 2, another; ***tašna***, twice as much.
*š-n-n* — *šanānu*, to strive; ***šāninu***, rival; ***šitannu*** (Gt-theme), striving.
*š-p-ʾ* — *šapû* C, to be silent; ***šuppû***, to silence; ***mušeppû***, silencing
*š-p-ʾ-l* — ***šupêlu***, to weaken.
*š-p-ḫ* — *šapāḫu*, to scatter; ***šuppuḫu***, to stir up.
*š-p-ṭ* — *šapāṭu* A, to issue orders; ***šipṭu***, decision.
*š-p-k* — ***šapāku***, to store; ***našpuku***, to be stored; ***našpaku***, granary; ***našpakutu***, storage.
*š-p-r* — *šapāru*, to commission someone to a task; ***šipru***, job, skill.
*š-q-ʾ* — ***šaqû***, to give to drink; ***mušesqû***, giving to drink; ***mašqītu***, watering place; ***šiqītu***, irrigation.
*š-q-l* — ***šaqālu***, to weigh out; ***šiqlu***, shekel.
*š-r-k* — ***šarāku***, to grant; ***šeriktu***, dowry.
*š-r-m* — *šarāmu* to cut to size; ***šurrumu***, to trim (or to cover) the horns of an ox.
*š-r-q* — ***šarāqu***, to steal; ***šarrāqānum***, thief; ***šarrāqu***, thief; ***šurqu***, stolen property.
*š-s-ʾ* — ***šasû***, to shout; ***šisītu***, call.
*š-ṭ-p* — *šaṭāpu*, to preserve life; ***šāṭipu***, caring.
*š-ṭ-r* — ***šaṭāru***, to inscribe; ***šaṭru***, inscribed.
*t-ʾ-r* — ***târu***, to return; ***turru***, to repay; ***mutēru***, returning.
*t-b-ʾ* — *tebû*, to attack; ***šutbû***, to remove; ***tībû***, attacking.
*t-b-k* — ***tabāku***, to pour out.
*t-b-l* — ***tabālu***, to carry away (probably a by-form of *abālu*, > *ʾ-b-l*).
*t-k-l* — *takālu* to trust; ***tukkulu***, to show reliability; ***tukultu***, faith.
*t-l-m* — ***šutlumu***, to bestow; ***talīmu***, devoted follower.
*t-m-ʾ* (*tmā*) — ***tamû***, to swear.

*t-m-ḫ* *tamāḫu*, to grasp; ***mutammiḫu***, grasping.

*t-r-ʾ* ***tarû***, to lead off.

*t-r-ṣ* *tarāṣu*, to reach out; ***šutruṣu***, to stretch; ***natruṣu***, to be stretched out.

*t-r-k* *tarāku*, to beat.

*ṭ-ʾ-b* (*ṭīb*) *ṭâbu* (*AHw ṭiābu*), to be good; ***ṭubbu***, to improve; ***muṭību***, making happy; ***ṭābu***, good.

*ṭ-b-ʾ* (*ṭbū*) ***ṭebû***, to sink; ***ṭubbû***, to cause to sink.

*ṭ-r-d* ***ṭarādu***, to send.

*ṭ-ḫ-ʾ* *ṭeḫû*, to be near; ***ṭuḫḫu***, to aggregate; ***ṭeḫḫu***, neighbour.

*ṭ-ḫ-d* *ṭaḫādu*, to be plentiful; *ṭuḫḫudu*, to make plentiful; ***muṭaḫ-ḫidu***, showing generosity.

*w-ʾ-r* *âru*, to advance (*AHw* 1471 *wâru*); ***u'uru***, to direct (see *CAD* s.v. *âru* A/2, 318).

*w-b-l* see also *t-b-l*; ***abālu***, to bring; ***bābilu***, bringing; ***šūbulu***, to remove completely from use; ***nābulu***, to be brought; ***biblu*** (A), marriage gift; *biblu* (B), flood-water (see *CAD*; cf. *AHw*, where only one lexeme is cited, with contrasting meanings, see s.v. 1 and 3); ***bubbulu***, flood; ***biltu***, rent; ***muttabbilu***, organizer (see *CAD* M/2, 302); ***šūbultu*** (= AHw *sēbultu*), consignment.

*w-l-d* ***alādu***, to give birth; ***ālidu***, progenitor; ***aldû***, seed-corn; ***tālittu***, young animal.

*w-p-ʾ* *apû*, to become visible; ***šūpû***, to display, make manifest; ***mušēpû***, making visible.

*w-q-r* *aqāru*, to become precious; *šūquru*, to hold in esteem; ***šūquru***, precious.

*w-r-q* *warāqu*, to become green; ***arqu***, green.

*w-s-m* *wasāmu*, to be associated with; ***simtu***, distinguishing symbol.

*w-ṣ-ʾ* ***aṣû***, to come out; ***šūṣû***, to bring out; ***mušēṣû***, bringing out.

*w-ṣ-b* *āṣibu*, to increase; ***ṣibtu***, interest.

*w-š-b* ***ašābu***, to dwell; ***šūšubu***, to allow to dwell; ***ašbu***, resident; ***aššābu***, occupant; ***šubtu***, dwelling.

*w-š-m* *wašāmu*, to mark (?); ***šimtu***, cattle-mark.

*w-š-r* *AHw wašāru*, to abase oneself (cf. *CAD ašāru* B, to be humble); ***uššuru*** (forthcoming in *CAD*, see *ašāru* C, to release), to prove innocent; ***utaššuru***, to be proved innocent, go away free (see *AHw* s.v. *wašārum* Dt, 2b); ***ašru* 2**, humble;

*w-t-r* *atāru*, to be much; ***utturu***, to exceed; ***šūturu* 2**, to make excellent; ***mušātiru***, making excellent; ***šūturu* 1**, exceptional; ***atru***, extra.

| | |
|---|---|
| *y-ʾ-l* | *eʾēlu*, to make a binding agreement (see *AHw*); ***eʾiltu***, debt. |
| *y-d-ʾ* | ***idû***, to know; ***uddû***, to find out; ***šūdû***, to make known; ***mudû***, acquainted with; ***mūdûtu***, knowledge. |
| *y-n-q* | *enēqu*, to suck; *šūnuqu*, to suckle; ***mušēniqtu***, nurse. |
| *y-š-r* | *ešēru*, to be straight; ***šūšuru***, to show straightforwardness; ***mušūšeru***, directing; ***muštēšeru***, keeping straight; ***mīšāru***, justice. |
| *z-ʾ-r* | ***zêru***, to hate; ***zāʾiru***, foe. |
| *z-ʾ-z* | ***zâzu***, to share; ***zittu***, share. |
| *z-b-ʾ* | *zebû*, to sacrifice; ***zību***, offering. |
| *z-k-r* | ***zakāru***, to state; ***nazkuru***, to be stated; ***zikru***, name. |
| *z-n-n* | *zanānu*, to care for; ***zāninu***, caring. |
| *z-p-r* | ***zapāru***, to leak, become rotten (of a boat, see *AHw*); cf. *CAD ṣabaru*, to list to one side; > *ṣ-b-r*. |
| *z-q-p* | ***zaqāpu***, to plant. |
| *z-r-ʾ* | *zarû*, to sow seed; ***zēru***, seed. |

# VERBAL FORMS

While it would have been too large a task to provide a descriptive grammar of the language of CH within these pages, a simple listing of the verbal forms that are actually attested may be a help in showing the literal meaning of certain sentences that has often had to be obscured in translation.

Whereas in the Glossary the derived themes of the verb (D, Š and N) were analysed as separate items, here they are grouped together with the basic G-theme (provided that the basic theme is actually attested in Akkadian). Secondary and tertiary themes (forms with *-t-* and *-tan-*) are separated, but without any notes on the function of the infix (such notes properly belong to a separate full grammatical commentary on the text).

Items are presented according to the standard order of the derived themes (G, D, Š, N). Within this framework the formal order adopted is: infinitive (inf.), stative (stv.), imperative (impv.), preterite (prt.), present-future (prs.); participles are excluded from this table. Within this scheme alphabetical ordering has been used, which normally (but not always) means that forms with additional affixes come after those without them.

***abālu***, to bring

| | | |
|---|---|---|
| G prt. | *lūblam* | L9 |
| | *ublam* | L138; 149; 156; 168 |
| | *ublu* | L163 |
| | *ublū* | L54 |
| prs. | *ubbalu* | §5.15 |
| | *ubbalū* | L169 |
| Gt | *itbal* | L45; 48 |
| | *itbalam* | L9; 9; 10; 10; 11; 45; 48; 169; 169 |
| Gtn | *attabbalšināti* | E7 |
| ***šūbulu*** | | |
| Š stv. | *šūbula* | L112, vnt.; L112, vnt. |
| | *šūbulu* | L112; 112 |

| | | |
|---|---|---|
| | *šūbuluma* | L112 |
| prt. | *ušābil* | L160; 161; 112, vnt. |
| | *ušābilaššu* | L112, vnt. |
| | *ušābilšu* | L112 |
| | *ušābilu* | L159 |
| Št | *uštābil* | L53; 55; 56; 160, vnt. |
| ***nābālu*** | | |
| N prt. | *ibbablušum* | L159; 160 |
| *abāru* | > *ubburu.* | |
| ***abātu***, to flee | | |
| ***nābutu*** | | |
| N prt. | *innabitu* | L136 |
| Nt | *ittābit* | L136 |
| ***adāru***, to fear | | |
| G prt. | *īdurma* | E19 |
| ***agāru***, to hire | | |
| G prt. | *īgur* | L242; 257; 258; 261; 268; 269; 270; 271; 272; 273; 275; 276; 277 |
| | *īgurma* | L26; 237; 239; 244; 245; 246; 247; 248; 249; 253 |
| | *īguru* | L249 |
| prs. | *iggar* | L274 |
| ***aḫāzu***, to seize | | |
| G inf. | *aḫāzim* | L144; 145; 148 |
| prt. | *aḫzu* | L166 |
| | *īḫuz* | L162; 166; 166 |
| | *īḫuzma* | L128; 144; 145; 146; 148; 163; 167; 175; 176a |
| | *īḫuzuši* | L176a |
| prs. | *aḫḫaz* | L159 |
| | *iḫḫassi* | L137; 156; 172 |
| | *iḫḫaz* | L141; 144; 145; 148; 161; 167 |
| | *iḫḫazu* | L151 |
| | *taḫḫaz* | L161 |
| | *taḫḫazani* | L142 |
| Gt | *ītaḫazma* | L167 |
| ***šūḫuzu*** | | |
| Š inf. | *šūḫuzim* | P22 |
| | *šūḫuzu* | P22, vnt. |
| prt. | *ušaḫḫazūšu* | L166 |
| Št | *uštāḫissu* | L188; 189 |
| | *uštāḫiz* | E19 |

***akālu***, to eat

| | | |
|---|---|---|
| G inf. | *akālim* | L133a; 134; 135 |
| prs. | *ikkal* | L171b; 178; 180; 181 |
| ***šūkulu*** | | |
| Š inf. | *šūkulim* | L57 |
| prt. | *ušākilu* | L57; 58 |
| Št | *uštākil* | L57; 58 |

***alādu***, to give birth

| | | |
|---|---|---|
| G stv. | *waldat* | L158 |
| prt. | *ūldu* | L146 |
| | *uldušum* | L119; 137; 138; 170; 171a |
| | *ūlid* | L147 |
| | *ūlissum* | L167; 170 |
| | *ūlissumma* | L162 |
| Gt | *ittalad* | L135; 146; 167; 173; 174; 175 |

***alāku***, to go

| | | |
|---|---|---|
| G inf. | *alākam* | L28 |
| | *alākišu* | L103; 250 |
| | *alākšu* | L26 |
| prt. | *illik* | L26 |
| | *illiku* | L25; 100; 101; 102 |
| | *lillikma* | E11 |
| prs. | *illak* | L2; 27; 28; 29; 30; 31; 40; 182 |
| | *illakā* | E22 |
| | *illakū* | L135 |
| Gt | *ittalak* | L12; 27; 30; 162; 163; 167; 176 |
| | *ittalkamma* | L280 |
| | *ittalku* | L30; 165; 166; 167; 170; 171a; 178; 179; 180; 181; 182; 183; 184 |
| Gtn | *ittallak* | L142; 149; 191; 191; 193 |

***alālu***, to hang

| | | |
|---|---|---|
| G prs. | *iḫallalūšu* | L21; 227 |
| ***naḫlulu*** | | |
| Nt | *ittaḫlalū* | L58 |

***amāru***, to see

| | | |
|---|---|---|
| G prt. | *līmur* | E11 |
| prs. | *immarūma* | L9 |
| Gt | *ītamar* | L100; 101; 102 |

***apālu***, to be responsible

| | | |
|---|---|---|
| G inf. | *apālam* | L256 |
| prs. | *ippal* | L100; 206; 279 |
| | *ippalma* | L66 |

| | | | |
|---|---|---|---|
| | | *ippalū* | L152 |
| | ***uppulu*** | | |
| | D prs. | *uppal* | L178 |
| ***apû***, to be visible | | | |
| | ***šūpû*** | | |
| | Š inf. | *šūpîm* | P3 |
| | stv. | *šūpât* | E24 |
| | prt. | *ušēpu, ušīpu* | P20, vnt. |
| | | *ušūpi'u* | P20 |
| | Št | *lištēpi* | E10 |
| ***arāku***, to be long | | | |
| | ***urruku*** | | |
| | D prt. | *lirrik* | E18 |
| ***arāru***, to curse | | | |
| | G prt. | *līrur* | E19; 27 |
| | | *līruršuma* | E32 |
| | | *līrurū* | E31 |
| ***arû***, to lead | | | |
| | G prt. | *līrūšu* | E27 |
| | Gtn | *littarrūšu* | E22 |
| *âru* > *u''uru* | | | |
| ***aṣû***, to go out | | | |
| | G inf. | *waṣâm* | L69+c |
| | | *waṣêm* | L141; 172 |
| | | *waṣêmma* | P3 |
| | stv. | *waṣiāt* | L143 |
| | | *waṣīma* | L142 |
| | prs. | *uṣiām* | L4 |
| | | *ūṣiamma* | L3 |
| | | *uṣṣī* | L172 |
| | ***šūṣû*** | | |
| | Š inf. | *šūṣîm* | L172 |
| | stv. | *šuṣâ* | E17 |
| | prt. | *lišāṣiaššuma* | E30 |
| | | *ušēṣīma* | L42; 44 |
| | | *ušēṣišināšim* | E3 |
| | | *ušēṣu* | [L69+c] |
| | Št | *ušeṣṣûšu* | L154 |
| | | *uštēṣi* | L15 |
| | | *uštēṣiam* | L16 |
| ***ašābu***, to dwell | | | |
| G | inf. | *wašābam* | L149 |

| | | |
|---|---|---|
| stv. | *ašbumma* | L69+c (later form for expected *wašbumma*) |
| | *wašbat* | L110; 130; 141; 151 |
| | *wašibma* | L112 |
| prs. | *uššab* | L5; 141; 171b |
| | *uššamma* | L148 |
| ***šūšubu*** | | |
| Š prt. | *ušešibma* | [L69+c] |

*ašāru* C > *uššuru*

***ašāšu***, to be in distress

| | | |
|---|---|---|
| ***uššušu*** | | |
| D inf. | *uššušim* | L116 |

***atāru***, to exceed

| | | |
|---|---|---|
| ***utturu*** | | |
| D prs. | *uwatterma* | §5.10 |
| ***šūturu*** | | |
| Š inf. | *šūturu* | E9 |
| prt. | *ušāterūšu* | P2 |

*balāṣu* > *palāsu*

***balāṭu***, to live

| | | |
|---|---|---|
| G stv. | *balṭat* | L148; 171b; 178; 180; 181 |
| ***bulluṭu*** | | |
| D prs. | *uballaṭ* | L129; 129 |
| Dt | *ubtalliṭ* | L215; 215; 221; 224 |

***balû***, to come, to an end

| | | |
|---|---|---|
| G prs. | *ibellû* | E30 |
| ***bullû*** | | |
| D inf. | *bullîm* | L25 |
| prt. | *ubelli* | E5 |

***banû***, to beget

| | | |
|---|---|---|
| G prt. | *ibni* | E29 |
| | *ibniušu* | P6 |

*baqāru* > *paqāru*

***bâru***, to be certain

| | | |
|---|---|---|
| ***burru*** | | |
| D prs. | *ubârma* | L23; 120; 240 |
| | *ubâršuma* | L126 |
| Dt | *ūtebbir* | L126 |

***bašû***, to exist

| | | |
|---|---|---|
| G prs. | *ibašši* | L48; 32; 32; 32; 134; 135; 151; 151; 139; 133a; 134; 135 |
| | *ibaššīma* | L48 |

| | | |
|---|---|---|
| | *ibaššīšum* | L66 |
| | *ibaššû* | L5; §5.15; E12 |
| ***šubšû*** | | |
| Š inf. | *šubšâm* | E20 |
| prt. | *ušabši* | E22 |
| | *ušabšû* | L267 |
| Št prt. | *uštabši* | L42; 49; 52;144; 255; 267 |
| ***nabšû*** | | |
| N prs. | *ibbaššû* | L5; 46; 49; 49; 50; 66; 66; 66; 77+f; E14 |
| Nt | *ittabši* | L48; 120; 152; 266 |
| ***dâku***, to kill | | |
| G prt. | *iddūk* | L266 |
| | *iddūkšu* | L244 |
| prs. | *idukkū* | L116; 210; 230 |
| | *idukkūšu* | §5.3a |
| | *idukkūšuma* | L21; 227 |
| ***šudūku*** | | |
| Š prt. | *ušdīk* | L153 |
| ***nadūku*** | | |
| N prs. | *iddâk* | L1; 2; 3; 6; 6; 7; 8; 9; 10; 11; 14; 15; 16; 19; 22; 26; 33; 34; 76+f; §5.3b; 109; 130; 229 |
| ***damāmu***, to weep | | |
| Gt | *liddammam* | E30 |
| ***damāqu***, to be good | | |
| ***dummuqu*** | | |
| D prt. | *lidammiqū* | E13 |
| ***danānu***, to be strong | | |
| ***dunnunu*** | | |
| D inf. | *dunnunim* | L53 |
| impv. | *dunnin* | L68+b |
| prt. | *udanninma* | L53; 229 |
| | *udanninuma* | L232 |
| prs. | *udannan* | L233 |
| | *udannanma* | L235 |
| ***dânu***, to judge | | |
| G inf. | *di'ānim* | E8 |
| prt. | *adīnu* | E14; 15; 19 |
| | *idīn* | L5; E23 |
| | *idīnu* | L5 |
| | *lidīn* | E16 |

***dâṣu***, to trick

| | | |
|---|---|---|
| G prs. | *idāṣma* | L227 |

***dâšu***, to thresh

| | | |
|---|---|---|
| G inf. | *di'āšim* | L268; 269; 270 |

***dekû***, to arrange

| | | |
|---|---|---|
| G prt. | *idkē*(!) | L11 |

***duppuru***, to be absent

| | | |
|---|---|---|
| Dt | *uddappir* | L30 |
| | *uddappirma* | L31 |

***ebēbu***, to be pure

***ubbubu***

| | | |
|---|---|---|
| D prs. | *ubbabma* | L266, vnt. |
| | *ubbamma* | L266 |
| Dt | *ūtebbibaššuma* | L2 |

***egû***, to be negligent

| | | |
|---|---|---|
| G prt. | *ēgu* | E2 |
| | *īgīma* | L236; 237 |
| | *īguma* | L125; 267 |
| Gt | *ītegīma* | L105 |

***elû***, to ascend

| | | |
|---|---|---|
| Gt | *ītelli* | L35; 37; 67+e; §5.7; [5.10]; [5.13]; 5.14; L113; 116; 177 |
| | *ītelianim* | L58 |
| | *ītellīma* | [§4.12] |

***ullû***

| | | |
|---|---|---|
| D prt. | *ullû* | E8 |

***šūlû***

| | | |
|---|---|---|
| Št | *uštēliašši* | L238 |

***emēdu***, to impose

| | | |
|---|---|---|
| G prt. | *līmussuma* | E24 |
| prs. | *immidū* | L172 |

***nenmudu***

| | | |
|---|---|---|
| N prt. | *innemdū* | L176a; 176a; 176b |

***enēšu***, to be weak

***unnušu***

| | | |
|---|---|---|
| Dt | *ūtenniš* | L254(!) |

***enû***, to change

| | | |
|---|---|---|
| G inf. | *enêm* | L5 |
| prs. | *inni* | L52 |
| Gt | *itēne* | L5 |

***epēsu***, to be a nuisance

***uppusu***

| | | |
|---|---|---|
| D prs. | *uppas* | L47; §5.15 |
| ***epēšu***, to do | | |
| G inf. | *epēšim* | L42 |
| impv. | *epuš* | L68+b |
| prt. | *īpuš* | L191 |
| | *īpušma* | L215; 218; 219; 224; 225; 228; 229; 233 |
| | *īpušu* | L148; 229; 232 |
| | *īpušū* | L176a |
| prs. | *ippeš* | L232 |
| | *ippešma* | L62; 63; [67] |
| | *ippešū* | L117 |
| | *ippušu* | §4.12 |
| Gt | *itēpuš* | [L68+a] |
| ***erēbu***, to enter | | |
| G inf. | *erēbim* | L177 |
| prt. | *īrubma* | L176 |
| | *īrubu* | L152;173 |
| prs. | *irrub* | L133a; 134; 177 |
| | *irrubu* | L151; 177 |
| Gt | *īterub* | L110; 133b; 136 |
| | *īterubma* | L135 |
| ***šūrubu*** | | |
| Š prs. | *ušerreb* | L145, vnt. |
| | *ušerrebši* | L145 |
| ***erēšu* A**, to demand | | |
| G prt. | *irriš* | L30 |
| ***erēšu* B**, to plough | | |
| G inf. | *erēšam* | L47 |
| | *erēšim* | L49; 253 |
| impv. | *ērišma* | L49 |
| prt. | *īrišma* | L43 |
| prs. | *irrišma* | L47 |
| ***esēpu***, to gather | | |
| G impv. | *esip* | L49 |
| ***esēru***, to press for payment | | |
| G prt. | *īsiršuma* | L66 |
| ***eṣēdu***, to harvest | | |
| G prs. | *iṣṣid* | L57 |
| ***ešēru***, to go straight | | |
| ***uššuru*** | | |
| Dt | *ūtaššar* | L20; 103; 130; 249; 227 |

| | | | |
|---|---|---|---|
| | ***šūšuru*** | | |
| | Št inf. | *šutēšur* | P22 |
| | | *šutēšuram* | E15 |
| | | *šutēšurim* | E8; 8 |
| | prt. | *lištēšer* | E16 |
| | | *uštēšer* | E12 |
| ***ešû***, to confuse | | | |
| | G prt. | *līši* | E23 |
| ***etēqu***, to pass by | | | |
| | ***šūtuqu*** | | |
| | Š prt. | *ūšetteq* | L118 |
| ***eṭēru***, to remove | | | |
| | G prt. | *līṭeršu* | E19; 24; 25 |
| | | *līṭeršuma* | E22; 29 |
| ***ezēbu***, to leave | | | |
| | G inf. | *ezēbim* | L137 |
| | | *ezēbša* | L141; 141 |
| | prt. | *īzib* | L61 |
| | | *īzibšim* | L150 |
| | prs. | *izzib* | L172; 138 |
| | | *izzibši* | L148; 138; 141 |
| | ***šūzubu*** | | |
| | Š prt. | *ušēzib* | L5 |
| | | *ušezzebūšunūti* | L177 |
| | Št | *uštēzib* | L151 |
| ***gamālu***, to care for | | | |
| | G prt. | *igmilu* | P17 |
| ***gamāru***, to complete | | | |
| | G prt. | *igmurma* | L61 |
| ***gullubu***, to shave | | | |
| | D prt. | *ugallib* | L226 |
| | | *ugallibu* | L227 |
| | prs. | *ugallabū* | L127 |
| | Dt | *ugdallib* | L227 |
| ***ḫabālu***, to exploit | | | |
| | G inf. | *ḫabālim* | P3; E8 |
| | Gt | *iḫtabal* | L34 |
| ***ḫabāšu***, to shatter | | | |
| | G prt. | *liḫbuš* | E28 |
| ***ḫabātu***, to rob | | | |
| | G prt. | *iḫbutma* | L22 |

| | | |
|---|---|---|
| ***naḫbutu*** | | |
| N prt. | *iḫḫabtu* | L23 |
| ***ḫalāqu***, to disappear | | |
| G inf. | *ḫalāq* | E20; 21; 23 |
| | *ḫalāqišu* | E20 |
| stv. | *ḫaliq* | L126 |
| | *ḫaliqma* | L126 |
| | *ḫalqu* | L9; [68+b]; 126; 240 |
| prs. | *iḫalliqu* | E24 |
| Gt | *iḫtaliq* | L20; 125 |
| ***ḫulluqu*** | | |
| D inf. | *ḫulluqim* | P3 |
| prt. | *liḫalliq* | E25 |
| | *uḫalliqu* | L53; 125; 232; 237 |
| Dt | *uḫtalliq* | L232; 236; 237; 263 |
| ***ḫarāṣu***, to deduct | | |
| G prs. | *iḫarraṣma* | L164 |
| ***šuḫruṣu*** | | |
| Št | *uštaḫriṣma* | §5.12 |
| ***ḫâru***, to choose | | |
| G prt. | *iḫīrma* | L155; 156 |
| ***ḫâṭu***, to discover | | |
| G prs. | *iḫiāṭ* | L186 |
| ***ḫepû***, to break | | |
| G prs. | *iḫeppe* | §5.11 |
| ***neḫepû*** | | |
| N prt. | *iḫḫepi* | L37 |
| ***ḫuppudu*** (D), to blind | | |
| D prs. | *uḫappadū* | L196 |
| Dt | *uḫtapda*(!) | L220, for *uḫtappid* |
| | *uḫtappid* | L196; 198; 199; 218; 247 |
| ***īdû***, to know | | |
| G inf. | *idû* | L206; 227 |
| prt. | *idī* | §5.7 |
| | *idû* | P14; §5.3b |
| | *idûma* | L130 |
| ***uddû*** | | |
| D prt. | *uweddīma* | L193 |
| Dt | *ūteddi* | L280 |
| ***šūdû*** | | |
| Š prt. | *ušēdīšumma* | L251 |

***itūlu***, to copulate

| | | |
|---|---|---|
| G inf. | *itūlim* | L129 |
| | *utūlim* | L131; 132 |
| prt. | *ittatīl* | L156; 157 |
| | *ittatīlma* | L130; 155 |

***izuzzu***, to stand

| | | |
|---|---|---|
| D inf. | *uzzuzim* | L253 |
| prs. | *izzazzu* | P5 |
| ***šūzuzzu*** | | |
| Š prt. | *lišzīz* | E26 |

***kabālu***, to be paralysed

| | | |
|---|---|---|
| ***kubbulu*** | | |
| D prt. | *ukabbilšīma* | L130 |

***kabātu***, to be important

| | | |
|---|---|---|
| G stv. | *kabtat* | E21 |

***kalû***, to retain

| | | |
|---|---|---|
| Gt | *iktalāšu* | L19 |

***kânu***, to be firm

| | | |
|---|---|---|
| ***kunnu*** | | |
| D prt. | *ukinnuma* | E1 |
| | *ukinnūšum* | P2 |
| prs. | *ukânma* | L106; 107; 116 |
| | *ukannūšima* | L108; 133b; 141; 194 |
| | *ukannūšuma* | L5; 42; 112 (error for *ukânšuma*); 113; 124; 255; 265 |
| | *ukânšūma* | L282 |
| Dt | *ukīn* | E8 |
| | *uktīn* | L3; 127 |
| | *uktīnšu* | L1; 2 |

***karābu***, to pray

| | | |
|---|---|---|
| G prt. | *likrubam* | E12 |

***karāṣu***, to snap off

| | | |
|---|---|---|
| ***kurruṣu*** | | |
| Dt | *uktarissu* | L161 |

***kasû***, to bind

| | | |
|---|---|---|
| G prs. | *ikassûšuma* | L155 |
| | *ikassûšunūtima* | L129 |

***kašādu***, to achieve

| | | |
|---|---|---|
| G prt. | *ikšud* | E12 |
| | *ikšudu* | P16 |
| | *likšudašu* | E32 |
| | *likšussu* | E23 |

| | | |
|---|---|---|
| Gt | *iktašassu* | L2 |
| | *iktašdam* | L27;135 |
| ***šukšudu*** | | |
| Š prt. | *ušakšidu* | P10 |
| | *ušakšidušu* | P10, vnt. |
| Št | *uštakšidaššu* | L32 |
| ***katātu***, to be low | | |
| ***šutaktutu*** | | |
| Št prt. | *uštaktitma* | E12 |
| ***kullu***, to hold | | |
| D prt. | *ukīl* | E7 |
| ***kullumu***, to explain | | |
| D prt. | *likallimšu* | E11 |
| | *likallimšuma* | E15 |
| | *ukallam* | L122 |
| ***lamādu***, to learn | | |
| G prt. | *ilmassi* | L155 |
| | *ilmassima* | L156 |
| prs. | *ilammadu* | E30 |
| Gt | *iltamad* | L154 |
| ***lapātu***, to touch | | |
| ***šulputu*** | | |
| Š inf. | *šulput* | E21 |
| ***lemēnu***, to be evil | | |
| ***lummunu*** | | |
| D prt. | *lilemmin* | E21 |
| ***leqû***, to take | | |
| G inf. | *leqêm* | L106; 113 |
| prt. | *ilqe* | §5.10; L120; 186 |
| | *ilqēma* | L49; 66; 5.15; L106; 185; 188; 254 |
| | *ilqû* | L47; 49; 51; §4.12; 5.12; L100; 101; 106; 107; 113; 120 |
| | *ilqušu* | L186 |
| | *ilqûšuma* | L190; 191 |
| prs. | *ileqqe* | L9; 9; 10; 12; 47; 60; 64; 66; §5.9; 5.9; 5.10; L104; 111; 125; 170; 172; 176a; 176a; 176a; 176b; 176b; 215; 216; 278 |
| | *ileqqēma* | L49; 50; 66; 142; 165; 171b; 172 |
| | *ileqqū* | L174 |
| | *ileqqūma* | L167; 178 |

| | | |
|---|---|---|
| | *ilteqe* | L34; 34; 105; 113 |
| | *ilteqēma* | §5.11; 5.12 |
| ***le'û***, to be capable | | |
| G prt. | *ile'i* | L28; 29; 54; 256; E15 |
| ***madādu***, to measure | | |
| G prs. | *imaddad* | L44; 56; 55; 58; 62; [65]; 63; 255 |
| ***magāru***, to agree | | |
| G prs. | *imaggarūšu* | L144 |
| Gt | *immaggar* | L66 |
| | *imtagar* | L149 |
| | *imtagarma* | L57 |
| ***maḫāru***, to be comparable | | |
| G inf. | *maḫārim* | P15 |
| stv. | *maḫar* | E28 |
| | *maḫir* | L264 |
| | *maḫru* | L165 |
| prt. | *imḫur* | L7; §5.13 |
| | *imḫurma* | L33 |
| | *imḫuru* | L6; 254(!); §5.13 |
| prs. | *imaḫḫar* | L75+e |
| | *imaḫḫaršu* | L266 |
| Gt | *imtaḫar* | L45; 46; 108; 108 |
| ***šumḫuru*** | | |
| Št | *uštamaḫḫar* | L145 |
| | *uštatamḫir* | L146 |
| ***maḫāṣu***, to fight | | |
| G inf. | *maḫāṣim* | L116; 245; 211 |
| | *maḫāṣišu* | L207 |
| prt. | *amḫaṣu* | L206 |
| | *imḫassuma* | L249 |
| | *imḫaṣma* | L209; 213; 240 |
| prs. | *imaḫḫaṣ* | L43; 44 |
| Gt | *imtaḫaṣ* | L195; 202; 203; 204; 205 |
| | *imtaḫaṣma* | L206 |
| ***namḫuṣu*** | | |
| N prs. | *immaḫḫaṣ* | L202 |
| ***malû***, to be full | | |
| G prt. | *imlāma* | L278 |
| ***mullû*** | | |
| D prt. | *limallīšuma* | E27 |

| | | |
|---|---|---|
| ***manû***, to count | | |
| G prs. | *imannûma* | L100 |
| | *imannûši* | L146 |
| Gt | *imtanûšu* | L190 |
| | *imtanûšunūti* | L170 |
| ***maqātu***, to fall | | |
| G prt. | *imqutma* | L229 |
| | *imqutu* | L232; 232 |
| Gt | *imtaqut* | L278 |
| ***šumqutu*** | | |
| Š prt. | *lišamqit* | E27 |
| ***marāru***, to hoe | | |
| G prs. | *imarrar* | L44 |
| ***maṣû***, to be equal | | |
| ***šumṣû*** | | |
| Š prt. | *ušamṣīši* | L178 |
| Št | *uštamṣīši* | L179 |
| ***mašāru***, to drag | | |
| Gtn | *imtanaššarūšu* | L256 |
| ***mâtu***, to die | | |
| G prt. | *imtūt* | L115; 116; 173; 194; 207; 210; 212; 214; 249 |
| ***šumūtu*** | | |
| Št | *uštamīt* | L218; 219; 225; 229; 230; 231; 245; 250; 251 |
| ***maṭû***, to be little | | |
| ***muṭṭû*** | | |
| Dt | *umtaṭṭi* | L65; 108; 264 |
| ***šumṭû*** | | |
| Š prt. | *ušamṭa* | L141; 143 |
| | *ušamṭâši* | L142 |
| ***mêšu***, to disdain | | |
| G prt. | *imēšma* | E19 |
| ***nabalkutu***, to overwhelm | | |
| N prs. | *ibbalakkatūnim* | L68+b |
| ***nabû***, to name | | |
| G stv. | *nabiat* | E19 |
| prt. | *ibbiū* | P2 |
| | *ibbû* | P3 |
| | *ibbûninnima* | E6 |
| *na'butu* > *abātu* B | | |

***nadānu***, to give

| | | |
|---|---|---|
| G inf. | *anadānim* | §5.2 (crasis for *ana nadānim*) |
| | *nadānam* | L178; 179 |
| | *nadānim* | L8; 66; §5.2; [L100] |
| prt. | *iddin* | L41; 46; 49; 50; 60; 64; §5.9; 5.9; 5.13; 5.14; L77+f; 104; 111; 117 |
| | *iddinam* | L9; E2; 4 |
| | *iddinma* | L45; 66; 69+c; §5.13; L100; 112; 112; 123; 124; 125; 144; 146; 160; 161; 194; 236 |
| | *iddinu* | L34; 35; 67+a; §5.7 (uncertain); §5.10; 5.13; [5.13]; 5.14; L105; 112; 113; 116; 123; 125; 159 |
| | *iddinūma* | L27 |
| | *iddinuši* | L171b, vnt. |
| | *iddinušim* | L171b; 172; 178 |
| | *iddinušum* | L9; 10; [69+c]; 107; 107; 165; 171b; 172 |
| | *iddinušumma* | L125 |
| | *iddišši* | L183; 184 |
| | *iddiššim* | L172 |
| prs. | *anaddikkum* | L160 |
| | *inaddin* | L5; 8; 38; 39; 40; 42; 43; 48; 49; 51; 57; 64; 67+a; 67+a; §5.15; L101; 106; 107; 112; 118; 120; 121; 122; 122; 124; 126; 150; 150; 171b; 178; 179; 182; 217; 221; 222; 223; 224; 225; 231; 235; 238; 242/3; 247; 248; 251; 252; 259; 260; 264; 267; 271; 272; 273; 273; [274]; 276; 277 |
| | *inaddinma* | L178; 281 |
| | *inaddinu* | L104;122 |
| | *inaddinū* | L177 |
| | *inaddinūma* | L54 |
| | *inaddinūši* | L184 |
| | *inaddinūšimma* | L137; 178 |
| | *inaddišši* | L146; 147 |
| | *inaddiššim* | L138; 139; 140 |
| | *inaddiššum* | L17; 67+a; 191; 228; 234; 239; 257; 258; 261 |
| | *inaddiššumma* | L191 |

| | | |
|---|---|---|
| Gt | *ittadin* | L34; 119; 255; 265 |
| | *ittadinma* | L102 |
| | *ittadnūšimma* | L178 |
| Gtn | *ittandin* | L117; 118 |
| ***nandunu*** | | |
| N prt. | *innaddin* | L32; 36 |
| | *innaddinma* | L29 |
| | *innaddinšum* | L30, vnt. |
| | *innaddinšumma* | L31, vnt. |
| | *innaddiššum* | L30 |
| | *innaddiššumma* | L28; 31 |
| | *innadnu* | L137 |
| | *innadnušum* | L41; 62; 112; 263; 264; 265 |
| ***nadû***, to knock down | | |
| G stv. | *nadû* | L2 |
| prt. | *addi* | E2 |
| | *iddīma* | L1; 2; 30; 44; 53; 55; 58; 136 |
| | *iddû* | L2; 43 |
| prs. | *inaddû* | L200 |
| | *inaddûši* | L108; 133b; 143 |
| | *inaddûšu* | L155 |
| | *inaddûšunūti* | L129 |
| Gt | *ittadi* | L43; 200; 201 |
| Gtn | *littaddi* | E27 |
| ***šuddû*** | | |
| Št | *uštaddīši* | L209; 211; 213 |
| | *uštaddīšu* | L103 |
| ***nandû*** | | |
| N prt. | *innadū* | L62 |
| prs. | *innaddi* | L25 |
| *nagāru* > *nakāru* | | |
| ***naḫašu***, to prosper | | |
| G prt. | *iḫḫiša* | E7 |
| ***nāḫu***, to be still | | |
| ***nuḫḫu*** | | |
| D prs. | *unaḫḫušu* | E30 |
| ***nakāpu***, to toss | | |
| G prt. | *ikkipma* | L250; 251 |
| ***nakāru***, to argue | | |
| G prt. | *ikkiru* | L107; 124 |

| | | |
|---|---|---|
| Gt | *ittakir* | L106; 120 |
| | *ittakiršu* | L107; 124 |
| | *ittakrūšu* | L123 |
| ***nukkuru*** | | |
| D prt. | *unakkir* | E14; 18 |
| Dt | *utakkaru* | E20; 32 |
| | *uttakkir* | L265; E19 |
| ***nakāsu***, to cut | | |
| G prt. | *ikkis* | L59 |
| prs. | *inakkis* | L282 |
| | *inakkisū* | L192; 194; 195; 205; 218; 226; 253 |
| Gt | *ittakis* | L246; 248 |
| ***namāru***, to be bright | | |
| G inf. | *nawārim* | E20 |
| ***nummuru*** | | |
| D inf. | *nuwwurim* | P3 |
| ***napāḫu***, to light a fire | | |
| ***nanpuḫu*** | | |
| N prt. | *innapiḫma* | L25 |
| ***napāšu***, to be relaxed | | |
| ***nuppušu*** | | |
| D prt. | *linappišma* | E11 |
| ***naqāru***, to pull apart | | |
| G prs. | *inaqqarma* | L235 |
| ***nasāḫu***, to tear out | | |
| G inf. | *nasāḫ* | E23 |
| | *nasāḫim* | L168; 168; 169; 191 |
| prt. | *assuḫ* | E4 |
| | *lissuḫ* | E16 |
| | *lissuḫšu* | E23 |
| prs. | *anassaḫ* | L168 |
| | *inassaḫ* | L168; 169 |
| | *inassaḫū* | L193 |
| Gt | *ittasaḫ* | L248 (or read *ittasak*) |
| ***nansuḫu*** | | |
| N prs. | *innassaḫ* | L158 |
| | *innassaḫu* | E30 |
| ***nasāku* A**, to throw away | | |
| ***šussuku*** | | |
| Š prt. | *ušassik* | E14; 18 |
| ***nasāku* B**, to wound | | |
| Gt prt. | *ittasak* | L248 (or read *ittasaḫ*) |

| | | |
|---|---|---|
| ***nasāqu***, to choose | | |
| G prs. | *inassaqma* | L60; 170 |
| ***naṣāru***, to watch | | |
| G stv. | *naṣratma* | L142; 143 |
| prt. | *iṣṣurma* | L133b |
| | *liṣṣur* | E14 |
| prs. | *inaṣṣar* | [133a] |
| | *inaṣṣarma* | L58 |
| | *inaṣṣarū* | L177 |
| ***našû***, to carry | | |
| G stv. | *našû* | L103 |
| prt. | *iššīma* | L25; 181 |
| Gtn | *ittanašši* | L4; 13 |
| | *ittanaššīši* | L148; 178 |
| ***naṭālu***, to see | | |
| ***šuṭṭulu*** | | |
| Š prt. | *lišaṭṭilšu* | E24 |
| ***nāṭu***, to hit | | |
| ***šuṭṭû*** | | |
| Š prt. | *lišaṭṭīšuma* | E29 |
| ***neḫelṣu***, to slip | | |
| ***šuḫluṣu*** | | |
| Š prt. | *lišḫelṣi* | E23 |
| ***nepû***, to seize | | |
| G prt. | *ippēma* | L115 |
| Gt | *ittepe* | L114; 241 |
| ***palāsu***, to look at | | |
| ***pullusu*** | | |
| Dt | *uptallisma* | L159 |
| ***palāšu***, to break into | | |
| G prt. | *ipluš* | L21 |
| prs. | *ipallašūnim* | L68+b |
| ***paqādu***, to entrust | | |
| G prt. | *ipqissum* | L253 |
| prs. | *ipaqqidūma* | L177 |
| ***paqāru***, to claim. | | |
| G prs. | *ipaqqarūši* | L150; 179 |
| ***napquru*** | | |
| N | *ippaqqar* | L118; 185; 187; 188 |
| ***parāsu***, to decide | | |
| G inf. | *parāsim* | E8 |

| | | | |
|---|---|---|---|
| | prt. | *aprusu* | E14; 15 |
| | | *iprus* | L5 |
| | | *liprus* | E16 |
| | prs. | *iparrasūma* | L168; 172; 177 |
| | ***naprusu*** | | |
| | N prs. | *ipparrasma* | L18; 142 |
| ***pasāsu***, to annul | | | |
| | ***pussusu*** | | |
| | Dt prt. | *uptassis* | E19 |
| ***pašāḫu***, to soothe | | | |
| | G prs. | *ipaššeḫū* | E30 |
| ***pašāru***, to trade | | | |
| | G inf. | *pašārim* | L104 |
| ***pašāṭu***, to remove | | | |
| | G prt. | *ipšiṭma* | E19 |
| ***paṭāru***, to redeem | | | |
| | G inf. | *paṭārim* | L32 |
| | | *paṭārišu* | L32; 32 |
| | prt. | *ipaṭṭar* | L32; 119; 281(!) |
| | | *ipaṭṭarišu*(!) | L32 (read *ipaṭṭaršu*) |
| | | *ipaṭṭaršu* | L32 (conjecture for *ipaṭṭarišu*!) |
| | | *ipaṭṭaršum* | L32, vnt. |
| | | *ipṭuraššuma* | L32 |
| | ***napṭuru*** | | |
| | N prs. | *ippaṭṭar* | L32 |
| ***pazāru***, to protect | | | |
| | ***šutapzuru*** | | |
| | Št prt. | *uštapziršināti* | E7 |
| ***peḫû***, to caulk | | | |
| | G prt. | *ipḫe* | L234 |
| | | *ipḫēma* | L235 |
| ***petû***, to open | | | |
| | G prt. | *ipte* | L55 |
| | | *iptēma* | L56; 120; 215; 218; 220 |
| | | *ipti* | L44, vnt. |
| | Gt | *iptete* | L44; 110 |
| | ***puttû*** | | |
| | D prt. | *upetti* | E3 |
| | ***naptû*** | | |
| | N prt. | *ippetû* | L53 |
| | Nt | *ittepte* | L53 |

| | | |
|---|---|---|
| ***puḫḫu*** (D), to exchange | | |
| G prt. | *upīḫ* | L41 |
| ***qabû***, to speak | | |
| G stv. | *qabû* | L26 |
| | *qabûma* | L26, vnt. |
| prt. | *iqbi* | L68+b |
| | *iqbīšum* | L49; 66 |
| | *iqbû* | L3 |
| | *liqbi* | E20 |
| | *liqbīma* | E12 |
| prs. | *iqabbīma* | L281(!) |
| | *iqabbûma* | L9 |
| Gt | *iqtabi* | L9; 9; 47; 69+c; 126; 141; 141; 142; 159; 160; 161; 168; 170; 171a; 192; 282 |
| ***qâlu* A**, to heed | | |
| G prt. | *iqūlma* | E18; 19 |
| | *liqūlma* | E15 |
| ***qalû* B**, to burn | | |
| G prs. | *iqallūši* | L110 |
| | *iqallūšunūtu* | L157 |
| ***qamû***, to set on fire | | |
| G prt. | *liqmi* | E28 |
| ***qâpu* A**, to entrust | | |
| G prt. | *iqīpma* | L107 |
| | *iqīpšu* | L253 |
| ***qâpu* B**, to crumble | | |
| Gt | *iqtūp* | L233 |
| ***qâšu***, to give | | |
| G prt. | *iqīšu* | P15 |
| ***qatû***, to end | | |
| ***šuqtû*** | | |
| Š prt. | *lišaqti* | E24 |
| ***qerēbu***, to be near | | |
| G stv. | *qerbu* | L13 |
| ***rabāṣu***, to crouch | | |
| ***šurbuṣu*** | | |
| Š prt. | *ušarbiṣ* | E5 |
| ***râbu***, to recompense | | |
| G inf. | *riābam* | L54 |
| prs. | *iriab* | L8; 53; 68+b; 125; 219; 232; 236; 237; 245; 246; 254; 263; 265 |

| | | | |
|---|---|---|---|
| | | *iriabbūšum* | L23 |
| | | *iriabbūšu* | L23, vnt. |
| | | *iriabšum* | L240 |
| ***rabû***, to be great | | | |
| | G prt. | *irbû* | L166 (conjecture for *iršû*) |
| | stv. | *rabû* | L202 |
| | ***rubbû*** | | |
| | D prs. | *urabba* | L60; 137 |
| | | *urabbāšu* | L29 |
| | | *urabbû* | L177 |
| | | *urabbûšu* | L190; 191 |
| | Dt | *urtabbīšu* | L185 |
| | | *urtabbû* | L137 |
| | ***šurbû*** | | |
| | Š | *ušarbiūšu* | P2 |
| ***ragāmu***, to claim | | | |
| | G prt. | *irgumu* | L126 |
| | prs. | *iraggum* | L162; 163; 175 |
| | | *iraggumū* | L171a |
| ***raḫāṣu***, to devastate | | | |
| | Gt | *irtaḫiṣ* | L45; 48 |
| ***rakābu***, to ride | | | |
| | ***rukkubu*** | | |
| | D inf. | *rukkubim* | L64 |
| | prt. | *urakkibma* | L65 |
| ***rakāsu***, to agree | | | |
| | G prt. | *irkusu* | L194 |
| | Gt | *irtakas* | L194 |
| | ***rukkusu*** | | |
| | D prs. | *urakkissu* | L253 |
| | Dt | *urtakkis* | L151 |
| | ***narkusu*** | | |
| | Nt | *ittarkasūma* | L109 |
| ***râmu***, to love | | | |
| | G prs. | *arammu* | E10 |
| | | *irammu* | L150 |
| ***raqû***, to hide | | | |
| | Gt | *irtaqīma* | L16 |
| ***rašādu***, to have foundations | | | |
| | ***šuršudu*** | | |
| | Š stv. | *šuršudā* | P2 |

| | | |
|---|---|---|
| ***rašû***, to possess | | |
| G prt. | *iršia* | E10 |
| | *iršû* | §5.10; 166 (perhaps read *irbû*); 176a; 176a; 176b |
| prs. | *iraššû* | L39; E11 |
| Gt | *irtaši* | L33; 235; 279 |
| | *irtašīma* | L191 |
| ***šuršû*** | | |
| Š | *ušarši* | E27 |
| | *ušaršīšināti* | E5 |
| | *ušaršīšu* | L145, vnt.; 163; E29 |
| | *ušaršīšuma* | L145 |
| | *ušaršûšu* | L137 |
| ***raṭābu***, to moisten | | |
| ***ruṭṭubu*** | | |
| D prs. | *uraṭṭab* | L48 |
| ***redû***, to pursue | | |
| G prt. | *irdeam* | L13; 109 |
| prs. | *ireddīšu* | L18 |
| Gt | *irtede* | L33 |
| | *irtediaššu* | L17 |
| ***re'u***, to tend | | |
| G inf. | *re'îm* | L261; 264; 265 |
| prt. | *lirē* | E18 |
| ***rîqu***, to be empty | | |
| G stv. | *rēqa* | E17 |
| ***sadāru***, to arrange | | |
| G prs. | *isaddarma* | L100; 104 |
| ***saḫāmu***, to be under pressure | | |
| ***suḫḫumu*** | | |
| D prs. | *usaḫḫamūši* | L172 |
| ***sakālu***, to appropriate | | |
| G prs. | *isakkil* | L141 |
| ***sakāpu***, to overturn | | |
| G prt. | *liskip* | E23 |
| ***sanāqu***, to supervise | | |
| ***sunnuqu*** | | |
| D prt. | *usanniqma* | L251 |
| ***sapāḫu***, to disrupt | | |
| ***suppuḫu*** | | |
| D prs. | *usappaḫ* | L141; 143 |

| | | |
|---|---|---|
| ***naspuḫu*** | | |
| N inf. | *naspuḫ* | E20 |
| ***sarāru***, to deceive | | |
| G stv. | *sar* | L13 |
| ***surruru*** | | |
| D prt. | *usarrirma* | L265 |
| ***sekēru***, to remove | | |
| G prt. | *liskir* | E22 |
| ***ṣabāru***, to become unstable | | |
| Gt | *iṣṣabar* | L235 |
| ***ṣabātu***, to seize | | |
| G inf. | *ṣabātiša* | L151 |
| stv. | *ṣabtu* | L9; 64; [133a] |
| prt. | *iṣbassuma* | L117; 119 |
| | *iṣbatma* | L17; 30 |
| | *iṣbatu* | L148 |
| prs. | *iṣabbatū* | L151; 151 |
| Gt | *iṣṣabassi* | L148 |
| | *iṣṣabat* | L9; 136 |
| | *iṣṣabtamma* | L109 |
| | *iṣṣabtuma* | L30 |
| | *iṣṣabtūšu* | L130; 155 |
| ***šuṣbutu*** | | |
| Š prt. | *ušaṣbitu* | E1 |
| ***naṣbutu*** | | |
| N prt. | *iṣṣabit* | L131 |
| Nt | *ittaṣbat* | L19; 22; 23; 129; 132; 158; 253 |
| ***ṣamû***, to thirst | | |
| ***šuṣmû*** | | |
| Š prt. | *lišaṣmi* | E23 |
| *ṣebû* > *ṣubbû* | | |
| ***ṣeḫēru***, to be small | | |
| G stv. | *ṣeḫerma* | L29 |
| ***ṣuḫḫuru*** | | |
| Dt | *uṣṣaḫḫir* | L264; 264 |
| ***ṣênu***, to load | | |
| G inf. | *ṣênim* | L237 |
| prt. | *iṣēnši* | L237 |
| ***ṣubbû*** (D), to observe | | |
| ***šuteṣbû*** | | |
| Št | *ušteṣbīma* | L233 |

| | | |
|---|---|---|
| ***šakāku***, to harrow | | |
| G | *išakkakma* | L43; 44 |
| ***šakānu***, to set | | |
| G prt. | *aškun* | P22 |
| | *iškun* | L68+b; 128 |
| | *liškunšum* | E27; 23 |
| prs. | *išakkanšimma* | L146 |
| | *išakkanma* | L122 |
| | *išakkanšu* | §4.12 |
| | *išakkanu* | §4.12 |
| | *išakkanūši* | L153 |
| | *išakkanūšum* | L61 |
| | *išakkanūšumma* | L13; 166 |
| Gt | *ištakan* | L137; 144; 145; 148; 168; 171a (perhaps read *iššakkan*); 172; 177; 191 |
| | *ištakanma* | L141 |
| | *ištakanšu* | L206 |
| ***šuškunu*** | | |
| Š prt. | *lišaškin* | E21 |
| ***naškunu*** | | |
| N prs. | *iššakkan* | L105; 117; 171a (conjecture for *ištakan*); 280 |
| ***šalālu***, to capture | | |
| ***našlulu*** | | |
| N prt. | *iššalilma* | L133a; 134; 135 |
| ***šalāmu***, to be safe | | |
| Gt | *ištalma* | L2, vnt. |
| | *ištalmam* | L2 |
| ***šullumu*** | | |
| D prs. | *ušallamma* | L125; 267 |
| | *ušallamšimma* | L138; 149; 156 |
| | *ušallamūšimma* | L172 |
| Dt | *uštallim* | L221 |
| ***šalû***, to leap | | |
| G prt. | *išliam* | L2 |
| prs. | *išalli* | L132 |
| | *išalliamma* | L2 |
| ***šâmu* A**, to purchase | | |
| G inf. | *šâmim* | §4.12 |

| | | |
|---|---|---|
| prt. | *ašâm* | L9 |
| | *išāmma* | §4.12; L278; 279 |
| | *išāmu* | L9; 10 |
| prs. | *išâm* | L67+a; §4.12 |
| | *išammu* | L40; 67+a; 177 |
| | *išammuma* | L39 |
| Gt | *ištām* | L7; 35; 37; 280 |
| ***našūmu*** | | |
| N prt. | *iššāmu* | L9 |

***šâmu* B**, to assign

| | | |
|---|---|---|
| G prt. | *išīm* | E12 |
| | *išīmam* | E4 |
| | *išīmu* | P16 |
| | *išīmūšum* | P1 |
| | *lišīmšum* | E20; 24 |

***šanānu***, to repeat

| | | |
|---|---|---|
| Gt inf. | *šitannu* | E24 |

***šanû***, to change

| | | |
|---|---|---|
| ***šušnû*** | | |
| Št | *uštašannāma* | §5.12; L101; 120; 124; 126; 160; 161 |
| | *uštašnama* | L120, vnt. |

*šapāḫu* (*AHw*) > *šuppuḫu* (*CAD*)

***šapāku***, to store

| | | |
|---|---|---|
| G prt. | *išpuk* | L121 |
| | *išpukma* | L120 |
| ***našpuku*** | | |
| N prt. | *iššapku* | L120 |

***šapû* C**, to be silent

| | | |
|---|---|---|
| ***šuppû*** | | |
| D inf. | *šubbîm* | E20 |

***šaqālu***, to pay

| | | |
|---|---|---|
| G prt. | *išqulu* | L9; 119; 278; 281; 281(!) |
| prs. | *išaqqal* | L59; §5.3b; L114; 116; 198; 199; 201; 203; 204; 207; 208; 209; 211; 212; 213; 214; 220; 241 |
| | *išaqqalma* | L119 |
| | *išaqqalšimma* | L156 |
| | *išaqqalū* | L24 |

***šaqû***, to be high

| | | |
|---|---|---|
| G prt. | *lišqi* | E27 |

| | | |
|---|---|---|
| ***šarāku***, to grant | | |
| G prt. | *išruk* | L165; 184 |
| | *išrukam* | E2 |
| | *išrukšim* | L150; 180 (conjecture); 181; 182; 183; 184 |
| | *išrukušim* | L178; 179 |
| | *išrukušu* | E17 |
| | *išukšim*(!) | L180 (read *išrukšim*) |
| prs. | *išarrakūšimma* | L184 |
| Gt | *ištarak* | L34 |
| ***šarāmu***, to trim | | |
| ***šurrumu*** | | |
| D | *ušarrim* | L251 |
| ***šarāqu***, to steal | | |
| G prt. | *išriq* | L6; 8; 259 |
| | *išriqma* | L253; 255 |
| | *išriqu* | L265 |
| Gt | *ištariq* | L14; 260 |
| ***šasû***, to shout | | |
| G prt. | *lissīma* | E25 |
| Gtn | *lištassīma* | E11 |
| ***šaṭāru***, to inscribe | | |
| G prt. | *ašturma* | E8 |
| | *ašturu* | E14; 15; 18; 19 |
| | *išṭur* | §5.12 |
| | *išṭuršim* | L182; 183 |
| | *išṭuršimma* | L178; 179 |
| | *išṭuršum* | §5.3a; L165 |
| | *išṭurušim* | L171b; 178; 178; 179; 179 |
| prs. | *išaṭṭar* | L38; 39 |
| Gt | *ištaṭar* | E19 |
| ***šebēru***, to break | | |
| G prt. | *išbir* | L248 (or read *ištebir*) |
| | *lišbir* | E19; 27; 26 |
| prs. | *išebbirū* | L197 |
| Gt | *ištebir* | L197; 198; 199; 246; 248 (conjecture) |
| ***šēmû***, to hear | | |
| G prt. | *lišmēma* | E11 |
| ***še'û***, to search | | |
| Gt | *ešte'īšināšim* | E3 |
| Gtn | *ištene'īma* | L125 |

*šubbû* > *šapû* C
***šuklulu***, to make complete

| | | |
|---|---|---|
| Š prt. | *ušaklilšum* | L228 |
| | *ušaklilušu* | P12 |
| | *ušaklilušum* | P12, vnt. |

***šupêlu*** (Š), to exchange

| | | |
|---|---|---|
| Š inf. | *šupēlam* | E20 |
| Št | *uštapal* | E19, vnt. |
| | *uštepēl* | E18; 19 |

***šuppuḫu***, to incite

| | | |
|---|---|---|
| D prt. | *lišappiḫaššum* | E20 |

***šutlumu*** (Š), to bestow

| | | |
|---|---|---|
| Š prt. | *ušatlimūnim* | E4 |

***tabāku***, to pour

| | | |
|---|---|---|
| G inf. | *tabāk* | E21 |

***tabālu***, to remove

| | | |
|---|---|---|
| G impv. | *tabal* | L49; 66 |
| prt. | *itbal* | L112 |
| prs. | *attabbalšināti* | E7 |
| | *itabbal* | L2; 2; 26; 41; 159 |

***takālu***, to trust

***tukkulu***

| | | |
|---|---|---|
| D prt. | *utakkilma* | L235 |

***tamû***, to swear

| | | |
|---|---|---|
| G prs. | *itamma* | L206 |
| | *itammāma* | L207; 227 |

***tarāku***, to beat

| | | |
|---|---|---|
| G prs. | *itarrakaššu* | §5.8 |

***tarāṣu***, to stretch

***šutruṣu***

| | | |
|---|---|---|
| Š prt. | *uštariṣma* | L127 |

***natruṣu***

| | | |
|---|---|---|
| N | *ittariṣma* | L132 |

***târu***, to return

| | | |
|---|---|---|
| G prt. | *ittūram* | L31 |
| | *ittūramma* | L27; 135; 136 |
| | *itūramma* | L30 |
| prs. | *itâr* | L41; 67+a; 37; [§4.12]; 131; 135; 136; 177; 186; 189;190 |
| | *itârma* | L5 |

| | | |
|---|---|---|
| ***tūrru*** | | |
| D stv. | *turrim* | L51; §5.10; 5.15 |
| | *tūrru* | L27; 28; 32 |
| | *turruma* | L27, vnt. |
| prs. | *utâr* | L43; 44; 48; 50; 62; 63; §5.12; L102; 104; 113 160; 161; 164; 278, vnt. |
| | *utârma* | L278 |
| | *utarrūšim* | L137 |
| | *utarrūšu* | L18; [§5.8] |
| | *utarrūšum* | §5.8 |
| | *utarrūšumma* | L27 |
| Dt | *litēr* | E25; 27 |
| | *litēršumma* | E26 |
| | *uttēr* | L107 |
| | *uttēršu* | L163, vnt. |
| | *uttēršum* | L163; 164 |
| ***tebû***, to revolt | | |
| ***šutbû*** | | |
| Š prs. | *ušetbûšuma* | L5 |
| ***ṭâbu***, to be good | | |
| G stv. | *ṭāb* | L264 |
| | *ṭāba* | P18 |
| | *ṭābu* | L178; 178; 179; 179; 182 |
| ***ṭubbu*** | | |
| D inf. | *ṭubbim* | P3 |
| prt. | *liṭīb* | E16 |
| | *uṭabbū* | L178 |
| | *uṭīb* | P22; E5; 12 |
| Dt | *uṭṭibbū* | L178 |
| ***ṭarādu***, to send | | |
| G prt. | *iṭrussu* | L100 |
| Gt | *iṭṭarad* | L26 |
| | *ittarad* | L26, vnt. |
| ***ṭebû***, to sink | | |
| G stv. | *ṭebiat* | L240 |
| ***ṭubbû*** | | |
| D prt. | *uṭebbû* | L237; 240 |
| Dt | *uṭṭebbi* | L236; 237; 240 |
| | *uṭṭebbīma* | L238 |
| ***ṭeḫû***, to be near | | |
| ***ṭuḫḫû*** | | |
| Dt | *uṭṭeḫḫi* | §5.12 |

***ubburu*** (D), to accuse

| | | |
|---|---|---|
| D prt. | *ubbirma* | L1 |
| | *ubbiršima* | L131 |
| Dt prt. | *ūtabbir* | L126, vnt. |
| | *ūtebbir* | L126 |

***u''uru***, to direct

| | | |
|---|---|---|
| D prt. | *uwa'eranni* | P22 |

*uzuzzu* > *izuzzu*

***zakāru***, to utter

| | | |
|---|---|---|
| G prs. | *izakkar* | L18 |
| | *izakkarma* | L20; 103; 131; 249 |
| ***nazkuru*** | | |
| N prt. | *lizzakir* | E10 |

*zapāru* > *ṣabāru.*

***zaqāpu***, to plant

| | | |
|---|---|---|
| G inf. | *zaqāpim* | L60; 61 |
| prt. | *izqup* | L60; 62 |

***zâzu***, to share

| | | |
|---|---|---|
| G prt. | *izuzzū* | L46; 54; 60; 77+f; 165; 165; 166; 167; 167; 170; 171a; 173 |
| | *izuzzūma* | L176a; 176b |
| prs. | *izâz* | L183 |
| | *izâzma* | L180; 181; 182 |

***zêru***, to hate

| | | |
|---|---|---|
| G prt. | *izērma* | L142; 193 |
| | *izēruma* | L136 |

# ENGLISH–AKKADIAN INDEX

This Index does not attempt to give every English word used as an equivalent for a given Akkadian word in the Glossary, but rather more of a key-word equivalent; so English verbs are not marked as such with 'to', and complementary words like 'be' and 'make' are placed after the key-word. Though somewhat crude in presentation and unsophisticated in detail, it may nonetheless prove helpful as a first step in identifying certain themes in the text and some apparently almost synonymous expressions. To link words in similar semantic fields it will be necessary to use this list together with the list of roots.

| | |
|---|---|
| abandoned ground | *nidītu* |
| ablaze | *napāḫu* |
| able | *leʾû* |
| above | *eliš* |
| abundant | *dešû* |
| account | *nikkassu* |
| accusing | *mubbiru* |
| acquainted | *mūdû* |
| acquire | *sakālu* |
| act | *epēšu* |
| additional | *elû* |
| | *elēnu* |
| adopted child | *tarbītu* |
| adoption | *mārūtu* |
| advance | *âru* |
| affliction | *liptu* |
| after | *arki* |
| afterwards | *arka* |
| | *arkānum* |
| | *arkānumma* |
| aggregate | *ṭuḫḫû* |
| agree | *magāru* |
| | *rakāsu* |
| agreed amount | *apšitû* |
| agreed rent | *kiṣru* |
| alight, set | *šuppuḫu* |
| alive | *balṭu* |
| although | *ela* |
| anarchy | *saḫmaštu* |
| and | *u* |
| anger | *aggu* |
| anger | *uzzatu* |
| angrily | *ezziš* |
| annul | *pussusu* |
| another | *šanû* 2 |
| answer | *apālu* |
| arable ground | *mēreštu* |
| arbitrator | *muštālu* |
| argue | *nakāru* |
| arm | *idu* |
| arrange | *dekû* |
| | *sadāru* |
| arranging | *muštakīn* |
| | *mušteṣbû* |
| ascend | *elû* |
| ascertain | *bâru* |
| assembling | *mupaḫḫiru* |
| assembly | *puḫru* |

| | |
|---|---|
| at | *ina* |
| attacking | *tību* |
| attain, allowing to | *mušakšidu* |
| attendant | *girsequ* |
| attentive, be | *šuteṣbû* |
| authority | *tašīmtu* |
| avert | *šūtuqu* |
| | |
| bad | *lemnu* |
| bandaging | *ṣimdu* |
| barber | *gallābu* |
| barley | *še'u* |
| barleycorn | *uṭṭetu* |
| basket | *pānu* 2 |
| basketmaker | *atkuppu* |
| beat | *tarāku* |
| because | *aššum* |
| beer | *pīḫu* |
| | *sību* |
| | *šikaru* |
| before | *lāma* |
| beget | *banû* |
| behaviour | *rīdu* |
| beloved | *narāmu* |
| below | *šapliš* |
| benefitting | *mudammiqu* |
| beseech | *emēqu* |
| bestow | *šutlumu* (Št) |
| bind | *kasû* |
| birth, give | *alādu* |
| bite | *nišku* |
| black | *ṣalmu* |
| blind | *ḫuppudu* |
| blood | *damu* |
| blow | *napāḫu* |
| boat | *eleppu* |
| | *māḫirtu* |
| boatman | *malāḫu* |
| body | *pagru* |
| | *zumru* |
| bonds | *kamîš* |
| bone | *eṣemtu* |
| bosom | *utlu* |
| both | *kilallān* |
| bow-maker | *sasinnu* |
| break | *ḫepû* |
| break | *šebēru* |
| breast | *tulû* |
| breathe freely | *napāšu* |
| brickwork | *libittu* |
| bridal gift | *terḫatu* |
| bride | *kallatu* |
| brightening | *munammiru* |
| brilliance | *šērtu* 2 |
| bring | *abālu* |
| bringing | *bābilu* |
| bringing out | *mušeṣû* |
| broad, be | *šadālu* |
| broken | *šebru* |
| bronze | *siparru* |
| brother | *aḫu* 1 |
| builder | *itinnu* |
| burgle | *palāšu* |
| burn | *qalû* |
| | *qamû* |
| butting | *munakkipû* |
| | |
| calamity | *lemuttu* |
| call | *šisītu* |
| capable | *lē'u* |
| captain | *ša ḫaṭṭātim* |
| captor | *ṣābitānu* |
| capture | *redû* |
| | *šalālu* |
| care for | *gamālu* |
| | *zanānu* |
| cargo, load as | *ṣênu* |
| caring for | *pāqidu* |
| | *zāninu* |
| carpenter | *naggaru* |
| carry away | *tabālu* |
| carry | *našû* |
| catastrophe | *karašû* |
| cattle | *littu* |
| | *sugullu* |
| cattle-herder | *kullizu* |
| cattle-mark | *šimtu* |
| caulk | *peḫû* |
| cease | *naparkû* |
| change | *enû* |

| | |
|---|---|
| cheek | *lētu* |
| chief | *ašarīdu* |
| choose | *nasāqu* |
| | *ḫâru* |
| circumstances | *arkatu* |
| citizen | *muškēnu* |
| city | *ālu* |
| city square | *rebītu* |
| claim | *baqrū* |
| | *baqāru* |
| | *ragāmu* |
| clarify | *burru* |
| clay figurine | *ṭīdu* |
| clean, be | *ebēbu* |
| cleanse | *ubbubu* |
| cloistered woman | *sekretu* |
| clothe | *šulbušu* |
| clothing | *lubūšu* |
| cohabit | *nenmudu* |
| come out | *aṣû* |
| command | *qibītu* |
| community | *babtu* |
| complete | *gamru* |
| complete, be | *gamāru* |
| complete, make | *šuklulu* |
| completion | *gamartu* |
| comrade | *rūʾu* |
| condemnation | *šērtu* 1 |
| conflict | *qablu* |
| | *tamḫāru* |
| | *tāḫazu* |
| confuse | *ešû* |
| confusion | *mišītu* |
| conquer | *kašādu* |
| consignment | *šūbultu* |
| contract | *riksu* |
| control | *sunnuqu* |
| controlling | *mukannišu* |
| convict | *kunnu* |
| copulate | *itūlu* |
| corpse | *šalamtu* |
| count | *manû* 1 |
| country | *ṣēru* |
| covet | *pullušu* |
| creator | *bānû* |
| creatress | *bānītu* |
| creature | *binītu* |
| credit | *qiptu* |
| creditor | *kāšišu* |
| crier | *nāgiru* |
| crown | *agû* |
| crumble | *qâpu* 2 |
| | *šuḫluṣu* |
| cry of victory | *irnittu* |
| cultivate | *erēšu* 2 |
| cultivated | *eršu* 2 |
| cultivation | *errēšūtu* |
| cultivator | *errēšu* |
| curse | *arāru* |
| | *erretu* |
| custody | *maṣṣarūtu* |
| custody, take into | *nepû* |
| cut off | *nakāsu* |
| cut to size | *šarāmu* |
| daily | *ūmišam* |
| damage | *miqittu* |
| | *nabalkattu* |
| | *pilšu* |
| darkness | *ikletu* |
| dates | *suluppū* |
| daughter | *mārtu* |
| daughter-in-law | *kallatu* |
| day | *ūmu* |
| death | *mūtu* |
| debt | *eʾiltu* |
| | *pīḫātu* |
| | *ḫubullu* |
| deceive | *sarāru* |
| deception | *sartu* |
| | *tuššu* |
| decide | *parāsu* |
| decision | *purussu* |
| | *šipṭu* |
| | *šīmtu* |
| decorate | *šulbušu* |
| decorating | *mušalbišu* |
| deduct | *ḫarāṣu* |
| defile | *šulputu* |
| deluge | *abūbu* |

| | |
|---|---|
| demand | *erēšu* 1 |
| demon | *asakku* |
| denigrate | *lummunu* |
| | *šumṭû* |
| denounce | *nugguru* |
| descendant | *liblibbu* |
| deserter | *nisiḫtu* |
| designate | *nabû* |
| desolate site | *tillu* |
| destiny | *šīmtu* |
| destroy | *ḫulluqu* |
| determining | *mušīmu* |
| | *šā'imu* |
| devastate | *raḫāṣu* |
| developing | *mušaddilu* |
| development | *teptītu* |
| devout | *na'du* |
| die | *mâtu* |
| difficult | *aštu* |
| difficulty, make | *epēsu* |
| diminish | *ṣuḫḫuru* |
| direct | *u'uru* |
| disappear | *ḫalāqu* |
| discover | *ḫâṭu* |
| discretion, grant | *šumṣû* |
| disdain | *mêšu* |
| disease | *la'bu* |
| | *murṣu* |
| | *pissātu* |
| diseased | *marṣu* |
| disloyal, be | *nagāru* |
| disposing | *mušassiku* |
| disrepute, cause | *ubburu* |
| disrupt | *sapāḫu* |
| distant | *rūqu* |
| distress | *ašāšu* |
| | *pušqu* |
| district | *pāṭu* |
| disturb | *suppuḫu* |
| ditch | *atappu* |
| divination | *bīru* |
| divorce settlement | *uzubbû* |
| do | *epēšu* |
| document | *ṭuppu* |
| | *kanīku* |

| | |
|---|---|
| | *kunukku* |
| donkey | *imēru* |
| doorway | *bābu* |
| double | *šušnû* |
| dowry | *šeriktu* |
| drag | *mašāru* |
| dragon | *ušumgallu* |
| dress | *labāšu* |
| drink, give to | *šaqû* |
| drink, giving | *mušesqû* |
| drink-seller | *sābû* |
| | *sābītu* |
| drop down | *šuddû* |
| duty | *ilku* |
| dwelling | *šubtu* |
| dyke | *kāru* |
| dynasty | *šarrūtu* |
| ear | *uznu* |
| earth | *erṣetu* |
| eat | *akālu* |
| effective | *pāti'u* |
| emptiness | *rīqūtu* |
| empty | *rīqu* |
| end | *qatû* |
| | *taqtītu* |
| end, come to an | *balû* |
| enemy | *ayyābu* |
| | *nakru* |
| enter | *erēbu* |
| entering | *ēribu* |
| entrust | *paqādu* |
| | *qâpu* |
| epilepsy | *bennu* |
| equal | *miḫru* |
| equal, be | *maṣû* |
| equally | *mitḫariš* |
| eternally | *matīma* |
| evermore | *dāriš* |
| evidence | *šībūtu* |
| exalted lady | *telītu* |
| exalted | *ṣīru* |
| exceed | *utturu* |
| excellent | *mušāter* |
| exceptional | *šūturu* |

exchange *puḫḫu*
exist *bašû*
expedition *ḫarrānu*
expenses *mānaḫtu*
expert *apkallu*
expire *malû* 1
explain *kullumu*
exploit *ḫabālu*
exploited *ḫablu*
extending *murappišu*
extolling *mušarbû*
extra portion *elītu*
eye *īnu*

face *pānu* 1
faith *tukultu*
fall *maqātu*
fallow ground *nidītu*
false evidence *sartu*
famine *bubūtu*
*ḫušaḫḫu*
famous *ṣurru*
famous, making *muṣīru*
fate, determining *mušīmu*
father *abu*
father-in-law *emu*
fault *ḫiṭītu*
favour *damiqtu*
*dumqu*
favourite *migru*
fear *adāru*
fees *idū*
field *abšinnu*
*eqlu*
fifth *ḫamšu*
fight *risbatu*
figurine *ṭīdu*
fill *mullû*
find *ṣabātu*
finger *ubānu*
fire *išātu*
fire, kindle *napāḫu*
firm, be *kânu*
first husband *ḫāwiru*
first time *ištiššu*
first wife *ḫīrtu*
five *ḫamiš*
fix securely *šuršudu*
flare up *nappuḫu*
flee *nābutu*
flesh *šīru*
flock *ṣēnu* 1
flood *mīlu*
flood-water *bubbulu*
flourish, making *mudeššû*
fodder *ukullu*
foe *zā'iru*
follower *talīmu*
following *arkû*
food *mākālu*
foodstuff *ukullu*
foot *šēpu*
forehead *nakkaptu*
former *maḫrû*
fortress *dannatu*
foster father *murabbû*
foster mother *murabbītu*
foundation *išdu*
founded, be *rašādu*
founder *mukīnu*
four *erbû*
fourth *rebû*
fraud *sikiltu*
free, be *šalāmu*
free, go away *uššuru*
freedom *andurāru*
friend *ibru*
from *ištu*
front *maḫru*
front, in *maḫra*
fugitive *munnabtu*
full *malû* 2
full, be *malû* 1
future *arkītu*

gardener *nukaribbu*
gate *abullu*
gather *esēpu*
generation *dāru*
generosity, showing *muṭaḫḫidu*

| | | | |
|---|---|---|---|
| ghost | *eṭemmu* | guiding straight | *muštēširu* |
| gift | *biblu* | half | *mišlu* |
| | *nudunnû* | half portion | *muttatu* |
| | *qīštu* | half-shares | *mišlānū* |
| give drink | *šaqû* | hand over | *šarāku* |
| give | *nadānu* | hand | *qātu* |
| | *qâšu* | | *rittu* |
| glad, be | *râšu* | hang | *alālu* |
| | *ḫadû* | hang loose | *ašāru* |
| gladdening | *muḫaddû* | happy, making | *muṭibbu* |
| glance | *niṭlu* | hard | *ašṭu* |
| go | *alāku* | harem | *gāgû* |
| go away | *âru* | harrow | *maškakātu* |
| go round | *saḫāru* | | *šakāku* |
| go straight | *ešēru* | harvest | *ebūru* |
| go up | *elû* 1 | | *eṣēdu* |
| goat | *urīṣu* | hate | *zêru* |
| god | *ilu* | have | *išû* |
| gold | *ḫurāṣu* | he | *šu, šû* |
| good | *damqu* | head | *qaqqadu* |
| | *ṭābu* | | *rēšu* |
| good, be | *ṭâbu* | heap | *gurunnu* |
| goods | *makkūru* | heap of grain | *karû* |
| | *šūbultu* | heaping up | *mugarrinu* |
| | *unūtu* | | *mukammeru* |
| goring | *nakkāpû* | hear | *šemû* |
| governance | *rē'ûtu* | heart | *libbu* |
| governor | *iššakku* | heed | *qâlu* |
| | *rabiānu* | heir | *aplu* |
| grain | *ašnan* | helper | *rēṣu* |
| | *karû* | herdsman | *kullizu* |
| | *še'u* | hero | *qarrādu* |
| granary | *našpaku* | | *qurādu* |
| | *qarītu* | hide | *pazāru* |
| grand, be | *rabû* 1 | | *raqû* |
| grant discretion | *šumṣû* | him | *šuāti* |
| grasping | *mutammiḫu* | hire | *agāru* |
| grass | *šammu* | | *igru* |
| great | *rabû* 2 | his | *šû* |
| greatly | *magal* | hit | *naṭû* |
| green | *arqu* | hoe | *marāru* |
| ground, abandoned | *nidītu* | hold | *kullu* |
| | *nidūtu* | | *tamāḫu* |
| ground, arable | *mēreštu* | holding | *mukillu* |
| group | *napḫaru* | holy | *ellu* |

| | |
|---|---|
| holy place | *ašru* |
| home | *šubtu* |
| horn | *qarnu* |
| hostility | *nukurtu* |
| house | *bītu* |
| household goods | *unūtu* |
| humanity | *awīlūtu* |
| | *kiššatu* |
| humble | *ašru* |
| hunter | *bā'iru* |
| husband | *ḫāwiru* |
| | *mutu* |
| I | *anāku* |
| if | *šumma* |
| ill | *marṣu* |
| illuminate | *namāru* |
| important, be | *kabātu* |
| impose punishment | *emēdu* |
| improve | *ṭubbu* |
| incite | *šuppuḫu* |
| increase | *utturu* |
| informer | *munaggiru* |
| inheritance | *aplūtu* |
| injury | *simmu* |
| innocent, be | *uššuru* |
| inscribe | *šaṭāru* |
| inscribed | *šaṭru* |
| inside | *qerbu* |
| inspire | *tukkulu* |
| insufficient | *īṣu* |
| intelligent | *ḫassu* |
| interest | *ṣibtu* |
| intrude | *palāšu* |
| irrigation official | *gugallu* |
| irrigation | *šiqītu* |
| job | *šipru* |
| judge | *dayyānu* |
| judgment | *dīnu* |
| judiciary | *dayyānūtu* |
| jug of beer | *pīḫu* |
| justice | *kittu* |
| | *mīšaru* |
| keep | *naṣāru* |

| | |
|---|---|
| kill | *dâku* |
| kind, be | *damāqu* |
| kindle | *napāḫu* |
| kindness | *tadmiqtu* |
| kindness, showing | *gāmilu* |
| king | *šarru* |
| know | *idû* |
| knowledge | *mūdûtu* |
| labourer | *agru* |
| | *ikkaru* |
| lady | *bēltu* |
| | *rubātu* |
| | *telītu* |
| land | *mātu* |
| lapicide | *parkullu* |
| law | *dīnu* |
| lay hold on | *lapātu* |
| leader | *etellu* |
| leadership | *ellilūtu* |
| leak | *zapāru* |
| leap | *šalû* |
| learn | *lamādu* |
| leather worker | *aškāpu* |
| leave | *ezēbu* |
| legal decision | *dīnu* |
| legislate | *dânu* |
| lengthening | *mušāriku* |
| lessen | *muṭṭû* |
| lie down | *rabāṣu* |
| life | *balāṭu* 2 |
| | *bulṭu* |
| | *napištu* |
| | *nīšu* |
| life, give | *bulluṭu* |
| life, preserve | *šaṭāpu* |
| light | *nūru* |
| like | *kî* |
| | *kīma* |
| limbs | *binātu* |
| lion | *nēšu* |
| live | *balāṭu* 1 |
| load as cargo | *ṣênu* |
| load of goods | *šūbultu* |
| lodger | *aššābu* |

| | |
|---|---|
| long, be | *arāku* |
| look at | *palāsu* |
| lord | *bēlu* |
| loss | *bitiqtu* |
| | *butuqqû* |
| | *ibbu* |
| | *rugummû* |
| lost property | *ḫulqu* |
| lost | *ḫalqu* |
| love | *ramû* |
| | *rēmu* |
| loving | *rāʾimu* |
| low, be | *katātu* |
| lustration | *šuluḫḫu* |
| | |
| malign | *kurruṣu* |
| man | *awīlu* |
| | *zikaru* |
| marriage-gift | *biblu* |
| | *nudunnû* |
| mass | *kiššatu* |
| master | *bēlu* |
| mattock | *mayyāru* |
| meadow | *ugāru* |
| measure | *madādu* |
| measure of area | *buru* |
| | *ikû* |
| measure of capacity | *kurru* |
| | *pānu* 2 |
| | *qû* |
| | *sūtu* |
| measure of length | *paršiktu* |
| measure of weight | *uṭṭetu* |
| merchant | *tamkāru* |
| message | *pû* |
| midst | *qablû* |
| | *qerbītu* |
| mighty | *gašru* |
| mina | *manû* 2 |
| mistress | *bēltu* |
| misuse | *uššušu* |
| moisten | *raṭābu* |
| month | *arḫu* |
| mother | *ummu* |
| mourn | *damāmu* |
| mouth | *pû* |
| much | *mala* |
| much, be | *atāru* |
| munificent | *munaḫḫišu* |
| murder | *nērtu* |
| murder, arrange | *šudūku* |
| muscle | *labānu* |
| | *šerḫānu* |
| | |
| name | *šumu* |
| | *zikru* |
| near, be | *qerēbu* |
| | *ṭeḫû* |
| neck muscle | *labānu* |
| neglected land | *nidītu* |
| neglecting | *mupparkû* |
| negligence | *mēgûtu* |
| negligent, be | *egû* |
| neighbour | *ṭeḫḫu* |
| | *itû* |
| net | *saparru* |
| new, be | *edēšu* |
| night | *mūšu* |
| nominate | *nabû* |
| nominee | *nibītu* |
| not | *ay* |
| | *la* |
| | *ul* |
| nurse | *mušēniqtu* |
| | |
| oath | *nīšu* 1 |
| obey | *šemû* |
| obeyed, one who is | *muštešmû* |
| observe | *ṣubbû* |
| of | *ša* |
| offering | *nindabû* |
| | *zību* |
| officer | *laputtû* |
| oil | *piššatu* |
| | *šamnu* |
| oldest | *rēštu* |
| omen | *ittu* |
| omniscience | *igigallu* |
| on | *eli* |
| one | *ištēn* |

| | | | |
|---|---|---|---|
| one-fifth | *ḫamuštu* | pig | *šaḫû* |
| one-sixth | *šuššu* | plan | *uṣurtu* |
| one-third | *šalšu* | planning | *mušteṣbû* |
| | *šuššān* | plant | *zaqāpu* |
| open country | *ṣēru* | pleasure, bringing | *murīšu* |
| open | *petû* | pledge | *kiššātu* |
| opening | *pītu* | | *nipûtu* |
| opening up | *pātiʾu* | plentiful, be | *ṭaḫādu* |
| oppress | *esēru* | plenty | *nuḫšu* |
| or | *lu* | | *ṭuḫdu* |
| oracle | *tērtu* | plough | *epinnu* |
| orchard | *kirû* | | *ḫarbu* |
| order, give | *uʾuru* | pollinate | *rukkubu* |
| organizing | *muttabbilu* | pollination | *tarkibtu* |
| orphan girl | *ekūtu* | portion, extra | *elītu* |
| other | *aḫu* 3 | possess | *rašû* |
| outside | *kamîš* | pour out | *tabāku* |
| overturn | *sakāpu* | power | *kašūšu* |
| overwhelm | *nabalkutu* | | *lēʾūtu* |
| ox | *alpu* | powerful lady | *telītu* |
| | *mīru* | praise | *tanattu* |
| | *rīmu* | pray | *karābu* |
| | | precious | *šūquru* |
| palace | *ekallu* | preserve life | *šaṭāpu* |
| paralyse | *kabālu* | press for payment | *esēru* |
| partnership | *tappūtu* | pressure, apply | *saḫāmu* |
| pass by | *etēqu* | previous | *pānû* |
| pasture | *aburru* | price | *šīmu* |
| | *merētu* | priestess | *entu* |
| | *šurbuṣu* | | *kulmašītu* |
| pathway | *kibsu* | | *nadītu* |
| pay | *apālu* | | *sekretu* |
| | *šaqālu* | | *šugītu* |
| pay attention | *šuteṣbû* | | *ugbabtum* |
| peace | *šulmu* | prince | *rubû* |
| peace, bringing | *mušallimu* | principal wife | *rabītu* |
| pelt | *šašallu* | problem, cause | *uppusu* |
| pen | *tarbaṣu* | profit | *nēmelu* |
| penalty | *arnu* | progenitor | *ālidu* |
| people | *ammu* | proper | *kīnu* |
| | *nišū* | property | *bīšu* |
| perfect | *gitmālu* | | *mimmû* |
| permit | *rašû* | | *numātu* |
| pester | *suḫḫumu* | property, lost | *ḫulqu* |
| physician | *asû* | property, stolen | *šurqu* |

| | |
|---|---|
| prosper | *naḫāšu* |
| prospering | *munaḫḫišu* |
| prostitute, sacred | *qadištu* |
| protect | *šupuzzuru* |
| protecting | *mušaršidu* |
| | *mušpazzir* |
| protecting spirit | *šēdu* |
| protecting statue | *lamassu* |
| prove innocent | *uššuru* |
| provide for | *ašāru* 1 |
| provided with | *šaknu* |
| providing for | *āširu* |
| providing | *mušaklil* |
| | *šākinu* |
| pull apart | *naqāru* |
| pull out | *nasāku* 1 |
| punish | *emēdu* |
| purchase | *šâmu* 1 |
| purchaser | *šāyyimānu* |
| pure | *ellu* |
| purifying | *mubbibu* |
| pursue | *redû* |
| quickly | *arḫiš* |
| quietening | *munēḫu* |
| radiance | *melammu* |
| rage | *aggu* |
| rain | *zunnu* |
| raising | *mullû* 2 |
| | *nīšu* 2 |
| ransom | *ipṭeru* |
| rape | *kubbulu* |
| rate | *ṣimdatu* |
| ration | *ipru* |
| rebel | *nābiḫu* |
| receive | *maḫāru* |
| reclaimed, be | *nabquru* |
| recompense | *râbu* |
| redeem | *paṭāru* |
| reed-bed | *apu* |
| reign | *palû* |
| reinstate | *šullumu* |
| relax | *nuppušu* |
| reliability, show | *tukkulu* |
| remove | *eṭēru* |
| remove | *pašāṭu* |
| renew | *uddušu* |
| renewing | *muddišu* |
| rent | *biltu* |
| repeat | *šanû* |
| report | *ṭemu* |
| reprobate | *sarru* |
| repurchase | *paṭāru* |
| reputation | *igirrû* |
| resident | *ašbu* |
| resplendent, make | *šūpû* |
| responsible, make | *uppulu* |
| restless | *galātu* |
| retain | *kalû* |
| return | *târu* |
| returning | *mutēru* |
| reviving | *muballiṭu* |
| revolt | *ešītu* |
| riches | *ḫiṣbu* |
| ride | *rakābu* |
| right side | *imnu* |
| rite | *parṣu* |
| ritual | *mû* 2 |
| rival | *kammālu* |
| | *šāninu* |
| rivalry, show | *šumḫuru* |
| river | *nāru* |
| rob | *ḫabātu* |
| robbed | *ḫabtu* |
| robber | *ḫabbātu* |
| robbery | *ḫubtu* |
| rope-maker | *kāmidu* |
| rotten, be | *zabāru* |
| ruined site | *tillu* |
| rule | *ūsu* |
| sacred prostitute | *qadištu* |
| sacrifice | *zību* |
| saving | *šāṭipu* |
| scalpel | *karzillu* |
| scatter | *šapāḫu* |
| sceptre | *ḫaṭṭu* |
| sealed document | *kanīku* |
| | *kunukku* |

| | |
|---|---|
| search | *še'û* |
| seat | *kussû* |
| secure | *kīnu* |
| securely | *šulmāniš* |
| see | *amāru* |
| | *naṭālu* |
| seed | *zēru* |
| seed-corn | *aldû* |
| seize | *lapātu* |
| | *nepû* |
| | *ṣabātu* |
| selected | *nasqu* |
| self | *ramānu* |
| sell | *pašāru* |
| seller | *nādinānu* |
| send | *ṭarādu* |
| serious | *kabtu* |
| serving | *muzzazu* |
| sesame | *šamaššammū* |
| set | *šakānu* |
| settlements | *dadmū* |
| shade | *ṣulūlu* |
| shadow | *ṣillu* |
| share | *zâzu* |
| | *zittu* |
| shatter | *ḫabāšu* |
| shave | *gullubu* |
| she | *šî* |
| sheep | *immeru* |
| shekel | *šiqlu* |
| shepherd | *nāqidu* |
| | *rē'û* |
| ship, drifting | *muqqelpītu* |
| short, be | *maṭû* |
| shout | *šasû* |
| show reliability | *tukkulu* |
| showing generosity | *muṭaḫḫidu* |
| showing kindness | *gāmilu* |
| shrine | *ašru* |
| | *gigunû* |
| shut off | *sekēru* |
| sick | *marṣu* |
| side | *aḫu* 2 |
| sign | *ittu* |
| | *simtu* |
| signal | *kannu* |
| silencing | *mušeppû* |
| silent, be | *šapû* |
| silent, make | *šuppû* |
| silver | *kaspu* |
| sinew | *šerḫānu* |
| sink | *ṭebû* |
| sink, cause to | *ṭubbu* |
| six | *šeššet* |
| sixth | *šeššu* |
| sixty | *šūši* |
| size | *emūqu* |
| sky | *šamû* |
| slave | *ardu* |
| slave-girl | *amtu* |
| slave-mark | *abbuttu* |
| slavery | *ardūtu* |
| slip | *neḫelṣû* |
| small, be | *maṭû* 1 |
| smith | *nappāḫu* |
| snap off | *karāṣu* |
| soldier | *rēdû* |
| | *ṣābu* |
| something | *mimma* |
| son | *māru* |
| soothe | *nuḫḫu* |
| | *pašāḫu* |
| sorcery | *kišpū* |
| source | *nagbu* |
| speak | *qabû* |
| spirit | *šēdu* |
| square | *rebītu* |
| stake | *gašīšu* |
| stand | *izuzzu* |
| stare | *balāṣu* |
| state | *zakāru* |
| statue | *lamassu* |
| | *ṣalmu* |
| stay | *ašābu* |
| steal | *šarāqu* |
| stele | *narû* |
| still, be | *nâḫu* |
| stir up | *šuppuḫu* |
| stolen property | *šurqu* |
| stone | *abnu* |

| | |
|---|---|
| stone-cutter | *zadimmu* |
| stonemason | *parkullu* |
| stop up | *sekēru* |
| storage | *našpakūtu* |
| store | *garānu* |
| store up | *gurrunu* |
| | *kummuru* |
| | *šubbuḫu* |
| store | *šapāku* |
| straight, be | *ešēru* |
| straight, keeping | *muštēširu* |
| street | *sūqu* |
| strength | *idu* |
| strengthen | *dunnunu* |
| stretch | *šutruṣu* |
| | *tarāṣu* |
| strike | *maḫāṣu* |
| | *šuṭṭû* |
| strive | *šanānu* |
| strong | *dannu* |
| | *eṭlu* |
| strong, be | *danānu* |
| submissive, be | *šutaktutu* |
| submit | *kanāšu* |
| substitute | *pūḫu* |
| suck | *enēqu* |
| sun | *šamšu* |
| superhuman power | *lē'ūtu* |
| superhumanly strong | *lē'u* |
| supernatural power | *kašūšu* |
| supervise | *sanāqu* |
| supplement | *nipiltu* |
| supplicating | *muštēmiqu* |
| support | *tummuḫu* |
| suppress | *šuppû* |
| surrounding | *muštasḫiru* |
| swear | *tamû* |
| symbol | *simtu* |
| tail | *zibbatu* |
| take away | *arû* |
| take | *aḫāzu* |
| | *leqû* |
| tariff | *maḫīru* |
| task | *šipru* |
| tear out | *nasāḫu* |
| ten | *ešir* |
| tend | *re'û* |
| tendon | *šašallu* |
| terminate | *bullû* |
| | *šuqtû* |
| that | *šî* |
| | *šiāti* |
| then | *inūmīšu* |
| thief | *šarrāqānum* |
| | *šarrāqu* |
| thirsty, be | *ṣamû* |
| thirty | *šalāšā* |
| this | *annû* |
| | *šû* |
| three | *šalaš* |
| thresh | *dâšu* |
| threshing place | *maškanu* |
| throne | *kussû* |
| throw down | *nadû* |
| throw out | *šussuku* |
| time | *adannu* |
| to | *ana* |
| tongue | *lišānu* |
| tooth | *šinnu* |
| toss | *nakāpu* |
| tossing | *munakkipû* |
| touch | *lapātu* |
| trader | *šamallû* |
| tree | *iṣu* |
| trick | *dâṣu* |
| trim | *šurrumu* |
| trouble | *gabaraḫḫum* |
| trouble-maker | *mugallitu* |
| trust | *qīptu* |
| | *takālu* |
| turmoil | *saḫmaštu* |
| | *tēšû* |
| twenty | *ešrā* |
| twice as much | *tašnā* |
| two | *šina* |
| two-thirds | *šittān* |
| unfortunate, be | *lemēnu* |
| unstable, be | *ṣabaru* |

| | | | |
|---|---|---|---|
| until | *adi* | widening | *murappišu* |
| utterance | *amatu* | widespread | *saphu* |
| | | widow | *almattu* |
| value | *emūqu* | wife | *aššatu* |
| verdict | *dīnu* | | *hīrtu* |
| verdure | *arqu* | wild | *kadru* |
| victory, granting | *mušakšidu* | wilderness | *ṣēru* |
| victory cry | *irnittu* | wisdom | *nēmequ* |
| villain | *mugallitu* | | *uršu* |
| violent | *ezzu* | wise | *emqu* |
| visible, be | *apû* | | *eršu* 1 |
| visible, make | *šuṭṭulu* | wish | *nizmatu* |
| visible, making | *mušēpû* | with | *itti* |
| | | | *qadu* |
| waggon | *ereqqu* | within | *qerbum* |
| waggon driver | *murteddû* | without | *balu* |
| walking | *āliku* | witness | *šību* |
| wall | *igāru* | woman | *awīltu* |
| war | *qablu* | | *sinništu* |
| water | *mû* 1 | womb | *sūnu* |
| watering place | *mašqītu* | wool | *šipātu* |
| way | *urhu* | work | *epištu* |
| weak | *enšu* | workforce | *ummānu* |
| weak, be | *enēšu* | working citizen | *muškēnu* |
| weaken | *šūpêlu* | world, areas of | *kibrātu* |
| | *unnušu* | worried, be | *šutaktutu* |
| wealth | *hegallu* | worship | *palāhu* |
| weapon | *kakku* | wound | *nasāku* |
| weariness | *tānēhu* | | |
| weaver | *kāmidu* | year | *šattu* |
| when | *inu* | you (fem. sing.) | *attī* |
| | *inūma* | you (masc. sing.) | *attā* |
| wherever | *ēma* | young animal | *talittu* |
| whip | *qinnazu* | young man | *eṭlu* |
| wicked | *raggu* | young | *ṣehru* |
| | *ṣēnu* 2 | young, be | *ṣehēru* |
| wide, be | *rapāšu* | young, very | *ṣehheru* |

# Akkadian–English Index

This is essentially a simple listing of the headings in the Glossary (with roots where appropriate), though many of the cross-references, especially those that concern freely variable phonemes, have been omitted here. Another difference is the primary listing for derived forms of verbs (D, Š and N themes) under their base forms, although the participles are still in principle treated as separate items, as they were in the Glossary.

The question arose of how best to mark homonyms, which *CAD* and *AHw* treat differently. It seemed best to follow the descriptive model of *AHw*, where any two words given an identical transcription are regarded as homonyms distinguished by a roman numeral (all references to *AHw* are shown here in decorative brackets); then to make a correlation with the capital letters and grammatical descriptions of the interpretative model favoured by *CAD* (shown here in rounded brackets). For the purposes of the list itself the homonyms that are found in CH (including those that arise from the decision to list derived forms of verbs and participles as separate items) are marked with Arabic numerals, and homonymous roots are marked similarly; this was done in order to avoid confusion with the roman numerals used in *AHw*.

Although this list was compiled as a necessary prerequisite to all the other lists in this book it was decided to place it here in final position, in the hope that it will help users to track down elusive words in the Glossary more quickly, and also more easily to find further information from *CAD* and *AHw* as required. Cross-references are marked with the sign >.

| | | |
|---|---|---|
| *abālu* (A) {*wabālu*} | *w-b-l* | to bring; Š *šūbulu*, to have brought |
| {*abāru* III} | *ʾ-b-r* | to encompass; D *ubburu*, to accuse (s.v. 2) |
| *abātu* (B) {*nābutu*} | *ʾ-b-t* 2 | to flee; N *nābutu*, to flee |
| *abbuttu* {I} | | slave-mark |
| *abnu* (A) | | stone |
| *abšinnu* {*absinnu*} | | > *šerʾu*, field |
| *abu* (A) {I} | | father |

| | | |
|---|---|---|
| *abūbu* | | deluge |
| *abullu* | | gate |
| *aburru* | | pasture |
| *adannu* {*adānum*} | | appointed time |
| *adāru* (B) {s.v. B} | *ʾ-d-r* | to fear |
| *adi* 1 (conj.) {s.v. B} | | as long as |
| *adi* 2 (A) {s.v. A} | | until |
| *adi* 3 (B) | | > *qadu* with |
| *agāru* | *ʾ-g-r* | to hire |
| *aggu* | | raging |
| *agru* | *ʾ-g-r* | labourer |
| *agû* (A) {I} | | crown |
| *aḫāzu* | *ʾ-ḫ-z* | to take |
| *aḫu* 1 (A) {I} | | brother |
| *aḫu* 2 (B) {II} | | side |
| *aḫu* 3 (adj.) {*aḫû* I} | | other |
| *aj* {*ai* I} | | > *ay*, not |
| *ajābu* {*ajjābu*} | | > *ayyābu*, enemy |
| *akālu* | *ʾ-k-l* | to eat |
| *aklu* A {*waklu*} | | > *ša ḫaṭṭātim*, captain |
| *alādu* {*walādum*} | *w-l-d* | to give birth |
| *alāku* | *ʾ-l-k* | to go |
| *alālu* (A) {II} | *ḫ-l-l* | to hang; N *naḫlulu*, to be hung |
| *aldû* | *w-l-d* | seed corn |
| *ālidu* | *w-l-d* | progenitor |
| *āliku* | *ʾ-l-k* | walking |
| *almattu* | | widow |
| *alpu* {I} | | ox |
| *ālu* {I} | | city |
| *amāru* | *ʾ-m-r* | to see |
| *amatu* (A) {*amātu*} | | > *awātu*, statement |
| *amīltu* | | > *awīltu*, woman |
| *amīlu* | | > *awīlu*, man |
| *amīlūtu* | | > *awīlūtu*, humanity |
| *ammu* {I} | | people |
| *amtu* | | slave-girl |
| *ana* | | to |
| *anāku* | | I |
| *andurāru* | | freedom |
| *annû* {I} | | this |
| *apālu* {I} | *ʾ-p-l* | to answer; D *uppulu*, to make responsible |
| *apkallu* | | expert |
| *aplu* {I} | *ʾ-p-l* | heir |
| *aplūtu* | | inheritance |

| | | |
|---|---|---|
| *apšītû* {*apšitûm*} | | agreed amount |
| *apu* (A) | | reed-bed |
| *apû* (A) {*wapû*} | *w-p-ʾ* | to be visible; Š *šūpû*, to make appear |
| *arāku* | *ʾ-r-k* | to be long; D *urruku*, to lengthen |
| *arāru* (A) {I} | *ʾ-r-r* | to curse |
| *arbaʾu* | | > *erbû*, four |
| *ardu* | | slave |
| *ardūtu* | | slavery |
| *arḫiš* | *ʾ-r-ḫ* | quickly |
| *arḫu* (A) {*warḫum*} | | month |
| *arka* {*warka*} | *ʾ-r-k* | afterwards |
| *arkānu* {*warkānu*} | *ʾ-r-k* | afterwards |
| *arkatu* {*warkatu*} | *ʾ-r-k* | circumstances |
| *arki* {*warki*} | *ʾ-r-k* | after |
| *arkītu* {*warkītu*} | *ʾ-r-k* | future |
| *arkû* {*warkû*} | *ʾ-r-k* | subsequent |
| *arnu* | | penalty |
| *arqu* {*warqu*} | *w-r-q* | green |
| *arratu* | | > *erretu*, curse |
| *arû* (A) {*warûm* II, *arû* VI} | *ʾ-r-ʾ* | to take away |
| *âru* {*wâru*} | *w-ʾ-r* | to advance; D *uʾuru*, to give an order |
| *asakku* (A) {I} | | demon |
| *asû* {I} | | physician |
| *aṣû* (*waṣû*) | *w-ṣ-ʾ* | to go out; Š *šūṣû*, to bring out |
| *ašābu* (*wašābu*) | *w-š-b* | to stay; Š *šūšubu*, to allow to dwell |
| *ašaridu* (*ašarēdu*) | | chief |
| *ašāru* 1 (A) {I} | *ʾ-š-r* | to organize |
| *ašāru* 2 (C) {*wašāru*} | *w-š-r* | to hang loosely, flee; Dt *uššuru*, to be let free |
| *ašāšu* {III} | *ʾ-š-š* | to be distressed; D *uššušu*, to maltreat |
| *ašbu* (B) {*wašbu*} | *w-š-b* | resident |
| *āširu* | *ʾ-š-r* | organizing |
| *aškāpu* | | leather-worker |
| *ašnan* | | grain |
| *ašru* 1 (A) {III} | *ʾ-š-r* | shrine |
| *ašru* 2 (adj.) {*wašru*} | *w-š-r* | humble |
| *aššābu* {*waššābu*} | *w-š-b* | occupant |
| *aššatu* | *ʾ-n-š* | wife |
| *aššum* | | because of |
| *ašṭu* {*wašṭu*} | | difficult |
| *atappu* | | canal |
| *atāru* {*watāru*} | *w-t-r* | to be much; D *utturu*, to exceed; Š *šūturu*, to make excellent |
| *atkuppu* | | basket-maker |

| | | |
|---|---|---|
| *atru* {*watru*} | *w-t-r* | extra |
| *atta* {*attā*} | | you (masc sing) |
| *atti* {*attī*} | | you (fem sing) |
| *awatu* {*awātum*} | | statement |
| *awīltu* {*awiltum*} | | woman |
| *awīlu* | | man |
| *awīlūtu* | | humanity |
| *ay* {*ay* I} | | not |
| *ayyābu* {*ajjābu*} | | enemy |
| | | |
| *babālu* | *w-b-l* | to bring |
| *bābilu* | *w-b-l* | bringing |
| *babtu* {*bābtu*} | | community |
| *bābu* | | doorway |
| *bāʾiru* {*bāʾeru*} | *b-ʾ-r* 1 | hunter |
| *balāṣu* | *b-l-ṣ* | to stare; > *palāsu*, to look at |
| *balāṭu* 1 (vb.) {II} | *b-l-ṭ* | to live; D *bulluṭu*, to give life to |
| *balāṭu* 2 (sbst.) {I} | *b-l-ṭ* | life |
| *balṭu* | *b-l-ṭ* | alive |
| *balu* | | without |
| *balû* {*belû* II} | *b-l-ʾ* | to come to an end; D *bullû*, to terminate |
| *bānītu* | *b-n-ʾ* | creatress |
| *banû* (A) {IV} | *b-n-ʾ* | to procreate |
| *bānû* | *b-n-ʾ* | creator |
| {*baqāru*} | *b-q-r* | > *paqāru*, to claim |
| *baqrū* | *b-q-r* | claim |
| *bâru* (A) {III} | *b-ʾ-r* 2 | to be certain; D *burru*, to declare |
| *bašû* | *b-š-ʾ* | to exist; Š *šubšû*, to produce; N *nabšû*, to be produced |
| *bēltu* | *b-ʾ-l* | mistress |
| *bēlu* {I} | *b-ʾ-l* | master |
| *bennu* (A) {I} | | epilepsy |
| *bibbulu* {*bubbulu*} | | > *bubbulu*, flood |
| *biblu* | *w-b-l* | marriage gift |
| *biltu* {I} | *w-b-l* | rent |
| *binâtu* {*binītu*} | *b-n-ʾ* | limbs |
| *binītu* | *b-n-ʾ* | creature |
| *bīru* (A) {III} | *b-ʾ-r* 2 | divination |
| *bīšu* {II} | *b-š-ʾ* | possessions |
| *bitiqtu* | *b-t-q* | loss |
| *bītu* | | house |
| *bubbulu* | *w-b-l* | flood |
| *bubūtu* (A) {II} | | famine |
| *bullû* | *b-l-ʾ* | > *balû*, to come to an end |

| | | |
|---|---|---|
| *bulluṭu* | *b-l-ṭ* | > *balāṭu*, to be alive |
| *bulṭu* | *b-l-ṭ* | life |
| *burru* | *b-ʾ-r* 2 | > *bâru*, to be certain |
| *buru* {*būru* III} | | measurement of area |
| *butuqqû* | *b-t-q* | loss |
| *dadmū* | | settlements |
| *dajjānu* | | > *dayyānu*, judge |
| *dajjānūtu* | | > *dayyānūtu*, judiciary |
| *dâku* | *d-ʾ-k* | to kill; Š *šudūku*, to arrange a murder; N *nadūku*, to be killed |
| *damāmu* | *d-m-m* | to mourn |
| *damāqu* | *d-m-q* | to be kind; D *dummuqu*, to show kindness |
| *damiqtu* {*damqu*} | *d-m-q* | favour |
| *damqu* | *d-m-q* | good |
| *damu* {II} | | blood |
| *danānu* {II} | *d-n-n* | to be strong; D *dunnunu*, to strengthen |
| *dannatu* | *d-n-n* | fortress |
| *dannu* {I} | *d-n-n* | strong |
| *dânu* {*diānum*} | *d-ʾ-n* | to legislate |
| *dāriš* | *d-w-r* | for ever |
| *dāru* {I} | *d-w-r* | generation |
| *dārû* | *d-w-r* | everlasting |
| *dâṣu* | *d-ʾ-ṣ* | to trick |
| *dâšu* {*diāšum*} | *d-ʾ-š* | to thresh |
| *dayyānu* {*dajjānu*} | *d-ʾ-n* | judge |
| *dayyānūtu* {*dajjānūtu*} | *d-ʾ-n* | judiciary |
| *dekû* | *d-k-ʾ* | to arrange |
| *dešû* | *d-š-ʾ* | to be abundant; D *duššû*, to make abundant |
| *dimmatu* | *d-m-m* | moaning |
| *dīnu* | *d-ʾ-n* | judgement |
| *dummuqu* | *d-m-q* | > *damāqu*, to be good |
| *dumqu* | *d-m-q* | favour |
| *dunnunu* | *d-n-n* | > *danānu*, to be strong |
| *duppuru* | *d-p-r* | to be absent |
| *ebēbu* | *ʾ-b-b* | to be clean; D: to cleanse |
| *ebūru* | | harvest |
| *edû* {III} | | > *idû*, to know |
| *edēšu* | *ʾ-d-š* | to be new; D *uddušu*, to renew |
| *egirrû* {*egerrû*} | | >*igirrû*, reputation |
| *egû* | *ʾ-g-ʾ* | to be negligent |
| *eʾiltu* | *y-ʾ-l* | debt |

| | | |
|---|---|---|
| *ekallu* | | palace |
| *ekūtu* (A) {*ekûtu*} | | orphan girl |
| *ela* (adv.) | | only |
| *elēnu* | *ʾ-l-ʾ* | in addition |
| *eleppu* | | boat |
| *eli* (prep.) | | on |
| *eliš* | | above |
| *elītu* {*ēlītu*} | *ʾ-l-ʾ* | extra portion |
| *ellilūtu* {*Ellilūtu*} | | leadership |
| *ellu* {I} | | pure |
| *elû* 1 (vb.) {IV} | *ʾ-l-ʾ* | to go up |
| *elû* 2 (B) {II} | *ʾ-l-ʾ* | upper |
| *ēma* | | wherever |
| *emēdu* | *ʾ-m-d* | to impose; N *nenmudu*, to join in cohabitation |
| {*emēqu*} | *ʾ-m-q* | to beseech ardently; Št > *muštēmiqu*, supplicating |
| *emqu* | *ʾ-m-q* | wise |
| *emu* | | father-in-law |
| *emūqu* | | value |
| *enēqu* | *y-n-q* | to suck; Š > *mušēniqtu*, nurse |
| *enēšu* | *ʾ-n-š* | to be weak; D *unnušu*, to weaken |
| *enšu* | *ʾ-n-š* | weak |
| *ēntu* {*entu*} | | > *ugbabtu*, priestess |
| *enû* | *ʾ-n-ʾ* | to change |
| *epēsu* | *ʾ-p-s* | to make difficulty; D *uppusu*, to cause a problem |
| *epēšu* {II} | *ʾ-p-š* | to act |
| *epinnu* | | plough |
| *epištu* | *ʾ-p-š* | work |
| *eqlu* | | field |
| *erbe* | | four |
| *erēbu* | *ʾ-r-b* | to enter; Š *šūrubu*, to bring in |
| *erēšu* 1 (A) {II} | *ʾ-r-š* 1 | to demand |
| *erēšu* 2 (B) {I} | *ʾ-r-š* 2 | to cultivate |
| *ēribu* | *ʾ-r-b* | entering |
| *eriqqu* {*ereqqu*} | | waggon |
| *errēšu* | *ʾ-r-š* 2 | cultivator |
| *errēšūtu* | *ʾ-r-š* 2 | cultivation |
| *erretu* {I} | *ʾ-r-r* | curse |
| *erṣetu* | | earth |
| *eršu* 1 (A) {I} | *ʾ-r-š* 3 | wise |
| *eršu* 2 (B) {II} | *ʾ-r-š* 2 | cultivated |
| *esēpu* | *ʾ-s-p* | to gather |
| *esēru* {III} | *ʾ-s-r* | to press for payment |

| | | |
|---|---|---|
| *eṣēdu* {II} | *ʾ-ṣ-d* | to harvest |
| *eṣemtu* | | bone |
| *ešēru* | *y-š-r* | to be straight; Š *šūšuru*, to show straightforwardness |
| *ešir* {*ešer*} | | ten |
| *ešītu* | *ʾ-š-y* 1 | disturbance |
| *ešrā* | | twenty |
| *ešû* {V} | *ʾ-š-y* 1 | to confuse |
| *etellu* | | leader |
| *etēqu* | *ʾ-t-q* | to pass by; Š *šūtuqu*, to allow time to expire |
| *eṭemmu* | | ghost |
| *eṭēru* {I} | *ʾ-ṭ-r* | to remove |
| *eṭlu* | | strong youth |
| *ezēbu* | *ʾ-z-b* | to leave; Š *šūzubu*, to get deposited |
| *ezziš* | *ʾ-z-z* 1 | angrily |
| *ezzu* | *ʾ-z-z* 1 | angry |
| | | |
| *gabaraḫḫu* | | trouble |
| *gagû* | | harem |
| *galātu* | *g-l-t* | to be restless; D > *mugallitu*, trouble-making |
| *gallābu* | *g-l-b* | barber |
| *gamālu* | *g-m-l* | to care for |
| *gamartu* (A) | *g-m-r* | completion |
| *gamāru* {II} | *g-m-r* | to complete |
| *gāmilu* | *g-m-l* | showing kindness |
| *gamru* {I} | *g-m-r* | complete |
| *garānu* {*qarānu*} | *q-r-n* | to store; D *gurrunu*, to store |
| *gašīšu* | | stake |
| *gašru* | *g-š-r* | strong |
| *gigunû* {*gegnû*} | | shrine |
| *girsequ͡û* {*gerseqqû*} | | attendant |
| *gitmālu* | *g-m-l* | perfect |
| *gugallu* (A) {I} | | chief irrigation officer |
| *gullubu* {II} | *g-l-b* | to shave |
| *gurrunu* | *q-r-n* | > *garānu*, to store |
| *gurunnu* {*qurunnu*} | *q-r-n* | heap |
| | | |
| *ḫabālu* (A) {II} | *ḫ-b-l* | to exploit |
| *ḫabāšu* {II} | *ḫ-b-š* | to shatter |
| *ḫabātu* (A) {I} | *ḫ-b-t* | to rob |
| *ḫabbātu* {I} | *ḫ-b-t* | robber |
| *ḫablu* | *ḫ-b-l* | exploited |
| *ḫabtu* | *ḫ-b-t* | robbed |

| | | |
|---|---|---|
| *ḫadû* {III} | *ḫ-d-ʾ* | to be glad; D *ḫuddû*, to gladden |
| *ḫāʾiru* | *ḫ-ʾ-r* | > *ḫāwiru*, first husband |
| *ḫalālu* | *ḫ-l-l* | > *alālu*, to hang |
| *ḫalāqu* | *ḫ-l-q* | to disappear; D *ḫulluqu*, to destroy |
| *ḫalqu* | *ḫ-l-q* | missing |
| *ḫamiš* | | five |
| *ḫamšu* (A) | | fifth |
| *ḫamuštu* | | one-fifth |
| *ḫarāṣu* {I} | *ḫ-r-ṣ* | to subtract; Š *šuḫruṣu*, to deduct |
| *ḫarbu* (A) {II} | *ḫ-r-b* | plough |
| *ḫarrānu* | | expedition |
| *ḫâru* {*ḫiāru*} | *ḫ-ʾ-r* | to choose |
| *ḫassu* | *ḫ-s-s* | intelligent |
| *ḫaṭṭu* {II} | | sceptre |
| *ḫâṭu* {*ḫiāṭu*} | *ḫ-ʾ-ṭ* | to find out |
| *ḫāwiru* | *ḫ-ʾ-r* | first husband |
| *ḫegallu* {*ḫengallu*} | | abundance |
| *ḫepû* {II} | *ḫ-p-ʾ* | to break; N *neḫpû*, to be broken |
| *ḫīrtu* | *ḫ-ʾ-r* | first wife |
| *ḫiṣbu* {I} | *ḫ-ṣ-b* | riches |
| *ḫiṭītu* | *ḫ-ṭ-ʾ* | fault |
| *ḫubtu* | *ḫ-b-t* | robbery |
| *ḫubullu* (A) {I} | *ḫ-b-l* | debt |
| *ḫuddû* | *ḫ-d-ʾ* | > *ḫadû*, to be glad |
| *ḫulluqu* | *ḫ-l-q* | > *ḫalāqu*, to disappear |
| *ḫulqu* | *ḫ-l-q* | lost property |
| *ḫuppudu* {II} | *ḫ-p-d* | to blind |
| *ḫurāṣu* | | gold |
| *ḫušaḫḫu* | | famine |
| | | |
| *iâti* {*jâti*} | | me |
| *ibbû* {*ibbûm*} | | loss |
| *ibru* | | friend |
| {*idu*} | | arm > *idū*, fees |
| *idû* {*edû* III} | *y-d-ʾ* | to know; D *uddû*, to find out; Š *šūdû*, to make known |
| *idū* {*idu* s.v. 9} | | fees |
| *igāru* | | wall |
| *igigallu* | | omniscience |
| *igirrû* {*egerrû*} | | reputation |
| *igru* | *ʾ-g-r* | hire |
| *iḫiltu* | | > *eʾiltu*, debt |
| *ikkaru* | | ploughman |
| *ikletu* {*ekletu*} | | darkness |
| *ikû* {II} | | > *buru*, measurement of area |

| | | |
|---|---|---|
| *ilku* (A) {I} | | feudal duty |
| *ilu* | | god |
| *imbû* (B) | | > *ibbû*, loss |
| *imēru* | | ass |
| *immeru* | | sheep |
| *imnu* | | right side |
| *in* {*ina*} | | at |
| *ina* | | at |
| *īnu* 1 (conj.) {*inu* I} | | when |
| *īnu* 2 (sbst.) {*īnu* I} | | eye |
| *inūma* | | when |
| *inūmišu* {*inūmīšu*} | | at that time |
| *ipru* | | barley ration |
| *ipṭirū* {*ipṭiru*} | *p-ṭ-r* | ransom |
| *irnittu* {*ernittu*} | | triumph |
| *iṣu* | | tree |
| *īṣu* | | insufficient |
| *išātu* | | fire |
| *išdu* | | foundation |
| *išītu* | | > *ešītu*, disturbance |
| *iššakku* {*iššiakkum*} | | governor |
| *ištēn* | | one |
| *ištiat* {*ištēn*} | | one |
| *ištīššu* {*ištiššu*} | | first occasion |
| *ištu* | | since |
| *išû* | *ʾ-š-y* 2 (?) | to have |
| *itinnu* (A) | | builder |
| *itti* | | with |
| *ittu* (A) | | omen |
| *itû* (B) | | neighbour |
| {*itūlu*} | *ʾ-ʾ-l* | to copulate |
| {*izuzzu*} (*uzuzzu*) | *ʾ-z-z* 2 | to stand; Š *šuzzuzu*, to erect |

| | | |
|---|---|---|
| *jâti* | | > *iāti*, me |

| | | |
|---|---|---|
| *kabālu* | *k-b-l* | to be paralysed; D *kubbulu*, to rape |
| *kabātu* | *k-b-t* | to be important |
| *kabtu* | *k-b-t* | serious |
| *kadru* | *k-d-r* | wild |
| *kakku* | | weapon |
| *kallatu* {*kallātu*} | | bride |
| *kalû* {V} | *k-l-ʾ* | to withhold |
| *kamāru* {III} | *k-m-r* | to heap up; D > *mukammiru*, heaping up |
| *kāmidu* | *k-m-d* | rope-maker; {weaver} |

| | | |
|---|---|---|
| *kamîš* | *k-m-ʾ* (*kmī*) | in bonds |
| *kammālu* | *k-m-l* | rival |
| *kanāšu* {I} | *k-n-š* | to submit; D > *mukannišu*, controlling |
| *kanīku* | *k-n-k* | sealed document |
| *kankallu* | | hardened soil |
| *kannu* (A) {I} | | potstand |
| *kannu* (B) {II} | | string |
| *kânu* (A) | *k-ʾ-n* | to be firm; D *kunnu*, to establish as true |
| *karābu* {II} | *k-r-b* | to pray |
| *karāṣu* | *k-r-ṣ* | to snap off; D *kurruṣu*, to malign |
| *karašû* {*karāšu* II} | | catastrophe |
| *kāru* (A) | | dyke |
| *karû* (A) | | heap of grain |
| *karzillu* {*karṣillu*} | | scalpel |
| *kaspu* | | silver |
| *kasû* {III} | *k-s-ʾ* | to bind |
| *kašādu* | *k-š-d* | to conquer; Š *šukšudu*, to enable to attain |
| *kašāšu* | *k-š-š* | to enforce payment |
| *kāšišu* | *k-š-š* | creditor |
| *kašūšu* | *k-š-š* | supernatural power |
| *katātu* | *k-t-t* | to be low {or to tremble}; Št *šutaktutu*, to be submissive {or to be worried} |
| *kî* {*kī*} | | like |
| *kibrātu* {*kibru*} | | areas of the world |
| *kibsu* (A) {I} | *k-b-s* | pathway |
| *kilallān* | *k-l-l* | both |
| *kīma* (prep.) | | like |
| *kīnātu* {*kittu* I} | *k-ʾ-n* | justice |
| *kīnu* | *k-ʾ-n* | secure |
| *kirû* | | orchard |
| *kiṣru* | *k-ṣ-r* | agreed rent |
| *kišpū* {*kispu*} | | sorcery |
| *kiššatu* (A) {I} | | mass of humanity |
| *kiššātu* | *k-š-š* | pledge for debt |
| *kittu* (A) {I} | *k-ʾ-n* | justice |
| *kitû* | | flax |
| *kubbulu* | *k-b-l* | > *kabālu*, to be paralysed |
| *kullizu* | | ox-driver |
| *kullu* {II} | *k-ʾ-l* | to hold |
| *kullumu* | *k-l-m* | to explain |
| *kulmašītu* | | priestess |

| | | |
|---|---|---|
| *kunnu* | *k-ʾ-n* | > *kânu*, to be firm |
| *kunukku* | *k-n-k* | sealed document |
| *kurru* (A) {I} | | measurement of capacity |
| *kurruṣu* | *k-r-ṣ* | > *karāṣu*, to snap off |
| *kussû* | | official seat |
| | | |
| *la* {*lā*} | | not |
| *labânu* {*labiānum*} | | neck muscle |
| *labāšu* | *l-b-š* | to dress oneself; Š *šulbušu*, to clothe |
| *la'bu* | *l-ʾ-b* | disease |
| *lāma* (conj.) | | before |
| *lamādu* | *l-m-d* | to learn |
| *lamassu* | | guardian spirit |
| *lapātu* | *l-p-t* | to lay hold on; Š *šulputu*, to overthrow |
| *laputtû* {*laputtāʾum*} | | officer |
| *lemēnu* | *l-m-n* | to be unfortunate; D *lummunu*, to denigrate |
| *lemnu* | *l-m-n* | bad |
| *lemuttu* | *l-m-n* | misfortune |
| *leqû* {II} | *l-q-ʾ* | to take |
| *lētu* {I} | | cheek |
| *leʾû* | *l-ʾ-ʾ* | to be able |
| *lēʾu* {*lēʾû*} | *l-ʾ-ʾ* | capable |
| *lēʾūtu* {*lēʾûtu*} | *l-ʾ-ʾ* | supreme power |
| *liʾātu* | | > *littu*, cattle |
| *libbu* | | heart |
| *libittu* | *l-b-n* | brickwork |
| *liblibbu* {*libbu; līpu*} | | descendant |
| *liptu* (A) | *l-p-t* | affliction |
| *lišānu* | | tongue |
| *littu* (A) {*lītu* II} | | cattle |
| *lu* {*lū*} | | or |
| *lubūšu* | *l-b-š* | clothing |
| *lummunu* | *l-m-n* | > *lemēnu*, to be unfortunate |
| | | |
| *madādu* (A) {I} | *m-d-d* | to measure |
| *magal* | | greatly |
| *magāru* | *m-g-r* | to agree |
| *maḫar* | *m-ḫ-r* | > *maḫru*, front |
| *maḫāru* | *m-ḫ-r* | to receive; Š *šumḫuru*, to show rivalry |
| *maḫāṣu* | *m-ḫ-ṣ* | to strike |
| {*māḫirtu*} | *m-ḫ-r* | moving upstream > *māḫiru* confronting |

| | | |
|---|---|---|
| *maḫīru* | *m-ḫ-r* | tariff |
| *māḫiru* | *m-ḫ-r* | confronting |
| *maḫra* | *m-ḫ-r* | in front |
| *maḫru* {II} | *m-ḫ-r* | front |
| *maḫrû* {I} | *m-ḫ-r* | former |
| *majjāru* | | > *mayyāru*, mattock |
| *mākālu* {*mākālum*} | *ʾ-k-l* | food |
| *makkūru* {*namkūru*} | *m-k-r* | property |
| *mala* {I} | | as much as |
| *malāḫu* (A) {I} | | boatman |
| *malû* 1 (vb.) {IV} | *m-l-ʾ* | to be full; D *mullû* 1, to fill |
| *malû* 2 (adj.) {I} | *m-l-ʾ* | full |
| *mānaḫtu* | *ʾ-n-ḫ* | expenses |
| *manû* 1 (vb.) {V} | *m-n-ʾ* | to count |
| *manû* 2 (A) {II} | *m-n-ʾ* | mina |
| *maqātu* | *m-q-t* | to fall; Š *šumqutu*, to bring down |
| *marāru* (B) {II} | *m-r-r* | to harrow |
| *markasu* | *r-k-s* | link |
| *marṣu* | *m-r-ṣ* | diseased |
| *mārtu* | | daughter |
| *māru* | | son |
| {*maruštu*} | *m-r-ṣ* | diseased > *marṣu*, (fem.) diseased |
| *mārūtu* | | adoption |
| *maṣṣarūtu* {*maṣṣārūtu*} | *n-ṣ-r* | custody |
| *maṣû* | *m-ṣ-ʾ* | to be equal; Š *šumṣû*, to grant discretion |
| *mašāru* | *m-š-r* | to drag |
| *maškakātu* | *š-k-k* | harrow |
| *maškanu* | *š-k-n* | threshing-place |
| *mašqītu* (A) | *š-q-ʾ* | watering-place |
| *matima* {*matīma*} | | eternally |
| *mātu* {I} | | land |
| *mâtu* | *m-ʾ-t* | to die; Š *šumūtu*, to cause death |
| *maṭû* 1 (vb.) {II} | *m-ṭ-ʾ* | to be too short; D *muṭṭû*, to lessen; Š *šumṭû*, to denigrate |
| *maṭû* 2 (adj.) {I} | *m-ṭ-ʾ* | small |
| *mayyāru* {*majjāru*} | *n-ʾ-r* (?) | mattock |
| *mēgûtu* {*mēgûtu*} | *ʾ-g-ʾ* | negligence |
| *melammu* {*melemmu*} | | radiance |
| *mēreštu* (B) {I} | *ʾ-r-š* 2 | arable land |
| {*merītu*} | *r-ʾ-ʾ* | > *mirītu*, pasture |
| *mêšu* | *m-ʾ-š* | to disdain |
| *migru* | *m-g-r* | favoured friend |
| *miḫru* (A) {*meḫru* I} | *m-ḫ-r* | equivalent |
| *mīlu* (A) | *m-l-ʾ* | flood |

| | | |
|---|---|---|
| *mimma* | | something |
| *mimmû* | | property |
| *miqittu* | *m-q-t* | damage |
| *mirītu* (A) {*merītu*} | *r-ʾ-ʾ* | pasture |
| *mīru* (A) {I} | | young bull |
| *mīšaru* (A) | *y-š-r* | justice |
| *mīšītu* {*mišītu*} | *ʾ-š-y* 1 | confusion |
| *mišlānū* | | half-shares |
| *mišlu* | | half |
| *mitḫāriš* | *m-ḫ-r* | equally |
| *mû* 1 (A) {I} | | water |
| *mû* 2 (B) {II} | | rite |
| *muballiṭu* | *b-l-ṭ* | reviving |
| *mubbibu* | *ʾ-b-b* | purifying |
| *mubbiru* | *ʾ-b-r* | accusing |
| *mudammiqu* | *d-m-q* | benefitting |
| *muddišu* | *ʾ-d-š* | making new |
| *mudeššû* | *d-š-ʾ* | making abundant |
| *mudû* {*mūdû*} | *y-d-ʾ* | acquainted with |
| *mūdûtu* | *y-d-ʾ* | knowledge |
| *mugallitu* | *g-l-t* | trouble-maker |
| *mugarrinu* | *q-r-n* | heaping up |
| *muḫaddû* | *ḫ-d-ʾ* | gladdening |
| *mukammiru* | *k-m-r* | heaping up |
| *mukannišu* | *k-n-š* | controlling |
| *mukillu* | *k-ʾ-l* | holding |
| *mukīnu* | *k-ʾ-n* | founder |
| *mullû* 1 | *m-l-ʾ* | > *malû*, to be full |
| *mullû* 2 | *ʾ-l-ʾ* | raising |
| *munaggiru* | *n-g-r* 2 | informer |
| *munaḫḫišu* | *n-ḫ-š* | munificent |
| *munakkipu* | *n-k-p* | tossing |
| *munammiru* {*munawwiru*} | *n-w-r* | brightening |
| *munēḫu* | *n-ʾ-ḫ* | quietening |
| *munnabtu* | *ʾ-b-d* | fugitive |
| *mupaḫḫiru* | *p-ḫ-r* | assembling |
| *mupparkû* {*naparkû* II} | *p-r-k-ʾ* | neglecting |
| *muqqelpītu* | *q-l-p-ʾ* | drifting |
| *murabbītu* | *r-b-ʾ* | foster mother |
| *murabbû* | *r-b-ʾ* | foster father |
| *murappišu* | *r-p-š* | extending |
| *murīšu* | *r-ʾ-š* | bringing pleasure |
| *murṣu* | *m-r-ṣ* | disease |
| *murteddû* {*redû* Gtn} | *r-d-ʾ* | driving |
| *musaru* | | > *mušaru*, measure |

| | | |
|---|---|---|
| *muṣīru* | *ṣ-ʾ-r* | making famous |
| *mušaddilu* | *š-d-l* | developing |
| *mušaklil* | *k-l-l* | providing |
| *mušakšidu* | *k-š-d* | granting victory |
| *mušalbišu* | *l-b-š* | decorating |
| *mušallimu* | *š-l-m* | bringing peace |
| *mušarbû* | *r-b-ʾ* | extolling |
| *mušāriku* | *ʾ-r-k* | lengthening |
| *mušaršidu* | *r-š-d* | protecting |
| *mušaru* | | surface measure |
| *mušassiku* | *n-s-k* | disposing |
| *mušātiru* | *w-t-r* | making excellent |
| *mušēniqtu* | *y-n-q* | nurse |
| *mušeppû* | *š-p-ʾ* | silencing |
| *mušēpû* | *w-p-ʾ* | making visible |
| *mušešqû* | *š-q-ʾ* | giving to drink |
| *mušēṣû* | *w-ṣ-ʾ* | bringing out |
| *mušīmu* | *š-ʾ-m* 2 | determining fate |
| *muškēnu* | | commoner |
| *mušpazzir* | *p-z-r* | protecting |
| *muštakīnu* | *k-ʾ-n* | arranging |
| *muštālu* | *š-ʾ-l* | arbitrator |
| *muštasḫiru* | *s-ḫ-r* | surrounding |
| *muštēmiqu* | *ʾ-m-q* | making supplication |
| *mušteṣbû* | *ṣ-b-ʾ* | arranging |
| *muštēširu* | *y-š-r* | keeping straight |
| *muštešmû* | *š-m-ʾ* | one who is obeyed |
| *mūšu* | | night |
| *mušūšeru* | *y-š-r* | keeping straight |
| *mutammiḫu* | *t-m-ḫ* | grasping |
| *mutēru* | *t-ʾ-r* | returning |
| *muttabbilu* | *w-b-l* | organising |
| *muttatu* (A) | | half |
| *mutu* | | husband |
| *mūtu* | *m-ʾ-t* | death |
| *muṭaḫḫidu* | *ṭ-ḫ-d* | showing generosity |
| *muṭību* | *ṭ-ʾ-b* | making happy |
| *muṭṭû* | *m-ṭ-ʾ* | to lessen |
| *muzzazu* | *n-z-z* | serving |
| | | |
| *nabalkattu* | *n-b-l-k-t* | burglary |
| *nabalkutu* {II} | *n-b-l-k-t* | to intrude |
| *nābiḫu* {*nābiʾu*} | *n-b-ʾ* 2 | rebel |
| *nabquru* | *b-q-r* | > *paqāru*, to claim |
| *nabšû* | *b-š-ʾ* | > *bašû*, to exist |

| | | |
|---|---|---|
| *nabû* (A) {II} | *n-b-ʾ* 1 | to nominate |
| *nābû* | *n-b-ʾ* 1 | nominating |
| *nābūlu* | *w-b-l* | > *abālu*, to bring |
| {*nābutu*} | *ʾ-b-d* | to flee |
| *nadānu* | *n-d-n* | to give; N *naddunu*, to be given |
| *naddunu* | *n-d-n* | > *nadānu*, to give |
| *naddû* | *n-d-ʾ* | > *nadû*, to throw down |
| *nādinānu* | *n-d-n* | seller |
| *nādinu* | *n-d-n* | giving |
| *nadītu* (A) | *n-d-ʾ* | devotee |
| *naʾdu* (A) | *n-ʾ-d* | devout |
| *nadû* {III} | *n-d-ʾ* | to throw down; Š *šuddû*, to cause to drop; N *naddû*, to be thrown down |
| *nadūku* | *d-ʾ-k* | > *dâku*, to kill |
| *nagāru* {II} | *n-g-r* | to be disloyal; D *nugguru*, to denounce; > *munaggiru*, informer |
| *nagbu* (A) | | source |
| *naggāru* {*nagāru* I} | | carpenter |
| *nāgiru* | *n-g-r* 1 | crier |
| *naḫāšu* | *n-ḫ-š* | to prosper; D *munaḫḫišu*, munificent |
| *naḫbutu* | *ḫ-b-t* | > *ḫabātu*, to rob |
| *naḫlulu* | *ḫ-l-l* | > *alālu*, to hang |
| *nâḫu* | *n-ʾ-ḫ* | to be still; D *nuḫḫu*, to soothe |
| *nakāpu* (A) | *n-k-p* | to butt; D > *munakkipû*, tossing |
| *nakāru* | *n-k-r* | to argue; D *nukkuru*, to change |
| *nakāsu* | *n-k-s* | to cut |
| *nakkaptu* | | forehead |
| *nakkāpû* {*nakkāpûm*} | *n-k-p* | goring |
| *nakru* | *n-k-r* | enemy |
| *namāru* {*nawāru*} | *n-w-r* | to shine; D *nummuru*, to shed light |
| *namḫuṣu* | *m-ḫ-ṣ* | > *maḫāṣu*, to strike |
| {*namkūru*} | *m-k-r* | > *makkūru*, property |
| *napāḫu* | *n-p-ḫ* | to blow; N *nappuḫu*, to flare up |
| *naparkû* {II} | *p-r-k-ʾ* | to abandon |
| *napāšu* (A) | *n-p-š* | to breathe freely; D *nuppušu*, to relax |
| *napḫaru* | *p-ḫ-r* | group |
| *napištu* | *n-p-š* | life |
| *nappāḫu* | *n-p-ḫ* | smith |
| *nappuḫu* | *n-p-ḫ* | > *napāḫu*, to blow |
| *napquru* | *b-q-r* | > *paqāru*, to claim |
| *naprusu* | *p-r-s* | > *parāsu*, to decide |
| *naptû* | *p-t-ʾ* | > *petû*, to open |
| *napṭuru* | *p-ṭ-r* | > *paṭāru*, to redeem |
| *naqāru* | *n-q-r* | to pull apart |
| *nāqidu* | | herdsman |

| | | |
|---|---|---|
| *narāmu* | *r-ʾ-m* | beloved |
| *narkusu* | *r-k-s* | > *rakāsu*, to agree |
| *narû* (A) | | stele |
| *nāru* (A) {I} | | river |
| *nasāḫu* | *n-s-ḫ* | to remove; N *nassuḫu*, to be removed |
| *nasāku* 1 (A) {I} | *n-s-k* 1 | to pull out; Š *šussuku*, to throw out |
| *nasāku* 2 (B) {*nasāḫu*} | *n-s-k* 2 | to wound; cf. *nasāḫu*, to remove |
| *nasāqu* A | *n-s-q* | to choose |
| *naspuḫu* | *s-p-ḫ* | > *sapāḫu*, to disrupt |
| *nasqu* | *n-s-q* | selected |
| *nassuḫu* | *n-s-ḫ* | > *nasāḫu*, to remove |
| *naṣāru* | *n-ṣ-r* | to keep |
| *naṣbutu* | *ṣ-b-t* | > *ṣabātu*, to seize |
| *naškunu* | *š-k-n* | > *šakānu*, to set |
| *našlulu* | *š-l-l* | > *šalālu*, to capture |
| *našpaku* (A) | *š-p-k* | granary |
| *našpakūtu* {*našpakūtum*} | *š-p-k* | storage |
| *našpuku* | *š-p-k* | > *šapāku*, to store |
| *našû* (A) {II} | *n-š-ʾ* | to carry |
| *nāšû* | *n-š-ʾ* | carrying |
| *našūmu* | *š-ʾ-m* 1 | > *šâmu*, to buy |
| *natruṣu* | *t-r-ṣ* | > *tarāṣu*, to stretch |
| *naṭālu* | *n-ṭ-l* | to look at; Š *šuṭṭulu*, to make visible |
| *naṭû* {IV} | *n-ṭ-ʾ* | to hit; Š *šuṭṭû*, to have beaten |
| *nazkuru* | *z-k-r* | > *zakāru*, to state |
| *neḫelṣû* | *ḫ-l-ṣ-ʾ* | to slip; Š *šuḫluṣû*, to allow to crumble |
| *neḫpû* | *ḫ-p-ʾ* | > *ḫepû*, to destroy |
| *nēmelu* | | profit |
| *nēmequ* | *ʾ-m-q* | wisdom |
| *nenmudu* | *ʾ-m-d* | > *emēdu*, to impose |
| *nepû* {*nepûm*} | *n-p-ʾ* | to seize |
| *nēpû* | *n-p-ʾ* | seizing |
| *neqelpû* | *q-l-p-ʾ* | > *muqqelpītu*, drifting |
| *nērtu* | *n-ʾ-r* | murder |
| *nēšu* {I} | | lion |
| *nibītu* | *n-b-ʾ* 1 | nominee |
| *nidītu* | *n-d-ʾ* | neglected land |
| *nidûtu* | *n-d-ʾ* | neglected land |
| *nikkassu* (A) | | account |
| *nindabû* | | offering |
| *nipiltu* | *n-p-l* | compensation |
| *nipûtu* {*nipûtum*} | *n-p-ʾ* | pledge |
| *nisiḫtu* {*nisḫu*} | *n-s-ḫ* | deserter |
| *nišku* | *n-š-k* | bite |
| *nišū* | | people |

| | | |
|---|---|---|
| *nīšu* (A) {II} | *n-ʾ-š* | oath |
| *nīšu* (B) {I} | *n-š-ʾ* | raising |
| *niṭlu* | *n-ṭ-l* | glance |
| *nizmatu* | *n-z-m* | wish |
| *nudunnû* | *n-d-n* | marriage-gift |
| *nugguru* | *n-g-r* 2 | > *nagāru*, to be disloyal; *munaggiru*, informer |
| *nuḫḫu* | *n-ʾ-ḫ* | > *nâḫu*, to be quiet |
| *nuḫšu* | *n-ḫ-š* | plenty |
| *nukaribbu* | | gardener |
| *nukkuru* | *n-k-r* | > *nakāru*, to argue |
| *nukurtu* | *n-k-r* | hostility |
| *numātu* {*numātum*} | | property |
| *nummuru* | *n-m-r* | > *namāru*, to give light |
| *nuppušu* | *n-p-š* | > *napāšu*, to breathe freely |
| *nūru* (A) | *n-w-r* | light |
| | | |
| *pagru* | | body |
| *paḫāru* {II} | *p-ḫ-r* | to assemble (intransitive); D > *mupaḫḫiru*, assembling (transitive) |
| *palāhu* | *p-l-ḫ* | to worship |
| *palāsu* | *p-l-s* | to look at; D *pullusu*, to covet; (otherwise read as *balāṣu*, to stare) |
| *palāšu* | *p-l-š* | to break into |
| *pāliḫu* | *p-l-ḫ* | worshipping |
| *palû* | | reign |
| *pānu* 1 (A) {I} | | face |
| *pānu* 2 (B) {II} | | basket |
| *pānû* | | previous |
| *paqādu* | *p-q-d* | to entrust |
| *paqāru* | *b-q-r* | to claim; N *napquru*, to be claimed; {or *baqāru* and *nabquru* (*b-q-r*)} |
| *pāqidu* | *p-q-d* | caring for |
| *parāsu* {I} | *p-r-s* | to decide; N *naprusu*, to be decided |
| *parkullu* | | lapicide |
| *parṣu* | *p-r-ṣ* (?) | rite |
| *paršiktu* {*parsiktu*} | | unit of measurement |
| *pasāsu* | *p-s-s* | to annul; D *pussusu*, to annul |
| *pašāḫu* | *p-š-ḫ* | to soothe |
| *pašāru* | *p-š-r* | to loosen, trade |
| *pašāṭu* | *p-š-ṭ* | to remove |
| *paṭāru* | *p-ṭ-r* | to repurchase; N *napṭuru*, to be redeemed |
| *pātiu* {*petû* II} | *p-t-ʾ* | opening out |

| | | |
|---|---|---|
| *pāṭu* | | district |
| *pazāru* | *p-z-r* | to hide; ŠD *šupuzzuru*, to protect |
| *peḫû* {II} | *p-ḫ-ʾ* | to seal up |
| *petû* {II} | *p-t-ʾ* | to open; D *puttû*, to solve; N *naptû*, to be opened |
| *pīḫātu* {I} | *p-ʾ-ḫ* | debt |
| *pīḫu* | | jug of beer |
| *pilšu* | *p-l-š* | burglary |
| *pissātu* | | disease |
| *piššatu* | | oil |
| *pītu* {I} | *p-t-ʾ* | opening |
| *pû* | | mouth, message |
| *puḫḫu* | *p-ʾ-ḫ* | to exchange |
| *puḫru* | *p-ḫ-r* | assembly |
| *pūḫu* | *p-ʾ-ḫ* | substitute |
| *pullusu* | *p-l-s* | > *palāsu*, to look at |
| *purussû* | *p-r-s* | decision |
| *pussusu* | *p-s-s* | > *pasāsu*, to annul |
| *pušqu* | *p-š-q* | distress |
| *puttû* | *p-t-ʾ* | > *petû*, to open |
| | | |
| *qablu* (B) {II} | | conflict |
| *qablû* | | middle |
| *qabû* {II} | *q-b-ʾ* | to speak |
| *qābû* | *q-b-ʾ* | speaking |
| *qadištu* | *q-d-š* | sacred prostitute |
| *qadu* | | with |
| *qalû* {II} | *q-l-ʾ* | to burn |
| *qâlu* (A) {I} | *q-ʾ-l* | to heed |
| *qamû* (A) {II} | *q-m-ʾ* | to burn |
| *qâpu* 1 (A) {*qiāpu*} | *q-ʾ-p* 1 | to entrust |
| *qâpu* 2 (B) {I} | *q-ʾ-p* 2 | to crumble |
| *qaqqadu* | | head |
| *qarītu* {I} | | granary |
| *qarnu* | | horn |
| *qarrādu* | *q-r-d* | hero |
| *qâšu* {*qiāšu*} | *q-ʾ-š* | to give |
| *qatû* {II} | *q-t-ʾ* | to come to an end; Š *šuqtû*, to terminate |
| *qātu* | | hand |
| *qerbītu* | *q-r-b* | interior |
| *qerbu* {II} | *q-r-b* | inside |
| *qerbum* {*qerbu* II} | *q-r-b* | within |
| *qerēbu* | *q-r-b* | to be near |
| *qibītu* | *q-b-ʾ* | command |

| | | |
|---|---|---|
| *qinnazu* {*qinnāzu*} | | whip |
| *qīptu* | *q-ʾ-p* 1 | trust |
| *qīštu* | *q-ʾ-š* | gift |
| *qû* (B) {II} | | grain measure |
| *qurādu* | | hero |
| | | |
| *rabāṣu* | *r-b-ṣ* | to lie down; Š *šurbuṣu*, to pasture |
| *rabiānu* | *r-b-ʾ* | governor |
| *rabītu* {cf. *rabû* I} | *r-b-ʾ* | principal wife |
| *rabû* {III} 1 | *r-b-ʾ* | to be grand; D *rubbû*, to grow crops; Š *šurbû*, to extol |
| *rabû* {I} 2 | *r-ʾ-b* | great |
| *râbu* {*riābu*} | *r-b-ʾ* | to recompense |
| *ragāmu* | *r-g-m* | to claim |
| *raggu* | | wicked |
| *raḫāṣu* | *r-ḫ-ṣ* | to devastate |
| *rāʾimu* | *r-ʾ-m* | loving |
| *rakābu* | *r-k-b* | to ride; D *rukkubu*, to pollinate |
| *rakāsu* | *r-k-s* | to agree; D *rukkusu*, to demand a contract; N *narkusu*, to congregate |
| *ramānu* | | self |
| *râmu* {II} | *r-ʾ-m* | to love |
| *rapāšu* | *r-p-š* | to be wide; D > *murappišu*, extending |
| *raqû* | *r-q-ʾ* | to hide |
| *râqu* {*riāqu*} | *r-ʾ-q* 1 | to be empty |
| *rašādu* | *r-š-d* | to be grounded; Š *šuršudu*, to fix securely |
| *rašû* {I} | *r-š-ʾ* | to possess; Š *šuršû*, to provide |
| *râšu* {*riāšu*} | *r-ʾ-š* | to be glad; D > *murīšu*, bringing pleasure |
| *raṭābu* | *r-ṣ-b* | to be moist; D *ruṭṭubu*, to moisten |
| *rebītu* | *r-b-ʾ* | city-square |
| *rebû* | | fourth |
| *redû* {I} | *r-d-ʾ* | to catch |
| *rēdû* | *r-d-ʾ* | soldier |
| *rēmu* {I} | *r-ʾ-m* | love |
| *rēṣu* | *r-ʾ-ṣ* | helper |
| *rēštû* | | oldest |
| *rēšu* | | head |
| *reʾû* | *r-ʾ-ʾ* | to tend |
| *rēʾû* | *r-ʾ-ʾ* | shepherd |
| *rēʾûtu* | *r-ʾ-ʾ* | governance |
| *rīdu* {I} | *r-d-ʾ* | behaviour |
| *rikistu* | *r-k-s* | contract |

| | | |
|---|---|---|
| *riksu* | *r-k-s* | contract |
| *rīmu* | | ox |
| *rīqu* {I} | *r-ʾ-q* 1 | empty |
| *rīqūtu* | *r-ʾ-q* 1 | emptiness |
| *risbatu* | *r-s-b* | fight |
| *rittu* | | hand |
| *rubātu* | *r-b-ʾ* | > *bēltu*, lady |
| *rubbû* | *r-b-ʾ* | > *rabû*, to be grand; *murabbû*, foster father |
| *rubû* | *r-b-ʾ* | prince |
| *rugummû* | *r-g-m* | loss |
| *rukkubu* | *r-k-b* | > *rakābu*, to ride |
| *rukkusu* | *r-k-s* | > *rakāsu*, to agree |
| *rūqu* | *r-ʾ-q* 2 | distant |
| *ruṭṭubu* | *r-ṭ-b* | > *raṭābu*, to moisten |
| *rūʾu* | | comrade |
| *sābītu* | *s-b-ʾ* | barmaid |
| *sābû* | *s-b-ʾ* | drink-seller |
| *sadāru* | *s-d-r* | to arrange |
| *saḫāmu* | *s-ḫ-m* | to be under pressure; D *suḫḫumu*, to pester |
| *saḫāru* | *s-ḫ-r* | to go round; Št > *muštasḫiru*, surrounding |
| *saḫmaštu* (A) | | turmoil, anarchy |
| *sakālu* (A) {I} | *s-k-l* | to acquire |
| *sakāpu* (A) {I} | *s-k-p* | to overturn |
| *sanāqu* (A) {I} | *s-n-q* | to supervise; D *sunnuqu*, to control |
| *sapāḫu* | *s-p-ḫ* | to disrupt; D *suppuḫu*, to disturb; N *naspuḫu*, to be scattered |
| *saparru* (A) {*sapāru* I} | | net |
| *sapḫu* | *s-p-ḫ* | widespread |
| *sarāru* | *s-r-r* | to deceive; D *surruru*, to deceive |
| *sarru* (A) {I} | *s-r-r* | reprobate |
| *sartu* | *s-r-r* | deception |
| *sasinnu* | | bow-maker |
| *sekēru* (A) | *s-k-r* | to shut off |
| *sekretu* | *s-k-r* | cloistered woman |
| *sību* | *s-b-ʾ* | beer |
| *sikiltu* | *s-k-l* | acquisition |
| *simmu* | | injury |
| *simtu* | *w-s-m* | symbol |
| *sinništu* | *ʾ-n-š* | woman |
| *siparru* | | bronze |
| *sugullu* | | > *littu*, cattle |

| | | |
|---|---|---|
| *suḫḫumu* | *s-ḫ-m* | > *saḫāmu*, to be under pressure |
| *suluppū* {*suluppu*} | | dates |
| *sunnuqu* | *s-n-q* | > *sanāqu*, to supervise |
| *sūnu* (A) {I} | | womb |
| *suppuḫu* | *s-p-ḫ* | > *sapāḫu*, to disrupt |
| *sūqu* | | street |
| *surruru* | *s-r-r* | > *sarāru*, to deceive |
| *sūtu* (A) | | grain measure |
| | | |
| *ṣabāru* (B) {I} | *ṣ-b-r* | to become unstable |
| *ṣabātu* | *ṣ-b-t* | to seize; Š *šuṣbutu*, to enforce; N *naṣbutu*, to be caught |
| *ṣābitānu* | *ṣ-b-t* | captor |
| *ṣābu* | | soldier |
| *ṣalmu* 1 (adj.) {I} | *ṣ-l-m* | black |
| *ṣalmu* 2 (sbst.) {II} | | statue |
| *ṣamû* | *ṣ-m-ʾ* | to be thirsty; Š *šuṣmû*, to allow to thirst |
| *ṣeḫēru* | *ṣ-ḫ-r* | to be small; D *ṣuḫḫuru*, to diminish |
| {*ṣeḫḫeru*} | *ṣ-ḫ-r* | very young |
| *ṣeḫru* {I} | *ṣ-ḫ-r* | young |
| *ṣēnu* 1 (sbst.) {III} | | flock |
| *ṣēnu* 2 (adj. A) {I} | | wicked |
| *ṣênu* {I} | *ṣ-ʾ-n* | to load as cargo |
| *ṣēru* (A) {I} | | open country |
| {*ṣiāru*} | *ṣ-ʾ-r* | to outshine; > *ṣurru*, to make famous |
| *ṣibtu* (A) {II} | *ṣ-b-t* | interest |
| *ṣillu* {I} | *ṣ-l-l* | shadow |
| *ṣimdatu* | *ṣ-m-d* | regulation |
| *ṣimdu* (A) {I} | *ṣ-m-d* | bandaging |
| *ṣīru* {I} | *ṣ-ʾ-r* | exalted (*CAD* Ṣ 210a) |
| *ṣubbû* (D) | *ṣ-b-ʾ* | to observe; Št > *mušteṣbû*, working to plan |
| *ṣuḫḫuru* | *ṣ-ḫ-r* | > *ṣeḫēru*, to be small |
| *ṣulūlu* | *ṣ-l-l* | shade |
| *ṣurru* {*ṣiāru*} | *ṣ-ʾ-r* | to make famous (perhaps denominative); > *muṣīru*, making famous |
| | | |
| *ša* | | of |
| *ša ḫaṭṭātim* | | captain |
| *šabaḫu* {*šapāḫu*} | *š-p-ḫ* | to scatter; D *šuppuḫu*, to stir up |
| *šadālu* | *š-d-l* | to be broad; D > *mušaddilu*, developing |
| *šaḫû* | | pig |

| | | |
|---|---|---|
| *šājimānu* {*šājjimānu*} | *š-ʾ-m* 1 | > *šāyyimānu*, purchaser |
| *šāʾimu* | *š-ʾ-m* 2 | determining |
| *šakāku* | *š-k-k* | to harrow |
| *šakānu* | *š-k-n* | to set; Š *šuškunu*, to have arranged; N *naškunu*, to be arranged |
| *šākinu* | *š-k-n* | providing |
| *šaknu* | *š-k-n* | provided with |
| *šalālu* (A) {I} | *š-l-l* | to take into captivity; N *našlulu*, to be taken into captivity |
| *šalamtu* | *š-l-m* | corpse |
| *šalāmu* {II} | *š-l-m* | to be safe; D *šullumu*, to reinstate |
| *šalaš* {*šalāš*} | | three |
| *šalāšā* | | thirty |
| *šalšu* | | one-third |
| *šalû* (B) {I} | *š-l-ʾ* | to submerge |
| *šamallû* | | trader |
| *šamaššammū* | | sesame |
| *šammu* | | grass |
| *šamnu* | | oil |
| *šamšu* | | sun |
| *šamû* (A) {I} | | sky |
| *šâmu* 1 (A) {I} | *š-ʾ-m* 1 | to purchase; N *našūmu*, to be bought |
| *šâmu* 2 (B) {*šiāmu*} | *š-ʾ-m* 2 | to determine |
| *šanānu* | *š-n-n* | to strive; Gt *šitannu*, to compete |
| *šāninu* | *š-n-n* | rival |
| *šanû* 1 (vb. A) {III} | *š-n-ʾ* | to repeat; Š *šušnû*, to double |
| *šanû* 2 (adj. A) {II} | *š-n-ʾ* | another |
| {*šapāḫu*} | *š-p-ḫ* | to scatter; D > *šuppuḫu*, to stir up |
| *šapāku* | *š-p-k* | to store; N *našpuku*, to be stored |
| *šapliš* | | below |
| *šapû* (C) {III} | *š-p-ʾ* | to be silent; D *šuppû*, to silence |
| *šaqālu* | *š-q-l* | to pay |
| *šaqû* (B) {III} | *š-q-ʾ* | to give to drink; Š *mušesqû*, giving to drink |
| *šarāku* (A) {I} | *š-r-k* | to hand over |
| *šarāmu* | *š-r-m* | to cut to size; D *šurrumu*, to trim |
| *šarāqu* (A) {I} | *š-r-q* | to steal |
| *šarrāqānum* | *š-r-q* | thief |
| *šarrāqu* | *š-r-q* | thief |
| *šarru* {I} | | king |
| *šarrūtu* | | kingship |
| *šasû* | *š-s-ʾ* | to shout |
| *šašallu* | | tendon, or pelt |
| *šattu* {I} | | year |
| *šaṭāpu* | *š-ṭ-p* | to preserve life |

| | | |
|---|---|---|
| *šaṭāru* {II} | *š-ṭ-r* | to inscribe |
| *šāṭipu* | *š-ṭ-p* | caring |
| *šaṭru* | *š-ṭ-r* | inscribed |
| *šāyyimānu* {*šājjimānu*} | *š-ʾ-m* 1 | purchaser |
| *šebēru* | *š-b-r* | to break |
| *šebru* | *š-b-r* | broken |
| {*šēbultu*} | *w-b-l* | > *šūbultu*, consignment |
| *šēdu* (A) {I} | | protecting spirit |
| *šēm* | | > *šû*, his |
| *šemû* {I} | *š-m-ʾ* | to hear |
| *šēmû* | *š-m-ʾ* | obeying |
| *šēpu* | | foot |
| *šerʾānu* | | sinew |
| *šeriktu* | *š-r-k* | dowry |
| *šērtu* 1 (B) {I} | | condemnation |
| *šērtu* 2 (D) {II} | | brilliance |
| *šerʾu* | | field |
| *šeššet* | | six |
| *šeššu* 1 (adj.) {s.v. 1} | | sixth |
| *šeššu* 2 (num.) {s.v. 2} | | one-sixth |
| *šeʾu* | | barley |
| *šeʾû* | *š-ʾ-ʾ* | to search |
| *šî* {*šī*} | | she, that |
| *šiāti* | | that |
| *šību* (A) {I} | *š-ʾ-b* | witness |
| *šībūtu* | *š-ʾ-b* | evidence |
| *šikaru* {*šikāru*} | | beer |
| *šimtu* | *w-š-m* | mark |
| *šīmtu* | *š-ʾ-m* 2 | destiny |
| *šīmu* | *š-ʾ-m* 1 | price |
| *šina* | | two |
| *šināti* | | these |
| *šinnu* (A) {I} | | tooth |
| *šipātu* {*šīpātu*} | | wool |
| *šipru* | *š-p-r* | task |
| *šipṭu* (A) {I} | *š-p-ṭ* | verdict |
| *šiqītu* | *š-q-ʾ* | irrigation |
| *šiqlu* | *š-q-l* | shekel |
| *širiktu* | | > *šeriktu*, dowry |
| *šīru* (A) | | flesh |
| *šisītu* (A) {I} | *š-s-ʾ* | call |
| *šitannu* | *š-n-n* | > *šanānu*, to rival |
| *šittān* | | two-thirds |
| *šu* (pron., p.152b) | | he of |
| *šû* 1 (adj., p.153b) {*šū*} | | his |

| | | |
|---|---|---|
| *šû* 2 (pron., p.155a) {*šū*} | | he, that |
| *šuāti* | | him |
| *šubbuḫu* | | > *šuppuḫu*, to stir up |
| *šubšû* | *b-š-ʾ* | > *bašû* to exist |
| *šubtu* (A) {I} | *w-š-b* | dwelling |
| *šūbultu* | *w-b-l* | consignment |
| *šūbulu* | *w-b-l* | > *abālu*, to bring |
| *šuddû* | *n-d-ʾ* | > *nadû*, to throw down |
| *šūdû* | *y-d-ʾ* | > *edû*, to know |
| *šudūku* | *d-ʾ-k* | > *dâku*, to kill |
| *šugītu* | | priestess |
| *šuḫluṣû* | *ḫ-l-ṣ-ʾ* | > *neḫelṣû*, to slip |
| *šuḫruṣu* | *ḫ-r-ṣ* | > *ḫarasu*, to subtract |
| *šūḫuzu* | *ʾ-ḫ-z* | > *aḫāzu*, to seize |
| *šuklulu* {II} | *k-l-l* | to make complete |
| *šukšudu* | *k-š-d* | > *kašādu*, to conquer |
| *šūkulu* | *ʾ-k-l* | > *akālu*, to eat |
| *šullumu* | *š-l-m* | > *šalāmu*, to be safe |
| *šulmāniš* | *š-l-m* | securely |
| *šulmu* | *š-l-m* | well-being |
| *šulputu* | *l-p-t* | > *lapātu*, to seize |
| *šūlû* | *ʾ-l-ʾ* | > *elû*, to go up |
| *šuluḫḫu* | | lustration |
| *šumḫuru* | *m-ḫ-r* | > *maḫāru*, to receive |
| *šumma* | | if |
| *šumqutu* | *m-q-t* | > *maqātu*, to fall |
| *šumṣû* | *m-ṣ-ʾ* | > *maṣû*, to be equal |
| *šumṭû* | *m-ṭ-ʾ* | > *maṭû*, to be short |
| *šumu* | | name |
| *šumūtu* | *m-ʾ-t* | > *mâtu*, to die |
| *šunu* | | they |
| *šupêlu* | *š-p-ʾ-l* | to weaken |
| *šuppû* | *š-p-ʾ* | > *šapû*, to be silent |
| *šuppuḫu* {*šapāḫu* D} | *š-p-ḫ* | to stir up |
| *šūpû* | *w-p-ʾ* | > *apû*, to be visible |
| *šupuzzuru* | *p-z-r* | > *pazāru*, to hide |
| *šuqtû* | *q-t-ʾ* | > *qatû*, to come to an end |
| *šūquru* | *ʾ-q-r* | very precious |
| *šurbû* | *r-b-ʾ* | > *rabû*, to be grand |
| *šurbuṣu* | *r-b-ṣ* | > *rabāṣu*, to lie down |
| *šurqu* (A) | *š-r-q* | stolen property |
| *šurrumu* | *š-r-m* | > *šarāmu*, to cut to size |
| *šuršû* | *r-š-ʾ* | > *rašû*, to possess |
| *šuršudu* | *r-š-d* | > *rašādu*, to be grounded |
| *šūrubu* | *ʾ-r-b* | > *erēbu*, to enter |

| | | |
|---|---|---|
| *šussuku* | *n-s-k* | > *nasāku*, to throw away |
| *šuṣbutu* | *ṣ-b-t* | > *ṣabātu*, to seize |
| *šuṣmû* | *ṣ-m-ʾ* | > *ṣamû*, to be thirsty |
| *šūṣû* | *w-ṣ-ʾ* | > *aṣû*, to come out |
| *šūši* | | sixty |
| *šuškunu* | *š-k-n* | > *šakānu*, to set |
| *šušnû* | *š-n-ʾ* 1 | > *šanû*, to repeat |
| *šuššān* {*šuššu*} | | one-third |
| *šuššu* (B) | | one-sixth |
| *šūšubu* | *w-š-b* | > *ašābu*, to dwell |
| *šūšuru* | *y-š-r* | > *ešēru*, to go straight |
| *šutaktutu* | *k-t-t* | > *katātu*, to be low |
| *šutbû* | *t-b-ʾ* | > *tebû*, to attack |
| *šutēmuqu* | *ʾ-m-q* | > *emēqu*, to be wise |
| *šuteṣbû* | *ṣ-b-ʾ* | > *ṣubbû*, to observe |
| *šutlumu* | *t-l-m* | to bestow |
| *šutruṣu* | *t-r-ṣ* | > *tarāṣu*, to stretch |
| *šūtuqu* | *ʾ-t-q* | > *etēqu*, to pass |
| *šūturu* 1 | *w-t-r* | exceptional |
| *šūturu* 2 | *w-t-r* | > *atāru*, to be excessive |
| *šuṭṭû* | *n-ṭ-ʾ* | > *naṭû*, to hit |
| *šuṭṭulu* | *n-ṭ-l* | > *naṭālu*, to see |
| *šūzubu* | *ʾ-z-b* | > *ezēbu*, to leave |
| *šūzzuzu* | *n-z-z* | > *izuzzu*, to stand |
| | | |
| *tabāku* | *t-b-k* | to pour out |
| *tabālu* | *t-b-l* | to carry away; cf. *abālu*, to bring |
| *tadmiqtu* | *d-m-q* | kindness |
| *tāḫazu* {*tāḫāzu*} | *ʾ-ḫ-z* | conflict |
| *takālu* | *t-k-l* | to trust; D *tukkulu*, to show reliability |
| *talīmu* | *t-l-m* | devoted follower |
| *tālittu* | *w-l-d* | young animal |
| *tamāḫu* | *t-m-ḫ* | to hold; D *tummuḫu*, to support |
| *tamḫāru* | *m-ḫ-r* | conflict |
| *tamkāru* | *m-k-r* | merchant |
| *tamû* {II} | *t-m-ʾ* | to swear |
| *tanattu* | *n-ʾ-d* | praise |
| *tānēḫu* | *ʾ-n-ḫ* | weariness |
| *tappûtu* | | partnership |
| *taqtītu* | *q-t-ʾ* | end |
| *tarāku* | *t-r-k* | to beat |
| *tarāṣu* {I} | *t-r-ṣ* | to stretch; Š *šutruṣu*, to stretch; N *natruṣu*, to be stretched |
| *tarbaṣu* | *r-b-ṣ* | animal pen |
| *tarbītu* | *r-b-ʾ* | adopted child |

| | | |
|---|---|---|
| *tarkibtu* | *r-k-b* | pollination |
| *tarû* {I} | *t-r-ʾ* | to lead off |
| *târu* | *t-ʾ-r* | to return; D *turru*, to repay |
| *tašīmtu* | *š-ʾ-m* 2 | authority |
| *tašna* | *š-n-ʾ* | twice as much |
| *tebû* | *t-b-ʾ* | to attack; Š *šutbû*, to remove |
| *telītu* | *ʾ-l-ʾ* | exalted lady |
| *teptītu* | *p-t-ʾ* | development |
| *terḫatu* | | bridal gift |
| *têrtu* | | oracle |
| *tēšû* {I} | *ʾ-š-y* 1 | turmoil |
| *tībû* | *t-b-ʾ* | attacking |
| *tīlu* | | desolate site |
| *tukkulu* | *t-k-l* | > *takālu*, to trust |
| *tukultu* | *t-k-l* | faith |
| *tulû* | | breast |
| *turru* | *t-ʾ-r* | > *târu*, to return |
| *tuššu* | *ʾ-š-y* 1 | deception |
| | | |
| *ṭâbu* {*ṭiābu*} | *ṭ-ʾ-b* | to be good; D *ṭubbu*, to improve |
| *ṭābu* | *ṭ-ʾ-b* | good |
| *ṭaḫādu* | *ṭ-ḫ-d* | to be plentiful; D > *muṭaḫḫidu*, showing generosity |
| *ṭarādu* | *ṭ-r-d* | to send |
| *ṭebû* | *ṭ-b-ʾ* | to sink |
| *ṭeḫḫu* | *ṭ-ḫ-ʾ* | neighbour |
| *ṭeḫû* {I} | *ṭ-ḫ-ʾ* | to be near; D *ṭuḫḫu*, to aggregate |
| *ṭēmu* | | report |
| *ṭīdu* | | clay figurine |
| *ṭubbu* | *ṭ-ʾ-b* | > *ṭâbu*, to be good |
| *ṭubbû* | *ṭ-b-ʾ* | > *ṭebû*, to sink |
| *ṭuḫdu* | | plenty |
| *ṭuḫḫu* | *ṭ-ḫ-ʾ* | > *ṭeḫû*, to be near |
| *ṭuppu* {I} | | document |
| | | |
| *u* | | and |
| *ubānu* | | finger |
| *ubbubu* | *ʾ-b-b* | > *ebēbu*, to purify |
| *ubburu* {*abāru* III} | *ʾ-b-r* | to bring disrepute (see *CAD* A/1 38b, s.v. *abāru* III) |
| *uddû* | *y-d-ʾ* | > *edû*, to know |
| *ugāru* | | meadow |
| *ugbabtum* | | princess |
| *ukullû* | | foodstuff |
| *ul* | | not |

| | | |
|---|---|---|
| *ullû* | *ʾ-l-ʾ* | > *elû* , to go up |
| *ulu* | | > *lu* or; *u* and |
| *ūmišam* | | daily |
| *ummānu* | | workforce |
| *ummu* {I} | | mother |
| *ūmu* | | day |
| *unnušu* | *ʾ-n-š* | > *enēšu*, to be weak |
| *unūtu* | | household goods |
| *uppulu* | *ʾ-p-l* | > *apālu*, to answer |
| *uppusu* | *ʾ-p-s* | > *epēsu*, to make difficulty |
| *urḫu* | | way |
| *urīṣu* | | goat |
| *urruku* | *ʾ-r-k* | > *arāku*, to be long |
| *uršu* {II; < *erēšu* II} | *ʾ-r-š* 1 | wisdom |
| *ūsu* | | rule |
| *uṣurtu* | *ʾ-ṣ-r* | plan |
| *uššuru* {*wašārum* Dt} | *w-š-r* | to prove innocent |
| *uššušu* | *ʾ-š-š* | > *ašāšu*, to be in distress |
| *ušumgallu* | | dragon |
| *utlu* | | bosom |
| *utturu* | *w-t-r* | > *atāru*, to be excessive |
| *utūlu* | | >*itūlu*, to lie down |
| *uṭṭatu* | | barleycorn |
| *uʾuru* | *w-ʾ-r* | > *âru*, to advance |
| *uznu* | | ear |
| *uzubbû* | *ʾ-z-b* | divorce settlement |
| *uzzatu* | *ʾ-z-z* 1 | anger |
| | | |
| {*wabālu*} | *w-b-l* | > *abālu*, to bring |
| {*waklu*} | | > *ša ḫaṭṭatim*, captain |
| {*walādu*} | *w-l-d* | > *alādu*, to give birth |
| {*wapû*} | *w-p-ʾ* | > *apû*, to be certain |
| {*warāqu*} | | > *arāqu*, to be green |
| {*wardu*} | | > *ardu*, slave |
| {*wardūtu*} | | > *ardūtu*, slavery |
| {*warḫu*} | | > *arḫu*, month |
| {*wâru*} | *w-ʾ-r* | > *âru*, to advance |
| {*wasāmu*} | *w-s-m* | > *asāmu*, to be fitting |
| {*waṣābu*} | *w-ṣ-b* | > *aṣābu*, to add to |
| {*waṣû*} | | > *aṣû*, to come out |
| {*wašābu*} | *w-š-b* | > *ašābu*, to dwell |
| {*wašārum*} | *w-š-r* | > *ašāru*, to hang loose; *uššuru*, to go free |
| {*watāru*} | | > *atāru* to be excessive |
| *zadimmu* | | stone-cutter; > *sasinnu*, bow-maker |

| | | |
|---|---|---|
| *zā'iru* {*zā'eru*} | *z-'-r* | foe |
| *zakāru* (A) {I} | *z-k-r* | to state; N *nazkuru*, to be stated |
| *zanānu* (B) {II} | *z-n-n* | to care for |
| *zāninu* | *z-n-n* | caring |
| *zapāru* | *z-p-r* | to become rotten; > *ṣabāru*, to be unstable |
| *zaqāpu* (A) | *z-q-p* | to plant |
| *zâzu* | *z-'-z* | to share |
| *zēru* {II} | *z-r-'* | seed |
| *zêru* | *z-'-r* | to hate |
| *zibbatu* | | tail |
| *zību* {I} | *z-b-'* | offering |
| *zikaru* | *z-k-r* | man |
| *zikru* (A) {I} | *z-k-r* | name |
| *zittu* | *z-'-z* | share |
| *zumru* | | body |
| *zunnu* (A) {I} | | to rain |